London: A Visitor's Guide
2016 Edition

Craig Cross

London: A Visitor's Guide
2016 Edition

Craig Cross

Published by Craig Cross, Tolworth, Surrey, United Kingdom

First edition published April 2014
This edition published July 2016

All text and photography copyright © Craig Cross 2016
Layout and design by Craig Cross

Street maps © OpenStreetMap contributors, using an Open Database License from www.openstreetmap.org/copyright

Craig Cross has asserted his right to be identified as the author of this work in accordance with the Copyright, Designs and Patents Acts 1988

All Rights Reserved. No part of this publication may be reproduced, stored in a retrieval system, or transmitted in any form or by any means, electronic, mechanical, photocopying, recording or otherwise, without the prior permission of the author and copyright owner

ISBN: 978-0-9955179-3-6

Also available as an eBook
ISBN: 978-0-9955179-5-0

This book is regularly updated and the author welcomes all suggestions and corrections. You can contact him through his blog at *http://www.londondrum.com/blog/*, or his Facebook page at *https://www.facebook.com/london.visitors.guide/*

Disclaimer: The author has made reasonable efforts to ensure the accuracy of all the information contained in this book; however, information about dates, times and prices changes frequently, and the author accepts no responsibility for any loss, injury or inconvenience sustained by anyone as a result of following the information or advice contained in this guide. You should always double-check the details with the various venues and companies before spending any money or making concrete plans

Table of Contents

Introduction	4
Landmarks & Attractions	7

    A p7 - B p15 - C p41 - D p69 - F p73 - G p74 - H p89 - I p119
    J p122 - K p125 - L p129 - M p147 - N p157 - O p168 - P p171
    Q p180 - R p182 - S p202 - T p228 - V p252 - W p255

Sightseeing Buses & Boats	265

    By road p265 - By rail p271 - By sea p275 - By air p285

Parades, Services & Seasonal Events	290

    Parades p290 - Church services p303 - Christmas p312

Places Further Afield	321
Example Itineraries	374

    For everybody p374 - For families p383

Top 10 Lists	389
Hotels	404

    Choosing a hotel area p404 - Hotel prices and facilities p405
    3-star hotels p407 - 4-star hotels p414 - 5-star hotels p425

Using London Transport	440

    Oyster cards p440 - Visitor Oyster cards p441 - Travelcards p443
    Contactless payment cards p445 - London Underground p456
    Train fares p447 - National Rail p455 - Buses p457 - Bus fares p457
    Minicabs and taxis p461 - Taxi fares p462 - Boris bikes p463
    River cruises p464 - Airports p468 - Heathrow p468 - Gatwick p469

Other Useful Information	473

    Calendar dates p475 - Typical prices p485 - Discount passes p485

Street Maps	494
Index	505
Get the eBook / Contact the Author / Visit the Website	511

Introduction

Big Ben, buses, umbrellas and rain... Welcome to London!

I suppose I'd better start by introducing myself, so we can get to know each other a bit better. Then you can tell me something about yourself as well, although obviously I won't be able to hear it because this is just a book, *but who cares!* Let's do it anyway.

I'll go first: *Hi.*

My name is Craig, and I'm just a normal everyday guy who happens to go to London a lot, because I love the place. I love pretty much everything about it: its buildings, its history, its traffic and noise, and even its dirty streets and wet weather. The only bits that I could happily do without are the crowds. If I could have the streets all to myself then that would be perfect, but I am happy to share them with you, though, because that's what this book is all about. We are going to become *travel companions*. I am going to show you around the entire city, and by the time you reach the end of the book we will be best buddies.

What you are holding in your hands are five hundred pages of reviews and views about attractions, palaces, parades, buses, boat rides, day trips, hotels, museums, galleries, churches, cemeteries, skyscrapers... pretty much everything. There are over two hundred reviews inside this guide, and I have been to every single one of them myself -- *honest!*

I've included all of the familiar favourites like Madame Tussauds, Tower Bridge and the London Eye; plus some of the more daring events like Prime Minister's Questions, a dinner at The Ritz, and a climb up Big Ben to stand five-feet from the bell. All of the popular children's attractions, museums and art galleries are in here, alongside lots of open-top buses and boats. I've also included a chapter full of day-trips to places like Oxford, Cambridge, Windsor Castle and Bath. And of course I'll describe all of the famous parades like Changing the Guard as well (no trip to London would be complete without a bit of pomp and pageantry). If you like Christmas then you're in luck, because I've reviewed everything from the Christmas lights and ice rinks, to the switching-on ceremony for the Trafalgar Square tree. I've also selected plenty of places that tourists rarely think of: like trudging up a distant hill for a sight of the skyline, listening to a court case at the Royal Courts of Justice, and nosing around an overgrown cemetery on a rainy day.

I've awarded all of the attractions a rating which goes from zero stars: ☆☆☆ (=rubbish), all the way up to three stars: ★★★ (=not rubbish). But bear in mind that these are my *personal* ratings, so if your interests are different to mine then take that into account. You will soon get to know what I like and dislike by reading the book -- I don't mind telling you when something is terrible. If a place deserves some praise then it will definitely get it, but if it sent me to sleep then I'll tell you that, too.

Most of the guidebooks on sale bombard you with names and dates that nobody wants to know, like who designed the roof, and how many bones and stones they found in a ditch fifty years ago, but I don't bother with any of that stuff. This guide is more of a travelogue than a textbook, because you're supposed to be on holiday, not at school. I may not have a degree in British history, but what I *do* have is a local's knowledge of which attractions are enjoyable, and which ones are a waste of your precious holiday time. What I try and do is walk through the door like a tourist, and then tell you exactly what I see. I queue up in the pouring rain, walk around for three hours, and then tell you whether it was worth getting soaked. I drag my suitcase around the hotels, faint at the minibar prices, and then tell you whether they forgot to re-stock the teabags. So it's not all sunshine and smiles in this book. This is not a travel brochure full of blue skies and happy kids. This is London how it *really* is. I have good days and bad days, good moods and blue moods, and you're going to be sharing my shoes for the next five hundred pages, which means you'll have to put up with all my bad jokes and anecdotes -- just like a *real* travel companion.

I've also been careful to include all of the usual information that you'll require to plan your stay like opening times, prices, street maps, and the number of hours that I think you'll need to set aside to properly enjoy each attraction. I do tend to take my time at each location, though, so you can probably knock off thirty minutes for every ninety if you're in a rush. (So if I say that something takes three hours, you can probably rush around it in two.) I hope that you will find my suggested itineraries useful as well -- I have put together two weeks' worth, to give you plenty of ideas about how to cram as much as possible into your holiday.

If you're a newbie to London then you might be interested in my big chapter explaining how to ride the buses, boats, taxis and trains. I totally understand that it can sometimes be a bit intimidating standing at a busy bus stop when you don't know what to do, and this chapter should help to calm your nerves. And after that comes another chapter filled with lots of handy practical info, like how to telephone abroad, how to post a letter, and where to find some free Wi-Fi spots. There's also a handy section about discount tickets and passes (because London can be *very* expensive).

Hopefully my book will encourage you to jump out of bed and explore London. If you're planning a holiday with friends or family then it should give you plenty of decent ideas. And if you're more of a solitary soul, like me, then I hope to be good company as you wander around the streets in the rain (and I apologise in advance for my terrible jokes).

If you enjoy my book then check out my blog at *londondrum.com/blog* and my Facebook page at *facebook.com/london.visitors.guide*, and let me know what you think. If you have any questions about the places that I've visited then feel free to drop me a line. I'll be happy to answer any questions.

Have fun!

Craig

Landmarks & Attractions

Abbey Road

ADDRESS Abbey Road, St. John's Wood
TRAINS Maida Vale, St. John's Wood (both zone 2) **BUSES** 139, 189 **TIME REQUIRED** 15 mins

Easy to get to? ★★★ Good for kids? ☆☆☆
Value for money? free Worth a visit? ★☆☆

I have two great passions in life: The Beatles, and zebra crossings. So a trip to Abbey Road is the perfect day out for me. And it's also the perfect place to watch some tourists getting shouted at by the London cabbies, which is always fun. You will witness more beeping horns and furious hand gestures around here than at any place in London. The Beatles famously sang that 'All You Need Is Love', but come rush hour in Abbey Road and all of that is abandoned. They have inadvertently turned this road into a battle-zone between the buses, bikes and Beatles fans.

But first of all you have to find the right zebra crossing. Good luck trying to find it if your only map is the album cover, because it has changed a bit since The Beatles' day. There are actually three different crossings just fifty feet apart now, plus another one further up the road, and the stripy white zig-zag lines and Belisha beacons make you think you've got the wrong one (they aren't shown on the cover). If you're lucky then you'll see a big bunch of tourists snapping away on their iPhones to guide you to the right spot.

If you find the pointy stone monument in the centre of the road and look straight down Abbey Road, then that is the same view as on the cover. The old Volkswagen has long gone now of course, and the black taxi is missing too. And there's an extra bus stop behind it. But you can still see the leafy green trees and the white wall of Abbey Road Studios. But it's a busy main road these days. If The Beatles had tried to snap the same shot today then they would have been run over in five seconds flat.

As I'm writing this I'm watching about fifteen camera clickers queuing up on the pavement, patiently waiting for their turn to march across. As soon as they sense the briefest of lulls in the traffic off they go, out of their starting traps, striding across in quads with their arms and legs at forty five degrees, like a row of paper dolls. When they reach halfway across they'll all pause and grin for ten seconds whilst their accomplice takes a picture from the pavement. That is when the road rage takes place. The cars will start bucking and agitating like angry broncos, impatient to get away. The drivers will have their hands hovering around their horns, ready to deliver a quick blast of trumpet if they take too long. But then reinforcements will arrive from the pavement -- four more fans will take their place in line. And then four more, four more... more and more. And this goes on and on, until the end of days.

A little farther down the path is Abbey Road Studios itself. You're not allowed to go inside without a reason, but you can still take a peek through the iron gate at the famous front door. Remember to check out the graffiti strewn posts, too, which are festooned with bazillions of lyrics and love notes like "I love you, John!", left by forty years-worth of music fans.

Albert Memorial

ADDRESS Albert Memorial, Kensington Gardens - map 6c **TRAINS** South Kensington (zone 1) **BUSES** 9, 10, 52, 70, 360, 452 **WEB** royalparks.org.uk/parks/kensington-gardens/things-to-see-and-do/memorials,-fountains-and-statues/the-albert-memorial **TIME REQUIRED** 15 mins

Easy to get to? ★★★ Good for kids? ☆☆☆
Value for money? free Worth a visit? ★★☆

There's a famous old story about Prince Albert that says he didn't want a fuss made after his death. "Don't build me a statue, for chrissakes," he said (I'm paraphrasing). "I don't want anything grand." So what did his missus do? She built him the flashiest statue in the capital! All I can say is that he must have been the world's greatest husband for Queen Victoria to stump up the money for this.

It's not an exaggeration to say that Albert has got the flashiest monument in London. I went to Windsor Castle the other day and saw Henry VIII's marker in St. George's Chapel -- one of England's greatest-ever kings -- and all he got was a stone slab in the floor. Churchill was awarded a solitary flagstone in Westminster Abbey. I suppose you could make a case for Nelson's Column being the granddaddy of statues, but even that is shorter than Albert's. I always find that fact a little bit hard to believe when I'm standing underneath the Albert Memorial, but apparently it's true: Nelson's Column is six feet shorter. That's what Wikipedia says, anyway (so it must be true). Maybe they've included the height of the steps as well.

When you look at the carvings and the ribbon of marble that runs around the base, you'll be forgiven for thinking that Albert was an emperor. It's like a *Who's Who* of world history. It starts off with famous builders like Christopher Wren and Cheops (the builder of the pyramids), and then moves onto artists like Raphael, Rubens, Titian and Turner. After that comes a library of writers like Homer, Dante and Shakespeare. It's all a bit strange really. Was Queen Victoria trying to compare her husband to these people? I don't think he sits very comfortably in that club.

There are probably about one hundred artists, writers, builders and thinkers immortalised around the base, plus a stone set of beauties higher up. After that comes another four scantily clad women, and what looks like a choir of golden saints and angels on the top (too far away for my poor eyes to see). And right in the middle is the figure of Prince Albert himself, all gilded in gold and looking like a god.

When I die, this is how I want to be remembered. This is how I deserve to be remembered.

Prince Albert's home at Kensington Palace is a short walk across Kensington Gardens.

Alexander Fleming Laboratory Museum

Landmarks & Attractions | 9

ADDRESS Alexander Fleming Laboratory Museum, St. Mary's Hospital, Paddington - map 1f **TRAINS** Paddington (zone 1) **BUSES** 7, 23, 27, 36, 205, 332, 436 **PRICE** Adult £4; Senior £2; Child £2 **OPEN** 10 AM to 1 PM (Mon-Thu) **WEB** imperial.nhs.uk/aboutus/ourhospitals/museumsandarchives **TEL** 0203 312 6528 **TIME REQUIRED** 30-45 mins

Easy to get to? ★★★ Good for kids? ☆☆☆
Value for money? ★☆☆ Worth a visit? ★☆☆

Alexander Fleming is the Nobel Prize-winning Scotsman who discovered penicillin. But he's also an extremely lucky doc who fluked his greatest achievement. That's how it seems to me, anyway, after visiting this museum -- he got lucky.

The way I understand it, he was just looking out of his pokey office window that overlooks the tatty shops and traffic of Paddington, counting down the clock until home time, and he either didn't clean his equipment properly (typical bloke), or left a window open, or left the top off his petri dish, but when he came back from holiday two weeks later he found that a bit of mould had contaminated his plate, and he was on the road to Oslo to pick up his Nobel Prize. *Nice one, Alex.* My hat's off to you, mate. You scored a point for the common man! This museum has managed to inspire me in a way that is not typical for an educational museum: it has shown me that you can fluke your way into fame at the ripe old age of forty four. So there is hope for me yet.

The museum occupies three tiny rooms at St. Mary's Hospital -- one of which was his original office. And the only way into them is through a few corridors of the hospital itself: those never-ending white tiled corridors that seem to go on forever and ever, past ward signs and toilets and chapels, past patients and nervous looking relatives trying to find the right room. Eventually you come across the shop, and get taken up to his office by a guide.

It's not quite like a time capsule -- it's more of a reconstruction. It does have a lot of his original items inside, but a good half of them are just contemporary copies. The desks are overflowing with dirty old test tubes and microscopes, and faded old notebooks and newspapers. Whilst you're standing there pretending to be interested, the guide delivers a monologue about how it all happened, before sitting you down in a little movie room to watch a ten minute documentary that looks like it was made in the 1970s. Then you step across the corridor to see one more tiny little room filled with photos and information boards. And that's it. You will be in and out in forty five minutes flat.

If you're interested in medicine then try the Florence Nightingale Museum, Science Museum and Old Operating Theatre.

All Hallows by the Tower

10 | London: A Visitor's Guide

ADDRESS All Hallows by the Tower, Byward Street - map 10b **TRAINS** Tower Hill, Tower Gateway DLR (both zone 1) **BUSES** 15, 42, 78, 100, RV1 **PRICE** Free **OPEN** 8 AM to 6 PM (Mon-Fri); 10 AM to 5 PM (Sat-Sun) **DENOMINATION** Church of England **WEB** allhallowsbythetower.org.uk **TEL** 0207 481 2928 **TIME REQUIRED** 45-60 mins

Easy to get to? ★★★ Good for kids? ★☆☆ Value for money? free Worth a visit? ★★★

People pass by this church without giving it a second thought, but please don't be one of them, because there's something very special in the basement that will make it worth a visit.

You'll find the church a short stroll from the Tower of London, directly opposite Tower Hill. That's where they used to set up the gallows every Saturday afternoon to give the crowd a bit of rowdy entertainment four hundred years ago. They gathered around here in their thousands to watch them stretch a few necks on the end of a noose, before the lifeless bodies were carted over to this church so their loved ones could weep in peace and carry them away, to wherever it was they dug their muddy hole.

So there's a lot of history attached to this place. It might not look it from the outside, but it's actually the oldest church still standing in the City of London. Samuel Pepys is supposed to have watched the Great Fire of London raging out of control from the steeple upstairs, and parts of the crypt are even older than the Tower of London next-door. Unfortunately it's also the unluckiest church in England because it's been blown up, burnt down and bombed, and only the tower and two of the exterior walls survive from olden times. The rest of it got obliterated by those damned Nazis in World War II. A lot of what you see today was rebuilt in the 1950s (it is immediately obvious which bits are old when you look at it). But don't give up on it just yet, because I promised you something amazing in the basement, and you won't be disappointed.

At the back of the church is a very narrow flight of stairs down to the crypt, where you'll find the holy of holies: a piece of tessellated Roman pavement that is still lying in the exact same spot where the Romans were standing 1,800 years ago. And that's not all, because the cramped little passage runs all the way under the church to a sunken chapel at the back.

It is the most unexpected thing that you can ever imagine. The whole thing is dimly lit and lined with Saxon stonework in the walls. They've got old roman bowls down there, ancient needles and keys, and silver and gold goblets from the 17th-century. There are a few interesting old pictures of London as well, plus some intricate little models of the church before it got damaged. They've even got an old crow's nest from one of Ernest Shackleton's Antarctic expeditions!

I'm not religious in the slightest, but this secret museum is one of the reasons why I love visiting London's churches.

If you like Roman history try the Museum of London. London's amphitheatre remains can be found at the Guildhall Art Gallery, and Billingsgate Roman House and Baths down the road. There's another church museum underneath St. Bride's.

Apsley House

Landmarks & Attractions | 11

ADDRESS Apsley House, 149 Piccadilly (Hyde Park Corner) - map 7d **TRAINS** Hyde Park Corner (zone 1) **BUSES** 9, 10, 14, 19, 22, 52, 74, 137, 414 **PRICE** Adult £9.20; Senior (over-60) £8.30; Child (5-15) £5.50; Infant (under-5) free; Family (2 ad+3 ch) £23.90; Price includes a voluntary donation **OPEN** 10 AM to 4 PM (Sat-Sun only, Nov-Mar); 11 AM to 5 PM (Wed-Sun only, Apr-Oct); Last entry 30 mins before closing **WEB** english-heritage.org.uk/visit/places/ apsley-house **TEL** 0207 499 5676 **TIME REQUIRED** 1-1½ hours

Easy to get to? ★★★ Good for kids? ★☆☆ Value for money? ★★☆ Worth a visit? ★★☆

I went back to Apsley House today. I've been here once before but I didn't fully appreciate it the first time around because I didn't know who the Duke of Wellington was (which says a lot about my education). But as I'm getting older I seem to be growing more and more patriotic, and swapping out my pop-star heroes for PMs and generals. When I was a kid it was all about John Lennon and Kenny Dalglish, but now I like Nelson, Wellington and Oliver Cromwell. We don't make people like them anymore because war isn't glorified in the same way that it was. If you shot ten thousand enemies in the old days then they would have given you a medal and a ticker-tape parade. They would have named a few streets after you and put up a statue. But if you do the same thing nowadays, all you get is a kicking from the leftie press and a parliamentary enquiry. I suppose that is progress, of sorts. Victory is for the losers. But who have we got left to chisel on a statue? Do you think we'll be walking around Tony Blair's house in fifty years time, with pictures of his Middle Eastern wars hanging on the walls? *Ha ha, I don't think so.* It's unthinkable, isn't it? The only public figure worthy of a stone statue these days is the Queen.

Imagine living Wellington's life... campaigning across Europe with a quarter of a million men, stacking up the victories one after the other, and then giving Napoleon a kicking at Waterloo. That would have been more than enough for most people, but then he decided to follow it up with a stint as Prime Minister as well -- *twice!* And to top it all off, he ended his career with twenty five years as Constable of the Tower of London. That would have been enough for me, just on its own.

When the Duke was living here he was at the edge of built-up London, hence its impressive address: No.1 London. But these days it's just the top end of Piccadilly, where all the cars come roaring around Hyde Park Corner. It's a beeping, screaming, busy rush of buses, cars and thundering lorries, overlooking one of the busiest junctions in London. If the Duke awoke from his grave today then he would move house in a flash, to somewhere more peaceful.

Once you get inside the imposing stone facade everything settles down into a nice quiet scene. It's pretty much the same as the day he died, with all the paintings and furnishings still in situ, and if you like old art and antiques (and gloating over the French) then you'll love it.

The first room is the Plate and China Room, stuffed with hundreds of porcelain plates and china cups and silver swords in scabbards, given to him by the grateful heads of Europe after he booted Napoleon off the throne. It reminded me of the trophy room at Wembley, and I was half expecting to see the FA Cup inside.

The ground floor is pretty bland after that, just a couple of entrance halls where they keep the reception desk and shop. But if you head downstairs then you'll find a little one-room museum that is well worth a visit. Alongside some old coins and medals is Wellington's own death mask. Apparently it was modelled on his face three days after he died, so it's all lopsided where his face had caved in. And boy-oh-boy did he have a big Roman nose! They must have used up a whole packet of plaster to craft that big conk. On the top shelf is the death mask of his nemesis, Napoleon.

I should probably pause at this moment to say a few words about Napoleon, because he's as much a star of this house as the Duke. Everywhere you go you will see the two of them sharing the limelight. If there's a picture of Wellington on one wall, then there will invariably be one of the French Emperor, too. It seems as if Wellington was truly obsessed with him. He chased this guy around Europe for years and years, and when he knocked him down the little French fella escaped and got the whole ball rolling again. When Wellington defeated him for the final time at Waterloo it must have left a gaping hole in his life. Who was his nemesis then? No one. So he surrounded himself with pictures and portraits to revel in his wartime memories. It seems a bit odd to me, though... imagine if Churchill had plastered Chartwell with pictures of Hitler!

The main stairwell is a good case in point. You can look up two storeys as the stairs wind their way around the wall, and right in the middle is a statue of Napoleon butt-naked, save for a fig leaf on his privates. It is undoubtedly impressive, but I'm not sure that I'd want to look at Napoleon's butt every time I traipsed up the stairs -- but each to his own, I suppose. Imagine if Churchill had a big statue of Hitler in his hall, saluting in his birthday suit. That would have been totally crazy, wouldn't it? What on earth was the Duke thinking?

You'll find the State Rooms on the first floor, decorated in deep reds and golds. I managed to latch onto the back of a guided tour here. The guy said some interesting things about the paintings on display but I learnt more from the audio guide, to be honest. What they need to do is hire an old soldier to do it, to inject a bit of life into it; because when he showed you a painting of a battle he said plenty about the painter, but nowt about the fight. Everyone was standing there in silence and listening intently to the bloke who was boring everyone silly. Not much fun, so I sneaked off after a while and went around myself.

The Striped Drawing Room is where a lot of the most interesting pictures are kept, including a very famous portrait of the young Duke in his red crimson tunic. Look out for Horatio Nelson as well, and William Pitt above the door. The best of the bunch is the long shot of Waterloo, at the very height of the fighting. It's one of the very few paintings in the house that depicts a live battle. Smoke is drifting across the hills from all the cannons blasting back and forth, turning the sky into a muddy, bloody brown, whilst waves of soldiers are rolling across the hills to join in the slaughter.

The most famous space in the house is the Waterloo Gallery. It reminds me an awful lot of the King's Gallery at Kensington Palace. The walls are stuffed with more of the Duke's loot: pictures that he either nabbed from the baggage trains, or had been given by the victors. He grabbed some real good ones, too: pieces by Rubens, Reynolds and Velázquez. The subjects jump around from kings and queens to religious scenes and landscapes. There's also a big portrait of Mary I (Bloody Mary) at the far end -- a strange queen to have hanging on his wall. But I suppose you can't be too choosy when you're looting them from a baggage train.

Keep an eye out for the big one of Charles I on horseback, too (you can hardly miss it). I'm sure that I've seen this painting about ten times before -- it's following me around London. You can see similar images hanging at Kensington Palace and the National Gallery.

The last little room on the tour is the Portico Dining Room, which has a nice little collection of curiosities in a cabinet. You can see a lock of Copenhagen's hair (the Duke's trusty horse), and Wellington's old telescope and false teeth. They've also got a walking stick that doubled-up as his hearing-aid (it sounds daft, but it's true!). And, of course, there are the inevitable pictures of Napoleon on the wall, except this time we've got Bonaparte's brothers and Josephine, too.

You can visit the Duke's tomb at St. Paul's Cathedral. There is more about the Battle of Waterloo at the Guards' Museum.

ArcelorMittal Orbit

ADDRESS ArcelorMittal Orbit, Queen Elizabeth Olympic Park, Stratford **TRAINS** Stratford (zones 2 and 3) **BUSES** 97, 339, 388 **PRICE** Observation deck: Adult £12; Senior (over-60) £10; Child (3-16) £7; Infant (under-3) free;

Family (2 ad+2 ch, or 1 ad+3 ch) £32 -- Observation deck plus slide: Adult £15; Senior (over-60) £12; Child (8-16, and 1.3m tall) £10; Family (2 ad+2 ch, or 1 ad+3 ch) £46 **OPEN** 11 AM to 5 PM (Mon-Sun, Oct-Mar); 10 AM to 6 PM (Mon-Sun, Apr-Sep); Slide opens 30 mins after opening time; Last entry 30 mins before closing **WEB** arcelormittalorbit.com **TEL** 0333 800 8099 **TIME REQUIRED** 45 mins

Easy to get to? ★★☆ Good for kids? ★★☆ Value for money? ★☆☆ Worth a visit? ★☆☆

What a crazy name for an attraction: *ArcelorMittal Orbit*. It sounds like a Russian space station. It doesn't look much like a space station though. It looks more like a tangled knot of Christmas lights, or a collapsed crane. It's all twisted metal and bent bits of pipe and wire.

The first time I clapped eyes on this thing I thought it was supposed to be a modern art sculpture, but it's actually an 80-metre high observation deck that overlooks the old Olympic Park. I remember when this whole area was heaving with people in 2012 -- you could hardly walk five feet without getting a flag waved in your face. All of the kids wanted to be like Mo Farah, but now they're just sitting in their prams being pushed around by fat mums. All of the community volunteers have disappeared. There are a few lazy planes doing circles in the sky and a class of noisy children on a school trip, but that's about it.

The only parts of Stratford I bother to visit are the train station, shopping centre and old Olympic Park. That is more than enough for me -- there is only so much concrete and glass that you need to see in one day. You don't have any choice but to visit the shopping centre, because when you exit the station you get sucked into it. It's colossal. It's like a shiny ghost town that spreads out everywhere, full of empty tables in empty cafes, big shops with no one in them, escalators with no one on them, and security guards with nothing to do but pick up a few bits of litter. When the only thing the security guards have to chase is a crisp packet in the wind, then that is when you know it's a ghost town.

I'm sitting in a coffee shop and I've got practically the entire place to myself (it's 9 o'clock). It reminds me of airport shopping in the early hours of the morning. I've hung around a few early morning terminals in my time, waiting for my lazy plane at 3 AM, and everything is equally sleepy here. Same dreamy music. Same handbag women dawdling at the clothes stores, fixing their already perfect hair in the glass. Every now and then I see a river of businessmen come streaming down the corridor towards the exit, but that is the sum total of life in the Westfield Shopping Centre: an occasional blast of action and then it's back to distant music and me. These are the sounds of silence: an occasional shoe squeaking on the polished floor, a cleaner wringing out his mop, and a high-pitched screech as a seat is scrapped across the lino.

There's not a lot to do at the Olympic Park other than climb the tower. You can walk around the outside of the stadium, I suppose, and stroll along the bland canal, but that's pretty much it. So I suppose I will have to climb the damn tower now (I have run out of excuses). Why do observation towers always have to be so high? It didn't look this tall when I saw it from the train station, but it looks gigantic now that I'm standing underneath it squinting in the sun.

It's changed a bit since the last time I came here. The observation deck obviously wasn't making them enough money, because they've decided to wrap a giant corkscrew slide around it as well. It's that little silver pipe in my photo. (I don't mean the thick grey band -- that's the walkway. I'm talking about the thin little tube that twists and turns around it.) I haven't paid for my ticket yet, but I can tell you right now that there is absolutely no chance of me riding it. I might be mad, but I'm not crazy. I'm not sliding down it, and that's all there is to it. You can call me a pansy if you want to, but it's easy for you sitting there in the comfort of your own home -- I'm the poor test pilot who has to risk my life sliding down a toothpaste tube at five hundred miles an hour. Apparently it takes forty seconds to ride it, and you go quicker than the speed of sound. One guy even burst into flames. Another kid actually travelled back in time -- that is how fast he was going.

I'll take the lift up to the observation deck and describe that (I can just about handle that) -- but I'm not riding the slide. No way. *I'm not doing it!* There are only two things that I refuse to do in London: climb up to the highest dome of St. Paul's, and this.

The observation deck is actually quite pleasant. It's basically just a big circular room with floor to ceiling glass, and they've got a couple of touchscreens dotted around to show you what's what. And for some strange reason that I have never fully understood, they've also installed a couple of funny mirrors like you find at the funfair.

Unfortunately the view is a bit bland, because Stratford is too far away from the centre of town to pick out anything interesting. The City is a quite long way away, and whilst you can easily see tall buildings like the Gherkin, Sky Garden and The Shard, anything smaller than a tower block is difficult to find. The dome of St. Paul's is easy enough, but you can't see Big Ben. You can't see the Tower of London or Tower Bridge either. The London Eye is practically impossible to make out unless you have telescopic eyes (even *I* had to consult the touchscreen for that one). Around to the south you can see the O2 Arena and Canary Wharf. See if you can spot the cable car -- that will give you a challenge. You can see the power station at Greenwich as well, but the Royal Observatory and Old Royal Naval College are frustratingly hidden behind some tower blocks.

If you're a West Ham fan then you can peer down into the Olympic Stadium, I suppose, but all you can see are the seats -- the pitch is hidden by the big white roof.

There are actually two different observation levels, one below the other, and the lowest one is where the daredevil tube riders line up to die. That is where I am cowering right now. Obviously I am standing as far away from the queue as possible, just in case they accidentally drag me into it by mistake, but even I can see the look of fear on the riders' faces. I can see them all fidgeting with their partners, clutching what looks like a giant sleeping bag -- the kind of vice-like clutch that turns their fingers white, and brings out the sharp edges of their bones. As they inch closer to the tube they bash a crash helmet onto their head, wrap their elbows up in protective pads, and place their sleeping bag (their body bag) onto a metal shelf by the lip. I can't help thinking that the silver shelf looks like a mortuary slab. Then they shuffle their backsides into it, crack a few jokes to try to convince their friends that they're not absolutely petrified... and disappear. They literally vanish in a nano-second. One second they're there, and the next second all that remains is the trailing end of a high-pitched scream.

Have you ever seen those pressurised toilets on an airplane? When you flush the lever on those things everything gets sucked outside at supersonic speed -- well, that's exactly what it's like. It's like being sucked out of an airplane toilet.

I really cannot stress enough how terrifying this ride is -- it's the scariest thing in London. I would definitely think twice before sending a little kid down it. If you'd prefer something a little less scary then you can try the open-air walkway instead -- it's that big band of grey that wraps around the tower in my photo. If you are feeling totally daft then you can follow it all the way down to the ground, instead of using the lift. The floor seems a little bit flimsy to me, but hey, I'm a total wuss when it comes to heights.

If you like tall towers then try the Sky Garden, Shard, London Eye, One New Change and St. Paul's Cathedral.

Bank of England Museum

ADDRESS Bank of England Museum, Bartholomew Lane, The City - map 5e **TRAINS** Bank, Cannon Street, Mansion House, Monument (all zone 1) **BUSES** 8, 11, 21, 23, 25, 26, 43, 47, 48, 76, 133, 149, 242 **PRICE** Free **OPEN** 10 AM to 5 PM (Mon-Fri); Closed (Sat-Sun); Last entry 15 mins before closing **WEB** bankofengland.co.uk/education/pages/museum/visiting **TEL** 0207 601 5545 **TIME REQUIRED** 60-75 mins

Easy to get to? ★★★ Good for kids? ☆☆☆
Value for money? free Worth a visit? ★☆☆

I don't suppose many tourists bother to visit this museum, but I've always had a soft spot for this place. It sounds quite boring on paper (a museum about money?), but if you are prepared to give it a chance then it's a decent way to wile away an hour. Once you've got past the security scanners and the big burly guards at the door, you can have a nice little wander through four hundred years of British history.

I'm not really interested in the history of money -- I like it because there's lots of architectural history on show. They have cabinets full of old drawings and photos of the city stretching back 250 years, and I'm a sucker for those old street scenes -- I like seeing how the city has changed over the centuries.

The first room concentrates on the building itself, beginning with the little mansion where it all began, and then on to John Soane's replacement. I always thought that Soane's solid stone building was the one we had today, but it turns out that his was largely knocked down and remodelled in the 1920s. The only visible bit that survives today is the curtain wall that runs around the outside. Normally I let out a little sigh when I discover that an old building has been demolished, but having perused the pictures I think I prefer the new one (don't tell anybody that I said that, though).

Then you move onto the history of the Bank of England itself, and there's a lot of serious sounding stuff about stocks and shares, the South Sea Bubble, and the invention of the National Debt. There's plenty of interesting British history mixed in with this period (i.e., a lot of wars), so it's not quite as dry as it sounds.

Some of the exhibits are actually quite historic, like the faded old papers signed by Nelson and Marlborough. They've got some old dividends signed by George Washington and his missus as well, and the paper accounts of the composer Handel. A couple of the old charters are practically work of arts.

The central room is decorated with scantily clad stone statues of classical ladies, and discusses how they defended the bank with muskets and guns, and locked up the boxes with chunky metal keys that probably weigh more than me. Then you come across everybody's favourite display...

Forget about doing the lottery every week. Forget about buying some Premium Bonds and going down the bingo with your gran, because here's your chance to steal a genuine gold bar. I am standing in front of it right now, and it is looking like a solid bar of sunshine. They are certainly very trusting with it, considering that there are so many shifty-looking tourists around (there are a few people in here that I wouldn't let within fifty feet of it -- including me). They even let you touch it!

You are supposed to feed your hand through a hole in the front and try and lift it up. Obviously I managed it easy-peasy, because I'm super tough, but I don't know how all those weedy bank robbers manage it in the movies, because it weighs about fifty thousand tonnes. In the movies they always chuck a couple into a bucket and then cart them off to a waiting van out the back, but trust me -- if they tried that with this one, then they'd give themselves a hernia. If they dropped this gold bar onto their foot then it would go straight through their foot, straight through the floor, and end up making a crater in the concrete.

The final section is like a *Who's Who* of British coins. You can have a walk down memory lane and see the shillings and sixpences from your youth, and the guineas and groats (you'll have to be pretty old to remember those). I can just about remember the halfpennies from the 1980s, but only because that was half a week's wages at Sainsbury's.

Museums like this are never going to appeal to everyone, and I'm sure that the majority of tourists will be bored silly by it. But if you enjoy your London history (like me), and you enjoy looking at old photos of the city (like me), then I reckon you'll enjoy it (like me).

Banqueting House

ADDRESS Banqueting House, Whitehall, Westminster - map 8d **TRAINS** Charing Cross, Embankment, Westminster (all zone 1) **BUSES** 3, 11, 12, 24, 53, 87, 88, 159 **PRICE** If bought online: Adult £6.10; Senior (over-60) £5; Child (under-16) free -- If bought at the door: Adult £6.60; Senior (over-60) £5.50; Child (under-16) free; Price includes a voluntary donation **OPEN** Usually 10 AM to 5 PM (Mon-Sun), but may close early for events; Last entry 45 mins before closing **WEB** hrp.org.uk/banquetinghouse **TEL** 0844 482 7777 **TIME REQUIRED** 1 hour

Easy to get to? ★★★ Good for kids? ☆☆☆
Value for money? ★★☆ Worth a visit? ★★☆

I have a theory that you can gauge the age of a person solely by the kind of artwork they like -- it's a bit like counting the rings on a tree trunk. When you're a kid you like cartoons and comics, and when you're a teenager (a hoodlum) you enjoy ankle tattoos and spray painting your name on the side of somebody's house. When you reach university it's all about modern art and Jackson Pollock, and then ten years later it's classical art and landscapes. That's the stage of life I am at right now: the adult phase. The phase that happily pays ten quid just to see a Rubens on the roof.

When you take up watercolour painting on a deckchair in your garden, that's when you have to start worrying. Because that's when you've entered the final phase of life: the one where you slowly run out of colours. You just sit there squeezing out every last flake of paint from your dried-up toothpaste tube of Cobalt Blue until you're dead.

So that's my theory.

Banqueting House contains the greatest work of art in London. But it's biggest claim to fame is probably what happened outside in the street, because this is where Parliament chopped off the head of Charles I after the English Civil War.

I know we're supposed to be too civilised for the death penalty these days, but if it was up to me I would bring it back in a flash, otherwise history is going to suffer. Imagine if -- instead of having his head chopped off outside Banqueting House -- Charles was just impeached and stripped of his titles after an in-camera court case. Or instead of chopping off the head of Anne Boleyn, Henry VIII was just granted a quickie divorce in Southwark Crown Court. William Wallace wouldn't have been sliced up in Smithfield -- he would have accepted a sixty grand a year seat in the Scottish Parliament. Let's be honest, let me be blunt: Royal history ended with the abdication. Elizabeth II is probably the first monarch we've ever had who hasn't done a single thing worth writing about. Whereas all of our other monarchs had wars and laws and religious persecution to keep them busy, the most exciting thing that's ever happened to Liz was a curtain fire at Windsor Castle.

But let's not get too depressed about it, because we still have plenty of great history to visit in London; and Banqueting House is one of the best, because this is where Charles spent his final five minutes on planet Earth. Imagine him pacing up and down and praying, and gathering his thoughts as the crowd waited and baited and bayed him in the street outside. What we now call 'Whitehall' looked a lot different in those days, because Whitehall Palace was still standing and most of its buildings were made of wood. Banqueting House rose above the lot in shining stone, and if you look at some old paintings of the palace and the park beyond, then you can usually see its shoulders poking above the rooftops. It's hard to get a sense of how grand it was in those days, because if you look at it now then it's just one more grand facade amongst the government offices, but back then it was the stand-out building in the street.

The whole place is staffed by doddery old ladies, who look like they could be friends with the Queen with their posh voices and flowery dresses and perm-white hairdos. But I wish they would make more of an effort to tell its story, though, because despite the incredible history of the place, you're only really here to see the Rubens on the roof. For the first part of the tour they just point you down an impressive looking hallway towards twenty school chairs arranged around a TV. You then have to sit there for ten minutes whilst you watch a potted history of the building.

This is my number one hate when visiting an attraction: being plonked in front of a telly. Who wants to spend a pocketful of money getting into an attraction, just to sit in front of a television set? You may as well just stay at home and watch the Discovery Channel. If they want to explain the history of the building then they should do it through a collection of historical objects, pictures and paintings, not a bleedin' TV program. But anyway, I digress... once you've twiddled your thumbs for ten minutes watching the video alongside a load of other strangers, you have to return to the till to pick up an audio guide, and then she sends you up a flight of stairs to the second room. To be perfectly honest, at this stage of the tour I thought it was a load of rubbish. But then I stepped through the door and saw the famous ceiling and everything changed...

I don't normally get bowled over when I see a piece of art, but this Rubens on the roof is huge. It really is impressive. And I say that as a middle-aged bloke who has no particular interest in art. So if *I* find it impressive then you I'm pretty sure that you will, too.

The room itself is basically just a double-height hall with a big red canopy throne at the end. That's all it is. There is nothing else inside it (apart from the chandeliers), so you are here to see the Rubens on the roof, and that's all.

Staring up at the painting doesn't half do your neck in, though. You'll be looking up for so long that your bones will fuse into position. Luckily they've placed some mirrored tables on the floor so you can look up by looking down. And they've also got a few beanie bags dotted around so you can lie down and listen to the audioguide -- but I'm too old to sit on those things. If I sat on one of those cushions then I'd never be able to get back up again.

If you like impressive old buildings steeped in politics, then you might enjoy a visit to the Guildhall and Mansion House.

Battersea Park Children's Zoo

Landmarks & Attractions | 19

ADDRESS Battersea Park Children's Zoo, Battersea Park **TRAINS** Sloane Square (zone 1) plus 20 min walk, or 137 bus **BUSES** 19, 44, 49, 137, 156, 170, 314, 319, 344, 452 **PRICE** Adult £8.95; Senior (over-60) £7.95; Child (2-15) £6.95; Infant (under-2) free; Family (2 ad+2 ch, or 1 ad+3 ch) £29 **OPEN** 10 AM to 5.30 PM (Mon-Sun, summer); 10 AM to 4.30 PM or dusk (Mon-Sun, winter); Last entry 30 mins before closing **WEB** batterseaparkzoo.co.uk **TEL** 0207 924 5826 **TIME REQUIRED** 1-2 hours

Easy to get to? ★★★ Good for kids? ★★☆
Value for money? ★★☆ Worth a visit? ★★☆

I'm normally a bit of a cynic when I see a sign like 'Children's Zoo'. I just assume that it's a cheapo zoo. A zoo with no animals in it. A zoo where they've taken out all the lions and tigers and tropical birds, and replaced them with a load of pigs and chickens and swings and slides. So that is what I was expecting this morning as I was walking over the Albert Bridge. I thought it would be a quick half-hour looking at a pen full of sheep and three thousand hyperactive school kids tearing around the place screaming their heads off, and then back into town for something to eat. I wasn't expecting much of Battersea Park Children's Zoo.

My hopes were kindled a little as soon as I entered the gate, because the first thing you see is a big monkey cage. I couldn't find many monkeys in it, though. Maybe they were having a lie-in or something. Considering that it's such a small zoo they have quite a nice collection of them: capuchins, tamarins and squirrel monkeys. Nothing very big though -- no chimps. No orangutans or gorillas. We are not talking *Planet of the Apes* here. These guys are not going to be taking over the world any time soon. Most of them are probably no bigger than my shoe. They've built some runs from one cage to another as well, so you can see them clamber up and over the wire bridges to the other side. You can also peer into their little hutches, and spy on what they're doing when they think that they're alone.

In the centre of the zoo is a big grass enclosure with a couple of corrugated iron Nissan huts in it (that's what they looked like to me anyway -- those places where they parked Spitfires in the war). I stood there for two minutes scanning the scene for enemy animals, until eventually one decided to poke his head out of the door. It was a wallaby. Or maybe it was a kangaroo. It was definitely something with big feet anyway. He didn't do much hopping around or jumping up and down, and he didn't even budge when the zookeeper tipped a crate full of food into his pen. So there's another animal getting paid to sit around all day doing nothing. *Sack him!* Put him on the first boat back to Australia.

The only animal that actually engaged me in conversation was an emu. He tried to stare me out and followed me around the fence for five minutes, strutting his stuff, but I was equal to the challenge. I stared deep into his eyes (into his soul) until eventually he had to admit defeat and skulk away.

The only other 'zoo-like' animals they have are meerkats (those skinny little guys that sell insurance on TV). They stand up on their hind-legs at the faintest gust of wind, to see what peril is coming round the corner. They seem like the most paranoid animal on earth, forever looking out for dangers that don't exist. They are quite cute, I suppose. But apparently they can rip your head off in two seconds flat. If you stumbled into the meerkat enclosure by mistake then you are basically dead... they will strip your skin off like a pack of piranhas until all that's left are a pair of dry eyeballs. That is what someone told me down the pub anyway.

The rest of the animals on display are pretty tame. In London Zoo they have penguins and flamingos, but in here they've got chickens and ducks. London Zoo has lions and tigers, but in here it's two fat pigs and a pony. They've even got some guinea pigs and rabbits on display -- the same kind that you might find in a pet shop. I'm guessing that they caught half of their animals from Battersea Park next-door, because there are lots of identical-looking birds and ducks roaming free outside, whilst the ones in here are all banged up, like prisoners, unable to escape. It reminds me of that POW camp in *The Great Escape*, where freedom is just fifty feet away at the tree line.

The rest of the zoo is filled with kiddie swings and slides, and a couple of cafes for a drink. It's not the biggest place in the world, and you'll probably be done inside an hour.

So... is it worth checking out? Well, it's not something that I'd recommend to tourists. If you're a tourist then you're definitely better off going to London Zoo. But if you have some restless toddlers or some children of primary school age who are stuck for something to do during half-term, then you can probably wile away an hour or two in here quite happily. It's definitely one for the little kids, though. If you drag your teenagers along then you'll embarrass the hell out of them and they won't talk to you for weeks.

If you like animals then try the London Aquarium and London Zoo.

Benjamin Franklin House

ADDRESS 36 Craven Street (near Charing Cross station) - map 8b **TRAINS** Charing Cross, Embankment (both zone 1) **BUSES** 3, 6, 9, 11, 12, 13, 15, 23, 24, 29, 87, 88, 91, 139, 159, 176, 453 **PRICE** Architectural Tour: Adult £3.50; Senior (over-65) £3.50; Child (under-16) free -- Historical Experience: Adult £7; Senior (over-65) £5; Child (under-16) free **OPEN** Architectural Tour: 12 PM, 1 PM, 2 PM, 3.15 PM and 4.15 PM (Mon only) -- Historical Experience: 12 PM, 1 PM, 2 PM, 3.15 PM and 4.15 PM (Wed-Sun) **WEB** benjaminfranklinhouse.org **TEL** 0207 925 1405 **TIME REQUIRED** Architectural Tour: 25 mins -- Historical Experience: 45 mins

Easy to get to? ★★★ Good for kids? ☆☆☆
Value for money? ★★☆ Worth a visit? ★☆☆

The Benjamin Franklin House is the kind of place you walk past without even realising that it's there. For something that's talked about as the "first American Embassy" you might be hoping for something a little bit grand, but it's basically just a regular townhouse in a side street off Charing Cross. Franklin was just a normal guy back then, a middle man between the government and the colonies, so he didn't have much cash to spend on rent.

The tour begins in the basement where they've got a couple of cabinets full of bones and medical equipment. Apparently the house used to have an anatomy school in it, after Franklin left, but there's not a lot else to show because it's passed through plenty of hands since the 1770s, and all of Franklin's stuff has disappeared. They only stripped it back to its original fittings relatively recently, so you're basically looking at the bones of the building. There are no original pieces of furniture inside... just a couple of modern chairs for the oldies to sit on. The only objects that remain true to Benjamin's day are the wooden walls and floorboards, and creaky old staircase. So you're walking on the same floor that he did, and climbing the same old stairs, but you can't see any pictures or paintings that hung on his walls. You can't see his toilet or his kitchen or anything else -- every single room is bare -- apart from one room that has just got a modern desk in it.

There are two different tours on offer: an Architectural Tour and a Historical Experience. I did the historical one, so that's what the following review refers to.

It begins with a very American guy giving you a quick little intro into who he was, and what he did, and then you get taken upstairs by Polly. Polly was Franklin's landlady's daughter, and she gets played by an actress in period dress (a very pretty actress!). The rest of the tour consists of Polly leading you around the rooms and having a chat with other actors' voices coming out of the speakers, to dramatise the events in Franklin's life. At the same time as all of this is going on they project a few slideshows onto the walls so you can view a few pictures and paintings.

It sounds a bit lousy but it was actually quite well done. The lady played the role of Polly very well -- you could tell that she was a proper actress (if she isn't an actress

then she should be). It's just a shame that the rooms are very plain.

I think I'd only recommend it if you're already interested in American history, and you want to learn about the build up to the War of Independence, because it will be very boring otherwise. And don't take any kids, for chrissakes, because they will be bored out of their skin.

If you enjoy this then you might like Dr. Johnson's House. It's a totally different subject, but a similar style of house.

BFI IMAX Cinema

ADDRESS BFI IMAX, 1 Charlie Chaplin Walk, Waterloo - map 9c **TRAINS** Waterloo (zone 1) **BUSES** 1, 4, 26, 68, 76, 77, 139, 168, 171, 172, 176, 188, 211, 243, 341, 381, 507, 521, RV1 **PRICE** Off-peak time (Mon-Fri before 5 PM): Adult £16; Senior (over-60) £12; Child (3-14) £12; Infant (under-3) free; Family (2 ad+2 ch) £46, or £33.90 with 1 ad+2 ch -- Peak time (Mon-Fri after 5 PM, and Sat-Sun): Adult £18.50; Senior (over-60) £13; Child (3-14) £13; Infant (under-3) free; Family (2 ad+2 ch) £50, or £37.80 with 1 ad+2 ch **OPEN** Usually 10 AM to 11.30 PM **WEB** odeon.co.uk/cinemas/bfi_imax/ 211 **TEL** 0330 333 7878 **TIME REQUIRED** 2-3 hours, depending on the film

Easy to get to? ★★★ Good for kids? ★★★
Value for money? ★★☆ Worth a visit? ★★☆

The BFI IMAX is quite an original looking building for a cinema. It's shaped like a big tin drum, wrapped around in glass.

I've never seen a 3D movie before. They've been out for quite a while now, but this is my very first one. I've come to see *The Hobbit: The Battle of the Five Armies*. The foyer is full of grungy kids in spectacles, and lots of people who wouldn't look out of place at a *Star Trek* convention (...christ almighty, am I talking about myself?). I can see one young couple that are obviously here on a date, because she has slapped on a face-full of make-up and was obviously hoping for something nice and romantic, but he's dragged her along to *The Hobbit* instead, ha ha. Sitting in the back row watching dwarves and orcs smacking each other around the head.

It's been a long time since I've been to the cinema and I'd forgotten what it smells like. It's like rolling back time to when I was a kid. As soon as you step into the foyer you get that warm popcorny smell and space-opera music blasting out of the speakers. They've got a little Costa coffee shop downstairs, and once you've bought your ticket you can head up to the second floor where the big screen is. That's where they keep all of their popcorn, drinks and sweets stands, and some sofa seats and tables. I'm not really a big fan of popcorn, but what the hell, *it's the movies!* It's obligatory to stump up for a big tub of hot popcorn and one of those two-feet tall cardboard cups of Coke that has got about half a tonne of ice in it -- even though I know that I'll need a wee halfway through the movie.

The cinema screen is absolutely huge. It's supposed to be the biggest screen in the UK, and it looks about three storeys tall. It's not very curved though... maybe it's a little tiny bit curved (it's too dark to see). Do you remember those fake 3D cinemas that we used to visit as kids, in the amusement parks, where we had to stand up in the centre of a 180-degree screen that wrapped around our field of view? (Do you remember those?) We'd stand there rocking and rolling and spewing and swaying as it took us up and down and round and round a roller-coaster track. Well, those screens were so lifelike that they actually made my stomach heave. But this one is nothing like that. It's just a huge, flat cinema screen about three storeys tall. It will be interesting to see how 3D they can make it.

When you are a little midget like me, the worse thing that can happen at a cinema is being stuck behind a basketball player. But you don't have to worry about that at the BFI IMAX. Each row is a couple of feet above the next one, so they would literally have to be about three metres tall to block your view. The flat pan of my seat is roughly at the head level of the seat in front -- so that is how much space you've got.

Five minutes in and they have finally told us to put the glasses on, just as the credits start to roll. (I had mine on already, so I must have been looking at the 2D adverts; that will explain why it wasn't very 3D!) And wow... this thing really pops out at you! It's as if the screen is five feet from your face all of a sudden. It seems to be hovering above the heads of the audience in front, and I feel like I'm sitting inside the movie... I can see landscapes stretching all the way to the horizon and people lumbering and jumping towards the screen. The weather effects are really good as well, settling over the scene in a haze. I can peer through the clouds at the forests and towns down below, and see wheeling birds and crows and snowflakes flying towards my face.

I've just had a quick look at the movie without the glasses on, just to be nosey, and unsurprisingly it looks totally rubbish. If you take the glasses off then everything looks out of focus and blurred. It is just about watchable (but only just), but it wouldn't be very enjoyable, and it would probably give you a major migraine as well. But the glasses aren't as bothersome as I thought, anyway. I can feel them pinching the bridge of my nose a little bit, but you soon forget all about that as the movie starts playing.

The Science Museum has another IMAX. The big cinemas are in Leicester Square.

Big Ben

ADDRESS Big Ben, Houses of Parliament, Westminster - map 8d **TRAINS** Westminster (zone 1) **BUSES** 11, 24, 148, 211 **PRICE** Free for UK residents, but you must write to your MP for a ticket (there may be a 6-month wait); Under-11s not permitted **OPEN** Tours at 9 AM, 11 AM and 2 PM (Mon-Fri); Extra tour at 4 PM (Mon-Fri, May-Sep only) **WEB** parliament.uk/ visiting/visiting-and-tours/tours-of-parliament/ bigben **TIME REQUIRED** 1½ hours

Easy to get to? ★★★ Good for kids? children under-11 not allowed Value for money? free Worth a visit? ★★★

I climbed up Big Ben today and stood next to the bell, which was pretty cool. But it's not as easy to get into the clock tower as it is to get into Parliament itself... which is a bit weird. You can't just turn up and ask for a tour. You have to write a letter to your local MP first and ask for a ticket. I did that way back in May, and got a place four months later -- so that shows you how far in advance you have to book (or maybe I just have a lousy MP!). They make you fill in a little spreadsheet with all your personal details as well, so the security people can check you're not a terrorist.

When you finally get the acceptance letter they make it sound a lot scarier than it actually is. First of all they insist that you bring two forms of ID with you (like a passport, driving license or utility bill). And then they ban everything from your camera to your phone. If you turn up one minute late, they say, then you won't be allowed in. And on the next page and they start talking about the stairs... no one with heart complaints, no one with breathing problems or vertigo can go, and pregnant women shouldn't even think about it. It's 334 spiral steps to the top, which is twenty more than The Monument (a stone obelisk in The City). And I remember having problems climbing that with my dodgy knees, so you can imagine how much I was looking forward to Big Ben after reading that letter. I was seriously starting to have second thoughts. But it turns out that I had nothing to worry about...

The meeting point for the tour is across the road in Portcullis House, where all the MPs have their offices. That is where you'll be frisked and have you photo taken. They'll also confiscate your bags and cameras (so no photos allowed). I thought that it was quite a good place to start the tour because it lets you have a little nose around an inaccessible building. You don't get to see much more than the open-plan foyer, though, but at least you can see the notorious trees. (So that's where all of our taxes are going -- the MPs are planting trees indoors!) Our guide even told us a little bit about the history and layout of Portcullis House, which was a bonus. After that you head straight through a tunnel to Parliament, passing right underneath the busy road.

The tour doesn't cover any part of Parliament other than the clock tower, it's strictly about Big Ben. And the first part is by far the hardest -- 115 steps to the first room. So rest assured that you don't have to climb all 334 steps in one go, which was certainly a relief to me. The guide splits it up into four stages with a long rest in-between where he does some talking. So when you get that scary letter warning you to write your will beforehand, just ignore it; if you've ever managed to climb up The Monument or St. Paul's Cathedral then you will find this easy-peasy.

The first part of the talk was all about the history of the building and the bell: who designed it, who built it, who installed it, etc. Our guide was pretty good and he went into plenty of detail, but there's not a lot to see in this first room: just a big poster on the wall and some seats were you can stop and catch your breath. There's not a lot to see when you're climbing up the stairs, either. It's basically just a load of tight windy stone steps, with some narrow windows every now and then to let in some light.

After that you head up another flight of stairs to the clock mechanism. This is a big old iron thing with cogs and wheels and pulleys, and a pendulum that disappears into a hole in the floor. The entire machine is enclosed inside this one room, with rods that disappear into the ceiling and walls to pull the clocks and bong the bells. Just before it struck half-past nine he warned us about a coming cacophony of noise, and he wasn't joking: when the whole thing whirred into action it scared the living daylights out of us. It was like being trapped inside a factory. Pulleys pulled, levers banged up and down, cogs clanked round and round, and the colossal bells sounded out tens of meters above our heads.

One interesting little thing that we saw in here were the pennies on top of the pendulum, to keep it in time. It sounds really low-tech, but every time they put a penny on top it speeds up the clock by 0.2 seconds. If you look closely then you can see a whole stack of them just sitting there, rocking back and forth on top.

After that bit of excitement you head up to the belfry to see the Big Ben bell itself. You actually get to stand inside the bell room, just six feet away from the hammer and bell. Whilst we were waiting for showtime he pointed out some interesting cracks in the casing and some mighty great holes, which apparently gives the bell its distinctive sound, and you can enjoy some fine views of the skyline, looking down upon Parliament and Whitehall.

But the highlight is obviously when the old guy goes off. When 10 o'clock came we were standing just six feet from the bell (no joke!). Our guide had handily dished out some earplugs beforehand, which we were obliged to wedge into our lugs, but it was still incredibly loud -- loud enough to make your bones vibrate. It made my eyes shake. I think a few of my teeth crumbled into dust as well. And it's not just Big Ben chiming either: there are several bells all around you (one for each note of the tune), all bonging and donging like tuneful thunder.

After that he takes you back downstairs and stops off at the huge clock faces, towering twenty feet from top to bottom. You can even see the shadow of the gigantic hands outside, passing across the panes of glass. Our guide pointed out a little peephole that can be popped out to clear the pigeons off the hands, but sadly he wasn't allowed to open it, otherwise we could have all stuck our heads out and sung a song.

And that was it, sadly. All that remained was for us to walk back down.

It's definitely worth jumping through all the hoops and writing to your local MP. How many people can say they've stood next to the Big Ben bell when it chimed ten?

If you enjoy the Big Ben tour then you might like a Houses of Parliament tour.

Billingsgate Roman House and Baths

ADDRESS Billingsgate Roman House and Baths, 101 Lower Thames Street, The City - map 10b **TRAINS** Monument (zone 1) **BUSES** 15, 35, 40, 43, 47, 48, 78 **PRICE** £8 **OPEN** Occasional weekends only. Keep checking this site for the dates: cityoflondon.gov.uk/things-to-do/visit-the-city/attractions/pages/roman-bathhouse.aspx **TIME REQUIRED** 45 mins

Easy to get to? ★★★ Good for kids? ☆☆☆
Value for money? ★☆☆ Worth a visit? ★★☆

I don't normally get up early on a Sunday morning... I didn't even know that Sunday morning existed. But they are opening up an interesting little place today so I thought I'd go and check it out.

Apparently there are some remains of an old Roman bathhouse in the basement of an office block in Lower Thames Street. That's where all the Roman wharves used to be, near the Tower of London today. It only opens up occasionally, so you've got to take your chance when it comes. If that means getting up early on a Sunday morning then so be it.

I've always thought it was a great shame that we didn't take better care of our Roman remains, because there's not a lot left of Roman London today. I blame Queen Boudicca and Adolf Hitler. If they hadn't come along and burnt it all down then we could still have the city wall, the forum, basilica and amphitheatre. But all we've got left nowadays are a few bits and pieces of the wall, a few disappointing blocks from the amphitheatre, and whatever statues they've managed to salvage for the Museum of London. There's supposed to be a Temple to Mithras down Queen Victoria Street, but I've never actually seen it myself because of all the building work going on. It's been boarded up behind wooden walls for the past few years, whilst they construct another office block behind. So that will probably end up in a city basement too. The closest that you can get to ancient Italy these days is a skip full of battered old pizza boxes round the back of Dominos. I suppose Little Venice sounds quite Italian. But that's about as Italian as a pair of chopsticks.

One hour later... well that was interesting. I've been inside and seen it now. It was housed inside a very boring office block, maybe the blandest building in the entire city. When you go inside you have to sign your name in a tatty old book and then they give you a quick little lecture about what you'll see downstairs. Then you all troop down a flight of concrete stairs in anticipation.

The remains are a good ten-feet below street level, and it feels like the cupboard door to Narnia when you're walking down those stairs -- it's like a portal to the ancient world. What treasures will you find down there? What will you see? Will there be gladiators? Will we see Caesar's bones and a few mosaics? Maybe some pastel frescos painted on the wall?

Er... no. What you find when you enter the gloomy chamber is a pile of broken bricks and smashed up stones, lined with wooden planks and metal poles and scaffolding for pathways. It's basically like a building site. In fact, if I stumbled across this place on a walk around London then I'd just assume that it was an abandoned building project. To my untrained eye it doesn't even look old. There are no mosaics, or anything like that. Apparently you can see a furnace, a hypocaust, a hot room, warm room and cold room, but what remains of the walls are very low-level, and the rooms are hard to pick out from your solitary vantage point. It's amazing that the archaeologists can even work out what they're looking at.

The most interesting exhibit for me was a little Saxon brooch that was found nestled amongst the collapsed roof tiles. Apparently a man from the 5th-century was rooting around the remains of this 1st-century bathhouse, and dropped his little bit of bling in the rubble. So in a way he was exactly like us: having a poke around the already ancient remains, to see what he could see. I wonder if he got up early on a Sunday morning, too?

If you like Roman ruins then try the Museum of London. You can see London's amphitheatre at the Guildhall Art Gallery, and there's a piece of old Roman pavement in All Hallows by the Tower. The city of Bath is also well-worth a day-trip.

Borough Market

ADDRESS Borough Market, Southwark Street, Southwark - map 10a **TRAINS** London Bridge (zone 1) **BUSES** 17, 21, 35, 40, 43, 45, 47, 48, 133, 141, 149, 381, 521, RV1 **OPEN** 10 AM to 5 PM (Mon-Thu); 10 AM to 6 PM (Fri); 8 AM to 5 PM (Sat); Closed (Sun); Note: The full market only operates Wed-Sat. There's a half market on Mon-Tue **WEB** boroughmarket.org.uk **TEL** 0207 407 1002 **TIME REQUIRED** 15 mins (but more if you plan to stop and eat)

Easy to get to? ★★★ Good for kids? ★☆☆
Value for money? free Worth a visit? ★★☆

Give McDonalds a miss today and come to Borough Market instead. This is a foodie market, for gourmet foodies... for people who like to pimp their dinner in nuts and sauces and make it look like a work of art.

Their burgers are huge! They are like solid footballs of meat. I'm guessing that the butcher has just cut the legs off a cow and dumped what's left straight onto his sizzling, smoky tray of flames. Five minutes in that furnace and it will be done. Put a bit of tomato sauce on top, a few grilled onions (no salad), and there's your dinner.

If you think the burgers are big then check out the cheeses... they are like solid stone sundials. It would take two of you just to carry one home. I suppose you could drill a hole through the middle and use it as a wheel. These are proper cheeses, covered in varicose veins and a white fluff of fungus. And what a variety of textures and colours: some of the wedges are creamy white and covered in bark, whilst other ones are roughed up like a sheet of sandpaper.

This place is hardcore: all the fish still have their heads, all the meat is covered in blood, and all the cheeses smell like they've been sitting in the sun for three weeks. There are lots of very strong aromas all around the place, and it reminds me of the perfume counter at Selfridges. Every time I walk inside that place my eyesight goes black and white from the toxic fumes, and it's the same in here -- you can tell the fish stall is coming from fifty feet away. They've got an oyster stall with tubs and buckets of shells that look like they've been sloshed straight from the sea -- they've still got the ocean foam on top. I can see a row of lobsters lined up like Red Army soldiers, slimy eels stretched out like striped ties in a suit shop, and a tray of vinegary whelks and winkles.

Check out the bakers and cake makers: they don't sell boring bread rolls like you buy in Tesco. These ones have been sculptured into swirling shapes, dipped into seeds, and brushed with a face-full of flour. Another stall is piled high with pies -- huge chunky pork pies and shoe-sized pasties.

The greengrocer has arranged his vegetables like flowers. It's all raspberries and apricots, pale pink turnips and a pine tub of cauliflowers, looking like the base of a wedding bouquet. He's got an old ship barrel full of deep green olives and nuts. It's so pretty you don't want to take anything out in case it ruins his display.

Try and find Maria's Market Cafe -- that's one of my favourite coffee stops in London. It's not a posh place. It's more like a builder's cafe with plastic checkerboard tablecloths and chunky mugs of tea. It's the kind of place that puts a bottle of tomato sauce on the table for your bacon sandwich.

British Library

ADDRESS British Library, 96 Euston Road, St. Pancras - map 3b **TRAINS** Euston, King's Cross St. Pancras (both zone 1) **BUSES** 10, 30, 59, 63, 73, 91 **PRICE** Free, but there may be a charge for temporary exhibitions **OPEN** 9.30 AM to 6 PM (Mon, Fri); 9.30 AM to 8 PM (Tue-Thu); 9.30 AM to 5 PM (Sat); 11 AM to 5 PM (Sun); Last entry 1 hour before closing **WEB** bl.uk **TEL** 0207 412 7332 **TIME REQUIRED** 45-60 mins

Easy to get to? ★★★   Good for kids? ☆☆☆
Value for money? free   Worth a visit? ★☆☆

If the Victorians had built the British Library 150 years ago then I'm guessing it would have been fantastic. But, alas, we built it ourselves, twenty years ago, so we ended up with this instead. *What a monstrosity!* It looks like a multi-story car park. It's three million bright red bricks, piled up into the first shape they could think of... the cheapest shape possible. Even the clock looks like something out of playschool. It really is ugly. It's even uglier than me, and that is saying something, because I am pretty ugly.

I am reminded of that story about St. Basil's Cathedral in Red Square... about how Ivan the Terrible loved it so much he poked the architect's eyes out so no one else could build anything as beautiful. Well, we should do the same thing with the bloke who built the British Library, but for the total opposite reason: so we don't ever again have to look at anything as bad.

Mercifully, once you step inside it starts to get a bit better. It opens up into a vast entrance hall with some bookcases spanning several floors. It's nothing to write home about, but it's certainly better than the outside.

The only interesting exhibits for a tourist are in a room called 'Treasures of the British Library', which is very dark and quiet inside, and even a little reverential. It's full of dimly lit display cases filled with books and faded manuscripts. They have some old music scores as well, by the likes of Beethoven, Bach and Mozart, and some handwritten scraps by The Beatles. The literature section has tomes by Ben Johnson and Shakespeare, and a few of Leonardo da Vinci's old notebooks, opened up so you can see his scribblings and pictures.

There are plenty of truly historic documents on show: like a letter from Galileo, written one month before his trial, and some pieces by Anne Boleyn, Elizabeth I and Mary I. They also own a letter from Charles I, written whilst he was banged up inside Carisbrooke Castle, and Admiral's Nelson's last letter to Lady Hamilton, written two days before the Battle of Trafalgar. Or how about Captain Scott's diary from his fateful voyage to the South Pole? The absolute holy of holies is a copy of the Magna Carta from 1225.

After that comes lots and lots and lots (and lots and lots) and lots of decorated bibles and religious texts. All very old and beautiful. And there are some early pamphlets from the dawn of printing too, plus some old maps and landscapes.

That's basically all that you can see as a tourist. You need to get hold of a 'Reader Pass' if you want to see inside the actual library itself -- and they vet everybody beforehand. You need to tell them which book you want, and why you need it, before they let you loose amongst the books; so it's not as simple as just turning up and sitting down for a read.

They are supposed to have a copy of every book every printed in Britain in here, so I wonder if my book is here? I doubt it. The only way I'll get catalogued in here is if I break in overnight and catalogue it myself (that's a good idea actually -- I might do that). I'm guessing that this book will probably sell about five copies at most... and I'm buying four of those for my family. So that means that you bought the fifth one -- *cheers*. But you shouldn't measure success by sales anyway, because it is a well-known fact that 95% of customers are idiots (obviously I don't mean you). Take Van Gogh for example -- the greatest painter who ever lived -- he didn't sell a single picture in his entire lifetime. His paintings just sat gathering dust on his mantelpiece until he shot himself, and it's the same with my guidebook. We are like two peas in a pod, me and Vince. The only difference between him and me is that I'm not nuts. Or maybe I am. I'm sitting in the British Library talking to myself.

If you're interested in literature then try the Charles Dickens Museum, Sherlock Holmes Museum and Dr. Johnson's House.

British Museum

ADDRESS British Museum, Great Russell Street, Bloomsbury - map 3f **TRAINS** Goodge Street, Holborn, Russell Square, Tottenham

Landmarks & Attractions | 29

Court Road (all zone 1) **BUSES** 1, 7, 8, 10, 14, 19, 24, 25, 29, 38, 55, 59, 68, 73, 91, 98, 134, 168, 188, 242, 390, X68 **PRICE** Free, but there may be a charge for temporary exhibitions **OPEN** 10 AM to 5.30 PM (Sat-Thu); 10 AM to 8.30 PM (Fri); Last entry 10 mins before closing **WEB** britishmuseum.org **TEL** 0207 323 8299 **TIME REQUIRED** 2½-3 hours

Easy to get to? ★★★ Good for kids? ★☆☆
Value for money? free Worth a visit? ★★☆

My idea of hell is spending all day in a big museum filled with stones, bones and busted cups and plates, whilst simultaneously trying to dodge an unstoppable army of hyperactive school kids running around shouting and snapping photographs of everything they see. If you throw in a few thousand tourists as well, then that is a perfect summation of the British Museum -- *it's hell on earth!*

Quality control goes right out of the window when it comes to museums. In an art gallery, the works generally have to be of a pretty high standard to get on the wall (unless it's modern art, of course). But in a museum, if it's old, it's in. If it's broken, it doesn't matter. They have marble statues with their heads missing, cracked vases with their handles snapped off, and a dusty pit filled with old bones and leathery skin.

Plenty of people love this place, and plenty of others just pretend to like it (to make themselves look clever), but I think it's one of those attractions that you are supposed to *appreciate*, rather than enjoy, because there are only so many pots and rocks that you can look at before you start to fall asleep. They've got more stones in here than on Brighton beach. The last time I saw this many bones was at the London Fashion Show. But I'm not a complete philistine, and I do like the building -- that is the highlight for me. The outside looks like something we copied from Rome. And when you step through the front door you'll be treated to the finest sight in the entire museum: the Great Court. This place used to be a giant open courtyard until Norman Foster came along and stuck a diamond sheet of glass on top. Now it's one of the brightest and whitest rooms in London, with the famous Reading Room in the centre. That's the circular room where Karl Marx used to come every lunchtime to write his *Communist Manifesto*. Unfortunately it's not possible to see his version of the Reading Room anymore because it's all been shipped over to the British Library, and they use the space for temporary exhibitions instead.

I've been to quite a few of their temporary exhibitions, and I must say that they are very hit and miss. The best ones are when they bring in objects from other museums around the world; but sometimes they will just assemble a lot of the British Museum's own items into a specific theme (like the afterlife), and then you are stumping up money to see stuff that might be on show for free six months later. And not all of the exhibitions take place in the Reading Room, either -- so if that's your sole reason for going then remember to check which room it's in first.

All of the big galleries lead off from the sides of the Great Court, and you can be walking around the place for days if you don't know where you're going. This museum is *huge*. In fact, let me spell that word again, incorrectly this time, so you can understand just how big it is: it is *huuuuge!* And what makes it even more confusing is that some of the countries span a couple of different floors, so when you think you've exhausted all of the Egyptian stuff downstairs you'll climb a flight of steps and find another six rooms full of sarcophagi.

The crowds can be suffocating at times. The Egyptian galleries are the worst, because everybody steams straight in there as soon as they step through the front door; and of course they all go straight for the one thing that you want to see: the famous Rosetta Stone. It's only a little slab of stone but it must have a hundred people crowding around it at the moment (and that's not an exaggeration). Imagine one hundred people and two hundred elbows, with fifty flashbulbs cracking and bouncing bright white light off the glass. That is your view of the Rosetta Stone.

But if you like Ancient Egypt then it's a must-see. Some of the wall paintings and artwork are so sharp and colourful that they look like they were painted yesterday. Some of the statues and monuments are colossal. They have huge walls lifted straight out of tombs, and gigantic temple fronts and gateways. I don't think the Assyrians will be too happy when they see how many of their city walls we demolished.

And then we come to the Greeks... *here we go*. (Get ready for a shouting match!) Yes, we did destroy half of your priceless Parthenon and cart it back to England, but we had the permission of the Turks, you see, who defeated you in war -- and all's fair in love and war. The Germans demolished half of London during World War II, and you don't hear us complaining about that (much). My own personal view is that I'm all for grabbing statues and trinkets, but when we find ourselves tearing down standing structures then that is a step too far. That is called looting. Our argument for keeping hold of the Elgin Marbles seems to be that we're protecting them from further damage (aren't we the ones you damaged them?), but most of them are already broken up and busted anyway. These things are not in pristine condition, and it's difficult to see how much worse they could be. There are very few figures that aren't already well-worn or busted. I suppose most of the damage occurred when the Turks were taking potshots at them with their cannons, but I don't think us chiseling them off the walls helped much.

But it's none of my business. The world is going to carry on spinning whoever has them, and we stole them fair and square. I don't think the Greeks quite appreciate how much time and effort it must have taken for us to dynamite those things off the walls and ship them back to Blighty. That was no easy feat -- and they want us to just give them back? *Those crazy Greeks!*

The European galleries are full of Saxon shields and swords, pots and boxes and farming tools, but the best bits are the treasure troves -- the silver plates from Mildenhall and Sutton Hoo. They have some interesting bodies of bones and leathery skin in there as well, still lying in their dying pose at the bottom of a bog.

Sometimes I think that this is my best chance of becoming famous: by dropping dead in a quiet field someplace, holding tight to a silver cup from Habitats, and then waiting for an archaeologist to dig me up in a hundred years. All you have to do is wear a pair of leather boots and a beaded necklace and he'll convince himself that you were a Saxon king to further his career. A few years later you'll end up in a glass case at the British Museum, exactly like this bloke. Museums are full of people like this... Stone Age losers whose bones happened to have lasted the longest because a big bully pushed them headfirst into a tar pit. Nobody dies a good death in a tar pit, do they? If you were thinking of topping yourself, then your first thought wouldn't be to drown yourself in a stinking hole of oil and sludge at the bottom of a swamp. So this guy clearly didn't have a good death. The village bullies were probably standing around pointing at him (like we are now), laughing at his predicament, as they watched him slowly sink beneath the putrid slime. And now we have immortalised his shame and compounded his embarrassment by nailing up a plaque beside his bones: *"This loser fell into a swamp!"*

I know we are all supposed to love and support Africa these days, and yes, Nelson Mandela is a saint and so is Mother Theresa and that Desmond Tutu fella, but I'm sorry... their historical artefacts are a load of pants. Mankind is supposed to have originated in Africa and all they have to show for it at the British Museum are a lot of sticks and spears and scary Halloween masks. They've nabbed a few wooden canoes, too, and what looks like a straw handbag, but that's about it -- it's all bone combs, beads and necklaces, and whatever basket weaves they've managed to salvage from the desert.

You might also enjoy the Victoria & Albert Museum and Sir John Soane's Museum.

Brompton Cemetery

ADDRESS Brompton Cemetery, Fulham Road **TRAINS** Earl's Court (zones 1 and 2), West Brompton (zone 2) **BUSES** 14, 74, 190, 211, 328, 414, 430, C1, C3 **PRICE** Free **OPEN** 8 AM to 4 PM (Nov-Jan); 8 AM to 5 PM (Feb, 2nd half of Oct); 8 AM to 6 PM (Mar, mid-Sep to mid-Oct); 8 AM to 7 PM (Apr, 1st half of Sep); 8 AM to 8 PM (May-Aug) **WEB** royalparks.org.uk/parks/brompton-cemetery **TEL** 0207 352 1201 **TIME REQUIRED** 1 hour
Easy to get to? ★★★ Good for kids? ☆☆☆ Value for money? free Worth a visit? ★☆☆

Is there a nicer place to walk than a graveyard in the rain? I'm pretty sure that the corpses prefer it, too -- the sun isn't much fun when you're six feet under. At least with the rain they can have a little taste of the outside world as it comes seeping through the coffin top. It must be the only drink they get all week: a thimble of dirty rainwater, filtered through the mud. It's not much of a life is it, being dead? I can't say that I'm looking forward to it.

I'm in a miserable mood this morning and I don't mind admitting it. I'm the kind of guy who draws the curtains when the sun comes up. I'm spending my free time sitting on a bench in Brompton Cemetery for chrissakes -- is that normal? Graves to the left of me, graves to the right, and no one is saying a word because they are all dead. This bench is nearly dead as well. Half the beams have been kicked in by the kids, and the bench is covered in a greeny-grey fungus. I notice the smell of wet wood and birds coughing in the treetops.

Cemeteries always remind me of going to the zoo: people gawping at the creatures in their cages, and here I am, gawping at the corpses in theirs. What a lazy life they lead. No TV, no radio. No more flowers, no more visitors... no one gives a toss about them any more because too much time has passed. That's when you're truly dead: when you're not even somebody's distant memory. Once the weeds have gotten hold and covered up your name, then you are truly finished. There's no coming back from that; you're being entombed all over again by the weeds and autumnal leaves.

I can hardly see where I'm stepping most of the time because the place is so thick with nettles and a mulchy slew of soggy wet weeds. Am I stepping on somebody's head? *Sorry ma'am*, I say. *Sorry sir*, I didn't mean to walk on your face. But maybe if you'd taken a bit more care of your pit then I would have seen you. They're a load of lazy bones, these corpses. Never get out of bed to do the housework, even on a nice day like today... they're wasting their whole lives away.

Not everybody in here is deceased. I can see a council worker having a cheeky fag and tapping happily on his knee as he relaxes on a bench. There are quite a few joggers all red-faced and puffing and panting as well. They will probably end up in here as well if they're not careful -- these graves are probably full of super-fit joggers.

I wonder how many people are buried here? Everywhere I look there are rows upon rows of graves and toppled over tombstones. Some of them have got big monumental crosses on top and big huge rooms like a mausoleum; but most of them are just dull stone slabs on the grass, slowly tilting sideways as their foundations give way. What a way to go, having your own gravestone topple into your coffin -- that's really rubbing it in. You truly know you're dead when your bones are crushed into dust by your own tombstone. Ouch.

It is very quiet now. I can hear a low rumble of buses on the street outside, and then it's just me and the breeze. That's the only thing that touches my face these days: the weather.

This grave has got a candle on it. It must have been here for a thousand years judging by the sorry state it's in. Poor old Leon Dunin Wolski. No one gives a toss about you any more, mate. I'm sorry to break it to you, but that's the brutal truth. Not even the groundsman has stopped by in a hundred years. If I had a lighter I might have brought your candle back to life, but I don't smoke... so that's it. Sorry, mate. Excitement over -- you can go back to sleep now.

Here's another tomb of William Taylor. He's been dead for twenty years, but he's still got fresh flowers on his grave. 'To a loving husband' it says, and I guess he was, because somebody obviously still cares for him (probably his mistress).

This next one has got a story to tell as well... it's surmounted by a framed marriage photo of them cutting the cake. Although it looks like a young couple in their twenties, the woman is already six feet under, all overgrown and forgotten. It doesn't look like the groom's been around since she died, so I guess he's found himself another woman. It didn't take him long to get over her death did it? I think you're better off without him, lady. You had a lucky escape there.

Do you know what all these corpses have in common? They all know whether God exists. They have all dropped dead and discovered the truth. I have my doubts about the Almighty, so I'm guessing that there are a lot of peed-off people in this cemetery... they've all been robbed of their promises and packaged up in boxes of rotting wood. It's like a train station to nowhere. No more trains to heaven, folks, it doesn't exist! You're stuck here forever... end of the line. The priests sold you a pup.

You might like to visit Highgate Cemetery.

Brompton Oratory

ADDRESS Brompton Oratory, Brompton Road, South Kensington - map 6f **TRAINS** South Kensington, Knightsbridge (both zone 1) **BUSES** 14, 74, 414, C1 **PRICE** Free **OPEN** Usually 7 AM to 7 PM (Mon-Sat); 8 AM to 8 PM (Sun) **DENOMINATION** Roman Catholic **WEB** bromptonoratory.com **TEL** 0207 808 0900 **TIME REQUIRED** 30 mins

Easy to get to? ★★★   Good for kids? ☆☆☆
Value for money? free   Worth a visit? ★★☆

It's darker in here than it is outside, and it's night outside. I'm sitting in the pews staring up at the altar wondering if there's anybody home. *Give me a sign!* Make the candles flicker on and off or something. Two thousand years ago he was curing lepers and turning water into wine, and now he can't even huff and puff a candle out. If I were God I would be going on TV every Saturday night just to prove that I still exist. But he doesn't seem to care anymore. He has lost interest in us. If we believe, we believe; and if we don't, he doesn't care -- he's run out of sons to spread the word. We bumped off the last one, so you can't blame him.

This church is beautiful, and any description I give here is not going to do this place justice. St. Paul's Cathedral is all airy and bright inside, but this place is dim and dark and full of silent shadows, and that's how a church should be. The dead don't want to sleep in the sunlight, they want somewhere like this. Somewhere that doesn't hurt their dried-up eyes.

I hate to think how much money they must have lavished on this place. There's gold, for sure, but that's not what makes it memorable. It's all dark, sooty stone and dirty dull creams. A bit of blue, too -- the same colour as a storm. Imagine a grey sky rolling in with rumbling thunder and enough wind and rain to end the world... that's the colour of this place. A brooding, moody building. The only light that I can find is coming from a few circular windows in the ceiling; the rest is just a rack of candles in the chapels.

Wear-worn faces stare down everywhere you look: on the statues, the mosaics and paintings, and even on the wooden carvings by the stall. But if they're trying to tell me something, then they're wasting their time: I'm a non-believer. The only person worth listening to in here is me. I reckon that's why people sit in here for hours on end, just to have a chat with the only person who cares: themselves.

There's an old woman kneeling in the side chapel praying for something she wants God to sort out. Put ten pence in the collection box love, and he'll do whatever you want. Isn't that how it works? And light a candle, too -- make a wish, like a kid blowing out the candles on his birthday cake. The statue of Jesus just looks down at her with his stone eyes and stony face, deaf and dead. She'd be better off asking her kids to fix whatever problems she's got. God never used to answer my prayers. He only answers your prayers if you've already provided the answers in the first place. But that's only fair, isn't it? You've got to help yourself to help yourself in this world -- He's not a miracle worker.

I can hear the sound of footsteps walking up the aisle behind me, and I can tell by their pace that they've only come in for a gander. It must be a businessman because he's wearing very squeaky shoes. Posh shoes, I am guessing -- Mister Posh Shoes. Then it's back to silence as he sits down in a pew. The only other sound that pervades the place is a quiet rumble around the room like distant traffic. It must be coming down the Brompton Road and straight in through the letterbox. It's a bit like those pigeons that fly around Waterloo station and get trapped inside the concourse: the sound has slipped inside and can't get out. I'm thinking of having a quiet cough, just to leave my mark on the place. Make a noise in here and it settles like dust for a hundred years.

I have noticed one of those confessional boxes off to the side. I remember being shoved inside one of those when I was a kid. I can't remember exactly what I did (I used to make my sins up just to keep him happy, because I was never naughty), but I do remember the punishment: *five Hail Marys*. That's not much of a punishment is it? If they started handing out proper sentences then maybe people would stop sinning. If I was a priest and somebody admitted to stealing a biscuit, I would knock his teeth out. Let's see you try and eat a biscuit with no teeth, I would say! They'd soon stop doing that. Do you know what a priest's problem is? He is too forgiving. Not everyone in the world is worth saving. (I'd make a lousy priest!)

There are four little chapels up the sides of the nave, and they are all beautiful in their own right and definitely worth a look. They all sport a little altar to some saint I don't know, staring down at a rack of wax candles. I'm sure they have an important story to tell, but their secret meanings are lost on me. For the past few years I have been meaning to learn the code, because churches are full of interesting architectural and literary references, but I am basically too lazy to learn. I will learn when I have to: on my death bed. I will do some last-minute swotting up before the big exam and try and blag my way into heaven. I'm just drawn to the chapel at the end, whose statue has been dressed up in real clothes -- it's a stone statue in a fabric outfit. A motherly bird and toddler... Mary and Jesus, I'm guessing. He's the one that I would pray to -- the boss. You may as well talk to the guv'nor.

A little kid has got the same idea and is kneeling in front of it, still dressed up in his school uniform and shoes. He only looks about eight years old, and his mum is watching and gently nudging him, making sure that he does it properly. Does he genuinely believe in Jesus? Kids will believe in anything that their mothers tell them is true -- even Father Christmas; so why wouldn't he believe in Jesus, too? But thirty years from now he'll be sitting where I am. And thirty years after that we'll both be buried in the floor.

If there ever comes a day when I need to find God, then this is the first place I'll start looking.

If you enjoy old churches then try Temple Church, St. Paul's Cathedral, Westminster Cathedral and Westminster Abbey.

Buckingham Palace -- Summer Opening

ADDRESS Buckingham Palace - map 7d **TRAINS** Green Park, St. James's Park, Victoria (all zone 1) **BUSES** 11, 211, C1, C10 **PRICE** Adult £21.50, or £30.50 with gardens; Senior (over-60) £19.60, or £27.50 with gardens; Child (5-16) £12.30, or £18.20 with gardens; Infant (under-5) free; Family (2 ad+3 ch) £55.30, or £79.20 with gardens **OPEN** 9.15 AM to 7.45 PM (Mon-Sun, end of July and Aug); 9.15 AM to 6.45 PM (Mon-Sun, Sep); Last entry 2¼ hours before closing **WEB** royalcollection.org.uk/visit/the-state-rooms-buckingham-palace **TEL** 0207 766 7300 **TIME REQUIRED** 2-2½ hours

Easy to get to? ★★★   Good for kids? ★★☆
Value for money? ★★★   Worth a visit? ★★★

I wonder how difficult it is to find an empty cupboard at Buckingham Palace, and hide in it without anybody seeing? I'll just wait until one of the tourists tumbles into a piece of furniture (because that always springs the guards into action) and then I'll jump behind a heavy velvet curtain until nightfall. Then when I hear the Queen tip-toeing past in her pyjamas I'll jump out and say hello, and bore her for five hours with my ideas about how we can improve England. I'm a taxpayer and I pay her wages, so the least she can do is offer me a cup of tea and a slice of cucumber cake. And after that she can take me to the Tower of London in handcuffs and shoot me.

Did you know that there's a secret door into her private apartments? I'm being serious -- I'll tell you about that later. Actually it's not so secret, because they tell you all about it on the audioguide. I've been to the palace so many times now that I know it better than my own house. I was walking round to see which bits of furniture they've moved.

Don't tell anybody that I said this, but I still get a little thrill whenever I'm waiting to go in (yeah, I know -- I'm sad). So that shows you how good it is: if it can still excite me after I've already seen it five thousand times then imagine what it's like for a first-timer. The queue can be horrendous, though. If you buy a ticket online then it's not quite so bad, because they put an entry time on it when you can breeze through the gate (I definitely recommend doing that). But even then you'll still have another twenty minutes in the waiting pen. It's a bit like being a lemonade bottle on one of those labelling machines, being bumped down the conveyor belt past all the robot hands and scanners: you have to go through all the X-ray machines and pat-downs and interrogations -- the security is super tight. I reckon they'd even strip-search the Queen.

Once you've made it inside the front door you can walk around at your own pace, listening to the history on the headphones. It's not the most riveting guide I've ever heard -- it describes what each room is used for and who designed the curtains, etc., but they only provide about two minutes talking for each room, so you're not going to learn a tremendous amount. Presumably they are trying to herd everyone through the rooms at supersonic speed so they don't hang around and dawdle.

The tour begins at the Ambassador's Entrance, which is the non-posh entrance for all the politicians. There are a few paintings and marble busts on display, but nothing particularly special. Then you come out to your first view of the interior courtyard, and up the steps into my favourite room of all: the Grand Hall. This is the first room that the VIPs see when they enter the Palace, and it's an absolute blinder. I would happily live out the rest of my days in this one room alone.

After that you head up the Grand Staircase with its golden balustrade, and into the tiny Guard Chamber and Green Drawing Room. Then it's into the Throne Room, which you've probably seen on the TV without realising it, because this is where most of their official photos are taken. This year it also contains a little exhibition of military medals, so you can see what all the gongs and ribbons look like. [Note: They always have a different exhibition each year, so what you see might be different to what I describe, but the actual rooms themselves are always the same.] After having a good look around I've decided that I want a CBE and an Order of Merit. If she's run out of those then I'll settle for an OBE, but I'm not having an MBE -- no way. That is what they give to old lollipop ladies and people who've been sweeping the streets for fifty years. Anyone who raises five quid on a curry night can apply for one of those trinkets. I deserve a knighthood or a dukedom at least, but I'll settle for fifty quid's worth of book vouchers.

After the Throne Room you come to the long Picture Gallery, which is hung with art by Rembrandt, Rubens, Vermeer and Canaletto. Then you move into the East Gallery and the Ball Supper Room.

The main exhibition always starts in the Ball Supper Room. In previous years I have seen the Queen's Coronation dress and Kate's wedding dress in here, and a collection of crowns and Faberge eggs, but this year they've decided to show you what goes on behind the scenes at a State occasion. It sounded quite interesting on paper, but in reality it's just a mock up of the wine cellar, pantry, dressmaker's room and admin office. I'd rather have just seen the unadorned Ball Supper Room on its own, to be honest, but luckily things improved tremendously from this point on.

After the Ball Supper Room comes the main Ballroom, which they've laid out as if for an actual State banquet. It really is spectacular, and it's the best that I've ever seen the room look. You can see how they lay the table out for the guests: everyone gets 46cm of tablecloth with five cut glasses (water glass, tasting glass, champagne glass and two wine glasses), plus three forks, three knives and spoons, a folded napkin and a spotlight. After that comes the saltcellar, mustard pot and pepper pot, and a butter dish with a couple of coins of butter. And somehow they have to squeeze a plateful of dinner in there as well (and the tomato ketchup). It reminds me of that scene in *Pretty Woman* when she was trying to learn which fork to use for which dish. All I know about dinner etiquette is this: keep your elbows off the table, and you don't wipe your teaspoon on your shirt.

The State Dining Room comes next (which is *not* where they hold the State dinners, confusingly), which has another little exhibition of gifts that she's been given by visiting Heads of State. She seems to receive a lot of porcelain plates from everyone she meets, so don't buy her plates for Christmas for chrissakes, because she won't thank you for it. (*"Oh no, not more plates! Stick them in the cupboard, Phil."*)

The White Drawing Room is one of my favourite rooms because it looks like the centre of the sun. Imagine a bright yellow room with garish gold all over the walls, and then scatter some sunflower seats around the walls and hang a ten-tonne chandelier six feet off the carpet... and that is what this room looks like. They really should hand out some sunglasses as you enter to protect your eyesight from the light. It's also where you'll find that secret door that I was telling you about earlier... there's a tall table with a mirror in the corner that swings open to reveal the Queen emerging from her private apartments -- *surprise!*

One thing that I have noticed this year is all the extra seats dotted around where the tourists can sit. Back in the old days (last year) you pretty much had to stand on your feet for the entire two hours, but now there seems to be a chair in every room. I actually think that's a shame, because I used to enjoy watching the tourists getting told off by the guards as they tried to sit on a priceless piece of French furniture.

The last part of the tour takes you down the Minister's Staircase and through the Marble Hall. The Marble Hall is like a twin to the Picture Gallery upstairs, and contains the Queen's collection of statues and sculptures. Then you head out of the Bow Room to the veranda out the back, where the gardens are laid out before you.

I always enjoy this bit the most, because you get to have a cup of tea in the tented cafe, and tell everybody that you've had a brew at Buckingham Palace. You might want to bring your chequebook along, though, because it's the kind of cafe that cuts its sandwiches into tiny triangles and then sells them for fifty quid each. All of the food seems to have a strawberry on top, and comes with a sprig of greenery that nobody knows if they can eat.

I think you get a better class of tourist at the palace. I noticed this when I saw my unshaven face reflecting in the shiny kitchen dustbin, and realised that everybody around me was wearing a floral dresses or a summer shirt, with cotton scarves and glasses on. Maybe they were all making an extra effort in case they bumped into the Queen. If they were, then they were wasting their time, because she always packs her bags for Balmoral when the palace opens up to the public, so she doesn't have to rub shoulders with her subjects. I don't blame her, though... imagine if ten thousand tourists came round your house and started touching all your stuff -- that would drive me nuts.

I normally go home after my cup of tea, but I stumped up an extra tenner for the garden tour this time, so I had to hang around for that to start. You always get to see a little piece of the garden even if you don't take the garden tour, because the exit path leads you round the southern edge of the grounds. But it's pretty plain. All they let you see is a load of green grass and woodland trees, plus a little pond. There are no flowerbeds or anything like that: no landscaping, no statues... just a two minute walk to the exit.

If you do the garden tour then you get to go round the northern edge instead, and past the Queen's private apartments at the side of the palace (you can't actually see into them -- you just look at them from the outside). The path runs roughly parallel to Constitution Hill, and up past Wellington Arch. You then round the bend at the western edge to the same exit as before.

Our guide was pretty good today. He was a posh guy called Mr Wild, and if the Buckingham Palace bosses are reading this then you should definitely give him a pay rise. He was exactly the kind of guy that you would imagine working at the Palace... a teeny-weeny bit posh, very friendly and quite funny too. He told us all about the famous flowers and shrubs, who built which building, and which Queen planted which tree, etc. But having heard the whole thing I think that it would mainly appeal to gardeners -- it was that type of tour. If you like your flowers, then you will learn a lot. Unfortunately you don't quite get to see the entire garden, because you are never allowed to leave the path and venture into the centre. But there is more than enough to make it worth a visit.

You might also like to visit the Queen's Gallery and Royal Mews.

Buckingham Palace -- Evening Tour

ADDRESS Buckingham Palace - map 7d
TRAINS Green Park, St. James's Park, Victoria (all zone 1) **BUSES** 11, 211, C1, C10 **PRICE** Adult £75 **OPEN** Usually 5.30 PM to 8 PM on selected dates between Sep-Jan - see website for dates **WEB** royalcollection.org.uk/event/exclusive-evening-tour-of-the-state-rooms-buckingham-palace **TEL** 0207 766 7300 **TIME REQUIRED** 2½ hours

Easy to get to? ★★★ Good for kids? ★★☆
Value for money? ★★☆ Worth a visit? ★★★

I thought I'd pop in and say hello to the Queen tonight, because they're putting on an evening tour of Buckingham Palace. It cost me £75 quid so it should be good. That's quite a lot of money to spend on a tour, so hopefully the Queen will be leading us around herself. If we end up with Prince Edward then I'll want a refund.

I'm sitting in St. James's Park at the moment, waiting for it to start (I always arrive at places far too early), surrounded by a pack of tourists snapping photos of the swans and ducks. They are running around on the bank splashing and flapping and squabbling over the food (the ducks I mean, not the tourists). All they get is photos, though. Flashlights and camera phones... no bread or biscuits for them today. I'm guessing that there must be five hundred ducks, at least. If they all turned nasty at once then there would be carnage. There is no way that us humans could fight that flock off; they'd outnumber us 100-to-1. We'd need Prince Philip to come down here and blast them to bits with his shotgun.

I've been to Buckingham Palace plenty of times in the past so I already know what it's going to look like inside. The big difference today is that we're going to get led around by an actual guide (a real human being!), instead of listening to some commentary on the headphones. And they've promised us a glass of bubbly at the end as well. That is what the ticket says.

Here's a tip: the next time you go to Buckingham Palace have a look at the flagpole. If the Union Jack is flying then you know the Queen isn't home. If it's the Royal Standard then you might see her poking her nose out of the net curtains. But it's the Union Jack today, which is no surprise: she doesn't want the hoi polloi running round her house while she's getting ready for bed, padding around in her slippers with her curlers in.

The daylight is fading now so I make my way to the palace. There's still quite a crowd of people standing outside the gates watching the guards march up and down. Some of them are doing mock soldier salutes and stamping on the spot in p*ss-take imitation. They are lonely old souls, those soldiers, standing on the same spot for hours on end, with their eyes trained upon the crowd. I wonder what thoughts go through their heads? They probably fantasise about testing their guns out on the tourists, or coming to the rescue of Her Maj in a terrorist attack. That's what I'd do: I'd be imagining the Nazis storming up the Mall in their Panzer tanks, and I'd fight the whole lot off with my ceremonial sword and bearskin hat. But all they do is march up and down, up and down, and up and down. And then up and down some more. And then up and down again.

It took me a little while to find the correct entrance to the tour because it's in a different place to the Summer Opening: you have to go into the Queen's Gallery gift shop, a few minutes down the road (worth remembering if you turn up late). Now we're all sitting in a cloakroom in a group of about thirty people waiting for the guide to arrive. It's a mix of young people, old people, and very old people. Some of them are posh, and some of them are not (me). Some of them are good looking, and some are not (me). Some of them are me (me) and some are not me (not me).

Now the guide comes in and she is a friendly grey-haired old lady. She looks like somebody's grandma. In fact, she is so old that she loos like somebody's grandma's grandma. She explains that the route is a little bit different today because there is some maintenance work going on inside the palace, so we're going to see an extra bit by the Chapel stairs and have our bubbly in a different place. We're also going to have a quick little stroll through the Queen's Gallery and see some of the works of art on display. Then she orders us out of our seats and frog-marches us through a few of the State Rooms at supersonic speed, before sitting us down in the famous Ballroom.

Now, I've seen this room plenty of times before, but it's still a blinder (it's where they hold all of the State Banquets and investitures). But this is the first time that I've ever seen it empty; because there's usually a big exhibition in here during the Summer Opening. But it's just our small little group and the guide this time, sitting here all alone in the vast Ballroom.

For the next twenty minutes she rattles through a talk on the history of the palace and its inhabitants. It's basically like a school lesson, with the teacher standing at the front of the class waving her arms about, whilst all the kids try and stifle their yawns. I admit that these lectures can often be a bit boring, but I happen to enjoy all of this Royal stuff, so twenty minutes of John Nash, Queen Victoria and the Duke of Buckingham is right up my street. She does a little Q&A session at the end as well. After that's all over she orders us up out of our seats again, and begins to lead us through the State rooms one by one.

The tour is a lot more fun when the palace is empty. You can really appreciate the vastness of the rooms when there's nobody around. Usually you are crammed in with a hundred people at least, all milling around and filling up every inch of carpet. But we are all alone with the guide tonight, walking the corridors like we own the place. It's all dimly lit, too, with warm yellow lamplights bringing out the velvet reds and golds. It sure does look pretty in the low light.

After the Ballroom comes the State Dining Room, the Blue Drawing Room, Music Room and White Drawing Room. It's the complete opposite of the Summer Opening route. It seems to be the exact same rooms, but in reverse order. I've already spoken about all of these rooms in my review of the Summer Opening, though, so I won't bore you with the same stuff twice. (I'd much rather bore you with some brand new stuff instead!) The guide carries on talking all the way through the walk, pointing about various pieces of furniture, etc., and she does a lot of talking about the art on the walls as well, working in some of the Queen's family history, because it's pretty much all portraits of long-dead kings and queens.

Then comes the Throne Room and Green Drawing Room, followed by the Picture Gallery, which is filled with pictures by Renoir, Rembrandt, Canaletto, Caravaggio, Titian and Vermeer.

After that comes the bit that everyone has been waiting for: bubbly time in the East Gallery (booze time at the palace). They set up a couple of tables with champagne glasses on (apple juice and water too, if that is your fancy), and dolly birds dished them out on silver trays. I would happily have swapped the bubbly for a sit down on a seat, but nobody was allowed to sit on the expensive furniture; so everybody ended up hovering around everyone else, chatting like it was date night. I've got no small talk whatsoever, so I just milled around like an idiot for twenty minutes looking at the art.

And there was one final treat to come... instead of walking out the back of the gardens like you usually do, you get escorted across the interior courtyard and straight out the front gate. They lead you across the parade ground where Changing the Guard takes place, and then throw you out the main gate where all the tourists gather to snap their pictures of the soldiers. One of them even mistook me for Prince William and screamed and tried to kiss me (that's not true).

So was it worth it? Well, *duh*. Of course it was! If I ever have to choose between an Evening Tour and the Summer Opening then it will be no contest: the Evening Tour will win hands down. It's just nice to be able to walk around the place without having a bazillion other people pushing past you, yakking with their mates. You also seem to learn a lot more of the history with a real human guide, instead of listening to some scholarly suit on the headphones.

The only downside is the cost. But if you don't mind stumping up a lot of money then definitely give it a go.

If you enjoy this tour then you might enjoy a Twilight Tour at the Tower of London.

Burlington Arcade

ADDRESS Burlington Arcade, 51 Piccadilly, Mayfair - map 8a **TRAINS** Piccadilly Circus, Green Park (both zone 1) **BUSES** 14, 19, 22, 38 **OPEN** 9 AM to 7.30 PM (Mon-Sat); 11 AM to 6 PM (Sun) **WEB** burlington-arcade.co.uk **TEL** 0207 493 1764 **TIME REQUIRED** 15 mins

Easy to get to? ★★★ Good for kids? ☆☆☆
Value for money? free Worth a visit? ★☆☆

Burlington Arcade is famous for its Beadles: they look like doormen dressed up in top hats and tails and are supposed to enforce a load of dopey rules like *No whistling! No singing!* and *No holding an open umbrella!* But if truth be told they are just a couple of old geezers who stand there staring at the traffic. When I was in there today, for example, a couple of kids tried to whistle a few tunes for a laugh (which is totally against the Burlington commandments), and what did they do? *Absolutely nothing.* Nowt. I was very disappointed. I thought they were supposed to come charging down the aisle with machine guns blazing and blow the kids to smithereens, but they didn't even break their gaze off the buses. But I bet if *I* whistled a tune, though, they'd beat the living daylights out of me. That is the kind of luck I have.

As for the shops, they're all posh and expensive boutiquey-like places. They are so expensive that even rich people can't afford to shop in them -- that is how expensive they are. I saw a cotton scarf on sale for seventy quid. No joke. And it wasn't even made out of wool! How is that supposed to keep you warm in the winter? Only rich people would buy a scarf that's made out of cotton. You can get second-hand Rolex watches (still ten grand a pop), five grand fountain pens, silk ties, bow ties, and the kind of pastel hats that women wear to Ascot. They have impossibly shiny bottles of perfume -- they look like toffee coloured whiskey in a crystal decanter. Pearl necklaces with beads the size of onions. Wallet-sized handbags that cost more than a house. Hand stitched leather shoes. Umbrellas with carved handles. Don't bother going in there for your groceries because the only food on sale is chocolate. The famous sweet shop at the end is decorated in gold -- all over. Every wall, shelf and spare inch of ceiling is covered in gold leaf -- and that is *not* an exaggeration. It's the shiniest shop in Britain.

I don't bother going in the shops anymore because they're the same size as shoeboxes, and I like to flit through life like I wasn't there -- I like to remain anonymous. I don't want to start up a conversation with the shop staff. As soon as you step through the door you are practically standing tiptoes with a saleswoman who will greet you with a cider-like *'Hello, Sir'*, or *'Hello, Madam'*, or *'How can I help you today?'* Obviously you can't admit to her that you're only there to be nosey, so for the next two minutes you basically have to pretend that you have a spare five grand to spend on a Rolex watch. She totally knows that you don't. And you know that you don't. Even the Burlington Beadles know that you don't. But this is the game that everyone plays down Burlington Arcade. She probably only gets one real customer each week, and she knows darn well that you're not him -- you're just another in a long line of nosey tourists who have come in to ooh and aah at the shiny objects on her velvety shelves.

The only thing that I can afford to buy is a tin of boot polish from the shoe-shine guy. He looks like one of those old-fashioned shoe-shiners you sometimes see in sepia-tinged photos of the steam train station. He's got a pot full of brushes and a chemistry set of oils and unguents, and you are supposed to sit there in the middle of the arcade whilst he buffs up your loafers and makes chit-chat about the weather.

Camden Town

ADDRESS Camden Town **TRAINS** Camden Town (zone 2) **BUSES** 24, 27, 29, 31, 46, 88, 134, 168, 214, 253, 274, C2 **TIME REQUIRED** 2 hours

Easy to get to? ★★★ Good for kids? ★☆☆
Value for money? free Worth a visit? ★★☆

I'm too old for Camden. You have to be under thirty and come here for the pubs and clubs and music, and cheapo markets.

There are three kinds of student in the world. The first type is the quiet ones, who sit at pine tables tapping out essays and letters into their laptop computers, next to a takeaway tub of nuts and salad. The second type walk around with bright blue hair and a steel bar through their nose, impatiently waiting for any kind of trouble to break out, with which they can show some solidarity (it doesn't matter what it is -- as long as they can shout at someone). And the third type are the wasters, the drinkers -- the happiest ones -- who spend their days doing nothing worth remembering, so have nothing to forget. You can see all three types in Camden. They live here for a few years before swapping their university clothes for a smart suit and shiny pair of shoes. As soon as they don the uniform of an adult they have to move out of town -- that seems to be the rule. And they are only allowed back in as day-trippers and tourists.

I'm sitting here watching some older ones desperately trying to delay their age by sporting a ponytail and a pork pie hat. They are the kind of people who splash aftershave over their designer stubble, and spend five minutes struggling to make a roll-up when they'd rather have a cigarette.

I will say this, though... Camden has got some of the craziest shop fronts in London. Have a walk down Camden High Street and you'll see huge shoes the size of rowing boats nailed to the roof, and playing cards that are bigger then a bedspread hanging off the wall. I can see scorpions and dragons and fifty-foot snakes, big yellow elephant heads, and even a naked lady wrapped around in black leather. One of the shops has got an airplane out the front (not a picture of a plane -- a twenty foot long model of one). It reminds me of the seaside -- one of those beachfront promenades selling buckets and spades and tacky tat to the tourists. It's all cheap T-shirts and Union Jack ashtrays, 99p umbrellas and mirrored sunglasses. Every shop seems to be selling beanie hats and clip-on cases for your mobile phone. If you want to buy a cigarette lighter with a marijuana leaf on it, then this is the place. If you want to buy one of those colourful bongs which look like a broken set of bagpipes, then come to Camden. Camden High Street is full of shops that have rails of hats and tat dangling from the top. *Get your Bob Marley t-shirts! Get your 'I Love London' shorts and shirts! Get some postcards, and a picture of the Pope smoking dope!*

It gets better when you reach the lock, because there are plenty of pavement cafes and posh pubs to have a sit-down. It's very nice around there when it's sunny, but if you make the mistake of coming at 8 AM on a cold January morning (like I did today) then bring a pair of gloves with you for chrissakes, because it's almost too cold to write anything down. My jaw has started aching from my chattering teeth. The ducks are dipping their webbed feet in the water before they get in, to check its temperature. The frozen leaves are hanging off the trees like crystal droplets on a chandelier.

The lock gates look nice from fifty feet away, but if you take a closer look then you'll see a rubbish dump of litter floating up behind. I can see tin cans and beer bottles, paper plates and polystyrene kebab cartons, two deflated old footballs, plus a chopped up forest of sticks and twigs and unwanted builder's planks. Don't let that put you off, though, because it's probably just too early in the morning for them to have emptied it (it's 8 AM). As soon as they open it up for a boat it will all flush away like a toilet.

There's one part of Camden that I definitely recommend you visit -- the market. Every guidebook ever written recommends Camden Market, but they rarely tell you that there's more than one. So lots of tourists step straight off the tube and end up in the tacky one down Camden High Street, and wonder what all the fuss is about. So here is my advice: ignore that one and find Camden Lock Market instead (by the lock), and especially Stables Market down Chalk Farm Road. Stables Market is the real beauty, because it's nestled amongst the railway arches. It's decorated with bronzed-models of horses, wooden stalls and fairy lights. I think it's worth a visit even if you're not buying anything.

Canary Wharf

ADDRESS Canary Wharf **TRAINS** Canary Wharf DLR, Heron Quays DLR, West India Quay DLR (all zone 2) **BUSES** 135, 277, D3, D7, D8 **TIME REQUIRED** 2-2½ hours

Easy to get to? ★★★ Good for kids? ★☆☆
Value for money? free Worth a visit? ★★☆

Canary Wharf is a sister to The City (the Square Mile), but the buildings are a lot taller and the people are a lot better looking. It's the closest that London ever gets to looking like New York.

This is where all the skyscrapers live. They don't allow very many of them to be built in central London in case they screw up the skyline, so they stick them out here in East London instead. I'm not usually a fan of all this glass and steel stuff, but they do look quite impressive when they're all collected together in one place. I like it when they start affecting the weather. They funnel the wind down their sides and along the street and create fierce little eddies that are strong enough to blow your wig off. Big strips of sun slice off the sides of skyscrapers and hit the ground at sharp angles, then suddenly disappear and plunge the pavement into darkness, before coming back bright like a nuclear sun around the next corner. One minute it's calm sunshine, and then it's a torrid wind and darkness. Then it's nice and bright again, then it's dark as night and hold-on-to-your-hat time. It's like you're walking between spring, summer and winter every ten steps.

The best photo-spot in the whole of Canary Wharf is from Cabot Square. This is where you can see the three tallest skyscrapers sitting in a row, like a long neck and pair of shoulders. The centre one, called One Canada Square, used to be the tallest building in Europe for about six months, and now it's not even the tallest building in London. It probably has a great view from the roof but you're not allowed to go up there unfortunately, because, like most of the buildings around here, it's filled with corporate banks and financial institutions.

The next best place to go is Reuters Plaza, which is a big open area filled with posh pubs and cafes. This is the banker's equivalent of Piccadilly Circus. But instead of having bright neon signs advertising Coke and iPhones, they've got a news ticker wrapped around the side of a building with all the latest stock prices on it. They've got a huge TV screen with the Bloomberg news too, so they can sit in the sun and not miss any share-moving news.

I like peering into all the posh lobbies around here, just to be nosey. You probably need a biometric swipe card to actually get inside them, so I just look through the windows. The best ones are the long cavernous halls with a little desk at the end of a shiny marble floor, staffed by one solitary blonde bird who looks like she's stepped off a Parisian catwalk. That's something that you'll notice as soon as you come to Canary Wharf: everyone looks like they've stepped out from the pages of a fashion magazine. I thought that it was illegal to hire someone based solely on their looks, but here is definite proof of the way the world really works. Long legs are better than ten GCSEs. Long legs will get you through more doors than an A-level. And they all have nice clothes, too. They are all wearing smart scarves and glasses. They have tight fitting suits and chunky gold watches and brown leather man-bags. Everyone seems to be smoking an e-cigarette. And they all look *busy busy busy*. I'm sitting here drinking my coffee but they're not even sipping it -- their jaws are talking numbers and discussing who to hire and who was heard saying what to whom and which bloke is not pulling his weight this week... lots of animated natter and office gossip going on. I get the impression that everyone is under intense pressure to do well. Everybody seems to be just one bad day away from getting the sack, and I thank my lucky stars that I'm just a lay-about writer.

Another thing that I like about Canary Wharf is all the water everywhere. This whole area used to be full of cargo docks so it's all wharves and quaysides now. You can't walk fifty feet without spying another little piece of river filled with buoys and boats. It does make it very cold and windy though, because the breeze is forever whipping around the corners of big buildings and screaming across the water tops. You can even see some seagulls and industrial cargo cranes that have been preserved and turned into a work of art. There are nowhere near enough big boats to make it look like a proper dock, though. All they've got left these days are pleasure craft and floats, festooned with fairy lights, that are doubling up as pubs and cafes.

The nicest boats that I could find today were in the Blackwall Basin and Poplar Dock. You should definitely have a walk around there if you've got the time because you get a great view of the skyscrapers. Keep on walking round until you reach the Blue Bridge, at least, because if you stand in the centre of that then you'll be staring straight down the length of West India Docks with its stooping cranes. Directly behind you will be the broad river and the O2 Arena beyond.

If you're going to Canary Wharf then how about catching a Thames Clipper boat?

Carnaby Street

ADDRESS Carnaby Street, Soho - map 3e
TRAINS Oxford Circus, Piccadilly Circus (both zone 1) **BUSES** 3, 6, 7, 8, 10, 12, 15, 23, 25, 73, 88, 94, 98, 139, 159, 176, 390, 453 **WEB** carnaby.co.uk **TIME REQUIRED** 10 mins

Easy to get to? ★★★ Good for kids? ☆☆☆
Value for money? free Worth a visit? ☆☆☆

You have to be in your sixties to remember the 60s, so I never saw this street in its hey-day. All I can do is tell you what it looks like now -- and it's nothing special. They've painted the shop fronts in pastel pinks and lemon yellows to try and brighten it up a bit, but it's just a long line of clothes shops with a couple of pubs and coffee bars.

The shops all flog the kind of gear that nobody dares to wear. But admittedly I'm too old to shop down here. In fact, the clothes that I'm wearing right now are probably older than most of the shoppers. But let's have a stroll along the street and see what we can buy...

Striped ties seem to be the fashion these days... either that or camouflaged khaki. The next shop along has got a velvet suit with plastic see-through shoes, topped off with swirls and twirls and a ribbon bow tie. Or how about this one: a pair of pyjama bottoms in the sequined style of 1970's disco. Another plastic mannequin is wearing that green beanie hat that Benny had in *Crossroads*. I particularly like this bright purple shirt with bobbles on the cuffs. And I would look great in that pair of pink trousers with tassels dangling from the ankles.

Do people really dress up in this stuff? Some of the furry hats could almost double up as a new hairdo.

Normally it takes me a whole six months to ruin a new pair of trousers, but you can buy some in Carnaby Street that are already wrecked -- to save you the trouble of having to wear them out. They come with big rips, patches and paint stains included. Whoever thought that idea up was an absolute genius, because they don't have to sell you new clothes anymore: they can just rip them to shreds and charge you double the price!

The Cenotaph

ADDRESS The Cenotaph, Whitehall - map 8d
TRAINS Charing Cross, Embankment, Westminster (all zone 1) **BUSES** 3, 11, 12, 24, 53, 87, 88, 159 **TIME REQUIRED** 5 mins

Easy to get to? ★★★ Good for kids? ☆☆☆
Value for money? free Worth a visit? ★☆☆

The Cenotaph is the one thing in London that you're not allowed to denigrate but I don't care -- I'm going to do it anyway. If I go to hell, then I go to hell. I'm probably going to end up there anyway, so it doesn't matter.

My biggest criticism of the Cenotaph is its location: they've marooned it on top of a tarmac island between two busy lanes of traffic. Hardly anybody goes over there to pay their respects because they don't want to get flattened by a thundering truck. The only time that people ponder on the war dead is during November, or when they glimpse it quickly from the window of a passing bus. And that's not right, is it? That's why they should shift it to the western edge of Horse Guards parade ground, opposite the Guards' Memorial.

I'm going to walk over and have a closer look...

The only hand salutes on show today are of the two-fingered variety (the road rage kind) as the cyclists get cut up by the cars. I can't see any glinting medals either -- just the glinting glass of a gigantic camera that's been set up to watch who's coming out of Downing Street. But here's the most depressing thing: a lot of the poppy wreaths have pooled up with stale rainwater. They look like a forgotten dog bowl outside the pub. An old bowl that's catching raindrops from the roof. All the green leaves have dried up and browned. Their handwritten words of remembrance have all run and smeared in the rain. Whatever kind words they wrote have now floated down the street.

That isn't remembering, is it? ...That is forgetting.

Charles Dickens Museum

ADDRESS Charles Dickens Museum, 48 Doughty Street - map 4c **TRAINS** Chancery Lane, Holborn, Russell Square (all zone 1) **BUSES** 7, 17, 19, 38, 45, 46, 55, 243 **PRICE** Adult £9; Senior £6; Child (6-16) £4; Infant (under-6) free **OPEN** 10 AM to 5 PM (Tue-Sun); Closed (Mon); Last entry 1 hour before closing **WEB** dickensmuseum.com **TEL** 0207 405 2127 **TIME REQUIRED** 1-1½ hours

Easy to get to? ★★★   Good for kids? ★☆☆
Value for money? ★★☆   Worth a visit? ★★☆

I went to the Charles Dickens Museum today, which wasn't bad at all. I'm not going to pretend that I'm a big fan of Dickens, because I'm not. I've never read any of his books. I still read *The Beano* -- that is my level. I watched Jim Carrey's animated movie of *A Christmas Carol* last year, and I vaguely remember the *Oliver!* musical from my youth, but that's about it. So when it comes to Dickens I'm much like the next man: I know who he is, and what he wrote, but don't ask me to explain the plot of *Bleak House* because I won't have a clue.

Whenever I think of Dickens I always think of debtors prisons and smoky old workhouses, and scruffy street urchins kicking stones along the road. But judging by his Bloomsbury townhouse Dickens must have been loaded! It's full of four-poster beds, pianos, comfy plush armchairs and oil paintings above the fireplace.

When you enter the front door you are given a little pamphlet-style book, which you are supposed to read whilst you're walking around the house. There is no audio-guide, which is unusual for a place like this, but the book is perfectly okay. It tells you what each room was used for, etc., and there are some extra placards propped up around the place to point out items of interest.

You get to see the whole house from top to bottom, and they've made a real effort to bring the rooms alive. The washtub room has got a line of dirty linen hanging from the ceiling, for example, and the comfy lounge has got a Dickens novel being played out the speaker, as if he was sitting in the room reading it.

The reception rooms and study are furnished with his bookcases and desks, and there are a couple of bedrooms upstairs with four-posters in. Glass cabinets display interesting little bits like his handwritten letters, scribblings and shaving kit. They've even got a lock of his hair and a letter he wrote to his doctor complaining of a dodgy downstairs (if you get my meaning).

At the top of the house is a little one-room museum containing a window frame from his old house (said to be the inspiration for *Oliver Twist's* burglary scene), and some iron bars from Marshalsea prison, where his dad got locked up for not paying his debts.

Even if you don't care too much about Dickens (like me), I think I would still recommend a visit. It's nice to have a little walk around Bloomsbury as well... a very pleasant part of town that still looks like Ye Olde London.

You might like to try Dr. Johnson's House and the Sherlock Holmes Museum.

Charterhouse

ADDRESS Charterhouse, Charterhouse Square, Clerkenwell - map 4d **TRAINS** Barbican, Farringdon (both zone 1) **BUSES** 4, 56, 153 **PRICE** Adult £10 **OPEN** Guided tour: 2.15 PM to 3.45 PM (Tue-Thu, plus some Sat) **WEB** thecharterhouse.org **TEL** 0207 253 9503 **TIME REQUIRED** Guided tour: 1½ hours

Easy to get to? ★★★ Good for kids? ☆☆☆
Value for money? ★★★ Worth a visit? ★★☆

I only discovered Charterhouse relatively recently because it's tucked away in a spot where no tourist ever goes -- a few minutes north of Smithfield Market. I don't think many Londoners even know that this place exists -- but what a surprise! It's like a cross between a Cambridge college and the cloisters at Westminster Abbey. One of the interior cobbled courtyards is very reminiscent of Hampton Court, with its dirty red and black bricks and muddy-coloured roof tiles.

The original 14th-century priory ended with Henry VIII's Dissolution of the Monasteries. The monks put up quite a spirited fight, though -- half of them were carted off to Newgate Prison and the Prior himself was dragged up to Tyburn and hung, drawn and quartered. So that was the end of them. *No more monks.* After that it was handed over to one of Henry VIII's courtiers, who knocked a lot of it down and built a Tudor mansion in its place.

Most of what remains today dates from this Tudor period (with a few alterations courtesy of Hitler's Luftwaffe), and the buildings have subsequently served as an almshouse and a school. The school moved out ages ago, so it's just a load of private flats and almshouses now -- home to a load of gentlemen pensioners. And it's one of these 'Brothers' that did our tour today. So he was basically showing us around his retirement home.

The Brothers are a bit like the Chelsea Pensioners at the Royal Hospital, I suppose, but without their heroic war record. The don't seem to be anybody special -- they're just normal everyday old blokes in need of financial support. He was telling us that anybody can apply to live there as long as they're over sixty and don't have pots of money. But they don't allow any women, though -- this is strictly an old boy's home. (I don't blame them. In my experience woman cause you nothing but misery, heartache and grief.)

When I arrived at two o'clock I found a group of ten people already waiting by the gate, bundled up for the cold. Then he led us straight into the chapel and sat us down in the warm, and launched into his history of the place.

To be honest, the chapel isn't all that impressive -- but I've been spoiled by the splendours of London's other churches and cathedrals. They do have a nice organ and a few tombs inside, but it was the history of the place that most impressed me.

The guy who built the Tudor mansion was called the Duke of Norfolk, and he led a very interesting life around the time of Elizabeth I. She even came to Charterhouse a few times, when she was planning her Coronation.

If you know the story of Elizabeth and Mary Queen of Scots, then you will know that they weren't exactly best buddies. Lets just say that they were polite pen-pals -- they said nice things in their letters, but terrible things behind each other's back. Elizabeth viewed Mary as her biggest threat after Spain, so when the Duke came up with the totally daft idea of marrying Mary behind her back, she wasn't very happy (she went nuts!), and she put him under house arrest -- in this very house. The guide even shows a few bits and pieces that he added to the building whilst he was banged up in London.

After the chapel he takes you into their Dining Hall, which is the Charterhouse equivalent of the Chelsea Pensioners' Hall at the Royal Hospital -- but nowhere near as grand (not even close). The Presence Chamber is probably the most impressive room, but it's the exterior of the building that I like the best.

The outside really is fantastic -- it's just like a Cambridge college, and you really get a sense of its great age. Unfortunately the Germans firebombed this area and wrecked a lot of the ancient ceilings, which is why the interiors aren't as grand as they might otherwise have been -- most of them are just plastered white with a few beams of wood. But when you stand outside you don't notice any of that, because everything has been sympathetically restored to look as good as new (or as good as old?).

Because I like the place so much, I made a promise to myself that I wasn't going to mention the truly awful new wing that they've recently added round the back... but I can't help it. I have to flag up bad architecture whenever I see it -- it's my mission. But there's no way that I'm going to waste a photograph on it. The guide explained that the architect was asked to design something "in keeping with its monastic surroundings", which made everyone burst into laughter. It's so bad that I'm hoping the Germans will come back and bomb it.

But that's just a very minor quibble. If you like old buildings then you should definitely take a look.

If you like this architecture then you check out Lincoln's Inn, or take a day trip to Hampton Court or Cambridge.

Chelsea Physic Garden

ADDRESS 66 Royal Hospital Road, Chelsea **TRAINS** Sloane Square, followed by a 15 min walk (zone 1) **BUSES** 170 **PRICE** Adult £9.90; Senior £9.90; Child (5-15) £6.60; Infant (under-5) free; Price includes a voluntary donation **OPEN** Garden, cafe: 11 AM to 6 PM (Tue-Fri and Sun, Apr-Oct) -- Garden only: 10 AM to dusk (Mon-Fri, Nov-Mar) **WEB** chelseaphysicgarden.co.uk **TEL** 0207 352 5646 **TIME REQUIRED** 1-1½ hours

Easy to get to? ★★☆ Good for kids? ☆☆☆
Value for money? ★★☆ Worth a visit? ★☆☆

Have you ever visited a garden that can kill you? The first thing that you notice when you step through the front door is a sign that says: "Some of these plants are highly poisonous -- Do not touch!" But here's the worrying thing: a lot of the vines and creepers are overhanging the path, like live wires on a construction site, so if you take that wording literally then it's pretty scary stuff! Obviously I kept my hands in my pockets the whole time, just to be safe. I don't want to get killed by a flower -- that is not the way that I want to die. I am sure they're just being ultra-careful, though, so they don't get sued -- surely they can't *really* be poisonous?

The Chelsea Physic Garden is quite a small patch of land inside an old brick wall, but they've managed to cram in a lot of plants. But it's all about the ones we use for food and medicines, though, rather than the ones we stuff inside a vase -- so don't go expecting much colour. You're not going to find a lot of pretty flowers like at Wisley and Kew. It's mainly green things like herbs and vegetables. Try and imagine a grandmother's garden, if she lived in the woods... the kind of place that you'd potter around in when you're eighty, feeding the frogs and robins. That is the Chelsea Physic Garden.

There are a lot of rockeries and slate walls all over place, and nicely raked paths and ponds. There are a couple of ramshackle greenhouses to have a nose around in, too, plus a butterfly garden (I couldn't find any butterflies -- maybe they'd all eaten the poisonous flowers and died).

They have a pretty little bamboo garden and some prickly cacti too (another plant that is dangerous). And you can learn about medicines and perfumes and vitamins and dyes. There are plenty of foodstuffs on show, like apricots and tomatoes, wild chillies, beetroots and parsnips. It's a bit like a greengrocers, I suppose. If you bring two slices of bread along then you can probably make yourself quite a decent dinner (but don't eat the poisonous ones for chrissakes -- I don't want you to die!).

It's a perfectly pleasant place to walk around, but it's definitely one for the adults only -- adults with white hair and creaking knees. The kind of place that you can come on a Sunday afternoon for a lazy stroll and a sit down, followed by a cup of tea and a slice of cake in the cafe.

If you enjoy the Chelsea Physic Garden then try a trip to Kew Gardens and Wisley.

Chinatown

ADDRESS Gerrard Street and Lisle Street, Soho - map 8a **TRAINS** Charing Cross, Leicester Square, Piccadilly Circus (all zone 1) **BUSES** 14, 15, 19, 22, 24, 38, 94, 176 **TIME REQUIRED** 15 mins

Easy to get to? ★★★ Good for kids? ★☆☆
Value for money? free Worth a visit? ★★☆

Special fried rice with stir-fry chicken pork balls, crispy duck and prawn crackers too, please, and some chop suey chow mien with oriental rice noodles plus two pieces of sesame prawn toast on a bun. And some tomato ketchup.

That is an example of what I might say when I have a Chinese takeaway. (Damn... I forgot the spring rolls!) But have you ever eaten a *real* Chinese meal? I mean one that's cooked in Chinatown? The Chinese Empire only stretches to two streets in London -- Gerrard Street and Lisle Street -- and it looks like one of those themed zones you find at amusement parks:

A big stone dragon? *check!*
A huge wooden pagoda with green roof tiles? *check!*
Red paper lanterns hanging from the lampposts? *check!*
Watercolour paintings of waterfalls and blossom trees? *check!*
Golden cats and pottery Buddhas? *check!*
Little old ladies with cigarette stained fingers mumbling to themselves? *check!*

You can tell who the real Chinese people are, because they're just hanging around the shop fronts smoking little roll-ups of sweet smelling... something (I'm not sure what). The tourists have the cameras, whilst the workers have stained aprons and are carrying boxes of vegetables on their heads. I can hear them talking Chinese as I'm sitting here, probably wondering who this English dipsh*t is, sitting on their doorstep.

The thing that I like most about Chinatown (and this is going to sound daft), is that it always seems to be just on the cusp of opening. No matter what time of day you come, whether it is 8 AM or mid-afternoon, everybody is still rushing around to get ready. Lorries are always reversing down the road with their drivers hanging their elbows out the window, beeping and tooting to the dawdling tourists. Metal shutters are always going up with a clack and a bang. The street is always filled with pallets of sacks of rice and pyramid piles of bin bags stacked up around the lampposts. Crushed up cardboard boxes and cheap boxes of fruit are getting in everybody's way -- it's like a street market without the stalls. One day this place will tidy up and open. *I like it!*

I'm doing a quick census of the shops and it seems to be 90% restaurants and 5% Chinese travel agents. There are a couple of fast-food joints as well, but not like McDonalds. The Chinese version of Kentucky Fried Chicken has got twenty dead chickens strung up in the window, all suntan brown with trussed up feet and strangled necks. I've decided that I'm going to try and buy a can of Coke. Nope... wait a minute... I've changed my mind. *I'm too scared.* Their supermarket doesn't look like Tesco's, so I'm not sure how it works. They haven't even got any shelves on the walls -- just a load of wooden pallets on the floor with rice sacks as big as dry concrete bags, and huge army-sized drums of cooking oil.

I like looking at all the Chinese medicine shops. Their windows are always full of pictures of bloated blokes with blotches and boils and big bald heads, but don't worry, it says, because if you eat this leaf then you will be cured. Just crush up this chicken bone and sprinkle it in your dinner and your rash will be gone in a week.

They certainly like a nice massage in Chinatown. Every other shop is offering a five minute lie down to loosen up your back -- but I'm guessing that it's the kind of massage that hurts. There are probably lots of karate chops and pummelling of fists involved. You go in with an aching back and come out in floods of tears.

Churchill War Rooms

ADDRESS Churchill War Rooms, King Charles St, Westminster - map 8d **TRAINS** St. James's Park, Westminster (both zone 1) **BUSES** 3, 11, 12, 87, 88, 148, 159, 211, 453 **PRICE** Adult £19; Senior £15.20; Child (5-15) £9.50; Infant (under-5) free; Family (2 ad+2 ch) £49.90, or £33.25 with 1 ad+2ch; Price includes voluntary donation **OPEN** 9.30 AM to 6 PM (Mon-Sun); Last entry 1 hour before closing **WEB** iwm.org.uk/visits/churchill-war-rooms **TEL** 0207 930 6961 **TIME REQUIRED** 2 hours

Easy to get to? ★★★ Good for kids? ★★☆
Value for money? ★★☆ Worth a visit? ★★★

Is it possible to feel nostalgic for something that you never experienced? Because that's what I felt like today when I visited the Churchill War Rooms.

I quite like World War II. It seems like a lot of fun. But obviously I say that as someone who has never fought a fight in his life. The closest I've ever come to war is watching *Rambo* on the telly.

It's very atmospheric down in the War Rooms. The corridors are cramped and claustrophobic, and dull and dusty lightbulbs drop down on wires from low-level ceilings. It's a warren of wooden doors with an artery of iron pipes running up and down the length, it's very easy to imagine the ceilings shaking and dust flooding the tunnels as a bomb drops on Whitehall.

It must have been pretty dark and smoky, too, judging by all the 1940s fag packets strewn around the desks. With all the dumb health and safety laws these days, they would probably make you stand outside in the street if you wanted a puff, even in the middle of an air-raid.

As you stalk the gloomy corridors you're holding tight to a big chunky audio-guide that looks like a 1980s mobile phone. You hold it up to your ear and it describes each room in detail with dramatisations of the meetings and conversations going on inside. The acting is pretty good. They've got a decent Churchill and a succession of plummy voiced generals and Air Force attachés. Some of the lowly nobodies get a look in as well, with diary extracts and interviews from the secretaries and staff.

The first room you see is the best of the bunch: the War Cabinet Room, where Churchill actually sat and directed the war. It still has the same arrangement of tables and chairs inside, and you won't believe how cramped it is. Winston's seat is right in the middle and the rest of them are practically on his lap. It's very cosy down there. So you probably had the twenty most important people in England sitting in thirty feet of office space.

Then you head past the top-secret scrambler room, which was cunningly disguised as the Prime Minister's bog. It even has one of those 'engaged' locks on the door so he wouldn't be disturbed whilst he was on the phone. I wonder what people thought, queuing up outside, when he came out an hour later with a satisfied smile on his face.

The route takes a detour through the Churchill Museum at this point. This is basically a big warehouse-like room with glass cabinets and display cases filled with TV screens and memorabilia. There are plenty of touch-table tops with maps and battle plans from the war as well. The objects on display are all top quality: they've got one of the captured Enigma machines, for example, and Churchill's bowler hat and cigar. You can check out his watercolours, paints and paintbrushes if you want, and one of his famous man-baby romper suits. There are stacks and stacks of stuff on show... everything from his dickie bow-tie and bottle of Pol, to his old army uniform and trusty gun.

There are lots of TV screens dotted around showing old news footage. One of the best (and the most moving) was the video of his State funeral, showing the long slow march to St. Paul's Cathedral. It seemed to be a very slow and somber affair, with the tolling bells of the church above the shuffling steps of the soldiers. You can see the young Queen filing in behind the Westminster statesmen, and old Clementine, too, in her black lace veil. Then they load him onto a boat and carry him up the Thames, past Tower Bridge and the stooping cranes, all bowing their heads as he passes by. And then a fleet of jets streak across the sky and you are reminded that he didn't die until the 1960s. It's a very moving video, and well worth a watch.

When you leave the museum you head back out onto the tour, and past the pokey little bedrooms of the detectives and generals. They don't look very comfortable... more like a prison cell. They are all kitted out with tubular bunk beds and scratchy camp blankets, with a tin p*ss-pot in the corner and a candle stub and shaving mirror. If the inhabitant was important then they got a little threadbare piece of carpet as well, just to brighten up the bare brick walls and the hot bright lightbulb hanging from the ceiling.

The Prime Minister's Dining Room is another sorry looking room, with a table and plates and a few watercolours on the wall. The table is set for two: him and Clemmie. I wonder what they had for tea? Clemmie's bedroom is next-door and is probably the nicest room in the whole building. She was given a pink bedspread, a comfy plush armchair and a dressing table, too. Winston certainly knew how to treat his missus.

The little kitchen is very nostalgic, and it reminded me of my great gran's cottage kitchen. You can see a tin sink and the copper pots and plates. There's a big metal stove with bread bins stacked up on the cupboards, and a plunger pump plus a rusty tin of floor wax propped up against the pipes. If you have a good look around then you can see a crate of booze in the corner, underneath the fire blanket, hidden away where no one can see it.

The Chief of Staff's Conference Room is quite well appointed, and much nicer than Winston's War Cabinet Room. They managed to bag themselves a lengthy table with some green felt cloth on top, and stack up some posh glasses and beakers for the drink. There are some huge campaign maps pinned against the wall as well, like wallpaper, with lots of little pinpricks in them, where they've been hatching up their battle plans. There's also a very famous doodle of Adolf Hitler on one of them, so make sure you listen to the audio-guide here! (You won't be able to spot it otherwise.)

It was at this point that I had a little sit-down and a rest in the cafe, where you can buy some sausage and mash and mugs of greasy tea. It's worth a look inside just to see all of the wartime posters on the wall, and listen to all the 1940s tunes playing out the wireless. It's all Dame Vera Lynn and *We'll Meet Again*, stuff like that... barbershop quartets and the Glenn Miller band. It was whilst I was in here that I noticed that my mobile phone didn't work -- I couldn't get a signal. So maybe I was deeper underground than I thought.

Most of the rooms from this point on are staffed by waxworks acting out their jobs; beavering away at the switchboards, answering phones, and tapping out letters on their clapped-out typewriters. You can almost hear the *tring tring tring* of Bakelite telephones vibrating on the desks. The typing pool is interesting, because nestled amongst the typewriters and pots of pens and pencils are two dolled-up young ladies fixing their make-up in the mirror... with a gas mask on the table. It makes you wonder what this place was really like all those years ago.

When you stumble across the 'Advanced Headquarters of the Home Forces' then you'll be amazed about how we ever won the war -- because this *Advanced HQ* is nothing more than a few small rooms with four desks in it, a few phones and a fire bucket.

The Map Room is the busiest room in the building, and looks like the nerve centre of our entire war effort. Maps as big as windows are pinned against the walls, and banks of phones are ringing off the hook. A line of waxwork men are having waxwork conversations with each other... all top-secret stuff. It's a good job their waxwork mouths don't work or we'd probably have to block our ears. There's a special red phone in there, too: a hotline to somewhere important? Meanwhile a posh Admiral is pinning new lines onto the map. The front has moved: the *Germans are coming!* Quick, pick up that waxwork phone and start shouting down it. Let Winston know the Nazis are coming. Tell him to light up a cigar.

I quite like the way that they've left all of the books open so you can peer through the glass and see what they say. From what I could see they're full of troop numbers, ship tonnage and sinkage. There are lots of nice little touches like the pencil stub tied to the top of the book with string, so nobody could walk off with it. See if you can spot the little packet of sugar lumps on the desk, waiting to be dunked in his cup of tea. Apparently these are all genuine items from the 1940s -- they shut the rooms down at the end of the war and they've lain undisturbed ever since.

The last room on the tour is the Prime Minister's bedroom. He had a big map of Europe on the wall, a p*ss-pot on the floor, and a cigar by his bed (who takes a cigar to bed?). He pinned up a load of terrain maps on the wall as well, so he can go to bed dreaming of troop movements. *Sweet dreams, Winston.*

One final note: I was always under the impression that the Cabinet War Rooms were deep underground like a concrete bunker, reinforced with beams of steel to withstand an atomic bomb blast, and accessed through a 10-level lift with fingerprint scanners and gun-guard guys patrolling the corridors. But maybe I've been watching too many Cold War movies, because no, it is nothing like that. It is literally just ten steps down from the pavement. It seems to be housed in the basement of the Treasury next-door! If Hitler had aimed his bombs a bit better then I'm sure he could have landed one on Churchill's bed.

You might also enjoy also Imperial War Museum, Bletchley Park and HMS Belfast.

The City (Square Mile)

ADDRESS The City stretches from Temple Bar to Tower Bridge - maps 4f, 5e, 5f, 10a, 10b
TRAINS Bank, Cannon Street, Mansion House,

Monument (all zone 1) **BUSES** 4, 8, 11, 15, 21, 23, 25, 26, 42, 47, 48, 78, 100, 133, 141, 149, 242, RV1 **WEB** cityoflondon.gov.uk/pages/ default.aspx **TIME REQUIRED** 1½-3 hours

Easy to get to? ★★★ Good for kids? ★☆☆ Value for money? free Worth a visit? ★★★

I thought I'd just hang around the Square Mile today. That's the area inside the old city walls that runs roughly from St. Paul's to the Tower of London. We confusingly call this area 'The City', or the 'City of London', which technically means that Big Ben and Parliament are not really in the City of London at all -- they are in the City of Westminster (the sister-city of The City, if you see what I mean). So now that you are thoroughly confused, I can carry on with the review...

If you'd like to make some new friends then try catching the tube from Waterloo to Bank at half-past eight in the morning, when all the bleary-eyed businessmen and women are rushing off to work. *Talk about a crush!* I have never seen such a busy station in all my life; you even have to queue up to get on the platform. Even when you finally reach the platform that is no guarantee of actually getting on the train. You advance a few rows forward every time a train leaves, until you're finally forced into a cabin by the advancing mass of commuters behind -- and that's when the fun really starts, because you're wedged in with a butter knife. They push people in like an ill-fitting puzzle piece, stuff them in, cram them through the tube train doors. You will get to know more than a few people intimately. And then you get shoved out the other end onto an airport-style travelator to the exit. *Welcome to London!*

When you get above ground you will be staring straight at one of London's finest buildings: the Royal Exchange. It's a big Corinthian-columned building that looks far too grand to enter (it's actually just a posh shopping centre). If this is your first visit to The City then get your camera out for some quick photos. Across the road from the Exchange is the Bank of England, and over the road from there is the third great facade: Mansion House -- home to the Lord Mayor of London.

I've seen it all before so I just headed straight for the next best place: Starbucks in Walbrook. And that's where I'm sitting right now, drinking my cup of bubbled gloop. This is another place stuffed with poorly-pressed business suits. You have to queue up for ten minutes behind fifty city calculators on their way to their office. Time is money to these people. Every five minutes standing in Starbucks is another ten grand down the plughole. They have deals to make, shares to sell, and losers to shout at. *We haven't got time to queue, god dammit!* Get out of my way, losers, they are saying. *Can't you see my elbows sticking in your ribs? That means MOVE!*

I would have made quite a good yuppie, I think. I was a bit too young for all of that (I was still at school in the 1980s), but I would have been one of the country's top yuppies, without a doubt. A Filofax in one hand, a big brick of a phone in the other, slicked-back hair like Don Johnson in *Miami Vice*, and listening to Duran Duran on my Sony Walkman. (Okay... maybe I would have drawn the line at listening to Duran Duran.)

I have been reading quite a few economic books recently about how the City really works, and with this new found insight (I have read about ten pages so far) I have decided that all of London's money men are a bunch of chancers, gamblers and crooks. Frittering away other people's money for a fat bonus and a laugh; which they then proceed to spend in Starbucks, it seems, on a frothy shot of custom coffee.

There is one guy opposite me right now, for example, laughing uproariously as he drains the last drop of someone's pension fund from his cup. And look at this guy... blowing all of my savings on a slice of lemon drizzle cake. These people are cold and ruthless and probably a little bit evil too. Some of them have lava-coloured fire eyes. Some of them have got hot smoke billowing out of their ears (I am getting carried away now). You have to admire them really. If I had been born ten years earlier then that could have been me, a raw recruit in Maggie's financial army. But instead I am just sitting here, nursing a cheapo cup of coffee as they hurriedly bundle past the window.

Is there such a word as 'smarm'? Because I have just seen a very suave guy smarming his way past some people in the queue. What a character this guy is: he is Mr Perfect. He has probably got a suit on under his suit, and a riverfront flat overlooking Tower Bridge. His bones are bright white and his heart beats in musical tunes. He gives off daylight in the morning. Says hello to everyone he meets. And when he opens his mouth butterflies come out. I wonder what kind of coffee he's going to buy? Because you can tell a lot about a man by the kind of coffee he drinks. If he has a choca-mocca-frappe-crappa-latte then he's a wannabe continental. If he has his coffee with ten sugars and half a bottle of milk then he's an Englishman. Let's see what he's going to have... come on... *hurry up!* Get a move on for chrissakes because my cup is getting cold. All I can tell from this distance is that the liquid is brown.

Back into the daylight now. One of the best benches in London is outside the Royal Exchange. You'll find a little forecourt with flowerbeds and statues of old soldiers and the Duke of Wellington (you will see him a lot on your travels around London). Have a sit down there for five minutes and watch the world go by -- this is my favourite place to sit in the whole of London. I think the workers have finally been summoned to their desks because it's 10 o'clock now. Oh no... wait a minute. I spoke too soon. It must be tea-break already because the streets are suddenly swarming with silk ties and Savile Row suits. I would love it if Londoners still wore the businessman's uniform of a bowler hat and briefcase, like they do on the Pathé news, but that seems to have fallen out of fashion now; although moustaches are making a comeback, I see. (And not just on the men -- I can see a few women with them, too.)

As pretty as this junction is, there's not a lot to actually *do*. You can have a look around the Royal Exchange if you like, and steam up the posh shops' windows with your breath (trust me, you won't be able to afford anything), but Mansion House is only accessible through a tour. And the only way to enter the Bank of England is with a fat wallet or a gun, and I have neither. They have a free museum about money if you're desperate for entertainment, but I don't recommend it for a regular tourist. So take a tip from me and go for a stroll down Lombard Street instead, to the left of St. Mary Woolnoth church. They usually have a little coffee caravan on the church steps if you fancy accompanying me on my coffee crawl. The last time I went on one of these coffee crawls I nearly had a heart attack from all the caffeine, so be careful.

There are a lot of nice buildings around this area, mixed up with a few modern monstrosities that went up after the war. Throgmorton Street is one of my favourites, which gives you a good idea of how Ye Olde London must have looked before it got demolished. You have to raise your eyes above the pavement to get the best of it, though, as there are some very ornate carvings, columns and clocks above the door-tops. There is also a very nice background soundtrack of beeping cars, black taxis and double-decker buses (a very underrated part of London life).

When you reach the end of Lombard Street you will be treated to three decent buildings. To your right is Christopher Wren's Monument, built to commemorate the Great Fire of London in 1666. If you are a total nut-job then you can spend the next thirty minutes climbing up the 311 steps to the balcony at the top. If you've drunk enough coffees then you might even want to run up. I am normal though, so I admired it from the street.

Over to the left is the so-called 'Cheese Grater' building. Apparently it looks like a cheese grater. I think it looks like a triangle. And straight ahead is the 'Walkie Scorchie' skyscraper. This is one of my favourite buildings in the entire city, but only because it can set your hair on fire. A few weeks after it opened it famously started to melt all of the cars in the road below, because the curved glass facade focused all of the sun's rays onto the pavement. So if it's sunny be extremely careful down there: I don't want you to burst into flames. (I won't be liable for that, by the way, so you can't sue me.)

Carry on walking in the same direction towards the Walkie Scorchie (down Fenchurch Street) and then take a left into Lime Street. You have just walked across the site of the old Roman basilica, although there's nothing left above ground to tell you (apparently there are a few bricks in a barber shop's basement, but it's out of bounds to the public). Take a quick left down Lime Street Passage, and then enter the Victorian-esque Leadenhall Market -- coffee stop number three.

After that little detour come back out the same way you came in, and continue up the rest of Lime Street, where you will be treated to two more nice buildings: the inside-out Lloyd's Building (you will understand what I mean when you see it) and the gherkin-shaped Gherkin. Or the pickle-shaped Gherkin, if you prefer. Personally, I think it looks more like an aubergine. You can't go inside any of these buildings unfortunately, but they are definitely worth a look.

Whilst you're in The City you can check out The Monument, Royal Exchange, Leadenhall Market and St. Paul's.

City Hall

ADDRESS City Hall, Queen's Walk - map 10d **TRAINS** London Bridge (zone 1) and a 10 min walk, or Tower Hill (zone 1) and a 15 min walk across Tower Bridge **BUSES** 42, 47, 78, 381, RV1 **PRICE** Free **OPEN** 8.30 AM to 5.30 PM (Mon-Fri) **WEB** london.gov.uk/ visiting-and-using-city-hall **TEL** 0207 983 4000 **TIME REQUIRED** 30 mins

Easy to get to? ★★★ Good for kids? ☆☆☆
Value for money? free Worth a visit? ★★☆

City Hall looks like quite a friendly little building from afar, but once you get within fifty feet it starts to look a lot more official. You start to wonder whether you're really allowed inside. It's all glass and steel with big burly guards inside the window. *Am I really allowed in there? Will*

I get told off if I walk through the door? You end up milling around the forecourt for five minutes as you watch the suited and booted people enter with their briefcases and phones. You can see the security people waving beeping machines over their clothes and rifling through their bags before they let them pass, and then you start sweating and having heart palpitations and panic attacks and start looking for the nearest bus stop. But of course you have nothing to worry about. Just go inside, the security guards were actually quite nice and happily answered all of my dumb questions. (*Where can I go? Can I take photos?*) If they let scruffy urchins like me inside, then you'll have nothing to worry about.

I quite like the building, although lots of people don't. At least they made an effort to be original. Most of the places they put up today are just brick and concrete boxes. But can you name another building that looks anything like City Hall? Nope. It is a one-off. And it's even more peculiar once you get inside because instead of having stairs, it has a huge ramp that runs around the interior of the window, giving you great views of the Thames as you wind your way around the floors. Unfortunately you are only allowed to go up to the second floor, though, where the council chamber is. Everything above that is out of bounds to the public. Apparently there was a time when you could wander all the way up to the roof for an exterior view on the balcony, but the Mayor put paid to that to save a bit of money. So the second floor is as high as you can go now -- Boo!

There's not a lot to see inside. There were no meetings on when I went, so I was stuck outside the council chamber peering in at the empty seats.

There's an exhibition space in the basement, but that was deserted, too. They've superimposed a huge satellite map of London on the floor, so I suppose you could try and find your house if you were truly bored. Apart from that it's just a little cafe downstairs, which was actually quite interesting. You can sit amongst the politician-types as they chat angrily on their phones, and punch buttons on their laptops like they're jabbing a finger in someone's eye. The people that I sat next to had a big black folder with three thousand Post-It notes falling out all over the place, arguing the toss about who's right and who's wrong, all whilst munching on their egg and sausage sandwiches. I wonder if the Mayor goes down there for lunch? Maybe he does.

So is it Worth a visit? Well... if you happen to be visiting Tower Bridge or HMS Belfast then it might be worth popping in, just to be nosey. Because both of those attractions are right next-door. You can get some decent photos of the City skyscrapers and the Tower of London across the river as well. But it's not worth planning your day around. It's a lot more interesting when there's an actual meeting on...

City Hall -- Mayor's Question Time

ADDRESS City Hall, Queen's Walk - map 10d
TRAINS London Bridge (zone 1) and a 10 min walk, or Tower Hill (zone 1) and a 15 min walk across Tower Bridge **BUSES** 42, 47, 78, 381,

RV1 PRICE Free **DATES** Once a month, usually during the third week - see website for the dates **WEB** london.gov.uk/about-us/london-assembly/public-meetings **TEL** 0207 983 4000 **TIME REQUIRED** Usually starts at 10 AM and lasts for 1-2 hours, but arrive early for a seat

Easy to get to? ★★★ Good for kids? ☆☆☆ Value for money? free Worth a visit? ★★★

I went back to City Hall again today to see Boris Johnson holding court at Mayor's Question Time. That's the big monthly meeting where all the London Assembly members get to badger him and shout at him for a couple of hours. They only hold it once a month, and it's always slap bang in the middle of a weekday (10 AM to 12 noon), so it's not the easiest of things to visit. But it's definitely worth doing if you can arrange it.

I got a bit unlucky with the buses today, because it took me thirty minutes to get to City Hall from Waterloo, so when I finally arrived the chamber was already packed out with the early birds. It was only ten minutes past the start, but the doors were slammed shut to latecomers. Luckily they still let you stand outside the chamber and peer in through the windows, so you can still see the Mayor and hear what he's saying through the big TV screens outside. It felt a bit like a day at the zoo... standing there with my nose pressed up against the glass, trying to get a peek of the prize exhibits inside.

Fortunately you don't have to wait too long on the outside, because as soon as a few people get bored and leave they let you take up their places. So within half-an-hour I was through the gate and into the inner sanctum. I still wasn't able to sit down, though. I was standing with all the latecomers at the back. It was another hour before I actually managed to sit down -- so make sure you get there early!

There are probably about 250 seats in total, and most of them seemed to be taken up by dopey-looking students with paper pads on their knees, biros sticking out of their mouths (and noses), looking bored and waiting for the playtime bell to ring. The rest of them were filled up with photographers, business-type people scribbling furiously into their notebooks, and one lady updating her Twitter feed every 0.5 seconds. At one point about fifteen kids from a local primary school turned up and got a mention from the chair, prompting all of the politicians to turn around and wave at them! (That's modern politics for you -- everyone has to be nice to the kiddies when there's a photographer around.)

Boris looked, sounded and acted exactly as you'd expect him to... all of his language and mannerisms were 100% present and correct. His trademark messy hair had a tufty lump of locks at right-angles to his head, and his battered down flat-top made him look dangerously like Donald Trump from a distance. I'm sure it must have taken him ages to get it looking that messy, because it was almost too messy. It looked like he'd styled it in a mirror.

The chamber is arranged for maximum uncomfortable-ness for the Mayor (if that's even a word). He is all on his own in a solitary seat, whilst a horseshoe of politicians stretches out around him. And after them come the baying crowd, sitting in four tiers of seats like a Roman amphitheatre. And there is no safety glass between the public and the Mayor either (unlike at the House of Commons), so there really is no escape for the poor fella. Everyone is facing him. Every camera is focused on him, and every word he says is amplified out of three billion speakers that are dotted around the room. They've even placed two huge TV screens off to the side with a couple of close-ups of his face, so you can see every bead of sweat that is rolling down his nose. It's like a police interrogation.

You had to feel a bit sorry for him, totally isolated at the front whilst they were all trying to do their best to trip him up and trick him into saying something stupid. But don't worry... because our hero was more than capable of holding his own against all of those nasty politicians. All he had to do when it got a bit lively was to trot out a witty one-liner and everyone was smiling again. He did crack a few funny lines, and let loose a lot of flowery speeches. He was surprisingly combative when it came to arguing his case. He certainly didn't mind talking over people and raising his voice if he thought that they were wrong. But most of the time he was totally serious, as you would expect. It was all party politics and policies, most of which washed straight over my head.

Here is a list of some of the subjects they covered, to give you a taste of what it was like: they talked about half-week travelcards, affordable housing, a third runway for Heathrow, and forcing developers to give up their land if they don't build on it. They also discussed an expansion of the hire bike scheme, extending the Northern Line to Battersea, and introducing rent controls for essential workers.

A tip: before you go inside the chamber look out for an A4-sized sheet of paper by the door that lists all of the questions. It's a good idea to pick one of those up, because the chairman doesn't always read the question out. Sometimes he just says "Question No.5", or whatever it is, and if you don't have the sheet with you then you won't know what it is they're blathering on about.

If you get bored of the politics then you can enjoy the view out of the back window. Straight across the river is the Tower of London, and towards the left are the Gherkin and the City skyscrapers. The chamber itself is at the centre of the 'teardrop', right inside the heart of the building, and you can see the spiral staircase winding its way around the floors above your head until it tapers out somewhere close to the dome.

The meeting overran a little bit today, and Boris ended up rushing out at 12:45. I thought it would have been fantastic if he ascended up the spiral staircase to his office at the top, with everyone applauding and cheering him in a series of ever-distant encores as he wound his way up the loop, but alas, it was a lot more boring than that. He just scooped up his rucksack from behind the lectern, roughly stuffed his folders into it, and disappeared out the back in a flash.

If you enjoy watching political debates then try the House of Commons, House of Lords, and Common Council at Guildhall.

Clarence House

ADDRESS Clarence House, The Mall - map 8c **TRAINS** Charing Cross, Green Park, St. James's Park (all zone 1) **BUSES** 8, 9, 14, 19, 22, 38 **PRICE** Adult £10; Senior (over-60) £10; Child (5-16) £6; Infant (under-5) free **OPEN** Guided tours between 10 AM and 4.30 PM (Mon-Fri, Aug only), and 10 AM to 5.30 PM (Sat-Sun, Aug only); Last tour 1 hour before closing **WEB** royalcollection.org.uk/visit/clarence-house **TIME REQUIRED** 1-1½ hours

Easy to get to? ★★★   Good for kids? ☆☆☆
Value for money? ★★★   Worth a visit? ★★☆

Clarence House is where Prince Charles lives with Camilla, in the Queen Mother's old house. So he basically lives in his grandmother's house. Imagine that... having to live in your 101-year-old grandmother's house and keep all her tables and chairs and pictures on the wall. No wonder the guy is a little bit nuts.

Every time I've been on this tour I've been the only young guy on it. My group today consisted of eighteen old people and me, and they were practically all English. The tourists all flock to Buckingham Palace and Windsor, and Clarence House is left with the ageing Brits. It seems to be much more for the older generation, this place, because it doesn't have the razzmatazz of the palace. So don't come here expecting to see a golden balustrade on the stairs, because it's still done up the same way the Queen Mother had it when she passed away.

It's a fairly short tour, but the plus point is that you get led around by a real human being rather than having to strap a pair of headphones to your bonnet. So there are plenty of opportunities to ask questions and learn little bits of info that you might miss with an audio guide. The old guy that led us around today certainly knew his stuff. He had the names and dates of everything dropping off the end of his tongue before we'd even got the question out of our mouths. One lady asked him about the antique fire-guard, of all things, and he even knew who built that.

But as good as the guide was, I think he spent a little bit too much time on the art. He slobbered over every single piece; but these aren't the kind of pictures that you'll find in an art gallery. We're not talking great works of art, here. These paintings are much more personal -- they're all family portraits and pictures of distant relatives, plus a collection of Windsor Castle watercolours.

Much more fun are the personal photographs that Charles' has dotted around the tables. In much the same way that you'd display a photo of your child's first day at school, he has photos of William and Kate's wedding day, and Harry dressed up in his first military uniform. You can see some faded pictures of his mother, too, (the Queen), when she still had kid-curls in her hair, and plenty of William when he was a cheeky little kid (when he still had hair). But I noticed that there wasn't a single picture of Diana anywhere -- he must have chucked them all out. Or maybe he's got them pinned to his dartboard upstairs? Perhaps Camilla 'accidentally' burned them with her cigarettes. But come to think of it... he didn't have any of Camilla either. *Strange.* But they are probably upstairs on his bedside table, because you only get to see about five of the reception rooms downstairs -- the private rooms on the second floor are all out of bounds to the public. Maybe that's where they keep the telly as well, because I didn't see one of those either.

Another nice thing about the tour is that there are no ropes or barriers anywhere. You can stroll around the rooms between the tables and chairs, an inch away from their knick-knacks and heirlooms. You certainly can't do that at the Palace.

I enjoyed having a nose around his bookcases. They seemed to be full of biographies of kings and queens and politicians. He had stacks of stuff about famous painters, too. There was a cabinet full of Dick Francis and PG Wodehouse novels, and a well-thumbed edition of *Peter Pan* that the Queen used to read when she was a kid.

After you've seen the rooms you are allowed to have a quick look at the garden, but it's basically just a big lawn with a tree in the middle. There's a vegetable patch off to the side, where he grows his grub in the mud and then gets his staff to cook it in the kitchens. Very eco-friendly, is our Prince. Then it's off to the shop to buy some organic teabags.

If you like the Royals then try Buckingham Palace, Kensington Palace, Windsor Castle and Hampton Court.

Cleopatra's Needle

ADDRESS Cleopatra's Needle, Victoria Embankment - map 8b **TRAINS** Charing Cross, Embankment (both zone 1) **BUSES** 1, 4, 6, 9, 11, 13, 15, 23, 26, 59, 68, 76, 87, 91, 139, 168, 171, 172, 176, 188, 243, 341, RV1, X68 **TIME REQUIRED** 5 mins

Easy to get to? ★★★ Good for kids? ☆☆☆
Value for money? free Worth a visit? ★☆☆

What's the oldest thing in London?

No, it's not Prince Philip. It's actually this big block of rock on Victoria Embankment: *Cleopatra's Needle*.

I must admit that I've never really looked at it properly before. It's one of those things that you just stare at from the warmth of a passing bus. But if you take the time to cross over the busy road and have a nose around then it's actually quite interesting. Did you know, for example, that this monument is even older than London itself? And I mean that *literally* -- because when the Romans built their first bridge across the Thames in 50 AD this obelisk had already been standing outside an Egyptian temple for 1,500 years. It's quite incredible, really.

Just think about that for a second... Cleopatra's Needle was already ancient before the Romans arrived. It was even ancient in Cleopatra's day -- she was born a millennium after it was built! She was as far removed from the Needle as we are from the Battle of Hastings.

It was originally carved by Thutmose III in 1450 BC, and chiselled with inscriptions by Ramesses II. Another 1,500 passed before the Romans shifted it to Alexandria to stand outside Cleopatra's Caesareum, which is where it obtained its name (although she was long dead by this time). A short time later it fell over and spent the next 1,800 years lying face down in the sand. If you check out all four faces then you can see that one side is slightly better preserved -- presumably that was the one that was face down in the desert.

That's where Napoleon and Admiral Nelson enter the story (what an amazing history!). Nelson beat back the French at the Battle of the Nile, and the grateful Egyptians gave us this long-toppled obelisk as a gift, but it was another sixty years before the Victorians finally worked out how to shift it. They probably wish they hadn't bothered -- because this thing is bad luck. It is bad news. (An Egyptian curse?) If you read the brass plaques around the side then you'll discover that six people died when the boat was caught in a storm on the way back to Blighty.

If you have a look around the base then you'll see a lot of pockmarks in the concrete. That's where it sustained some shrapnel damage in World War I. Most people believe that the first bombing raid in London was during the Blitz, but it was actually when a wave of wooden fighters came over in 1917. I wonder what Thutmose III would have thought 3,500 years ago, standing in his flip-flops in the desert, if he had a flash forward to its apocalyptic future of fire and flames and Germans dropping dynamite on it from the sky?

So that's the story of the Needle. Personally I think that it deserves a much better spot than it has, because you can hardly see it behind the leafy trees. How about the centre of Leicester Square instead? Then we can shift that Shakespeare statue to stand outside the Globe.

If you like Egyptian archaeology then try the Petrie Museum, British Museum and Sir John Soane's Museum.

Clink Prison Museum

ADDRESS Clink Prison Museum, 1 Clink Street, Southwark - map 10a **TRAINS** London Bridge (zone 1) **BUSES** 17, 21, 35, 40, 43, 45, 47, 48, 133, 141, 149, 381, 521, RV1 **PRICE** Adult £7.50; Senior £5.50; Child (under-16) £5.50; Family (2 ad+2 ch) £18 **OPEN** 10 AM to 9 PM (Mon-Sun, Jul-Sep); 10 AM to 6 PM (Mon-Fri, Oct-Jun); 10 AM to 7.30 PM (Sat-Sun, Oct-Jun); Last entry 30 mins before closing **WEB** clink.co.uk **TEL** 0207 403 0900 **TIME REQUIRED** 30-45 mins

Easy to get to? ★★★ Good for kids? ★★☆
Value for money? ★★☆ Worth a visit? ★★☆

The Clink was a proper prison. The kind of prison that actually punished you. These days our prisoners get a colour TV and a PlayStation. Back then all they got was typhoid. Not that I've ever spent a night in prison, of course -- although I have spent a couple of nights in the Covent Garden Travelodge, which isn't very far off.

There's hardly anything left of the original prison anymore. All that remains of the medieval gaol is a solitary wall that survived the fire of 1780, so you're not walking around anything historic. You can't sit in the same cells that they did. It's basically just a mini-version of the London Dungeon.

It begins with a few gloomy monks chanting at the dungeon door, and then you walk around a few dimly lit rooms with fake flames and orange lightbulbs illuminating the walls, etc. Every time you turn a corner you'll meet a waxwork prisoner propped up in the corner, lamenting and repenting and posing for photos. The decoration is quite well done, I suppose -- you can tell they've made a proper effort to mess it up. It's all sawdust in the corner, oak beams and wagon wheels, and a constant song of crying kids and blokes moaning, bells tolling, chains clanking, flames crackling, and little pigs squealing and squeaking out of the speakers.

As you walk around you can learn a bit about the prison's history from the placards on the walls. It's all very basic, but it's a decent little taster for the tourists. They describe some of the famous criminals and what happened to them as well.

The best bit is obviously the torture equipment. I'm a huge fan of torture. Don't tell anybody that I said this (because it's a supposed to be a secret) but I've even dug a dungeon in my basement so I can torture anyone who gets on my nerves (which basically means everybody). I've certainly learnt a lot of fantastic new techniques at this museum. I think my new favourite form of torture is definitely the Oubliette, because it appeals to my laziness. You simply dig a hole and kick them in it, and then wait for them to die -- nice and simple. The Morning Star is more for psychos. It's a solid metal mace that you swing ten times around your head and then smash into their skull (it makes a lot of mess, that one). Or how about the Scold's Bridle? -- a cage for their face. You wrap a birdcage around their head and then tighten it up until their bones splinter through their cheeks. Some of the other forms of torture are too gruesome to mention. But how about the poor guy who was boiled to death at Smithfield? That will teach him to serve up poisoned porridge!

The gibbet is another of my favourites. That's when you wedge somebody into a metal cage and hang them from a lamppost until the birds have pecked them to death. It says on the plaque that we didn't finally abolish this practice until 1832, which sounds a bit late -- that's only five years before the Victorian period. I wonder if it's possible to bring that back again? Wait a minute... *I've just had a fantastic idea!* The Clink Prison could offer a babysitting service for our kids. We could drop them off in the morning, stick them in a gibbet, and then pick them up a week later.

The big difference between this place and the London Dungeon is the cost -- the Clink is a lot cheaper. But it's also a fraction of the size. The London Dungeon is more like a guided tour with acted-out scenes, whereas the Clink is just a museum with waxwork figures. It's also a lot less frightening for your kids.

You might like the London Dungeon and Madame Tussaud's Chamber of Horrors. Or how about a Jack The Ripper Tour, or a Ghost Tour around Hampton Court?

Courtauld Gallery

ADDRESS Courtauld Gallery, Somerset House, Strand - map 9a **TRAINS** Charing Cross, Embankment, Temple (all zone 1) **BUSES** 6, 9, 11, 13, 15, 23, 91, 176 **PRICE** Adult £7; Senior (over-60) £6; Child (under-19) free; Price includes a voluntary donation; Temporary exhibitions cost extra **OPEN** 10 AM to 6 PM (Mon-Sun); Last entry 30 mins before closing **WEB** courtauld.ac.uk/ gallery **TEL** 0207 848 2526 **TIME REQUIRED** 1-1½ hours
Easy to get to? ★★★ Good for kids? ☆☆☆
Value for money? ★★★ Worth a visit? ★★☆

I've found a nice place to have coffee today: it's on the forecourt of Somerset House. If you walk through the arch then it's directly on the left. It has to be a sunny day, though -- it's no good when it's raining, because you have to do a bit of people watching on the forecourt. They usually have some fountains spraying water ten feet into the air, but they must have switched them off today, because it's just a lot of tea drinkers and security guards lounging around in the sun.

I'm sitting here waiting for the Courtauld Gallery to open. This is the gallery that all the tourists miss. They tick off the National Gallery and the Tate, but if you ask them about the Courtauld then they'll say, *What? Where is that? Never heard of it!* I've never been here either, and it's supposed to be quite impressive. Apparently there are some real works of art inside -- the kind of stuff that actually took some skill to paint.

They've switched the fountains on now (just as I'm finishing my coffee). They go straight up like a rocket and then collapse over the top. All of the kids immediately make a beeline for them and dance around the edges like they're dicing with death. Their mum's faces immediately go into panic mood: *Don't get too close to it, or you'll die!* Too late. They have been touched by the poison and no amount of washing will get that water off.

Into the gallery now... At first sight it seems quite similar to the National Gallery. It's the same sort of art that's on display in there, except there's a lot less of it, and it costs more money to get in. So my first impression is this: go to the National instead, which doesn't cost a penny.

The first room is full of golden altarpieces and religious crucifixions. Then it's upstairs to a room full of Rubens. I'm a little bit surprised at how many famous names they've got on display. After the Rubens you come to an Impressionist section with works by Renoir, Degas, Manet, Monet and Gauguin. Not forgetting Seurat and Van Gogh, of course. They have plenty of pictures by Romney and Gainsborough as well.

The only pictures that I actually recognise (bearing in mind that I am no lover of art) are the straight-on shot of a busty barmaid in a Parisian bar, who isn't as pretty as I remember from my school days, and that one by Van Gogh with his head all bandaged up. He looks surprisingly content, considering that he's just chopped his ear off -- although he *was* nuts, I suppose. I wonder if that's where Quentin Tarantino got the idea for his ear-slicing scene in *Reservoir Dogs?* That would make Van Gogh Mr Blonde, I suppose. Or would it make Van Gogh the LA gun cop...? Hmmm... it's probably not important anyway. I shouldn't be thinking about Quentin Tarantino movies whilst standing in front of a priceless piece of art -- I should be concentrating on the colours and the texture of the brush strokes and other high-brow stuff like that.

Upstairs is where they keep the pieces by Cézanne and Matisse. And I'm not just talking about one or two paintings -- they have ten big canvases by Cézanne alone! I'm starting to think that their Impressionist collection is even better than the National's (seriously). I don't recall the National having as many pieces by each artist.

But after that it starts to go downhill, methinks, because you reach the modern art section with works by Kandinsky and Ben Nicholson. That's when they abandon the skilful stuff and resort to playschool paintings.

The gallery is still worth a visit, though. It's not the biggest place in the world, but if you like your Impressionists then you should definitely give it a go.

If you enjoy this try the National Gallery, Tate Britain and Wallace Collection.

Covent Garden

ADDRESS Covent Garden - map 8b **TRAINS** Charing Cross, Covent Garden, Leicester

Landmarks & Attractions | 65

Square (all zone 1) **BUSES** 4, 6, 9, 11, 13, 15, 23, 26, 76, 87, 139, 172, 243, 341, RV1 **WEB** coventgarden.london **TIME REQUIRED** 45-60 mins (but more if you plan to stop and eat)

Easy to get to? ★★★ Good for kids? ★★☆
Value for money? free Worth a visit? ★★★

I thought I'd do a spot of people watching in Covent Garden today. Obviously I'm only going to watch the women, though (that goes without saying -- I am a bloke, after all). But it's a bit wet and gloomy this morning, so there aren't many people about. The sky is dark and water is emptying out of it. The raindrops are like rocks, and don't even break on the pavement.

Everybody is hurrying under cover to get out of the wet. Umbrellas as big as dustbin lids are doming over their heads, bashing against brollies as they bundle past the others... it's like a big game of conkers. They are dangerous weapons, umbrellas. They might look pretty, but when you have a whole wall of them coming towards you at head-height it's like facing down a cavalry charge. The ones who haven't armed themselves (with brollies) are protecting their hair with whatever they've got: a supermarket plastic bag or a soggy wet newspaper.

I'm just sitting here enjoying the show -- this is my kind of weather. Some people like the sunshine, and some of us like the rain. I spend the next twenty minutes watching the pretty women walk past the coffee shop window and occasionally manage to make eye contact with one of them; usually when I have the coffee cup covering up my face. Or I might be in the middle of smiling about something, and they'll start smiling too, thinking that I was smiling at them (I wasn't). Such is how first impressions are made: the whimsy that happens to be sitting on your face at any given moment. They think you're being flirty, but in actual fact you were just recalling the time your dog fell in the river.

I make a quick dash across to the Piazza and find that everything is still in the process of opening up. Baristas are cleaning and steaming out their coffee machines, and beeping trash trucks are carting away the bin bags full of rubbish. Street cleaners are sweeping up last night's revelry. But once it gets going this place is packed. This is one of the meeting spots of London, like Trafalgar Square and Piccadilly Circus. People come here for their lunch and a nose around the shops, trying to find a way to waste their cash.

Covent Garden is extremely popular with the tourists, and now that I stop to think about it I'm wondering why that is. It only has one real attraction inside: the London Transport Museum; and that's hardly the city's biggest pull. The Royal Opera House is around the back, and St. Paul's church is worth five minutes of your time, but that's pretty much it. So why is it so popular? I dunno. It has some nice little shops inside, I suppose, plus an undercover street market, but if I'm honest the only time I ever come here myself is to have a wee -- there are some toilets next to the church (which are few and far between in London).

You can usually find some free street entertainers outside St. Paul's church, juggling balls and swallowing swords, doing flips and magic tricks. Crowds of people gather around and enjoy the show for twenty minutes, and then disappear as soon as the hat gets passed around. But it must be a bit early in the morning for all of that... because all I can see right now are a load of old drunks kipped out on the steps, clutching crumpled-up tins of Diamond Light. They are holding out their hands for money, but it's a tough crowd around here. If you want some money then people will expect a show -- *this is Covent Garden, mate!* If you want some notes then you'll have to earn them. People don't want to hear your sob stories, they want you to sing a song.

I don't think much of the shops in the piazza. It's full of little boutiques and markets stalls selling overpriced tat to the tourists. Carved candles and big chunks of coloured soap, wooden pipes and piddly pots of posh jam -- stuff like that. Put it this way: it's not the kind of place where you'll come to do your weekly shop.

Let me have a walk around and I'll tell you some of the things they've got on sale...

I can see posh perfumes and watches, silver pewter teapots and little china teddy bears, framed prints of pressed flowers, old army berets and decorated thimbles, coffee beans and tea-leaves in brown paper bags, miniature Russian dolls, and smelly coloured candles. So you can basically buy everything under the sun... but none of it is useful. If you were wandering along in the desert and stumbled across one of these shops then you wouldn't be very happy.

Gasp! Gasp! Do you have a glass of water?

Er... no. I'm afraid not.

What about a picture of a dog made out of old jumper buttons?

Now that we *can* do! And it's only twenty five quid!

So this is a great place to buy gifts -- stuff that you can give away to your friends when you get back home so you won't have to keep it yourself. And remember to bring your wallet as well, because even the fivers cost a tenner here -- that is how expensive it is.

Covent Garden is also home to a more traditional market (Jubilee Market), with lots of tented stalls selling scarves and hats and second-hand trinkets. If you want to get one of those corny 'My brother went to London' t-shirts, or a 'Keep calm and carry on' poster, then this is the place to find it. (Although Camden Market is probably better.)

I still can't find any street entertainers anywhere, and it's getting on for 10:30 AM now. *Where are they all?* There are two places where you can usually find them, and the main one is on the courtyard outside St. Paul's church (not to be confused with St. Paul's Cathedral -- if somebody gave you directions to St. Paul's and you ended up here then you're in totally the wrong place!). If you want the best viewing spot then try and wedge yourself onto the balcony of the Punch & Judy pub, overlooking the square. It gets jam-packed in the afternoon and early evening though, and is probably not worth the hassle. Even if you manage to get a spot by the balcony, you'll lose it as soon as you try and fight your way back to the bar.

The second place where you can see some entertainment is downstairs in the Piazza (near the *Nauticalia* shop). That's where I'm sitting at the moment. It's a bit more upmarket down here because it's all opera singers and string quartets. And it's not just a load of two-bit tunesters, either -- they are proper warblers doing Mozart, Beethoven and Verdi. As I'm writing this they are belting out Vivaldi's Four Seasons on three violins and a cello. Five minutes ago they had a big bird up there singing Puccini.

Because the Piazza is undercover the sound really echoes loudly around the room. It's almost like a concert hall -- real top-notch stuff. I like watching the expressions on their faces as they play the piece. Every time she hits a top note she screws up her eyes tight like a tourniquet, squeezing out every last drop of the note, mouth pursed tight like she's sucking on a sweet. I think there must be a whole different event going on inside her head... inside her skull's movie dome she's dreaming of singing in the Royal Albert Hall, but in reality it's just us lazy coffee drinkers in Covent Garden. I almost never give buskers any money (too tight), but I must be in a good mood today because I dipped a fist into my pocket and brought up... ten pence. She gave an acknowledging nod as I dropped the coins into the bucket, thinking that it was more.

There are still no signs of any buskers in the main square, and it's nearly noon-time now, so I guess I'll have to make my own entertainment today. Oh no... wait a minute... I spoke too soon because here he is -- he's moved into the North Hall to escape the rain. I've found a very shouty magician with bright blue spiky hair; sort-of like a cross between Paul Daniels and Sid Vicious (if you can imagine such a thing). His tricks aren't up to much but his jokes are quite funny. He made a Coke can float and two hundred people laugh.

Twenty minutes later... I've just stood and watched his entire show from start to finish and it was quite good. He dragged a chubby guy out of the crowd and ordered him to lie face up on the ground, and then stripped down to his Union Jack pants and juggled sharp knives over his face. Now *that's* entertainment! His big finale was lying on a bed of nails whilst the big fella walked on top. The whole thing was laugh out loud funny and well worth twenty minutes of my time.

Cutty Sark

ADDRESS Cutty Sark, King William Walk, Greenwich - map 11c **TRAINS** Cutty Sark DLR (zones 2 and 3) **BUSES** 129, 177, 180, 188, 199, 386 **PRICE** Adult £13.50; Senior (over-60) £11.50; Child (5-15) £7; Infant (under-5) free; Family (2 ad+2 ch) £35, or £24 with 1 ad+2ch; Price includes a voluntary donation **OPEN** 10 AM to 5 PM (Mon-Sun, Sep to mid-Jul); 10 AM to 6 PM (Mon-Sun, mid-Jul to end of Aug); Last entry 45 mins before closing **WEB** rmg.co.uk/ cutty-sark **TEL** 0208 858 4422 **TIME REQUIRED** 1¼-1½ hours

Easy to get to? ★★★ Good for kids? ★☆☆
Value for money? ★☆☆ Worth a visit? ★★☆

If you're planning on visiting Greenwich for any reason whatsoever, then take my advice and catch a boat from Westminster Bridge. Tube trains should be banned to Greenwich, because you're missing out on the best bit: the river ride. It takes about an hour to float from Big Ben to Greenwich pier, and if it's boiling hot weather like it was today and you get the cold wind in your face, it's great. So get a boat. If I discover that you caught a train, then you will be in big trouble. When you disembark at Greenwich pier the Cutty Sark will be right in front of you -- you can actually see the mast towering up as you come in to dock.

When I was a kid it used to be beached inside a dry concrete pit by the water's edge, and all the stale rainwater would collect in the corners in a dirty stew of sticks and polystyrene cups. *Ah, nostalgia!*

But these days it appears to be floating on top of a big blue greenhouse of glass.

It's quite clever the way they've done it. Imagine a half-bubble of glass with a boat dropped on top. It just sits on the surface like its sailing on the sea, and then you can descend into the basement and see it hanging in mid-air above you, like a giant chandelier. The only other place that you can view a boat from such a unique angle is on the bottom of the seabed.

As I'm sitting here minding my own business, waiting for the doors to open, a party of fifty school kids has turned up -- noisy ones. And three teachers, too -- even noisier than the kids -- all marching around like stressed-out sergeant majors. They're trying to marshal their adolescent army into a tidy line, but not having much luck. It's a very unfair fight. The three teachers are armed with nothing but raised voices and pointed fingers, whilst the fifty kids have malfunctioning ears and deadly mocking laughter. I wonder if they still have a plank onboard this boat? Or was that just on pirate ships? Are you even allowed to make criminals walk the plank these days? Probably not... I never understood the point of a plank anyway. Why bother blindfolding them and making them walk five feet on a bendy bit of wood? Why not just shoot them? Or fire them out of a cannon, or something. Throw them over the side and let the sharks eat them. Who cares whether they can balance on a bit of wood?

Part of me would quite like to be a sailor. Half of my head wants to stow away on a boat and never come home. But then I have a stroll around the Cutty Sark and learn that life onboard wasn't much fun. They've stacked up a few sacks and bags and crates of cargo to give you a taste of the cramped space, but most of it is empty today, and filled up with flashing TV screens showing scenes of the sloshing sea. They've got a little sit down cinema as well, projecting a very basic documentary onto the back of some old tea chests to tell you what it did and where it went. I like sitting here and listening to all of the sounds floating out of the speakers: you can hear the creaking hull and brass bell ringing on top, and a few seagulls flapping around outside.

The next deck includes a few interactive table tops and push-button models for the kids (not very exciting) and some scale models of the ship. They also have a small collection of original artefacts on show including a lifebelt, a barometer and a bell, but not a lot else. The middle deck seems rather sparse and empty to me -- they should have put some more cargo boxes in there.

The top deck is by far the most interesting. What a beautiful deck. It's all polished planks and warm woods, and coils of rope that look like iron cables. The masts are towering fifty feet at least, and I'm struggling to see where they finish because their pointed tops are puncturing the sun. The river is only fifty feet away and the seagulls are wheeling and circling the ship, and if you shut your eyes you can almost believe that you're sailing somewhere exciting. I can only imagine what the masts must have looked like with their white sails billowing -- what an amazing sight! Why don't they put them back on again? This ship has got no clothes on. But even without its skin the bones are beautiful.

How on earth did the sailors manage to climb to the top of those masts? They must have been mad. You would require balls of steel to even attempt it today -- so imagine what it must have been like when the boat was rolling around on the South China seas.

You can have a nose around a couple of the crew cabins and see the five-foot bunkbeds where they slept (you'd have to chop your feet off to fit inside). You can also look inside the beautiful saloon with its tea-coloured wood and hanging lamps of polished brass -- it even has a cast iron fireplace in it. Did they not have health and safety laws in the 19th century? I don't think I'd fancy lighting a fire on a wooden boat. That just shows you how soft and lily-livered we've become these days, because the only time this boat ever caught fire was actually right here in Greenwich, on this very spot, when some hoodlums torched it in dry dock.

The end of the tour takes you down into the concrete pit underneath the ship. As you come down the stairs you can see the whole thing suspended above you like a storm cloud in the sky. It is huge. If you stick a pair of wings on it then it would bigger than a jumbo jet. It seems far too heavy to be hanging from the roof. It reminds me of that big Blue Whale they've got suspended from the ceiling at the Natural History Museum. The final exhibit down there is a collection of colourful figureheads, but there's not a lot else. Just a lot of screaming kids and nattering families in the cafe.

If you like boats and you've got time for a day trip, you can try Chatham Dockyard.

Design Museum

ADDRESS Design Museum, 28 Shad Thames, Butler's Wharf **TRAINS** London Bridge and a 15 min walk, Tower Hill and a 15 min walk (both zone 1) **BUSES** 42, 78, 188, 381, RV1 **PRICE** Adult £13; Senior (over-60) £10.40 (Wed only, with ID); Child (6-15) £6.50; Infant (under-6) free; Price includes a voluntary donation **OPEN** 10 AM to 5.45 PM (Mon-Sun); Last entry 30 mins before closing **WEB** designmuseum.org **TEL** 0207 403 6933 **TIME REQUIRED** 1 hour

Easy to get to? ★★★ Good for kids? ☆☆☆
Value for money? ☆☆☆ Worth a visit? ☆☆☆

The way that the Design Museum operates is through a series of temporary exhibitions, so I can't guarantee that what you'll see will be the same as what I saw today. But hopefully you'll have better luck, because what I saw was rubbish.

I hate using the word *rubbish* in a review because it's such a lazy way of describing something, but on this occasion it's a perfect fit -- because it was rubbish! I've actually been to plenty of places that were far worse than the Design Museum, but I always let them off the hook because they were free (you expect a bit of rubbishyness when it's free), but what wound me up about this place was the price -- they charge you a totally ridiculous amount to get in. Thirteen quid is a crazy amount to pay for the slim pickings they have inside.

The first floor was full of women's dresses. Not famous dresses, worn by famous people, but just some standard shop-bought dresses on a plastic mannequin. Some of them were brave and outrageous, I suppose (huge feathers and neon stripes, etc.), but most of them were just the same stuff you'll see walking down the high street: a pair of dungarees, some high-heeled shoes, a lady's business suit.

I think they must have realised that it was a bit poor because they tried to pad it out with photographs. So instead of seeing Margaret Thatcher's actual blue suit, you just got to see a photo of it, plus a photograph of Jackie O wearing some sunglasses. They gave you photos instead of objects. That was it. It took me fifteen minutes to walk around the whole lot, and five of those were spent sitting down writing this.

The second floor focused on wearable tech. This one looked like an Apple Store. It had a long wooden table with some iPads and iPhones on top, coupled with some sensors that can measure your blood pressure and heart rate. It just seemed like one big advert to me. One of the exhibits was for a baby app, for example, which dished out child advice to new parents, but it just seemed like something you'd buy for 99p in the App Store. Another one was called iHealth, which allowed you to type your sugar intake into your phone. *Woopie-doo!*

The third floor is where they kept all of their best stuff... if you can call a stackable chair and a bike light their best stuff. Okay, so I admit that a stackable chair is quite a handy piece of design, but do you really want to come to a museum to see one? Or how about a brick? I suppose it fits the bill as another great piece of design... but it's a brick. You can't charge people an entry fee to see a brick! How about an early inkjet printer (you've probably got one of those gathering dust in your loft). Or a plastic wastepaper basket? Or a potato peeler? Or twelve teapots? *I kid you not, folks.* That is what you can see when you stump up thirteen quid to enter the Design Museum: a display case containing twelve teapots. If you gave me eighty quid and a shopping trolley then I could recreate this entire display with a ten minute trip to Argos.

I was assuming that the museum would be full of amazing inventions. They could have displayed a succession of designs to show how things have changed over the years... early telephones to modern mobile phones... early black-and-white TVs to modern-day 3D ones... early gramophones and crystal radios to Sony Walkmans and iPods... but there was none of that. It was just a random collection of disparate objects: this is a razor... this is a potato peeler... this is a teapot... this is a brick...

The most amazing thing to me was how packed the place was -- *and it was!* It was genuinely busy. As I was walking around I felt a bit like that kid in the crowd who was trying to draw everyone's attention to the emperor's new clothes. *It's just a teapot, you idiot! It's just a shoe!* That is what this place does -- they take a teapot and shine a load of lights on it and voila! ...an instant museum exhibit. All they have to do is put a plaque up saying how wonderful it is and people will believe them, because they don't want to admit to themselves that they've just wasted half a day of their holiday.

Take my advice: if you want to learn about the history of design then visit the V&A Museum instead, or the Science Museum, which are both a hundred times better, and free.

I suppose I'd better end this review by saying something positive, so here it is: there's a long river walk outside the front door which is worth a look, because you get a great view of Tower Bridge and the city skyscrapers behind.

Downing Street

Landmarks & Attractions | 71

ADDRESS Downing Street, off Whitehall - map 8d **TRAINS** Charing Cross, Embankment, Westminster (all zone 1) **BUSES** 3, 11, 12, 24, 53, 87, 88, 159 **WEB** gov.uk/government/organisations/prime-ministers-office-10-downing-street **TIME REQUIRED** 10 mins

Easy to get to? ★★★ Good for kids? ★☆☆ Value for money? free Worth a visit? ★★★

If I was Prime Minister the first thing I would do is knock down every atrocious new building that has gone up since the war (with my bare hands, if necessary), and then I'd open up the Port of London again and bring back the trams. Unfortunately I've left it a bit late to start a political career, because if you want to become a politician these days then you need to slave away as an MP's office boy for five years. That's how David Cameron started out -- by polishing Norman Lamont's shoes and making sure that his tea was constantly topped up with whiskey. So that's what I'm doing today: I've bought myself a box of tea bags and I'm off to No.10 to see if the Prime Minister needs a new tea boy.

There are a few things that you need to know about the famous Downing Street door before you try and storm inside. The first one is this: it's not made of wood. It's actually a bulletproof, black slab of armoured steel, so the chances of you shoulder-barging it down are zero. Not even a tank could put a dent in that thing. And secondly, it hasn't got a letterbox. So you can't squeeze yourself in disguised as a petition. And thirdly, there are about fifty million gun toting policeman with twitching fingers just itching for an excuse to shoot you (and they will). So basically what I'm saying is this: don't bother trying to infiltrate the headquarters of our country's leader, because you've got no chance. That place is a fortress. Just stare through the gate like everyone else.

I've probably peered down the street about a million billion times before (at least), but I've never once seen the Prime Minister come out. *Not once*. I'm starting to think that he doesn't actually live there. But even if he did pop his head outside then the odds of you actually catching his attention are basically zero, because not only do you have to peer through the big black iron gate -- over the shoulders of a big burly copper pointing a machine gun at your face -- but you are simultaneously being wedged in by ten thousand tourists snapping away at the postman, thinking he's the Queen.

I got a bit lucky this morning because a delivery guy came in with a trolley full of parcels, and the gun cop opened the gate for a few minutes so he could come out and shake them. As I was standing there watching him jostle them up and down I was thinking, thank Christ there aren't any bombs inside, otherwise we would have all been blown up! He even put one up to his ear so he could have a listen to it. Now... I don't claim to be an explosives expert, but I'm pretty sure that bombs only go tick in the movies, so I don't know what he was expecting to hear. But it gave me a better view of the front door than I've ever had, anyway, but there were still no signs of life. We probably could have rushed the gate pretty easily and overpowered the police (maybe taking a bullet or two) but by the time I'd geed up the tourists to give it a go, the moment had passed. I guess the Japanese Kamikaze spirit died in World War II.

You can just about make out the famous front door on the righthand side of the street. You need to look for a door with an iron arch and a lamplight on the top. You are viewing it from a very shallow angle, but if the PM did happen to stand on the doorstep then you would easily see him. It's too far away to throw any tomatoes at him, though (believe me, I've tried).

Did you know that you can also see the back-end of Downing Street? All you have to do is walk through the central arch of Horse Guards, towards St. James's Park, and it's behind that big brown brick wall on the lefthand side of the parade ground (where the gun cops are standing). Unfortunately the view is even worse that way, but at least you won't have as many tourists to contend with.

Big Ben and the Houses of Parliament are a short walk down the road.

Dr. Johnson's House

ADDRESS Dr. Johnson's House, 17 Gough Sq, The City - map 4e **TRAINS** Chancery Lane, Blackfriars, Temple (all zone 1) **BUSES** 4, 8, 11, 15, 17, 23, 25, 26, 45, 46, 76, 172, 242, 341 **PRICE** Adult £4.50; Senior (over-60) £3.50; Child (5-17) £1.50; Infant (under-5) free; Family (2 ad+any ch) £10 **OPEN** 11 AM to 5 PM (Mon-Sat, Oct-Apr); 11 AM to 5.30 PM (Mon-Sat, May-Sep); Closed (Sun) **WEB** drjohnsonshouse.org **TEL** 0207 353 3745 **TIME REQUIRED** 1 hour

Easy to get to? ★★★ Good for kids? ☆☆☆
Value for money? ★★☆ Worth a visit? ★☆☆

You might know that Samuel Johnson was a London wit, who wrote a dictionary, but after that you're probably struggling. So why would you bother to visit his house? *Hmmm... that's a toughie.*

It's supposed to be a perfectly preserved Georgian townhouse, but to be honest I was a little underwhelmed. The problem is that it's too sparsely decorated... there's not enough *stuff* in it, and I didn't really feel as if I was being transported back in time. Where are all his belongings? And his books, papers and letters? They have a small selection on show, but the rooms aren't exactly overflowing with items.

They seem to have decided that unless an item has an evidential connection with Johnson, then it doesn't belong in the house. There are a few wooden tables and chairs dotted around (none of which are of any particular interest -- they are all plainly made) and some dim and dark portraits hanging on the walls, but that's pretty much it. If I was in charge I would have filled the house with period furniture to bring a bit of life to it. The bedroom hasn't even got a bed in it. They don't show you the kitchen or the bathroom, either, so there's no cooking equipment. No bath tub. No nothing.

If you don't fancy splashing out on the audio guide (which costs extra) then they've placed a few essays on the tables for you to read, but that's about it as far as Johnson's writings are concerned. Apart from a dictionary which you can leaf through, all of his other works are safely locked up inside a bookcase. Why don't they put some glass cabinets against the walls so you can read his words? They don't have to be originals, do they?

They need to put some Madame Tussauds' waxworks in there as well: lounging around in their Georgian clothes, with some period music playing out of the speakers. They need to bring the house alive a bit more, because it's just too damn *dull*.

If you're expecting a Samuel Johnson museum then you're going to go home disappointed. You're really there to see the house.

You might like to try the Charles Dickens Museum, Sherlock Holmes Museum and a tour of the Globe Theatre.

Florence Nightingale Museum

ADDRESS Florence Nightingale Museum, St. Thomas's Hospital, Waterloo - map 9c **TRAINS** Waterloo, Westminster (both zone 1) **BUSES** 12, 53, 76, 77, 148, 159, 211, 341, 363, 381, 543, 507, C10, RV1 **PRICE** Adult £7.50; Senior £4.80; Child (5-15) £3.80; Infant (under-5) free; Family (2 ad+up to 3 ch) £18, or £13 with 1 ad+up to 3ch **OPEN** 10 AM to 5 PM (Mon-Sun); Last entry 30 mins before closing **WEB** florence-nightingale.co.uk **TEL** 0207 620 0374 **TIME REQUIRED** 30-60 mins

Easy to get to? ★★★   Good for kids? ☆☆☆
Value for money? ★☆☆   Worth a visit? ★☆☆

I was quite brave today. I had to swallow my male pride and venture somewhere a bit girly -- the Florence Nightingale Museum. I live my life by the rule of Clint Eastwood, you see; always asking myself: "What would Clint Eastwood do?" And he definitely wouldn't be seen dead in here, nosing around a museum about a 19th-century nurse. So it took a lot of courage and bravado on my part, of which I am quite proud.

Of course, I jest (but only a little). The Florence Nightingale Museum is one of those tiny little museums that caters to a very select audience: *nurses*. Who else is going to want to come here? Kids? Tourists? Funnily enough, when I left the place a huge group of Japanese camera-clickers walked in, so maybe it has a bigger appeal than I thought.

My only recollection of Florence Nightingale prior to today was from those sepia-tinged photos: a bossy old nurse with a serious face, and I was half-expecting the museum to be equally ancient, filled with dusty old cabinets and orange bottles and bandages. But it was actually quite modern inside, with a lot of bright TVs showing photos and documentary videos. There are lots of info screens dotted around with headphones dangling down so you can have a listen to the commentary. It reminded me a little bit of the Churchill Museum in the Cabinet War Rooms, if you've ever been there. It has the same kind of feeling to it, except on a much smaller scale.

The museum is quite tiny (it's basically just one big room, split up into different sections), so its focus is very narrow. It's just about Florence -- her life, her clothes, her possessions, and the changes that she made to nursing. They also have a section on her love life (not very happy), and her dealings with Queen Victoria and the Government.

I definitely think that they missed a trick by not describing the wider war. If they had a few cabinets about the Crimean War then maybe the museum would appeal to men. A few bits and pieces about the weapons and the battles, and how the casualties piled up, etc. That is where she made her name, after all. But there's nothing like that. It's all *Florence, Florence, Florence,* which is a bit like the Churchill Museum failing to mention World War II.

I am reminded of the medicine exhibition at the Science Museum... now that is interesting. They've put together some life-size mock-ups of surgeries and treatment rooms throughout the ages, so you can see what the conditions were really like. I appreciate that the Florence Nightingale Museum is probably too small to include anything like that, but that's the kind of exhibit that makes it interesting. This place is just words and photos.

If Florence is your chief focus, then okay, give it a go, and you will probably enjoy it. But for everyone else it's just a quick half-hour and out the exit.

You might like the Old Operating Theatre and Alexander Fleming Museum.

Garden Museum

ADDRESS Garden Museum, Lambeth Palace Road, Lambeth - map 8f **TRAINS** Lambeth North (zone 1), Vauxhall (zones 1&2) **BUSES** 3, 344, 360, 507, C10 **OPEN** Closed until 2017 **WEB** gardenmuseum.org.uk **TEL** 0207 401 8865 **TIME REQUIRED** 45-60 mins

Easy to get to? ★★★ Good for kids? ☆☆☆
Value for money? ★☆☆ Worth a visit? ★☆☆

I'm not much of a gardener. I like weeds, not flowers. The last time I ventured into my own garden was to pick up a dead fox and throw it in the bushes. I noticed it at the weekend and for the first few days I was hoping that it was just asleep and having a snooze, but eventually I crept up on it and knocked it with a stick and it was rock solid, like a block of concrete. Rigor mortis had claimed it, and it took me five minutes to lever it up with a spade because its decomposing bodily juices had glued it to the grass. I honestly thought that I was going to have to get the shears out of the shed and chop all of its hair from underneath, to try and work it loose.

That was a nice story, wasn't it?

That was my gardening story.

I wonder if they'll have any stories like that at the Garden Museum? I doubt it but you never know. They might do. I hope so. They might have a few spades and shears, though, because this place is full of garden implements and horticultural books. But the reason that I came here myself is not for any of that, but because I thought it was housed inside the grounds of Lambeth Palace (but more on that later).

The first room is a big biography about a famous gardener called Russell Page. They've collected together a few of his old scribblings and stuck up some photographs of his landscaped grounds. They have a little movie playing, too. If you like watching *Gardener's World* then I suppose you might like it. If you prefer *Rambo* then you probably won't.

It gets a lot more exciting upstairs, because that's where you'll find their impressive collection of old hoes. They have a display case full of saws and shears and watering cans as well. The excitement doesn't end there, though, because they also have a rusty wheelbarrow, a few gnarly old walking sticks and... *wait for it*... a tin full of slug pellets (that was my favourite). And if you're a big fan of lawnmowers then you're in luck, because they have **two** of those. And some gnomes. It's as if somebody has come along and donated the contents of their grandad's shed.

The only bit that's actually worth seeing is outside, because that's where you'll find the grave of Captain William Bligh, of *Mutiny on the Bounty* fame. There's a pretty little ornamental garden out there as well, but don't turn up expecting Kew Gardens -- it's probably only about fifty feet across with a few privet hedges in the middle. It's more like a kitchen garden, I suppose, with a few tables and chairs for the cafe customers. But at least you can have a good look at the back gable of the church.

As I mentioned at the beginning, I only really came here to see inside Lambeth Palace, and that was very disappointing -- because you can't go in there! You can't go in the red-brick gatehouse either. I was under the impression that the museum was housed inside Lambeth Palace itself, but it's actually housed inside St. Mary-at-Lambeth church next-door (the grey stone building to the right of the gatehouse). I don't know why I thought that -- probably because I'm an idiot. And whilst the church is certainly old, it's not actually a church anymore, because it was de-consecrated and taken over by the gardeners, who have proceeded to completely wreck the interior -- there is no other way to describe it. I'm surprised they were allowed to get away with it. They've covered up the stonework with some pine walls and plank floorboards, and built a little shop where the pews are supposed to be. Instead of candles and statues they've got a rack of gardening books and postcards. Instead of an altar they've got a payment desk.

It's almost as if they have tried to weed out every piece of history and sanitise it. If you were hoping to learn something about the old archbishops and the events that took place next door then you will go home disappointed, because God doesn't live here anymore -- they've kicked the old fella out. Alan Titchmarsh has taken over. That's who these people are praying to now: he who brings forth life from dirt. He who raises the trees and brings the flowers into bloom. Alan's army has torn down the crucifixes, and erected some bean poles in their place.

They do have quite a nice cafe, though. I will admit that.

A tip: if you do decide to visit the Garden Museum then have a walk along the river from the Waterloo side of Westminster Bridge to Lambeth Palace, because you'll be treated to one of the finest views of Big Ben and Parliament.

If you enjoy the Garden Museum then you might like the Chelsea Physic Garden.

Geffrye Museum

ADDRESS 136 Kingsland Road, Shoreditch
TRAINS Hoxton (zones 1&2), Old Street, and a 15 min walk (zone 1) **BUSES** 67, 149, 242, 243, 394 **PRICE** Free **OPEN** 10 AM to 5 PM (Tue-Sun) **WEB** geffrye-museum.org .uk **TEL** 0207 739 9893 **TIME REQUIRED** 45-60 mins

Easy to get to? ★★★ Good for kids? ☆☆☆
Value for money? free Worth a visit? ☆☆☆

This had better be good because it's quite a long walk. You have to get a tube train to Old Street and then traipse your way through an ugly bit of London for fifteen minutes. But when you finally arrive it's quite a nice surprise... because one minute you're on a busy main road and then all of a sudden it's peace and quiet in a countryside courtyard. All of the brown brick almshouses are wrapped around in ivy and it really is pretty. There are some big huge trees shading the lawn and it reminds me of a Cambridge college. Let's hope the inside lives up to the exterior...

The first room is just a short line of wooden chairs... so it doesn't bode well. After that you get a few plates and knives and forks. Then it picks up a bit with a reconstruction of a Tudor room.

A ha... I see how this place is arranged now. They begin with a few examples of Tudor furniture, before moving on to a mock-up of the room. Then they move onto the next period in time and follow it with another mock-up of the room. And you keep moving through history like that, so you can see how the room has changed over the last 400 years.

Quite a neat idea... but unfortunately it's all rather dry and boring. None of the reconstructions are original to the almshouse, so it's just a collection of disparate objects they've assembled from each period. You get to see a few tables and chairs and writing desks, for example, and china cups and teapots, and different coloured floorboard planks. You can follow their changing tastes in wallpaper too. Most of the objects aren't even real, but are modern copies in a similar style.

Once you get up to the 1900s you may as well just be walking around a big branch of IKEA. Who wants to spend a day looking at an office chair from the 1970s? And the 1980s? And the 1990s? (You can do all of those.) You can look at a ten-year-old sofa too, and a rug and a lamp and a telephone from 1965.

If you've got a particular interest in furniture then you might want to give the museum a try... but not before you visit the V&A, which is a million billion times better. They do have a nice little cafe though, but it seems to be a hangout for pushchair mums and their toddler kids.

P.S.: I always feel a little bit guilty slating a place when it's free, because at least they don't have the cheek to charge an entrance fee like some places -- but what the hell. Just because it's free doesn't mean it's any good.

If you're interested in historical furniture then try the Victoria & Albert Museum and Wallace Collection.

Globe Theatre -- Guided Tour

ADDRESS Globe Theatre, 21 New Globe Walk, Bankside - map 9b **TRAINS** London Bridge, Southwark (both zone 1) **BUSES** 11, 15, 17, 23, 26, 45, 63, 76, 100, 344, 381, RV1 **PRICE** Adult £15; Senior (over-60) £13.50; Child (5-15) £9; Infant (under-5) free; Family (up to 2 ad+3 ch) £41 **OPEN** Tour during theatre season (mid-Apr to mid-Oct): Every 30 mins from 9.30 AM to 5 PM (Mon); 9.30 PM to 12.30 PM (Tue-Sat); 9.30 AM to 11.30 AM (Sun) -- Tour outside theatre season (mid-Oct to mid-Apr): Every 30 mins from 9.30 AM to 5 PM (Mon-Sun) -- Museum: 9 AM to 5 PM (Mon-Sun) **WEB** shakespearesglobe.com/exhibition/about-the-exhibition-and-theatre-tours **TEL** 0207 902 1400 **TIME REQUIRED** 45 mins for the tour, plus 45-60 for the museum

Easy to get to? ★★★ Good for kids? ★☆☆
Value for money? ★★☆ Worth a visit? ★★★

I consider myself to be reasonably well educated. I'm not quite on the Albert Einstein level, but put it this way: I went to school. I'm not thick. I can do all the usual stuff: I can tie my shoelaces, I can count to ten, I can recite the alphabet backwards, I can say "please can I have a ham sandwich" in French... and that's pretty much all you need to know in life. So here's my take on Shakespeare: I don't mind reading about him and his Tudor times, but his plays are too much hard work. I actually tried to read them all once. I think I slogged through the four biggies plus a couple of others, but then I just gave up because it was like trying to decipher pig Latin: I could see that it made sense underneath (sort of), but I couldn't be arsed to sit there and work it all out -- some of the phrases would have baffled Alan Turing.

If your thinking is similar to mine then here's my advice: the Globe Theatre Tour is still worth a visit anyway. It really doesn't matter if you don't like his plays, because it doesn't focus on his words. They don't stand there singing his sonnets. It's much more about the man himself, and the history of his original playhouse.

It begins with a quick little look at the museum before meeting the tour guide downstairs (don't worry if you have to rush around the museum, because they give you endless time to see it at the end). Our guide was a very nice lady who looked a lot like Taylor Swift. She may even have *been* Taylor Swift. She also had the remarkable ability to show off all thirty-two of her pearly white teeth at once, even whilst she was busy talking to us. She spoke like she was posing for a photo. I got the feeling that she was a wannabe actress who wanted to jump up on stage and sing us a song, because some of her theatrical demonstrations were good enough for a spot in the cast.

There were about thirty people in our tour group but don't worry if you're deaf, because everyone has to wear a pair of headphones. Taylor Swift stood there talking about ten feet from our face, whilst simultaneously broadcasting it through the headphones, so we could hear everything she said as clear as a bell.

The first thing she did was take us outside onto the veranda and told us all about Southwark and what a hellhole it was in Shakespeare's day. Apparently it was stinking crime den full of bear-baiting pits, violent drunks and very friendly ladies (if you know what I mean)... not a lot different to today then (only joking, ha ha). Then she told us all about the Clink (the local nick), and all the traitors' heads that were stuck up on spikes by London Bridge. She really set the scene well, and it's a wonder that Shakespeare spoke in such flowery prose with all of that going on around him.

The tour gets really interesting once you get led inside for a look at the stage. The layout is pretty standard for a theatre, but what sets the Globe apart from everywhere else is the roof: because there isn't one! It's totally open to the sky. At the front of the stage is a pit where seven hundred cheap people stand (the 'groundlings'), and then you've got three levels of balcony seats wrapped around the yard.

Now... this is where I need to give you some advice, so pay attention. I have been on this tour several times now, both during the theatre season (mid-April to mid-October), and outside it (mid-October to mid-April), and I definitely recommend the latter. That's because they frequently have rehearsals on during the theatre season, and no one is allowed to make a noise once you step inside the theatre space -- not even Taylor Swift. She basically just sat us down and let us look around, but her lips were zipped up tight to avoid disturbing the rehearsal. The precious actors were busy choreographing their movements and couldn't be interrupted, you see. Apparently waving their arms around in circles is so tremendously difficult that if anybody makes even the slightest noise then it will put them off and unravel all their preparations. I had to hold my breath for a whole ten minutes. I was even afraid to move my eyes in case they made a squeak. At one point I thought they could hear my thoughts. It was so silent I could even hear my neighbour's heart beating. When I came on this tour before, she sat us down in the balcony and had a long chat about the stalls and the stage, pointing out all the decorations and explaining how the trapdoors work, etc., but Taylor Swift was forced to recite all of that outside today, and we had to try and remember it all when we came inside. But that's just a very minor quibble, because it's still definitely worth going -- I still enjoyed it.

I won't reveal exactly how the theatre operates here, because you'll get a much better taste by reading the review I wrote whilst watching *Julius Caesar* (read it!). So just trust me when I say it's a theatre like no other, and whilst the guided tour gives you a perfectly good idea of what it's like to see a play, it's not a patch on seeing one for real.

Once the rehearsal was over Taylor took us down into the pit and let us stand next to the stage. And that was basically it. Tour over. It was just a quick forty-five minutes of history before heading back to the beginning. Taylor Swift then said her goodbyes and let us loose in the museum, which you can walk around at your own pace.

It's actually quite a good little museum but it will probably appeal more to London history buffs than theatre nuts, because whilst there's plenty about Bankside, the old Rose Theatre and the timeline of the Globe, there's not a tremendous amount of detail about Shakespeare himself, other than a section on his acting company. It's just bit and pieces -- odds and sods. They've got a copy of his will on show, for example. They've also got a couple of cabinets filled with archaeological pots and bowls. After that it's all theatre props and costumes, and how they created the sound effects in Tudor times. If you're a kid then they've also got a little stage area where you can dress up in actor's clothes and have your photo taken by your mum and dad. (I suppose crazy adults might want to dress up as well.)

The final section explains how they built the modern day theatre using centuries old methods, and gives a well-deserved pat on the back to Sam Wanamaker, who's forty year vision (and, let's be honest, his sheer indomitable will when faced with British bureaucracy!) helped to get the new place built.

So is it Worth a visit? In short: *yes*. And I'm not just saying that because the guide looks like Taylor Swift. It's definitely interesting, but it's not a patch on seeing a play being performed for real. They've got quite a good gift shop as well, if you're looking for some Shakespeare presents.

Shakespeare fans might also enjoy a day trip to Stratford-upon-Avon.

Globe Theatre -- Watching a Play

Landmarks & Attractions | 79

ADDRESS Globe Theatre, 21 New Globe Walk, Bankside - map 9b **TRAINS** London Bridge, Southwark (both zone 1) **BUSES** 11, 15, 17, 23, 26, 45, 63, 76, 100, 344, 381, RV1 **PRICE** £5 to £45 **OPEN** It's open to the weather, so plays are shown from mid-Apr to mid-Oct only - see website **WEB** shakespearesglobe.com/ theatre/whats-on/ globe-theatre **TEL** 0207 401 9919 **TIME REQUIRED** Usually start in the early afternoon and last for 2-3 hours

Easy to get to? ★★★ Good for kids? ★★☆
Value for money? ★★★ Worth a visit? ★★★

I'm sitting in the Globe Theatre waiting for *Julius Caesar* to start, watching them assemble the set. The stage is very close to the seats, with three floors of balconied seats wrapped around the yard in a circle. I am sitting in the middle level. The seats aren't exactly the comfiest in town... they are like wooden church pews and they don't have any back rests (unless you sit in the back row... but that will ruin your view). You can buy a plush red cushion to sit on if you want and they are only a quid each -- I definitely recommend it. Apparently that's how they used to do it in Shakespeare's day: touting out cushions in the foyer before the show starts.

The theatre is supposed to be a perfect replica from Elizabethan times. The whole place is made of wood, with whitewashed plaster walls and mock-Tudor beams holding it up. And it's completely open to the weather as well; there are even a few pigeons flapping around the rafters, peering down at us from the moss-coloured thatched roof. The balcony seats have got a little bit of cover above, but it won't protect you very much if the rain comes in sideways. It says on the ticket that the actors don't stop for anything -- not even howling gales and downpours. I would quite like to see a hurricane funnelling down the wooden-O, just to see what they do. We've already had a bit of a drizzle, and the staff just carried on regardless. The punters tugged up their hoods and didn't seem to care. So that is something to be aware of if you stand in the central yard: you will get wet. And you won't get a refund!

That is where the paupers stand -- the low-life nobodies who can't afford a pew. It's basically just a big concrete floor surrounding the stage. In Shakespeare's day it would have been filled with wet mud and sawdust, and people's spit and piss (seriously!) but these days it is dry concrete. You have to stand up for the entire show down there, shoulder to shoulder with hundreds of other punters. If you've got a short wife or a short kid then trust me: they won't be able to see a thing. So get there early and elbow your way to the front otherwise they will just be staring at someone's shoulders all day. The stage rises up to about head height, so you can just about rest your arms on the front edge if you raise them above your neck. Lots of people are doing that. The staff doesn't seem to mind about the standees encroaching upon the stage.

I can see a bloke wandering around the yard with a big wicker basket selling nuts and tubs of juice. There are a few people munching on doorstop-sized pork pies as well, and gripping polystyrene cups of hot coffee.

The set itself is quite nicely decorated. They are still assembling it at the moment, and the stagehands are all dressed up in Elizabethan togs, carrying big beams and placards around. They are busy nailing up marble tiles and stone-style walls, and hanging chiselled tablets on the roof. They've got a few faux-marble columns and a Romanesque balcony too. There are a few doors and arches into the backstage area, and a trapdoor for the ghosts to come out.

Okay... here we go: the show is starting now and loads of Elizabethan-style minstrels have bounded out and are diddling some tunes around the exits. There are a few doors dotted around the sides and back of the yard, and all of the musicians are parading in from those. In they come all cheering and singing... banging tambourines and little flutes too, and it is quite a May Day atmosphere. Then the cheers go up as the actors come in... straight through the packed-out yard and up onto the stage. Lots of shouting out: "Clear off you plebs!" and "Get out of the way!" The yard has become part of the show, and the audience is playing the part of a Roman crowd. Pretty soon everyone is shouting and clapping for Caesar.

Out he comes with his retinue in tow, waving and kissing the crowd like he was a real life Emperor. They had a few stooges in the yard cheering "Caesar!" to get the crowd going, but it was like a genuine parade, and the stand-up punters had the best seat in the house. Fanfares and trumpets and drums are playing up on the stage, and it makes me wonder why they don't build all theatres like this -- it is brilliant!

The play is well under way now, and the actors are shouting out their lines from the stage. They didn't have any electric lights and microphones in Shakespeare's day, and they haven't got any today either. They are just standing there in the daylight and shouting out their stuff across the punter's heads. It is very clear and easy to hear though; the stage is very close to the seats so you can hear the words as clear as a bell.

But hearing it and understanding it are entirely different things. When I was younger I went through a phase of trying to educate myself by reading through the classics. That didn't last long (about two weeks). I think I managed *Hamlet* and *Macbeth* and that was it, and it's every bit as impenetrable in the theatre as I remember it on paper. Shakespeare is hard enough to understand in a book, but when you've got actors firing it at you in a madman's chunter it is very difficult to keep up. And it hasn't been Hollywood-ised or dumbed down for the tourists either, this is the real McCoy: straight out of the Folio and onto the stage. If your English isn't 100% then good luck trying to understand it.

The way they are involving the crowd has led to some very funny scenes -- like when we had a Roman legion fighting for their lives on stage, and then storming off through the yard to the back of the theatre. A couple in the crowd were a bit slow to shift, and got a deafening bellow of "MOVE!" at the point of a sword. They soon moved -- very funny! They also had a scene where the rioters ripped a poor gent's entrails from his stomach. Bright red blood sprayed out across the crowd, and then she chucked his 'naughty bits' at their feet: cue lots of groaning and hearty laughter from the crowd.

As soon as the play ended the whole cast bounded out and did the most unexpectedly boisterous dance I have ever seen. It was like New Year's Eve and our last night on Earth all rolled into one -- very good! It was a really good show, and I certainly enjoyed it.

Now that the show is over I can give you a little piece of advice about where best to sit for a decent view. Try and sit in the middle gallery, where I was, but avoid the three bays closest to the stage, because your view will be obscured by the supporting columns (so don't go in blocks A, B, C, N, P or Q). If you are in the upper gallery then try and avoid the first four bays, because the stage roof juts out across the top (so don't go in blocks A, B, C, D, M, N, P or Q). And if you are in the lower gallery then just avoid the first two bays (A, B, P and Q). If you are standing in the yard then it doesn't matter, because you can just walk around wherever you want.

If you enjoyed watching some Shakespeare then how about a day trip to his birthplace at Stratford-upon-Avon?

Golden Hinde

ADDRESS Golden Hinde, Clink Street, Southwark - map 10a **TRAINS** London Bridge (zone 1) **BUSES** 17, 21, 22A, 35, 40, 43, 44, 47, 48, 95, 133, 149, 214, 501, 505, 510, 513 **PRICE** Self-guided tour: Adult £6; Senior £4.50; Child (4-16) £4.50; Infant (under-4) free; Family (4 people, including at least 1 ch) £18 -- Guided tour: Adult £7; Senior £5; Child (4-16) £5; Infant (under-4) free; Family (4 people, including at least 1 ch) £20 **OPEN** 10 AM to 5.30 PM (Mon-Sun) **WEB** goldenhinde.com **TEL** 0207 403 7276 **TIME REQUIRED** 45-60 mins

Easy to get to? ★★★ Good for kids? ★★☆
Value for money? ★★☆ Worth a visit? ★★☆

The first time you clap eyes on the Golden Hinde you'll think that it's a joke. It's supposed to be a full-size replica of the boat that carried Francis Drake around the world, but it's tiny! It's like a decorated rowing boat -- I'm serious. I actually read the leaflet from cover to cover just to make sure that it really is full-size -- and it is. How on earth did Drake manage to spend two years cooped up in this little thing?

It's difficult to believe that a crew of thirty people lived in this little tub, sailing around the seven seas weighed down by barrels of fish and biscuits, and a hold full of Spanish silver. It must have been incredibly uncomfortable. But there must be plenty of room in it though, because I was surprised to learn that this little copy has actually surpassed the original and sailed even further than Drake. It's been all around the girdle of the earth, up and down the coast of America, Asia, Japan, Africa... even to the moon and back. And when you step inside and see how cramped it is you'll be gobsmacked.

The only real bedroom is at the front (for Drake), and the rest had to make do with a sleeping mat on the floor. The cabins below the deck level are all at shoulder-height -- and I am not exaggerating when I say you have to stoop down to walk through them. You almost have to bend your waist at 90° to walk along, or you'll bump your barnet on the beams above your head. I reckon if I spent more than six hours on this thing then I'd be doubled-up with a crippling bad back. How did they manage it? They must have all been midgets and kids; there is no other explanation.

The ladders are pretty lethal too. They are the kind that goes straight down into oblivion. If you're old, or young, or unfit like me, then the boat becomes an obstacle course.

When you first step onboard you are basically left to your own devices. You can explore every inch of the ship in your own time. The only thing that you are banned from doing is climbing up the rigging to the crow's nest at the top; but you'd have to be a total nut-job to do that anyway. That is probably why they don't have pirate ships these days: because they'd never get the crow's nest past health and safety. They wouldn't allow any cannonballs onboard either, in case you dropped them on your foot. (I found it quite amusing when they issued me with an A5 health and safety sheet before I boarded the boat. No smoking it said... no running, don't bang your head, be careful on the stairs... is this a genuine 16th-century document, I wondered? Francis Drake would have a good hearty laugh at that.)

There are no audio-guides or anything like that. Just a little map that tells you the names of all the different sections. There are a few placards dotted around which tell you a few bits and bobs, but I got the impression that it's mainly aimed at kids. There are no genuine artefacts onboard, no museum pieces. It's all replicas. But it's very well kitted out with cannons and barrels and a dining table for the officers. You can even lie down in Francis Drake's quarters and have a little kip. You can quite happily spend an hour of your time pretending to be a pirate, clambering up the little ladders to the half-deck and forecastle; steering the ship's wheel and descending into the hold to peer out of the portholes.

I don't like to boast, but I think I would have made quite a good pirate. I even had a budgerigar when I was little -- called Buzzby -- which is kind-of like a parrot, and I've got a hook for a hand as well (no I haven't).

I was pretty lucky with the timing because when I finished at 11 o'clock a big army of school kids bundled up. It's a very small boat, and having a pack of rabid hoodlums running around screaming their heads off would certainly try my patience -- they'd all be walking the plank inside five minutes. Or I'd stuff them inside a cannon and fire them up the Thames. And that is actually one thing that I've noticed every time I walk past the boat... it always seems to be crewed by a gang of hooligans from the local schools. I think that is one of the reasons why I've never bothered to board it before. So if you're going to go, take my advice and go when it opens.

If you like boats then how about catching one to Greenwich to see the Cutty Sark?

Green Park

ADDRESS Green Park - map 7d **TRAINS** Green Park, Hyde Park Corner (both zone 1) **BUSES** 2, 8, 9, 14, 16, 19, 22, 36, 38, 52, 73, 82, 148, 436 **PRICE** Free **OPEN** 24 hours (Mon-Sun) **WEB** royalparks.org.uk/parks/green-park **TEL** 0300 061 2350 **TIME REQUIRED** 20 mins

Easy to get to? ★★★ Good for kids? ☆☆☆
Value for money? free Worth a visit? ★☆☆

Green Park is the great un-loved park of London. No one has ever said: *"I know, let's take the kids to Green Park for the day"*. No one goes there on a sightseeing tour. No one takes photographs of it and nobody wants to scatter their ashes in it. They couldn't even be bothered to give it a proper name: Green Park. That's like calling an orange and orange just because it's orange. But it certainly is apt: it is definitely green. There is nothing here but green leaves and the smell of wet wood.

The canopy of trees is very thick in places, and it makes it look like early evening in the winter. Raindrops are trickling on my wet bench from the drip-drying trees. It's what's leftover from the rain. This seat is practically a sponge: all of its paint has flaked away and its rotten wood is crumbling up like a half-eaten fruitcake. I love the old fashioned lamplights that are lining the path as well -- it all adds to the moody gloom. Obviously there must be some lightbulbs inside, but I'm not entirely sure without going up close: the sodium glows are shivering and flickering like they're battling against the wind.

While you're here check out Constitution Hill on the south side of the park, because on the other side of that huge brown brick wall is Buckingham Palace Gardens. Someone took a potshot at Queen Victoria's carriage along here once, but inexplicably missed (she was a big target in those days). Someone else had another go a couple of years later and missed again. So they had another go (third time lucky?)... and missed again. I've almost died a few times on Constitution Hill myself, whilst dodging the bicycles on the speedway cycle lane. They tear down here with fire and flames coming off their wheels like they're racing Bradley Wiggins.

They've built a few memorials at the top end of Constitution Hill to liven it up a bit. There's an impressive monument to Bomber Command near Wellington Arch, and four concrete obelisks for the forces of the British Empire. There's also a rather plain-looking piece for Canada, close to the Canada Gate.

A word of advice: if you see any deckchairs don't sit on them, because they charge about a thousand pounds per hour (which is a slight exaggeration, but not by much). Tourists are forever sitting in them thinking that they're free -- and why not? It's only a seat. But they are forgetting that this is London: where even sitting down costs a fortune. A warden will come along before long and kick them out.

Greenwich Hill

ADDRESS Greenwich Hill, Greenwich Park - map 11f **TRAINS** Cutty Sark DLR (zones 2&3), and a 25 min walk **BUSES** 53, 54, 177, 180, 188, 199, 202, 286, 380, 386 **PRICE** Free **OPEN** 6 AM to 6 PM (Mon-Sun, Nov-Feb); 6 AM to 7 PM (Mon-Sun, Mar and Oct); 6 AM to 8 PM (Mon-Sun, Apr and Sep); 6 AM to 9 PM (Mon-Sun, May and Aug); 6 AM to 9.30 PM (Mon-Sun, Jun-Jul) **WEB** royalparks.org.uk/parks/greenwich-park **TEL** 0300 061 2380 **TIME REQUIRED** 30-45 mins

Easy to get to? ★★☆ Good for kids? ★★☆
Value for money? free Worth a visit? ★★☆

You might want to give Tenzing Norgay a quick ring before you climb up Greenwich Hill, just in case you need a Sherpa to carry you the final fifty yards. It doesn't look like very high when you're standing at the bottom, but trust me, this is a proper hill. Think about it: it's got an observatory at the top for chrissakes -- and they don't put telescopes on top of a molehill. They put them at the top of a mountain. By the time you walk to the top you'll be two days older and you'll need another shave.

Or maybe I'm just very unfit...

There are three hills worth climbing in London: Parliament Hill, Primrose Hill and Greenwich Hill; and this one has got by far the best view. You are right at the bottom of the Isle of Dogs and can see the river bending right round to The City. From left to right you've got The Shard, St. Paul's Cathedral, the Walkie Scorchie and

Gherkin, and then on to the skyscrapers at Canary Wharf. Then you can look down the slope towards the National Maritime Museum and Old Royal Naval College, before heading east towards the Millennium Dome and the cable car. (You will have to move along the brow of the hill to see the whole collection.)

I always like to pick out a few hard landmarks to give you a test... so see if you can spot the BT Tower and Tower Bridge. If you manage to spot Tower Bridge without looking at the plaque then very well done -- because it's nowhere near the place you think it will be. (I was looking to the right of the Gherkin.) The hardest one of all is the London Eye. You might have to use the observatory telescope to see that one.

Whilst you're at the top of the hill you might like to visit the Royal Observatory.

Guards' Museum

ADDRESS Guards' Museum, Wellington Barracks, Birdcage Walk - map 8c **TRAINS** St. James's Park, Victoria, Westminster (all zone 1) **BUSES** 11, 24, 148, 211, 507 **PRICE** Adult £6; Senior (over-65) £3; Child (under-17) free when accompanied by an adult **OPEN** 10 AM to 4 PM (Mon-Sun); Last entry 30 mins before closing **WEB** theguardsmuseum.com **TEL** 0207 414 3428 **TIME REQUIRED** 1 hour

Easy to get to? ★★★ Good for kids? ☆☆☆
Value for money? ★★☆ Worth a visit? ★★☆

I like the Guards' Museum, but you probably need a particular interest in military history to appreciate it. It's quite similar to the Household Cavalry Museum in Horse Guards, but it's double the size and a lot better done. If you've only got time for one or the other, then definitely choose this one.

It leads you through the history of the five regiments of the Foot Guards from the English Civil War right up to modern day Afghanistan, and covers everything in-between from the Battle of Blenheim and Waterloo, to the Crimea and World War II. You've got some of the biggest names in British military history here: the Duke of Marlborough, Duke of Wellington and Monty from El Alamein.

A lot of it is quite personal, like the mementos from the dead (some of whom died as recently as Afghanistan). And there are plenty of medals, weapons and uniforms too. They've even got some stuff that they captured from the enemy. A lot of it looked pretty rubbish to be honest... rusty old wooden rifles and blowpipes firing darts, but then again, I've never been on the wrong end of one!

Other pieces really bring you close to the fighting -- like the tattered Colours and blood-stained uniforms. There are some especially good pieces from Waterloo, like the gate chain from the Hougoumont farmhouse, and a nice selection of paintings, battle maps and scale models of the fighting fronts.

Whether you like this museum or not is going to depend entirely on how much you're into British military history. I think it will probably appeal to old soldiers and middle-aged blokes. There's nothing for the kiddies.

A tip: after you've been to the museum it's worth having a little look along Birdcage Walk, to see the big white building behind the black railings. This place is called Wellington Barracks, and it's home to the modern-day Foot Guards. If you're lucky (or you're prepared to wait around for a while) then you'll see the military being put through their paces on the parade ground, marching up and down and practising their drills. It's a bit like watching a mini-Changing the Guard ceremony, complete with the military bands and music. If you're ever walking through St. James's Park and hear some military music filtering through the trees, then this is probably where it's coming from.

The modern-day Foot Guards take part in Changing the Guard at Buckingham Palace. You might like to watch the ceremony at Horse Guards as well.

Guildhall -- Guided Tour

ADDRESS Guildhall, Guildhall Yard, The City - map 5e **TRAINS** Bank, Mansion House, St. Paul's (all zone 1) **BUSES** 8, 11, 21, 23, 25, 26, 43, 76, 100, 133, 141, 242, 388 **PRICE** £7; Must be booked in advance **DATES** Usually once a month - see website for dates **WEB** cityoflondonguides.com/tours/guildhall **TIME REQUIRED** Usually 10.45 AM to 12 noon, plus 1 hour for the Common Council

Easy to get to? ★★★ Good for kids? ☆☆☆
Value for money? ★★★ Worth a visit? ★★★

I went on a guided tour of the Guildhall today. It's a real good-looking building. If Errol Flynn ever gets round to doing another swashbuckling movie about Robin Hood and has to ride to the rescue of his curly-headed mate, this would be the perfect place to do it. He could ride down King Street into Guildhall Yard, chop off a few heads, and storm into the medieval chamber in his poncy pair of tights and he'd feel right at home. It's just a shame that they have allowed a few modern buildings to encroach upon its space. Why do they do that? I was walking down the side of St. Paul's this morning and they've got a few red-brick office blocks a stone's throw from the dome. If I were the Mayor of London I'd bulldoze them things down and chuck the bricks into the sea.

I blame the Nazis. If they hadn't bombed half of the city in the Blitz we'd have streets and streets of olden stuff. But instead we've got Errol Flynn mixing it with city suits and Starbucks.

But anyway... enough about that... the Guildhall Tour. I'm sitting in the Guildhall Art Gallery at the moment waiting for it to start. It's worth arriving an hour early just to have a look around the gallery because they've got the remains of London's Roman amphitheatre in the basement. And it's totally free as well, so it's a decent way to while away an hour before the Guildhall guide turns up.

Once the tour gets started she takes you on a little stroll outside to see St. Lawrence Jewry (one of Christopher Wren's City churches) and points out the big ring of grey bricks on the forecourt. You might have ignored those if you didn't know what they signify, but they mark out the ring of the original amphitheatre that you just saw in the gallery basement. So if you travelled back in time to 70 AD you'd be standing slap bang in the middle of the pit with 2,000 people baying for your blood.

Then she turns her attention to the Guildhall itself and talks about its history and its reconstruction after the Great Fire of London. She also points out that the Victorian front doesn't match the back. Apparently the dopey architect decided to use a different kind of stone so the facade is creamy white, whilst the medieval hall is dirty brown. I hadn't really noticed that before but she's right -- it doesn't match.

After that you head inside to the Great Hall. It really is fantastic to look at... much better than Mansion House which I visited the other day. The place is hanging with ancient faded flags and shields from the City's livery companies, and huge statues of the great and good stare down from the sides. You've got Winston Churchill, Wellington, Nelson and Pitt, plus a couple of Lord Mayors that I've never heard of. And high up on the balcony are the two big statues of Gog and Magog -- the legendary giants of the ancient city.

After that you head down some stairs and into the crypt, with a ceiling slung low and decorated with stained glass windows of famous Londoners like Samuel Pepys and Chaucer. Then it's back up top and through a few good-looking committee rooms. The final room is another highlight: a huge gothic-style library with more stained glass windows, heavy tapestries hanging down, and huge oil paintings of the modern day royals on the walls.

Banqueting House, Mansion House and the Royal Courts of Justice also have some very impressive interiors.

Guildhall -- Common Council

ADDRESS Guildhall, Guildhall Yard, The City - map 5e **TRAINS** Bank, Mansion House, St. Paul's (all zone 1) **BUSES** 8, 11, 21, 23, 25, 26, 43, 76, 100, 133, 242, 388 **PRICE** Free **DATES** Usually once a month, except Aug - see website **WEB** democracy.cityoflondon.gov.uk/ielistmeetings.aspx?cid=223&year=0 **TIME REQUIRED** Usually 1 PM to 2 PM

Easy to get to? ★★★ Good for kids? ★☆☆
Value for money? free Worth a visit? ★★★

Every month-or-so they hold a big meeting inside the Guildhall which is open to the public. It's called the Common Council and is attended by the city bigwigs and Lord Mayor of London in her golden chains and robes.

The Guildhall is another one of those intimidating-looking buildings that seems out of bounds to you and me, but it's actually really easy to get inside. You don't enter it through the big doors on the front facade though. If you stand in the courtyard and look to the left then you'll see some modern offices with a strange pepper-pot building out the front. If you head through the glass doors to the left of that then you can pass your bags through security. Round the corner is a little glass corridor that you can follow into the Great Hall.

The meeting today started at 1 PM but it's definitely worth getting there half-an-hour early so you can have a quiet look around the hall. The public is allowed to sit on about eight rows at the back, whilst the council occupies the front half of the hall beyond the barrier. Right at the top is the table where the Lord Mayor of London sits, surrounded by an arc of Aldermen on either side.

These are the people who run the City of London, but their writ doesn't run much further than the old city walls, so you're not going to hear anything of national importance. You can pick up a paper by the door that lists all of the questions under consideration, and the subjects up for discussion today include such riveting stuff as on-street parking, local libraries, and the adoption of the West Smithfield Area Enhancement Strategy.

There are still fifteen minutes to go before the start but it's slowly starting to fill up with people. It seems to be a mix of bowler-hatted ushers (no joke), judge-like people in their white wigs and gowns, and business leaders with smart suits and briefcases. And these aren't your £100 suits from M&S either -- we're talking Savile Row and Jermyn Street here. These people look like the movers and shakers of the City -- the kind of people who shave every day and take phone calls every five minutes. *Buy! Sell! Buy! Sell!* Gordon Gecko will probably stroll in soon.

There's a big hubbub rising up as show time draws near. Lots of chat and expectancy in the air. I was imagining it to be a really dry meeting with lots of people fast asleep, but it actually looks like quite a lively scene.

All of the smart suits are walking into the business end of the chamber now, away from the area where the public sits. There are a load of folks sitting at the top table in gold chains and ruffle wigs. The Aldermen of London have taken their places, but wait... wait a mo... here she comes, the lady Lord Mayor of London!

She marches down the centre aisle in her traditional garb and gold chains of state, whilst a parade of ceremonial suits leads her to her seat. Everyone stands up to see her process to the stage like the Queen. Then everyone bursts into a loud round of applause as she takes her place. Then we're allowed to sit down again and the judge-like ringleader bangs his gable on the table to start the meeting.

They are plodding their way through the questions now, in-between taking votes. I won't bore you with the details beyond this point, suffice to say that the best bit is definitely over. Apart from a quick little speech at the start, the lady Mayor has remained silent throughout. After an hour the public got kicked out so they could discuss some secret stuff in private.

A tip: You're not allowed to take any photos in the chamber once the meeting has started, so if you want to get a shot of the Mayor in her robes of State then it's best to wait outside in the courtyard, where her limo idles over. She left the building at 2 PM today, and you have a quick thirty-seconds before she disappears into the car.

If you enjoy political meetings then try Mayor's Question Time at City Hall. You can also attend Prime Minister's Questions at the House of Commons.

Guildhall Art Gallery

ADDRESS Guildhall Art Gallery, Guildhall Yard, The City - map 5e **TRAINS** Bank, Mansion House, St. Paul's (all zone 1) **BUSES**

8, 11, 21, 23, 25, 26, 43, 76, 100, 133, 141, 242, 388 **PRICE** Free, but there may be a charge for temporary exhibitions **OPEN** 10 AM to 5 PM (Mon-Sat); 12 noon to 4 PM (Sun) **WEB** cityoflondon.gov.uk/things-to-do/visit-the-city/attractions/guildhall-galleries/pages/guildhall-art-gallery.aspx **TELEPHONE** 0207 332 3700 **TIME REQUIRED** 1-1½ hours

Easy to get to? ★★★ Good for kids? ★☆☆ Value for money? free Worth a visit? ★★★

Romans: metal skirts, bright red sandles, and feathers in their hats. They don't sound very tough, do they? But these guys used to fight each other by the Guildhall. That's where they used to have their amphitheatre -- a short walk from Costa's coffee shop. Obviously Costa's wasn't there back then. I don't know what was there two thousand years ago (maybe Starbucks), but bits of the amphitheatre are still hidden in the basement of the Guildhall Art Gallery.

Before you go inside remember to have a look at the big black ring of bricks on the forecourt, because that marks out the diameter of the amphitheatre underneath. It always looks a bit small to me... it's more like a big wrestling ring. If the Coliseum is the Wembley Stadium of amphitheatres, then London's must have been a Sunday morning kick-about pitch.

When you get inside you have to spend a bit of time admiring the art first. Upstairs is where they put on their temporary exhibitions, which at the moment is all about Victorians. But you didn't come here to see that (trust me on this). Downstairs is much better, because that's where they keep all of their London scenes and landscapes. If you like your London history then this will be a treat, because you get to see what London was like before we modernised it. They've got pictures of old London Bridge in its hey-day (my favourite piece of architecture in the whole history of the city), and the old city burning in the Great Fire. There are some decent river scenes and pictures of the pageants, too, and some interesting old views of famous London landmarks like Covent Garden and the Leadenhall. Sometimes the streets have changed so much around these places that it's difficult to recognise them. If you don't know what the streets look like now then maybe it's a waste of time, but if you can spot the differences then you'll get a lot of enjoyment out of it.

My favourite picture is probably *The Heart of the Empire*, which gives you a good idea of how St. Paul's really dominated the skyline a hundred years ago -- back when God was the tallest man on the planet. If you're standing in front of it whilst you're reading this, can you see that brown brick building in the centre of the picture? (With all the shop awnings along the pavement?) The next time you're in the vicinity of Mansion House have a look at what we replaced that with, and then have a little cry. We knocked that beauty down in 1994 and replaced it with a Toy Town office block.

After you've seen the pictures you can head down to the basement for the main attraction... the remains of London's Roman amphitheatre.

When you enter it through two very heavy wooden doors the room is all dark and gloomy, and dimly lit in yellow. There isn't very much of it left anymore, just a small section of the entrance way and a thin sliver of the circle. They found a couple of guardrooms as well (or maybe some animal pens), but what walls remain only rise to a few feet. But it's still quite impressive to stand there and wonder what it must have been like all those years ago. I think I would have made quite a good gladiator. I'm not exactly Superman but I think I can take out a lion -- how difficult can it be? I've killed a few spiders in my time, and they've got more legs than a lion.

They've added some atmosphere by pumping in the sounds of the crowd. (I wish they would play the sounds a bit louder, though, because it hardly drowns out the sound of the air conditioning pipes.) But they've also decided to decorate the background with bright green neon lights, which is totally out of keeping with the scene. They've dressed the gladiators in the space-age style of *Tron* (huh?). Why can't they just have a colourful painting of the arena instead? They've tried to be too clever, and ended up with something daft. That's what happens when you put a load of architectural artists in a room and ask them to do some brainstorming -- they should have just asked me to do it.

You can learn about Roman London at the Museum of London. There are more remains at the Billingsgate Roman House and inside All Hallows by the Tower.

Handel House Museum

ADDRESS Handel House Museum, 25 Brook Street, Mayfair - map 2f **TRAINS** Bond Street, Oxford Circus (both zone 1) **BUSES** 6, 7, 10, 13, 23, 73, 94, 98, 137, 139, 159, 390 **PRICE** Handel House and Hendrix flat: Adult £10; Senior £10; Child (5-16) £5; Infant (under-5)

free -- Just one house on its own: Adult £7.50; Senior £7.50; Child (5-16) £3; Infant (under-5) free **OPEN** 11 AM to 6 PM (Mon-Sat); 12 noon to 6 PM (Sun); Last entry 1 hour before closing **WEB** handelhendrix.org **TEL** 0207 495 1685 **TIME REQUIRED** 1 hour

Easy to get to? ★★★ Good for kids? ☆☆☆
Value for money? ★☆☆ Worth a visit? ★☆☆

I'm at an age now where I don't mind listening to a bit of classical music every now and then, so I actually know who Handel is, believe it or not -- he's the guy who wrote the theme tune music for Champions League football. Or was that Puccini? I can never remember. He did the music for *Coronation Street* anyway, or the coronation music -- something like that.

Handel is technically a German but the English still love him because he used to live in London whilst he was writing music for George II. We even buried him in Westminster Abbey for chrissakes -- that is how much we love the bloke. He comes in at No.3 in our all-time list of favourite German musicians (behind David Hasselhoff and the Scorpions).

All of his tunes seem to be very jaunty and jolly, so I'm guessing that he was a fat fella who liked his drink. It is very happy music -- you can put it on and the sun will come out. If your kids are fighting then play them a bit of Handel and five minutes later they'll be hugging each other like nothing happened.

When you get inside the front door you are pointed straight up the stairs to the first room -- the rehearsal room. They don't provide an audio guide or anything like that -- you just walk around the rooms reading the little plastic cards that they've got dotted around the tables.

The rehearsal room is home to a huge harpsichord but it was all quiet today, and that's why I'm going to have my first little moan -- I was looking forward to hearing some actual music. It sounds daft, but parts of the house are quieter than a library. I only heard one solitary song the whole time I was there, and that was only coming out of one room. Why don't they have his music blasting out all over the place? From every room and every corridor? That seems like a total no-brainer to me. One of the rooms contains a couple of personal CD players which you can stick on your head and listen to, but that's pretty much it -- it's all hush hush on the headphones so no one can hear. If you've ever heard Handel's *Music for the Royal Fireworks* then you'll know it needs to be played loud. You need to throw open the windows and blast it across Mayfair. People come here because they love Handel, and they want to hear a few of his tunes. It's like going to the Van Gogh museum and not seeing any of his pictures.

Maybe you'll get lucky and hear some live music coming from the rehearsal room, because they put on a lot of concerts in the house (check out their website for the dates). I think you're better off coming to a concert, if I'm honest, because there's not much else to see.

The house looks very much like it would have done in his day, with creaky wooden floorboards and a few oil paintings and drawings on the walls, but none of them look original to the house -- they just depict people that he would have known. There are hardly any pieces of period furniture either -- just a few fireplaces and wooden shutters on the windows. The only room that is properly furnished is his bedroom at the top, which has got a plush red bed and chamber pot. There are next to no personal possessions on show, just a few of his music scores.

The information boards are certainly detailed and well worth a read, but if you came here to see how he lived then you're going to go home disappointed. I would have liked to have seen a Georgian kitchen with a roaring fireplace and hunks of bread and bloody meat on the table, and a tin bath downstairs where he had a wash (like they do in the Charles Dickens Museum). Even if the objects are all replicas it doesn't matter, because it would bring a bit of life to the place. It's too darn quiet.

Somebody needs to buy this place a radio and a few Handel CDs, so they can stick them on and liven the place up a bit -- maybe I'll post them a present at Christmas.

Note: Jimi Hendrix used to live in the flat next door (you can see a blue plaque on the wall outside), and they are planning to open it up to the public in 2016. Unfortunately that's a bit too late for this review, but hopefully it will be a bit better than Handel's house.

The most stirring place to listen to Handel is in Westminster Abbey (they play the Coronation Anthem on the audioguide whilst you're standing by the altar).

Harrods

ADDRESS Harrods, 87-135 Brompton Road, Knightsbridge - map 7c **TRAINS** Knightsbridge (zone 1) **BUSES** 9, 10, 14, 19, 74, 137, 452, C1 **OPEN** 10 AM to 9 PM (Mon-Sat); 11.30 AM to 6 PM (Sun) **WEB** harrods.com **TEL** 0207 730 1234 **TIME REQUIRED** 45-60 mins

Easy to get to? ★★★ Good for kids? ★☆☆

Value for money? free Worth a visit? ★★★

The first thing that you need to know about Harrods is that they've got bouncers on the door. Not big burly ones with blue tattoos on their faces... I mean little old guys in olive green gloves and frock coats and boaters. When I was young (many moons ago), I remember trying to get inside whilst wearing ripped jeans. And this was way before ripped jeans were a fashion statement -- they were just ripped, for real. And the old bouncer guy on the door wouldn't let me in! So that was the last time I went to Harrods until the other week. These days I am a bit better dressed, so I got in easy-peasy. I'm not even sure they have a dress code any more anyway, judging by some of the other scruffs walking around, so maybe they have relaxed the rules. They let me in, for starters -- so that is clear evidence of a drop in standards.

It's worth a visit to just to have a look at the building. Check out all of the lightbulbs on the outside. There are thousands of them (literally thousands). If you come back at nighttime the whole place is lit up like a Christmas tree. It looks like Chevy Chase's house in the *Christmas Lampoons* movie.

Apparently this is where Buckingham Palace gets all of their groceries from, but I've never seen the Queen walking around with her shopping trolley. They had a bit of a falling out a few years ago when Mohamed Al-Fayed was in charge, because he always blamed the Palace for Princess Diana's car crash (in which his son also died). He even had a cheesy statue of them in the foyer, locked in a big kiss; but he flogged the shop off to some rich Arabs in 2010, and I'm guessing they chucked it in the bin because it was rubbish. (Sorry Diana, but you know it's true!)

Landmarks & Attractions | 91

The confectionary hall is like Willie Wonka's Chocolate Factory. But instead of a load of orange Oompa Loompas running around you've got movie-star staff that look like catwalk models. The sweets look like they have been magicked up by elves in some factory out the back -- I'm looking at them right now, salivating. They've got orange segments dipped in dark chocolate for two quid a go. Stem gingers and decorated truffles; rose cream fondants with rose paper petals. Bright pink macaroons for three quid fifty (about the same size as a button) and little whipped cones in edible gold paper (probably made of real gold).

Even the tea bags cost a fortune. You can forget about buying a bargain box of Typhoo or PG Tips in here. What we are talking about here are tea leaves carried down from the top of a Peruvian mountain by little old women, and then saddled on a train of donkeys through jungles and deserts and stormy seas, before getting sifted into loose leaf silver caskets. They've got breakfast tea, morning tea, afternoon tea, early afternoon tea, late afternoon tea, evening tea... if you like tea then you are sorted. Everything seems to come wrapped in a bow or a decorated metal tin.

All of the food halls are fabulously ornate. The fish and meat room comes with a cast of butchers in blue-and-white striped aprons and straw hats. They've got a sit-down caviar bar as well, if you feel like sampling some of that. Next-door they have all of the exotics fruits on show: flat peaches and dates direct from Jordan, coconuts from Thailand, pomegranates from Peru and nuts from all over the place (too many to mention). The carrots in here are actually straight (they must stretch them out) and the potatoes look like they have stepped straight out of the shower. I have never seen such a clean and polished potato in all my life. Their button mushrooms are whiter than my teeth! And don't even get me started on the lettuces... their green leaves look like they have been styled by a hairdresser.

If you want something affordable then check out the boulangerie. They've got some bread rolls in there that are so overstuffed with ham and salad and cheeses that they look like they are about to explode. Have you ever tried to pack your suitcase before going on holiday, only to have to sit down on it to get it shut? Well, that is what the bakers must have done, to get so much food inside their sandwiches.

I thought I might be able to afford something in the stationary section but the fountain pens were 400 quid a pop. They've got some really nice pads and notebooks too, all leather bound with delicate golden braid.

The Egyptian Hall is worth a look. That is where they keep all the women's clothes and handbags, so I didn't stick around very long, but it's full of carved stone columns and obelisks, with decorated palms and mosaics all over the place. I especially like the way that you can see their craftsmen hard at work, stitching together custom-made handbags for the ladies. Don't just look at the first Egyptian thing you come across and leave, though. Because what you need to see is the Egyptian escalator in the middle of the shop -- wow! It's the centrepiece of the store.

It's September at the moment so they are starting to put out all the Christmas decorations. There are stacks and stacks of shortbread biscuits and Turkish Delight, with posh mince pies and brandy pies and rich Christmas puds. All of the baubles seem to be handmade and chiseled in feather-leaf wood. They are fifteen quid a pop, though (for just one bauble), but they could have come straight from a little Bavarian workshop they are so pretty. The stockings are all thick and knitted by grandmas, not glued together by factory kids. They've got a roaring fireplace in there as well -- like you'd get in Queen Victoria's day. This is how Charles Dickens would decorate his tree.

After a lot of looking I finally manage to find a coffee place that doesn't seem too expensive... it's called *Ca'puccinos*, one level down from the street; and it's staffed by very pretty women and guys in pin-striped suits. I only ordered a coffee but it came with a slice of cake and set me back a new note.

And last but not least... your little sightseeing trip should definitely include a look inside the toilets and the lift. Yes, I am being serious... the toilets and the lift. If you want to have a wee in luxurious surroundings then this is where to do it (the toilets, I mean -- not the lift). They've got one of those gents in the corner who sprays perfume onto your hands in case you tinkled on your fingers.

You might like to try Fortnum & Mason in Piccadilly, and Selfridges in Oxford Street.

Hayward Gallery

ADDRESS Hayward Gallery, Southbank Centre - map 9a **TRAINS** Waterloo, Embankment (both zone 1) **BUSES** 1, 4, 26, 59, 68, 76, 139, 168, 171, 172, 188, 243, 341, 521, RV1 **OPEN** Closed until 2017 **WEB**

Landmarks & Attractions | 93

southbankcentre.co.uk/venues/hayward-gallery **TEL** 0844 847 9910 **TIME REQUIRED** 45-60 mins

Easy to get to? ★★★   Good for kids? ☆☆☆
Value for money? ☆☆☆   Worth a visit? ☆☆☆

The Hayward Gallery is quite difficult to review because it doesn't have a permanent art collection. What they tend to do is devote the entire space to a single theme, or a single artist, and then swap it over for something else every few months. So whatever exhibition I describe to you now will have disappeared by the time that you arrive. But seeing as they only ever show stuff by contemporary artists, whatever you see is probably going to be just as rubbish (I hate modern art!).

Let me describe the current exhibition to you now, so you can understand what I mean. This will give you a good idea about the quality of the 'artwork' inside the Hayward Gallery.

Can you remember that scene in *Die Hard*, when Bruce Willis was crawling through a ventilation shaft on his knees and elbows? Well the first piece was exactly same as that -- except that we were playing the role of Bruce Willis, and we could walk through it instead of crawl. It sounds totally daft but it's true -- the first piece was just me walking through a big metal tube. Apparently that is what passes for art in the 21st century. It was more like something you'd find at a funfair.

The other installations were so dumb that they defy parody. Try and imagine three gigantic poles revolving around like a washing line, with big red and white toadstools on top. That was artwork number two. The next room contained a huge pile of red and white pills. That was literally it -- just a load of red and white plastic pills tipped onto the concrete floor.

Artwork number four consisted of two hospital beds inching their way across the concrete on electronic wheels, plus a bench full of virtual reality specs. I was hoping that the view through the specs might prove to be interesting but after queuing up for five minutes it turned out to be a load of pixelated white tree trunks.

Then they had that old chestnut that has been done a million times before: TV screens containing close-up views of peoples' faces. Then we had some flashing TV screens with more faces on them. Plus a room full of bemused people wondering why on earth they paid fifteen quid for a ticket (except that bit wasn't art -- that was reality).

It was like a sixth-form art show by C-grade students.

Every time a customer hands over fifteen quid at the front door I can imagine the bosses laughing their heads off out the back -- *ha ha ha, another punter fleeced!*

But as I said... the exhibitions only hang around for a little while, so maybe you'll have better luck than me.

If you like contemporary art then try the Tate Modern and Saatchi Gallery.

Highgate Cemetery

94 | London: A Visitor's Guide

ADDRESS Highgate Cemetery, Swain's Lane, Highgate **TRAINS** Archway (zones 2&3) and a 25 min walk **BUSES** 143, 210, 271, C2, C11 **PRICE** East Cemetery: Adult £4; Child (under-18) free -- West Cemetery tour (including entry into the East): Adult £12; Child (8-17) £6; Under-8s not permitted; Weekdays must be booked in advance; Weekend are on a first-come, first-served basis **OPEN** East Cemetery: 10 AM to 5 PM (Mon-Fri, Mar-Oct), 10 AM to 4 PM (Mon-Fri, Nov-Feb), 11 AM to 5 PM (Sat-Sun, Mar-Oct), 11 AM to 4 PM (Sat-Sun, Nov-Feb); Last entry 30 mins before closing -- West Cemetery: Guided tour at 1.45 PM (Mon-Fri, Jan-Dec), and every 30 mins from 11 AM to 4 PM (Sat-Sun, Mar-Oct) or 11 AM to 3 PM (Sat-Sun, Nov-Feb) **WEB** highgatecemetery.org **TEL** 0208 340 1834 **TIME REQUIRED** East Cemetery: 1½-2 hours -- West Cemetery: 1½ hours

Easy to get to? ★★☆ Good for kids? ★☆☆ Value for money? ★★☆ Worth a visit? ★★☆

Is there a nicer place to walk than a graveyard in the rain? I'm pretty sure that the corpses prefer it too -- the sun isn't much fun when you're six-feet under. At least with the rain they can have a little taste of the outside world as it comes seeping through the coffin top. It must be the only drink they get all week: a thimble of dirty rainwater, filtered through the mud. It's not much of a life is it, being dead? I can't say that I'm looking forward to it.

Highgate Cemetery is split into two sections: the East and West, and you can only get into the western half on a guided tour (I am doing that later today). But I thought I'd check out the eastern half first and see if it's worth the money. Neither section is free. You have to stump up some money whichever one you pick, but you have to book the guided tour in advance which is a bit of a hassle, because it books up really quick. But here is a word of advice: be careful which train station you arrive at. Their website suggests getting off at Archway instead of Highgate because it's closer, but they neglect to tell you that you will have to struggle up Highgate Hill. And trust me -- it's a hill. A proper climb. The kind of climb that requires a Sherpa. It takes about 20-25 minutes to get to the cemetery, after which you will probably need a grave yourself.

The East Cemetery is supposed to be the lesser of the two, but it still struck me as being impressive as soon as I stepped through the gate. All of the plots on the very first bend are monumental, and chiseled with scenes that wouldn't look out of place in Westminster Abbey. Blocks the height of buses... carved with Latin scripts and marbled columns. Take this guy here as an example (I am looking at him right now, as I'm writing this): his tomb is making me jealous. He's given himself a crowd of women across the top, all weeping and wailing like he's their long lost love. But they are stone women. And he is a bone man. Whatever loving he's done in the past it is over now.

Now I've come across two ninety-year-olds buried in the same concrete box. Can you imagine that? Spending seventy-odd years with the same woman in life, and then all eternity on top. What do you think the symbolism of a faded name is? Because I've noticed that his name has worn out, whilst his wife lives on in bright white letters. That doesn't bode well, does it? The poor, downtrodden husband who is not allowed to speak... still being dominated by his battle-axe wife. "In affectionate remembrance of Maude", it says, "and her loving husband" who shall remain nameless. I'm guessing that he's regretting boxing himself up in the same bedroom now.

Jesus Christ... I just got a scare as a fox burst out of the undergrowth and bounded over some stones ten steps from where I'm standing, before disappearing into the trees. I guess he's not used to seeing living people here. I had another little shiver five minutes earlier when I looked out across the woods and saw the back of somebody's head. Was it a real person? A thought went through my mind that it might have been a punter in a moment of private prayer, so I just stood there waiting for him to finish. But he didn't finish. It turned out that I was standing like a statue, staring at another statue waiting for it to do something.

I probably shouldn't spend so much time in graveyards (seeing as we're all going to end up there for eternity anyway), but how can you see a scene like this and not think that it's beautiful? The more they let it go, the more beautiful it gets. Everything is ruined -- the trees are overgrown, the branches are snapped and cracked, the gravestones are cracked and shattered, too. If you drop a bit of rain in here, and turn the sun down a few notches so it's early evening, then this is my perfect scene. No flowers, just weeds, old trees and the breeze.

Everybody gets buried twice in here: the first time in a concrete box and then once again in a knotted tangle of nettles, weeds, and prickly black berries. The gardeners have clearly given up in some places, and who can blame them? It's not as if the dead will complain. In many ways they are the perfect customers. They hand over their ten grand, and then you don't hear a peep out of them ever again. You've just got to remember to dig their hole deep enough so they can't get out. That is what would worry me if I were a gravedigger. I'd be digging down another twenty-feet at least, just to make sure they can't crawl out and ask for their money back.

The gardeners can't get near some of them anyway, as they've got big thick thorns around them, like chunky chains around their property to keep out the burglars. You'd literally need a chainsaw to pass it. They say that you can't take it with you... but this guy here has clearly given it a bloody good go, because even in death he is jealously guarding his territory. This is my space, he says -- my turf -- and no one is allowed in. Well, okay then, we won't come in. You can just have the weeds and leaves for company.

A few of the plaques have obviously received a lot of loving care and attention, but the vast majority are lying down cracked and broken and busted, and tilting over to the side as subsidence drags them down. I'm looking at a tomb right now, which even seems to be open! The headstone has toppled over and cracked a chasm in the pit below. It's a bit too dark to see clearly... but there appears to be some dirty planks of wood and a crinkled crisp packet down there. Maybe she got buried with her favourite snack? Or perhaps it was just washed down into the grave by the rain. But that's how you get remembered, isn't it? When I leave here today I will have totally forgotten the names of all of the rich people with their thousand-pound tombs, but I will still have a soft spot for poor Lucy Edwards, buried in a broken box with a bag of cheesy Wotsits.

The most famous grave in the East Cemetery is Karl Marx, but did you know that he's actually got two tombs? The original one is deeper into the middle, and is worth seeking out with the map if you don't mind leaving the path (you will be given a map when you enter). If you manage to find it then congratulations -- it's not easy. It's just a very faded slab of smashed stone, and much more in keeping with his working class roots. Another one worth seeking out is for the Victorian novelist George Eliot, who is surely too famous to suffer the nettle-strewn tomb that she's been lumbered with. I guess no one loves you when you're dead. Not enough to do the weeding anyway.

I quite liked Jeremy Beadle's (from *Beadle's About* -- do you remember him?). If anyone was going to jump out of their grave and try and scare you, then it would be him. But no... Beadle is not about. Not anymore anyway.

Douglas Adams has got quite a poignant little tomb. One of his *Hitchhiker's Guide To The Galaxy* fans has come along and stuck a pot of pens and a box of Lemsip on top, and I think that it's the little thoughtful touches like these that mean the most... I saw another one just now that had a cold cup of tea on it. I suppose his mate must have sat down for five minutes and had a Thermos flask of tea with him. I really wanted to tip the tea all over the soil, otherwise how is he supposed to drink it? But you can't fiddle will things like that, so I left it alone. He's probably lying in his tomb shouting and swearing at his buddy for being so thoughtless. (The cynical side of me just thinks that a workman put it down and forgot about it, whilst he was busy relieving himself against the tombstone.)

I dont know who's buried under this lot, but they had a fair few knick-knacks on top of their box. Candles and lanterns, flowers and fir cones... all dusted and watered and neatly arranged. I'm guessing that it's a lady under there. Maybe a lady who's scared of the night? Hence all the bright lights and lanterns on top of her grave. Nobody ever comes to light them, though -- you only get so much love when you're dead. They'll place some wax candles on your grave, but don't expect them to catch the bus up to Highgate every night to light them. Once the sun goes down you're on your own.

I like the foreign graves the best -- especially the Poles and the Italians. They seem to have a bit more love in them than the British ones. The most emotion that we can muster is a chiselled line about "falling asleep" and "much missed". But the other countries actually put portraits on top: proper photo frames so you can see their faces. That's how you remember someone isn't it -- by staring into their eyes, and having a conversation with their face. We Brits are too reserved for that, even in death. We just brush a bit of grass down and stare at the mud.

Before I leave the East Cemetery I just want to do something with you... for when you come and visit. I want to find a lonely old grave that hasn't received a visitor in years, so we can both stand there and toast his health together. Are you up for that? Let's stand over his bones and shake hands through the pages of this book.

Okay... I have found a perfect one. This is how you get there: grab a map from the main gate and follow the path towards Karl Marx, but take a right straight after the grave of Richard Smith (marked as 'R Smith' on the map). Have a walk down that overgrown path, and keep looking towards the right. You will have to keep your peepers peeled because it's two tombs back from the front of the path, but hopefully you will catch sight of a headstone with a handshake on top. It's got a carved cross at the peak. I can't even make out the name on it because it is so faded and worn. Is it *William* something? Let's call him Bill. This guy is a nameless nobody and we are probably the only visitors he's had in a hundred years. But that handshake seems like the perfect place for this writer and reader to stop and say hello. I'm guessing that Bill is a smoker so I bury a fag a few inches down.

Two hours later: I have just finished my guided tour of the West Cemetery, and it is easily the best cemetery I have ever been too. That place is amazing -- I think I have just discovered where I want to spend my dead days. And maybe some of my living ones too. (I can't wait to die now -- that's how great it is!) The only problem is the cost... they are selling burial plots for forty grand a piece in there; so maybe my kids will have to forgo their inheritance -- ah well. Tough luck, kids. I will just tell them that I blew the lot on a hole in the ground.

There were about twenty people in my tour group, which consisted mainly of old tourists in tailored shorts and middle-aged women. And the guide was an elderly gent of sixty-plus years, which gave him a vested interest in the subject matter (he even told us about the plot he'd just purchased for him and his missus!). But he was the perfect guide for a tour like this -- you don't need comedy and Hollywood in a graveyard. He was slow talking and slow walking, which gave you plenty of time to enjoy the views. It was a bit like a sunny Sunday stroll after lunch... and very pleasant it was too.

The West Cemetery is a little bit smaller than the eastern half, so you get to see a fair-sized chunk of it in the sixty-minutes that it takes to walk around. The main difference between the two is the monumental set pieces. The eastern cemetery is all graves and tombstones, but the western half has got big buildings too. He takes you up the Egyptian Avenue, for example, which is guarded by two giant obelisks. Then you come to the Circle of Lebanon which is a solid ring of stone doors surrounding a grassy hill, topped off by the spookiest tree in London. (If you have ever read *The Lord of the Rings* and can recall the Barrow-downs, then come back here in the fog and re-live the scene.)

After that he drags you right inside the catacombs. This dead place is dank and black, save for a shaft of light shining through the skylight. All of the alcoves are stacked with rotting coffins, piled up high to the ceiling. Some of the alcoves haven't even been topped off with concrete, so you can see the coffins sitting silent on the shelves. (So there's basically just a sliver of wood between you and the bones -- very spooky!) If the catacomb door suddenly slammed shut then you'd basically have a heart attack -- no doubt about it. You'd just run around screaming until you passed out. It's a bit like a morgue I suppose: those ones that you see on the TV, where they have cupboards of corpses in the walls. Imagine that... but replace all of the shiny metal walls with rotting wood. And then turn off all of the lights. And add some spiders and flies and heat up the dusty air another ten degrees. *Welcome to the catacombs.*

Whilst he is leading you around all of these terrifying places, he is busy telling you the history of the cemetery, and stopping off at a few of the famous names to tell you their life story. There are nowhere near as many famous people in the West Cemetery compared to the eastern one, which is a bit surprising. The only people that I can remember off the top of my head are Michael Faraday, the bloke who invented postage stamps, and the guy who started Crufts. One of the most recent ones that you might remember is Alexander Litvinenko -- that Russian guy who was poisoned by polonium. (And no, before you ask, his grave *doesn't* glow in the dark.)

So in conclusion then... is the cemetery worth a visit? Bearing in mind that Highgate isn't exactly in the centre of town, and will probably use up an entire afternoon of your holiday, would I recommend a visit? Well, the western half is easily the best cemetery I have ever been to, but I wouldn't beat yourself up too much if you can't get a tour ticket. If you want to go midweek then you'll have to book at least a week in advance, although you can just turn up at the weekend and hope for the best (you don't need to book for that). The East Cemetery is a bit more laid back... you can just pay a few quid at the gate. I would definitely try for the western half, but if truth be told I would be just as happy walking around the eastern bit. But then again I am a morbid kind of bloke, who likes to spend his free time in a cemetery.

If you enjoy walking around cemeteries then try Brompton Cemetery.

HMS Belfast

ADDRESS HMS Belfast, Queen's Walk - map 10b **TRAINS** London Bridge (zone 1) **BUSES** 42, 47, 78, 381, RV1 **PRICE** Adult £16; Senior £12.80; Child (5-15) £8; Infant (under-5) free; Family (2 ad+2 ch) £42, or £28 with 1 ad+2 ch; Price includes a voluntary donation **OPEN** 10 AM to 5 PM (Mon-Sun, Nov-Feb); 10 AM to 6 PM (Mon-Sun, Mar-Oct); Last entry 1 hour before closing **WEB** iwm.org.uk/visits/hms-belfast **TEL** 0207 940 6300 **TIME REQUIRED** 2½ hours

Easy to get to? ★★★ Good for kids? ★★☆
Value for money? ★★☆ Worth a visit? ★★★

I wouldn't mind joining the Navy for six months and sailing around the world on a boat. Six months in Hawaii would be nice... maybe stopping off at the Bahamas and the Caribbean for a few days. As long as there's not an actual war going on then it would probably be quite fun. I could be that good-looking guy in the movies who presses all the buttons on the bridge. As soon as they've decided what to shoot I could tell everyone to stand back and then press the button and retire to my cabin to listen to Mozart for the rest of the day (with my little dog -- submarine captains always seem to have a little dog for some reason).

HMS Belfast is an old battle cruiser from World War II that's been moored up by City Hall. But here's a word of advice: leave the high-heels at home because you'll struggle with the stairs. This is a war ship so there's no room for proper staircases. What they do is weld some metal rungs between two lengths of pipe and make you tiptoe down them backwards. They are so horrendously steep that you can't even come down them facing the front, because your feet are too long for the rungs. It is literally like stepping off the edge of a cliff. (Did they not have health and safety laws during World War II?) The last time I visited this ship I remember my knees were playing up and I was very close to giving up and going home. (*Call the war off! Tell the Germans to stop shooting! The fighting will resume once we've installed some proper stairs!*)

Luckily my knees are okay today so I should be fine (not that you care).

One of the reasons why I like this boat so much is because it is fully staffed by a crew of waxwork sailors, and they've got a few Royal Navy guys walking around in uniform too. Sometimes you even mix them up with the waxworks. I walked into a communications room filled with computers and radios and heard the sound of someone going "bravo, niner, you are cleared for loading" (or something like that), and assumed that it was just a tannoy recording to set the scene, but then I turned the corner and found myself face-to-face with a guy doing his day job! I think he was an officer judging by his plummy posh voice and the stripes on his jacket. There are loads of people like that all over the ship. I saw one of them polishing a torpedo. Another one was checking out the dials on the bridge. It's almost like being aboard a working boat.

You can pretty much walk wherever you want and explore every deck from top to bottom. You don't have to do it in any particular order, you just punch a number into your audio guide when you wander across a room, and it will tell you what it was used for. You can visit the mess, the cabins, the chapel and engine rooms, the gun turrets and armoury, the bridge and the dentist... it's never ending. Even the mundane stuff like the baker's and sail maker's workshop have been properly kitted out to look exactly as they were in their hey-day. It's almost like a little city with every kind of amenity you need. They've got a little tuck shop-style canteen selling 1940s groceries like Bovril and Lifebouy soap (remember Spangles?). They definitely had a soft-spot for Kit-Kats during World War II because the shelves are stuffed full of them. They've got a little hospital ward and an operating room too, with a waxwork patient being sliced up by a waxwork doctor (I hope he knows what he's doing -- he seems half asleep to me).

The audio guide is about as detailed as you'd wish it to be: along with the descriptions they've got recollections from the wartime crew and memories of what life was like on board. I suppose we should be grateful that HMS Belfast led a lucky life, because there are plenty of recollections to go around. If they re-ran the war then this is the boat you want to be on.

The mess deck is pretty fantastic with the hammocks strung between the walls and the sounds of conversations and card games coming out the speakers. These waxworks are noisier than the humans! You can see them playing dominoes and writing letters back home, laughing and kipping in a quiet corner with one arm dangling out the bunk whilst their mouths are lolling open. I'm always complaining about traffic noise in my hotel rooms, but jesus christ... these guys have got their hammocks strung above the actual machinery! Imagine sleeping two inches from ten more sailors and five inches from a burning steaming machine pumping out oil and smoke and water.

The whole boat is alive with the sounds and noise of life on board. When you go into the Operations Room for example, you get a flood of radio messages and helicopters flying high overhead, and people barking out the commands. All the lights are flashing and the radar screens are spinning and it feels like something serious is about to kick off.

I love the period music being piped out of the speakers too -- they've got old World War II tunes and Dame Vera Lynn floating through the cramped metal corridors and it gives you a real nostalgic feeling.

If you descend deeper down into the boat then you can see all of the engine rooms. You have to be super skinny to make your way through this bit because the pipes are two inches from your face. It's like an obstacle course: you have to walk along a little chain gangway suspended halfway between the floor and the ceiling.

The deepest you can go is the shell room below the water line. Hopefully they are all duds because they've got a couple of hundred lying around where any idiot can fiddle with them. You can see racks and stacks of them and where they fed them up the tubes to the big guns at the top. I hate to think what it must have been like working down here... can you imagine? In a boiling hot claustrophobic metal box filled with deafening clanks and bangs and the rocking and rolling of the boat, surrounded by fire and flames if you make a mistake. They've got a couple of water extinguishers dotted around if the worst happens, but something tells me they won't be much help if two hundred shells blow up.

At the top of the boat is the Admiral's Bridge, where you can have a sit down in his seat and pretend that you've spotted the Bismarck sailing past London Bridge. They've got one of those rotating radar screens with orange blips on it (German tourists?). I'm not sure what all the other buttons and levers are for, but I still pressed them anyway. Nothing happened. Nothing blew up. So I tried pressing them harder but again nothing happened. I pressed them again. And again. And again. And again. *Work, damn you!* I wanted to blow something up but they must be duds.

The highest you can go is up to the Director's Control Tower (the turret that sits above the main deck guns). Once you get up there you'll be surprised how high you've climbed -- it's probably at the same height as a four-storey building. You get some good views of Tower Bridge and the Tower of London from up there.

There's nothing like standing on the open deck of a battleship with the cold wind in your face and the Arctic rainwater coming in sideways and getting you drenched. It was pelting down with rain today so I felt like I was rolling around in the North Sea. I didn't stay up there for too long because I didn't want to get swept overboard and die. I just had a look at the cannons and the anchor. The anchor on this boat is bigger than a family-sized car -- it must weigh more than a skip full of concrete. How does this boat even float? It's covered in industrial-sized pipes and skyscraper girders everywhere you look. The bones of this boat are made of steel.

Unsurprisingly they have plugged up the barrels of the guns to stop the kids dropping bananas down them. The big ones at the front seem to be pointing towards St. Paul's Cathedral, which is a bit worrying -- I hope they haven't loaded them by mistake. (Can you imagine the trouble they'd be in if they accidentally blew up St. Paul's?) While you're on the deck try and find the A-Turret and step inside there -- what a smell! It's like a burning oil smell and it feels like the guns have been firing all morning.

After that you can go into a little mess hall-style canteen for a sit-down and a pot of tea, and watch some old newsreels on the telly.

You might enjoy a day trip to Chatham Dockyard to see HMS Ocelot and HMS Cavalier.

Horse Guards

ADDRESS Horse Guards, Whitehall - map 8d
TRAINS Charing Cross, Embankment, Westminster (all zone 1) **BUSES** 3, 11, 12, 24, 53, 87, 88, 159 **TIME REQUIRED** 20 mins

Easy to get to? ★★★ Good for kids? ★☆☆
Value for money? free Worth a visit? ★★★

When people talk about Horse Guards they usually think of the gravel parade ground where the military bands do Beating Retreat, but the best section is actually the small courtyard that faces onto Whitehall. That's where you'll find all the horses and foot soldiers.

Everyone loves a horse. Especially when it's got a soldier on top. If you put a soldier with a shiny sword on top of a horse then you can keep the tourists happy all day. When the horses are out between 10 AM and 4 PM this place is packed full of happy, snapping, camera clicking visitors, all taking it in turns to tiptoe up to the horse and hoping it doesn't kick them in the goolies. It's probably the most dangerous thing they do all week: standing two feet from a military horse whilst their buddy blinds it with a camera flash. Everyone takes it in turns to walk up and have their photo taken two inches from its feet, like they are best buddies all of a sudden. Up they go, smiling and laughing and grinning with their cameras clicking, while the soldier is just sitting there with a big two-foot sword in his hand that he's not allowed to use. This goes on all day, every day. Just a million billion people and him, snap snap snapping away on their cameras.

And it's even worse for the Foot Guards (the standing soldiers), because they haven't got an animal tank to sit on. You used to be allowed to stand side-by-side with those guys but they don't allow that anymore. They are all safely stationed behind a wire chain these days, and if you step behind the line then you will get barked at -- *loudly*. They have to stand there all day watching the tourists do limp-wristed salutes and getting laughed at to smile and say cheese by a mob of foreign students. Students always laugh when they salute a soldier -- have you noticed that? That's because most of them are socialists. People don't realise that these guys are actual soldiers -- they are not actors dressed up in a suit. Half of them have probably spent six months in Afghanistan or wherever, and then they come back here and get taken for granted outside one of London's tourist hot spots. Or maybe they are grateful for the easy gig? At least you don't get shot at in London. If I had a choice between Afghanistan and Whitehall then I know which one I would choose (neither).

You might notice a couple of machine gun coppers standing inside the courtyard whenever the troops are out -- another sad sign of the times. It really is coming to something when the army needs a bodyguard.

You might be wondering why the soldiers are standing there at all -- surely it can't just be to entertain the tourists? Once upon a time this building used to be the headquarters of the British Army, and the Household Cavalry still retain a stables in the building. The rest of them moved into the Ministry of Defence building further down the road and abandoned their desks to the bureaucrats. So most of the windows around the parade ground will have a civil servant in these days, occupying the same rooms that Wellington wandered around all those years ago.

Have a walk through the central arch and stand in the centre of the parade ground. Can you see that grand facade on the left? That's Admiralty House. Back when Horse Guards was the headquarters of the army this building was home to the navy. Nelson would have been in and out of here around the same time that the Duke was walking around Horse Guards.

The best building for me is the one next door: the ugly one -- that brown concrete box that looks like an eyesore. Sometimes it's covered in green ivy, sometimes in red ivy, but most of the time it's just a pile of dirty brown breezeblocks. I usually want to knock down all the ugly buildings but I'm prepared to make an exception for this one because of its interesting history. This is the Citadel, and Churchill ordered it to be built so the Admiralty could have a bomb proof operations centre during World War II. So here is definite proof of how close we came to invasion in 1941: they must have been truly desperate to build this. If you look up at the top righthand corner then you can even see some holes where the soldiers would have positioned their machine guns.

The rest of the buildings around the parade ground are nice looking, but rather uninteresting for a tourist (even for a London nerd like me). But on the far right-hand side of the parade ground, just before you hit the road, is the most interesting brick wall in Westminster. I am talking about that dark brown brick wall with a big black gate in it. You will probably see a couple of serious-looking policeman standing nearby holding automatic weapons across their chests, because on the other side of that wall is the garden of No.10 Downing Street.

No.10 itself is further back and out of sight, tucked away in the corner behind that white building, so you can't see what the Prime Minister is doing. I suppose you could bring a big step-ladder and a pair of binoculars with you and try and peer over the wall, but I don't recommend that -- those gun cops will shoot you.

You might like to time your visit to coincide with the Changing the Guard ceremony and Dismounting Ceremony.

Household Cavalry Museum

ADDRESS Household Cavalry Museum, Horse Guards Parade, Whitehall - map 8d **TRAINS** Charing Cross, Embankment, Westminster (all zone 1) **BUSES** 3, 11, 12, 24, 53, 87, 88, 159 **PRICE** Adult £7; Senior (over-60) £5; Child (5-16) £5; Infant (under-5) free; Family (2 ad+3 ch) £18 **OPEN** 10 AM to 6 PM (Mon-Sun, Apr-Oct); 10 AM to 5 PM (Mon-Sun, Nov-Mar); Last entry 45 mins before closing **WEB** household cavalrymuseum.co.uk **TEL** 0207 930 3070 **TIME REQUIRED** 45-60 mins

Easy to get to? ★★★ Good for kids? ☆☆☆
Value for money? ★★☆ Worth a visit? ★☆☆

If I told you that there's a museum 500 feet from Downing Street with some horses and a stable inside, then you'd probably think that I was mad. Well, I'm not mad. (Well, actually, I *am* mad -- but that's not the point.) Even most of the locals don't realise that there's an 18th-century stable down Whitehall. They all know where Horse Guards is, but they rarely stop to think who the actual 'horse guards' are -- they're soldiers from the Household Cavalry, made up of two different regiments: the Life Guards and Blues & Royals.

The mounted sentries that occupy the famous horseboxes are from the Household Cavalry. If you're lucky enough to see them change over shifts then you can stand there and watch them enter the stables through a big door on the righthand side of the courtyard (where the foot guard is standing). When you enter the museum you can see these exact same horses being groomed through a plate glass window. That's where I am standing right now: watching the soldiers talk to the horses.

The horses are huge -- and I mean *huuuuge*. They might have skinny little legs but their bodies are bigger than a concrete barrel. They're just standing there staring at the wall whilst the soldiers are walking around with all their gleaming gear on, in various states of undress, getting ready for their sentry duty. It's a bit like peering into a football changing room at half-time -- you can see what's going on behind the scenes. I can see one guy sitting on a bench polishing his golden buckles, whilst another one is tightening up his leather braces. They're all acting totally oblivious to the tourists taking photos of them. I guess they must be used to it.

That window is definitely the best thing about the museum. The rest of it will only appeal to military enthusiasts. It's literally just two rooms filled with old uniforms and weaponry, and a bit about the Battle of Waterloo. They've got some old medals, saddles and swords, trumpets, bugles and buttons, and some dusty old muskets and guns. The regiments date back 300 years to the reign of Charles II, so they've accumulated pretty much every kind of memento going. They've got pipes and prayer books, canes and cards, and display cases full of shiny finery. Some of their plumed helmets must be two feet tall at least, like a giant haircut, with feathers bursting out the top like an ornamental fountain. The French must have seen those peacocks coming from miles away. Another cabinet explains in great detail what equipment they need to shine their shoes.

Their uniforms become a lot drabbier when you reach the First World War: everyone seems to be dressed up in the colour of mud. Happily for the horses they were replaced by armoured cars and tanks by the 1940s. Nobody goes to war on a horse anymore. It's all about pomp and pageantry these days, parading up and down for the tourists. They're a bit like pampered supermodels now -- they just stand there eating sugar lumps while some poorly paid humans brush their hair and polish their shoes so they can strut around outside, whilst crowds of people snap photographs of them. If you took these catwalk horses to war then they'd complain about the dirt.

If you're interested in horses then try the Royal Mews.

Houses of Parliament -- Summer Opening

ADDRESS Houses of Parliament, Westminster - map 8d **TRAINS** Westminster (zone 1) **BUSES** 11, 24, 148, 211 **PRICE** Adult £25.50; Senior (over-60) £21; Child (5-15) £11; Infant (under-5) free; Young kids not advised due to the walking **OPEN** Timed tickets every 15-20 mins between 1 PM and 5.15 PM (Mon, Aug); 9 AM to 5 PM (Tue-Fri, Aug to 2nd half of Sep) **WEB** parliament.uk/visiting/visiting-and-tours/tours-of-parliament/guided-tours-of-parliament **TEL** 0207 219 4114 **TIME REQUIRED** 1½-2 hours

Easy to get to? ★★★ Good for kids? ★☆☆
Value for money? ★★★ Worth a visit? ★★★

I got absolutely soaked on the way to Parliament this morning. Do you know when you're so wet that your socks are squidging in your shoes? That is how wet I was.

Once you've negotiated the gun cops at the gate, armed with sub-machine guns, grenades and rocket launchers (I exaggerate only slightly) you head into Westminster Hall where you wait for the guide. This is without a doubt the best waiting room in London, and it also happens to be the only room in the building where you're allowed to take photos. After that it's strictly phones off and cameras away, so get snapping. Westminster Hall is the oldest part of the palace and dates back to the 11th-century. It's the same place where they tried Guy Fawkes, Thomas More and Charles I -- and now they're using it as a waiting room for the tour! Remember to check out the golden plaques on the floor, which show you the exact spots where famous events took place. It's quite astonishing to think that you can stand in the actual spot where Charles I sat in his seat, shortly before getting the dreaded news from Olly Cromwell.

Our guide turned out to be a bloke called Colin, who not only looked like a Colin but had the encyclopedic knowledge of a Colin as well. He was one of those geeky guys who knew everything about everything, and everything else as well. He gave us a little test too, whilst he was counting up the heads, asking us who our local MP was. Luckily I knew who mine was -- Ed Davey -- but you could see some of the people squirming in their seats whilst they tried to dredge the name out of the depths of their head. After that little bit of fun he took us on a 5-minute trek through the heart of the palace, past all the good rooms and halls without saying a word. You literally pass through the whole lot without learning a thing. This can be a little disconcerting if you've never been on the tour before, but don't worry: he's just taking you to the far end of the building where the tour begins.

You pretty much follow the same route that the Queen takes at the State Opening of Parliament, starting at the Norman Porch and Robing Room. It's a lovely looking room, but I found the decorations a bit bizarre. They've got murals of King Arthur and his knights, complete with Lancelot, Merlin and Camelot -- it's like something out of a fairy tale. If there was a picture of Indiana Jones on the wall then it wouldn't look out of place. After that you go into the Royal Gallery where the pictures return to reality: two huge ones of Nelson's death and Wellington's victory at the Battle of Waterloo. Apparently the French President was supposed to give a speech in here once, but refused to do it because of the beating his Napoleon was getting on the walls.

Everywhere you look (and this goes for the entire building) are statues and paintings of British kings and queens, PMs and politicians. Every famous name from the last 1,000 years can be found in some place or another. Queen Victoria gets the most because she built the place, but our present Queen is there alongside Edward the Confessor, Henry VIII, Churchill, Nelson, Wellington and Thatcher.

After that comes the Prince's Chamber, where they have some fantastic portraits of the Tudors and Stuarts, and then you hit the first highlight: the House of Lords.

You won't believe the amount of gold and decoration in the House of Lords. The place is absolutely covered in it, and the seats are stretched in plush red leather. Just remember not to sit down, because one lady in our group decided to take the weight off her feet and got a real roasting from the tour guide. Apparently she hadn't "earned the right" to sit there, and her crimson cheeks went the same shade as the seat.

The tour goes right down the centre of the room, five feet from the golden throne. You get to stand at the far end as well, where the Commons come and stand at the State Opening, whilst they are listening to the Queen's Speech; so you get exactly the same view as they do, crammed behind that little wooden fence.

After the House of Lords you leave the Royal half of the palace and head towards the Commons, and this is where the decor starts to get a bit drab. The Royal half of the palace is all reds, golds and chestnut browns, whereas the Commons has to make do with light browns and green. I'm not saying that it looks cheap -- because it still looks great -- but it definitely suffers in comparison with the Lords. The nobles used up all the money on the precious metals, you see, and the Commons had to make do with the wood.

First up is the Peers' Lobby and Peers' Corridor, and then you enter the Central Lobby, which is the room you always see on the 10 o'clock news (where the journos interview the politicians). The final room before the House of Commons itself is the Members' Lobby, which is full of busts and statues of famous politicians. Lloyd George, Churchill, Thatcher and Attlee get the biggest ones, whilst the less famous (or less well-remembered) PMs get smaller spots. Anthony Eden, for example, gets shunted off into a corridor. I quite liked this room because they've left part of it in ruins. If you look at the arch that leads into the chamber then you can see some bomb damage from the war. Apparently the Luftwaffe totally demolished the House of Commons and a bomb blasted debris out of the arch. Churchill decided to leave it in a sorry state as a sober reminder.

The tour then enters the House of Commons from the back, from behind the Speaker's Chair, and proceeds down one of the sides. So you are standing a short distance from where the Prime Minister usually sits.

It's amazing how small the House of Commons is. It is tiny! Colin said that it measures the same size as a tennis court, which seems a bit small too me, but it's not far out. Honest to god -- it is so small that you'll think they've cut it in half. You can really imagine how intimidating it must be when all the opposition benches are shouting back at the PM trying to drown him out. It must be absolutely terrifying.

Once again, you are not allowed to sit down on the seats because you "haven't earned the right" (although I'm not sure any of the MPs deserve to sit down either!). In fact, that is something that I should warn you about on the tour... it is very heavy on your tootsies. The whole thing lasts for about 75 minutes and you can only sit down once (for about two minutes). So if you've got dodgy knees like me then be prepared for some aching bones at the end.

Colin's dialogue was very thorough throughout, but I really do think that you need an understanding of British history to get the most out of it. And that is not me being pompous... the names, dates and events are fired at you so thick and fast that it's practically impossible to remember anything unless you already know it in advance. You might recognise a few famous names like Guy Fawkes and Henry VIII, but he goes into detail about practically every monarch we've ever had, plus the Prime Ministers too, and famous events from the Magna Carta and English Civil War, through to the battles against Napoleon and introduction of the Welfare

State. It's a whistle-stop tour through a thousand years of English history.

One annoying little criticism though, is that your tour is constantly competing with other groups for floor space. You end up being pushed into a little corner of the room whilst three more groups occupy the others, and all four guides are jabbering on at once. Luckily Colin had a big mouth so I had no problems hearing him, but I did feel a bit sorry for the tours being led by little old ladies.

After the Commons you head down St. Stephen's Hall and back into Westminster Hall. Then it's off to the cafe for a cup of tea.

If you can't make the Summer Opening then don't worry... they also offer guided tours on most Saturdays.

Houses of Parliament -- Saturday Guided Tour

ADDRESS Houses of Parliament, Westminster - map 8d **TRAINS** Westminster (zone **1) BUSES** 11, 24, 148, 211 **PRICE** Adult £25.50; Senior (over-60) £21; Child (5-15) £11; Infant (under-5) free; Young kids not advised due to the walking **OPEN** Timed tickets every 15-20 mins between 9 AM and 4.15 PM (Sat only) **WEB** parliament.uk/visiting/visiting-and-tours/tours-of-parliament/guided-tours-of-parliament **TEL** 0207 219 4114 **TIME REQUIRED** 2 hours

Easy to get to? ★★★ Good for kids? ★☆☆ Value for money? ★★★ Worth a visit? ★★★

You might be under the impression that you can only have a tour of Parliament during the Summer Opening, but that's not true. There are actually three more ways to sneak a peek inside. The first way is to stand as an MP and get 50,000 people to vote for you at the next General Election. But granted, that is probably too much hassle if you're only here on holiday. The second way is to write a letter to your local MP and ask him for an invite. He is then duty bound to stick your name down for a free guided tour. (And I swear to God that is true -- it's called a Member's Tour, because it's sponsored by a Member of Parliament.) But that's not much use if you live abroad because you won't have a local MP. So the third way, and definitely the easiest way, is to just go along on a Saturday.

The MPs don't like working at the weekends you see, and disappear off to their constituencies, so they let the public have a walk around instead. All you've got to do is buy a ticket online before you go -- easy-peasy. Or you can get from the ticket office by Portcullis House on the same day -- but then you are running the risk that it will already be full up.

I've never been on a Saturday tour before, and I'm curious as to whether it's identical to the one at the Summer Opening. I've got a sneaking suspicion that it is... but I will let you know. I am standing outside at the moment waiting to go in. The entrance is directly opposite the back end of Westminster Abbey, where all the gun cops stand around discussing who to shoot. Luckily I've got a very angelic-looking face so they let me in.

The first thing you have to do once you get inside is get undressed, and I'm not even joking. The security is super tight and they make you take off your coat and belt so they can put them through the scanner. So if you've got baggy trousers then watch out, because they are going to fall down around your ankles. After that you head into Westminster Hall for a sit down. This is the room with a hammer-beam roof that dates back a thousand years. Remember to check out the plaques on the floor as well because lots of people miss those -- they mark out the spots where famous events took place, like the trial of Thomas More and King Charles I.

After that you get frog-marched through the palace at a thousand miles per hour to the Norman Porch at the far end. Then she slowly makes her way back describing all of the rooms in detail. I have already described the rooms in my review of the Summer Opening though, so I won't bore you with the same stuff again. Just have a read of my previous review, because the rooms are exactly the same.

Because I've been here plenty of times before, none of the rooms are new to me, but they still manage to knock my socks off every time I see them. I think this is the fourth time I've traipsed through the building, but I still get a little thrill whenever I walk into the House of Commons. There can't be a person on earth who isn't secretly thinking *wow!* as he's walking through that chamber. You see this room on the news, and here you are standing five feet from the spot where the Prime Minister sits -- how can you not get a little thrill from that? If that doesn't float your boat then how about getting close to the golden throne where the Queen sits at the State Opening of Parliament? Or standing under the bomb-damaged arch where Winston Churchill glares down at you with his hands on hips?

The guide I had today was probably the best I've ever had. She was very detailed like a school teacher, and she explained a lot of the workings of Parliament that I've never heard before. It will probably bore your kids silly though (it bored a lot of the adults I was with too), but it's very good if you're interested in politics.

The tour turned out to be identical to the one at the Summer Opening, but with one minor change: you get taken into a room where the Lords hold a few of their meetings. It's called the Moses Room and has a few huge paintings on the wall, but it's nothing special. She also allowed us to take some photos in St. Stephen's Hall, which was a bonus (you are usually only allowed to take photos in Westminster Hall).

If I had to recommend choosing either a Saturday tour or the summer one then I think I'd plump for the Saturday tour; because even though it is still pretty busy, it's a lot less busy than the Summer Opening (which is packed solid like sardines). That means your guide can take a bit more time explaining things because the rooms don't get as crowded with other groups.

If you're interested in Parliament then how about watching a debate in the House of Commons? You can also arrange an invite to Prime Minister's Questions.

Houses of Parliament -- Saturday Audio Tour

ADDRESS Houses of Parliament, Westminster - map 8d **TRAINS** Westminster (zone 1) **BUSES** 11, 24, 148, 211 **PRICE** Adult £18.50; Senior (over-60) £16; Child (5-15) £7.50; Infant (under-5) free; Young kids not advised due to the walking **OPEN** Timed tickets every 15-20 mins between 9 AM and 4.15 PM (Sat only) **WEB** parliament.uk/visiting/visiting-and-tours/tours-of-parliament/guided-tours-of-parliament **TEL** 0207 219 4114 **TIME REQUIRED** 2 hours

Easy to get to? ★★★ Good for kids? ★☆☆ Value for money? ★★★ Worth a visit? ★★★

This is the only event that I haven't yet attended at the Houses of Parliament -- an audio tour. I've done everything else that a tourist can do: I've climbed up Big Ben, been to see the PM, fell asleep in the House of Lords, seen the protesters banging pots outside, seen the Queen trundle up in her carriage -- this is the last one. So after this they should give me a badge or a balloon to mark my achievement... maybe put a statue of me up in Parliament Square. Yeah, that's a good idea. Knock down Abraham Lincoln and put me up there instead. What did he ever do for London? I bet he never went on a Saturday tour of Parliament -- twice. I bet he never had to sit listening to Neil Kinnock droning on in the House of Lords for two hours. If anyone deserves a statue it's me.

I've already written about the Saturday tour once already so I don't want to bore you with the same stuff twice (I'd rather bore you with some all new stuff), so have a quick read through that one before you start on this one, because the rooms you see inside are identical. The Saturday guided tour and the Saturday audio tour are exactly the same -- the only difference is that you're in a group with a human guide on the first one, whilst the audio tour makes you stroll around on your own with some headphones.

I should add a little caveat to that... because sometimes the tour route is shortened when they are using the rooms. If you visit the week before the State Opening of Parliament, for example (like I did), then they'll miss out all the Royal stuff from the Norman Porch through to the Royal Gallery. Unfortunately that includes some of the best-looking rooms in the building, so you might want to give them a ring before you book. (I still think it's worth attending even without these rooms, but you'll definitely be missing out a fair-sized chunk.)

I quite enjoyed the audio tour because you get to walk around Parliament unaccompanied. Obviously you can only stick to a particular route -- it's not a complete free-for-all (if you jump over the ropes then the police will probably pump a hundred bullets into you). But it does make you feel quite important having a wander around the corridors whilst everyone else is being shepherded around by the tour guide. The politicians desert the House at the weekend you see, so there's nobody there apart from the guards and the guides and the groups and the cleaners, plus a few suited staff pottering around to check you're not misbehaving.

You get lots of extra detail on the audio-guide that is not included on the guided tour. There are sections on the State trials in Westminster Hall, for example (about William Wallace, Guy Fawkes and Charles I), and some interesting info about the 1834 fire. I also learnt a lot about St. Stephen's Hall that I never knew before. But whether you actually find any of this stuff interesting is another matter entirely, of course -- not everybody is going to enjoy a ten minute monologue about the Parliamentary committees. But at least it gives you a reason to sit down and look around the rooms for a while -- something that you don't have time for on a guided tour.

I apologise for this rather short review but you really need to read the other one first, because that's where I describe the route and all of the rooms. Remember... the two routes are identical -- *literally!*

But before I go, let me just give you an answer to the most important question: which one is better, the guided tour or the audio tour?

Well... I think I'd definitely recommend the guided tour to a tourist -- simply because it's a lot easier being led around by someone and listening to what they have to say. But on a personal level I think I prefer the audio tour. I've already done the guided tour about ten million times so it makes a nice change being able to walk around the place on my own. You also get a bit more time to stop and look at the walls and windows.

You might enjoy a tour of Big Ben as well. You can also ask your local MP for an invite to see Prime Minister's Questions.

House of Commons

ADDRESS Houses of Parliament, Westminster - map 8d **TRAINS** Westminster (zone 1) **BUSES** 11, 24, 148, 211 **PRICE** Free **OPEN** Usually 2.30 PM to 10.30 PM (Mon); 11.30 AM to 7.30 PM (Tue-Wed); 9.30 AM to 5.30 PM (Thu); 9.30 AM to 3 PM (some Fri) -- Note: The Commons doesn't sit in first week of Jan, one week in mid-Feb, last week of July, whole of Aug, mid-Sept to mid-Oct, one week in mid-Nov, and last two weeks of Dec **WEB** parliament.uk/visiting/visiting-and-tours/ watch-committees-and-debates/debates **TIME REQUIRED** 5-60 mins for the queue, plus 30-60 mins inside

Easy to get to? ★★★ Good for kids? ★☆☆

Value for money? free Worth a visit? ★★★

Apparently the best things in life are free. That's what they say, anyway (the people with money). But in this case it happens to be true: because you can come to the Houses of Parliament and sit in the House of Commons for nothing. You don't even need a ticket or any ID. And yes, I know that sounds totally ridiculous, but trust me when I say it's true. You might have to wait an hour to get inside, but once you've bagged yourself a seat you can basically sit for as long as the chamber is open. [Note: You do require a ticket if you want to visit between 12 and 1 PM on a Wednesday, because that's Prime Minister's Questions. Check out my separate review for details.]

Whenever I visit the Houses of Parliament I always like to begin my day with a five-minute sit-down in Parliament Square, to watch the pigeon protestors defecate on the statues' heads. This is a great reminder not to think too highly of our politicians, I think -- because these people are not role models. Just because we pay them sixty grand a year doesn't mean they deserve it. When you're sitting in the public gallery you won't see people cheering and clapping and blowing kisses at them. People don't swoon at them, like kids do at a pop concert. The seats will be full of people peering down at the performing MPs, trying to spot a few famous faces off the telly.

When you're ready find the visitor entrance, which is roughly halfway along the front side of Parliament, and ask the nice lady at the barrier if you can "go inside the House of Commons". She will then give you a piece of green card (nicely laminated -- very hi-tech). If you ask for the House of Lords then she'll give you a red card instead. All you have to do is show the card to the gun cop on the gate, and he will then deliver a totally redundant speech about all the things you're not allowed to take inside: scissors, swords, knives, guns, bombs, ballistic missiles, tactical nuclear weapons, etc. Then you get a little visitor's pass to hang around your neck and pass through some airport-style security. After you've negotiated all of that you can finally head into Westminster Hall.

Westminster Hall is a thousand years old -- literally. It is *genuinely* a thousand years old. (That's even older than me.) But seeing as I've already written about it ten thousand times in my previous reviews of the Houses of Parliament tours, I won't bore you with the same stuff again. Just head straight to the end and turn left up the stairs. This will take you into the splendour of St. Stephens Hall. This is the waiting room.

If you're unlucky then you might have to join a lengthy queue here, which might add on anything from five minutes to an hour. They don't have very many seats inside the public gallery, you see, and people can basically stay for as long as they like. So if it's already full then you just have to wait patiently for a space to open up -- which could take ages. It's a bit like waiting for a space to open up in a multi-story car park: there really is no knowing how long it will take. But I've visited the Commons five or six times and I've never had to wait longer than thirty minutes. Don't be too worried about the queuing, though, because from the moment you step into Westminster Hall you will be immensely impressed by the decor. You can trust me on this. I know I'm rather biased because I love London, but if the decoration inside Parliament doesn't knock your socks off then you may as well just go home now. Even if you only get as far as St. Stephen's Hall and bail out because of the queue, I would still definitely recommend a visit -- that's how good it is.

When you're finally allowed to proceed a guard will give you a little piece of paper that you have to fill in with your name and address, and then he'll show you where to head next (through the door and turn left, and then up the stairs to the Strangers Gallery). The last time I came here they confiscated your camera and mobile phone at this point, but they seem to have relaxed the rules now. They still confiscate your camera but they let you keep hold of your phone (even if it's got a camera on it, which sounds a bit daft). They even let you type on it whilst you're sitting in the gallery -- but they'll kick you out if you start taking phone calls and snapping photos. Photography is a definite no-no. Taking photos will get you kicked out quicker than your camera flash. Remember to have a quick look on the cloakroom desk as you walk past because that's where you'll find a copy of the Order Paper. It's a big white thing about A4 size, and it lists all of the subjects that are up for discussion that day. If you don't grab a copy when you walk past then you won't be able to get one inside the chamber (don't worry, it's free).

The first time that you enter the House of Commons is one of those highlights you'll remember forever. It will probably mean much more to a Brit, because we're used to seeing this room on the news every night, but it's still going to be a memorable moment for a tourist. Put it this way: I've been here a load of times now, and I still get a little thrill whenever I step through the door.

The public gallery is at the back of the Commons, looking down upon the MPs heads. It runs around the sides of the room as well but you're not allowed inside those areas: you're strictly limited to the ten rows at the back. The gallery on the far side of the room is reserved for the journalists and court reporters. You can see the Speaker's chair directly ahead, the bewigged clerks sitting below him, the front benches where the Prime Minister and the Leader of the Opposition sit, and the central table where all the books are stacked up, but you can't see anything further south than that.

Unfortunately this is where it starts to get a bit boring because you have to sit here listening to the politicians. There are only nineteen MPs present in the chamber today, none of whom I recognise, and all I've heard so far is John Bercow droning on about Parliamentary privilege. He's just banging on and on and peeling the paint off the walls. It's quite warm in here and the MPs are lounging around waiting for him to stop talking. One guy is happily flapping his tie back and forth over his shoulder. Another lady is lazily arranging the folds of her skirt across the top of her knee. Another Labour guy has spent the last two minutes staring up at the forest of microphones hanging from the ceiling. I've never noticed those before actually: there must be a hundred of the things just dangling from the top like streamers. Hmm... interesting.

This is our government. These are the people who run the country. Sitting here fighting off their pins and needles by making little circular shapes with their ankles. The green seats around them are strewn with plastic folders and typed-up letters.

Is Bercow still talking? He certainly loves to talk. Maybe that's why they call him the Speaker: because that's all he ever does. It reminds me of 3 PM on a Friday, five minutes before we were let out of school. We're all waiting for the teacher to stop talking so we can go home.

When you finally get tired of trying not to fall asleep then I recommend seeking out the little gift shop and cafe. They sell some nice Parliamentary souvenirs in there.

You can also watch a debate inside the House of Lords, City Hall and Guildhall.

House of Commons -- Prime Minister's Questions

ADDRESS Houses of Parliament, Westminster - map 8d **TRAINS** Westminster (zone 1) **BUSES** 11, 24, 148, 211 **PRICE** Free for UK residents, but you must write to your MP for a ticket (and wait up to four months for a spot); Unclaimed tickets are handed out at the visitor entrance from 11.30 AM (but you will need to be extremely lucky) **DATES** Wed only - except for when the Commons is in recess during the first week of Jan, one week in mid-Feb, last week of July, whole of Aug, mid-Sept to mid-Oct, one week in mid-Nov, and last two weeks of Dec **WEB** parliament .uk/visiting/visiting-and-tours/watch-committees-and-debates/question-time **TIME REQUIRED** 12 noon to 12.30 PM, but you will need to arrive before 11 AM

Easy to get to? ★★★ Good for kids? ★☆☆ Value for money? free Worth a visit? ★★★

It's a bit of a rigmarole getting into Prime Minister's Questions (PMQs). It's only on once a week, for just half an hour on a Wednesday, and you can't simply turn up and queue like you do on any other day of the week. What you have to do is write a begging letter to your local MP three months in advance and ask for an invite. I told mine that if he came up with a ticket then he'd have won a voter for life.

Obviously I lied. The chance of me voting for my bloke is close to zero -- he's useless! But he did deliver on my ticket, though, so fair play to him.

I sent my letter off at the beginning of January and got a spot in April, so that shows you how much forward planning you need to do: a few months at least. If all goes according to plan then you'll end up with a headed letter from your MP's office, which you can use to get past the gun cops on the gate.

Security is super tight today because there's a state visit from the Irish president taking place, and there's a battalion of machine-gun coppers standing outside the entrance, all eyeing me up and wondering whether they can shoot me. I smile widely and they let me through -- thank Christ for that. Then I get a thorough pat down and a frisk inside and tiptoe past the scanners and metal detectors. Even Harry Houdini would have trouble sneaking something through security today.

Once you're through security you head into Westminster Hall and on to St. Stephen's Hall and Central Lobby (that's where they do all of the interviews on the ten o'clock news). Have a look around for the Reception Desk, and right next-door to that is the Admissions Order Office. Head in there and swap your headed letter for a proper ticket at one of the windows. (You don't need any ID, just the letter.) Then all you've got to do is fill in a form with your personal details on (name, address, occupation, embarrassing birthmarks, etc.), and then you can relax.

The session starts at noon, and you need to grab your ticket by 11:30 at the latest, otherwise they'll assume that you don't want it and dish it out to the public standing at the gate. (Important note for tourists: you might be wondering how on earth you can write a letter to your local MP when you don't even live in Britain. Well, this is how you do it: you have to wait by the gate at half-past eleven and hope that some of the tickets go unclaimed. The odds of that happening, though, are very slim.)

I've got another thirty minutes to wait until they let everyone up to the gallery, so I spend my time looking around Central Lobby. It's a very beautiful room but it's quite a small space, and it rapidly fills up with another two hundred to three hundred people. At 11:27 precisely the policemen suddenly stand to attention and everybody gets ordered out of the centre. What is going on? Then he shouts out 'Hats off!' and the Speaker parades in with his posh togs, off to open Parliament. The Sergeant-at-Arms comes first, holding the ceremonial mace, and then the Speaker John Bercow follows through, grinning and waving at the crowd and clearly enjoying being the centre of attention. Immediately after that there's a big bundle into the Admissions Office again, and they finally let you up the back stairs into the public gallery. At this point you have to hand over all of your mobile phones and cameras because there's no photography allowed in the chamber.

It's 11:35 now, and PMQs doesn't start for another twenty-five minutes, so for the first half-hour you have to yawn your way through departmental questions. There's hardly anyone famous in the chamber yet, just a load of bureaucrats and faceless suits that nobody knows. It's a bit like watching an orchestra tuning up before a classical concert starts. Any minute now the curtain will go up and the main players will bound out onto the stage.

They've erected a big thick glass screen between the public and the chamber, which is a bit annoying -- presumably to prevent us throwing tomatoes at the politicians. So we are looking down on the MPs from above, spying through a plate-glass window, whilst the sound is piped in through the speakers. It's a very curious effect, and removes you a little bit from the action. You can see them speaking and moving about below, but their voices are floating in from the sides and behind. You can hear a general hubbub of supplementary voices as well, because no one bothers to keep quiet when the other MPs are talking. There is lots of muttering and chuntering on the back benches. People interrupt, shout, wave, make faces, and generally make plain their disdain for the opposition.

I find it childishly amusing that the Speaker John Bercow doesn't fill up his chair -- his head doesn't quite reach the top. He's got three wigged clerks in front of him and a few suited henchmen to the side, and he's resting his palms on the side of the seat like Marlon Brando in *The Godfather*.

Things are starting to build up to the start... still no sign of the PM, though. I guess he's going to make a grand entrance with party poppers, streamers, and balloons. Oh, wait a minute... here he comes. Dave has arrived to a general cheer from the Tory side. He's sneaked in from behind the Speaker's chair and sat down without fanfare. He's got a pair of spectacles on too -- he never wears those on TV; he'll probably take them off in a minute. Now he's pouring out a glass of water and puffing out his cheeks, geeing himself up for the fight.

Here comes Ed Miliband and Ed Balls now, who both sit down with a *whump*. I've just spotted Nick Clegg, Danny Osborne, and Harriet Harsperson, too -- the whole gang is in today. The only bloke missing is George Osborne.

Twelve o'clock arrives, and here we go; it's show time. *Ding ding for round one.* They've turned the microphones up to maximum, and it's shaking the glass.

Cameron is very combative straight off the bat; he must be in a bad mood this morning -- he isn't taking any prisoners today. I've just noticed that he's taken his spectacles off, too, so I was right: he doesn't want to look nerdy on the telly.

Up comes Ed Miliband to huge cheers, as if they're welcoming a boxer to the ring. He is rising to his feet, and so am I. *BOO! BOO! You suck, pal!* I shout, but he doesn't hear me over the cacophony of noise. The amount of sound in this place is incredible. The benches are doing more booing than me, cheering and jeering and waving their arms about like it's the Second Coming. If you've never been to the House of Commons before, then you might have expected our politicians to behave impeccably, with great gravitas and dignity. Well... you'd be wrong. Let me explain to you what it's really like: imagine a room with two hundred blokes in it, all arguing about who's right, when all of them are wrong. That's pretty much what it is: two hundred ten-year-olds in Savile Row suits.

Miliband kicks off with some questions about Maria Miller (a disgraced MP who resigned this morning). Everything is aimed at Dave, though; that's all Ed cares about, pinning the blame on David Cameron. Someone else does something wrong, but it's all Dave's fault apparently. The noise bubbles up every time he spouts out a question; he's getting a big din of noise just for talking. The Speaker has had enough and jumps out of his chair, barely any taller when he's standing up, and points to a load of Brownies in the balcony in an attempt to shame everybody into silence. Doesn't work. Noise keeps coming.

It really is a bear pit down there, and I don't envy them their job at all -- it must be incredibly intimidating. They've got five rows of shouting MPs behind them and another five benches bearing down in front; plus a couple of rows of journos and the public glaring down from the balcony. Not to mention all of the microphones and cameras hanging from the ceiling -- what an arena! The noise is bashing about their ears from all directions, and they can hardly get a word heard. Now I know why they pipe the sound in through the speakers: because we wouldn't be able to hear anything otherwise.

It's a good bit of knockabout entertainment. They shout out their slogans and bat away the replies like they're idiotic lies. What a load of ham actors! Both of them have a good line in gags, too, straight out of the playground and into Parliament. It reminds me of being back in the sixth-form common room at school -- every time somebody stands up to say something it's all shouting and howling and rolling their eyes. I'm surprised that they don't go the whole hog and fake faint, in mock shock and horror.

Every now and then we get a question that invokes total silence, like something on Ireland, Israel, or a terrible murder that has taken place. The MPs might be childish, but they know when to hush up. Thankfully that doesn't last very long, and the verbal punch-up continues straight after.

I've noticed that the MPs have a curious habit of lying back in their seats every time someone rises up to speak, as if they're having a five-second power-nap. Apparently that is because there are some little speakers buried in the back of the chair, and they are trying to have a listen to what's being said. That is how loud this place is: they can't even hear one another speaking from fifteen feet away!

At 12:30 PM the whole thing comes to an abrupt halt, and with the Speaker's final 'Order! Order!' everybody files out. Everyone is up and out in five seconds flat, probably off for a cup of tea somewhere, which is where I am going, too.

Remember to bring some money with you for the end, because they've got a nice little cafe adjoining Westminster Hall, and a little gift shop selling Parliament chocs and coffee cups.

If you like political debates then try a visit to the House of Commons, House of Lords and Mayor's Question Time at City Hall.

House of Lords

ADDRESS Houses of Parliament, Westminster - map 8d **TRAINS** Westminster (zone 1) **BUSES** 11, 24, 148, 211 Price Free **OPEN** Usually 2.30 PM to 10 PM (Mon-Tue); 3 PM to 10 PM (Wed); 11 AM to 7.30 PM (Thu); 10 AM to 3 PM (some Fri) -- Note: The Lords doesn't sit in first week of Jan, one week in mid-Feb, last week of July, whole of Aug, mid-Sept to mid-Oct, one week in mid-Nov, and last two weeks of Dec **WEB** parliament.uk/visiting/visiting-and-tours/watch-committees-and-debates/debates **TIME REQUIRED** 5-30 mins for the queue, plus 30-60 mins once inside

Easy to get to? ★★★ Good for kids? ★☆☆
Value for money? free Worth a visit? ★★★

Come on Big Ben, speed up son! I've been sitting in Parliament Square for the last half-an-hour waiting for 11 o'clock to come. I've already been to see the MPs debating in the House of Commons so I thought I'd give the House of Lords a try today. The Commons is usually open by mid-morning, so silly old me thought that the House of Lords would open up at the same time. But I forgot that they are all 80-year-old peers and need two hours to get out of bed. So here I am sitting in Parliament Square trying to waste away a bit of time.

The square has been tidied up quite a lot during the last 12 months. There are no more big wire mesh fences all over the place. No more protesters either -- they've kicked them all out. Good! It was starting to look like a messy old cub camp with pots and pans and tatty old tents about the place. I don't understand why they let them live here in the first place. I'm all for free speech, but only if you've got something interesting to say. Moaning about the Iraq war ten years after we left is just plain daft. If you want to bang on about Tony Blair all day, then go and do it outside his house and leave Parliament Square alone!

Big Ben has just bonged his bell and sounded out the hour, so off I go...

Security was a lot tighter today than it's been in the past. I even had to remove my belt. I was a bit worried that my trousers were going to fall down but they stayed up, thank god. After that they let you walk through Westminster Hall on your own, and you take a seat in St. Stephen's Hall. The queue for the House of Lords is usually a lot shorter than the Commons. It was supposed to be 45 minutes today (for the Commons), but I got called through to the Lords after two minutes. You just have to fill in a little card with your name and address, and then you get taken up a few flights of stairs to the Stranger's Gallery. Be advised that you have to hand over all your mobile phones and cameras at this point, and then you head through for a pick of the seats.

When I went to the Commons it was packed with people but the Lords is a lot more boring (supposedly) so no one was there, and I pretty much had my pick of the seats. But I don't think that it's boring at all -- I'd happily visit either.

I am sitting inside the chamber now and it's much better than the Commons. Big black statues of ancient kings stare down from the walls and great stained glass windows decorate the sides. The ceiling is gold, the chandeliers are gold, the railings are gold, and the seats are plush red leather. The whole place has been decorated to within an inch of its life.

There are a lot more famous names in here as well, because the peers are largely made up of grandees that should be sitting at home with the wife. They should be retired really, but after forty years of small talk with the missus they have run out of stuff to say, and end up coming in here every day instead. The MPs in the Commons don't do that: they have got other things to do, so their chamber is largely empty. The Lords is full of old people having a natter. It's a mixture of old men with white hair, old women with white hair, old men with walking sticks, old women dripping in pearls, and bishops with their white frocks on. There is also a very fine collection of moustaches on display. I can't see any young people though. Are there any young ones? They all look over fifty to me. But I'd rather be ruled by people with a bit of common sense and experience. There should be a rule that no one is allowed to stand for parliament until they're suffering from arthritis.

Another big difference between the Lords and the Commons is that there is no bullet-proof screen between the public and the peers. I guess no one wants to threaten the peers because there's no point: they haven't got any legislative power. It would be like taking pot-shots at pillows.

The discussion is all about Gibraltar and the behaviour of Spain. Everyone is up in arms about it and they want to know what we're doing to beat down Johnny Foreigner. What have we done? (Not a lot.) Why don't we send in the ships? (Because we don't have any left.) Why don't we drop a bomb on Madrid? (My idea.) *Let's burn all our Julio Iglesias records!* The talk soon moves onto a different subject -- teacher training for kids who can't read.

Wait a minute... who do I spy here... is that Alan Sugar? I think it is! Yup, it's definitely him: I recognise his gruff mannerisms. He's got his hand clamped around his face like a tightened vice. It looks like he's trying to hold his jaw in place to stop it falling off. It's nice to see that he actually turns up and contributes. I thought he might be one of those stay-at-home peers who collect all the pay and perks and don't bother with the rest. But here he is, holding onto his face as he listens to something that he's not remotely qualified to comment upon. Much like the rest of the chamber, I'm guessing.

I've just spotted Norman Tebbit too, staring up at the public gallery. His thoughts are somewhere else, it seems. I wonder what he's dreaming about. Maybe he's dreaming of Maggie and past glories.

An anonymous bloke has been talking for ten minutes now and I've just realised that I haven't heard a single word he's said (too busy writing this). His words are floating around my ears without ever going in. I wonder if everyone else is the same? A room full of people and he's still talking to himself. I'm still not listening to him, even now. I listened just long enough to note that I haven't been listening, and then I stopped listening again. That just about sums up the House of Lords for you: the Commons does all the important stuff, whilst the House of Lords just sits and talks to the walls.

Alan Sugar has decided that enough is enough and walked out (he's probably got some people he needs to fire or something), and even old Norman has gone off for a cup of tea. I take that as my cue to leave and stroll out through Westminster Hall. They've got a little gift shop in there if you want to buy someone a box of posh chocs, and there's a little cafe too if you fancy a cup of coffee.

If you're interested in political debates then try Prime Minister's Questions, Mayor's Question Time at City Hall, and the Common Council at Guildhall.

Hunterian Museum

ADDRESS Hunterian Museum, 35-43 Lincoln's Inn Fields, Holborn - map 4e **TRAINS** Holborn, Chancery Lane (both zone 1) **BUSES** 1, 11, 26, 59, 68, 76, 168, 171, 172, 188, 243, 521, X68 **PRICE** Free **OPEN** 10 AM to 5 PM (Tue-Sat) **WEB** hunterianmuseum.org **TEL** 0207 869 6560 **TIME REQUIRED** 30-60 mins

Easy to get to? ★★★ Good for kids? ★☆☆
Value for money? free Worth a visit? ★★☆

Come and see the severed head of Winnie the Pooh! If that doesn't want to make you want to visit the Hunterian Museum, then nothing will. I'm not sure that I'd recommend it to tourists, though. It's more for medical students, I think, and for local Londoners who've already seen all of the obvious attractions, and are searching around for something a bit different.

It's basically a big collection of human bones and sliced-up animals. They pickle up bodies and stick them in a jar. They've dissected birds and bees (literally -- even bees!) and slit open their throats and stomachs, so you can see all of their muscles and blood and bones. Some of them are truly gruesome. They have glass jars with hairless rodents and a foetal pig. They have bottles on show with severed heads in them (bird's heads) -- they've simply sliced through the throat and pickled it. They have a chimp's head too -- just his head in a bottle, complete with his fur. The museum is housed inside the Royal College of Surgeons, you see, so it's all about the anatomy. It's there for the students. And people who like horror movies.

The worst ones are the pickled humans. You might think that I'm joking, but I'm not -- they have actually taken some unborn babies and pickled them throughout every stage of development. You can follow them along from conception to birth, watching their faces forming onto blobby heads, then their arms and legs stretching and bending into limbs, and finally into a fully formed stillbirth that didn't quite make it. (I don't recommend this museum for kids!). If that doesn't tickle your fancy, then how about their huge collection of tumours?

What makes the museum most interesting for the casual visitor are all the freaks and weird ones. They have skeletons of deformed humans, and a giant Irish circus showman. One poor guy seemed to have a skull the same size as a beachball. They even have the skull of Winnie the Pooh. *I'm being serious!* There used to be a brown bear in London Zoo that inspired A. A. Milne to write his children's tale. Well... you can see the bones of his severed head at the Hunterian Museum (I don't remember that being in his bedtime book).

I see this place as a sister to the Natural History Museum, because that place displays the animals with their clothes on (with their feathers and fur), whilst the Hunterian strips off their skin and shows you their blood vessels and bones.

I also think it's worth a visit just to have nose around the building itself (the Royal College of Surgeons). You have to pick up a security pass to get through the barriers, and then you walk up some very grand stairs lined with paintings of talented docs.

If you enjoy looking at dead animals then try the Natural History Museum.

Hyde Park

ADDRESS Hyde Park - maps 6b, 7a **TRAINS** North side: Lancaster Gate, Marble Arch (both zone 1) -- South side: Hyde Park Corner, Knightsbridge (both zone 1) **BUSES** North: 2, 6, 7, 10, 16, 23, 38, 52, 73, 74, 82, 94, 137, 148, 274, 390, 436, C2 -- South: 2, 9, 10, 16, 19, 22, 52, 73, 74, 82, 137, 148, 414, 452, C2 **OPEN** 5 AM to midnight (Mon-Sun) **WEB** royalparks.org.uk/parks/hyde-park **TEL** 0300 061 2000 **TIME REQUIRED** 1-2 hours (depending on how far you wish to walk)

Easy to get to? ★★★ Good for kids? ★★☆
Value for money? free Worth a visit? ★★☆

I don't get on very well with the sun. Put it this way: we're not friends. If I'm going to be walking around a park for two hours then I usually like to do it in the rain -- but it's sunny today. It's hot enough to boil the tears off my cheeks. So if I wilt halfway round then you'll understand why, because Hyde Park is a lot bigger than it looks on a map.

I'm starting off at Speaker's Corner, opposite Marble Arch -- famous for its free speech and hecklers. Wannabe politicians and the world's worst orators bring their stepladders along and start shouting at the crowds, sharing their wit and wisdom and weirdo conspiracy theories, but I've never seen anyone here except for Sunday lunchtimes. The only people giving speeches today are a few pigeons and squirrels. I can hear a cyclist ringing his bell at a few dawdling walkers, but that's about it.

Head out into the middle of the park and try and get away from the roads. You need to try and block out all the traffic noise by filtering it through the tree leaves. People claim that Hyde Park is so vast it's like walking in the countryside, but there's nowhere that you can't see a building. Cranes are constantly peeping over the tree line. There's always someone running or walking their dog or pushing their pushchair kids. It's very hard to hide from humans in London. If you take away the lake then it's actually quite a flat and featureless place. There are only three kinds of tree in here: green, brown or dried-up and dead. It does have quite a lot of wildlife, though. I've just noticed a lot of bird houses nailed up on the tree trunks. You'll also see plenty of horses if you keep your eyes open. There's a dusty red path along the top and bottom edge where they get their daily exercise, and a couple of empty paddocks were they get trotted around by the riders. One of the paddocks has even got a couple of jumps inside. But I don't think these horses are going to win the Grand National any time soon. We're not talking Red Rum, here. They're more like plodding donkeys, in training for a career down the seaside carrying fat kids in flip-flops.

As you're walking along the top edge keep an eye out for Victoria Lodge. Head through the road gate towards the street outside, but at the very last second have a look left through the railings. What can you see? I can't see very much today because it's all overgrown with weeds, but if you peer through the greenery then you might be able to make out a few midget gravestones. This is a Victorian pet cemetery, full of dead doggies and moggies. Women sure do love their dead pets, don't they? I'm guessing that they must have been women who buried them. Women bury their pets like they're one of the family -- men just flush them down the toilet.

If you carry on walking around the edge then you'll come to Buck House -- another spooky little place which looks like a haunted cottage. I don't know if it actually is haunted, but trust me when I say I'm not going anywhere near to find out. It *looks* haunted, and that's enough for me -- it looks like it's filled with spider's webs, darkness, and evil. The last time I walked past this place I was overcome with a deep dread and terror and I had to sit down and have a beer (several beers, in fact).

At the top of the lake is the Italian Gardens. This is quite a pleasant place for a sit down: four stone pools and a few spouting fountains, decorated in water reeds and lily greens. I'm sitting here listening to a six-foot fountain having a fit of spurting spasms and it's actually quite violent. It's like an Icelandic geyser or a busted road pipe. The ducks don't seem to mind: they're just sitting under the spray like it's a bathroom power shower.

It's hard to believe when you see the size of it, but the Serpentine is actually a man-made lake. There used to be a river running down through Bayswater but Queen Caroline (George II's wife) had it dammed up so she would have somewhere to sail her pleasure boats. That's royalty for you. They couldn't get away with that these days. But it created a great home for the birds, I suppose. It's quite a multicultural little town, this lake: you've got ducks and dogs and swans and coots and flies. London is just a big melting pot of races and religions, isn't it? Feathers, fur, webbed feet, no feet; as long as you're happy eating soggy cigarette ends and stale breadcrumbs off the concrete then you're welcome in our town. They are probably the best-fed birds in Britain because everybody seems to bring a loaf of bread with them. Every five paces you'll see a little old lady carrying a supermarket carrier bag, crunching up some crumbs and scattering them around her feet for the fowl. Every bird in London must have got a whiff of it because they're coming down in their thousands for a massive slap-up meal (of bread). What happens if you're a bird and you don't like bread? We humans have got a very fixed idea about what animals like to eat. If you're a bird then you get bread. Monkeys get bananas and mice get cheese. Horses get sugar lumps and rabbits get lettuce, and if they don't like that then *tough*. Dogs are totally different though: because dogs get a fully-cooked roast dinner with Sunday veg and gravy (at least, they do in my house).

There are two big cafes in Hyde Park. The Serpentine Bar & Kitchen is at the eastern end of the lake, and you'll find the Lido on the southern side. The first one is definitely the best because you can pick a seat outside and stare down the length of the lake. From this perspective it's almost like an ocean -- it's vast! The ducks are sitting in the bay preening their feathers (cleaning their engines) getting ready to sail away... they're just stocking up on a few more flies and then they'll be off on their adventures. I think I'll just stand here and watch them sail away. It's a bit like standing on the Albert Dock, watching the iron liners disappear over the horizon. I can see a load of pigeons as well, but they never seem to go in the water. Can pigeons even swim? They just stand on the bank staring at their big brother ducks sailing away to distant shores, waving them goodbye with their wings.

The prettiest parks are St. James's Park and Regent's Park. You might also like to visit Kensington Gardens next-door.

Imperial War Museum

ADDRESS Imperial War Museum, Lambeth Rd - map 9e **TRAINS** Elephant & Castle (zones 1&2) and 15 min walk, Lambeth North (zone 1) and 10 min walk, Waterloo (zone 1) and 15 min walk **BUSES** 159, 360, 109, 344, 360 **PRICE** Free, but there may be a charge for temporary exhibitions **OPEN** 10 AM to 6 PM (Mon-Sun); Last entry 30 mins before closing **WEB** iwm.org.uk/visits/iwm-london **TEL** 0207 416 5000 **TIME REQUIRED** 2-3 hours

Easy to get to? ★★★ Good for kids? ★☆☆
Value for money? free Worth a visit? ★★☆

I quite like World War II. It seems like a lot of fun, getting a boat across the channel and giving the Hun a good seeing to, etc. *Take that Hitler! Take that you evil Nazis!* Maybe I watch too many old war movies, but my visit to the Imperial War Museum today just made me like it even more. I am from the generation where the Nazis were just the bad guys in *Indiana Jones*, and not the rowdy rabble rampaging across Europe killing millions of Jews, so war has still got the derring-do of *Commando* comics to me. I think if I had a time machine I'd travel back to the year 1925. That seems like the perfect year to be born: still young and dumb enough to look forward to the war, and not too old to forget the sixties.

The entrance hall has been totally redesigned from the last time I came. They've still got the big green V2 rocket and Spitfire hanging from the ceiling, but now they've added a flying V1 and a Harrier Jump Jet as well. Lord knows how they managed to hang that up there (maybe they flew it up vertically?). Unfortunately they've also moved the collection of tanks and field guns they had parked up on the floor... but maybe I'll come across them later.

The big new exhibit that they are currently plugging is all about the First World War. Normally I would just skip straight past this room because I'm not a big fan of the Great War (I think that's because it lacks the panto villain and hero of Adolf Hitler and Churchill), but this new gallery is very good indeed. And it certainly doesn't shy away from showing the dirty side of war.

It covers everything from the early recruiting posters and queues of happy kids eager to sign up, to the military tactics and medals given out to the dead. There are plenty of weapons and uniforms on show, lots of battle maps and tactical plans, and loads of mementos from the guys who did the fighting.

Many of the exhibits are very imaginatively displayed, and really bring home how horrendous it must have been. They've put a couple of German machine guns up, for example -- just simple little machine guns doing a crossfire -- but they've traced the spray of bullets with solid rods of metal. It sounds a bit rubbish when I describe it like that, but believe me: anyone standing in front of that is dead, simple as that -- cut to ribbons. When you combine that with all the bomb blasts and awful screeches and rat-a-tat rifles they've got blasting out of the speakers, it makes you happy you were born sixty years later. Another good exhibit is a walkthrough trench that has got a full-size tank lumbering up and over the edge. I'm glad they've moved the tank here instead of sticking it in the entrance hall, because when you're standing underneath that metal monster, trapped between the dirty walls of mud, it makes you realise what little hope they had.

The next floor is home to their World War II collection, starting with the Home Front. They've got some mock-ups of people's parlour rooms and kitchens with all the old stoves and wirelesses, which you can tune-in and listen to the BBC news. They've got lots of old wartime sing-songs playing out of the speakers as well, and if you're of a certain age then I'm sure you'll love it -- a trip down memory lane. The last time I came here they actually had a full-size house built from top to bottom, and you could climb the stairs and roam around every single room, but sadly that has disappeared now.

Then you move onto the WWII-era tanks and jeeps -- proper old battle tanks like the Sherman and Mark II. Whenever I see an old war movie they always have a scene where the soldiers are lounging around on the tank tracks, sitting up there puffing on a skinny little cigarette as they trundle through the towns, and I almost want to jump up and do it too. But you can't go inside them unfortunately, or even look inside them, which is a bit of a shame, so I had to settle for standing up close.

Another interesting machine is a one-man submarine. It is unbelievably small and the pilot must have had to lie down on his stomach to drive it through the water, in a space not much bigger than my shoe. Imagine slicing through the pitch black and freezing sea for five hundred miles on a suicide mission. He must have been nuts. They've got the wreckage of a Japanese plane as well, plus the cockpit of a Lancaster bomber. They don't have a lot of information on the actual battles though, or on the personalities involved. They definitely did the last time I came, but they seem to have whittled it all down so they can focus on the machines. If you want a good grounding in the Second World War then I recommend going to the Churchill Museum inside the Churchill War Rooms instead -- there's plenty of good stuff in there. (The Imperial War Museum and the Churchill War Rooms are actually run by the same people, so maybe they've made a conscious decision not to double everything up.)

The next level moves onto atomic bombs and nuclear bombs, and a mangled strut of steel from the World Trade Centre.

I'm not sure that it's such a great idea having a nuclear bomb as one of the exhibits, because there are a lot of school kids running around the place. And you know what kids are like: they will have a fiddle with all the buttons whilst their teachers aren't watching, and the next thing we know London will disappear in a choke of rubble and dust. I am assuming that they must have disarmed the bombs before putting them on display, because there is bound to be a dumb health and safety law that says you can't have a live atomic bomb on show.

The next floor is the one that I don't even want to write about because it's so depressing -- the Holocaust Exhibition. Let me give you some advice: don't take your kids in. And don't take any adults in either. That is how depressing and awful it is. They've got a big sign outside that warns you it's not suitable for children, but there's stuff in there that's not even suitable for me. They've got pictures of the dead and dying, and people who are so starved and skinny that their bones are bursting through their skin. I saw a picture of a Russian bloke so desperate to flee the camp that he jumped onto a barbed-wire electric fence. Another one showed a firing line: a split second before they pulled the trigger. One victim seemed to be begging and crying for his life, whilst another one just stood and smiled and suggested that they get on with it, to give him some relief. It was probably the happiest day of his life.

I thought their most profound exhibit was a huge model of Auschwitz that's about fifty feet long (and that's not an exaggeration). They have every little detail done to perfection, from the big train driving in to the tiny bits of razor wire wrapping around the barbed wire fence. Thousands of tiny people are disembarking off the train (literally thousands), and when you walk up to the end of the model you are confronted by the little building where they burnt the bodies. If it portrayed anything but Auschwitz then you'd think it was the best model railway you'd ever seen. But instead it's the worst.

If there's just one little criticism that I can make of the Imperial War Museum, then it's this: they've got a habit of removing my favourite displays. The last time I came here they had a much better trench exhibition and an Anderson air-shelter scene, where you could actually walk through a full-sized bombed-out street. They have both vanished now. And I have already mentioned that excellent 1940's house that has disappeared. I am guessing that they decided those exhibits didn't suit the museum's chief focus anymore: which is the awfulness of war. That's the main aim of this place now it seems -- to drum it into our brains that war is not very nice. They don't want to celebrate our victories anymore, they want to apologise for them. But I'm not a member of that 'all war is bad' brigade, who wring their hands and roll their eyes whenever somebody dares to mention the British Empire. And yes, I am well aware that the Holocaust was a truly horrendous event, which should never-ever be forgotten, but how about telling us something about Dad's Army or Dame Vera Lynn for a change, instead of showing us yet another case full of dead Jews' shoes?

And there's nothing for the kids either -- you can't even climb inside the vehicles. I remember when my parents brought me here as a child I walked out thinking it was pretty cool, but I'm not sure it would have the same appeal now.

This is how I would sum the place up: in the past it made you want to join the army. Now it makes you want to join the priesthood.

If you like World War II then you will enjoy the Churchill War Rooms, Bletchley Park, HMS Belfast, and the RAF Museum.

Jack The Ripper Tour

ADDRESS Starts by Trader's Gate Souvenir Shop (outside Tower Hill Station) - map 10b
TRAINS Tower Hill (zone 1) **BUSES** 15, 42, 78, 100, RV1 **PRICE** Adult £10; Senior £7; Children (3-16) £5; Infant (under-3) free **OPEN** Tours at 3.30 PM (Mon-Sun, Apr-Sep) and 6 PM (Mon-Sun during Apr-Sep, but Tue, Thu-Sun only during Oct-Mar) **WEB** goldentours.com/jack-the-ripper-walking-tour **TEL** 0207 630 2028 **TIME REQUIRED** 1½-2 hours

Easy to get to? ★★★ Good for kids? ☆☆☆
Value for money? ★★☆ Worth a visit? ★★☆

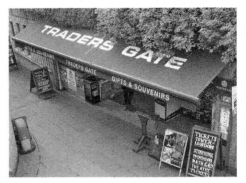

I'm actually a bit scared sitting here, waiting for the Jack the Ripper Tour to start. I could die tonight. Apparently this guy knows all there is to know about the case, so I'm wondering if he was in on it. Think about it... they never caught Jack the Ripper did they? And here is some bloke who supposedly knows all about the murders and the grisly ways they met their maker. It all sounds a bit suss to me.

When I came here the other day I saw his tour leave with about twenty people on it, and when it came back two hours later there was no one left (seriously!). I reckon he bumps them off one-by-one as you walk around, reliving his Victorian thrills under cover of his walking tour. But I have seen through his disguise -- I have him sussed. I will solve this 150-year-old mystery tonight, or die in the attempt!

The tour starts outside the Trader's Gate Souvenir Shop by Tower Hill station, but it's worth turning up an hour early to have a nose around the area. You can do a full lap around the Tower of London's curtain wall, and have a little stroll along the river for some good views of Tower Bridge and City Hall.

Our group is about fifteen people big tonight, made up of all ages and nationalities. Disappointingly, the tour guide turns out to be quite a young bloke and at first sight he doesn't seem to be very steeped in Ripper-lore. He's a bit of a 'geezer'. I've had plenty of tour guides who were friendly, and some who were funny, but never one who seems to be angry at authority like this bloke. I reckon it might be part of his act though... he is building up modern-day Whitechapel like it's present-day Baghdad. Every time a police siren streams past his eyebrows shoot halfway up his forehead, like another murder has just taken place. But these are the streets that we'll be walking in five minutes time, so I'm guessing he's trying to trying to set the scene and scare us. *Stay in a group, people -- keep close!* We don't want to get separated in case we get beaten up by the locals.

He begins with a little description of the area, and how it's been a magnet for immigrants and never-do-wells since the Middle Ages. Then he leads us up onto Tower Hill to see the spot where they executed all the traitors. Then he sets off towards St. Botolph's church and that is when he starts to get into gear. I realise now that he is actually pretty darn good (which will teach me not to judge a book by its cover). I was expecting the usual touristy fare, you see... an old guy with a big bushy beard dressed up in a Sherlock Holmes outfit, creeping down the streets on tippy-toes. But this guy's style is like we're talking down the pub. And he doesn't mince his words either. Our group has got a few 12-year old kids in it but he doesn't hold back. I hope they've had the birds and bees speech at school, because they'll be going home with stories of whores, brothels, lynchings and god knows what else -- every nightmare under the sun. If they didn't know what a prostitute was before, then they definitely do now. They won't need their mums and dads to explain it to them on the way home, that is for sure. He's describing each death in detail, right down to which bit of the body was thrown where (it's gruesome). If you can't stomach the thought of someone's stomach being draped across their shoulders, or their kidney being chopped up and posted to the police, then maybe this tour isn't for you.

He paints a good word picture on the steps of St. Botolph's church, about how the ladies got picked up by the punters. Pretty ladies, these: women with their teeth missing and boils as big as noses on their noses. That's when he introduces us to the murder victim Catherine Eddowes, and describes her typical day... showing us where she had her fumbles, and even the original police station where she spent a few hours on her fateful day. And he takes you to the brick wall in Mitre Square where she ended up a bloodied corpse with her entrails hanging out.

If I have a little criticism then it's this: he could do with a few more photos of the victims, because the only one he's had so far was of Mary Kelly (that famous final photo of her dying pose, laid out on the bed with her guts on show). And all he did for that one was pass around a little image on his mobile phone. I think your imagination needs all the help that it can get on a tour like this because the route is much changed from its Victorian heyday. A lot of the murder sites got bombed out in the war so all that's left are a few old houses on one side of the street. Mary Kelly's final spot is a multi-story car-park, for example. A lot of the other ones he didn't even bother taking us too because there's no point: the streets don't even exist anymore. But luckily there's just enough stuff still standing to give you an inkling of what it must have been like all those years ago. It's not the prettiest part of town, but there are some atmospheric little alleyways and squares.

You get to see a lot of nice-looking pubs as well, only to discover that they were once brothels. When he points up to the big windows on the first floor you realise what they were used for.

Along the way he tells you all about the suspects, and the evidence for and against their guilt. He dispels plenty of myths too, about the fake letters and long-cloaked costume that he was supposed to have worn. He never actually gets around to saying who did it though, because nobody knows. He just leaves a few names dangling in the air for you to think about on the way home.

Despite my silly first impression, it turned out to be a very worthwhile, wordy, and educational tour. No one jumps out in fancy dress, or anything like that. You learn about the case, and that's it. Then you go home and have a few nightmares. The only disappointing bit was a fat American woman who was yak yak yakking to her husband the whole way through, about what they were going to do for the rest of the week. I was hoping Jack the Ripper would leap out and make her his sixth victim.

If you enjoy being scared try the London Dungeon, Clink Prison Museum, and a Ghost Tour of Hampton Court Palace.

Jewel Tower

ADDRESS Jewel Tower, Abingdon Street, Westminster - map 8d **TRAINS** Westminster (zone 1) **BUSES** 11, 24, 148, 211 Price Adult £4.70; Senior (over-60) £4.20; Child (5-15) £2.80; Infant (under-5) free; Family (2 ad+3 ch) £12.20; Price includes a voluntary donation

OPEN 10 AM to 6 PM (Mon-Sun, Apr-Sep); 10 AM to 5 PM (Mon-Sun, Oct); Closed (Mon-Fri, Nov-Mar); 10 AM to 4 PM (Sat-Sun, Nov-Mar); Last entry 30 mins before closing **WEB** english-heritage.org.uk/visit/places/jewel-tower **TEL** 0870 333 1181 **TIME REQUIRED** 30 mins

Easy to get to? ★★★ Good for kids? ☆☆☆
Value for money? ★☆☆ Worth a visit? ☆☆☆

Oh dear... I think this might be the worst attraction in London. The last time I came to the Jewel Tower the first room was full of whiteboards detailing the history of parliament, with some big glass cabinets showcasing the Speaker's old robes, but they seem to have done away with all of that now. I remember it being badly out of date (talking about a current Government that had long since departed), so whilst it certainly could have done with a bit of a spruce up, they didn't have to bin the whole lot!

All they've got now is a wooden model of the original Palace of Westminster and a handful of boards about its history. If you're a London buff like me then it's quite interesting to see what the palace used to look like before it burnt down, but I don't think many tourists will be writing postcards home about it. (I don't mean to be a smart arse but they've actually made quite a sizeable error on it as well -- because their circa 1400 model of

Westminster Abbey includes the two huge towers at the western end, which weren't added until the 1720s.)

A handful of other boards include a few paragraphs about what the Jewel Tower was originally used for (Edward III's treasure house) and a side room stores a few boxes of silver plates and weights and measures. Then you head downstairs to the third and final room which is basically... empty. Just a bit more about weights and measures and some stuff about the important documents that were kept inside. You don't actually get to see any of the documents though -- just a few facsimiles of them.

I'm guessing that if you read every single piece of information in the building then it would take you no more fifteen minutes -- that is how little information there is. The only reason that I stayed longer was because I had to write this.

It's a shame, because this place could be so much better than it actually is. If you read my blog from a few years ago then you can see what I thought of it back then (I thought it was pretty lousy then too) -- but they have managed to perform a miracle and make it even worse! All of that history of Parliament is gone. The Speaker's clothes -- gone. Thirty minutes of my life -- gone.

If you've got a few quid and half-an-hour to spare, or it's pouring with rain outside and you don't want to get wet, then maybe you can pop inside and have a look. But everyone else should just take a photo of the front and move on.

If you're interested in early coinage then try the Bank of England Museum.

Kensington Gardens

ADDRESS Kensington Gardens - maps 6a, 6c
TRAINS North side: Bayswater, Lancaster Gate, Queensway (all zone 1) -- South side: High Street Kensington (zone 1) **BUSES** North side: 70, 94, 148, 390 -- South side: 9, 10, 17, 45, 49, 52, 63, 70, 452 **OPEN** 6 AM to dusk (Mon-Sun) **WEB** royalparks.org.uk/parks/kensington-gardens **TEL** 0300 061 2000 **TIME REQUIRED** 1½ hours

Easy to get to? ★★★ Good for kids? ★☆☆
Value for money? free Worth a visit? ★★☆

I always think of Hyde Park as stretching all the way from Park Lane to Kensington Palace, but it actually stops at the Serpentine. Anything west of that is called Kensington Gardens. But it's obviously the same place so I think it's a bit daft, but hey... I'm not in charge (I should be).

Apart from the lake, the Albert Memorial and Kensington Palace, it's actually quite a flat and featureless place. There must be ten thousand trees at least, but they never look like a wood. They've spread them out like single strands of hair on a bald head. They need to clump them up a bit and turn them into a forest. How difficult is to move a tree? How many people will it take to pull one up and carry it to the lake? If we try it one stick at a time then it won't take very long. I'll carry a branch, that young couple can carry a leaf. Those squirrels can carry the acorns -- we'll have it done in no time.

The lake is a magnet for pushchairs, ducks and dogs. If people have a pet then they'll walk it, and if they don't then they'll feed the ducks instead. Or they'll bring their boyfriends.

Halfway around the western edge you'll find a statue of Peter Pan. JM Barrie only lived over the road, and one night he had the bright idea of sneaking up a statue. He did it while the park was shut, so all the kids would think it magically appeared overnight. You'll find another spot for the kids in the northeastern corner: the Princess Diana Memorial Playground. Princess Di loved kids, so it full of swings and slides and sandpits. But not many people know that she was an even bigger fan of pirates -- hence the big pirate ship in the middle of it. I'd love to be able to show you a photo of it, but there's no way I'm standing there taking photographs of little kids playing in a children's playground, because I'll probably get arrested. Keep an eye out for the famous Elfin Oak as well -- it's covered in carved and coloured fairies, ladybirds and butterflies.

The rest of the lake is lined with benches of death. That's what I like to call the benches with memorials on them -- the benches of death. They're like a row of tombstones by the water. But they all seem to be devoted to dogs, because they all have inscriptions like "To Harvey, a great companion -- 1986 to 1999". That can't be for a child, can it? And it's too young to be an adult. So it must be for someone's mutt. Another ones says: "Topsy, Scarlett and Chloe", and that just has to be a dog, because you can't call a kid Topsy -- that would be cruel.

To the west of the lake is the Round Pond. This is one of the coldest places on earth. This pond is colder than the North Pole -- no joke. All of the wind in the world seems to funnel into this circle and scream across the top. I can see people holding onto their hats, and other ones holding onto their hair. Some are even holding onto their *heads*, lest they get ripped off the top of their necks. People are walking around like sailing ships, with their coats pressed back like a struggling sail in a storm. My eyes have actually started watering! I can't look into this wind anymore because my eyeballs will fall out. Everyone is crying from the cold, but up in the air it's bright blue sky and not a cloud in sight. The birds don't care, they are just flapping around from person to person looking for the handouts.

There are two highlights in the park. One of them is Kensington Palace (obviously), and the other one is the Albert Memorial opposite the Royal Albert Hall. This is easily the finest monument in the whole of London, and when you first clap eyes on it you'll think that he must have been our greatest-ever king. But he was just the Queen's other half, that's all. Just a bloke with a moustache. Even Queen Victoria didn't get a monument as good as this one. But sons don't build monuments for their mothers, like their mothers build ones for their husbands.

You'll find the palace along the western edge of the park. This is where William III and Mary used to live after the Glorious Revolution, but you probably need to know your British history to have heard of them. Queen Victoria used to live in it as well, while she was still a princess. (If you've never heard of her then you really should have paid more attention at school!) But these days most people associate it with Princess Diana, who carried on living here after Prince Charles dumped her for Camilla. You might remember the golden gates being festooned with flowers after her death. Nowadays it's home to Prince William and Kate (I refuse to call her Catherine -- that's not her name!). A couple of other minor Royals are allowed to live here as well, but nobody knows who they are.

You have to pay to see inside the palace itself, but you can have a nose around the gardens for free if you like, and there's a posh Orangery if you'd like something to eat.

Whilst you're here you can visit Kensington Palace, the Albert Memorial, and Princess Diana Memorial Fountain.

Kensington Palace

ADDRESS Kensington Palace, Kensington Gardens - map 6a **TRAINS** High Street Kensington, Queensway (both zone 1) **BUSES** 9, 10, 49, 52, 70, 94, 148, 390, 452 **PRICE** If bought online: Adult £15.40; Senior (over-60) £12.60; Child (under-16) free -- If bought at the door: Adult £16.50; Senior (over-60) £13.70; Child (under-16) free; Price includes a voluntary donation **OPEN** 10 AM to 6 PM (Mon-Sun, Mar-Oct); 10 AM to 5 PM (Mon-Sun, Nov-Feb); Last entry 1 hour before closing **WEB** hrp.org.uk/kensington-palace **TEL** 0203 166 6000 **TIME REQUIRED** 2 hours

Easy to get to? ★★★ Good for kids? ★☆☆
Value for money? ★★☆ Worth a visit? ★★☆

I made the soggy wet trek over to Kensington Palace today, trudging through the park in the muddy flooded fields. I walked a few muddy footprints all over the palace's shiny floors as well which I was a bit embarrassed about. It's a good job that Queen Victoria doesn't live there anymore or there would have been hell to pay.

The palace is broadly split into three different sections that cover their own king or queen. You can do them in any order you like, but I plumped for the one upstairs first. That's the one which follows the lives of Queen Victoria and Prince Albert -- the palace's most famous residents. I got the impression that the palace must have been emptied of furniture at some point, and is slowly recovering its stuff, because a lot of the rooms were quite sparsely decorated. There were still plenty of historical items to look at though, so that's not meant as a criticism, but there were nowhere near as many objects on show as somewhere like Buckingham Palace, for example. It doesn't seem very *lived in*, if you know what I mean. You get told that this room housed so-and-so, but where are their chairs? Where is their bed? It's just bits and pieces dotted around.

The objects upstairs include Queen Vic's jewellery and dresses, books and bible. They've got a big dolls house too, and a little toy box for their six billion kids, filled with choo-choo trains and tin drums with tassels. The dresses are quite enlightening because Queen Victoria seems to be a midget. You could almost wear her dresses as a skirt. Albert wasn't exactly Arnold Schwarzenegger either, judging by his military uniform. He was probably about the same size as one of Arnie's arms.

As you would expect, there are plenty of portraits hanging on the walls and some old black and white photos of the Queen in later life. I think she was quite a looker when she was young -- I think Albert got a bit lucky there. Luckily for him he dropped dead before she got old though, because the photos of her looking mean and moody in her seventies are the complete opposite (that was her 'fat Elvis' period). Boy oh boy was she a misery! She looks like she spent the last few decades of her life chewing a wasp. They've got a room full of her black fat mourning dresses as well -- she seems to have liked the colour black after Albert died. She was the Johnny Cash of the Victorian age. It's all black black black. Black dresses, black hats. Black thoughts. She was probably the world's first emo-Goth. I can understand her being upset for a little while, but thirty years is pushing it. For god's sake snap out of it woman! Pull yourself together. If I was there I would have just given her a slap round the chops and told her a few of my jokes. That would have cheered her up.

The second part of the palace is the King's State Apartments, which covers the Georgian period and a bit of William and Mary. The King's Gallery is the stand-out room -- a bit like the Waterloo Gallery at Apsley House, if you've ever been there -- or a poor man's version of the Picture Gallery at Buckingham Palace. The room is nice enough, with a few marble busts and deep velvet reds and woods, but the pictures aren't quite up to scratch. They've got the famous one of Charles I on horseback, striding through an arch, but the bloke on sentry duty explained that it was just a copy of the one at Buckingham Palace.

As you venture further into the apartments you come across some increasingly spectacular spaces, all decorated in the same deep reds and golds. And as you're walking around they've got some jaunty Georgian music playing in the background -- baroque tunes by Handel, which perfectly suits the mood. The Cupola Room was my favourite. The ceilings are groaning under the weight of giant chandeliers, whilst garish golden statues stare down from alcoves in the walls. Put it this way: it's not the kind of place you'd come for a quiet lie-down -- but it's all right if you want to impress the neighbours next-door.

Next up are the Queen's Apartments, overlooking the Sunken Garden out the front. They had a big exhibition of royal dresses from the Queen's own wardrobe today, plus a few bits from Princess Margaret and Princess Diana. It was quite well done I suppose but I'm a bloke, and dresses + bloke = boredom. It's like going clothes shopping with your missus: you're just willing it to be over so you can go and watch the telly. The dresses are all set up in dazzling display cases of brilliant glass, all shining white with spotlights on the ceiling. There are lots of copies of *Vogue* and *Harpers* on the wall as well, featuring front covers of the Queen and royal ladies, with little videos beamed upon the whitewashed walls of Diana dancing with John Travolta and meeting Michael Jackson. I don't think she dated very well... she looks very 80s with her bouffant bob and shoulder pads.

This is how I would sum up Princess Diana... she had a couple of nice hairdos, but she was a bit of a fruit loop. It's not often a pretty young bird gets ousted by a chain-smoking old granny, but that is basically what happened to poor Princess Di. So we can only imagine what she was must have been like behind closed doors; she must have driven Prince Charles nuts for him to boot out a beauty like that.

The best bit about the dresses exhibition was hearing two old biddies walking around moaning about the clothes. They were going "Oooh I wouldn't wear that," and "I wouldn't wear those jewels. What does she look like!"

The rest of the Queen's Apartments focus on William and Mary. Whereas all the Georgian areas of the house are brushed in garish gold, William's bits are all dark and moody browns, with autumnal colours and birdsong playing out the speakers. It seems like they've tried to turn it into a magical enchanted palace, with paper toys spinning in the stairwells and model birds flapping down the corridors. You can hear whispered conversations drifting out of a gramophone (the 'gossip of court'), and in one room they've gone totally Narnia-nuts. It's all done up like a creepy forest with twisting branches on a bed of dying autumn leaves. Prickly strings of holly wind their way around the fence posts, whilst wooden boxes sit precariously in the boughs, filled with paper-cut kings and queens, their faces peeping out of lamp-lit windows. It's all very special looking, but I'm not exactly sure what it's got to do with William and Mary -- it's more like an art piece. If you could walk around it at night then you'd probably think you were dreaming.

The other Royal homes worth visiting are Buckingham Palace, Windsor Castle, Hampton Court and Clarence House. You can also try Kew Palace at Kew Gardens.

Leadenhall Market

ADDRESS Leadenhall Market (entrances in Gracechurch St, Lime St, Leadenhall Place, Whittington Ave) - map 10b **TRAINS** Bank, Monument (both zone 1) **BUSES** 25, 35, 40, 47, 48, 149, 344 **OPEN** Shops: 10 AM to 6 PM (Mon-Fri), but you can walk through 24-hours a day **WEB** cityoflondon.gov.uk/things-to-do/leadenhall-market **TIME REQUIRED** 5 mins (but more if you plan to stop and eat)

Easy to get to? ★★★ Good for kids? ★☆☆
Value for money? free Worth a visit? ★★★

This is how I imagine Victorian England to be. This is the London of glitter-covered Christmas cards and 19th-century novels. It's all top hats and monocles and bookshops selling Dickens. Alas, it's not quite like that in real life... but it's not very far off. It's all warm reds and butter-coloured yellows, with star-covered ceilings and fancy iron frames.

The best time to see it is definitely when the sun has given up and gone home a few hours early; when you've been walking through the wet forever; when the clouds are sitting five feet off the floor, and everyone is barging past you to bundle on the bus. Trust me: that's the best time to have a wander through Leadenhall Market. When you're cold and tired and skirting around the edge of a bad mood, and all you want to do is see somewhere pretty.

It has a decent pub and a sandwich shop (the kind of sandwich shop that will sell you a sausage between two slices of bread), and there's an old shoeshine guy with a cupboard full of brushes and bottles of polish. But it always seems to be packed full of rich city workers because the financial district is just around the corner. When the lunchtime bell goes they roll out of their banks and their billion dollar business meetings to grab a quick cup of cappuccino coffee. Half of the floor will be packed full of leather shoes and office gossip. The other half will just be the tourists strolling through, staring up at the roof as the tin drum raindrops batter it with bullets.

Leicester Square

ADDRESS Leicester Square - map 8b
TRAINS Charing Cross, Leicester Square,

Piccadilly Circus (all zone 1) **BUSES** 14, 19, 24, 29, 38, 176 **TIME REQUIRED** 20 mins

Easy to get to? ★★★ Good for kids? ★★☆
Value for money? free Worth a visit? ★★★

Everybody who comes to London ends up here at some point -- they'll have a wander around the West End to see the bright lights of Piccadilly Circus and get sucked into Leicester Square along with a million billion other people. It's where you'll find all the big cinemas and nightclubs. It's where the nightlife is. The pubs have punters spilling out onto the streets, and shops sell cheapo theatre tickets to West End shows.

There must be a thousand people milling around me this afternoon, all trying to decide what to do with their evening. It's all noise, boys, the lost, wasted, wasters, tourists. Everyone seems to be sitting here and waiting for the sun to go down. I used to come here on a Saturday night when I was still the right side of thirty. Not to do anything in particular, but just to do... *something*. When you're twenty it's better to do something rather than nothing. You wander across from Waterloo, have too many drinks around Soho, and then nod off on the train home. Nothing's changed -- the pubs are still packed-out with young drunk drinkers and theatre goers in sober suits and shoes. These are some of the busiest pubs in London but you can't get served because they're all five people deep at the counter. By the time you've spilled and splashed your armfuls of pints back to the table there'll be a trail of lager on the carpet. That is assuming you can even get a table in the first place, of course (which you won't). You'll be lucky to even get a piece of floor to stand on -- that is how busy they are.

But during the daytime... well that's a different story. I quite like this place in the morning. It's the leafy green trees in the middle that make it, and the spouting fountains surrounding the Shakespeare statue. There's really no need for any extra water today (it's raining again) but they're still bubbling away regardless. We're just sitting here listening. Me and the pigeons. The homeless dudes are sitting here, too (one of them has just tried to ponce a cigarette off me) -- those beer can dudes who drink cider for breakfast. This is the life, isn't it? Forget the nightlife. Forget the bright lights. Just have a sit by the fountains and admire the buildings on the eastern edge -- plus the ones running down to Piccadilly Circus. You don't really notice them at night because of all the billions of bodies blocking them out, but there are some very fine buildings around Leicester Square.

Ten minutes later I'm still sitting here, mindlessly idling some time away. I am engrossed in the fountains. One guy has decided to tempt fate, and is currently standing with his legs akimbo right over the top of a docile fountain, laughing, while his mates are egging him on with their camera phones at the ready. This guy has obviously got no fear. Any minute now the fountain is going to spray up into the sky and send him into space. *Please, oh please*... nope. He has chickened out with just seconds to spare. What a shame... I would have quite liked to have seen him get drenched. Meanwhile the stony-faced Shakespeare just looks on with two pigeons sitting on his head, bird crap dribbling down his face in the rain. I wonder what couplet he would have come up with to describe that?

Do you want to join me for a coffee? I'm sitting in that little corner cafe opposite the Vue cinema. It's just a crappy little cafe, nothing special -- it's so plain it hasn't even got a proper name, just 'Espresso Bar' -- but I've always had a soft spot for this place. If you have a few days to waste then you can camp out in one of these seats and watch practically the entire population of London walk past the window.

Here comes the rain again -- but much harder this time. The tourists are suddenly pulling out their plastic macs and rushing to get them on over their folded arms and elbows, all whilst being shouted at by their panicking mum. *Quick, kids! Quicker! They're going to get wet... jesus christ. Get a move on, kids! Their dad has started joining in the shouting now. Too late. They're dead. They got wet.* It's only rain, mate. You're in London now, you'd best get used to it!

Whilst you're here you might like to visit Piccadilly Circus and Chinatown.

Leighton House Museum

ADDRESS Leighton House Museum, 12 Holland Park Road, Kensington **TRAINS** High Street Kensington (zone 1) Kensington Olympia (zone 2) **BUSES** 9, 10, 27, 28, 49, C1 **PRICE** Adult £10; Senior (over-60) £8; Child (12-17) £8; Child (under-12) free **OPEN** 10 AM to 5.30 PM (Mon, Wed-Sun); Closed (Tue) **WEB** rbkc.gov.uk/subsites/museums/leightonhousemuseum1.aspx **TEL** 0207 602 3316 **TIME REQUIRED** 45-60 mins

Easy to get to? ★★★ Good for kids? ☆☆☆
Value for money? ★★☆ Worth a visit? ★★☆

The Leighton House Museum is the architectural equivalent of opening up a brown paper bag and finding a diamond inside. This guy was an artist, and he lived inside a work of art.

Don't be put off by the photo of the front. This house will never win any awards for the outside. It's not until you get beyond the entrance hall that you'll understand what all the fuss is about. The kind of words that sprang to mind when I first entered the rooms were *Sultan's palace*, *Turkish bath* and *Arabian nights*. What do those three phrases conjure up for you?

Downstairs is decorated with those oily-looking lapis lazuli blue tiles that shimmer like a nighttime rainbow. It's all mustard yellows and Persian carpets. There are bronze nudes and peacock feathers, and marble columns carved from a muddy coloured storm. Everything is dim and dark and lined in gold. The only sound that you can hear is the tinkling drip from an indoor fountain.

I've got to admit that I'd never heard of Frederic Leighton before I visited his house, but it turns out that he was a very famous Victorian painter -- good enough to be ennobled and buried at St. Paul's. There aren't very many of his pieces inside, though, because they all got sold off after he passed away. It's quite a sad story actually, and highlights the pitiful way we treat old architecture. The interior was allowed to die a death before the Germans nearly finished it off by dropping a bomb on one end, and practically everything you see today was recreated from photos. But it's been so well done that you'd never guess.

Unfortunately the upstairs rooms pale in comparison. Apart from some fairly interesting artwork on the walls, the decorations don't come close to replicating what came before. I'm guessing that they ran out of money halfway through the rebuild, because its obvious that the decorators decided that less is more. Downstairs it's the total opposite: *more is more*. Downstairs is like looking at money. Upstairs is like looking at savings. But I'd happily pay the entrance fee just to see those few rooms at the start.

The downstairs is truly unique, and well worth a visit.

If you like this then try Sir John Soane's Museum and 18 Stafford Terrace.

Lincoln's Inn

ADDRESS Lincoln's Inn, Holborn - map 4e
TRAINS Chancery Lane, Holborn (both zone 1)
BUSES 8, 25, 242, 521 **PRICE** Walk around the grounds: Free -- Guided tour: £3 **OPEN** Walk around the grounds: 7 AM to 7 PM (Mon-Fri) -- Guided tour: 2 PM to 3 PM (1st and 3rd Fri of each month, except Aug); Note: No tours between May 2016 and Jan 2018 **WEB** lincolnsinn.org.uk/index.php/tours-and-visits
TEL 0207 405 1393 **TIME REQUIRED** Walk around: 20 mins -- Guided tour: 1-1½ hours

Easy to get to? ★★★ Good for kids? ☆☆☆
Value for money? ★★★ Worth a visit? ★★☆

Do you know what the most annoying thing in the world is? (Maybe not *the* most annoying, but it's definitely up there in the top ten.) It's when you visit a great looking building only to find a load of scaffolding framing up the front. That's what happened to me today at Lincoln's Inn. Apparently they're having a big round of building works over the next few years and it's going to look like a building site. Fortunately for me the best building was still unencumbered by metal make-up, but there's a picture of the end gable that I couldn't include. They'd even wrapped the trees up!

Lots of Londoners don't even know that that Lincoln's Inn exists -- and its only two minutes from Fleet Street. You'll find it round the back of the Royal Courts of Justice. It's one of the four Inns of Court. The other three Inns can be found nearby -- Gray's Inn, Middle and Inner Temple (near Temple Church). Back in Tudor times these Inns of Court were regarded as the country's third university after Oxford and Cambridge, and every single barrister in the country has to belong to one of them -- even today. If you walk around the grounds then you'll find it full of suits and blokes with briefcases. It's like a little campus, I suppose, consisting of a chapel, some chambers (digs) and a hall.

If you just want to have a stroll around the grounds and have a sit down in the sun, then that's free, but if you want to look inside the buildings themselves then you'll have to join a guided tour. Unfortunately they only lay on a couple every month (unless you want to arrange a private one for a pot full of money), so it's not always an easy thing to visit, but if you're a fan of old architecture then I definitely recommend finding the time.

My tour started in the undercroft of the chapel. I always arrive at places far too early, so I was milling around for fifteen minutes making small talk with the others (I'm useless at small talk). To make matters worse, they all turned out to be American lawyers. Then a nice lady came along and introduced herself to us, and made us recite our names and CV that was a bit embarrassing, because mine is basically blank. The Americans' CVs were full of Ivy League degrees and words like 'Harvard' and 'Yale'. Mine was just a few years putting out the peas at Sainsburys. Then she went around the circle again, asking us what interest we had in the law. (*What was this, a police interrogation?*) I have no interest in the law whatsoever (I've watched a few episodes of *The Bill* on the telly) -- I was strictly there for the architecture -- but I didn't want to appear rude so naturally I just lied through my teeth and told everyone that I absolutely loved the law. Then I remembered that I was with a bunch of lawyers, so they probably could have told straight away that I was lying -- ah well.

Then she took us into the old Tudor Hall and launched into a long monologue about how solicitors, barristers and QCs in England are trained. The Old Hall reminded me a little bit of the Great Hall at Hampton Court, but on a much smaller scale. It had a wooden roof, long wooden tables, candle chandeliers, and huge oil paintings of high court judges and Lord Chancellors hanging at angles on the walls. It even had a huge Hogarth on the back wall.

Next up was the chapel itself, which contained some of the finest stained glass I have ever seen -- and that is not hyperbole. I've been to plenty of religious buildings and the strained glass in here trumped the lot. It was almost like an oil painting on glass, and the paint and the saints were incredibly intense and colourful.

Each room gets better and better as you progress along the tour. The New Hall dates back to the 1840s and reminds me of the interior of the Guildhall -- it's all deep reds and chestnut-coloured browns, full of gold plates and oil paints. They had it all dressed up for a posh dinner when I went -- the kind of dinner where everybody gets three knives, four forks and five clear-cut glasses each.

It has a huge fresco on the back wall and heraldic shields decorating the walls, including plenty of ex-prime ministers who all seemed to be lawyers in a previous life. Everyone from Thatcher and Asquith, to Chamberlain, Disraeli and Blair passed through here at one time or another.

If you like Lincoln's Inn then check out Charterhouse, and the Middle and Inner Temple by Temple Church.

Little Venice

ADDRESS Centred around Maida Avenue and Warwick Avenue, Paddington - map 1c
TRAINS Warwick Avenue (zone 2) **BUSES** 6, 18, 46, 187, 414 **TIME REQUIRED** 30-60 mins
Easy to get to? ★★★ Good for kids? ★☆☆
Value for money? free Worth a visit? ★★☆

Little Venice is a pretty place with canals and houseboats. It's up past Paddington, about two minutes from the Edgware Flyover.

When you're coming out of Paddington station and making your way under the thundering flyover the first thought that enters your head will not be the Italian city of Venice -- you can trust me on this. Paddington is 95% concrete and 5% bin bags. Happily by the time you reach Warwick Avenue it starts to slow down and pretty up a bit. That's where Little Venice really starts -- at the bridge by Warwick Avenue.

I've never been to the real Venice but I'm guessing that it looks a little bit better than this. That's not to say that it isn't nice -- because it is. But in a leafy green, Sunday-stroll kind of way. The prettiest stretch is definitely up the far end of Blomfield Road and Maida Avenue (which run either side of the same canal). This is the picture postcard place that everyone comes to see. The boats must be semi-permanent because they're all rigged up with electricity and have patio tables and chairs on the towpath. You probably won't believe it's as twee as this, but these are all things I'm seeing this morning: chopped logs and fairy lights wrapped around the railings; empty bird feeders dangling from the spindly winter trees; rusty coloured water-cans and ornamental benches. I've just had a quick little look inside a porthole and seen a collection of china teapots and pottery frogs -- that is a perfect example of what this place is all about. It's the kind of place where old grandmas and grandpas might leave out a saucer of milk for the robins. I can see one guy sitting on an upturned plant pot, threading his shoelaces in his shoes. It's that kind of place -- nice and relaxed. Every day is Sunday. Everybody has breakfast at eleven in the morning and talks to their neighbours. That is Maida Avenue.

But then you cross over the bridge and everything turns into concrete (I'm talking about the junction between Warwick Avenue and Westbourne Terrace, where the two canals meet.) This place has a few ugly ducklings in the water -- the kind of ducks that never turn into swans -- and some stooping, drooping trees that trail their wooden fingers in the water, but it's mainly a place to catch a canal bus up to Camden. The most popular one is Jason's Canal Trip (check out my separate review -- it's well worth a try), but there's also a cheapo waterbus on the opposite side. Or you can grab a cup of tea from the little houseboat cafe.

Don't bother going any further into Delamere Terrace. The ornate blue bridge might look tempting, but it's actually an iron curtain hiding a waterway of doom. The overgrown towpaths don't have fallen twigs and flower petals over there -- they have old Coke cans and cigarette ends. They have weeds instead of flowers. A punctured football instead of a swan. During the summer months the water is bright green from all the algae floating on top. The boat owners down Maida Avenue have arranged a parade of country knick knacks on top of their roofs, like candle lanterns and a bag of wood chippings, whereas these ones use them as a dumping ground for their empty Calor Gas bottles, giant blue tarpaulins, and torn plastic sheets. Maybe I'm being a bit harsh, but you'll definitely notice a difference. These houseboats are more like sheds that have been dumped in the water. There's no way that these things can float on the open sea -- they're just sucked into the mud on the bottom.

Maida Avenue is still very nice, though -- and well worth a visit.

Whilst you're here you might enjoy a boat ride to Camden with Jason's Canal Trip.

London Aquarium

Landmarks & Attractions | 135

ADDRESS London Aquarium, County Hall, Westminster Bridge Road - map 8d **TRAINS** Waterloo, Westminster (both zone 1) **BUSES** 12, 53, 59, 76, 77, 148, 159, 211, 341, 381, RV1 **PRICE** If bought online: Adult £19.98; Child (3-15) £14.41; Infant (under-3) free; Family (2 ad+2 ch, or 1 ad+3 ch) £62.15 -- If bought at the door: Adult £23.50; Child (3-15) £16.95; Infant (under-3) free; Family (2 ad+2 ch, or 1 ad+3ch) £70.64 **OPEN** During school term: 10 AM to 7 PM (Mon-Sun); During school holidays: 9 AM to 8 PM (Mon-Sun); Last entry 1 hour before closing **WEB** visitsealife.com/london **TEL** 0871 663 1678 **TIME REQUIRED** 1½-2 hours

Easy to get to? ★★★ Good for kids? ★★★
Value for money? ★★☆ Worth a visit? ★★★

There are quite a few aquariums in London, but the Sea Life Centre at County Hall is by far the biggest and the best. (The other ones are inside London Zoo, Chessington World of Adventures, plus a tiny little one at Kew Gardens.)

Your visit will begin with a walk across the top of their shark tank, on foot-thick glass. I have to be honest and admit that I don't like this bit, and I am always very careful to check it for cracks beforehand (because you can never be too careful). I noticed that all the parents were making their kids run across as well. The staff guy assured us that it was perfectly safe, but these are proper sharks we are talking about here... not toothless tiddlers who are just going to swim up and give you a kiss. If you fall inside that tank then you can basically say goodbye to your arms and legs. I actually started screaming and they had to sedate me, and this was only two minutes from the front door -- not a good start!

The first big tank that you come across is an open-top pool full of flat fish. I'm pretty sure that you were allowed to stick your hand in and touch them the last time I came, because I remember a big brute of a guy jumping like a jessie when one of them brushed up against his skin. But I'm guessing that the fish must have complained to their HR department, because you can't do that anymore.

After that comes the first multi-story tank and it is absolutely colossal, filled with mountainous rocks and towering columns of stone. They've put a load of bones inside too (a full-size skeleton of a whale), and they've got some big fish that look like they lived in dinosaur times: big chunky fellas with heads the size of a concrete block. There's a glass tunnel underneath that takes you straight through the centre, and you can stand there for five minutes as all the flatfish float six inches above your head -- it's actually quite magical.

The next tank is even better. It's probably about three storeys tall and has a lot of Easter Island heads inside. This is where those sharks live (the same ones that you saw at the start).

This is actually one of things that I like most about the arrangement of the place: you keep coming across the same tanks as you wind your way up through the building. After that scary shark walk at the start you ride a lift down to the basement, and then you walk your way back up through the floors viewing the same tanks at different levels.

I could stand in front of these tanks all day. It's very relaxing watching fish swim round and round. There doesn't seem to be very many rules of the road, I've noticed. Quite often a big swarm of tiddlers will be racing around in formation, and then a big shark will come smack through the middle of them, going the opposite way, scattering them all around the rocks. It's as if he's driving the wrong way down a one-way street; but I suppose when you're a shark you can do what the hell you like. Some of the guys have got wise and just hang halfway up the water like a life buoy, trying to stay out of trouble.

There are plenty of coral tanks and tropical tanks too. Some of the fish inside those are so brightly coloured that they must have been down the tattoo shop before it opened, to get their skin dyed. It's all purples and pinks and sunshine orange. Some of them look like they have been charged up with electricity, with lightning blue lines blazing down their side.

Another thing that I really like about the London Aquarium is that the zones have been very decoratively themed. One minute you'll be walking through wooden walls of logs and stone, and then a cave-like rock place, and then a lushly-coloured Aztec jungle with bright green vegetation, Inca carvings, Buddhist statues, hanging vines and waterfalls. It's almost like stepping onto the set of *Indiana Jones* with the jungle cheeps and thunderstorms piped in through the speakers. They've got a few crocodiles and reptiles in there too, which makes a change from looking at the fish.

The final section worth seeing is the arctic zone. The last time I came here they had the corridors chilled down to minus-five degrees, but I guess someone must have died of hypothermia because they've dialled the heating back up again now. Right at the end of the corridor is where you'll find Penguin Beach, which is basically just a little pool of water with about five penguins in it, with some fake snow for them to stand on. I felt a bit sorry for them to be honest, because they were just standing there staring at the back wall: a painted scene of distant clouds and icebergs. He looked a bit like a criminal staring out of his prison bars at a thin sliver of sunshine in the sky, dreaming that he was five feet from the Bahamas. I suppose he was imagining himself diving over those icebergs and into the friged, frozen sea. It reminded me of that final scene in *The Truman Show* (that Jim Carrey movie, have you seen it?), when he finally reaches the edge of the world and just stands there banging on the exit, wailing to be let out. What a lousy life they lead.

London Zoo has an aquarium. Chessington World of Adventures has a smaller one, and Kew Gardens has a tiny one.

London Canal Museum

ADDRESS 12-13 New Wharf Road, King's Cross **TRAINS** King's Cross (zone 1) **BUSES** 10, 17, 59, 91, 259, 390 **PRICE** Adult £4; Senior (over-60) £3; Child (5-15) £2; Infant (under-5) free; Family (2 ad+up to 3 ch, or 1 ad+up to 4 ch) £10 **OPEN** 10 AM to 4.30 PM (Tue-Sun); Last entry 30 mins before closing **WEB** canalmuseum.org.uk **TEL** 0207 713 0836 **TIME REQUIRED** 30-60 mins

Easy to get to? ★★★ Good for kids? ☆☆☆
Value for money? ★★☆ Worth a visit? ☆☆☆

Did you know that London used to buy its ice from Norway? That sounds a bit daft doesn't it, but apparently we did. (I thought that was what Scotland was for?) We used to sail it into the docks and then ship it down the Regent's Canal in big barges so the rich people could eat their ice cream in the summer.

And here is something else that is interesting: Did you know that Leonardo Da Vinci invented the lock gates that they use in Camden Lock? (And that is true!)

They are just two of the many amazing facts that you can learn at the London Canal Museum.

It's only a little place with two big rooms, but it's all right if you've got forty minutes to waste. I don't mind these little museums... I call them 'homemade' museums, built by interested locals rather than professionals (you can tell by the homemade state of the exhibits). As long as you don't go in there expecting too much then you can usually find a couple of things worth looking at.

The museum is all about the birth of the canals and how the boatmen plied their trade. You learn a bit about the barges and how they worked them up and down the river, and there are some interesting bits and bobs about the docks as well, with some old photos of London before the war.

Upstairs they go into a lot more detail about the design of the boats and all the different cargos they carried, and there are plenty of watercolour paintings and old black and white photos from the early days of Regent's Canal.

I don't mind looking at all this stuff myself, because I quite like seeing old photos of London, but I'm not sure that it will interest a tourist. (Actually, let me re- phrase that: it definitely *won't* interest a tourist.)

The big surprise is out the back, where they let you open a door onto a genuine dock where a couple of barges are moored up. It's not the prettiest dock in the world (it might even be the ugliest!), and you can't go inside any of the barges (because they are real barges -- and belong to other people), but I must admit that I was surprised to find an actual dock at the museum.

It's definitely not the kind of museum that you'd want to visit whilst on holiday, or with your kids, but if you're a local with a particular interest in the waterway then it might be worth doing on a Sunday afternoon. I'd much rather visit the Museum of London in Docklands though, which is a hundred times better -- and free.

If you enjoy this place then try the Museum of London Docklands as well.

London Dungeon

ADDRESS London Dungeon, County Hall, Westminster Bridge Road - map 8d **TRAINS** Waterloo, Westminster (both zone 1) **BUSES** 12, 53, 59, 76, 148, 159, 211, 341, 381, RV1

PRICE If bought online: Adult from £18.95; Child (4-15) from £16.50; Infant (under-4) free -- If bought at the door: Adult £25.95; Child (4-15) £20.95; Infant (under-4) free **OPEN** During school term: 10 AM to 5 PM (Mon-Wed, Fri); 11 AM to 5 PM (Thu); 10 AM to 6 PM (Sat-Sun) -- During school holidays: 11 AM to 8 PM (Thu); 9.30 AM to 7 PM (Fri-Wed); Last entry same as the closing time **WEB** thedungeons.com/london **TEL** 0871 423 2240 **TIME REQUIRED** 1½ hours, plus 15-45 mins for the queue

Easy to get to? ★★★ Good for kids? ★★★
Value for money? ★☆☆ Worth a visit? ★★☆

I hate the London Dungeon.

I actually hate it... in the same way that cats hate dogs. I know that's a very strong word to use about something that is supposed to be fun, but there you go -- that is the truth. The scariest thing about the Dungeons, for me, is the thought of having to visit it. I went there a couple of years ago and the best bit was walking out of the exit; so when they announced they were going to move it from Tooley Street and rebuild it at the County Hall, I knew that meant I was going to have to visit it again... *aaargh! My worst nightmare!*

As you're queuing up for the show to begin you can hear a soundtrack of moans and groans and blood curdling screams coming from deep inside the building. They are not actors doing that -- that is the actual sound of tourists as they discover how much it costs to take a family inside. That is probably the scariest thing about the whole place for an adult: the price. You can see dads walking around with pained expressions on their faces, as if they have just undergone some horrific form of torture. The mums don't care -- the dads are paying. The kids don't care either. The first bit of torture for the dads is stumping up ninety-five quid for a family of four.

When I was taken to the Dungeons as a child (many moons ago) I remember it being more like a museum, where you could walk around at your own pace looking at all of the gruesome exhibits; but it's not like that anymore. It's more like a guided tour, in which you get led from scene to scene in a big group of about twenty people. I've visited it a couple of times now, and to be fair to them, the show isn't as bad as I remember it from two years ago: the Tooley Street Dungeon was definitely worse. The County Hall one starts off in a dark warren of smelly cells, where you can hear all the prisoners clanking and banging their chains behind the doors. It's all fiery red lanterns and dirty cobbled streets. It does set the mood quite nicely I suppose -- I'll give them that. Then you get taken through the rooms by actors in gruesome suits and costumes. A lot of it depends on how good the actors are, and they were pretty good today -- I will give them that as well. A couple of them really got into character and had the whole room smiling and laughing at their gags.

Let me just warn you about something, in case you're a bit of a scaredy cat: it is extremely dark inside (even darker than dark) and some of the noises are incredibly loud. You will have invisible bangs and cracks and screams and squeals going off two feet from your face, and I reckon they've pumped in some smells too. There is no let up to the darkness for ninety-minutes -- no bright scenes at all -- it's pretty relentless.

I was thankful today that my group had a lot of kids in it, because they always seem to get picked on as the victims. Practically every scene involves the actor singling out a stranger (or two) to get shouted at, stabbed at, strung up, locked in a cage... you get the idea. It is a very interactive show, and the odds of you having to say something along the way are quite high. And because we were a British group, we all just stood there hugging the walls hoping not to be picked, because it's embarrassing having to scream whilst they're pretending to spoon out your brains. I'm not exactly the life and soul of a party, so this wasn't much fun for me (that's why I hate the place). But of course everybody is different: and I am sure that some people will absolutely love being the centre of attention.

Let's see if I can remember all of the scenes...

It starts off with a scary lift down to the docks, which shakes about a bit and lurches left and right. Then you have a nice little boat ride through Traitor's Gate, where you meet Henry VIII and Anne Boleyn. This bit will blow your eardrums out and spray you with water, but it's quite a fun start if you don't mind being deaf and drenched. Then you meet one of Guy Fawkes' co-conspirators hiding in the tunnels underneath Parliament. I thought that this guy deserved an Oscar for his acting, because he was brilliant. Someone will get picked on at this point, and ordered to carry a warning letter into the next scene. That's where you'll meet Guy Fawkes himself (well... just his head) and witness Parliament being blown up. Then you have to brave the plague, and watch somebody getting sliced up by the doctor. Then you'll be walking through the foggy streets of Whitechapel where Jack the Ripper cuts up his victims. There's a good little scene in a pub here, where you'll meet Jack the Lad himself. Then it's into Mrs Noggin's pie shop and Sweeney Todd's barber shop.

After that comes my least favourite scene of all: the Kangaroo Court. You are either going to like this scene or loathe it, because what they do is stick a few people in the dock and laugh at them. Every time I've seen it (which is a couple of times now) I've ended up feeling very sorry for the poor tourist who can't speak decent English, can't understand why she's being laughed at, and clearly had no wish to be singled out.

After that you enter Newgate Prison and the final ride, where you get strapped into a seat and drop ten metres to your death -- and the exit... hooray!

So how does it compare to the old London Dungeon in Tooley Street? Well... I still hated it, but I'll put that down to me being a misery. It was definitely better than the old one. The scenes, sounds and decorations are a lot better, and there were parts of the show that actually made my heart pump. The rides are still basically the same with a few little tweaks (they've got rid of that awful 3D laser-zapping one though, which is a definite improvement). But at the end of the day it's still just a long walk from scene to scene, standing at the back of the crowd and trying to avoid getting hauled onto the stage.

On their website they recommend that your kids are over the age of eight, and I think that's probably about right. Some of the scenes are definitely scary enough to make a little kid cry.

Why not try the Clink Prison Museum and Chamber of Horrors at Madame Tussauds?

London Eye

ADDRESS London Eye, outside County Hall, Westminster Bridge Road - map 8d **TRAINS** Waterloo, Westminster (both zone 1) **BUSES** 12, 53, 59, 76, 77, 148, 159, 211, 341, 381, RV1 **PRICE** If bought online: Adult from £19.35; Senior from £16.65; Child (4-15) from £13.95; Infant (under-4) free; Family (2 ad+2 ch) from £66.60 -- If bought at the door: Adult £23; Senior £20; Child (4-15) £17; Infant (under-4) free; Family (2 ad+2 ch) £80 **OPEN** Closed (middle two weeks of Jan); 10 AM to 8.30 PM (last week of Jan-Mar); 10 AM to 9.30 PM (first half of Apr); 10 AM to 9 PM (second half of Apr); 10 AM to 9 PM (Sun-Thu, May-Jun); 10 AM to 9.30 PM (Fri-Sat, May-Jun); 10 AM to 9.30 PM (Sat-Thu, Jul-Aug); 10 AM to 11.30 PM (Fri, Jul-Aug); 10 AM to 8.30 PM (Sep-first week of Jan) **WEB** londoneye.com **TEL** 0871 781 3000 **TIME REQUIRED** 30 mins for the ride, plus another 30-60 mins for the queue

Easy to get to? ★★★ Good for kids? ★★★
Value for money? ★★☆ Worth a visit? ★★★

Normally I don't like heights but the London Eye is a bit of fun, isn't it? As long as you don't think about it too much then you'll be fine. I made that mistake today, as I was waiting to get on. I can't for the life of me work out how it's standing up. What exactly is holding the wheel on, apart from those flimsy little spokes? I'm being serious: the next time you're standing on the Southbank see if you can work out what is holding the wheel up, and why the whole thing doesn't just topple face-first into the river. (It's probably best to do that *after* you've been on it, though, so you don't freak yourself out.)

It doesn't seem all that high when you're sitting underneath it in the queue. The wheel is turning at a nice sedentary rate above your head, and no one is banging on the windows screaming to get out. So it seems safe. But then it starts getting nervy when they do the bomb search in the queue. They have a little metal detector looking for knives too. Oh *my god* you are thinking... not only might the flimsy thing collapse into the river and drown us, but we might get blown up and stabbed too!

Normally the queue snakes all the way to Timbuktu and back, so I waited until the end of September when all the kids were back at school and the tourists had gone home, so I only had about ten people in my pod today. There's not a lot inside the pod itself; there are no maps or telescopes or anything like that. No parachutes either. All they've got is a little wooden bench in the middle for the jelly-legged people to sit on.

You can definitely feel it moving, that is for sure. There's a very slight wobble as it slides along the track, and every now and they'll be a bigger wobble. Don't ask me why it wobbles, because I don't know. It's like turbulence, I suppose. Or maybe one of the nuts has fallen off. Or one of the main chains has broken -- I don't know. But you soon settle down and after a while you don't even notice it. Then you can start snapping your camera at all of the views.

The first few minutes are a bit of a snooze-fest because you are still close to the ground and the best stuff is hidden behind the metal wheel structure. All you've got to look at is Charing Cross station and Waterloo Bridge. Once you've risen up above the rooftops you get an interesting perspective on Horse Guards Parade, and Buckingham Palace can be seen nestling beyond the trees of St. James's Park. See if you can spot the top of Nelson's Column too, for some bonus points.

The best photo that you can get is undoubtedly of Big Ben and Parliament. It's probably the finest view of either from anywhere in London -- and I genuinely mean that. The City (the Square Mile) is a bit too far away for any decent shots. St.

Paul's is just a tiny little dome above the rooftops. I couldn't see the Gherkin anywhere, but it might have been hiding behind another skyscraper. I couldn't see Tower Bridge or the Tower of London either. The farthest thing that I could recognise was the curved arch of Wembley Stadium.

I must admit that I was expecting the view to be better from the top. In my mind's eye I had visions of being able to see all the way to the Thames Barrier, but you can't even see The O2. I wanted to see France. I wanted to see the Statue of Liberty. I wanted to look back through time to the day I was born. Considering that you can see the all the way to the moon just by looking up, I thought we'd be able to see a little bit further than the Circle Line.

Whatever you do... don't go when it's raining. Take that tip from me. Because you're basically standing inside a giant goldfish bowl, and when it rains the water runs around the curved glass and messes up all your photos. And don't go when the sun is low in the sky either (like early evening, before it gets dark) because you'll get a bright haze in your lens which will mess up your shots. I reckon the best time to ride it is around lunchtime or early afternoon, when the sun is directly overhead.

Once you've finished on the wheel then you can have a look inside their 4D cinema. You can find it inside the ticket hall (entry is included with your ticket). It's not the greatest movie in the world but it's worth a try if you've got nothing better to do.

But what is a 4D cinema, I hear you ask? That sounds a bit hi-tech. According to Einstein's *Theory of General Relativity* the 4th-dimension is a merging of space and time to create *space-time*. In order to see the full expanse of space-time we would need to travel outside of our present, and into what we humans call our past or the future (but these are actually both the same thing, and encompass a single solitary point in time and space). So it comes as something of a surprise when they hand you a pair of cheapo plastic specs at the entrance. Apparently that is all you need to enter the 4th-dimension.

It's basically just a 3D fly-through of the city skyline, past the London Eye and Houses of Parliament, and across the top of Tower Bridge. Some noisy kids then blow bubbles at the screen and fire pop guns in your face. And they blow a bit of cold air through the vents when a snow scene comes up. That's it. It might be worth ten minutes if you've got some kids.

If you like good views of the skyline then try the cable car, Sky Garden, Shard, and the topmost dome of St. Paul's Cathedral.

London Film Museum

ADDRESS London Film Museum, 45 Wellington Street, Covent Garden - map 8b
TRAINS Charing Cross, Covent Garden, Leicester Square (all zone 1) **BUSES** 1, 4, 6, 7, 8, 9, 10, 11, 13, 15, 19, 23, 24, 25, 26, 29, 38, 55, 59, 69, 73, 77A, 91, 98, 134, 139, 168, 171, 172, 176, 188, 242, 243, RV1 **PRICE** Adult £14.50; Senior (over-65) £9.50; Child (5-15) £9.50; Infant (under-5) free; Family £38
OPEN 10 AM to 9 PM (Thu, Aug to mid-Sep);

10 AM to 7 PM (Fri-Wed, Aug to mid-Sep); 10 AM to 6 PM (Sun-Mon, mid-Sep to Jul); 10 AM to 7 PM (Sat, mid-Sep to Jul); Last entry 1 hour before closing **WEB** londonfilmmuseum.com **TEL** 0207 836 4913 **TIME REQUIRED** 1 hour
Easy to get to? ★★★ Good for kids? ★★☆
Value for money? ★★☆ Worth a visit? ★★☆

What is your favourite film? Hmm... I think mine is... er... I think I will plump for *Star Wars*. *Star Wars* is the only film in history where everybody knows at least five characters; even if you hate *Star Wars* you will still know a few of these: Darth Vader, Luke Skywalker, Hans Solo, Chewbacca, Yoda, R2D2, Princess Leia and Jabba the Hut. I like it so much in fact, that I have actually modelled myself on some of the characters: I'm short (like Yoda), hairy (like Chewbacca), fat (like Jabba), ugly (like Princess Leia), and I wear a plastic black cape and airtight head helmet whenever I step outside (like Darth Vader).

You won't see anything about *Star Wars* when you go to the London Film Museum though, because they've dedicated the entire building to *James Bond*. The special exhibition has been running since March 2014 and shows no sign of closing down -- it's even possible that it will stick around forever. (On their website it says that it will remain open "until further notice", which isn't very helpful.)

The museum is basically just a big collection of bikes and cars and vehicles from the James Bond movies, with the relevant movie clips projected onto the wall beside them. That is it. So you've got Roger Moore's Rolls Royce from *A View To A Kill*, for example, and Sean Connery's flash black number from *Goldfinger*. I think the Pierce Brosnan-era ones are the best because they're a bit more hi-tech and you can see all of the little panels that fold out for the rockets and guns. Do you remember that remote controlled car he drove from the back seat in *The World Is Not Enough?* They've got that one in here. (Still in one piece though... didn't he send it crashing off the top of a car park?). They've got that little black motor boat he flew out of the side of the MI6 building as well, which is pretty cool.

There was no sign of that daft invisible car from *Die Another Day* though (but maybe I just couldn't see it). They should have put a plaque up next to an empty wall, just for a laugh.

There are lots and lots of vehicles, from *Dr No* all the way up to the Daniel Craig. And they aren't replicas either -- these are the real deal that were used during filming, so some of them are fifty years old. (It made me feel quite old myself -- can you believe that *The Living Daylights* came out thirty years ago? I still remember that theme tune by A-Ha.)

It was nice to see that they hadn't forgotten Timothy Dalton (everyone else has). They've got that Aston Martin that slides across the ice, and even that cello case he sat on to slide down the mountain.

There are plenty of motorbikes and little copter planes too, and even that rickety little taxi from *Octopussy*. Do you remember Roger Moore's Citroen 2CV from *For Your Eyes Only*? I've just been watching some clips of him in action and he's not exactly Jason Bourne is he? If he had a fist fight with Daniel Craig then he'd last about two-seconds. I like his submarine car from *The Spy Who Loved Me* though -- they've got that on show too.

One of the best things about the exhibition is being able to watch all of the old movie clips and hear all of the chases and fights and explosions pumping out of the speakers. I've had the *James Bond* theme tune rattling around my head ever since, because they played it non-stop the whole way round.

If you like James Bond then you will obviously love it, but if you are expecting a proper 'film museum' then be aware that there is nothing else here apart from the 007 stuff. It's not like Planet Hollywood where you can see a few famous props and costumes hanging up from other movies. You are not going to see John Travolta's first toupee or anything like that. They haven't got Dorothy's red shoes or Marilyn's white skirt. It's literally just the James Bond exhibition, and that's it.

The museum space itself is not very big. There is a tiny little bit upstairs with a few bits and bobs, and then it's just the basement room below, which takes about thirty minutes to walk around if you look at all of the exhibits. I tend to take my time with these things, but even I was finished inside forty-five minutes. I padded out another fifteen minutes with a sit-down in the coffee shop.

You can learn more about film-making at the Warner Bros. Studios (aka. Harry Potter Tour).

London Zoo

ADDRESS London Zoo, Regent's Park - map 2b **TRAINS** Baker Street (zone 1) and a 30 min walk or 274 bus; Camden Town (zone 2) and a 15 min walk; Regent's Park (zone 1) and a 20 min walk **BUSES** 274, C2 **PRICE** If bought online: Adult £26.70; Senior £24; Child (3-15) £19.40; Infant (under-3) free; Family (2 ad+2 ch, or 1 ad+3 ch) £82.65; Price includes a voluntary donation -- If bought at the door: Adult £28.10; Senior £25.29; Child (3-15) £20.39; Infant (under-3) free; Family (n/a - online only); Price includes a voluntary donation **OPEN** 10 AM to 6 PM (Mon-Sun, Apr-Aug), 10 AM to 5.30 PM (Mon-Sun, Sep-Oct), 10 AM to 4 PM (Mon-Sun, Nov-Mar); Last entry 1 hour before closing **WEB** zsl.org/zsl-london-zoo **TEL** 0344 225 1826 **TIME REQUIRED** 3-4 hours

Easy to get to? ★★☆ Good for kids? ★★★
Value for money? ★★☆ Worth a visit? ★★★

I'm watching the giraffes getting fed at the moment. The zookeeper is walking around sweeping up all the leaves that he's dropping off the branches. He's a funny looking fella (the giraffe I mean, not the zookeeper). He's got two bony tufts coming out the top of his head and a neck that's longer than his legs. I think God must have been having an off-day when he came up with that. Or maybe he got his sheets of paper mixed up in the wind and couldn't be bothered to sort them out. And what's going on with his camouflaged skin? What is the point of trying to camouflage yourself when your neck is ten-feet long? Nobody is going to miss that sticking out the treetops.

I'm having a good look around the whole zoo today and taking my time, and I've discovered a few new places that I've never seen before, like the fruit bat room. It's a spooky room all dark and quiet inside... except for the sound of their tiny claws scrapping along the wire fence. You can hear them cheeping in the dark, hanging by their toes with their beady white eyes staring out of the glass. Some of them are wrapping their wings around their skinny girths exactly like Dracula does when he's sleeping in his coffin. Creepy looking things! Let's get the hell out of here before they suck out my blood.

Now I'm passing 'Into Africa'. They've got a very strange looking half-zebra half-horse monster that I reckon must have been bred for a bet. He's got the stripy legs of a zebra and the body of a donkey. He decided to hide his head inside the shed and I don't blame him, because when he came out everyone laughed at him. I feel a bit sorry for the warthogs as well, because I'm guessing that they belong in the mud. They certainly have a lot of mud, but it's all bone dry and flaking away in the wind. The whole place is a dust bowl, and if I have one criticism of London Zoo then it's about the lousy state of some of the cages. I've already walked past a couple that had danger signs up saying "Beware of deep water"... inside a bone dry river of dust.

The only thing I know about warthogs is from watching old Mafia movies. If you starve them for a month and chuck a human in the pit they will eat them whole -- bones included. It's a great way of getting rid of dead bodies apparently. They don't mention any of that on the placard though: just some boring stuff about where they live.

After that I crossed over the canal to the Snowdon Aviary. Have you ever seen the Snowdon Aviary? It reminds me of that scene in Jurassic Park when the kids run into that cage of pterodactyls. Once you've heaved open the heavy blocking door and parted the curtain of chains it's just you and two hundred ravenous birds. If they get vicious then you are basically doomed because you're trapped inside a big wire mesh bird cage. Luckily the birds are all quite friendly: ducks and gulls and cranes and that kind of thing. You're not going to come face-to-face with any buzzards or vultures or man-eating eagles with ten-foot talons. At least, I hope not, because I'm in here right now! There are quite a few sparrows and pigeons in here too, I've noticed; I suppose they must have flown in through the mesh and can't get out.

Now that I've stopped for a while and taken the time to look around, I have decided that some of the birds do actually look a bit dangerous with their long pointy bills just perfect for poking out my eyeballs, so I give them a wide berth. I much prefer the peacocks -- very nice. They are the supermodels of the bird world. Way out of my league.

The Blackburn Pavilion is another walkthrough bird exhibit, but this time it's filled with tiny little tropical birds with brightly coloured plumage. And the building is worth a look just for its architecture. If Jules Verne had ever built an aviary then this is what it would have looked like. It's all red wrought iron and green steel, with sandy coloured walls and a noisy waterfall inside.

Don't forget to go inside the Butterfly House as well. Yeah, I know what you're thinking... boring boring butterflies zzzz zzzz. But it was actually one of my favourite exhibits. Imagine a very warm greenhouse filled with tropical plants and foliage, and a soundtrack of jungle drums pounding out the speakers. And all around you flying and fluttering through the sky are thousands of colourful butterflies, flittering past your face, brushing up against your hair... and straight into a poor toddler's face who promptly bursts into tears, ha ha. Of all the scary animals that they've got in the zoo it was the butterflies that made her cry. There are so many flying around that you have to be careful not to tread on them.

The aquarium is quite large but the fish are only a few inches long. The longest one they've got on display is probably about three feet. There are no sharks or anything like that. Nothing that could kill you if it fell out the bath taps. It's just everyday angel fish and catfish, and pretty little tropical fellas swimming around the coral.

The 'Bug House' is a bit better. It's full of stuff that you might find crawling around my kitchen: beetles, spiders and maggots. They've also got a little ant colony carrying leaves from one end of a stick to the other. It reminded me of those old flea circuses that you sometimes see in the movies; but let's face it, a box full of ants isn't the best zoo exhibit.

The Reptile House is full of snakes and lizards. Patience pays off in this place because you have to wait a while before they come out to play. Some of the snakes are thicker than a rubber tyre, all coiled up in a circle three-feet wide. They could probably crush the life out of you in ten-seconds flat and yet here they are, snoozing fast asleep, like butter wouldn't melt in their mouths -- but I am not fooled. These guys are pure evil and would crush your stomach if given half a chance. Luckily they are entombed behind a thick sheet of glass or I would have run away very fast (I hate snakes).

Next up was the 'Rainforest Life' room which is a big building done up like the Amazon rainforest. As soon as you enter it you are hit by the heat and a sheen of misty white water being pumped from the ceiling. It really is hot in there but it's very well done. They've got rainforest plants and a carpet of ferns on the floor, and spindly little branches for the monkeys to sit on. The place is filled with little tamarins and big ugly sloths, and it's all open-plan so the monkeys are loose in the room (no joke!). You are standing there frozen in fear whilst they balance on the balcony and run along the banisters, and across the treetops stretched above your head. Everywhere you look is a creature cheeping or scrabbling about for somewhere to sit. They don't stand still for a second (they won't pose for photos). I would imagine that it would be quite painful to have a sloth drop on your head, but these guys only move at 2mph so you've got plenty of time to see them coming. Every now and then a warm cloud of spray will come drifting out the pipes to keep the atmosphere hot and humid. It gets quite oppressive after a while and I'm glad I'm not a monkey.

The scariest exhibit in the zoo is definitely the 'Nightlife' room. Forget about lions and tigers: if you want to confront your fears then this is the place to do it. This is the place where Hollywood comes to dream up new nightmares. We are talking about rats as big as dogs in here. And beetles like armoured hamburgers. When I tell you that it is dark, what I actually mean is that it is *darker* than dark -- totally pitch black like midnight in space. All you can hear is the quick sound of rats' feet scurrying around the corners of the floor. They drip-feed it out of the speakers so you're not sure whether they have been let loose in the room... and it's too dark to see! But unfortunately unless you've remembered to bring your army-issue night-vision goggles with you you'll be hard pressed to see anything inside the display cases (that's how dark it is).

The gorillas are definitely my favourite animals, and they are satisfyingly huge. You wouldn't want to jump in and stroke them, put it that way. When they come up to the glass all the kids start screaming because they think they're about to die. I was in there for a good twenty minutes today just watching them watch me, and I have come to the conclusion that they are actually humans in disguise. Everything they do, from the expressions on their face, to the way they sit, stand up, pick at their nails, and scratch the side of their face, is exactly the way that we would do it too. I could almost read their minds and share their thoughts by the expression on their faces.

It seemed like one guy had resigned himself to his fate. I am captured, he said. He didn't look too happy -- not like those monkeys in the PG Tips advert. I've got a theory that monkeys don't actually like bananas. The reason that they eat them all the time is because that's all we give them: it's either bananas or starve. But the truth is that they are sick to the back teeth of eating bananas 365 days a year and that is why he was sitting there staring at me like a moody teenager. He was saying, please mate, no more bananas for chrissakes. If I eat another banana I'm going to turn into one. Give me a bowl of Pedigree Chum or something, but not bananas!

As I was walking out of their enclosure I suddenly noticed the big moat around it and the double doors marked "Exit in emergency only". It made me wonder what the emergency might be... there can only be one.

Apparently if a bird leaves a little present on your head that is supposed to be very lucky. That is what everyone tells me anyway, when a bird shats on my head. So I was thinking: what if you want to be really, *really* lucky? Well, I have the solution. All you've got to do is visit the 'Meet the Monkeys' enclosure at London Zoo, which is home to loads of little squirrel monkeys; and you can watch them clamber up the trees and ropes all around you, with no barriers between you and them. You are literally face-to-face with the little blighters, and that will make it especially easy for them to deposit a 'present' on your head -- bringing you good luck for the rest of the day.

Onto the tigers now. They've had a nice new enclosure built since the last time I came here. It's certainly a lot bigger and more lush than the old one. The old stripy guy was particularly lazy today though, and decided to have a kip on the far side of the grass where we struggled to see him. I was going to try and tempt him out by throwing one of the annoying school kids in, but he was too fat to pick up.

The lion's pen is not quite on a par with the tigers, but it still looks quite wild and forest like. They've got a big moat around it (good), big thick concrete walls (good) and some electric fences too (good idea). There's a family of four or five living inside it, including one guy with a very impressive mane (he definitely needs a haircut). They steadfastly refused to move as well, despite much encouragement from the crowd. But I suppose when you're a lion you can do what the hell you like. Back in the old days they would train them to jump through flaming hoops, or ask one of the dopey tourists to put their head inside their jaws -- why don't they bring that back again? So what if a few lions died, and a few tourists got their head bitten off -- that's showbiz! After standing around for five minutes waiting for them to move from their snooze I walked back through the petting zoo (pigs, sheep, boring) and the camels. I don't know what was wrong with the camels... it looked like they had the hump to me.

Next up was the Mappin Terrace. This zone looks absolutely fantastic when you first clap eyes on it. It's a huge desert-style mountain range that rises up about fifty feet (I'm useless at judging heights, but it certainly looks like a mountain). I assumed that there were going to be some lions or brown bears lazing on the summit, but all I saw were two emus and a wallaby. Maybe the emus had scared the lions off? Their river was bone dry too. But I guess they live in Australia so they must be used to it.

My final stop of the day was watching the show at Penguin Beach. There were about a hundred of them in total all waddling around the edge of the pool chasing the keeper with his big bucket of fish. Meanwhile a pretty blonde bird (of the human variety) trotted out an excitable speech for the millions of school kids sitting down in the stands. I only went there for a sit down because I had been on my feet all day, but it turned out to be quite a nice way to end the day.

I normally recommend three hours for a trip to the zoo, but after looking at my watch on the way out I saw that I was there for four (...four hours very well spent).

There are more animals at Chessington World of Adventures, Battersea Park Children's Zoo and the London Aquarium.

Madame Tussauds

ADDRESS Madame Tussauds, Marylebone Road, Marylebone - map 2c **TRAINS** Baker Street (zone 1) **BUSES** 13, 18, 27, 30, 74, 82, 139, 205, 274, 453 **PRICE** If bought online: Adult £23.10; Child (4-15) £20.16; Infant (under-4) free; Family (2 ad+2 ch, or 1 ad+3 ch) £86.52 -- If bought at the door: Adult £33; Child (4-15) £28.80; Infant (under-4) free; Family (2 ad+2 ch, or 1 ad+3 ch) £123.60 **OPEN** During school term: 9.30 AM to 5.30 PM (Mon-Fri); 9 AM to 6 PM (Sat-Sun); During holidays: 8.30 AM to 7 PM (Mon-Sun); Last entry 1 hour before closing **WEB** madametussauds.co.uk/london **TEL** 0871 894 3000 **TIME REQUIRED** 2 hours

Easy to get to? ★★★ Good for kids? ★★★
Value for money? ★☆☆ Worth a visit? ★★☆

I finally succumbed to the inevitable and went to Madame Tussauds today. I've been putting it off for two years but it had to be done, so I did it. It's done. So now I don't have to go again for another ten years -- *thank God*.

The queue outside is totally nuts. Every time I go past on the bus it stretches for miles and miles as far as the eye can see -- all the way down the Marylebone Road. I tried to count the amount of people when I turned up this morning, but I don't know any numbers high enough. When I finally made it through the front door I thought the queue had ended, but then it carried on snaking its way around the inside as well -- it just goes on forever and ever and ever and ever. It's never-ending, even when you get to the end. Why is it so popular? Apparently it's the most visited attraction in the capital, but I haven't got the faintest idea why.

It reminds me a little bit of the Natural History Museum. That place is full of stuffed animals, and this one is full of stuffed humans. They've taken a load of famous people, embalmed them in wax, and then put them on display for everyone to gawp at.

The first room that you enter is full of Hollywood movie stars. You can have your photo taken with Brad Pitt and George Clooney if you want, and then try and fool your friends back home that you met them in real life (they won't be fooled). I must admit that the models are quite realistic, and they even have a couple of fake tourists standing around. They had one woman set up to look like she was taking a photograph of one of the waxworks, and I stood there like an idiot waiting for her to finish her snap. I was starting to get a little bit annoyed about how long she was taking and it's a good job I didn't hit her, because her head might have fallen off.

I liked ET in his bike basket, and Arnie dressed up as the Terminator. The Bruce Willis one was pretty good, too. They've also got Bruce Lee and Bruce Springsteen on show, so that is three different Bruces -- and it's not often that you see a collection of famous Bruces. The only ones missing were Bruce Forsyth and Ken Bruce from Radio 2.

For some reason David Beckham got placed next to all of the Hollywood legends, and he seemed to be quite popular with the lady visitors, with big queues forming for a photo. Victoria Beckham was there as well, for the blokes (no queues). And they've got a nice model of Audrey Hepburn in full Holly Golightly mode. Sadly I don't think Audrey would have lasted long in Hollywood these days -- not unless she had a gun and bigger tits.

After that you move on to the pop stars and sport stars. If you're under five, then you can have a sit down with One Direction. If you're over five then you can punch Justin Bieber in the face. There are plenty of big names like Jimi Hendrix and The Beatles. Kylie Minogue and Beyoncé get a prominent spot as well (primarily because they look good in hot pants). I couldn't recognise many of the other singers... I guess I'm getting old. One of them didn't have many clothes on, so I'm guessing that was Rihanna.

A lot of my favourite people were missing which was a bit disappointing. They've got Michael Jackson and Frank Sinatra, for example, but no Des O'Conner. And they've got political giants like Nelson Mandela, Gandhi, and President John F. Kennedy, but there's no sign of Nick Clegg.

They've got a decent collection of royals with the Queen, Phil, Will, Kate, and that bloke with the big ears. Even Diana gets a look in (but on a separate stage, of course -- they can't place her next to the real royals!). In fact, that's one of the most amusing things about the whole place... seeing which models get lumbered with a lousy spot. I'm sure that Churchill would be delighted to know that they've stuck him next to Adolf Hitler, for example. Whilst David Cameron gets to pose in front of No.10 with his arch-nemesis Boris Johnson. I couldn't see Ed Miliband anywhere, but I think I spotted him flipping burgers out the back afterwards, so he is still hanging around somewhere.

Obama bagged the biggest set with a huge Oval Office and a desk, whilst Margaret Thatcher was left with one of the worst waxworks on display (it really is awful). They've still got the old pope, too -- the one who decided to quit. Where's the new guy? I guess he was too busy saying prayers to have his waxwork done. There's no Jesus either. No God. No Satan. No Father Christmas. And no sign of Darth Vader or Captain Kirk -- none of my favourites. And where's Johnny Cash? How can you have Justin Bieber and not Johnny Cash?

The Chamber of Horrors has changed a lot since the last time I came here as a child -- it's been turned into a 'living exhibit' now, with costumed actors. You descend some cold stone stairs into the blackest of black, all the time with a thumping heartbeat playing out of the speakers and dark red lights bathing the place in blood. And then you walk through a few rooms filled with very loud bangs and doors slamming. Actors occasionally jump out from behind the curtains and go Boo! at you (literally). And you can see a few prisoners swinging from the rafters and toothy dogs barking as you pass.

It's all very tame, but it will probably scare the pants out of your kids. I even saw a little kid crying on the way out, being comforted by his mum (true!). She didn't look too happy, either.

Next up is the 'Spirit of London' ride, which is definitely worth a look. I actually thought that this was the best thing in the entire place. First of all you have to queue up through an old wooden library (yes, more queuing) and get into a little black taxicab. Then it drives off on a little track past scenes from London's history. It starts off in Elizabethan times with pipe-playing musicians and tights-wearing nobles, and Shakespeare sitting at his desk. Then comes the plague and the Great Fire of London, and Christopher Wren rebuilding St. Paul's Cathedral. The taxicabs are constantly twisting and turning all the time to show you the sights, up and down and round and round, but it's not like a funfair ride. It's very slow and pleasant.

After the Industrial Revolution it conveniently skips straight past the Blitz and on to the Swinging Sixties (just in case there are some German tourists watching), and the whole thing ends with a big knees-up outside Buckingham Palace with some soldiers, coppers, a motor-biking old granny and some city-suited gents in a rowing boat (don't ask).

It was quite entertaining, and it was definitely the most enjoyable part of the day; but it was ruined a tiny little bit by their blatant attempts to make some more money out of you. They have obviously realised that once you're strapped inside the taxis you're a captive audience, because they have plastered the backs of the cabs in front with billboard ads for West End shows. It totally ruins the mood. In fact, the whole place is a lot like that... every ten steps you take they are trying to flog you some extra stuff. *Pose for a photo,*

sir? Would you like some sweets, madam? They have erected big cinema stands selling Coke and crisps and popcorn in every exhibition space, and people armed with cameras are constantly harassing you to stand and pose for a picture, which you can purchase as a framed photo at the end. So if you thought it was a bit pricey spending thirty quid to get in, then that's nothing... you can easily spend another thirty quid just walking around the displays.

Their final money-making wheeze was to herd everyone through the shop like sheep, whether you wanted to go or not, just to suck the final few pennies from your wallet. The only escape from Madame Tussauds is past shelves of tat and tills. (They had a waxwork of entrepreneur Richard Branson in there as well, which I thought was a nice touch!) And then they parade you past a coffee shop as well. Then the guards strip search you at the exit just to make sure that all your money is definitely gone, before they finally agree to let you leave (okay, I made that last bit up).

To be fair to the place, it is pretty huge. There is quite a lot to see, and the Spirit of London ride was definitely fun. But let's be honest... it's basically an attraction where nothing happens. You just walk around looking at wax models of people you've seen on the telly. They don't move, and they don't talk. They just stand there like lemons, whilst all of us lemons hand over a week's wages for the privilege of looking at them.

I'm filing this one under 'money pit'.

Mansion House

ADDRESS Mansion House, The City - map 5e **TRAINS** Bank, Cannon Street, Mansion House, Monument (all zone 1) **BUSES** 8, 11, 21, 23, 25, 26, 43, 47, 76, 133, 141, 149, 242 **PRICE** Adult £7; Senior £5 **OPEN** Usually every Tue

(except Aug) - see website for dates **WEB**
cityoflondonguides.com/tours/mansion-house
TIME REQUIRED Usually 2 PM to 3.30 PM

Easy to get to? ★★★   Good for kids? ☆☆☆
Value for money? ★★☆   Worth a visit? ★☆☆

I went on a tour of Mansion House today, where the Lord Mayor of London lives. Our tour group consisted of about 25 old people and me. Some of them were even older than old -- older than the building itself, so maybe that's why the security was so lax. The security guy just seemed to stuff our bags through the scanner and let everyone through the gate. I had my camera, phone, money and keys, guns, knives and bazooka with me, and not a single beep went off. I'm sure the old people had a few metal hips and canes too, but this X-ray machine didn't want to know. Maybe the machine was asleep.

Once you're through the security you have to stand around in a little cloakroom for ten minutes, filled with marble busts of long dead Mayors.

The tour begins in the entrance hall, which also happens to be the only place where you're allowed to sit down. The guide then launches into a very wordy speech which rattles along at a steam train pace for the next sixty minutes. Not a lot of people know the history of the Guilds and the Lord Mayors of London, so most of the facts she fires at you are brand new and like a scattergun they come, rat-a-tat-tat, from Magna Carta all the way up to the present day: about the building, its history, the aldermen, the art and architects... my head was stuffed with so much stuff it's all fallen out and I can't remember any of it. I could see people's faces slowly starting to lengthen as she battled on and on, their lids and chins getting dragged down by gravity. Their ears were listening, but their eyes had other ideas.

She also spoke at length about the current Lord Mayor, what his role is, and how he came to be elected. Everyone thinks that the Lord Mayor of London is the same guy as in City Hall, but of course it isn't -- he's the *Mayor* of London (Greater London) whereas the Lord Mayor looks after the Square Mile.

The Lord Mayor only holds onto his job for twelve months at a time but they actually let him live in Mansion House, which is some perk! You don't get to see any of his private rooms though; it's strictly about the 'State Rooms' below. There are only five rooms on the tour, but two of them are absolute stunners. You might have seen one of them on the telly already -- the Egyptian Hall. That's where the Chancellor gives his annual address to all the bankers and money men. But the first room you see is an interior courtyard that used to be open to the sky. Now it's all roofed over and decorated with huge white columns and crystal chandeliers. As an entrance hall it would work extremely well, but that little pokey place you started is the main way in. The grand facade that you can see from the street is almost never used, she said. Even the Queen has to come in the side way. It seems like a terrible waste to me. It's as if they bricked up the front steps of St. Paul's, and sent everyone through the Crypt.

The next stop is in the boardroom, which is used for official city meetings. Like most of the rooms and stairwells on the tour, its walls are decorated with pretty

Dutch landscapes and dusty old portraits of the Aldermen and Mayors.

Then comes the highlight -- the Egyptian Hall. This room is three storeys tall and reminded me a little bit of Banqueting House. It has a line of Corinthian columns down each side and a minstrel's gallery running around the top. Marble statues of mythical gods look down from the golden alcoves, and stained glass windows brighten up each end. The windows tell the story of the City, from the signing of the Magna Carta and the Peasant's Revolt, all the way up to the economic charters of Elizabeth I. It's a monumental space and one of the best rooms in the city.

The tour lasted for one hour exactly. But it was a long hour because most of that was standing on the spot listening to her talking about paintings and plasterwork.

If you like old historic buildings then try Apsley House, Banqueting House, the Guildhall and Royal Courts of Justice.

Marble Arch

ADDRESS Marble Arch, Oxford St - map 2e
TRAINS Marble Arch (zone 1) **BUSES** 2, 6, 7, 10, 16, 23, 36, 73, 74, 82, 113, 137, 148, 159, 274, 390, 414, 436 **TIME REQUIRED** 5 mins

Easy to get to? ★★★ Good for kids? ☆☆☆
Value for money? free Worth a visit? ☆☆☆

If you're expecting Marble Arch to compare with the Arc de Triomphe in Paris, or the Arch of Constantine in Rome, then forget it -- you're going to be extremely disappointed. The best arch in London is Wellington Arch, at the top of Constitution Hill, but Marble Arch was never supposed to be anything other than the Queen's front gate.

One hundred and seventy years ago (a bit before my time) Buckingham Palace was just three wings around a courtyard, and Marble Arch was the ceremonial gateway into middle. It stood roughly where the forecourt is today (where they do Changing the Guard). But when Queen Victoria started churning out the babies she decided to expand the palace by building a fourth wing -- that entire front wing where the famous balcony is. Marble Arch obviously looked a bit daft then, so they shifted it brick-by-brick to the corner of Hyde Park.

What a demotion! It's just a dirty roundabout at the end of Oxford Street. The concrete courtyard is home to a load of mangy old pigeons, and tired old homeless geezers.

All of the benches are covered in raindrops and pigeon sh*t (not a nice combination) -- I have never seen so many pigeons. They used to live in Trafalgar Square until the Mayor of London scared them off with sparrow hawks, so now they've settled down here instead -- it's like one of those migrant camps you see on the news. They hog all of the benches and sit there preening their falling-out feathers. The rest of the benches are filled with office workers and homeless people on a begging break, having a quick five-minute kip before resuming their day job down Oxford Street.

What else can I see? The rest of the square is decorated with dustbins and parked-up council vans, and damp flags on the flag poles, looking like dirty pairs of pants on a washing line.

Here come some rubbish lorries... three of them have just pulled in to the square and unloaded an army of yellow-bibbed council workers with grabbers and plastic bags. They are all gloved-up like a chemical warfare unit. They have spread out around the square and cleaned out the dustbins in sixty seconds flat, and then piled back onto the lorries and gone. *Wow*. Did I really just witness that? I have never seen a man empty a dustbin so fast. Normally you'd have to nag at him for a few days.

Here's something interesting that I've just remembered... apparently if you walk through the central section of the arch then you can get arrested for treason (a throwback to its days in front of the palace). Why not give it a go? But if you get arrested then you can't blame me -- I did warn you first. Bear in mind that the penalty for treason is *death*. (You still can't blame me!)

Whilst you're here you might like to try and find the two little plaques that are buried in the road nearby. The first one is on a traffic island a little further west, down the Bayswater Road, and is supposed to mark the original location of the Tyburn Tree. The Tyburn Tree is not a tree trunk -- it's actually a euphemism for a set of wooden gallows. A few hundred years ago this end of Oxford Street was the darkness on the edge of town (as Bruce Springsteen would say), and they carted up the condemned from Newgate Prison to tie their heads to the end of a rope. Plenty of people have died at this spot. Thousands of low-lifes and scum, and hundreds of innocents, too. And probably a fair few have been knocked down by the buses in modern times, because the traffic around here is terrible.

The second plaque is supposed to show the final resting place of Oliver Cromwell, after Charles II dug up his bones and hanged them, in revenge for beheading his dad. Can you imagine the difficulty he had in hanging a corpse that had already been rotting in the ground for two years? You have to take your hat off to Charles for giving it a go. I've probably visited Marble Arch about a million times in my life (at least), but I have never once managed to find this plaque. And you can believe me when I say that I have hunted high and low for it. I am starting to think that it doesn't actually exist... but maybe you will have better luck.

While we're here, I'm just going to say a little something about the Edgware Road, because no guidebook ever spares a thought for this place. And the reason for that is this: it's ugly. It's even uglier than me, and that is really saying something, because I am pretty ugly. I used to think it was a total dump, too, but I've actually softened to it now (it's still ugly, though).

The first time you come down here I guarantee that you will think it's a total disaster. There is not a single nice piece of architecture down here -- not one! It's all concrete office blocks and council towers. It's full of Iranian cafes and Lebanese restaurants. All of the shop signs are in that Middle Eastern cursive script, and I haven't got a clue what most of them sell. They are a few Turkish travel agents and Arabic hair salons dotted around, and plenty of mentions of Damascus and Beirut, but to sum it up as simply as possible: if you're English, then you're a foreigner. But come down here at night and you'll see it in a whole different light.

If you ever stay in a Paddington hotel then this is where you'll be getting the bus every night -- probably the No.23 from The City. That's when you can stare out of the window and into the windows of the restaurants. They are full of colourful fairy lights and decorations. Old men sit outside the front doors sucking on those long teapot-like tubes (bongs, we used to call them). I can see them stubbornly sitting outside in their hats and coats, sucking on those tendril-like tobacco tubes, in between the shivers, because it's about minus ten degrees tonight. English OAPs have a pint down the British Legion, whilst these Middle Eastern guys settle for a puff outside their pavement cafes, discussing whatever it is that old men discuss. Other cafes are full of mustachioed men with collars and ties. They are the Middle Eastern equivalent of those Mafia cafes you see in the movies, where fat Italians stand in the doorway, guarding the big guy at the back. How come other countries have a cafe culture, and we don't? We need to invent one, because we're missing out.

Whilst you're here you might like to cross over the road and see Speakers' Corner.

The Monument

ADDRESS The Monument, Monument Street, The City - map 10a **TRAINS** Bank, Cannon Street, Monument (all zone 1) **BUSES** 17, 21, 43, 48, 133, 141, 149, 521 **PRICE** Adult £4; Senior £2.70; Child (under-16) £2; Note: Under 13s must be accompanied **OPEN** 9.30 AM to 6 PM (Mon-Sun, Apr-Sep); 9.30 AM to 5.30 PM (Mon-Sun, Oct-Mar); Last entry 30 mins before closing **WEB** themonument.info **TEL** 0207 626 2717 **TIME REQUIRED** 45 mins

Easy to get to? ★★★ Good for kids? ★★☆
Value for money? ★★★ Worth a visit? ★★☆

I climbed up The Monument yesterday -- never again. I'm done with stairs. I'm not climbing up any stairs ever again. You have to go through the little door at the front where a little old lady is wedged into a cubbyhole about the size of a shoebox. Then she points you to the stairs and that is when you start to have second thoughts.

The little leaflet says there are only 311 steps to the top, but I think they must have miscounted because it seemed like ten times that to me. They wind up tightly for a million miles and it just goes on forever and ever. I thought I was going to come out onto the surface of the moon, that is how long it took me to climb it. After two minutes my heart was pounding loud enough to make a sound -- it was the drumming percussion to my shuffling huffs and puffs. My chest was thumping, my legs were shaking, my head was sweating... and people do this for fun? *Seriously?*

It wouldn't be so bad if it was all one-way traffic, but you frequently have to hug the stone wall to allow a descending stream of sightseers to squeeze past. And if they happen to be a bit on the chubby side (i.e., if they're Americans), then it can even be a little scary. As soon as the people above me heard my size 9 shoes slapping on the stairs below they quickly hogged the wide section of the spiral, forcing me to tiptoe gingerly around the narrow bit. If you stumble on the way past then down you'll go, like a marble in *Kerplunk*, bouncing down to the bottom of the column until you're just a skin bag full of dust.

Happily there are plenty of alcoves on the way up where you can have a sit down and catch your breath, but they get fewer and fewer as it tapers up towards the top. By the time you get to the top you will basically be dead. Apparently suicidal people used to come up here and hurl themselves off the top, but I reckon a few of them must have died just climbing up the stairs. I certainly thought I was dying -- and I'm being serious! I thought it was the end. My eyesight was turning black and white. I was telling myself to just keep climbing, godammit -- keep climbing towards the light. If I was going to die then I was damn well going to do it at the top.

It took me nine minutes to climb it, and that was followed by another ten minutes of me collapsed against a wall trying to think happy thoughts and slow my heart down.

Eventually I had recovered enough to look at the view and it was a bit disappointing, to be honest, because it's a very small space on the balcony (a lot smaller than it looks from the ground), and you're trapped inside a wire mesh. It's a bit like being a budgie in a birdcage. I seem to remember there being a couple of coin-operated telescopes in the corners the last time I came up here, but they've disappeared now. And there are no plaques of the skyline to show you what's what, either.

The Monument used to be one of the tallest buildings in The City for a few hundred years, but now it's barely creeping up to the shoulders of the big ones. They would have to build some tiptoes on the bottom of the column for it to see above the rooftops.

Would you like a game of I-Spy while you're up there? See if you can spot these landmarks: I'm not giving you any points for Tower Bridge, because that's far too easy. But how about City Hall and the Tower of London? Southwark Cathedral is a bit more of a challenge. And how about the Golden Hinde on Bankside? Greenwich is very difficult -- you will need to know what the power station looks like to spot that.

You can't see Big Ben because it's hidden behind an office block (unless I'm going blind), but you can see the Victoria Tower at the other end of Parliament. And if you can spot the top of Westminster Cathedral then you're a genius (and I do mean the *cathedral* -- not the abbey). The London Eye is easy-peasy, and so is St. Paul's, but how about Cleopatra's Needle? That is my final challenge to you -- I'm not letting you head back down until you see the Needle.

The walk back down is a lot easier, thank God. And when you stumble, half-dead, back to the counter the lady will be waiting to give you a little certificate, so you can prove to the world that you were dumb enough to climb it.

If you like climbing tall buildings then try the Sky Garden, The Shard, St. Paul's, and Westminster Cathedral's bell tower.

Museum of London

ADDRESS Museum of London, 150 London Wall, Barbican - map 5e **TRAINS** Barbican, St. Paul's (both zone 1) **BUSES** 4, 8, 56, 100, 172, 242, 521 **PRICE** Free, but there may be

Landmarks & Attractions | 155

charge for temporary exhibitions **OPEN** 10 AM to 6 PM (Mon-Sun); Last entry 20 mins before closing **WEB** museumoflondon.org.uk/london-wall **TEL** 0207 001 9844 **TIME REQUIRED** 2 hours

Easy to get to? ★★★ Good for kids? ★☆☆ Value for money? free Worth a visit? ★★☆

This is probably my favourite museum in London, but of course I am a big fan of London. The more you know about the city the better it gets. You need to know what it looks like today, to be amazed at pictures of its past.

The collection begins in the prehistoric era, which is basically just a load of bones and stones. If a cabinet is full of bones and stones then I don't even bother stopping, as a rule. I've got my own bones and stones in the garden, and I don't need to see three thousand more. (Yeah, I know, I'm a philistine. But does anyone really find this stuff interesting? A bone's a bone, isn't it -- they haven't changed in a million years.) The one redeeming feature is all the animal skeletons that they've dug up in the capital: skeletons of rhinos, elephants and some mammoth teeth too. It turns out that London used to be better than a Kenyan safari. They've also got some fierce looking spears that probably ended up sticking out of someone's head.

It starts getting better when you reach the Roman era. They've got intricate little models of Londinium's basilica, forum and the wharves, and it's hard to believe that it was real. It actually looks like Rome! I always curse Boudicca for burning it all down in 60 AD, because it would be fantastic if we still had some of this stuff standing.

As you would expect for the Roman era, there are lots and lots and lots (and lots) and lots, and lots (and lots) of busted pots and plates and statues. They've also got a few wooden timbers and mosaics as well, and a pile of coins and jewellery. Don't forget to have a look out of the window at this point... because you can see the remains of London's city wall downstairs in the street.

Then you move into the medieval era, which has plenty of religious treasures from the Dissolution of the Monasteries. I always curse Henry VIII as well (along with Boudicca), for knocking down some of our finest spiritual buildings. If you are a big fan of broken cups and smashed up statues then you will love this section. The Museum of London must have one of the best collections of broken crockery in the UK. And they've got a gruesome movie about the Black Death as well, if you're a big fan of the plague.

After the medieval section comes my favourite bit: all about the Tudors and Stuarts. This area covers William Shakespeare and the English Civil War. They've got a nice little exhibition about the Great Fire of London here (albeit very small), where you can see some burnt timbers and bricks that they've dug up from the City. I always curse the Great Fire of London (along with Henry VIII and Boudicca), for destroying some of London's finest buildings. They've got a few decent displays about the theatres as well, and if you're a saddo like me then you'll be smiling when you see two plates from the famous 'Copperplate Map'. This is also the era when you'll start to see some early paintings of the London skyline, and it's interesting to see what changes have taken place.

Then comes the Georgians. My favourite part of this section is an original cell door from Newgate Prison. Have a close look at that wall with all the prisoners' scribblings on it... that's a proper punishment, being shut up in that dark crate, scratching your name into the wood with your fingernails so someone won't forget you're dead. It's ironic, isn't it, that these are the people we remember: the low-lifes and scum, who didn't have a penny to their name, whilst the rich men's tombs get buried in nettles and weeds and disappear. No one bothers to read their names.

Next up is a life-size Victorian shopping street. There are about ten shop fronts in total, with the sounds of street-life pumped in through the speakers. The windows are stuffed full of Victorian goods... toys and cards, fags and tobacco, powder and snuff, pots full of crackers and biscuits, top hats and tails, wigs and bodkins, and even a little post office, pub and public urinal.

After that comes a few bits on the Blitz and the 1960s... but this isn't very well done, I don't think. It's basically just a collection of paintings and photos and not a lot else. You can see some people sleeping in the subway when the Germans came to town (and pictures of the rubble-strewn streets after they left). I always curse the Germans (along with the Great Fire of London and Henry VIII and Boudicca), for destroying some of our finest buildings. And they've got a few early motor cars and home computers from the 1980s. But it seems to be much more about Britain by this point, rather than the city of London, so it doesn't interest me so much.

The final thing worth seeing is the Lord Mayor's golden coach, which he uses every year at the Lord Mayor's Show. I'm not sure what the Queen thinks of it, because I think it's definitely better than her own State coach (which you can see at the Royal Mews).

Learn more about the history of London at the Museum of London Docklands.

Museum of London Docklands

ADDRESS Museum of London Docklands, No.1 Warehouse, West India Quay **TRAINS** Canary Wharf DLR, West India Quay DLR (both zone 2) **BUSES** 135, 277, D3, D7 **PRICE** Free, but there may be a charge for temporary exhibitions **OPEN** 10 AM to 6 PM (Mon-Sun); Last entry 20 mins before closing **WEB** museumoflondon.org.uk/docklands **TEL** 0207 001 9844 **TIME REQUIRED** 1½ hours

Easy to get to? ★★☆ Good for kids? ★☆☆
Value for money? free Worth a visit? ★★☆

I've known about this place for a while but I could never be bothered to get the train to Canary Wharf (I'm very lazy). But today I thought what the hell and I gave it a go.

I wish I'd come here before now, because it's really good. I think you have to be a bit of a London history buff to appreciate it though, because there's not a lot for tourists. There's not all that much for kids either. But I'm not saying any of that to put you off: because I actually found it really interesting.

The museum is all about life along the River Thames and especially the Docklands area, and starts off with a bit about the Roman and Viking settlements. You can see how it was built up and burnt down, and built up and burnt down, and built up and burnt down some more, and then you come to the first good bit: a huge model of the Old London Bridge. Have a read of my review of St. Magnus the Martyr church and you will see why I love this building so much. To call it a bridge is almost an insult. This thing was a town on water and I never tire of seeing models of it. This one solitary model made the whole trip worthwhile for me (but I am a bit of a saddo when it comes to the bridge).

Another good display is a life-size reconstruction of a quay. You can walk through a dark and dingy street past the stacked-up barrels and counting house, with the sounds of the sea and seagulls piped in through the speakers. Try and imagine the kind of place that Jack the Ripper stalked at midnight -- that's the kind of place it is.

They talk a lot about the docks and merchants after that, and the cargos they brought back from the Caribbean. There is a big exhibition about the slave trade too. To be honest my eyes always glaze over when it comes to stuff about the colonies because it feels like I'm being preached too (apparently slavery was bad), but they certainly give it a thorough discussion if that is your interest.

After that we move on to the building of the new bridges and the really huge docks in Queen Victoria's day. They've got a nice little model of St. Katherine Docks too, which doesn't seem to have changed much over the years (apart from the Starbucks in the middle).

They've got another walk through street after that which is even better than the first one, and even darker and scarier too -- it's almost pitch black! (It's like something from the London Dungeon.) You can peer into the chandlers and supply merchants and see your shadow growing on the sooty arch as you pass by the pub and print sellers. The noises they've got playing out of the speakers greatly add to the atmosphere with sea shanties and old hags shouting and clock bells in the fog -- it really is good and I almost wish I had a time machine so I could travel back and experience it for real.

Next we come to the Industrial Age with bits about shipbuilding and the big old steamships. Then you watch it all go up in flames when you learn about the Blitz and the firestorms that swept across the East End. There are lots of photos in this section of the devastation and bombed-out buildings, and crackling fire and air-raid sirens playing out the speakers.

Finally you come to the fifties and beyond, when they start to build the modern-day docks and DLR. They've got some nice information about Canary Wharf too and how they built it up as a rival to The City.

So, to sum it all up... I definitely recommend this for locals but I'm not sure it will be much fun for tourists. If you like London history then it's a good place to visit after the Museum of London, because it covers completely different ground.

St. Magnus the Martyr has a model of Old London Bridge. You can learn more about the canals at the London Canal Museum.

National Gallery

ADDRESS National Gallery, Trafalgar Square - map 8b **TRAINS** Charing Cross, Embankment, Leicester Square (all zone 1) **BUSES** 3, 6, 9,

11, 12, 13, 15, 23, 24, 29, 87, 88, 91, 139, 159, 176, 453 **PRICE** Free, but there may be a charge for temporary exhibitions **OPEN** 10 AM to 6 PM (Sat-Thu); 10 AM to 9 PM (Fri) **WEB** nationalgallery.org.uk **TEL** 0207 747 2885 **TIME REQUIRED** 2 hours

Easy to get to? ★★★ Good for kids? ☆☆☆
Value for money? free Worth a visit? ★★☆

Do you know what the nicest thing about the National Gallery in the evening is? The peace and quiet. I was walking here from Leicester Square five minutes ago and it was all busy busy busy. Pavements heaving, people jostling bustling barging elbows out, hurrying everywhere, cars all over the place, sirens blaring, damn pigeons in the way. And then you walk through the gallery double doors and it's all quiet like a library. Just a lot of people shuffling around in silence, tip-toeing to and fro, looking at the art.

I can understand why people come in here for their lunch break. It must make a nice change of pace from answering the phone all day, signing this and that, and getting shouted at by the suits in the office. You can come in here and have a think for a bit, on the comfy plush poofees. In fact, most of the people in here aren't even looking at the art, now that I come to study them. Sure, their eyes might be staring at the walls, but their brains are on other things. Daydreaming about their missus or what they're having for tea tonight. Some of them are just tourists, ticking off the gallery box on their 'must-do in London' list. But others are clearly here for the paintings. You can see them peering up close at the colours and brushstrokes. I suppose it must mean something to them. I don't get the attraction myself. It's just a picture of a place, isn't it. Or a portrait of a bloke I don't know -- no different from looking at a picture in a magazine. Imagine if you went to see *The Sound of Music* at the cinema and they paused it on a shot of the mountains, and you just sat and stared at it for ten minutes, admiring the scenery -- people would think that you're a bit daft. But that's what they do in here all day: just sit staring at a landscape where nothing happens. The leaves don't drop, the wind doesn't blow. No one is moving, just snoozing. Like a photo in a magazine. But it's nice and quiet anyway, and that's what I came for.

I'm in a room full of portraits at the moment. People in tight trousers, white wigs and ruffles around their necks. I'm sure they looked great in their day, but it's just silly suits and fancy dress now. Can you imagine walking down Whitehall in a pair of white tights and a ruffle these days? You'd get beaten up or arrested before you made it to Horse Guards. I wonder how we will be remembered in 100 years time? Will they be taking the mick out of our trousers too? That is why you should always have your portrait done from the neck up -- so they can't laugh at your garb in a century from now. Not that I will ever end up in here, of course. I'm a total nobody... too ugly for a picture on the wall.

The next room is full of angels and saints and Jesus on the cross. They don't seem to be too fussed about clothes in here: the angels are all stark naked. I wonder if that's the first thing they do when you get up to the pearly gates: nick all your clothes. They probably have to make sure that you're not bringing in any contraband -- they don't want people sneaking weapons into heaven. When was the last time you saw an angel wearing a coat? Or Jesus, for that matter? I don't know about you, but I would quite like to see a painting of Jesus in a jumper. Surely he can't have worn the same old toga for 33 years.

There are also quite a lot of paintings of people getting stabbed. I thought saints were supposed to be the good guys? But they all seem to be getting shot and stabbed and strung up and arrested by the Romans. Even Jesus managed to get himself banged up on Death Row. But then he escaped out of the cave and ascended up to heaven, so I suppose he got away in the end. *Ha ha, you can't catch Jesus!* He's like Harry Houdini, escaping out of a locked box. Wait a minute... does that mean that he's still technically on the run? That is probably why there hasn't been a Second Coming yet: because he's afraid of getting banged up by the Romans. He hasn't served out his original sentence yet. If he came back down to earth again then he'd be like Ronnie Biggs.

Imagine if Jesus did come back down to earth and repeated the exact same story all over again... it just wouldn't have the same impact as 2,000 years ago. He'd be turning water into wine and we'd be going, "So what? I saw Paul Daniels make an elephant disappear last week. Haven't you ever heard of David Blaine, mate? He can levitate five feet in the air!" He needs to update his tricks -- he'd be trying to cure lepers with prayers and we'd be going "just take him down the hospital mate, and the doctor will give him a dose of antibiotics." And we wouldn't nail him up on the cross either, because capital punishment was abolished in 1965. Can you imagine the end of the Bible without the crucifixion? Imagine if the Bible's big ending was just him doing 100 hours community service picking up litter along the side of the M3. Nope... it just wouldn't work. So that's why there hasn't been a Second Coming yet: Jesus knows about showbiz, and he knows that it would be a massive anti-climax.

Another thing that I have noticed about religious paintings is this: it's all tears and jeers. It's never "Oh look Jesus is here, hooray!" It's always some poor bedraggled old woman crying and weeping and kneeling at his feet to beg his forgiveness. You never see Jesus on a day off, or out on the town with his mates. He's always on the job, or got six-inch nails sticking out of his hands and blood pouring down his face. Who wants to look at that all day? So instead of seeing him at the Last Supper all the time, how about having him making some toast in the morning? Or taking his dogs out for a walk?

I'm in the Impressionist section now looking at my favourite painting. Even though I'm a total Philistine I do still have a favourite piece of art: it's Vincent Van Gogh's *A Wheatfield with Cypresses*. I like it because it's all lively sky and windy. It looks like a winter's day out on the moors somewhere. It's the kind of place where you'd end up if you got horribly lost on a Sunday stroll.

One minute you're walking through the countryside having a chat with your missus, and the next thing you know you're out on the moors with the wind and the wolves, and it's 5 o'clock, and you've got nothing to eat or drink. *Oh no, my mobile doesn't work either! What am I going to do? I'm doomed!* Tree leaves are blowing and a hurricane is scraping the skin off your face, and it's actually quite pretty. Just me and the trees -- that is what this picture means to me. I wouldn't object if it was hanging on my toilet wall at home. I can't afford to pay fifty million quid for it, though. I can probably scrape together about a hundred pounds -- tops. I wonder how much they'll sell it for? There's no harm in asking, I suppose. (I asked, and they said no.)

I've just stumbled upon another picture that I recognise, but only because I like my Tudors: *The Execution of Lady Jane Grey*. I always feel sorry for this girl because she was quite pretty, and she was forced into doing something silly and now look where she has ended up -- on the end of an axe. I think the characters are hamming it up a bit though -- they are overacting outrageously. Swooning and feinting with hands all limp. Even the executioner looks a bit worried for her health. And who ever heard of an axe-man wearing poncy pink tights? I'm sorry, but no. I'm not having that. If I ever have my head chopped off and the axe-man comes waltzing in wearing pink pants and a red felt hat then I will make a quick dash for the door. I want someone tough to do it.

My final stop is at the Turner's. He was quite handy with a paintbrush. I like the way he couldn't be bothered to paint the detail. He just went, *right*... a bit of white, green and blue -- let's just luzz a load of colour on and mix it up a bit. Chuck in some bright white sunshine and call it a day. He can't be arsed to paint the blades of grass or the leaves on the trees. Let's just get the colours down, he says, and stick it on the wall.

If you like this then try the Courtauld, Wallace Collection and Tate Britain.

National Maritime Museum

ADDRESS National Maritime Museum, Romney Road, Greenwich - map 11f **TRAINS** Cutty Sark DLR (zones 2&3) **BUSES** 129, 177, 180, 188, 199, 386 **PRICE** Free, but there may be a charge for temporary exhibitions **OPEN** 10 AM to 5 PM (Mon-Sun, Sep to last week of Jul); 10 AM to 6 PM (Mon-Sun, last week of Jul and Aug); Last entry 30 mins before closing **WEB** rmg.co.uk/national-maritime-museum **TEL** 0208 858 4422 **TIME REQUIRED** 1½-2 hours

Easy to get to? ★★★ Good for kids? ★☆☆
Value for money? free Worth a visit? ★☆☆

I rode the boat to Greenwich this morning and then had to decide what to do once I arrived. There are quite a few places to try in the town, but I plumped for the National Maritime Museum. I briefly thought about going to the Royal Observatory instead, but that would have involved walking up the big hill and actually doing some exercise; so that was out (I'm having a bad knees day). When they move it down the hill, I will give it a go.

I do like the National Maritime Museum, but given Britain's rich history of war on the waves, and the fact that we won just about every battle we ever fought, it always seems a bit sparse on content to me. Where's the rest of it? I suppose we must have sunk it all. All you'll find downstairs are some ship's figureheads, a titchy model of Nelson's Column, a gilded barge from Georgian times, two old industrial engines, a few scale models and a silver speedboat. That is practically it. That is downstairs done... unless you like looking at old paintings of the River Thames. Luckily I do, but I'm not sure how interesting they will be to a tourist.

If you like your London history then check out that giant panorama of the city and see how much it's changed. Can you see Marble Arch, still standing in front of Buckingham Palace? It gives you a good insight into how many ships came into the Pool of London as well -- what a sight that must have been! That is the kind of sight I dream about.

Upstairs is where you'll find all the moralising lessons about the evil Empire (the British Empire). Apparently we were a bunch of whalers and slavers and money-grabbing capitalists who brought nothing but pain and misery to everyone we ever met. Obviously, I apologise wholeheartedly for my part in this. I may have been born 170 years after slavery was abolished, but in this touchy-feely world of ours every generation has to apologise anew for their ancestor's behaviour.

Walking through those rooms is like wearing a hairshirt. It's like slapping a cat n' nine tails down your back, and I think it gets a bit grating after a while. Yes we did some questionable things (even awful things), but Jesus Christ, *come on!* The whole of Europe was playing the game in those days. And didn't we do some impressive things as well? Can't we hear about some of those, for a change? When they talk about the East India Company and the beginnings of global trade with the colonies, for example, they illustrate it with a whip and pair of rusty old leg-irons. Everything always comes back to that. The Romans never have this problem: you never hear the Italians apologising for throwing the Christians to the lions two thousand years ago. I've never once heard the Norwegians say sorry for sending the Vikings raping and pillaging and burning down Yorkshire. Maybe we should demand some compensation from them; then we can pass it on to the Americans for stealing their cotton crops. Then the Americans can pass it on to the native Americans for stealing their land. Then the native Americans can pass it back to the Norwegians for killing the original Viking settlers. (Did you know that the Vikings discovered America before the Brits?) Then maybe everyone will be happy.

Most of the other exhibits are timepieces, clocks and watches, with some guns and flintlock muskets. They've got a lot of maps and sacks and paintings of famous sailors as well. They also have Captain Bligh's sword and coconut cup, from *Mutiny on the Bounty* fame, which he used to measure out the rations when he was stranded on a rowing boat.

After you have thoroughly depressed yourself with a stroll through that section, you are treated to an environmental lecture about how much rubbish gets thrown into the sea -- *yawn*. (What's that got to do with British naval history?)

At this point of the review you might be thinking that it's not worth a visit... but you'd be wrong, because I have saved the best for last. There aren't many museums in London that can sell themselves with a single display case, but the National

Maritime Museum is definitely one of them, because they've got hold of the actual uniform that Nelson was wearing at the Battle of Trafalgar. It seems almost unbelievable to me that this thing still survives, because this is the *actual* uniform that he was wearing onboard HMS Victory the day that he was shot. You can even see the torn up fluff where the bullet entered his shoulder. A French marksman was supposedly stationed high up in the mast of the neighbouring boat, and shot down at the Admiral as he was striding around the deck. When you remember that both boats were rolling around in the sea and covered in gunsmoke, it was probably the greatest shot in history (or the luckiest). In hindsight, he probably should have removed his Admiral's hat and medals before stepping out on deck -- the marksman would have seen him sparkling like a Christmas tree.

If I had to choose the most spine-tingling exhibit in the whole of London then this is probably it. When you stop and stare at the *actual clothes* he was wearing that fateful day -- one of the most famous days in British history -- it gives you goosebumps. Well, it gave me goosebumps anyway.

If you don't mind a day trip then try the dockyards at Chatham and Portsmouth.

National Portrait Gallery

ADDRESS National Portrait Gallery, St. Martin's Place, Trafalgar Sq - map 8b **TRAINS** Charing Cross, Embankment, Leicester Square (all zone 1) **BUSES** 3, 6, 9, 11, 12, 13, 15, 23, 24, 29, 87, 88, 91, 139, 159, 176, 453 **PRICE** Free, but there may be a charge for temporary exhibitions **OPEN** 10 AM to 6 PM (Sat-Wed); 10 AM to 9 PM (Thu-Fri); Last entry 15 mins before closing **WEB** npg.org.uk **TEL** 0207 306 0055 **TIME REQUIRED** 1½-2 hours

Easy to get to? ★★★ Good for kids? ☆☆☆
Value for money? free Worth a visit? ★★☆

The National Portrait Gallery is probably my favourite gallery in London because it appeals to history lovers as well as art lovers. It's all about the sitters, not the painters. Admire the people, not the paintings. But that's not to say that the paintings aren't good, because they are -- they still have pieces by Hockney and Holbein, etc. -- but if they need a picture of a British hero and all they can find is an incomplete prep, then that's what they'll put up.

It's like walking through a *Who's Who* of British history -- a Panini sticker book of portraits. They've got every royal from Henry to Harry to Hotspur, with Anne Boleyn and Wallis Simpson along the way. If you want to see the face of every monarch we've ever had, then this is the place. A lot of them are very famous pieces -- the big pictures of Elizabeth I are maybe the most famous portraits in London. They cover all of her contemporaries as well: people like William Cecil, Walter Raleigh, Shakespeare and Drake (considering that he was such a tough bloke, Francis Drake is wearing the dandiest outfit I have ever seen!).

They've got actors, writers, scientists, musicians, military generals... everyone from Christine Keeler to Bernard Montgomery, via Michael Faraday and the big beard of WG Grace. You can see Samuel Pepys, Christopher Wren and

Nelson, mixing it with Paul McCartney and Sir Tim Berners-Lee.

You can have a lot of fun just walking around trying to recognise the faces before reading the plaque. I'm all right with the 20th century politicians, but I do struggle with the Stanley Baldwins of this world (the bank managers of Downing Street). You can't mistake the wild hair of the early Liberals and Labour guys, or the oily moustaches of the top hat Tories. Stanley Baldwin could probably spend all day standing in front of his portrait and still no one would recognise him, but imagine if you heard the *tap tap tap* of Chamberlain's ivory cane on the parquet floor!

Apparently there used to be a rule that you had to be dead for at least ten years before you got a spot on the wall, so the trustees could tell whether you've truly earned a place. But that rule was dumped in the interests of making more money. So whilst upstairs you've got people like Elgar and Handel, downstairs it's Eddi Reader and Blur. Upstairs are Disraeli, Gladstone and William Pitt, and downstairs is Mo Mowlam. Upstairs is Samuel Johnson, and downstairs is Gok Wan (no joke!). They've got a ten minute video of David Beckham too, which is just him lying on a bed trying to fall asleep. Why can't they just sit him down and paint his face? We just don't paint portraits like we used to.

Search out the long shot of Arthur Balfour leaning against a wall. Can you imagine a commission like that these days? Nowadays you're much more likely to get an abstract jumble of colours or something shocking: hence the plethora of unrecognisable skulls and celebrities posing in their underwear. Artists are always looking for an angle these days: some other kind of message that they wish to impart. In the old days (upstairs) the aim of the game was to create a good likeness, and the better the likeness the better the painting. And they'd put them in a pose which told us something about the sitter -- was he a thinker? a romantic? a bit moody? The artist tried to show us something about their character by the way he posed. But if you look at all the present day stuff it seems as if the likeness is often the first thing to get dumped. The artist doesn't tell us anything about the subject at all -- not even what he looks like. It's much more about his own style of painting. I don't think the artist even cares whether his portrait looks like the person concerned anymore -- he'd much rather the viewer walk away talking about them (the artist) rather than the sitter. Maybe that's why there are so many photos in the present day section? Because that's the only way of recording what the subject actually looks like.

But listen to me... jeez. You'd think I didn't like the place by the way I'm talking. But I do! It's their collection of modern art that I don't like. If you stick with the past then it's well worth a visit.

The National Gallery is next-door. The Courtauld and Tate Britain are also good.

Natural History Museum

ADDRESS Natural History Museum, Cromwell Road, South Kensington - map 6e **TRAINS** South Kensington (zone 1) and a 10 min walk **BUSES** 14, 49, 70, 74, 345, 360, 414, 430, 710, C1 **PRICE** Free, but there may be a charge for temporary exhibitions **OPEN** 10 AM to 5.50 PM (Mon-Sun); Last entry 35 mins before closing **WEB** nhm.ac.uk **TEL** 0207 942 5000 **TIME REQUIRED** 3 hours

Easy to get to? ★★★ Good for kids? ★★★ Value for money? free Worth a visit? ★★★

I used to quite like dinosaurs when I was a little kid. That was my big interest as a child: dinosaurs... and Ian Rush and Kenny Dalglish. I used to like Michael Jackson as well, but I don't admit to that anymore. Obviously I'm a lot older now so I have totally grown out of dinosaurs (I like *Star Wars* instead), but you can imagine how many times I've been to the Natural History Museum... millions. If you're a kid who grows up near London then this is one of the first places that your parents drag you to during the holidays because it's educational. They do a "fun day out at the museums" which involves getting a train to Waterloo and then a bus to South Kensington (the tube is too scary for mums). Then you run around the Natural History Museum and the Science Museum for four hours whilst your mum tells you not to press all the buttons.

Well, I am going back today... and I am damn well going to press all of the buttons! I am a grown man now for chrissakes, and my mother isn't here so I can press whatever the hell I like. If I want to press the buttons then I will; but I'll have to fight my way past all of the school kids first because there's a whole army of them outside. You've got to be careful with kids these days because they are more heavily armed than the police -- I'm glad I'm not a teacher. In my schooldays the worst weapon we'd face was a thwack from a plastic ruler, but now they come tooled up with razors and blades and hand grenades. (I exaggerate only slightly.)

But anyway... I am in now. The one thing that everybody knows about the Natural History Museum is that they've got a big huge dinosaur skeleton standing in the entrance hall. But did you know that it's actually a fake? His name is Dippy and he's not a real Diplodocus at all -- he's just a replica. I only found that out today and it took the gloss off it a little bit, but he still looks mighty fine facing down the hordes as they storm through the door. Luckily he's a vegetarian so you don't have to worry about getting eaten (unless you're a vegetable).

Sometimes I have a hard time believing that dinosaurs actually existed because they look totally impossible. They've got a prehistoric sloth off to the side, for example, which looks bigger than a Mini Metro (no joke!). They've got a huge Triceratops which could probably charge down a Challenger tank and flip it over. Some of the animals are just... nuts. It's almost as if they came with weapons attached to their face... huge knives coming out of their thumbs and six foot horns like lances on their head. Imagine trying to catch your dinner in 1 million BC when it came with armour plating and ten-tonne feet. It would be hard enough trying to bring it down with a gun -- and all they had was a sharpened stick!

I quite like the way that they've arranged the dinosaur room... it's very dark and moody inside and they send you up onto a walkway to look at all the dinosaur bones from above, before doubling-back and doing the whole lot again from below. They've got plenty of full-size skeletons and lots of half-exposed bones still buried in the rock. They've got lots of fossilised footprints and dinosaur eggs as well, and a couple of animatronic Velociraptors for the kids; but wait until you get to the very end for the big surprise... because that's where you'll come face-to-face with a life-size Tyrannosaurus Rex!

You'll round a corner into a darkened swamp, with misty purple lights drifting over the trees, and then he'll swing his great big head around and roar at the crowd of screaming toddlers. I'm pretty sure that it's a robot. I don't think it's real. I waited around for five minutes to see if he'd rip the head off one of the school kids, but no luck. They probably would have fought back and stabbed him anyway -- you know what kids are like these days.

My favourite part of the museum is the mammals. It might sound boring on paper but trust me -- it is good. It's basically like a modern-day zoo, except everything in it is dead. And it's not just their bones either, we're talking life-size specimens with big teeth, eyeballs and fur. Imagine if your favourite cat had died and you had it sitting stuffed on your mantelpiece -- that is exactly what it's like.

They've got every kind of animal in the world from rats and cats and kangaroos, to elephants, rhinos, bison and sheep. They've got galloping horses, giraffes, lizards, leopards, polar bears, panda bears, brown bears, zebras, camels, snakes, bats... the list just goes on and on. See if you can find Guy the Gorilla from London Zoo (the apes and monkeys are in a completely different section, so it's not easy -- you can pretend you're hunting them down as you walk around. It will be like a poor-man's safari.)

They usually have a collection of birds on show with a Dodo and hundreds of colourful tropical finches, but that seems to have disappeared now. I did manage to find a sign saying the area is being redeveloped though... so I'm sure they will return at a later date.

After that comes the creepy crawly section where you can see ants and bugs and slugs and locusts. They've got an ant farm as well, where you can see the little fellas traipsing their way across a big log carrying bits of leaf to build their nest. They seem to be the only animals in the entire building that are still alive (although I imagine it would be quite difficult to stuff an ant).

It will probably be around this stage of the tour that you'll be thinking you're getting close to the end. Well... you'll be wrong. You'll wander into the entrance of the Earth Hall and go *woah!* It's a big huge escalator rising up through the centre of a planet, past a molten core bubbling with thunder and noise and pulsating with flames and lava, and it's easily the best escalator in London. (Yes, I am that sad -- I have a favourite escalator.)

When you reach the top you can learn about volcanoes and earthquakes. There's some stuff about glaciers, canyons and caves as well. It's mainly all pictures and info boards in this section but they've got a few interesting bits and pieces dotted around -- they've got a curled up body from the ruins of Pompeii, for example, and a rather silly simulation of the powerful Kobe earthquake in Japan (easily the worst simulation in London). You are supposed to stand on the floor whilst the building shakes all around you, but the floor hardly shakes at all, and all you get are a few pots and pans and boxes banging about on the walls. If that was the worst earthquake in Japanese history then it was a piece of cake! It was so pathetic that I actually thought it seemed a bit insensitive, considering that the real earthquake killed 6,500 people. But that is what it's like in our health and safety sensitive world -- they want to show people the power of a devastating earthquake, but have to neuter it in case someone falls over and sues them for scuffing a shoe. God help us if we ever suffer a real earthquake.

After that comes a small section on the solar system, and what the different planets are made of, followed by a room full of jewels and gems and precious metals. This turned out to be a lot more interesting than it sounds, because they've got everything from wood and rock and marble, to iron, quartz and gold. If you want to see some rubies and sapphires and emeralds and diamonds then this is the place to go. The gold ore is a surprise because it looks like a dull piece of sparkly stone. It's a bit like the ugly duckling I suppose (a bit like me)... on the outside it might look rough and ugly (like me) and dirty and dusty and cut up and ruined (like me) and loved by no one (me) and worth next to nothing (me), but once you've polished it up it suddenly becomes the most beautiful thing in the universe (me!) and coveted by women all around the world (me!) and worth bazillions (me!).

Probably the most overlooked and under-appreciated part of the museum is the museum itself -- the building. You don't notice it when you're a kid because you are too busy running around screaming your head off, but when you take some time to look up above the display cases you'll see that it's every bit as impressive as a palace or a church. There are statues of animals everywhere you look -- they are climbing up the columns and across the tops of arches, wrapped around the banisters and guarding the tops of doorways. They don't have statues of saints in here: they have gorillas and Griffins and winged dragons. I could quite easily lapse into my usual boring rant here, about how we don't build anything of this quality anymore, but it's true: we don't. (I am on the verge of a rant, but I will reign myself in.) But I'll just say this one thing: if this museum didn't already exist then it would be impossible to create, because as soon as you killed your first animal or felled your first tree you'd have three thousand Greenpeace protesters marching past the front door. Genocide used to be about people -- now they use the same word about oak trees and chickens. If Charles Darwin had set out on the Beagle today, and Greenpeace discovered that he was keeping a load of captured animals on board, they would have stormed his boat and let them loose.

If you want to see more dead animals in glass jars then try the Hunterian Museum.

Nelson's Column

ADDRESS Nelson's Column, Trafalgar Square - map 8b **TRAINS** Embankment, Charing Cross, Leicester Square (all zone 1) **BUSES** 3, 6, 9, 11, 13, 15, 23, 24, 29, 88, 91, 139, 159, 176, 453 **TIME REQUIRED** 5 mins

Easy to get to? ★★★ Good for kids? ★☆☆
Value for money? free Worth a visit? ★★★

I read in a book that Hitler planned to uproot Nelson's Column and transport it back to Berlin after he beat us in World War II. That's what we should have done -- we should have nicked the Brandenburg Gate and put it across the top of Whitehall. We missed our chance there, ah well. Too late now. We'll know better for next time.

The tourists have got their selfie-sticks are out in force today. I can count about twenty people brandishing their flagless flags, waiting the right time to pull the trigger and shoot. They look like an infantry line of muskets and rifles. They are all lined up around the base of Nelson's Column practising their smiles inside the little two inch camera window... making sure the wind isn't messing up their hair... rearranging their lips to show their teeth a bit better... making sure the landmark is right behind them so they can prove they were really here, and then... get ready... *oh darn it!*... now somebody has selfishly walked into their camera shot so they will have to start all over again.

They've been standing here for two minutes now and they haven't looked at the column once. All they've done is stare at themselves in the mirror, but that's modern tourism for you: it's just a great big treasure hunt. They visit a location and take a photo of themselves standing in front of it. Then they chuck the photo in the cupboard and never look at it ever again. They probably won't even bother to print it off. No one visits a place just to sit down and stare anymore -- so do me a favour and take ten minutes to stare at the scene. Put your smile away for five minutes and sit in the seats around the edge of Trafalgar Square and listen to the noise. *You're in London!*

It's quite an impressive column. It's very tall, that is for sure, which is what you want in the middle of a square. And it's got somebody worthy of a column on top: Horatio Nelson. It's very hard to build something like Nelson's Column these days because we don't produce any more heroes. Churchill could have pulled it off, but even he would have looked a bit incongruous with his bowler hat and cigar puffing out his mouth. He is a statue man, not a column one. So who else could we put up there? Marlborough and Wellington, and that's about it. Certainly nobody else from the last two hundred years. We just don't produce people like Nelson anymore.

If you ask someone about Nelson today then they'll probably say, *er... he's that boat guy, that bloke with a pirate patch over his eye? That bloke with one arm?* They might vaguely recall the Battle of Trafalgar if they paid attention at school. It's funny, isn't it? You can stand on top of one of the tallest monuments in London, and have its grandest square named after your most momentous battle, and 95% of people still won't have a clue what you did to achieve it. *This is Admiral Nelson, people!* One of the greatest Britons who ever lived.

He might also have been the vainest (he wasn't into modesty), so he would have loved standing on top of that column. If ever a man was destined to stand on top of a column, it's him. The Duke of Wellington would have been happy standing at the bottom, but not Nelson. I've read stories about him wearing all his medals at once. He even wore his medals on the day he got shot, striding around the deck of HMS Victory, painting a nice shiny target on his jacket for the French sharpshooters to aim at. They would have seen those garish gongs glinting through the gun smoke. If you go to the National Maritime Museum and look at the uniform he was wearing that day, then you can even see where the bullet ripped a hole a couple of inches above his medal crosshairs -- vanity did him in.

The four bronze plaques around the bottom of the column represent his four most famous victories: St. Vincent in 1797 (where he still had two arms, but one eye); the Nile in 1798 (one arm, one eye); Copenhagen in 1801 (one arm, one eye, lost a shoe); and finally his death scene at the Battle of Trafalgar.

168 | London: A Visitor's Guide

Kids are forever climbing on top of the giant lions around the base. It's one of the unwritten rules of London that if you're still a kid then you're duty bound to climb on their back and have your photo taken by your worrying mum. I haven't got the faintest idea why they do it, because those things are colossal. I wouldn't climb on one anymore than I would a real lion, because if you slip off you are going to crack your nut on the concrete. Maybe I am just getting old.

If you're interested in Nelson then try the Nelson exhibit at the National Maritime Museum. You can also visit HMS Victory in Portsmouth Historic Dockyard.

Old Operating Theatre

ADDRESS 9A St. Thomas Street, Southwark - map 10c **TRAINS** London Bridge (zone 1) **BUSES** 17, 21, 35, 40, 43, 47, 48, 133, 141, 149, 343, 381, 521, RV1 **PRICE** Adult £6.50; Senior £5; Child (under 16) £3.50; Family (up to 2 ad+4 ch) £13.90 **OPEN** 10.30 AM to 5 PM (Mon-Sun) **WEB** thegarret.org.uk **TEL** 0207 188 2679 **TIME REQUIRED** 30-45 mins

Easy to get to? ★★★ Good for kids? ☆☆☆
Value for money? ☆☆☆ Worth a visit? ☆☆☆

This is a strange old place. It's a very modern street outside, with busy cars and concrete offices, but as soon as you're through the door it's straight up some winding wooden stairs like a castle turret. There are thirty-two very steep stairs up into an atmospheric little loft with wooden rafters and creaky old floorboards. It reminds me of my grandad's old attic. It's the kind of place that birds might roost. And it's just you and a few tourists nosing around the old tables and displays.

The museum is all about doctors and medicines in the early 19th-century, and the cabinets are full of gruesome treatments like worm cakes and maggot wash. (I think I'd rather be ill than have the cure!) They've got a lot of torture equipment too: vice-like forceps and blunt blades. Some of the forceps are big enough to pull a football out. Then there's all the tubes and trumpets and funnels that they used to stick up your... I won't say where (I don't want to spoil your dinner).

They've got a wonky old apothecary table, full of dusty old bottles and baskets of snuff and seeds and weeds and leaves. Pickled hearts and human kidneys too, and a nice slice of uterus, if that is your fancy. It reminds me of a witch's kitchen: like a little old cottage that you'd stumble across in the woods. All that is missing is a big cauldron to cook up her dinner.

They can probably cure anything up here. *Are you bald?* Have a few seeds of this, and you'll be a werewolf within a week. *Have you got an insightly birthmark?* Just rub some of this freeze-dried bat's dung on it, and it will disappear before you go to bed. *Do you have nightmares?* No problem... just swallow some of these crushed up elephant's bones, and I promise it will be sweet dreams for you.

The second room is also the last room (there are only two real rooms) -- the old operating theatre itself. It's like a little amphitheatre I suppose, made entirely of wood. The students stood on the balconies at the back looking over a couple of tables in the centre, and that's where the poor patient must have sat.

Try and imagine what it must have been like to lay naked on that table, whilst two hundred people stood around the balconies watching you scream! There was no general anaesthetic in those days, so you would have been wide awake whilst the doctor chopped all your bits up. As the blood and tears filled up your eyes all you'd see is a semi-circle wall of ghouls staring back at you. People died in that room. People got worked on and chopped up and cut and sliced and held down tight so they couldn't jump about. Imagine that wooden floor washed in sloppy blood... people slipping and sliding and trying to teach the new recruits some science as the poor bugger on the table was writhing and crying out in agony. *Keep still, man!* Stop writhing about for chrissakes! I'm trying to teach some students here!

So is it Worth a visit? Well... I'm glad that I saw it because I'm nosey like that, but unless you've got a particular interest in medicine then you're better off spending your money elsewhere. The price is a bit silly for just two rooms, and you'll be probably be out of the door in thirty minutes.

If you're interested in medicine then try the Florence Nightingale Museum and Alexander Fleming Laboratory Museum.

Old Royal Naval College

ADDRESS Old Royal Naval College, King William Walk, Greenwich - map 11d **TRAINS** Cutty Sark DLR (zones 2&3) **BUSES** 129, 177, 180, 188, 199, 286, 386 **PRICE** Free **OPEN** Grounds: 8 AM to 11 PM (Mon-Sun); Painted Hall and Chapel: 10 AM to 6 PM (Mon-Sun, last week of May-Sep); 10 AM to 5 PM (Mon-Sun, Oct-third week of May) **WEB** ornc.org **TEL** 0208 269 4747 **TIME REQUIRED** 1 hour

Easy to get to? ★★★ Good for kids? ☆☆☆
Value for money? free Worth a visit? ★★★

My favourite moments at the Old Royal Naval College all involve me walking around in the sun (because it's always sunny here) and hearing classical music drifting out of the open windows. If ever a place was made for classical music then it's this place. You feel like there should be some Regency dandies walking around the gravel paths, and people with big white wigs and parasols. This is Christopher Wren country. He certainly earned his wages when he designed this place.

Do me a favour: the first time you come here make sure you are sitting on a boat from Big Ben. You have to see the two wings from the middle of the river to get the full effect. When the boat pulls into the pier you will have the Cutty Sark on your right and the college on your left. Resist the temptation to walk inland and have a stroll along the waterfront instead. When you round the corner of the first wing the whole vista will open up and there's your first photograph, right there.

Back in the old days this was where we trained all of our sailors and admirals and captains, and you can just picture them can't you... strolling around the grounds in their smart white uniforms and shiny stiff caps (I'm thinking of Richard Gere in *An Officer And A Gentleman*). But all you see nowadays are the tourists and teachers and music students carting around their big bassoons and trumpets and drums, because the righthand-side is home to the

Trinity College of Music (that's where all of the classical music comes from).

It is certainly worth walking around the whole of the grounds, but there are only two real rooms that you can look inside. You will find them on the inside middle of each wing -- the famous Painted Hall and Chapel.

The Painted Hall dates back to a time when the college was a hospital and a retirement home for naval seamen. It was supposed to be their dining hall until Hawksmoor made it too good to ruin. As soon as he finished the paintings they kicked out the eaters and used it for balls and important events. I feel a bit daft describing it -- because it's one of those rooms that you really have to see to believe. It's like trying to describing a pretty woman on paper... yes she's get blonde hair and blue eyes, but so did Margaret Thatcher, and you wouldn't put her on the cover of *Vogue*. Sometimes it's better just to say nothing and let you be gobsmacked when you walk through the door.

So let me just say this one thing: Hawksmoor spent nineteen years painting this one solitary room and it earned him a knighthood... so that goes some way to describing how grand it is.

The Chapel pales in comparison but it's still one of the prettiest religious rooms in London. It's not the painting that impresses, but all the carved plasterwork on the ceiling (did I really just say that?). It looks like one of those Wedgwood china teapots, with a raised white design on a pale blue background.

Whilst you're here you might like to visit the Cutty Sark, National Maritime Museum and Royal Observatory.

One New Change

ADDRESS One New Change (round the back of St. Paul's) - map 5e **TRAINS** St. Paul's (zone 1) **BUSES** 4, 8, 25, 56, 100, 172, 242, 521 **PRICE** Free **OPEN** Shops: 10 AM to 7 PM (Mon-Wed, Fri); 10 AM to 8 PM (Thu); 10 AM to 6 PM (Sat); 12 noon to 6 PM (Sun) -- The restaurants, bars and roof terrace stay open later **WEB** onenewchange.com **TEL** 0207 002 8900 **TIME REQUIRED** 20-30 mins

Easy to get to? ★★★ Good for kids? ★★☆
Value for money? free Worth a visit? ★★☆

I don't normally recommend visiting a shopping centre on a day out, but One New Change is no ordinary shopping centre -- because this one has got an open-air observation deck on the roof.

You can find it round the back end of St. Paul's Cathedral (it's that big dark-glass building across the street). But whatever you do, don't climb up the stairs or use the escalators... because if you do that you'll be missing out on a treat. What you need to do is find the central lift and have a ride in that instead. As you rise up the building you can stare out of the window and see the back end of St. Paul's climbing up with you. When you're about level with the bottom of the dome you can step out onto the roof and take in the skyline. They've got a little cafe up there too, but you don't have to go in it if you don't want. You can just walk over to the barrier and peer over the edge.

The last time I came here I inexplicably described the view as being a bit so-so (I must have been in a terrible mood!) but I have totally changed my tune since then, because now I think it's well worth a visit. Maybe I just like looking at St. Paul's more than I used to, because I'd happily stare at that pile of bricks for thirty minutes. I actually like looking at the lines and the decorations on the sides of buildings now (I'm starting to lose my mind). I don't watch pretty women anymore... I stare at the stones and the rooftops. And standing up here in the breezy wind is a great way to see the stuff you can't glimpse from the street -- it's almost like your prize for riding the lift. I think that's one of the reasons why I don't like modern skyscraper architecture... because it invariably looks the same all the way up to the top. If you've seen the bottom three floors then you've seen the whole lot -- they don't bother putting carved columns and gargoyles on the 50th floor because there's no point. The most you'll get is a load of aerials and satellite dishes. Compare that with the green dome and golden cross of Christopher Wren's attempt...

You get a great view of the dome -- in fact, it's probably the best view of the dome from anywhere in the City. You also get a nice view of The Shard and the top half of the London Eye. If you can't see the Tate Modern across the river then you need to get your eyes tested, but see if you can spot the top of Parliament and the Ministry of Defence building (you will really need to know your London for that one). I will give you some bonus points if you can pick out the top of Westminster Cathedral... and I do mean the Cathedral, not the Abbey!

If you really want to show off then try and find the line of Fleet Street. [Hint: you need to look for the spire of St. Dunstan's.] If you follow that along then it will lead you to the clock hanging off the side of the Royal Courts of Justice. You're not allowed to go home until you locate that.

The best free view is at the Sky Garden.

Parliament Hill

ADDRESS Parliament Hill, Hampstead Heath
TRAINS Hampstead (zones 2&3), and 20 min walk **BUSES** 214, C2, C11 **TIME REQUIRED** 1-1½ hours

Easy to get to? ★☆☆   Good for kids? ★☆☆
Value for money? free Worth a visit? ★★☆

I thought I'd have a stroll up Parliament Hill today. It's about time I did some exercise. The last time I did some proper exercise was about five thousand years ago, when Parliament Hill was still covered in ice and snow.

You have to prepare yourself for a bit of a trek because Hampstead train station is about a mile away from the lookout point, and some of that is trudging up a hill. So come out of the station and head down the slope, along Hampstead High Street, and take a quick left up Flask Walk. This pretty little lane is full of cottage shops selling summer clothes and sesame seed snacks. I get the impression that nothing bad ever happens down here. No one drops litter, no one gets mugged. Even the rainclouds blow over so they don't have to urinate on the flowers. Then it merges into a leafy street with picture postcard gardens and old-style lantern lampposts. It has a really nice village-feel to it, with uneven streets and wonky old brick walls. Pink quilts of petals and dropped blossom have fallen on the pavement, and everywhere is the Sunday sound of birds and people banging hammers, doing bits of DIY.

I hope it's sunny when you decide to come, because that's when you're going to get the best out of this place.

Keep walking nice and slow up Well Walk, where people are strolling about with little yappy dogs and flip-flops. I spy an old guy taking his parcel to the postbox... he looks older than the trees. Everything seems to be covered in lilac and lavender or wrapped around in ivy. I'm guessing that a team of grandmas is in charge of the decor.

See if you can spot John Constable's house as you walk along (look out for the blue plaque on the wall).

After 10-15 minutes you should reach the boundary of the park, so get ready for a sudden mood change. Because soon you'll be marching downhill on a stony, muddy path, winding its way through a dark and gloomy wood. The path is walled-in by nettles and fat trees, armoured-up in leaves and chains of thorns. It's all sawn-off tree trunks and cracked boughs, buzzing with moths and midges darting around your eyes. Every fifty-feet you'll come across a big felled giant, like a boat of wood, a shipwrecked log -- riddled with barnacles of fungi and ferns. They remind me of some burnt-out tanks on the road to Berlin. They are the broken bones of the wood, being feasted on by flies. I wonder how long they have been lying there.

It's quite a spooky scene actually. All of the sunlight seems to be sitting above the canopy of trees, waiting for permission to enter. It's as if the time-zone changes fifty-feet above your head. Up in the sky it's still sunny Sunday morning, but down here on earth it's gloomy Monday.

Eventually you'll come across a little green field on the right -- keep going past that (you are nearly there). Fifteen minutes after entering the wood the trees will split and you'll be seeing your first sight of skyline. You'll hit the open air and discover that you have climbed the hill without even realising it. The whole brow of the mound is covered in wispy tall grass and pacing through it is a bit like trudging through a deep drift of snow.

There's not much point in me giving you any more directions, because there are about a million different dusty paths to follow (none of them signposted). Just keep aiming in the same general direction around the brow of the hill, and eventually you will see your goal. It's a mound that looks like no other, and you will know straight away that you have found the right one. It rises cleanly out of the woods like a bald head out of a jumper. If you pick the right path then you'll see the top of The Shard rising out of the top as you climb it, like someone is poking a needle through the skin of a balloon. Then you'll have the whole of London laid out before you, from Canary Wharf in the east (in the west -- because you're looking south from Hampstead), all the way to Westminster.

They've got a few benches and a silver plaque to help you pick out the landmarks, but half of the fun is in trying to tease them out of the skyline. It was very sunny today so all of the colours were drowned out, but I could still see Canary Wharf with ease, and the Gherkin and The Shard too, but St. Paul's took a little longer (it's still easy though!). And what about the Houses of Parliament? If you can spot that without looking at the plaque then give yourself a pat on the back (they label it as 'Victoria Tower' on the plaque). The farthest thing that I could see today was the tall mast at Crystal Palace, which is about ten miles away.

So then... here comes the million dollar question: which view is better, Parliament Hill or Primrose Hill? I would have to say that Parliament Hill is better, without a shadow of a doubt. The walk is far nicer too, but Primrose Hill is a lot closer to the centre of town, so it won't take up so much of your day. [Note: There are no refreshments at the top of either, so you definitely need to bring a drink.]

If you enjoy climbing up hills, then try Primrose Hill and Greenwich Hill.

Parliament Square

ADDRESS Parliament Square, Westminster - map 8d **TRAINS** Westminster (zone 1)
BUSES 11, 24, 148, 211 **TIME REQUIRED** 10-20 mins

Easy to get to? ★★★   Good for kids? ★☆☆
Value for money? free Worth a visit? ★★★

Parliament Square has changed a lot over the last few years. When Ken Livingstone was in charge (a leftie mayor) he was happy for it to descend into a messy cub camp of bleeding hearts and long-haired liberals, who'd plant their homemade banners and placards railing against whichever war was their flavour of the month. Who is the bad guy today? they'd ask. *Israel?* Yeah... Woo hoo! Let's have a shout about them. *George Bush?* Yeah, we hate George Bush and Tony Blair and Maggie Thatcher the milk snatcher! Arrest them all for war crimes! And they'd shout down their loudhailers and smash their pots and pans about on the pavement and it was just... *awful*. It was actually quite embarrassing.

I might be talking a load nonsense here -- and this is going to make me sound very middle-aged and unsympathetic -- but it sometimes seemed to me that protesting in Parliament Square was just a fig leaf for begging. It became a job for drop-outs and rebels. That is how they would spend their days. They would set up their posters and placards and beg for 'donations' from passers-by, and the police would be powerless to act because they'd all start banging on about free speech. It wouldn't look very good if the police started silencing the public fifty feet from Parliament, would it? So they got more and more confident and moved in with their camping stoves and tents. You could see all of their dirty plates and cutlery and rubbish all over the place -- Lord knows what the tourists must have thought of it all, just fifty yards from Big Ben.

But then Boris came along (a Tory mayor) and sanity was restored. It was like spring had come: all the grass grew back -- *literally*. He must have passed a law that prevented people from sleeping overnight, because all the tents came down in a flash.

So I've only got one thing left to moan about now, and that's the subject of the statues -- I don't know who half of them are. I mean, who the hell is Ian Christian Smuts? Where is Gladstone? And where is Pitt? Even the totally inoffensive Attlee is nowhere to be seen. And what about Walpole? Surely he deserves a place as our first-ever PM. [Note: If you're looking for Disraeli then he is there, but he is confusingly called Beaconsfield -- because he was the Earl of Beaconsfield.]

Personally I would like to see Maggie Thatcher up there as well, but I know that is totally impossible: someone would just come along and knock her head off within a week.

If you're looking for the greatest parliamentary champion of all-time -- Oliver Cromwell -- then you'll find him shunted off to the other side of the road, sunk into a walled-off pit that you can't approach. And that's the problem with living in PC Britain -- we're too scared of upsetting people. We can't honour Thatcher in case it upsets the students and the miners and the Scots. And we can't give Cromwell pride of place in case it upsets the Irish. So we're stuck with people that either everyone loves, or nobody knows. That's why Abraham Lincoln and Mandela went up in Parliament Square: because they are totally safe. No one ever has a bad word to say about those fellas. If you come back in ten years time then we'll probably have a statue of Ghandi and Mother Theresa too -- no more British Prime Ministers though. [An amusing note: a couple of months after I wrote this review they unveiled a brand-new statue in Parliament Square. Guess who it was? It was Ghandi! And I'm not even joking -- you can find him near Abraham Lincoln.]

Abraham Lincoln is the one that really gets my goat because he's got the biggest statue in Parliament Square. *Why?* Why did we do that? He's an American for chrissakes. Take it down and stick it in Grosvenor Square instead, along with all the other American statues. Somewhere that we don't have to look at it. I don't mind Nelson Mandela so much, but he's already got another one just half-a-mile away on Southbank. Why do we have to have so many foreign leaders taking up space in Parliament Square? Haven't we got enough worthies of our own?

But listen to me... I'm having a huge old moan here, without telling you any of the good stuff! The last thing I want to do is put you off going to Parliament Square, because it's one of the must-see sights in London. So forget the statues and do what I do... focus on the buildings.

The best photograph of Big Ben can be shot from the middle of the grass (or halfway across Westminster Bridge). If you want to hear the ding dong bells then you don't have to hang around for the hour, because he sounds out four notes at quarter-past, plus an extra four notes every fifteen minutes after that. So it's four notes at quarter-past... eight at half-past... then twelve and sixteen on the hour (which is the full tune). The full tune is then followed by the famous bongs that count out the hour. If you want to set your watch then you have to listen for the first bong after the full tune. *Confused?* I probably could have explained that a bit better but all true Londoners know this stuff from birth -- you will have to learn!

If you follow the road down to the far end of Parliament then you can see the Jewel Tower across the street. If you're lucky then you might be able to see a few politicians being interviewed on the lawn as well, because that's where all the dolly birds gather with their news camera crews. The Jewel Tower is a rare survivor from the original Palace of Westminster (the biggest survivor is Westminster Hall, at the Big Ben end of Parliament).

While you're here you can look the Houses of Parliament and Westminster Abbey. Downing Street is just down Whitehall.

Petrie Museum

ADDRESS Petrie Museum, University College London, Bloomsbury - map 3c **TRAINS** Goodge Street, Russell Square (both zone 1) **BUSES** 10, 14, 24, 29, 73, 134, 390 **PRICE** Free **OPEN** 1 PM to 5 PM (Tue-Sat) **WEB** ucl.ac.uk/museums/petrie **TEL** 0207 679 2884 **TIME REQUIRED** 45-60 mins

Easy to get to? ★★★ Good for kids? ☆☆☆
Value for money? free Worth a visit? ★☆☆

The Petrie Museum of Egyptian Archaeology is situated right inside the grounds of University College London so you have to stroll past all the students to get to it. It is student central around there and you feel like a fish out of water amongst all the scruffy kids. Luckily I am even more scruffy than them, so I don't think they noticed the interloper within their midst. And being a university museum, it keeps very strange opening hours. I'm guessing that it must be staffed by the students themselves because when I walked up to the door at 11 AM and pressed the buzzer by the window, he snoozily said that he doesn't open for another two hours. I think I must have disturbed his sleep. So here I am, sitting waiting for the place to wake up.

That could have been me once, believe it or not (you are going to find this hard to believe), because I actually won a place at UCL to study Egyptology. But being a dumb idiot, I quit the course before it started. I didn't even bother to turn up for the first day. I wonder what job I would have ended up with? There's not much demand for Egyptologists in London. If I played my cards right I could have had my own pyramid by now. That's why I'm still sitting here, waiting for the place to open, because I've got a lingering interest in anything Egyptian.

One hour later... well that was a waste of time! When you read their website they give you the impression that the shelves are all dark and dusty and stacked with magical artefacts from a Hammer House horror movie. I quote: "Lighting within the museum is less than ideal, and we offer the visitors the loan of torches". Well, it's not like that at all... it's just a couple of school-like rooms filled with tall glass cabinets and they are all very brightly lit.

They've got two wooden sarcophagi at the far end, but that's about it for the big stuff. We are not talking Tutankhamun's tomb here. There is nothing on show that Indiana Jones would want to steal. How can I best describe it? It's the kind of stuff that you might find on an ancient Egyptian skip -- cracked cups, pots, busted bowls and bits of broken pottery. I'm sure that it must be very interesting if you're a scholar or a student, but for everyone else it's just odds and sods.

They've got piles and piles (and piles) and piles (and piles) and piles of brooches and bangles and beads. They've got some game boards and pieces too, and some stone ducks and seashells. A lot of combs and bone cutlery, and the inevitable collection of stones and broken bits of flint. They've got some funerary stele too, and quite a lot of stone slabs with carvings and hieroglyphs on, but nothing that's going to knock your socks off.

My favourite part of the collection was a cabinet full of death masks... people's portraits painted on crumbling shaves of wood. Some of the colours are still fresh like a daisy and could have been painted last week. It's quite interesting to stare at a lifelike face from two thousand years ago, complete with a dodgy-looking moustache and beard. It's probably the closest we'll ever get to an ancient Egyptian photograph. Judging by the picture, I don't think us humans have changed much in two thousand years; we still have a short back and sides at the barbers, and are too lazy to shave our stubble off.

So to sum up: don't bother going unless you're a scholar. If you're a tourist with an interest in Egyptology then you should definitely head for the British Museum instead. But don't get me wrong... I'm not having a moan. This museum is clearly meant to be an educational place for the university, and not a stop on the tourist trail. So if you come with that in mind then maybe you will like it.

There is more about Egypt at the British Museum and Sir John Soane's Museum. And don't forget Cleopatra's Needle!

Piccadilly Circus

ADDRESS Piccadilly Circus - map 8a **TRAINS** Leicester Square, Piccadilly Circus (both zone 1) **BUSES** 3, 6, 12, 13, 14, 19, 23, 88, 139, 159, 453 **TIME REQUIRED** 10 mins

Easy to get to? ★★★ Good for kids? ★★☆
Value for money? free Worth a visit? ★★★

I arrived at Piccadilly Circus nice and early this morning, or so I thought, so I could get there before all the tourists came flocking -- it didn't work. There were bazillions of them already... they were like the pigeons in Trafalgar Square, all sitting on the steps waiting for something to happen. It must be the most popular place in London for foreigners to congregate I reckon. They must have it written on their plane ticket that they have to descend on the place as soon as they step off the airplane.

There's not actually a lot to do at Piccadilly Circus, surprisingly. Once you've taken a photo of Eros and the neon lights then you are pretty much done. They've got the Ripley Museum on the corner, if you fancy that (I don't recommend it though -- read my review), but apart from that you may as well join the tourists sitting on the steps.

Piccadilly Circus was probably the first part of London that I got to know well as a kid because they had a big Tower Records on the corner (gone now), and an HMV in the Trocadero Centre (also gone); and when you're 16 years-old they are where you do your weekly shop. Forget food and groceries -- who needs food? It was all CDs and DVDs (videos in my day). Burger King has disappeared too -- it's Barclays Bank now. The only things that have remained the same are the neon lights, the fountain and the crowds. And me. I'm still here.

I know this sounds a bit daft, but there are no benches at Piccadilly Circus -- not a single one. It's full of traffic lights and litter and pigeons and tourists. Personally I would get rid of all the tourists and put a few benches in. And I would shoot the pigeons. But the litter can stay.

Whenever I come here during the day it's always heaving with traffic and tourists, and when I come here at night it's exactly the same thing, because they all flock here to see the neon lights and Eros.

Eros is to London, what the Manneken Pis is to Brussels: it's how you tell people you've been to England. You take a selfie in front of the bright red Coca Cola sign, and everyone thinks that you've 'done' London. That sign is right up there alongside Big Ben and Tower Bridge as one of the must-see sights in the city. Coca Cola has constantly hogged the biggest spot ever since I can remember. I wonder how many bottles that sign sells? If I advertised my guidebook up there how many do you think I would sell? I would probably quadruple my sales figures overnight. I'd be selling... what... four copies? Or maybe even five copies a week -- I'd be rich!

As for the Eros fountain... well... that has been the source of many, many arguments, and I am in the mood for a right old ding-dong so let's have an argument right now -- come on, between you and me. Let's have it out! (This may end up in a fist fight.)

I will begin: *He's not Eros.*

I don't care what you think you know, or what anybody has told you, or how many guidebooks you've read saying that he is, because I am telling you right now that he is not Eros. Just because he's stark naked and holding a bow and arrow does not make him bloody Eros. Robin Hood carried a bow and arrow and no one thought that he was Eros did they?

Okay: now it's your turn. Tell me why you think it's Eros. Obviously I can't hear what you're saying so you can blather on all day and it doesn't matter, because I am not going to pay any attention anyway. I am the Londoner. I am the expert on Greek Gods. So I am right and you are wrong and that is all there is to it -- he's not Eros!

So who is he then? Well, the correct answer is the Angel of Christian Charity (whoever that is). But if you try and enlighten the tourists they won't believe you -- they don't want to. They bring their wives and girlfriends along to hold hands and have a kiss and a cuddle under the fountain, thinking that the Greek God of Love will shower them with a lifetime of wedded bliss. But he won't. Because it's not him. It's the Angel of *Charity*, so the most he'll bestow is five years of happiness followed by fifty years of misery. After which she'll probably die of old age and you'll get dementia in an old peoples' home. But if you try telling that to the tourists they won't listen; they just burst into tears. (I'm thinking about giving up writing and becoming a tour guide.)

Sometimes I wonder what Eros would look like if we built him today. He wouldn't have a bow and arrow, would he? -- because we don't use those any more. He'd probably have a machine gun. I've never understood what is so romantic about Eros anyway. If I was in love with somebody then the last thing I'd want is a chubby little kid coming along firing arrows at her. If I wanted to fire arrows at her then I'd damn-well do it myself -- I don't need a 5-year-old hitman in nappies.

The other argument that everyone has is whether his bow is pointing down Shaftesbury Avenue. There is an urban myth that Eros (although it's not Eros -- but I'm not getting into that again) is "burying his shaft" up Shaftesbury Avenue. We've got Stephen Fry to thank for this cock-and-bull story because he gave it as one of his answers on QI. But I am telling you right now that it's not. It's actually pointing in the complete opposite direction towards the southern half of Regent Street -- the part that leads down towards the Duke of York's Column. And I should know, because I am standing underneath the damn thing as I'm writing this! So if anybody tries to tell you something different then just tell them they're talking nonsense.

Have you ever been to a wood at night and heard the bats cheeping in the trees? Well Piccadilly Circus is a bit like that, only the buildings are the trees, and the car horns are the bats. Honest to god there is a horn blasting every ten-seconds in this place -- it is one of the busiest junctions in London. All the main roads come and bundle up into a knot -- you've got Leicester Square to the east, Trafalgar Square down Haymarket, the West End up Shaftesbury Avenue, and the grand facades of Regent Street curving off to the north. And then there's Piccadilly of course, with the Royal Academy and Ritz Hotel disappearing into the west.

Postman's Park

ADDRESS Postman's Park (entrances in St Martin's Le-Grand and King Edward St) - map 4f **TRAINS** St. Paul's (zone 1) **BUSES** 4, 8, 25, 100, 141, 172, 242, 521 **OPEN** 8 AM to 7 PM, or dusk (Mon-Sun) **WEB** cityoflondon.gov.uk/things-to-do/green-spaces/city-gardens/visitor-information/pages/postman's-park.aspx **TIME REQUIRED** 15 mins

Easy to get to? ★★★ Good for kids? ☆☆☆
Value for money? free Worth a visit? ★☆☆

This isn't the kind of place that you'd make a detour for; it's just a nice little piece of green to see if you happen to be visiting the Museum of London (because it's next-door). It's situated in the middle of some posh office blocks and you can have a peer into the windows and watch all the workers lounging around at their desks, having a lazy stare out of the window, with their minds on other things. There are some plants and trees and benches as well, so you can have a quiet sit down and escape the noise for five minutes.

The reason you need to come here is not for the plants, but for the covered wooden walkway at the back. Have a closer look at that, and you will see a collection of creamy green and blue ceramic tiles nailed up on the wall. They are all more than a century old, and commemorate fifty-four brave souls who gave up their lives to save others. It's like a hall of fame for heroes, I suppose. Dead heroes.

Each tile includes a couple of sentences to explain how they met their grisly end. There are quite a few blokes who threw their mates to safety, before getting flattened by a steam train. Another lady battled up a burning staircase to save her mother, only to get roasted alive in the fire. One poor guy got swallowed up in quicksand, as he tried to drag some kids from the pit. It's all really cheerful stuff -- the perfect place to eat your lunch.

My favourite tale is about a woman who tried to extinguish some flames in her inflammable dress only to -- you guessed it -- die in the fire. One guy fell through some ice in Highgate Pond, and another one got blown up in a sugar factory. There are stories about runaway horses... kids tangled up in seaweed... sinking ships... suicidal lunatic women... you name it, it's here.

It's all quite depressing really, now that I come to think of it. Maybe you shouldn't come here after all.

Primrose Hill

ADDRESS Primrose Hill (north of Regent's Park) **TRAINS** Camden Town, Chalk Farm (both zone 2) **BUSES** 274 **OPEN** 5 AM to 5 PM (Mon-Sun, Jan); 5 AM to 6 PM (Mon-Sun, Feb); 5 AM to 7 PM (Mon-Sun, early Mar, early Oct); 5 AM to 8 PM (Mon-Sun, late Mar, Sep); 5 AM to 9 PM (Mon-Sun, Apr, Aug); 5 AM to 9.30 PM (Mon-Sun, May-Jul); 5 AM to 5.30 PM (Mon-Sun, late Oct); 5 AM to 4.30 PM (Mon-Sun, Nov-Dec) **WEB** royalparks.org.uk/parks/the-regents-park/things-to-see-and-do/primrose-hill **TIME REQUIRED** 45-60 mins

Easy to get to? ★★☆ Good for kids? ★★☆ Value for money? free Worth a visit? ★★☆

The first time you clap eyes on Primrose Hill you'll kid yourself that it's an easy climb. The way that people talk about it, I was half expecting there to be snow on top and mountain goats clinging to the side. But trust me: once you start climbing you'll wish it had a cable car, because this hill is a *lot* steeper than it looks. It's the kind of hill that makes you turn around and look at the view halfway up, just so you can have a couple of minutes rest. Then you'll sit down and re-tie your already tight shoes so you can catch your breath. But when you finally reach the summit (five hours later, if you're unfit like me) you'll be looking down on the whole of London. You'll have an uninterrupted view from the London Eye to Canary Wharf.

They've put a few benches on the top and a metal plaque to help you pick out the places, but where's the ice cream van? There's no burger van either. If you want a drink then you'll have to bring it with you.

Now we're up here shall we have a game of I-Spy? I'll shout out some landmarks and you have to find them.

If you can't see The Shard then you need to get your eyes tested, so we'll skip that one. The London Eye and St. Paul's are extremely easy as well, so we'll forget those. But how about the Gherkin and Canary Wharf? The Houses of Parliament are quite hard, and Westminster Cathedral will really test you (and I do mean the *cathedral* -- not the abbey). If you really want to show off then try and find the ArcelorMittal Orbit, because that's too new to even appear on their plaque (you'll have to be fairly knowledgeable to even know what that is).

After you've seen the buildings you can turn your attention to the humans, because you can see all sorts of puffed-out people up here: people in running shoes and women in high heels; people with stopwatches and people with giant tripods and zoom lens cameras. One guy has just chucked his frisbee off the summit and the wind has lifted it fifty feet in the air, and dumped it halfway down the hill. It's very popular with joggers and dogs as well... and mountain climbers. I'm standing next to a bloke who has dressed himself up like Edmund Hillary, complete with spiked shoes and a ski pole. He's staring out from the summit like he's conquered the top of the world. *Er...* you're only ten minutes from Camden, mate.

You might enjoy the views from Greenwich Hill and Parliament Hill as well.

Princess Diana Memorial Fountain

180 | London: A Visitor's Guide

ADDRESS Princess Diana Memorial Fountain, Hyde Park - map 6d **TRAINS** Hyde Park Corner (zone 1) and 15 min walk, South Kensington (zone 1) and 15 min walk **BUSES** 9, 10, 52, 452 **OPEN** 10 AM to 4 PM (Nov-Feb); 10 AM to 6 PM (Mar, Oct); 10 AM to 8 PM (Apr-Aug); 10 AM to 7 PM (Sep) **WEB** royalparks.org.uk/parks/hyde-park/things-to-see-and-do/memorials,-fountains-and-statues/diana-memorial-fountain **TIME REQUIRED** 10 mins

Easy to get to? ★★★ Good for kids? ★★☆
Value for money? free Worth a visit? ☆☆☆

Some people believe she was stuck in a loveless marriage, shunned by the Royal Family and hounded by a relentless press... while other people think she was a bit of a fruitcake. I couldn't possibly comment (well, okay... I thought she was a fruitcake as well). But there is one thing that I am definitely sure about: she didn't deserve to be lumbered with a memorial as poor as this. But that's what happens when you annoy the Queen: you end up with a concrete river as your tombstone. Most of the royals get a six-foot statue in the street or a polished plaque in Westminster Abbey -- Diana got a concrete water drain fifty feet from the cafe toilets. Even I deserve a monument better than this, and I'm a total loser.

If it was just supposed to be a normal fountain, built as a garden ornament or a work of art, then okay -- fair enough. But it's supposed to be a memorial to *Princess Di*. It doesn't make you think of her, though, or remember her, so as a memorial it's a total fail. If it wasn't for a picture of her face by the gate then you wouldn't even know what it was -- you'd just think it was something they'd put up for the kids.

Let me explain to you exactly what it is... so you can fully appreciate how rubbish it is. It's basically just a big circle of stone on a flat field, like a half pipe in the grass. The water is pumped out from the top and burbles and gurgles it's way over the ruts and gullies to the drain, whilst pushchair mums sit on the side and paddle their feet, dads kick giant inflatable footballs about, and excited kids run around like they're competing for last place in the Olympics. On a sunny holiday it's not unlike a child riot. It's about as peaceful as Armageddon. Thank God they didn't bury Princess Diana in the middle because she'd never get any peace.

I think they should demolish the whole thing and build a fountain in the middle of the Round Pond instead. At least then it would actually have something to do with her -- because it would be visible from Kensington Palace, where she lived.

If you like Princess Di then you might like to visit her home at Kensington Palace.

Queen's Gallery

Landmarks & Attractions | 181

ADDRESS Queen's Gallery, Buckingham Palace - map 7d **TRAINS** St. James's Park, Victoria (both zone 1) **BUSES** 11, 211, C1, C10 **PRICE** Adult £10; Senior (over-60) £9.20; Child (5-16) £5.20; Infant (under-5) free; Family (2 ad+3 ch) £25.20 **OPEN** Timed tickets between 10 AM and 5.30 PM (Mon-Sun, Oct-Jul); 9.30 AM and 5.30 PM (Mon-Sun, Aug-Sep); Last entry 1¼ hours before closing **WEB** royalcollection.org.uk/visit/the-queens-gallery-buckingham-palace **TEL** 0207 766 7300 **TIME REQUIRED** 1-1½ hours

Easy to get to? ★★★ Good for kids? ☆☆☆
Value for money? ★★☆ Worth a visit? ★★☆

This is my third gallery in one day: the Courtauld, Saatchi, and now the Queen's Gallery; and for somebody who doesn't like galleries that is like going to the dentist three times in a row. But I've got a feeling that I'm going to like this one because it's full of Royal stuff, and I've got a soft spot for the Queen.

The gallery is round the side of Buckingham Palace, next-door to the Royal Mews. It's actually part of the palace building itself and when I went on an evening tour of Buckingham Palace a while back, she walked us through the gallery on our way to the start, so there must be a locked door somewhere which takes you into the inner sanctum. But don't ask me where it is because I haven't got a clue. (And even if I did know, I still wouldn't tell you because to be honest you look a bit shifty to me, and if you broke into the palace and started rifling through the Queen's knicker drawer guess who would get the blame -- *me*.)

A word of warning: when you visit the gallery you get a timed ticket because it's so busy. I arrived at 1 PM today and wasn't allowed in until 3.15 PM -- so that shows you how busy it is (something to bear in mind if you're planning an itinerary).

The gallery is usually split into two sections, with a temporary exhibition at the start, followed by a few rooms from the main collection. So if I describe a picture to you here the chances are that it will have gone by the time you visit. At the time of writing they've got a big collection of Georgian treasures. It's all Royal portraits and battle maps, with some Hogarth cartoons and flintlock guns. They've got an audio guide as well, so you can learn a little bit about the paintings and painters.

The most interesting exhibits for me were the old maps of London, showing how it used to look in the 17th-century (I'm a sucker for old London maps). You can pick out a few familiar buildings like Banqueting House and St. James's Palace, but it's surprising how much else has changed. Can you imagine a time when St. Martin-in-the-Fields actually was in the fields? Or when Westminster Abbey was without its two big towers?

The most impressive pieces come after the temporary exhibition, where they showcase some stuff from the Royal Collection. And they are spectacular. They are what I call 'proper art', from the days when painters could actually paint -- none of this modern art rubbish. Even the rooms themselves are worth looking at. The decorations are all deep greens and golds, with rich wood and marble -- exactly how a palace's gallery should be. Some of the frames are thick and chunky gold about five inches fat -- they must weigh a tonne. They've got some original furniture from Buckingham Palace's State Rooms too (I recognise it from the summer tour).

My favourite paintings are by Canaletto. He has the knack of making London look like Venice, and the River Thames like the Tiber. It's only when you see the dome of St. Paul's rising above the rooftops that you realise where he's sitting.

It's not the biggest gallery in the world. To be honest I thought there would be more on show than there actually was, but I guess that most of the Royal Collection is already hanging on the walls of Buckingham Palace and Windsor Castle. That's where all the best works are, so if you want to see the meat of the Queen's collection then you'll have to stump up for the tours. If you forget the temporary exhibition for a minute (four rooms), then there are really only two rooms that I'd happily pay to see -- but they are blinding rooms. And that is coming from someone who doesn't usually like art galleries... so they must be good!

You can see more of the Royal Collection at Buckingham Palace, Kensington Palace, Windsor Castle and Hampton Court.

Regent's Park

ADDRESS Regent's Park - maps 2a, 2b, 2c, 2d **TRAINS** Baker Street, Great Portland Street, Regent's Park (all zone 1) **BUSES** 2, 13, 18, 27, 30, 74, 82, 113, 139, 189, 274, 453, C2 **OPEN** 5 AM to 5 PM (Mon-Sun, Jan); 5 AM to 6 PM (Mon-Sun, Feb); 5 AM to 7 PM (Mon-Sun, early Mar, early Oct); 5 AM to 8 PM (Mon-Sun, late Mar, Sep); 5 AM to 9 PM (Mon-Sun, Apr, Aug); 5 AM to 9.30 PM (Mon-Sun, May-Jul); 5 AM to 5.30 PM (Mon-Sun, late Oct); 5 AM to 4.30 PM (Mon-Sun, Nov-Dec) **WEB** royalparks.org.uk/parks/the-regents-park **TEL** 0300 061 2000 **TIME REQUIRED** 2 hours

Easy to get to? ★★★ Good for kids? ★★☆ Value for money? free Worth a visit? ★★☆

I'm watching two ducks having a fight. It's quite exciting. They are skimming the lake and flapping and scrapping and squawking and it's definitely going to end in bloodshed. Somebody is going to go home with a dead duck for dinner tonight. It was quite relaxing sitting here by the flower beds and fountains until those two hoodlums came along.

They've got a lot of ducks in here. I'm pretty sure they're ducks. They are definitely birds anyway. Maybe there's only one type of bird but with different outfits on. The mallards like a shiny green waistcoat with orange waterproof boots, whilst others have gone for a dark brown tweed or a smart black suit (the coots). The unfussy pigeons prefer a simple grey suit and bright red socks -- I think of them as the businessman of the bird world. They are the old men you see tumbling off the trains every morning in fraying suits and scuffed-up shoes.

This is actually quite a decent place to come if you want to do a bit of bird watching (of the feathered variety, I mean). They've got ducks, geese, herons... all sorts. Eagles, vultures, buzzards, pterodactyls (I made those ones up). The best looking bird in here is the swan. If you had to marry a bird for a bet then it would definitely be a swan -- no doubt about it. They've even got their wedding dresses on ready to walk down the aisle. It's a bit of a lousy life though, isn't it... now that I've been sitting here for five minutes I'm starting to feel a bit sorry for them. They've basically got themselves all tarted up for nothing. They just float around waiting for somebody to chuck them a bit of bread, and when an old woman finally obliges a quick little duck steams across and steals it. They've got a lot in common with prisoners, I think (I have just realised this) because that's all they eat: bread and water. Stale bread and water: the feast of swans and Wormwood Scrubs. And they both wear tags around their ankles as well. I came here thinking that they'd make a beautiful bride, but just five minutes later I see them for what they really are: narcissistic criminals surviving on soggy stale bread with electronic tags around their ankles. How the mighty have fallen.

Queen Mary's Gardens is the prettiest part of the park and is famous for its roses. They've got a couple of big circular beds but it looks a bit bland today. All I can see are green canes and threatening thorns -- it must be out of season. But I've been here enough times in the past to know that it's usually a riot of colour.

I always wonder why we associate roses with romance, because if you think about it, there are only two types of plant that hurt you when you handle them: nettles and roses. And then we go and give them to our missus: *here you go, my love... here is a token of my undying love (but be careful when you touch it because it might draw blood).*

Queen Mary's Gardens is where you'll find the nicest cafe in the park. There are actually five of them dotted around the grounds but the Garden Cafe is definitely the best. That's where you can have a proper sit down meal and a coffee (it's like a big restaurant). This is the place to take your grandmother on a Sunday. Show her the roses and park her wheelchair up in the cafe for a cup of tea afterwards. Then push her in the lake.

The best thing about Regent's Park is the boating lake. It doesn't seem very big when you first clap eyes on it, but if you take the time to walk around the whole circumference then you'll be trotting along for a good thirty minutes. They've got some little blue boats at the top end that you can hire out with your kids, and a big bandstand on the inner curve. If you came here in 1982 then the place would be littered with corpses and dead horses -- this is where the IRA detonated one of their terrorist bombs that killed some soldiers (not soldiers holding guns -- soldiers holding trumpets on the bandstand). They've still got a plaque and poppies around the base today.

I've just been watching a load of people on the pedal boats and I have decided that they are death traps best avoided. They are using them like bumper cars, bashing into their buddies and trying to sink them. It's like a Toy Town version of the Battle of Trafalgar. The poor husbands are doing all the pedalling and look totally knackered, whilst their kids are shouting Faster! Faster! The mums just look scared stiff and wish that they'd stayed on the bank. You can see them secretly praying for the ordeal to end. It looks to me like you need two people to pedal or you'll just go round and round in circles (there are two sets of pedals), but some of them are magically managing to go in a straight line with just one -- I cannot understand how that is possible.

I'm at the second cafe now -- the Boathouse Cafe. This is the rubbish one. Lots of noise. Big queues. This is where you come to pay for the boats so it's full of families and kids and pigeons and litter sweepers. It's a self-service place with very few seats inside and three thousand hyperactive children running around the patio. One of the toddlers has just tripped over on the concrete and is screaming so loudly that the birds are fleeing from the trees. Don't bring your grandmother here for chrissakes, or she'll push you in the lake.

The northern half of the park is where the pretty stuff comes to an abrupt end. It's just a flat and featureless pasture of grass and sports fields. You'll see a little hill in the middle with a building on top --

that is cafe number three. Even if you don't fancy a drink it's still worth climbing the hill just for the distant view of London Zoo.

The zoo occupies the northern corner of the park and you can walk along the southern edge and have a sneaky little look at some of the animals. I absolutely love the zoo. I've been there about a million times and it's one of my favourite places in London, so I'm quite happy sneaking a peek at the cages. The most obvious attraction is the big desert mountain range on the far left -- that's called the Mappin Terrace. It looks like it should have some lions and tigers grazing on top, but it's actually full of wallabies and emus (it's their 'Outback' zone). If you stick around long enough then you should be able to see some wandering around the flat bit at the bottom. The brown brick building next door is called the Mappin Pavilion, but you won't be able to see anything in there (unless you can see through walls).

After that come a couple of cages full of furry brown ferret-like creatures (they are too far away for me to see what they are -- but see if you can do it). A little further to the right is a small patch of grass underneath some netting -- that is a tiny section of the 'Tiger Territory'. If you cross your fingers then you might get lucky and see some stalking around (most of the territory is hidden behind the wall though, so it will be a long shot).

The concrete building with the green pepper pots on top is the famous old elephant house, but they got rid of the elephants ages ago and it's full of bearded pigs these days (which you won't be able to see). The mud-filled paddock next-door is home to the camels. If the big beasts are outside then you'll have a great view of them from the path... this is probably the best view of the zoo from the park.

After that are a few goats in the children's zoo, plus the sandy coloured meerkats zone. Then there are a couple of largely invisible bird cages (invisible... but not inaudible!). If you then turn left down the eastern edge of the zoo then you can get a glimpse of the Bugs house and some llama-like guys in a muddy pen, plus a very distant view of the penguins.

So there you go... you weren't expecting that, were you! There are a surprisingly high number of animals that you can see for free from the path, and it's well worth strolling up to the northern edge of the park to have a look. [Note: you can see even more cages from the opposite side, but I will write about those in my Regent's Canal review.]

If you're walking the same route as me then you will now be heading south down a broad avenue on the eastern edge of the park. This will take you to the fourth cafe out of five -- the Smokehouse. This one does burgers and sausages and hot dogs. A bit further on is another little coffee shop and some ornamental gardens. I saw Tony Benn down here once, so keep your peepers peeled for him (although he's dead now, so you probably won't see him).

Ripley's Believe It Or Not!

Landmarks & Attractions | 185

ADDRESS Ripley's Believe It Or Not!, Piccadilly Circus - map 8a **TRAINS** Leicester Square, Piccadilly Circus (both zone 1) **BUSES** 3, 6, 12, 14, 19, 23, 38, 88, 94, 139, 453 **PRICE** If bought online: Adult £20.21; Child (4-15) £14.96; Infant (under-4) free; Family (2 ad+2 ch, or 1 ad+3 ch) £59.96 -- If bought at the door: Adult £26.95; Child (4-15) £19.95; Infant (under-4) free; Family (2 ad+2 ch, or 1 ad+3 ch) £79.95 **OPEN** 10 AM to midnight (Mon-Sun); Last entry 1½ hours before closing **WEB** ripleyslondon.com **TEL** 0203 238 0022 **TIME REQUIRED** 2 hours

Easy to get to? ★★★ Good for kids? ★★☆
Value for money? ☆☆☆ Worth a visit? ★☆☆

This is another one for the 'big waste of money' file. You have to stump up nearly thirty quid to get in! You'll get a couple hours of amusement out of it, for sure, but that doesn't mean I would encourage you to blow thirty quid to see it. The only reason they can get away with charging that much is because it's on the corner of Piccadilly Circus and the dopey tourists don't realise how much money they're spending -- it's a tourist trap.

The idea behind Ripley's is this: all of the exhibits are supposed to be a bit weird and freakish, like a shrunken skull and five-legged sheep. Apparently this Ripley fella was a real-life Indiana Jones who used to scour the globe for as many oddities as he could lay his hands on, so he could fleece all the tourists out of thirty quid when he got back home. But the problem with the museum is that most of the stuff on display is not weird at all. What's weird about Charles II's glove? And Henry VIII's shoe? They've got a little piece of meteorite on show as well, which is basically just a boring bit of rock -- and alongside that is a signed photograph of five astronauts. What's weird about that?

Some of the other exhibits are totally ridiculous... like a bowl of cold water, chilled down to minus 10°C. The idea behind that one is that you can put your hand inside and imagine how cold the sea was when the Titanic sank. Wow. (I paid 30 quid for this?)

A lot of the paintings on display are truly awful... portraits painted in hamburger grease, for example, and famous faces made out of gum balls. There was a picture of the queen made out of pennies, and a matchstick model of Tower Bridge. Yawn.

One section of the museum is devoted to torture (in case you're bored and feel like doing yourself in). They've got an Iron Maiden and a ball and chain, etc., and some poor geezer sitting in an electric chair waiting for you to press the button. If you want to see some real torture equipment then go to the Tower of London (or even the London Dungeon, which I hate) -- don't go to this place.

One of the most disappointing things about the museum is that a lot of the truly weird stuff just consists of a photo. Take the Elephant Man, for example. He is certainly weird enough to be in the Ripley Museum, but all you get is a picture and a little placard to tell you who he is. That's it. *A photo.* It gets a bit better when they bring out the waxworks. They've got mock-ups of the world's ugliest woman, the world's hairiest man, and some poor guy who can pop his eyeballs out of his sockets. They've got a life-size model of the world's tallest man too, and the world's tiniest midget. They've also got a little zoo of messed-up animals -- chickens with an extra pair of drumsticks, etc. None of them are real though, I don't think (they are not stuffed), they are just models.

Oh yeah... don't forget the very exciting 'Mirror Maze'. This is basically the same as the mirror maze in the London Dungeon, except that it's not quite as good because there's none of the scary stuff alongside it. You are supposed to stroll around the darkened room trying to find the exit, but all of the walls are mirrors so it looks as if the boundary extends for a million miles. It took me about two minutes.

So, to sum it up... if the entry fee was ten quid then I might have recommended it, but charging thirty quid for this is ridiculous.

If you enjoy this then you might also like the Clink Prison Museum, London Dungeon and Madame Tussauds.

Roman Bath

ADDRESS Roman bath: 5 Strand Lane - map 9a -- Whitefriars Monastery: Magpie Alley (off Bouverie Street), The City - map 4f **TRAINS** Roman bath: Temple (zone 1) -- Whitefriars Monastery: Temple, Blackfrairs (both zone 1) **BUSES** Roman bath: 1, 4, 6, 9, 11, 13, 15, 23, 26, 59, 68, 76, 87, 91, 168, 171, 172, 188, 243, 341, 521, RV1, X68 -- Whitefriars Monastery: 4, 11, 15, 23, 26, 76, 172 **PRICE** free **TIME REQUIRED** Roman bath: 10 mins -- Whitefriars Monastery: 10 mins

Easy to get to? ★★★ Good for kids? ☆☆☆
Value for money? free Worth a visit? ★☆☆

Before you get too excited... it's not really a Roman bath. It might not even be a bath, but that's what people call it (that's what they used to think it was). These days the experts have deduced that it's probably a 17th-century plunge pool for Arundel House... or a 17th-century water cistern... or part of a garden feature... or maybe a few other things... so basically they haven't got a clue. The only thing that they can definitely agree on is that it's not a Roman bath. That doesn't mean that we're going to stop calling it one though. As far as we Londoners are concerned it is still a Roman bath, and who cares what the experts think!

The really interesting thing about this place is not what it is, or how old it is, but how you find it. Because there is absolutely no way in the world that you can stumble upon this place by accident -- somebody has to tell you it is there so you can seek it out and find it (it's fun!).

The easiest way to locate it is by going down Surrey Street, which cuts between Temple Place and the Strand. Halfway along there is an entrance into Surrey Steps -- look for a very fine-looking archway in that red brick building (it's not a road, it's just a dark alley through an arch). It is quite spooky down here -- the kind of place where Charles Dickens might kill off one of his characters -- but if you creep down the steps and turn right then you will be in Strand Lane. The bath is behind those railings on the righthand side.

Once you actually get there then the excitement is all but over, because the remains themselves are nothing special (especially when you remember that they're not even Roman). You just stare through a big window into a basement, where you can just about make out a brick-lined hole in the floor. There is a push button light on the wall if it's too dark. The window was dripping in condensation when I went today, so I could hardly see anything.

If you fancy going on another little archaeological adventure after that, then head back out onto the Strand, walk to the right for five minutes, past the Royal Courts of Justice into Fleet Street, and turn right when you find a place called Bouverie Street. Halfway along that road is a turning called Magpie Alley. Walk through there and down the gated steps at the end (don't worry, you are allowed), and you will find some more secret bricks that hardly anyone knows about. These are the remains of a 14th-century crypt at Whitefriars Monastery.

Henry VIII demolished it during the Reformation, and we buried the rest underneath a law firm, or a financial firm (something like that -- they all wearing suits through the window). But it's still an interesting little find, don't you think? London is full of interesting little remains like this. I'll scatter a few more throughout the book.

You can see some genuine Roman remains at the Billingsgate Roman House, and in the Guildhall Art Gallery basement.

Royal Academy of Arts

ADDRESS Royal Academy of Arts, Piccadilly - map 8a **TRAINS** Green Park, Piccadilly Circus (both zone 1) **BUSES** 14, 19, 22, 38 **PRICE** Adult from £11.50; Senior (over-60) from £10.50; Child (under-16) free; Price includes a voluntary donation **OPEN** 10 AM to 6 PM (Sat-Thu); 10 AM to 10 PM (Fri); Last entry 30 mins before closing **WEB** royalacademy.org.uk **TEL** 0207 300 8000 **TIME REQUIRED** 1 hour

Easy to get to? ★★★ Good for kids? ☆☆☆
Value for money? ★☆☆ Worth a visit? ★☆☆

I've always been slightly confused by the Royal Academy of Arts. This is probably going to sound totally daft, but I've never been entirely sure whether it's free to go inside with some extra paid-for exhibitions (like all the other big galleries in London), or whether you have to pay for the entire thing. Even now, whilst I'm standing inside the front door, I'm still not 100% sure! Given its history, if any gallery in London should own a permanent collection then it's this one; but if they do, then they never seem to show it. All they ever seem to offer is a series of paid-for exhibitions.

The exhibitions don't hang around for very long either, so what I describe to you now will have disappeared by the time you arrive. So maybe it would be more useful if I just described their favourite style instead. Mercifully they don't seem to like modern art, because most of their shows are of a classical nature (what I describe as "proper painting"). They also showcase a lot of photography, sculpture and architectural pieces.

Personally I think that the building is better than the exhibitions -- it's worth a quick walk down Piccadilly just to peer into the courtyard. The exhibition that I saw today was just a load of collages and boxes with assorted bits and bobs inside... like marbles and bottles and wire and wood. The artist seemed to like cutting up maps and adverts as well, and mix them with pictures of budgies and ballerinas.

I don't think I'm ever going to understand art.

So the most important thing to take away from this review is this: the Royal Academy doesn't have a big art collection like the National. It doesn't even have a small one like the Courtauld. It's really just a series of temporary exhibitions housed inside an impressive building.

Royal Albert Hall -- Guided Tour

ADDRESS Royal Albert Hall, Kensington Gore, South Kensington - map 6c **TRAINS** South Kensington (zone 1) and 10 min walk **BUSES** 9, 10, 52, 70, 360, 452 **PRICE** Adult £12.25; Senior £10.25; Child £5.25 **OPEN** Usually every 30 mins from 9.30 AM to 4.30 PM (Mon-Sun), but the timings vary due to the events **WEB** royalalberthall.com/tickets/tours-and-exhibitions/grand-tour **TEL** 0845 401 5045 **TIME REQUIRED** 1-1½ hours

Easy to get to? ★★★ Good for kids? ☆☆☆
Value for money? ★★☆ Worth a visit? ★★☆

I've never been inside the Royal Albert Hall before and I'm quite looking forward to it. The closest that I've ever come to the auditorium is watching *Last Night of the Proms* on the telly -- when they all stand up waving the Union Jack like we've just won the World Cup. It's definitely one of London's best-looking buildings from the outside, so let's hope it's pretty on the inside too.

You don't have to splash out on a concert ticket to see the stage, because they lay on regular guided tours throughout the day. Most of the events are in the evening, so if you want to play it safe then you should roll up first thing in the morning because they sometimes cancel the ones after lunch to prepare the room for that evening's gig. I arrived at half-past nine today and I'm currently sitting in the nice little cafe waiting for it to start.

Okay... it's all over now. The whole thing lasted for about an hour and it was pretty good. I always hate writing reviews after it's all over, but if I tried to scribble it all down whilst I was walking around then I would have probably fallen down the stairs. So you'll have to forgive me for that!

For such a big building there wasn't a lot to explore, to be honest. You don't get to see very many rooms for the money -- but I think I would still recommend it because the main auditorium is worth the entry cost alone.

Our little group had ten people in (there is a maximum of 20 on any one tour), and we were led around by a Billy Bragg-style guy who was quite entertaining. He was friendly enough, had some decent jokes, and told us all we needed to know about the history of the building. He kicked it off with a walk around the interior corridors, stopping at some of the photos on the walls to show you what kind of events they hold. Then he took us into one of the foyers for a peek out of the window at the exterior wall. It's a very impressive building to look at from the outside, all red bricks and terracotta, and he spent some time explaining what changes have been made to it over the years.

There was plenty of historical info about Queen Victoria and Prince Albert, and how the Prince came up with the plans after counting up the proceeds from the Great Exhibition. In fact, I would say that the focus of the tour was more about its history than the music, which suited me down to the ground. Sadly Albert died before the Hall was complete, so you learn a lot about how Queen Victoria turned it into a big memorial for him. That is reinforced by some good views of the

Albert Memorial as you walk around the windows.

After that he takes you to the meat and potatoes of the tour, into one of the balcony boxes, and all of a sudden you find yourself looking out over the whole auditorium from a few floors up. It really is impressive... all deep reds and warm browns, and bathed in pink and purple light. It's a bit like a Roman amphitheatre I suppose, with every seat looking inwards towards the stage. We were sitting up there for a good fifteen minutes-or-so, and whilst he was busy describing how the Hall is used we could see all of the roadies and engineers setting up the stage for the evening's show. They were all running around testing out the mikes and lights, doing booming sound-checks and constructing the runners for the camera tracks. That was quite interesting in itself.

One interesting little tidbit of information that he provided was about the big brick chimney on the forecourt (have you ever seen it?). It's a bizarre looking thing and I have always wondered what it is for. Well apparently there used to be a big steam engine in the basement which powered up the organ, so every time there was some music playing in the Hall they'd have a big cloud of steam rising out of the chimney! Sadly it's all been converted to electricity these days, so we don't get any more smoke shows.

After that you are allowed to peek inside the Royal box where the Queen sits (you are not allowed to sit in it though), and then it's straight across the Royal stairs and into the Royal Retiring Room. This is where the Queen comes for her pre-show cup of tea.

Then you go up another few floors to the gallery that runs around the top of the auditorium, directly under the roof. I've never seen a space like this before and I thought it was fantastic. It's basically a big stand-up corridor that runs around the entire circumference, where people can peer over the edge at the show going on below. It's a bit like the stalls, I suppose, but instead of having them in front of the stage, the Royal Albert Hall has got them in the heavens. You get a pretty decent view from up there too (something to bear in mind if you need a cheap ticket).

Royal Albert Hall -- Proms Concert

ADDRESS Royal Albert Hall, Kensington Gore, South Kensington - map 6c **TRAINS** South Kensington (zone 1) and then a 10 min walk **BUSES** 9, 10, 52, 70, 360, 452 **PRICE** £7.50 to £95 **DATES** Usually mid-Jul to mid-Sep - see website for dates **WEB** bbc.co.uk/proms **TEL** 0845 401 5045

Easy to get to? ★★★ Good for kids? ★★☆
Value for money? ★★★ Worth a visit? ★★★

I'm sitting on the steps of the Royal Albert Hall at the moment, waiting for the doors to open. I've bought myself a ticket to a Proms concert. It's quite nice out here in the evening. The sun is just about to head home and duck down behind the terracotta rooftops, and everyone is dressed up in nothing much at all -- it's very hot today. I thought it was going to be all shirts and ties and suits and boots but it's more like sandals and flip-flops. It doesn't look like a classical crowd -- not your typical Mozart fans, I don't think. Not that I know much about classical music... it's all violins and kettle drums, trumpets and tin whistles, and a bald bloke waving a stick in the air. That is all I know about classical music.

I'm going to Proms #16 by the Borusan Istanbul Philharmonic Orchestra. They are playing something by Balakirev and Islamey (nope, I've never heard of them either), Prokofiev, Mozart, Handel and Holst. And the *Queen of Sheba* by Respighi.

Okay, I'm in... I've got myself a nice seat in the Grand Tier. Try and imagine one of those little balcony boxes where the Muppets sit -- that's me. I'm one of those cantankerous old codgers in *The Muppets*. We've got the sound of cymbals and tubas tuning up (how do you tune a cymbal?), and a little cough cough splutter splutter of animated chatter as the crowd comes in. I hadn't realised they could do this, but they've actually taken out all of the central seats and made it standing room only downstairs, like a pop concert. That seems a bit weird for a classical gig (I'm up in the balcony so I don't care). But I don't suppose it really matters if you can't see the musicians at a Proms concert. It's all about the noise, isn't it -- it's not as if the conductor is going to suddenly rip his top off and start strutting around the stage like Mick Jagger.

The crowd is mostly middle-aged and above: 50% bald heads and grey hair. There are probably quite a few wigs around too. There is no dress code whatsoever. The crowd is sitting down on the floor waiting for show time. Some of them are lying flat on their backs on puffed-up pillows. It's all very civilised at the Royal Albert Hall.

There is a lot more standing room available at the top of the dome as well, if you want a cheaper ticket, because the very highest level hasn't got any seats. How can I explain it best? -- It's a bit like a running track that runs around the top. People just stand up there and peer over the edge. I can see them up there now, all leaning on the barrier.

The so-called 'Grand Tier' is definitely the best place to sit, methinks, especially if you get a seat at the front. Maybe the level above will be okay too (if you get a seat near the front). I wouldn't bother going any higher than that though, because it would be like staring down from the side of a mountain. The seats are so steep up there that you'll have to strap yourself in. I wouldn't fancy sitting or standing in the central pit either, because it's too much like Brighton beach on a summer's day, with everyone fighting over five-feet of personal space. Nope... the Grand Tier it is. And my box number is pretty good too (box number 12). Don't go any further round the circle than 10 or 11, because you'll be too side-on to the stage.

The orchestra has started to wander onto the stage now. Some of them are skipping in with little flutes and piccolos, whilst some poor sods are dragging in ten-tonne double basses. Two big harps have come on now, taller than a double-decker bus. Now the violins are tuning up. It's getting very difficult to tell which bit is practice and which bit is a song. It all sounds good to me.

It's definitely close to show time now because they've stopped messing around and are playing proper songs... still no sign of the conductor though.

Here we go... the principal violinist has come out to wild applause. And then the conductor comes out in his penguin suit and the whole place erupts. We are all on our feet clapping like mad, but I haven't got a clue why. I am just clapping along for the hell of it. (I am secretly clapping for the cleaner at the side of the stage.) Then the lights go down and up comes the first note...

At first the sound doesn't seem particularly loud, but at various moments in the tune it rumbles up into a roar like a bone-shaking thunder. Some of it is quite violent, with sharp shrieks and wailing; whilst at other times they have it turned down lower than your ears can hear.

Even if you don't like the music there is still plenty to look at. Everybody's bodies are bobbing about in unison, the music bows darting back and forth in a swish swish swish. It's as if they've all had a thousand cappuccinos before the show. Arms and elbow pumping left and right and up and down, carrying the tune like a piston. The conductor is almost dancing off his podium -- he's possessed. He's been overtaken with wild, exaggerated movements, like a ham actor, or a puppet with out of control strings. It's not just his hands that are flying about, he's got his arms and legs in motion too. It's as if his body is made of rubber all of a sudden, with two tubular arms snapping around like wind socks in a hurricane. To my untrained eye his movements don't seem to correspond with the music, and it's hard to make out what he's ordering the band to do. When he waves his stick in the air, what does that mean? And when he jabs it towards their faces, what does he want them to do? He's just prancing about and nobody is paying a blind bit of notice. They are all too busy reading the actual music. He reminds me of that Bez bloke in the Happy Mondays, who got wheeled out every show to give the punters something to look at.

I like the way he flounces out for a tea break at the end of every song, whilst everyone in the orchestra has to sit in silence with hands on laps. I think that's probably because he just wants some extra claps every time he comes back. This guy certainly likes his claps.

I'm trying to decide which instrument I'm going to play, in case they ask me up onto the stage. It's probably going to be one of the easy ones at the back. Maybe a tambourine, or a triangle. I reckon I could just about manage one of those without screwing it up. I mean, how talented do you have to be to hit a triangle with a stick? That's the one they give the thick kids at school. They have certainly got some strange instruments up there. One girl is playing the wooden clappers. It looks like she's smacking two cheese boards together.

I like the way the principal violinist has got her own lackey to turn over the songbook. Everyone seems to have their own political level. The orchestra might look pretty in their penguin suits and cocktail dresses, but I reckon behind the scenes it is a seething sea of jealousies. When the curtain comes down it's all cat-fights and back stabbings, as they jostle for the best seat on stage. That's why a lot of the tunes are so pounding and angry, because they are playing out the private battles in their heads. Every time they attack a note they are plunging the bow into the back of their neighbour's neck. It's an orchestra of enemies, being led by a stick wielding nutter at the front. That is what I imagine anyway, to liven it up. Whilst they are playing out the tunes, I am playing out the fights.

The show has come to a close now, and this orchestra certainly knew how to milk the applause... they basically just stood there for five minutes whilst we fed them a banquet of claps. We were wilting and losing people to exhaustion but still they stood on. It's as if we had to charge them up with claps, to get them off the stage. Once the clap-o-meter hit a million they eventually relented and let our tired hands have a rest.

Royal Courts of Justice -- Guided Tour

ADDRESS Royal Courts of Justice, Strand - map 4e **TRAINS** Chancery Lane, Holborn, Temple (all zone 1) **BUSES** 1, 4, 11, 15, 23, 26, 59, 68, 76, 91, 168, 171, 172, 188, 243, 341, 521, X68 **PRICE** Adult £12; Senior (over-60) £10; Child (under-14) £5; Note: Tickets must be booked in advance **DATES** Tours at 11 AM or 2 PM on occasional dates - you need to email or telephone for the dates **WEB** justice.gov.uk/courts/rcj-rolls-building/rcj/tours **TEL** 0778 975 1248 **TIME REQUIRED** 2 hours

Easy to get to? ★★★ Good for kids? ☆☆☆
Value for money? ★☆☆ Worth a visit? ★☆☆

I turned up an hour early and of course I'm soaked to the skin. What is going on with the weather lately? It's raining every day and night. I turned up at the Royal Courts of Justice and I had to squelch past security, dripping through the scanners like a fish out of water.

It's quite a sight once you get inside. The first thing you see is the colossal entrance hall and it's like a cathedral. Strong stone architecture, stained glass windows towering three storeys above your head, and huge oil paintings of long dead judges staring down at you from the walls in their gowns and wigs. It's almost worth committing a crime just to come inside the court.

The sounds you hear are all deep echoes of distant bangs and voices... things going on in other parts of the building... all carrying through the corridors and bouncing off the walls. It's a bit like being inside a church, where every whisper you make is amplified and shouted back by the bricks.

There is no one around today, and I'm not sure why. It must be a holiday or something because there's nobody about -- there are just a few members of the public shuffling around. Are they on trial for something? They sure do look guilty. But with the way I'm dressed at the moment they're probably think exactly the same thing about me. I'm pretty scruffy sitting here with my fingerless gloves and two-week old beard. I get stared at by a few kids and mums strolling past... don't walk too close to that bloke, they are thinking as they nudge their kids away... we don't know what he's done. I can tell by the looks on their faces that they think I am a criminal. Lord knows what they think I have done. You can relax, lady -- I am just here for the guided tour, *honest!*

I've still got half an hour to go before the tour starts so I seek out the cafe. This must be where the criminals come for their final cup of freedom tea. It's just a little pokey place but it's worth seeking out for the route -- you have to walk down the cathedral-like nave and through the big double doors into what looks like a crypt. It's got a load of thick carved columns about five-feet apart, holding up a low vaulted roof. It would be a great place to have some tombs but of course it's empty. As is the cafe. As is everywhere, in fact. This place is like a ghost town today.

I actually used to work in a court, believe it or not, when I was still young and good looking (a long time ago now). I was one of those stenographers who had to sit at the front and note down every umm and ahh. You need quick fingers tap-tap-tapping away at the speed of light for that job, but boy-oh-boy was it boring as hell -- the most boring job I have ever had. The most interesting case I worked was about a bloke who stole a biscuit from Tesco's. But I'm guessing that the crimes they have in this place are a lot better than that -- murderers, explosions, terrorist plots, crimes against humanity... real meaty stuff. It makes you wonder who'll be walking (or stalking) the corridors. Pol Pot? Idi Amin? I might brush shoulders with a mass murderer whilst the guide is pointing out some pictures -- I'd better be on my guard. Luckily I know some karate moves in case a shifty low-life gets too close for comfort. If Slobodan Milosevic comes round the corner then he'll be getting a swift kick in the nuts.

We've been ordered to take a seat by the security scanners now, so it looks like show time is close... Our little tour group consists of me, two chatty Americans and a bookwormish couple dragging their kids along for some education. I have a good look around the entrance hall while I'm waiting. It's reminiscent of the Natural History Museum, I think. Imagine that building in grey, instead of brown, and with judges instead of dinosaurs. There are some really impressive statues dotted around the alcoves, and some dark and dingy paintings of court life hanging on the walls. All the signs are written in mock-gothic script too, it's like a medieval Disneyland.

Our guide turns out to be a nice lady called Sue who has been working here for ten thousand years. She's basically like your long-lost mum, grey-haired and friendly, and she's marched us off to one of the courtrooms and sat us down; and that's where I am right now, secretly writing this while I'm pretending to listen.

We are thirty minutes into the tour now and my attention is starting to wane. It's not so much a tour... it's more like a lecture. She's got a nice conversational style and everyone is free to ask some questions, but it's very heavy going. She's led us through the history of the place (the building and the architecture), and now she's charging on through the court process and function of the judiciary.

The court room is very nice though. It's all wood-panelled walls and old bookcases filled with leather-bound legal tomes. It's got a vaulted ceiling and stone gallery balconies, a hanging chandelier and a big ticking clock. It's a bit like walking onto the set of *Rumple of the Bailey*.

It turns out that they don't do murders here after all. This is a Civil Court, so it's all divorces, adoptions and libel cases, with a bit of boring bankruptcy, asylum and deportation cases thrown in. So I've learnt something at least -- I've learnt that it's safe to walk the corridors without getting jumped on by a mass murderer.

...I do like Sue and she is a good guide, but this speech is going on and on and on and on. When is the actual tour going to start, Sue? I'm guessing that when people come on a tour of the Royal Courts of Justice, then what they really want to do is go on a tour of the building. Not listen to Sue banging on about everyone she's ever met in the few decades she's been here. Eighty minutes later we finally get up and have a walk around. *Eighty minutes!* If I knew it was going to take that long then I would have come in my pyjamas and had a kip. So be advised: you have to sit through nearly an hour-and-a-half of monologue before you get to see some of the building.

The actual 'tour' bit of the tour lasts for just half-an-hour and consists of some corridors, a moderately impressive painted room, and then up to a balcony where they're housing a collection of mannequins wearing judges wigs and robes, and then back down to the main hall again... plus the crypt-like place (which we already saw when we had a cup of tea). And that's basically it. The only courtroom you see is the one where you've been sitting for the last eighty minutes snoozing through her legal lecture.

Eighty minutes of talking, followed by a quick thirty minutes of tour. But hey, the guide was a genuinely lovely lady, so you can't be too critical. But take my advice... unless you've got a special interest in learning about the judiciary then it makes more sense to just come in and have a walk around yourself. A large part of the building is open to the public anyway, and they provide you with a little leaflet at the front desk for a self-guided tour. Doing it that way means you can spend a nice hour walking around at your own leisure, taking your time to see all the stuff, without having to wade through eighty minutes of school lessons wondering when the home time bell will ring.

You can go and see where all the lawyers are trained at Lincoln's Inn.

Royal Courts of Justice -- Watching a Trial

ADDRESS Royal Courts of Justice, Strand - map 4e **TRAINS** Chancery Lane, Holborn, Temple (all zone 1) **BUSES** 1, 4, 11, 15, 23, 26, 59, 68, 76, 91, 168, 171, 172, 188, 243, 341, 521, X68 **PRICE** Free **OPEN** Building: 9 AM to 4.30 PM (Mon-Fri) -- Court cases: 10.30 AM and 1 PM, and 2 PM to 4.30 PM (Mon-Fri); Note: Under-14s not permitted in the courts **WEB** justice.gov.uk/courts/rcj-rolls-building/rcj/faqs **TIME REQUIRED** 1-1½ hours

Easy to get to? ★★★ Good for kids? Under-14s not permitted Value for money? free Worth a visit? ★★☆

I'm back in court again... off to see the judge this time. I've got my toothbrush and my pyjamas all packed in case he wants to put me away. I should be all right though -- I'm only here to watch a trial. I came on a tour the other day so I thought I'd come back and see the real thing.

I'm sitting in the same little cafe as last time, but there are actually some people in here now. It's a work day today so there are lots of lawyers and briefs and guilty people milling around. One guy has still got his white wig on like they wear inside the courtroom. He's just queuing up like everybody else, waiting to buy his cup of tea. I wonder why they make them wear those silly wigs and gowns? The solicitors are much better dressed with sharp suits and Blackberrys, haircuts all slicked back like Don Johnson in *Miami Vice*. Educated voices too -- I can hear them gossiping behind me and it's all *oh yah, ha ha, Jamie's off to Manchester*. His judgment has gone against him apparently, whatever that means, and he needs to recharge his juices. He doesn't sound too disappointed though. But I don't suppose he cares because he's only the brief. It's the criminal who actually has to go to prison isn't it -- he's downstairs in the cells while we're up here drinking medium lattes from the coffee shop.

I'm going to have a walk through the courts in a minute and pick a place to sit.

It's very easy to get this far: all you have to do is stroll through security (past the security scanners and a pat down from the guard) and straight past reception. On the other side of the desk is a wooden display case showing every case that's playing today. It's a bit like reading through the *TV Times*: this case is rubbish, this one's all right, I might stay in for that one. To be honest it was all gibberish to me. It's all written in legalese and makes about as much sense as a page full of scribble. When I was here on the tour the other day I found out that all of the cases are listed in order of seniority, so if you want to see the best judge then pick whatever's listed on the left.

Note: You should bear in mind that the Royal Courts of Justice is a Civil Court, and they very rarely have juries (they only appear on appeals). The kind of cases that they do have are very quiet, detailed affairs about property, finance, family disputes, divorces and immigration. There are no big Hollywood bust-ups about murders, bombings and bank robberies. So if you are expecting it to be like one of those courtroom dramas on TV then you are going to go home disappointed.

I must admit that I was a little bit intimidated standing outside the courtrooms, plucking up the courage to go inside. The place is a maze of long empty, echoing corridors, and you can walk the whole length of them and not see a soul. It's just you and the sound of your own footsteps on the stone floors. When you finally tip-toe up to a wooden court door there is invariably no one around to ask what to do. There are no bouncers on the door or anything like that. No ushers. No one there to stamp your ticket. It's just a big shut door and you, facing each other off in a cold cavern corridor. And on the other side of that big wooden portal is the judge -- someone who has the power to lock you up if he doesn't like your face. And what makes it even worse is that there are some tiny little windows at the side so you can peer inside and see them all talking, discussing the case and hearing evidence. *Oh Christ*, you think to yourself, *this is far too scary*. It's very easy to chicken out at this point, and I wouldn't blame you if you sheepishly turned tail and fled, but this is where you need to steel yourself and pluck up some courage. Just take a deep breath, my lad, you can do it. Man up! What's the worst that can happen? Even if the judge locks you up in prison, you'll probably be out in five years anyway.

The rule for entering the courts is that the public can just come and go as they please, without even having to wait for a lull in proceedings. That sounds slightly dubious, but trust me -- it's true. We live in a country of open justice, and they take the rule quite seriously. So I just booted open that big oak door and stormed inside like I owned the place (no I didn't). No one even looked in my direction. No one cares. You just take a seat at the back and they carry on blathering on about whatever it is they are talking about. It's as if you don't exist.

A word of advice before you head in: remember to turn off your mobile phone for chrissakes, because you will definitely get scolded by the judge if it rings. Especially if it's one of those annoying ringtones.

I ended up in Court 14 which is a real good-looking court (I think they are all pretty much the same, from what I could tell). It's full of leather seats and wood-panelled walls, green velvet curtains and creaky old bookcases filled with dusty legal tomes. The lawyers are all wigged-up in their black gowns, and the judge looks like a million dollars in his bright red sash.

There are also plenty of suited solicitors lounging around, taking notes.

I don't think I'm allowed to tell you the actual details of the case, so you'll just have to imagine what happened next. But let me sum it up for you in one word: boring. It's not like it is in the movies, where the briefs smash their fists down on the table and the judge shouts out *Order! Order!* whilst the defendant screams out that he's been framed. It's just a quiet room in which a few suits discuss legal mumbo jumbo.

Unfortunately I never got to find out what happened at the conclusion because after half-an-hour the lawyers wanted to discuss some legal points in private. So the judge ordered all the nobodies out (ie, me). I listened at the keyhole though, ha ha (no I didn't).

Royal Exchange

ADDRESS Royal Exchange, The City - map 5e
TRAINS Bank, Cannon Street, Mansion House, Monument (all zone 1) **BUSES** 8, 11, 21, 23, 25, 26, 43, 47, 48, 76, 141, 149, 242 **OPEN** Shops: Usually 10 AM to 6 PM (Mon-Sun) -- Bars & Restaurants: Usually 8 AM to 11 PM (Mon-Sun) **WEB** theroyalexchange.co.uk **TEL** 0207 283 8235 **TIME REQUIRED** 15 mins

Easy to get to? ★★★ Good for kids? ☆☆☆
Value for money? free Worth a visit? ★★★

I've been meaning to go inside the Royal Exchange for yonks, but never got past the front door. It's another one of those intimidating buildings that looks like it's out of bounds to the likes of you and me. It looks like you need a reason to go inside. What is it? Maybe it's a big bank, or a courthouse, or a city business filled with big wigs smoking fat cigars. You would never guess what it really is from the outside. Do you know what it actually is? It's a shopping centre! I kid you not. It's the poshest shopping centre in London.

You won't find Tesco's or Poundland in here, though. Back in the old days (400 years ago) the shops around the edge were selling simple foodstuffs like fruit and veg and coffee. But now it's a bit more upmarket: it's all diamond rings and handbags. You wouldn't want to come in here to do your Sunday shop, that is for sure -- not unless you want to live on truffles and white wine all week. It's full of boutiques like Tiffany's, Gucci and Paul Smith. They've got leather goods, jewellers, watch makers, smokes and pipes, fine art dealers and beauty treatments. But I'm pretty sure that the only people who use beauty shops like these are the ones who are already beautiful. The people who buy a watch in here have probably got their own staff to wind them up. I had a nose through the windows but of course they didn't have any price tags on. You know how the old saying goes -- if you need to ask the price then you probably can't afford it. That is pretty much the rule in here.

Here is a list of some of the things they sell:
A can of coke? *no*. A ham sandwich? *no*.
A champagne flute and salmon pâté on a little poncy piece of French toast? *yes!*
A copy of The Sun? *no*. A packet of fags? *no*.
A copy of Tatler and a silver tin of menthol snuff? *yes!*

A pair of plastic flip-flops? *no.* A pair of Jimmy Choo shoes for 10 grand a pop? *yes!*

You get the idea. If you've got more money then sense, then this is the place to spend it.

I thought I'd try and buy a cup of coffee because they've got a big cafe on the ground floor, taking up the central space. But it's not really like Costas or Starbucks. It's more like a wine bar with pretty waitresses in pencil-thin skirts and ponytails. The waiters are all waltzing around with silver trays balanced on upturned palms, dropping off cappuccinos and cupcakes to the suited and booted patrons. Practically everyone I can see is smartly dressed in black suits and power outfits, hobnobbing and networking with their business buddies, showing off their latest electronic gizmos. This must be where the City businessmen come for canapés, or whatever it is you are supposed to eat in a Savile Row suit. One of them is twirling his car-keys around his fingers like Clint Eastwood twirls his gun, showing off his key fob to anyone who wants to look (just me).

I can see them looking over and thinking "who is that scruffy oik taking photos of us", and sure enough a nice lady comes over and forbids me from taking any more photos.

So is it worth a look inside? Er... I don't think so, no. You should definitely have a look around the outside because that is fantastic, but unless you're wearing a suit and you've got a gold credit card in your wallet, give it a miss and go to Starbucks instead. Much more welcoming!

If you're looking for some posh shops then try Burlington Arcade.

Royal Hospital

ADDRESS Royal Hospital, Royal Hospital Road, Chelsea **TRAINS** Sloane Square (zone 1), and a 10 min walk **BUSES** 11, 137, 170, 211, 360, 452 **PRICE** Self guided tour: Free -- Guided tour (10 or more people, booked at least a month in advance): Adult £12; Child (6-15) £7 **OPEN** Great Hall: 10 AM to 12 noon, and 2 PM to 4.30 PM (Mon-Fri) -- Chapel: 10 AM to 4.30 PM (Mon-Fri) -- Museum: 10 AM to 4 PM (Mon-Fri) -- Guided tours at 10 AM and 1.30 PM (Mon-Fri, but must be booked in advance) **WEB** chelsea-pensioners.co.uk **TEL** 0207 881 5200 **TIME REQUIRED** 1½ hours

Easy to get to? ★★☆ Good for kids? ☆☆☆
Value for money? free Worth a visit? ★★☆

How do you fancy spending a few hours walking around an old people's home? I thought not. Actually it's better than it sounds... because this is the Royal Hospital in Chelsea, one of Christopher Wren's old buildings. That's where all the Chelsea Pensioners live. You might have seen them shaking their money tins down the old King's Road, wearing black caps and red tunics, looking like they have just come home from a Napoleonic War.

I'm not sure what hoops they had to jump through to qualify for a room in this place -- it's the country's grandest retirement home -- but I'm guessing that it must have been pretty spectacular. They wouldn't get in just because they're good at bingo, that is for sure. They'd need a distinguished army career probably, and plenty of medals on their chest. Maybe have an arm or a leg blown off as well... something like that.

It's hard to imagine these old fellas running around with guns and grenades, but that is what soldiers do isn't it? They might look cute in their buttoned-up tunics, but these aren't your everyday grandads -- these are grandads of war. Fighting grandads. Grandads that blow up tanks and parachute in behind enemy lines.

The main gate is along the Royal Hospital Road, and once you get inside you are basically on your own, and you can walk around at your own leisure. There is no leaflet or map, or anything like that. So what you need to do first of all is walk towards the right, along the main facade. Head through the big central porch and you'll find a large wooden door on either side. These are the two rooms that everyone comes to see. On one side is the chapel, and on the other side is the Great Hall. Apart from the little museum and shop, these are pretty much the only rooms that you're allowed to enter, but when you take in all the gardens and the grounds as well then there is more than enough to fill up ninety minutes.

The chapel is nice enough I suppose, but it's not going to knock your socks off. I think Christopher Wren saved his best work for the exterior. He was probably sick of building churches by this time (he'd already done fifty of them). It's full of dark carved oak and there is a nice painted scene behind the altar. If you're lucky then you'll find a Chelsea Pensioner in there chatting with the visitors, telling them a little bit of its history. (He might be doing a guided tour though, which you have to pay for in advance, so don't join the crowd or he might kick you off.)

The thing that always impresses me most about old churches is the silence. To get the best out of it you need to be sitting there in the dark, with the rain beating on the windows, and then hear some footsteps echoing up the aisle to light a candle. I was in Brompton Oratory a while ago and it seemed like the clouds had seeped inside the walls -- that's how moody and broody it was. This place isn't going to feel anything like that because it's too white and bright, but it's still worth a visit.

I had high hopes for the Great Hall because that's where the Duke of Wellington was laid in State, but it's much the same as the chapel really -- a bit so-so. It's basically a big dining hall now and the kitchen staff were still tidying up the tabletops and sweeping crumbs off the floor, which kind of ruined the mood a bit. The tables were furnished with deep green lampshades and chunky knives and forks. There were a load of bowls filled with croutons too, that no one wanted to eat. This isn't the kind of place that serves up two slices of toast and a mug of Typhoo tea for breakfast. It's more like salmon pate and a pile-high plate of bacon and eggs.

It reminded me a little bit of the dining hall at my old school, because they've got old oil paintings of kings and queens glaring down at you from the side, and big boards full of the battles they fought. My old school had a big list of ex-headmasters and school captains to inspire the pupils, and this place has got dead men who did their duty.

Now head out of the other door and into the three-sided courtyard and colonnade. This was definitely my favourite space and is very reminiscent of Kensington Palace. It uses the same style of red and brown bricks that Wren used over there. There's also a rather bizarre statue standing in the middle, of King Charles II. It's all gilded over in gold and he's togged up like a Roman emperor, complete with a short skirt and laurel leaves. I've never seen a British king look like that before... he looks like he's off to a fancy dress party.

After that you can check out the museum and shop. The museum is just a tiny little three-room affair filled with uniforms, citations and racks and racks of medals on the walls. There must be a few thousand of them at least, all donated by the Pensioners. The best exhibit was a little mock-up of their bedroom. I can't say that I know what a prison cell looks like inside, but it must be of a similar size. It's almost like a dorm room at university. It is very nice and cozy and comfortable though, and I would be quite happy to live in it.

As you're walking around the grounds you can't help but bump into a few of the Pensioners. This is, after all, where they live. I know it sounds stupid but I wasn't really expecting them to be proper OAPs -- I don't know why. But they are all shuffling around with walking sticks and mobility scooters. You can straight away tell that they are ex-army by the way they talk and hold themselves. It's almost like they are still in the forces... still living the dream... waiting for the Queen to call them up again. Once a soldier, always a soldier. 99% of them are men (there's about 350 of them), but I did notice one woman too, so I guess they have started letting in the ladies.

And oh yeah, like a lot of old people once they start talking you can't shut them up. They have so many stories to tell that I recommend bringing an extra pair of ears with you. They are so polite and friendly that you have to just stand there and listen until they chat themselves out.

Charterhouse is another impressive home for old folks.

Royal Mews

ADDRESS Royal Mews, Buckingham Palace Road, Victoria - map 7d **TRAINS** St. James's Park, Victoria (both zone 1) **BUSES** 11, 211, C1 **PRICE** Adult £9.30; Senior (over-60) £8.50; Child (5-16) £5.50; Infant (under-5) free; Family (2 ad+3 ch) £24.10 **OPEN** Closed (Jan, Dec); 10 AM to 4 PM (Mon-Sat, Feb-Mar, Nov); 10 AM to 5 PM (Mon-Sun, Apr-Oct); Last entry 45 mins before closing **WEB** royalcollection.org.uk/visit/royalmews **TIME REQUIRED** 1 hours

Easy to get to? ★★★ Good for kids? ☆☆☆
Value for money? ★★☆ Worth a visit? ★☆☆

You really have to be a fan of the Royals to like this place. Either that or you need to love horses, because there's not a lot to see inside. I'm a bit of a Royal nut, but even I would skip this one.

After you've emptied out all of your pockets for the super-tight security, the first things you see are a couple of wooden stalls where the horses are groomed. I saw two of them munching on their nosebags, eating whatever it is that horses eat -- sugar lumps, I'm assuming. Horses have a very particular diet once in captivity: sugar lumps and carrots.

After that you enter the interior quadrangle that seems to double up as a staff car park. Presumably they exercise the horses in it, but every time I've been here in the past (including today) it has been jam-packed full of modern day cars. People seem to live in the flats around the top, so it's where they park all their buggies and bikes and vans.

As you walk around the quadrangle you can peer into the gated stalls where they keep all the black and gold coaches. Each one has a single State coach inside, along with a big placard to show you what it's used for. They've got the State Landau used by Queen Victoria, for example, and the one that carries the Imperial Crown on parade (and yes, the crown really does get a carriage all to itself). They've also got the Irish State Coach that carries the Queen to the State Opening of Parliament, and the one that carries all the Royal brides to their weddings (to their doom). The newest coach was built by the Aussies for the Queen's Diamond Jubilee, and it really is a beauty. They've also got a shiny Rolls Royce on show.

Obviously you're not allowed to sit in any of them. The stables are extremely small so you can't even walk around them. You literally just stare through the stable door and snap a few photos of the front. It's all rather disappointing really -- hence why I said you need to be a big fan of the Royals to enjoy it. Imagine how much money they could make if they tied a couple of donkeys to the front and allowed the tourists to ride them down The Mall. They could charge 20p a go -- they'd make a fortune!

After that comes the glory of glories: the famous Gold State Coach. This is the fairytale coach that carried the Queen during her Coronation in 1953. You won't believe the size of this thing when you first clap eyes on it -- it's bigger than a tank (no joke!). My photograph definitely doesn't do it justice. They've set it up with four waxwork horses and accompanying riders, all dressed up in their white wigs and finery. If I ever have to pick just one object to represent Britain, then this will probably be it.

There's not much to see beyond the coaches. As you exit the building you can peer into their Riding School, where the horses are trotted around a dusty parade ground, but it's really just a quick glimpse through an open door. I've never once seen a horse in there -- and I've been here three times.

If you enjoy this then you might also enjoy a visit to the Household Cavalry Museum.

Royal Observatory

ADDRESS Royal Observatory, Greenwich Park - map 11f **TRAINS** Cutty Sark DLR (zones 2&3), and a 25 min walk **BUSES** 53, 54, 177, 180, 188, 202, 380, 386 **PRICE** Observatory: Adult £9.50; Senior (over-60) £7.50; Child (5-15) £5; Infant (under-5) free; Family (2 ad+2 ch) £22, or £15 with 1 ad+2ch; Temporary exhibitions may cost extra -- Planetarium: Adult £7.50; Senior (over-60) £6.50; Child (3-15) £5.50; Infant (under-3) free; Family (2 ad+2 ch) £20, or £15.50 with 1 ad+2ch **OPEN** 10 AM to 5 PM (Mon-Sun); Last entry 30 mins before closing **WEB** rmg.co.uk/royal-observatory **TEL** 0208 858 4422 **TIME REQUIRED** 2-3 hours

Easy to get to? ★★☆ Good for kids? ★★☆
Value for money? ★★☆ Worth a visit? ★★★

When I was a kid I always wanted to be a spaceman. Well, actually that's not quite true: I wanted to be Darth Vader. So I've always had an interest in the Royal Observatory. I don't think people quite realise how serious it is though. They turn up thinking it's going to be full of spaceships and entertainment for the kiddies but it's actually more for the adults. It's all antique watches and clocks and period furniture from the days of

Christopher Wren. The only bit that's suitable for children is the planetarium.

Once you've paid your money you'll enter the forecourt of Flamsteed House. That's the red brick building that you can see perched on top of Greenwich Hill. Check out that big red ball on top of the spire -- what's that for? Well, that is how the ships in the river used to tell the time. The captains would sit in their ships and wait for the ball to drop down the pole, and that would signal the start of the hour. Clever huh? If you want to set your watch these days then you'll have to wait until 12.55 PM, when it will start rising up the mast. At 1 PM it wall fall down and signal that it's time for lunch.

The interior of Flamsteed House has been restored to how it looked when the original Astronomer Royals were in residence, so it's full of old chairs and tables and dusty old paintings of serious looking men. The Octagon Room is right at the top, where they set up their telescopes. Sadly it hasn't got any telescopes inside it today, just a couple of old grandfather clocks and paintings of Charles II.

Downstairs you'll find a museum full of antique clocks and telescopes, including the first four timepieces by John Harrison which helped to solve the longitude problem. To be honest I thought all of this stuff was quite dry. It didn't help that the place was crawling with about six billion school kids running around shrieking and wailing and ooh-la-la-ing in my earhole. I must have picked the day when the whole of France had come over for a school visit. And whilst they are undoubtedly very important exhibits... they are just clocks. As are the quartz clocks and atomic clocks, and wind-up watches and grandfather clocks that make up the rest of the exhibition.

Do you see what I mean now... when I say that this place isn't very Good for kids? Because so far we haven't seen a single thing that will interest them, and you're probably wondering why I've awarded it my "good for kids" symbol on the index. Well, that's because of the next section -- the planetarium.

But before you get there though, you have to take a little stroll across the courtyard to the famous Meridian Line: the line that splits the hemispheres in two. This is where we slice our days in half and make midnight.

I read in the newspaper a while ago that the French are trying to persuade the UN to scrap GMT and convert the world to atomic time instead. *Huh? What???* They should ban their school kids from coming over -- that's what I would do. No more noisy French kids allowed until the French president gives up his megalomaniac plan to dominate time!

It's possible to buy a ticket just for planetarium alone if you want to, and skip everything that I mentioned before, which will save you a few pennies. They've got a small astronomy exhibition attached as well, but I didn't think it was very good to be honest (it's too small) -- the space exhibition at the Science Museum is far superior. But there are a few push-button displays and hands-on exhibits to keep your kiddies amused before the show starts.

The planetarium is great -- there isn't a kid in the world who doesn't like planetariums. I remember going to the big one in Madame Tussauds when I was a child but they've shut it down now, so this is the only one left in London.

My timings were a big tight today so I had to settle for the first show available, which unfortunately turned out to be a bit of a kiddie-style one with shout-out answers for the audience, but they lay on a whole programme ranging from fun to serious. So you might want to check the timings on their website first and pick an adult one. Our show started off by showing the stars that are visible tonight, and went on to explain the constellations, zodiac and ecliptic. The pictures that fill the screen are much larger than you'd imagine... I was just expecting a field of little stars but you actually get pictures of planets shooting out of the void and spinning and filling up the entire room. They had some good shots of the moon too, and the Milky Way, dust clouds, and standout shots from the Hubble telescope. One of the best bits was when they made it seem as if we were all standing on the surface of Mars, with a horizon full of real-life stills from the planet's surface.

The whole screen wraps around you 360° and you can sit back and relax in your reclining seat, staring straight up into the darkening dome. You don't have to worry about getting a dodgy seat behind a basketball player because the entire show takes place directly above your head. It's a bit like sitting inside a giant upturned teacup.

If you like astronomy then check out the space gallery at the Science Museum.

Saatchi Gallery

ADDRESS Saatchi Gallery, Duke of York's HQ, King's Road, Chelsea **TRAINS** Sloane Square (zone 1) **BUSES** 11, 19, 22, 49, 137, 211, 319

PRICE Free **OPEN** 10 AM to 6 PM (Mon-Sun); Last entry 30 mins before closing **WEB** saatchigallery.com **TIME REQUIRED** 1 hour
Easy to get to? ★★★ Good for kids? ☆☆☆
Value for money? free Worth a visit? ★☆☆

The only thing that I know about Charles Saatchi is what the lovely Nigella Lawson said in the newspapers: that he's a bit of a bully (...allegedly). So a little piece of me is very happy to see that he has squandered so much of his hard-earned cash on a lot of rubbish art. Ha ha -- somebody definitely saw him coming!

"Look!" they grinned. "It's Charles Saatchi with his big fat wallet... What can we flog him today?"

"I know," suggested a cheeky charlatan. "Let's find some deflated old footballs and stick them on a shelf, and charge him six thousand quid for it -- he's a sucker for stuff like that." (And yes, that really *is* a piece of art in here.)

A lot of the artwork on show just appears to be graffiti -- the same kind of scribble that you might find on a tube train wall. Other ones just seem to be an excuse to finish up a pot full of paint. The artist has just bought himself a huge canvas and smeared red paint all over it... that's it. I'm guessing that the size alone was supposed to make it impressive. But if that were true then people would be queuing up to stare at a whitewashed wall.

I'm not a fan of how he's arranged his collection either, because he's just plonked a few pieces in each room. It's like a minimalist gallery full of minimalist art -- it's all wall. I've never understood minimalism myself. Why is something better when there's nothing there? It doesn't work like that in other walks of life... if they served you up a minimalist meal of two peas on a plate then you'd ask for your money back. And you'd soon get tired of listening to a minimalist song. So why is minimalist art any different? We want Turner to paint the entire sky, not a single raindrop. We want him to paint the steamships and the sea and the driving rain, not settle for a single splodge of blue -- but that's what minimalist art is all about.

Gone are the days when you'd look at a picture and admire the artist's skill with a paintbrush. Contemporary artists would much rather be thought of as being clever with their head. It's all about the *message* these days. If you are commissioned to do a piece about global warming then you can forget about painting a rainforest... Saatchi would never show anything like that. You'd be better off sticking an ice cube on a plate and filming it melt. Art has gone backwards.

The most disappointing thing about this gallery is that there are no famous names on display. (Although, admittedly, I don't know much about contemporary art.) If you are expecting the gallery to be full of Andy Warhol's and Piet Mondrian's then forget it -- go to the Tate Modern instead. There are no Pollock's... just b*llocks. He claims that he's trying to champion the up-and-coming artists, but the cynic in me thinks he's just buying up a load of cheapo art, by painters that nobody has ever heard of, so he can stick them in his gallery and increase their value.

If you're a fan of modern art then try the Tate Modern and Hayward Gallery.

St. Bartholomew-the-Great

ADDRESS St. Bartholomew-the-Great, West Smithfield - map 4f **TRAINS** Barbican, Farringdon, St. Paul's (all zone 1) **BUSES** 4, 8, 17, 25, 45, 46, 56, 63, 153, 242, 243, 341, 521 **PRICE** Adult £4; Senior £3.50; Child £3.50; Family (2 ad+up to 3 ch) £10; Extra £1 to take photos **OPEN** 8.30 AM to 5 PM (Mon-Fri, mid Feb-mid Nov); 8.30 AM to 4 PM (Mon-Fri, mid Nov-mid Feb); 10.30 AM to 4 PM (Sat); 8.30 AM to 8 PM (Sun) **DENOMINATION** Church of England **WEB** greatstbarts.com **TEL** 0207 600 0440 **TIME REQUIRED** 30-45 mins

Easy to get to? ★★★ Good for kids? ☆☆☆
Value for money? ★★★ Worth a visit? ★☆☆

It's nice and cold this morning. Everything is pin sharp and my cheeks feel as if someone has been slapping them with a plank. Do you remember when you used to do sports at school (cross-country runs) and your fingers would get so frozen that you couldn't do up your shirt buttons? Well, that is how I feel this morning.

St. Bartholomew-the-Great is a bit of a bugger to find at the moment because they seem to be rebuilding the whole of London around St. Bart's Hospital. Everything looks totally different -- it's a warren of orange boards and hard hats and scaffolding, and blokes holding big stop signs directing the traffic around huge holes in the ground. But once you stumble into the right street you will stand back and love it the moment you clap eyes on its checkerboard walls. This church just looks old -- it looks older than old. But wait until you step inside...

The first thing that hits you when you tiptoe through the door is the wonderfully thick smell of incense... is that what it's called? I'm not very good with the terminology of churches, but you get smothered in that thick smog of God and it's the scent of Christmas. It coats your throat in a religious syrup. What on earth do they burn to create that wonderful smell? Old Bibles and prayer books? Please don't tell me that there's a crematorium around the back...

I choose a pew and sit down. I decide on the loser's pew at the back, where the priest can't see you. In the cinema the back row is always full of couples holding hands, but in a church it's full of sinners: the people who look the other way when the collection plate comes around, or who want to slip out quick if their kids start crying.

Everything is quiet and low and barely even there -- the lights are all fading in and out like sleepy eyelids, just illuminating a few faces of the saints in the oil paint. The sounds are all whispers coming from locked off chapels. A couple of spears of sunshine are falling through the windows in the roof, but it may as well be night-time at noon. Shut the front door and put a guard on the door because the sunlight is not coming in here today. It's four quid to get in here, sunshine. No cameras allowed and no sunshine either.

No noise and no movement. This is where we come for a sit down and a think. To ponder on our miserable little lives and beg God to make them better. He doesn't care though -- he doesn't give a stuff. Take it from me: he's had 2,000 years of us begging for aid every day and he's fed up with it. There's only so much he can take.

I'm guessing that after we stapled Jesus to a tree he decided, *Right, I made a big mistake here.* Then he started sending pain and pestilence to wipe us out. First of all he sent a flood, but Noah saw that coming. Then he sent a few plagues, but we cured them with the NHS. Then he went on an all-out attack with Adolf Hitler, but he was no match for Winston Churchill. So ever since then he's been reduced to blasting bad weather at us with hurricanes and tornados and earthquakes, but we are proving too tough to kill. We are the immortal ones, not him. We are winning this war! Am I the only one who sees it?

And as if to prove my point... here I am in his holy house, blaspheming like crazy, and I'm not hearing a peep from the big fella. Maybe he's got better things to do than waste his time on a total nobody like me.

That's why I don't bother praying, because it's a complete waste of time. The things that I would pray for are impossible to repair anyway. You really *would* have to be a miracle worker to sort out my screw-ups.

What a beautiful place, though. I don't mind people believing in God if they carry on building churches like this. The walls are all old stones and dark woods, lit with golden lamps and candlesticks. You don't have to be a genius to see that it's six hundred years old because some of the stonework is practically a ruin. I see dirty, weathered stones and blackened organ pipes. I see heavy velvet curtains around the balcony to muffle the musician's coughs. I see deflated leather cushions that people have been kneeling on since time immemorial -- they've squeezed all the air out of them till there's nothing left. (That's why I could never be a Christian -- because of all that kneeling down they have to do. My knees couldn't take it.)

I believe in God now. Forget everything that I said before -- I have changed my mind in the last five minutes. I believe in God again, if it means free entry into this place every Sunday. I'll just stare at the walls whilst everyone else is listening to the priest.

After all, it might be true... *right?*

Is it really so far-fetched that an omnipotent old man is up there watching over us... who managed to fashion the entire universe out of nothing but dust and crumbs? He probably had lots of help anyway -- he wouldn't do the whole universe on his own, would he? Not in seven days -- that's just daft. That was probably an ancient typo. It's a bit like when people ask: "Who built St. Paul's?" and we say: "Christopher Wren". He's the guy who gets all the credit, but we all know that he didn't do it on his own -- he had a lot of help. And it's like that with the universe: God probably had a whole army of priests and bishops and nuns and Eastern Europeans to help him out -- he was just the foreman. He was the guvnor. He got the pope in to do all the decorations. The nuns did all the gardening. The choirboys did all the colouring in. The vicars just kept everyone fuelled up with tea and sandwiches. I haven't got a clue what Adam and Eve contributed (probably nothing) -- maybe I can find a holy man and ask him.

I look at my watch and realise that I've just spent the last thirty minutes sitting here in the dark, writing about God Almighty -- it must be this place that gets your head ticking over.

Brompton Oratory, St. Bride's and Temple Church are also quite beautiful inside.

St. Bride's

ADDRESS St. Bride's, Fleet Street, The City - map 4f **TRAINS** Blackfriars, St. Paul's (both zone 1) **BUSES** 4, 11, 15, 23, 26, 45, 63, 76, 172 **PRICE** Free **OPEN** 8 AM to 6 PM (Mon-Fri); 10 AM to 6.30 PM (Sun) **DENOMINATION** Church of England **WEB** stbrides.com **TEL** 0207 427 0133 **TIME REQUIRED** 30-45 mins
Easy to get to? ★★★ Good for kids? ☆☆☆
Value for money? free Worth a visit? ★★★

There are so many churches in London that it's impossible to see them all. But let me give you a piece of advice: St. Bride's is one of the ones that you need to visit. You'll find it tucked away inside a little courtyard off Fleet Street, hemmed in by the houses. It's so tightly guarded by houses that's it practically impossible to get a decent picture of the outside.

I sometimes use this place as one of my coffee stops when I'm strolling up to St. Paul's, because there's a little tea cart outside the front porch. The guy is always sitting on his stool reading his book, wrapped up in a hat that is two sizes bigger than his head. It's the kind of tea that melts your teeth. The steam that rises off the top is practically a flame.

It's only a tiny little church inside, but it's not far off being St. Paul's Cathedral. Christopher Wren was a busy boy in the 1670s, because not only did he build the cathedral, he also found time to build him fifty two little brothers. The decoration is amazing (although not original to Wren). Everything is made out of carved wood and marble. The only paint they could find was gold paint, and they've covered every jut and column top in it. It's the kind of place that makes you get up early on a Sunday morning to sing songs about a guy that you don't even believe in. I wish he did exist -- he *should* exist! Then I could come here and praise the guy who built it.

But wait... there's more. Adolf Hitler clumsily dropped a bomb on it during the war, and demolished everything except for the steeple and the outer walls, but he made up for it by uncovering a hidden crypt. And much like the little museum that's hiding underneath All Hallows by the Tower, this one similarly goes unnoticed by 95% of Londoners. If you took a poll of everyone walking down the street, then I guarantee that hardly any of them will have heard of this crypt. But what a place! It's full of tombstones and wonky walls, and a tessellated pavement that dates back to Roman times. They've got solid stone masonry on show from the Saxon period. They've got archaeological pots and pennies, medieval stonework, and decorated floor tiles from before the Great Fire of London... it's just like a time capsule. There's nearly two thousand years of history hiding quietly beneath this church.

There's another church museum in the crypt of All Hallows by the Tower.

St. James's Park

ADDRESS St. James's Park, Westminster - map 8c **TRAINS** Charing Cross, St. James's Park, Westminster (all zone 1) **BUSES** 3, 11, 12, 24, 29, 53, 88, 91, 148, 159, 211, 453 **OPEN** 5 AM to midnight (Mon-Sun) **WEB** royalparks.org.uk/parks/st-jamess-park **TEL** 0300 061 2350 **TIME REQUIRED** 45-60 mins

Easy to get to? ★★★ Good for kids? ★☆☆
Value for money? free Worth a visit? ★★☆

I had a nice sunny stroll around St. James's Park today, which was very pleasant. I think it's a toss-up between this one and Regent's Park as the best park in London, but I'm going to plump for St. James's. Regent's Park has got London Zoo and a boating lake, but it's too far north to have a walk around. You're never passing it unless you're already there, whereas St. James's is a stone's throw from Trafalgar Square and Parliament. If you want to have a sit down for half-an-hour and eat your lunch then it's perfect.

I had a wander around the whole lot today... I sat on the grass, tried out the cafe, met all the ducks, said hello to the pigeons, and even had a wee in the toilets. You need to take your time in a park, I reckon. It's no use running around to see the sights, because there aren't any. Not unless you like looking at the plants. The best place to sit is on the northern edge of the lake, where the thousand-strong army of ducks assembles its troops. It's like the Roundheads assembling their soldiers on Parliament Hill. They've got Canada geese, coots, mallards, and some tough as nails swans, all fighting over the little bits of bread that people drop on the concrete. There are hundreds of these beating, flapping, squawking winged-things, all jumping up and down to get the tourists' attention. They're not scared of humans at all -- there are some herons as well (the poor man's flamingo) -- and a few squirrels, brave enough to get within a few feet.

Once you're bored of watching the birds following each other up the path you can switch your attention to the humans. They all act in a similar manner... following their tour guide as he marches from place to place. The geese all follow their boss bird as he ruffles his feathers and sticks his neck out, and the tourists all follow their guide as he sticks his umbrella in the air, waving his arms about to keep everyone in line. The ducks are pecking at the breadcrumbs on the pavement, and the people are chomping on their last crisp crumbs in the packet.

There are two specific places in the park that are worth searching out: and the first one is a celebrated view of Buckingham Palace. You'll find it on the bridge across the centre of the lake. If you stand right in the middle of that then the Palace can be seen right at the eastern end... but with a ruddy great tree obscuring one whole half. I know that we are supposed to be living in enlightened times when it comes to chopping down trees, but if you gave me a chainsaw then I would happily fell that monster -- it's ruining the view! If you turn around 180° then you can get an even better view of a fountain through the trees and the buildings around Horse Guards.

The second place worth searching out is a little cottage at the western end of the park (directly opposite Horse Guards). It's called Duck Island Cottage and it's surrounded by little vegetable patches and wild flowerbeds. I don't think anyone actually lives there though -- it might even be haunted. The place is made out of wood and if you peered inside then I reckon you'd find it solid with cobwebs.

If you hear a marching band as you're walking around the park then it's probably the soldiers trooping down The Mall for Changing the Guard. The Mall stretches along the northern edge of the park and you can follow it all the way down to Buckingham Palace. So if you're planning on seeing the ceremony then may I recommend a spot of lunch in the park afterwards. They've got a big cafe at the western end called 'Inn The Park', and some little kiosks dotted around selling hot dogs and ice creams and that kind of thing. You can tell that it's a posh park because they sell lattes and frothy coffees instead of milkshakes.

During the summer months they set up a load of deck-chairs on the northern edge -- but don't sit down in them unless you've got some coins with you, because you'll be accosted by a warden wanting money (they are quite expensive). I always feel quite sorry for those guys, but on the other hand I find it quite amusing, too, because they spend an hour every morning putting out hundreds of deckchairs in sunny spots, and then all the tourists come along and plonk their butts down in them like they are free. They haven't got the faintest idea that they have to pay for them, so the warden has to run around all day kicking them out.

What a job that must be... patiently explaining to an endless stream of tourists that he wants some money or they'll have to stand up. *This is London, folks!* You have to pay for everything over here, even the seats.

St. John's Gate (aka. Museum of the Order of St. John)

ADDRESS St. John's Gate, St. John's Lane, Clerkenwell - map 4d **TRAINS** Barbican, Farringdon (both zone 1) **BUSES** 55, 153, 243 **PRICE** Self-guided tour: Free -- Guided tour: Donation of £5 **OPEN** Self-guided tour: 10 AM to 5 PM (Mon-Sat); 10 AM to 5 PM (Sun, Jul-Sep only) -- Guided tour: 11 AM and 2.30 PM (Tue, Fri and Sat) **WEB** museumstjohn.org.uk **TEL** 0207 324 4005 **TIME REQUIRED** Self-guided: 30-45 mins -- Guided tour: 1½ hours

Easy to get to? ★★★ Good for kids? ☆☆☆

Value for money? free **Worth a visit?** ★☆☆

Every now and then you'll be walking around London and come across an amazing place that you never knew existed -- and St. John's Gate is one of those places. It looks like a castle gatehouse dropped in the middle of some shopping streets and office blocks.

Whenever I see it I always wonder what London would have been like if we didn't knock half of it down. I've seen a million pictures and paintings of all the stuff we wasted (and all the buildings that the Germans bombed), and you can't help but feel a little wistful. Occasionally you come across a little snapshot of how it might have been before the hammers got busy on the bricks, and it's like finding a faded photo of your grandad in the back of a book, or an old newspaper stuffed underneath the floorboards. That's what this building is: a little snapshot of our city before modern life started throwing its weight around.

Inside is a little museum about the Monastic Order of the Knights Hospitallers of St John (you will know them better as the Knights Templar). Clerkenwell Priory was the Order's headquarters in England -- and St. John's Gate is the largest bit still standing. It's not the biggest exhibit in the world (it's only two rooms and a corridor), but it's still worth a quick look if you've got thirty minutes to spare.

They've got some illustrated manuscripts and a few suits of chainmail armour in there. The rest is just a load of plates and pots and vases, some old coins, plus a few oil paintings and portraits. You can also see some more of the gatehouse masonry when you step inside.

The museum begins with the Order's adventures during the Crusades, when they set up a hospital in Jerusalem to look after the pilgrims. After they got kicked out of the Holy Lands they moved onto Rhodes and Malta, until Napoleon sent them packing back to England. Queen Victoria revived the Order in the 1880s, and these days we know them as St. John's Ambulance, who are about as far removed from the Knights Templar as you could possibly get (you can tell that from the displays -- the Knights have got swords and shields and armour, whilst the modern guys make do with peaked caps and bandages).

Once you've seen inside the museum remember to have a little stroll down the road to the Priory Church (it's a totally separate building -- the nice guide behind the desk will give you directions). The church itself is nothing much to look at anymore because it was rebuilt after the war, after the Germans decided that they didn't like it, but you're not here for that -- you are here to see the creepy Norman crypt downstairs. It's a very low room with concrete arches that press down upon your head, and I'm not sure that I'd want to sit through a Mass here -- it seems a bit oppressive.

Remember to check out the tomb in the chamber on the left -- is that not the most gruesome tomb you've ever seen? Most people want their effigy to show them at their best, but this bird has gone for a face that looks like a starved skull, and ribs jutting through her chest like a famine victim.

If you have an interest in the Knights Templar then check out Temple Church.

St. Katherine Docks

ADDRESS St. Katherine Docks (behind Tower Bridge) **TRAINS** Tower Gateway DLR, Tower Hill (both zone 1) **BUSES** 15, 25, 42, 78, 100, RV1 **WEB** skdocks.co.uk **TIME REQUIRED** 45-60 mins

Easy to get to? ★★★ Good for kids? ★☆☆

Landmarks & Attractions | 209

Value for money? free Worth a visit? ★★☆

St. Katherine Docks is an interesting little place to visit, but unless you already know it's there it's very easy to miss -- it's tucked away behind the Guoman Hotel at Tower Bridge. It's not the kind of place that I'd make a detour for, but it's a nice enough place to stop if you happen to be visiting the Tower of London or Tower Bridge and you fancy a cup of tea.

It's basically a string of marinas all linked together by wooden walkways and towpaths, and you can have a stroll around the pathways past the rows of boats all floating in the dock. One hundred years ago this area used to be a car-park of cargo ships (the Port of London), offloading their goods before Tower Bridge, but these days all of the big warehouses and wharves have been turned into million pound flats (although I'm guessing that even a million would be cheap -- it's probably at least three times that). But it's the boats that make the place worth visiting. If you took the yachts away then it wouldn't be half as pretty. Everywhere looks better with a boat out the front, doesn't it? It's like putting tinsel on a Christmas tree -- all of a sudden it looks rich, and ten times as smart. It turns into the kind of place that you'd want to stop and have a sandwich... sit and watch what people are doing with their day. It's a people-watching place: that's what it is.

I like peering into all of the posh offices from the wooden walkway around the water. You can see them sitting at their desks punching numbers into the computers, with their frappuccinos and mocha chocolate lattes hovering around their mouths. One hand is typing away as good as gold (doing what it's paid to do), whilst the other hand is busy feeding their face. You can see rows and rows of desks stretching out around the office, each with its own little worker inside, and some little cubicles for the middle managers too. A few paces further on and you come to another window, but this time it's a posh office for the bosses, complete with a polished pine table and leafy green plant pot. You'd think that they'd be able to afford some metal blinds for the window, but no -- the nosey public can still stand outside and watch what they're doing. You can see them all sitting around the table discussing something important, holding out their power-thumbs and pointing to the whiteboard. I wonder what they are talking about? They are probably making million-pound decisions in there, whilst just one window along all of their poorly-paid staff are busy surfing the internet and drinking coffee and gossiping and pretending to be busy. I can see them skiving! Ha ha. Lazy workers... I was one of them once. I was getting paid peanuts for doing as little work as possible (nothing's changed). Shall I bang on the manager's glass and grass them up? *Nah*.

My photo isn't going to do this place justice today because -- you've guessed it -- it's raining again. So try and imagine my photo with a bit of colour in it. Paint that grey sky blue. Visualise some bright white light bouncing off the boats and a string of bunting flapping off the mast. Picture some pretty ripples in the water and some scantily-clad women lounging around on the decks -- that is what this place is like in the sun. Imagine that it's Monaco, and then turn the dial down a few notches (about 1000 notches). That is St. Katherine Docks.

I'm trying to count up all the boats but there are far too many. There must be about 100-or-so... maybe a little more. The top-of-the-range ones are big wooden ships with 20-foot masts and top-deck cabins for the captain, and at the bottom of the scale are breezy little weekend affairs that would get tossed over on a wave. The big ones are probably all corporate -- hired out for staff parties and jollies -- whilst the little ones are owned by white-haired retirees, sailing around the coast and fighting off the pirates. I would quite like to own a boat, I have just decided. I can picture myself sailing to the sun and back. The only problem is, I can't swim. Is that going to be a problem? How often do these things spring a leak? I'm always amazed at how some of these bigger boats can float. How heavy are they? They must weigh more than a double-decker bus, and yet here they are, sitting on the water like a sponge.

There's one boat here today that really is something special. It's about thirty feet tall, all pristine and shining white. Everything is rigged to perfection, with ropes wound up in pretty little coils, rain glistening off the cabin like dewdrops on ice. I would quite like to walk down the gangplank and peer inside the portholes to see how the other half lives, but the jetties are out of bounds to the public. You probably need to flash a gold credit card to step foot on those.

Who needs to go all the way to Monaco and the south of France when you've got St. Katherine's Docks? What has Monaco got that Docklands hasn't, apart from a load of French people?... Boats? (it's got plenty of them)... Water? (it's got that too)... Rich people? (got some of those as well)... Starbucks? (it's got two of them!)... Sunshine? (well, okay... it hasn't got much of that).

So what else is here? -- Well, there are lots of nice little cafes, restaurants and bars. And there's a cake shop and a store selling nautical gifts and memorabilia. There's also a coin-operated launderette for some reason -- which seems a little out of place. And a couple of art dealers selling oil paintings and pastels too. I tried to spy the prices but there weren't any tags on show (a sure sign that they are expensive). The highlight, though, is definitely the Dickens Inn. It's probably the best-looking pub in London, and wouldn't look out of place on the side of a Swiss mountain. It's like one of those Austrian hotels that you see on Ski Sunday. The front is all wooden balconies and hanging baskets, spilling over with pretty little flowers and strings of green leaves (at least, it would be if it was summer. But I have been here plenty of times to know it's being a bit modest today). Inside it's like an old country pub, all dark and dingy and done up in warm stone and wood. The only downside is that it gets incredibly busy and usually has a bouncer by the door. (I hate bouncers -- I'm always too ugly to get in.)

St. Magnus the Martyr

ADDRESS St. Magnus the Martyr, Lower Thames Street, The City - map 10a **TRAINS** Bank, Cannon Street, Monument (all zone 1) **BUSES** 17, 21, 35, 40, 43, 47, 48, 133, 141,

Landmarks & Attractions | 211

149, 521 **PRICE** Free **OPEN** 10 AM to 4 PM (Tue-Fri); Closed at weekend except for Sunday services **DENOMINATION** Church of England **WEB** stmagnusmartyr.org. uk **TEL** 0207 626 4481 **TIME REQUIRED** 20 mins
Easy to get to? ★★★ Good for kids? ☆☆☆
Value for money? free Worth a visit? ★★☆

Do you know which is my favourite building in London? Go on, have a guess...
No, you're wrong -- it's not St. Magnus the Martyr (it was a trick question!). Have another guess.
Nope, wrong again -- guess again.
Nope! -- Have one more guess and then I will tell you.
Wrong again -- you are totally useless at guessing.

It is actually London Bridge. But I don't mean the modern-day monstrosity that leads up to The Shard, I mean the fantastic medieval one that used to have a street full of houses and churches on top.

If you've never seen a picture of it then try and imagine picking up an entire street and dropping it across the river, complete with overhanging houses and horses, carts and markets and muddy pavements packed with traders and beggars and soldiers and scum. And then imagine a big gatehouse drawbridge in the middle and a tower at the Southwark end spouting bloody spikes and severed heads, and a raging, roaring torrent of water storming underneath. That, my friend, is what I'm talking about when I say *London Bridge*.

And this thing actually existed! This bridge was one of the longest-standing structures in the city's history, dating all the way back to 1176. By the 1750s it wasn't half the bridge that it was in its heyday, because all the buildings got demolished to make the roadway wider (so it was just a normal flat bridge by then). Shortly before Queen Victoria took the throne somebody had the bright idea of knocking it down and building something worse, and we sold that off to the Americans in the 1970s (they transported it brick by brick to a lake in Arizona). The boring replacement that we see today was opened in 1974. But it's still incredible to think that the original one stood for more than 650 years. For comparison, the modern-day Tower Bridge has only been standing for around 125 years.

So why am I telling you all of this, in a review about St. Magnus the Martyr church? Well, it's because this church marks the spot where the bridge came to an end on the City side. When you enter the church through the porch you are walking on the patch of ground where the roadway used to be. It's not quite as old as the original bridge though, because the first church got wiped out in the Great Fire of London. What you are looking at today is Christopher Wren's rebuild in the 1670s, with a few modern adjustments (courtesy of our German friends in the Luftwaffe).

But that's not the reason why I like this church so much... step inside...

Just inside the door is a big glass box with a thirteen-foot model of the original bridge. Have a good look at that, and then you will understand why I like the bridge so much. It's a really lively scene packed with people running up and down the streets with their houses hanging precariously over the edge -- they are all propped up with struts and it's a wonder that they never collapsed into the Thames. It must have been incredibly dark and gloomy with all the two-story houses blocking out the sun. It's a dirty motorway of horses and carts and traders and kids and dogs and chickens and sheep and soldiers and mud and squalor, all shoulder-to-shoulder like it's rush hour at Waterloo. Check out the great big gatehouse halfway along, and that unbelievably grand church built in the middle of the roaring river. How on earth did they build that?

It's almost like something out of a fairytale. How fantastic would it be if that structure still stood?

But it doesn't.

Ah well. St. Magnus the Martyr is quite nice though (I suppose I should say a few words about the church while I'm here). My entire focus has been on the model so far, but now that I've stopped to look around I have realised that the church is actually quite beautiful. It's got that lovely smoky incense smell like a perfumed fog, and a hushed rumbling sound that is on the very edge of hearing -- the kind of quiet that you only get inside big buildings. (Do you know what I mean? Probably not. How can you describe a sound that isn't there?)

The decor is all dark wood and stained glass. There are plenty of plaques on the wall and tombstones on the floor; but their names are getting rubbed out by the footsteps. The pattern is wearing off their blankets, and soon they'll be sleeping under plain stone sheets. I wonder how many people are buried under the floor? There are probably more people under the floor than in the pews -- it's literally just me and a fidgety old bird in a tatty coat. She's doing that furious nodding thing that crazy people do. She's having an animated natter with somebody, but as I look around I realise that there's nobody here. Is she talking to me? Maybe she's talking to God. Maybe she thinks *I* am God. (I think that I'm God as well sometimes -- so maybe we're both crazy.) I'm guessing that she's homeless by the way she's dressed, but she's probably thinking the same thing about me.

Every now and then we hear a loud bang and a crash coming from the organ on the balcony above our heads. I think there's a workman up there doing some DIY. Either that or God has dropped something.

It's just one big room really -- there are no side chapels. They've got some smaller altars in the corners with purple curtains and candlesticks. And they've got a model of a big ship too, all rigged up like it's ready to set sail at the Battle of Trafalgar. No explanation as to why it's there -- just another model on display for us sinners to look at, like the Airfix Jesus on the altar.

There's another model of London Bridge at the Museum of London Docklands.

St. Martin-in-the-Fields

ADDRESS St. Martin-in-the-Fields, Trafalgar Square - map 8b **TRAINS** Charing Cross, Embankment, Leicester Square (all zone 1) **BUSES** 3, 6, 9, 11, 12, 13, 15, 24, 29, 87, 88, 139, 159, 176, 453 **PRICE** Free **OPEN** 8.30 AM to 1 PM, and 2 PM to 6 PM (Mon, Tue, Thu, Fri); 8.30 AM to 1.15 PM, and 2 PM to 5 PM (Wed); 9.30 AM to 6 PM (Sat); 3.30 PM to 5 PM (Sun); Classical concerts between 1 PM and 2 PM, and evenings **DENOMINATION** Church of England **WEB** stmartin-in-the-fields.org **TEL** 0207 766 1100 **TIME REQUIRED** 15 mins

Easy to get to? ★★★ Good for kids? ☆☆☆
Value for money? free Worth a visit? ★★☆

This place is famous for helping out the homeless, and whenever you come in here you'll find a few of them kipping in the pews. There are two guys in here at the moment, gently resting their heads against the stone cold columns. The rain is knocking on the window and they've still got their hoods zipped up. I suppose when you're homeless you expect it to rain wherever you go, even indoors. A couple of religious do-gooders have crept up on them and seem to be asking them questions and offering some help, but they haven't shifted an inch from their slumbering pose, and it's obvious that they just want to sleep. *Thanks for your interest,* he's saying in his head, *but do please get lost.*

It's very quiet in here. Ten steps outside the front door is the busy traffic of Trafalgar Square, but in here it's nothing... just a quiet tapping of water on the window. I can see trails of grey rain drizzling down the glass in rivulets. It's like runny grey paint. The droplets are racing down the window until they splatter on the bottom, like suicidal jumpers falling off a rooftop. They've got a very strange stained-glass window in here -- its almost like boiled metal (you will understand what I mean you see it). They must have got it from a bomb-damaged disaster zone. It's all mangled and bent.

There are no artworks in here, no paintings, but there's plenty of ornate plasterwork and a Royal coat of arms above the altar. This is the parish church of Buckingham Palace, you see, (which is just down The Mall), so they've spruced up the edges in gold. The altar just seems to be a solid block of marble, and they've got some fancy chandeliers and a dark wood organ at the back.

I wonder if the Queen comes here every Sunday? I wonder what she's pray for? Good health and a skateboard for Christmas -- the same as the rest of us.

Here we go... the silence has been shattered by a piano tuner. They hold classical concerts in here every lunchtime and evening, and it looks like he is getting ready for a show. He has already busied himself setting up the instruments by the altar, and now he's starting to thump out the same note over and over, a deep drumming *thud thud thud* as he listens to the vibrato. Twenty times he's banged on this key in three-second intervals. You can't call it a tune... it's a barrage of war drums. It's the same note they play in horror movies before the bad man comes to slit your throat. Surely it must be a sin to make a din like that in church?

He has driven the homeless people back onto the streets.

Remember to have a nose around downstairs in the crypt. They've got a surprisingly big cafe and exhibition space down there (they are even bigger than the church upstairs). They've got a little gift shop as well, selling church books and religious knick-knacks. The thing that I like most about this cafe is that you can practically always get a seat, because not many people ever think to come down here.

St. Paul's Cathedral

ADDRESS St Paul's Cathedral, Ludgate Hill, The City - map 4f **TRAINS** Blackfriars, Cannon Street, Mansion House, St. Paul's (all zone 1) **BUSES** 4, 11, 15, 23, 25, 26, 100, 242 **PRICE**

If bought online: Adult £15.50; Senior (over-60) £13.50; Child (6-17) £7; Infant (under-6) free; Family (2 ad+2 ch) £38 -- If bought at the door: Adult £18; Senior (over-60) £16; Child (6-17) £8; Infant (under-6) free; Family (2 ad+2 ch) £44; Price includes a voluntary donation **OPEN** 8.30 AM to 4.30 PM (Mon-Sat); Last entry 30 mins before closing; It's only open for worship on Sundays **DENOMINATION** Church of England **WEB** stpauls.co.uk **TEL** 0207 246 8348 **TIME REQUIRED** 2-2½ hours

Easy to get to? ★★★   Good for kids? ★★☆
Value for money? ★★★   Worth a visit? ★★★

I went to St. Paul's Cathedral today and climbed all the way to the top (nearly), and I'm bloody knackered now -- they need to get a lift installed for lazy people like me. They should get Christopher Wren back to design a lift. I'm surprised he didn't put one in in the first place -- I thought he was supposed to be a good architect.

One of the things that I have always liked about St. Paul's is the lousy piece of street planning outside the front door. As you walk up Ludgate Hill you'll be expecting to see the entire grand facade blocking off the top like a big barn door, but with the way the street curves around the brow all you get is the centre portion with the side chopped off. It's the worst piece of street planning ever and it must have driven Christopher Wren nuts! But I don't suppose the surrounding shops were as tall in his day.

They do a similar trick when you enter the front door, because all you see is a little bit of the aisle. It's not until you pay your money and enter the Nave that you'll stand back and say "wow". You'll be standing in the same spot for ten minutes before you even switch the audio-guide on. Some buildings are just worth standing still and looking at.

I feel like a stalker. How long can you stand and stare at something before you get arrested?

I'm not a big fan of the audio guide, if I'm honest. I thought I'd better give it a go just to make sure I got all the history, but I ended up tuning out for large parts of it. The one at Westminster Abbey was too short but at least it was interesting. The one at St. Paul's has got too much about religion and not enough about the bricks. I know that sounds a bit daft (and I do realise that it's a cathedral!), but it was almost like they were trying to convert you through the headphones, imploring you to sit down and revel in the glory of God. It's full of lines like "May God go with you", "Take time to reflect on God" and "Our main purpose is to worship God". You do learn lots of nice stuff about the architecture though (the way he constructed the domes is an eye-opener) and a crazy line about the cost. Did you know that the cathedral only cost £143 million in today's money? That might sound like a lot but that is £20 million cheaper than Gareth Bale and Ronaldo! Why are our priorities so warped these days that we'd rather watch two footballers knocking in a few goals than build another St. Paul's?

Have you seen Portcullis House opposite Big Ben? That cost an unbelievable £235 million. So on the one hand we've got St. Paul's for £143 million, and on the other we've got Portcullis House for £235 million. It doesn't make sense, does it? Where on earth does all the money go these days, if it doesn't go on the bricks? They must blow it all on fees. I think it must have something to do with the timeframe as well, because they want everything completed last week so they can start earning their money back. If Christopher Wren turned up and told them that he needed thirty five years to complete just one cathedral then he'd be laughed out of town.

And don't get me started on the modern art... *Too late!* You've got me started now. They've erected two new war memorials on either side of the Nave and they look like intergalactic space stations -- no joke. Have we lost the ability to do traditional sculpture? I'll tell you how art works these days: they create rubbish like this and then cover up the fact that it's not very good by applying a layer of 'hidden meaning' to it (which nobody can see). And the public are supposed to stand there and say: "Oh yes, isn't this twisted piece of metal wonderful!" Who needs the skills of Grinling Gibbons and Michelangelo, when you can just pull a piece of structural junk out of some rubble and paint it white? I will say one thing, though: art is very democratic these days, because they've opened it up to the talentless masses. Art is the one discipline where you don't need to be any good at it in order to be successful.

You shouldn't get angry in a cathedral... what's wrong with me? Just ignore it and count to ten...

Let's sit underneath the dome and look up instead. That is all the art that I need to see. These seats underneath the dome are worth the entry fee alone. I've been sitting there for fifteen minutes and I'm quite happy. I could have sat here for another fifteen but my neck has started to get stiff from staring straight up. They have a few choral tracks on the audio guide that you can sit and listen to whilst you're looking, and that is my advice to you: just loop through those tunes until your neck gives out.

Once you've plucked up some courage you can head for the stairs and the half-hour traipse to the top of the dome. The first level is the Whispering Gallery, at a mere 257 steps, which even I could climb. This one looks down onto the interior of the Cathedral floor (where you've just been sitting), and it gets its name because you're supposed to be able to whisper to the wall and hear it clearly round the other side; but since I was on my own, and both of my ears were stuck to my head, I couldn't really test that out. But I think you'd be hard pressed to hear your partner above the hundred other people all doing the same thing anyway -- you couldn't even hear a whisper if they were standing five feet from your face!

After that you need to steel yourself for another 119 steps to the Stone Gallery. This is where it starts to get hard, because these stairs are of the stone windy type (like a castle turret), and I was extremely happy to get to the top. When you step through the door you'll find yourself at the very bottom of the exterior dome (which is a bit confusing... but there are actually two different domes, one inside the other). I have managed this one okay in the past so I forced myself to do it today, but my legs were definitely complaining halfway up.

You get a great view of The Shard and the City skyscrapers from up here. See if you can spot the top of Tower Bridge (which is easy) and the golden urn at the top of The Monument (a bit harder). The White Tower at the Tower of London might take you a while as well. Then look for the Globe (easy) and the London Eye and Parliament. I will give you some bonus points if you manage to spot the top of Westminster Cathedral -- and I do mean the 'cathedral', not the abbey!

If you're fitter than Superman then you can try and climb another 150 steps to the Golden Gallery. This one takes you to the very top of the exterior dome, with even better views over the city. But unfortunately there's no stone tunnel to climb this time. There are no wide wooden steps either. What you have to do for this one is tiptoe up a rickety old iron thing that goes straight up vertically, with fabulous views of the solid concrete floor far, far below. To make things even worse the stair-treads are like an iron lattice, and totally see-through, so you can see the exact spot on the floor where your blood stain will be in two minutes time. Even Edmund Hillary would think twice about climbing them (I'm being serious!). Needless to say, I chickened out -- I don't mind admitting it. I know that I'm supposed to be writing a review for you, but I'm not insane. Anyone who climbs those stairs is clearly as mad as a box of frogs.

My problem is that I am a total wuss when it comes to heights, and I always think that I've picked the day when the whole edifice is going to come tumbling down on my head. The fact that it has been standing quite happily for 350 years doesn't matter. It even stayed standing when the Germans were dropping bombs on it during the Blitz, but I don't care -- it still looks totally unsafe and there is no way you will ever get me onto that death trap!

The final place to visit is the Crypt downstairs, containing the tombs of Nelson and the Duke of Wellington.

Nelson died first so he was given the plum spot in the centre, which is a better setting than many of our English kings and queens were given. The height of the tomb coupled with the way it's lit makes him almost like a saint. I would go so far as to say he's got the grandest burial in London after Edward the Confessor and Henry VII.

The Duke of Wellington's tomb doesn't disappoint either. Whilst Nelson's bed is fancy like the dandy man he was, the Duke just gets a no-nonsense block of stone. The Duke didn't do small talk and his tomb doesn't either. His coffin is like his character. I think this guy was the greatest Englishman who ever lived and it gives you a strange feeling standing five feet from his bones.

If you walk to the chapel at the far end then you'll find the graves of famous painters like Turner, Reynolds and Millias (Constable is on the other side). You'll also find the most surprising tomb of all -- to Sir Christopher Wren. The surprise is not that he's buried here, (that is obvious), but the fact that they made so little fuss of his grave! It's basically just a simple slab of black tucked quietly away in the corner. But I suppose he gets the Cathedral as his headstone.

The other big churches in London are Westminster Abbey, Westminster Cathedral and Brompton Oratory.

Science Museum

ADDRESS Science Museum, Exhibition Road, South Kensington - map 6f **TRAINS** South Kensington (zone 1), and 10 min walk **BUSES** 14, 49, 70, 74, 345, 360, 414, 430, 710, C1 **PRICE** Museum: Free, but there may be a charge for temporary exhibitions -- Flight simulators: Adult £5-6; Senior £4-5; Child £4-5; Family (4 people with up to 2 ad) £15-17, or £12-14 for 3 people with up to 2 ad -- IMAX: Adult £11; Senior £10; Child £10; Family (4 people with up to 2 ad) £30, or £27 for 3 people with up to 2 ad **OPEN** During school term: 10 AM to 6 PM (Mon-Sun) -- School holidays: 10 AM to 7 PM (Mon-Sun); Last entry 45 mins before closing **WEB** sciencemuseum.org.uk

Landmarks & Attractions | 217

TEL 0870 870 4868 **TIME REQUIRED** 2½-3 hours, plus 1 hour if you watch an IMAX film

Easy to get to? ★★★ Good for kids? ★★★ Value for money? free Worth a visit? ★★★

If you are anything like me, then you will love learning about industrial-sized pistons and pipes and steam traction engines dating from the years 1715 to 1904. So when you walk into the Science Museum it will be like walking into heaven.

The first hall is like a big factory floor filled with iron turbines, pumps and pulleys, huge wheels and squeals and wheezing noises as they go up and down and round and round. You can hear metal shrieks and tin whistles coming from the speakers as if they are still alive. If you're into Victorian engines then you'll have a great time. If you're not into Victorian engines (which is 99% of us, I'm guessing) then head straight through the door towards 'Exploring Space'.

If you like astronomy then this place is great (albeit quite small). They've got some full-sized models of famous shuttles and ships in here, like the Huygens space probe that landed on Titan, and that ill-fated Beagle Explorer that bounced to death on Mars. I quite liked the Nazi V2 rocket in there as well. Not because I'm a Nazi (I hasten to add!), but because it kicked off our trip to the moon. Did you know that the Nazi V2 was the first man-made object to make it into space? And it took the first photo of the earth from space as well -- they've got a copy of it on display. Where would we be without those evil rocket-building Nazis, huh?

Best of all is their life-size model of the Apollo 11 lunar lander (the one that took Armstrong to the moon). It looks a bit flimsy to me and it's amazing that it ever made it off the launchpad -- it's covered in gold tin foil and looks about as sturdy as a Kit Kat wrapper. I'm not sure that I'd want to climb the stairs even now, while it's sitting safely on terra ferma (they probably wouldn't let you anyway -- health and safety).

The space gallery also contained the only hands-on exhibit that I dared to touch (because there was no one around to see me). I had to put my hands through a glass tube into some bulky astronaut's gloves, and then try and tighten up some nuts and bolts. I don't mean to boast, but it was actually quite easy. Maybe I should give NASA a ring and offer them my services.

After that comes the 'Making of the Modern World' gallery. This huge room contains some very famous vehicles like the Puffing Billy, Stephenson's Rocket and Model T Ford. It's a bit like Madame Tussauds for vehicles, I suppose -- the machines don't actually do anything, you just walk around going *oh, I remember that from school! and my grandad used to have one of those...* It's probably more for the boys, this place, because I don't reckon many girls will get a kick out of a Rolls Royce Merlin engine.

Less interesting are the early looms and printing presses, typewriters, sewing machines, sundials, gas ovens, vacuum cleaners, radios and toasters... they've got lots of model trains and planes on the upstairs balcony too, if that is your fancy. And oh yeah... I can't leave without mentioning the car park on the wall -- they've stacked up six minis on top of each other. Don't ask me why, because I haven't got a clue.

I found the 'Information Age' section a bit dull but if you're into the history of computers and communications then you might like it. It's full of early telephones and computers. The worst thing about this room is that it makes you feel extremely old because one of the display cases contains examples of early home computers like the BBC Micro and Commodore 64 -- I remember those from when I was a kid! (The BBC Micro even had a paper strip across the keys from the space game Elite -- I used to like that game!) They had a Casio keyboard too. Jesus christ... my life has become history already. Imagine how much money we could have raised if we hadn't flogged all of these 'museum exhibits' off at a car boot sale. That just goes to show you... be careful of that busted junk you've got in your loft, because tomorrow it might end up in the British Museum.

The third floor is where they keep all of the planes. And I don't mean piddly little models either -- I mean full-size aircraft that have been dropped in from the sky (they must have a canopy roof that peels back, because there's no way that they could have carried them up the stairs). They've got quite a nice collection too: a big business jet, a Spitfire, Hawker Hurricane, Messerschmitt, Vickers Vimy... all the way back to the early biplanes built with string and wood. They're worth seeking out just for the total surprise of walking into a hangar full of planes, three floors up.

The medicine section on the fourth floor is probably my favourite part of the museum. And yeah... I know exactly what you're thinking: *the medicine section?* You are probably thinking the same thing as me: that a medicine section sounds as boring as hell but it actually turned out to be really good. The bit that made it interesting wasn't the cabinets full of bottles and pills and needles, but the life-size mock-ups of doctors' surgeries throughout the ages. They've got everything from Roman field hospitals and navy doctors amputating legs on the deck of a warship, to a plague-ridden street scene in the scummy part of Rome. A lot of them are full-size as well: they've got X-ray rooms... intensive care units... and a full-size operating theatre too, complete with waxwork surgeons fiddling with a waxwork patient.

I finished the day off with a forty-minute movie in their 3D IMAX cinema. It's been a while since I've visited the big BFI IMAX in Waterloo but it looks about the same size to me (maybe just a teeny-weeny bit smaller). They've got a selection of different films playing throughout the day but a lot of them seem to be for the kids. I'm still quite young looking, but I don't think I could pass for an 8-year-old, so I plumped for *Hidden Universe*. It was okay -- it wasn't the greatest 3D movie I've ever seen (it contained a lot of fluff that had nothing to do with space) but it was an okay way to waste forty minutes of my life. I get the impression that most of their 'movies' are more like documentaries -- the same kind that you might find on the Discovery Channel; so it's not as good as watching an actual 3D Hollywood movie, but your kids will probably enjoy it nonetheless.

Their second cinema tries to go one better by showing *4D films*; and if that sounds a bit daft then there is a very good reason for that: because it is daft. If you thought that a four-dimensional movie was theoretically impossible in a three-dimensional world then you are wrong, because it turns out that 4D is exactly the same as 3D, except with some soapy bubbles and warm water sprayed in your face.

My movie was called *Legend of Apollo*, and I can describe it for you in one word: rubbish. Actually, it was so bad why don't you let me describe it in two words instead: it was *really* rubbish. When the rocket takes off the seats shake about a bit and air is blown in your face. This is supposed to simulate what the astronauts experienced when they took off in Apollo.

They also blow some bubbles around the auditorium for some reason (I still haven't worked that one out -- is it supposed to be smoke? Maybe we should give Neil Armstrong a ring and ask him). Then you land on the moon (more shaking) and get out and have a walk around on the lunar surface (more shaking). Then the rocket takes off again (more shaking) and enters the earth's atmosphere (more shaking) and lands in the sea (water gets sprayed in your face). And then everyone gets up and goes to the cafe for a cup of tea.

P.S.: There is one more thing that you should be made aware of before you go to the Science Museum, in case you're under the impression that it's free (which it is). They perform quite a hard sell on you when you walk through the door. Gone are the days when they'd just put a glass cabinet by the door and ask for a donation. That was far too polite. What they do these days is funnel everyone through a manned barrier with a money slot on the side, and if you don't want to donate then you basically have to look this person right in the eye and say: "No thank you, madam" -- which will make you feel like Ebenezer Scrooge. All they need to do is rig up some flashing lights and a big neon arrow with 'miser' written on it and your humiliation will be complete.

Listen, Mister Science Museum man... either it's free, or it's not. Either you want an entry fee, or you don't. But don't bully the poor tourists into handing over a fiver because they don't understand what a 'voluntary donation' is (they aren't exactly the first two words that you learn in English lessons!).

I actually don't mind stumping up the money, because even if you hand over the suggested donation of £5 it's still a bargain day out compared with most other London attractions. But it's a very aggressive way of asking for a voluntary donation. The Tower of London even has the cheek to add our donation straight onto the ticket price! They don't even bother asking you anymore -- they just add it straight on. If you don't want to donate then you are supposed to let them know before you pay; and how many people are going to have the balls to do that? It's a bit like forcing a load of soldiers into a helicopter, parachuting them behind enemy lines, and then telling them if they don't want to fight then they're welcome to walk home.

Another P.S.: They've got a very good gift shop at the Science Museum. It's full of science books and fun little gadgets -- perfect stocking filler gifts for Christmas.

If you enjoy the Science Museum then you might like the Royal Observatory as well.

The Shard

ADDRESS The Shard, London Bridge Street, Southwark - map 10c **TRAINS** London Bridge (zone 1) **BUSES** 43, 48, 141, 149, 521 **PRICE** If bought online: Adult £25.95; Child (4-15) £19.95; Infant (under-4) free; Family (Sun only, 2 ad+2 ch, or 1 ad+3 ch) £74.95 -- If bought at the door: Adult £30.95; Child (4-15) £24.95; Infant (under-4) free; Family (Sun only, 2 ad+2 ch, or 1 ad+3 ch) £79.95 **OPEN** Timed tickets from 10 AM to 10 PM (Mon-Sun, Apr-Oct); 10

AM to 7 PM (Sun-Wed, Nov-Mar); 10 AM to 10 PM (Thu-Sat, Nov-Mar); Last entry 1 hour before closing **WEB** theviewfromtheshard.com **TEL** 0844 499 7111 **TIME REQUIRED** 1-1½ hours

Easy to get to? ★★★ Good for kids? ★★★ Value for money? ★★☆ Worth a visit? ★★★

I don't like heights. I'm not a bird, I'm not a pilot. And I haven't got a death wish. So why would I want to go a mile up into the sky just to look out of a bleedin' window? There are plenty of decent windows at ground level. Why can't I just go up to the second floor and look out of that window? But no, apparently I had to ride the lift all the way up to floor six-billion-and-eight, which is taking the mick -- is there even any oxygen up there, I said? Am I going to be able to breathe? But that is what I was forced to do today for this review, against my wishes. Luckily the building didn't fall down and I am still alive to tell you the tale, so here goes.

The 'View from the Shard' is London's highest observation deck, at a mere thirty quid a go. Thirty pounds just to look out of a window! But what a window -- even I admit that the view is pretty fantastic. But if you're a family of four then you'll probably have to take out a Wonga loan to pay for it. Even the guidebook was a tenner. When you walk in the front door you can certainly see where they've spent the money. The foyer is very hi-tech, like a space station, with huge HD screens all over the place showing you picture-perfect cloudless views from the top.

The first thing they do after you hand over the money is make you stand up against one of those giant movie green-screens, so they can try and flog you a picture of yourself when you come back down, magically inserted into a view of the skyline. What a waste of money, I thought. You could just snap the same picture of yourself when you get to the top! Needless to say I still bought one, because I'm an idiot.

Then they lead you to the lift, and that is when the fun starts...

If I told you that this lift travelled faster than the speed of sound, then I wouldn't be very far off the mark. I swear to God that if the brakes weren't working, then this lift could probably launch you into space. If a suicidal bloke jumped off the top of the building, then I reckon you could ride the lift all the way down and catch him -- that is how fast it goes.

Before the lift attendant has even had time to shut the door you are already at level 32. All of a sudden he tells you to get out, and you wonder what you've done wrong. If it wasn't for the fact that my ears popped like dynamite then I would have sworn we hadn't moved. At level 32 you have to get out and enter a second lift to level 68. That is where the first observation deck is.

I admit it... I was a bit jelly-legged when I first stepped out onto the floor. I had to wait 15 minutes before I could even go near the window (true!). I always think that I've picked the day that the building's going to fall down around me. But of course, I am a wimp -- there is nothing for you to be worried about, unless you're a wimp like me. The building doesn't sway about like the Eiffel Tower, and the first observation deck is totally enclosed in floor-to-ceiling glass, so you can't hear any noise or feel the wind in your face. It feels pretty solid and well built. I think the odds of it falling over are pretty slim, but you never know. Once you've got used to the height then you can walk around the entire floor for uninterrupted views of the London skyline.

They've got a few telescope-like machines dotted around the place, but they are more like TV screens. You don't look through the optic with these -- you just point it at a spot and the picture pops up on the screen. I think it's much better just to use your eyes. They helpfully point out the direction of all the sights on a sign above the window, and half of the fun is trying to pick them out amongst the bazillions of city buildings stretched out below you.

It really is very high. You probably knew that already, just be looking at it. But let me stress the point again -- it is very high indeed. I remember when I went to St. Paul's Cathedral I chickened out of climbing to the very top because the level below was already too high for my bladder. But when I looked down upon St. Paul's today, it just looked like a little Lego building miles below me. The buildings which you already know are high, just seem like midgets. Imagine being in an airplane flying over London, coming in to land at Heathrow with all the buildings streaming past your window at two miles out -- that is how high it is.

When your jelly legs are feeling a bit more solid you can venture up another four floors up to level 72. There's no lift this time, just a few flights of stairs, and this will take you out onto the open-air deck. As you can see from the photo, it's actually open to the weather -- you can reach beyond the window and touch the raindrops before they fall out of the clouds. I actually had a conversation with the birds up here -- that is how high it is. You are standing in the sky.

Surprisingly, it's not that windy. I had visions of me being blown over the edge by a force ten gale, like a crisp packet in the wind, but it's actually quite pleasant. The panes of glass around the edge are still taller than a human, so it's not possible to stick your head over the edge and look down, but I wouldn't recommend doing that anyway because the wind would rip your head off. The first things to go would be your teeth, quickly followed by your lips and eyeballs as the hurricane-strength wind spaghettified your face. The scariest thing is when a plane flies nearby and you can hear the roar of the engines.

So what was the view like? It was extremely sunny when I went this morning, so I didn't have any clouds or rain to frustrate my camera, but unfortunately the bright light made it very hazy. I couldn't even see as far as Canary Wharf -- it was totally hidden in the bright-light haze. The triangle top of One Canada Square was just about visible if I squinted and I knew where to look. I had no chance of seeing the Millennium Dome. I couldn't even see the bend of the river at the Isle of Dogs. Tower Bridge was almost lost in a bright white sheen, and my pictures of it look like they've been taken through a net curtain. In the other direction I could easily make out the London Eye, Big Ben and the Houses of Parliament, but Buckingham Palace and the London parks were lost in the sun. The tall chimneys of Battersea Power Station were about the furthest landmark I could see to the west.

So the view was a tiny-weeny bit disappointing, if I'm honest. The literature makes out that you can see as far as forty miles, which I'm sure is true, but obviously a lot depends on the weather. Maybe you'll have better luck than me. If I had to go again then I'd probably go in the late afternoon or early evening, when the street lights are just beginning to turn on.

If you like views of the skyline then check out the Sky Garden and London Eye. You can also climb to the top of St. Paul's.

Sherlock Holmes Museum

222 | London: A Visitor's Guide

ADDRESS Sherlock Holmes Museum, Baker Street, Marylebone - map 2c **TRAINS** Baker Street, Marylebone (both zone 1) **BUSES** 13, 74, 82, 113, 139, 189, 274 **PRICE** Adult £15; Child (under-16) £10 **OPEN** 9.30 AM to 6 PM (Mon-Sun) **WEB** sherlock-holmes.co.uk **TEL** 0207 224 3688 **TIME REQUIRED** 1-1½ hours

Easy to get to? ★★★ Good for kids? ★☆☆
Value for money? ★★☆ Worth a visit? ★★☆

If you've got a magnifying glass and a deer stalker hat, then get them out right now and put them on. Stick one of those long wooden tobacco pipes in your mouth as well, and settle down in front of a roaring fire and let me tell you all about the Sherlock Holmes Museum.

The first thing you need to know about the Sherlock Holmes Museum is this: it is chockablock with tourists every hour of the day. This place is always busy. Every time I walk down Baker Street there are about three million people standing outside having their photo taken with the Victorian copper on the door. I think the rest of the world really does want to believe that English people wear bowler hats and drink cups of tea, whilst reading Shakespeare and Sherlock Holmes. When you go to America what is the first thing you do? -- you eat a hamburger. And when you go to France what is the first thing you do? -- you buy a string of onions. And it's the same in England... as soon as they step off the plane they want a bit of Sherlock Holmes and a cup of tea please.

I've always wondered why Sir Arthur Conan Doyle sited Sherlock Holmes in Baker Street. Have you ever been to Baker Street? It's not exactly the prettiest street in London. It's just a concrete street of shops and offices, with buses and lorries thundering round from Regent's Park. And stuck at the top end of it is this little piece of Victoriana, looking like something that belongs in Bloomsbury. The museum is not even in the right house -- did you know that? The real 221b Baker Street is a few doors down.

Okay, so my interest is peaked now... I'm going to do a bit of detective work (on Wikipedia) and find out why he chose that house. Imagine if Sherlock Holmes had Wikipedia in the 1890s -- he would have saved himself a lot of hassle. Right... here we are... apparently 221b Baker Street didn't even exist in Conan Doyle's day; the street was only half the length that it is now. It wasn't until the 1930s that it reached all the way up to 221, and then the Abbey National moved in and grabbed it. The Sherlock Holmes Museum was a bit slow off the mark, and had to settle for a shop a few doors down. But when the bank moved out in 2005 they bagged themselves sole use of the address. So that's what happened... *mystery solved*. This detective lark is easy!

The first room is basically just a big shop selling all kinds of tourist tat. Books, DVDs, tea-cups, pens, pencils, pipes... you name it, they've got it. It's all decorated like it would have been in Sherlock's day (if he had a tourist tat shop), and the staff are dressed up like they've just stepped out of the pages of a Sherlock Holmes novel. It certainly does look the part.

From then on you just walk around the house at your own leisure. There's no audio-guide or anything like that, all you get is a little A4 leaflet that covers the basics. All the rooms are set out exactly as they are in the novels. I don't profess to be an expert, but it seemed to be pretty well done to me. You can walk around his first floor study, his sitting room, his bedroom and the landlady's room. Right in the rafters you've got a little lavvy too, but I guess he must have bought a lot of takeaways because there doesn't seem to be a kitchen.

All of the rooms are fit to bursting with objects related to his books. I suppose that is one of the fun things about the house if you're already a fan... you can hunt around the rooms for the 'clues'. The desks and tables are absolutely stuffed with papers and pens and the people around me were cooing and aaahing every time they spotted a prop. You can have a sit-down in his fireside armchair as well, and try on his deerstalker hat. People were even having a puff on his pipe (no tobacco in it though -- not these days. Health and safety!).

I'm pretty sure that half the people walking around the house believed him to be real, judging by the way they were talking. Tourists were pointing out the places he sat (no he didn't), the things he wrote (no he didn't) and the objects he owned (he's fictitious!). I suppose that is testimony to how well the thing is done: he is as real to them as Father Christmas is to me.

At the top of the house is a collection of Madame Tussauds waxworks, dressed up as characters from his stories. They've got a spooky looking Moriarty in there, a man with a twisted lip, and a dying Grimesby Roylott lying spread-eagled on the floor.

If you're already a fan Sherlock Holmes then I'm sure you'll love it. And if you don't, well... it's a decent enough way to pass an hour of your time.

You might also like the Charles Dickens Museum and a tour of the Globe Theatre.

Sir John Soane's Museum

ADDRESS Sir John Soane's Mus., 13 Lincoln's Inn Fields, Holborn - map 4e **TRAINS** Holborn (zone 1) **BUSES** 1, 8, 59, 68, 91, 168, 171, 242, 243, 521 **PRICE** Free **OPEN** 10 AM to 5 PM (Tue-Sat); Closed (Sun-Mon); Last entry 30 mins before closing **WEB** soane.org **TEL** 0207 405 2107 **TIME REQUIRED** 1-1½ hours

Easy to get to? ★★★ Good for kids? ★☆☆ Value for money? free Worth a visit? ★★★

A word of advice: If you see some people milling around outside then don't walk through the door, or an old bloke will lambast you for jumping the queue. Sir John Soane's Museum must be the only museum in London where you have to queue outside for ten minutes before they let you through the door. Lots of people fell foul of that rule whilst I was waiting, but once you get inside you realise why they do it: the house is so small and pokey that they can only fit about fifty people in it.

The first room that you enter is a spacious dining room with a big picture of the main man on the wall. The rest of the rooms are tiny. Some of them are no more than a few feet across (no joke), and the walls are crammed full of shelves and hooks and anything else that can hang an ancient piece of tat. Honest to God, you will never have seen a house like this. This guy was a kleptomaniac. He picked up bits of concrete from Egypt, Greece, Italy and everywhere else on planet earth. He's got millions and bazillions of vases, statues, heads, legs, cups, jugs, plates, slates, books and boxes stacked up from the floor to ceiling in every room of the house. Imagine if you tried to cram the entire contents of the British Museum into a three story townhouse -- that is what this place is like. If you are a part-time cleaner then trust me when I say you don't want to do the dusting in this house, because you will be there until kingdom come.

You'll come across the first true treasures a few rooms into the tour: paintings by Canaletto and Hogarth. But that's when the size of the building lets him down, because there must be about thirty-odd paintings crammed into a space no bigger than my shed. The only way that I can describe the crazy arrangement is like this: imagine if you nailed the spine of a book onto a wall, so the pages flapped out into the room. That is what it is like. Except the flaps all have paintings on. It's a totally stupid way to display the works of art, because every time you open a flap you are hiding one of the others. I never got to see the Canaletto because the guide had another panel open that was covering it up. And there's no room to move for a better view either -- there were six people in that room and it was like squeezing into a tube train on a Saturday night.

After that you come to a fantastic little room that looks down upon the sarcophagi of Seti I. The balcony around it is crammed with ancient knick-knacks all overhanging the edge, so I guess they must be cemented into place to stop them falling off. If someone stumbled on his shoelaces then the whole lot would come raining down on the poor buggers below. I actually sucked in my breath a little bit the first time I saw it because I'm quite a clumsy so-and-so, and I had visions of crashes and bangs and shouts and screams as my elbows went to work.

When you finally get down into the crypt you can see the sarcophagi up close. And I really do mean up close, because the surrounding wall is no more than a foot away from your face. And that is both the biggest problem and the biggest charm of this place: you can never really stand back for a decent view. The pathway around the balcony, for example, is so small and skinny that you have to squeeze in your stomach and fold up your bones and wait for the people to shuffle past before you can continue. If you want to stop and take your time then you may as well forget it, because you will very quickly have a conveyor belt of people bunching up behind.

Apart from the famous paintings and the sarcophagi of Seti I, the other artefacts on display are basically bric-a-brac -- that is how I would describe them. But I'd still definitely recommend a visit simply to see how tightly he's arranged the place -- that's where the real interest lies.

There's more Egyptian archaeology at the British Museum and Petrie Museum.

Sky Garden

Landmarks & Attractions | 225

ADDRESS Sky Garden, 20 Fenchurch Street, The City - map 10b **TRAINS** Bank, Cannon Street, Monument (all zone 1) **BUSES** 25, 35, 40, 47, 48, 149, 344 **PRICE** Free, but you must book a timed ticket on their website **OPEN** 10 AM to 6 PM (Mon-Fri); 11 AM to 9 PM (Sat-Sun); Last entry 1¼ hours before closing **WEB** skygarden.london **TEL** 0207 337 2344 **TIME REQUIRED** 1 hour

Easy to get to? ★★★ Good for kids? ★★★ Value for money? free Worth a visit? ★★★

I like skyscrapers. Anything that blocks out the sun is good. Anything that can create a mini-whirlwind down on the pavement is good. But this one has got another trick up its sleeve because it can channel the power of the sun into a tightly focused jet of death -- *and I'm not even joking!*

When the building opened in early 2014 everyone was very interested in the curved facade; especially when it started focusing the sunshine like a giant concave mirror. Cars parked in the street got so hot that their bodywork blistered (true!). So this building has real power: the power to melt metal; the power of death and destruction and fiery flames! If the devil ever came to London then this is where he would live. Its official name is 20 Fenchurch Street, but everyone calls it the Walkie Scorchie (because it looks like a walkie-talkie) -- I call it Dr. Evil's HQ.

You can guess what happened next though... the bosses started having panic attacks and nightmares about the building burning up humans in the street, so they got the builders back in to fix it. So you don't have to worry anymore because it is totally safe -- Boo! But that's okay because it's got another little surprise at the summit: a three-story greenhouse looking out over the London skyline. And that is where I am headed today -- to the Sky Garden.

The security for it is totally over the top. First of all you have to order a ticket on their website (even though it's free), and then take some photo ID along with you so they can match it up with your personal details -- which basically means taking your passport if you're a tourist. You don't even have to do that for Parliament! But I jumped through their hoops because I wanted to see the plants, and when I stepped out on the 35th floor all was forgiven.

The landscaped gardens are arranged around a big open courtyard with seats and a cafe in the middle, and there's another level on top with a seafood brasserie. The windows stretch all the way around so you have a 360-degree view of the skyline.

The south side just looks across to the top of The Shard, whilst the north side gives you a great view of the Gherkin and the Cheesegrater building. But it's the views on either side that will knock you out. The west side looks straight down the Thames past St. Paul's and the London Eye, whilst the east side drops you straight down on top of the Tower of London. You get a really good birds-eye view of it, and Tower Bridge too, with the skyscrapers of Canary Wharf in the far distance.

Hey! I've got an idea... let's have a little competition between you and me. See if you can spot Buckingham Palace (for 10 points), Big Ben (20 points), Primrose Hill and St. Pancras station (you will need to know London really well for those), the British Museum (very hard!), the Royal Courts of Justice (easy-peasy) and Wembley arch. If you can pick out the Old Royal Naval College at Greenwich and Alexandra Palace as well then give yourself a pat on the back. It's a lot harder than it sounds because they don't have any telescopes to look through. And they haven't even bothered to put up any of those silver plaques to pinpoint the places, so you might want to bring a map of London with you to give you some clues.

As for the plants... I was a bit underwhelmed to be honest. It wasn't exactly a lush rainforest. I was hoping that it was going to be like one of those greenhouses at Kew, with palm trees and vines creeping all the way up the side, but it was basically just a bank of mud with some piddly little cacti and flowers out of season. They did have a bit of that misty spray coming out of the pipes, though, to make the place all wet and humid. There were no animals or birds either. No monkeys swinging through the trees. No venomous snakes curling around the branches. No big spiders to worry about.

I am assuming that I caught it out of season though, because it would be totally daft of them not to have any tropical plants, so I am prepared to give them the benefit of the doubt on that -- maybe you'll have better luck than me.

Another thing worth noting: they do have an exterior balcony but they weren't letting anyone onto it today. There was no explanation as to why not, but I'm guessing that it was too windy.

If you enjoy climbing up towers then check out The Shard and ArcelorMittal Orbit.

Speakers' Corner

ADDRESS Speakers' Corner, Hyde Park (north-east corner) - map 7a **TRAINS** Marble Arch (zone 1) **BUSES** 2, 6, 7, 10, 16, 23, 30, 36, 73, 74, 82, 94, 98, 113, 137, 148, 159, 274, 390, 414, 436 **OPEN** Best at 12 noon on a Sunday **TIME REQUIRED** 30 mins

Easy to get to? ★★★ Good for kids? ☆☆☆
Value for money? free Worth a visit? ★☆☆

I've been meaning to go to Speakers' Corner for ages now... and then I went and picked the worst day possible. It rained when I was going there, rained whilst I was watching, and rained all the way home as well. It was just a dirty grey sky tipping water onto my head for three hours.

I turned up at 10 AM first of all, and there was absolutely no one there. Not a soul. Just me and a bloke cycling his bike over the grass. Then I went back at 11 AM and it was just me and two women walking their dogs. I was soaking wet by this time so I nearly went home, but I had a little stroll down Oxford Street and then trudged back at noon and thankfully it was starting to fill up by then. So my advice to you is this: go at 12 noon, on a Sunday, because there will be nobody around otherwise. The only things that make speeches outside of those hours are the birds in the trees.

Legend has it that you can stand up and say whatever you want, about whatever you want, without fear of prosecution, but apparently that is a total load of cobblers -- you are still subject to the same laws as everyone else in London. There are no special laws here at all. It's just a patch of grass in the park where people come and stand on stepladders.

I was there for about sixty minutes and I saw a grand total of two speakers. One of them was a Muslim cleric, who was a real barrel of laughs (not), and the other one was an old professor-like guy talking about the United Nations. He was actually quite good and had about 100 people listening. The Muslim guy had five (I counted them). The gist of his speech was this: *Allah... Islam... Mecca... sins... the Koran.* I gave him five seconds of my time and then went and listened to the other guy.

Now this was when it started to get a bit more interesting, because there was a very lively heckler butting in every ten-seconds, trying to drown him out. The old guy was standing on his little fold-up ladder and had a big booming voice, and he was trying to reform the UN right there and then, in Hyde Park, in the drizzling rain. He was arguing that the UN is an unelected, unaccountable body of faceless bureaucrats and that it should introduce a second elected chamber forthwith, which we -- the members of the public -- can vote for. That was his plan. Yeah, I know what you're thinking... zzz zzz boring! But it was actually quite a nice and lively debate because he was very good at involving the crowd. He was pointing to the assembled masses and challenged them to name their local MP and Euro MP, which of course most of them couldn't do. Then he picked on a gaggle of Austrian tourists and that's when the heckler piped up.

His jokes were pretty lousy. This guy didn't have a lot of wit. He spent two minutes telling everyone that Hitler was from Austria, for example, and blaming the tourists for starting World War II. But the sheer relentlessness of his heckles did eventually become quite amusing, because the crowd were trying to get him to shut up so they could listen to the speech.

I think this is probably what makes Speakers' Corner so entertaining: because everyone is entitled to speak, even if they're idiots. (And let's be honest... most politicians are idiots.) The old guy was obviously an old pro at doing this kind of thing and didn't mind being heckled at all -- in fact, he even engaged the heckler in his dopey views. And whilst the heckler was obviously a nobhead, nobody in the crowd got angry about it -- they just went along with it, sometimes taking issue with his jokes, but most of the time just turning back to the speech. People were piping up from the crowd too, asking the old guy questions and suggesting why it wouldn't work. The Austrians started arguing that a Brit bloke can't ask for more accountability in the UN, when our government can't even be bothered to take part in Brussels. It was more like a conversation than a speech, with the old guy acting as chairman.

So did I learn anything? Nope. But it was quite nice to see a lively and vocal debate going on in the park without anyone getting angry.

If you enjoy debates then try the House of Commons, Mayor's Question Time, and Common Council at Guildhall.

Staple Inn

ADDRESS Staple Inn, Holborn - map 4e
TRAINS Chancery Lane (zone 1) **BUSES** 25, 46, 242, 341, 521 **TIME REQUIRED** 15 mins

Easy to get to? ★★★ Good for kids? ☆☆☆
Value for money? free Worth a visit? ★☆☆

This is not the kind of place that you'll bother with as a tourist because it's not good enough to visit on its own, but if you have nothing better to do on a rainy afternoon, and you fancy a walk down Holborn, then you'll be treated to one of the best buildings in The City.

When you first clap eyes on it you'll think to yourself: 'There is no way that this is real'. You'll think that it's a Disney reconstruction, or something like that; but believe it or not this is a genuine Tudor house that dates all the way back to the mid 16th-century. This place saw the English Civil War and the Great Fire of London. It lived through the Restoration, the Napoleonic wars and the Blitz. 450 years of fire and bombs can't knock this thing down.

This is how London *used* to look, folks -- all black and white beams with crooked floors and wonky windows. This is the London of Elizabeth I and Shakespeare -- the London of fairytales and Victorian Christmas cards. Now it has a mobile phone shop in the middle of it.

Don't just stand in the street and stare at it from the front, because you'll be missing out on two lovely little courtyards behind. If you look in the middle of the building then there's an ornate gateway that you can walk through. This will take you into a secluded square with red brick buildings and shady trees. The next arch beyond that will take you into a little garden that Dickens described in his novel, *The Mystery of Edwin Drood*. I'm not going to mention the modern-day monstrosity that blots one whole side of that scene (too late, I just did). I'm making a list of all the architects who should be arrested for crimes against London -- and the guy who built that is No.8.

There are some more Tudor-style fronts in Fleet Street.

Tate Britain

ADDRESS Tate Britain, Millbank, Westminster - map 8f **TRAINS** Pimlico (zone 1), Vauxhall (zones 1&2) **BUSES** 2, 36, 87, 88, 185, 436, C10 **PRICE** Free, but there may be a charge for temporary exhibitions **OPEN** 10 AM to 6 PM (Mon-Sun); Last entry 45 mins before closing **WEB** tate.org.uk/visit/tate-britain **TEL** 0207 887 8888 **TIME REQUIRED** 1½-2 hours

Easy to get to? ★★★ Good for kids? ☆☆☆
Value for money? free Worth a visit? ★★☆

Tate Britain is the one gallery that I've never bothered to visit before today. And the reason is this: I'm lazy. Yeah I know it's a dumb excuse, but it's true. They need to knock it down and move it closer to the train station. You've either got to get off at Vauxhall and walk across the bridge (I'm not doing that), or get a tube to Pimlico (not doing that either), or walk it from Big Ben (don't be daft -- with my knees?). But I can't write a book about London and leave out Tate Britain, can I? So it had to be done. I hope you are happy.

I decided to take the trek across Vauxhall Bridge because at least you can pretend to be a spy. On the southern side of the bridge is the Lego-like MI6 Building, where James Bond lives, bristling with about a billion CCTV cameras. If you ever need to get yourself arrested for a bet, then just prop a ladder against that wall and the Men in Black will be on you in five-seconds flat. (I don't recommend doing that, by the way. If you get yourself arrested then I'm not bailing you out.)

Tate Britain is full of British art, hence the name. No foreigners allowed. My knowledge of British art runs to about five people at most: Turner, Constable, Gainsborough and, er... who else... I'm struggling now. Does Tony Hart count? And Francis Bacon! So that's four. And Damien Hirst -- but you can hardly call him an artist. All he does is pickle things -- he's more like a fishmonger.

I've been walking around for fifteen minutes now and the collection seems to be quite mixed up inside. They've lumped a load of religious pieces and classical landscapes in with the portraits... it's all in the same room. And some modern art as well. The next room has got a lot of black and white photographs of London next to some pencil sketches of clouds, and a sci-fi temptress climbing up the stairs.

I must say that the building is rather nice -- that is the real artwork for me. I'd rather look at the ceiling than the frames. Give me a decent ceiling over sculptures any day of the week. It's not quite on a par with the National Gallery (what is?), but it comes a close second. Most of the rooms have got a huge concrete canopy arching over your head, and you can run your eyes along the lengthy corridors to a painting far away -- far enough away to shrink it down to the size of a postage stamp. The only noise I can hear is the sound of stilettoed footsteps on creaky old floorboards.

Okay, here we go... here is the first silly piece of art. I've just walked into a huge empty room and there's a plaque at the far end that says: "Martin Creed uses commonplace objects, simple gestures and everyday actions in his work". And the piece is called: *Work No.227: The lights going on and off.*

See if you can guess what's in here. Go on, have a guess...

Yup, you're right. There's a light in here that's going on and off. *That's it.* A huge cavernous room with a blinking light in it. You can recreate this work of art right now, in your front room, just by flicking the switch on and off. Nobody's going to call you an artist though. This is exactly why I find art galleries boring -- silly pieces of art like this.

Okay... now we're back onto solid ground again, with a room full of classical pieces. There are some apocalyptic scenes by John Martin that are worth a look. They've got tiny trains of angels lining the clouds and mountains as the skies fall down. There are some good landscapes too, full of chugging and puffing chimneys and ships, rusting on the docks. They've got some atmospheric old horse carts wobbling along the cobbled streets too -- it's like something out of Dickens.

I've just come across a famous piece by John William Waterhouse: *The Lady of Shallot.* I used to quite fancy this lady at school but she looks a bit moody now. I think she's lost her paddle or something because she's just sitting in her canoe waiting for somebody to save her. Is she looking at me? *Sorry love,* I say -- *I'm busy.*

I've got things to do. I've got a book to write.

She is actually very beautiful... now that I've taken two minutes to rekindle my schoolboy crush. Who cares about all the fancy brushwork and colours when you've got a pretty face to stare at. She hasn't changed a bit -- unlike me. I wonder if she still recognises me? *Jesus Christ... look at the state of me.* She hasn't seen me for twenty years and I roll up looking like a tramp. I feel a bit embarrassed now, and I start brushing down the front of my hair to make myself look a bit more presentable. She's still patiently waiting in her canoe for me to save her. *Hold on a minute, babe!* Don't fall in for chrissakes, because I'll never forgive myself. *Use your hands to paddle a bit closer to the bank... I can't jump that far* (she must think that I'm an Olympic athlete or something). *Oh, sod this.* Now I've suddenly remembered why we split up twenty years ago -- she's too much hard work.

I'm whizzing through the modern art section now, because I hate modern art -- the standard has dropped dramatically in here. Here are some examples of the work on display: a floor full of bricks, a shelf full of seashells, a black square and a copy of *The Sun*. Or how about a load of old car doors lying on the floor? Or a TV clip of a tree? I've stumbled across an L.S. Lowry hidden amongst the sculptures -- that is how crazy the layout of this place is. There is no rhyme or reason to it. But it's a good reason why you should explore every room because you never know what you're going to find.

Now I've found some pieces by Francis Bacon and David Hockney... at least these guys could paint. Sticking a brick on the floor is not art. That's like a footballer playing football without using his feet. You have to use a pencil, some paint or a paintbrush to call yourself an artist. Putting a French beret in a box will never be art -- not in my book anyway.

Now here's a picture that I *do* like. It's by an Italian though, so I'm not sure how it managed to sneak in here, but who cares, because it's a big view of Horse Guards by Canaletto, painted in the mid-18th century. That's right up my street, because I love old pictures of the city. If you ever come to the Tate then here's an idea: have a look for that picture and stand in front of it, picking out the edge of Banqueting House. Then you and I will have shared a special moment together -- because we both stood and stared at the same thing. We will have connected through the pages of my book.

If you like J.M.W. Turner then you're in for a treat, because the Clore Gallery is totally devoted to him. I was going to try and count up all of his pictures but I lost track at fifty. With a collection this size there are bound to be a few clunkers, but it's quite interesting to see his unfinished stuff and simple little sketches, to see how rough and ready his preparatories were. They've got a room full of Constables as well, if you like your English landscapes.

Before I finish... Do you remember that piece by Martin Creed that I mentioned earlier, about the blinking light? I've just realised that it was the exact same light that's hanging in all of the other rooms too -- so he didn't even design that! He's basically just emptied out an entire room and put a twiddle on the switch. I'm obviously in the wrong job -- the next time I write a book I'm just going to fill it up with blank pages, then everyone will hail me as a literary genius!

If you like this then you'll probably enjoy the National Gallery, Courtauld Gallery and Wallace Collection.

Tate Modern

Landmarks & Attractions | 231

ADDRESS Tate Modern, Bankside - map 9b
TRAINS Southwark (zone 1) **BUSES** 45, 63, 100, 344, 381, RV1 **PRICE** Free, but there may be a charge for temporary exhibitions
OPEN 10 AM to 6 PM (Sun-Thu); 10 AM to 10 PM (Fri-Sat); Last entry 45 mins before closing
WEB tate.org.uk/visit/tate-modern **TEL** 0207 887 8888 **TIME REQUIRED** 1½-2 hours

Easy to get to? ★★★ Good for kids? ☆☆☆
Value for money? free Worth a visit? ★☆☆

I promised myself that I would come here with an open mind, but I know I'm going to laugh at the modern art. It's so bad, it's good. A Coke can on the street is just a piece of rubbish, but in here it's an exhibit... *literally*. A pile of clothes on your bedroom floor is a mess, but in here it's a movement. If they hung a sign around the light switch people would stand there with their thumbs on their chins saying how wonderful it is -- it's that kind of place.

In the old days (bear with me while I have a rant), in the old days painters painted pictures of *stuff* -- people, places and plants. Now they paint pictures of blobs and blotches and spots. Surely one of the reasons that we enjoy art is because we recognise that the artist possesses a talent that we lack? When you look at a Rembrandt you are amazed at what he's done, because it looks better than a photo. How the hell did he do that? *That is amazing!* It's not like that nowadays though -- it's all about the deeper meaning. As long as it has a special message in it then who cares what it looks like. Pile up some dead leaves and you've got yourself a powerful ecological statement with just five minutes of work. They used to paint a picture of a leaf -- now they just put a real one on a plate. They used to do portraits of people's faces -- now they just skin a dead man's head and pickle it in the fridge.

When a student has no artistic talent whatsoever the teacher just tells them to snap a black and white photo of a dead tree, or a crying kid, or film themselves blinking at the mirror in slow-mo. Or they'll nail some beer cans to the wall and splatter them with paint and call it something like: *Youth Crying Out In Anguish Against The Capitalist Hegemony*. That's the Tate Modern for you -- it's full of pictures like that. It's the world's biggest sixth form college art show, dotted with an occasional big name piece like Warhol or Picasso.

So that's what I think.

It's no good me giving you a route through the building because it's colossal -- it used to be a power station. And it still looks like a power station, right down to the industrial sized chimney in the middle. The stomach of the building is where the turbines used to be, but now it's just a vast abandoned chasm. The room is so huge that the only thing they can fill it with is nothing. And it's surprising how much nothing they can squeeze into it. But what else can they do with a space that large?

The first room that I entered today had a couple of Piet Mondrian's on the wall. He's the guy who had a love for misaligned lino. He was like a blind kitchen fitter. After that came a mashed-up Picasso face, a melted Dalí face, and a quizzical my face.

Get five crayons and scratch about on a piece of paper for five minutes, and that is what I'm looking at right now. If you gave an elephant a few paintbrushes and promised him a sticky bun then this is what he'd come up with. If my nine year-old niece came home with that then I wouldn't even stick it on the fridge. I'd get her enrolled into some art lessons quick, before the teachers kicked her out of class.

Here's another great one: a white curtain called *The Penelope*. This one is supposed to evoke "the tension and isolation felt by someone coping with AIDS through reference to a classical story of deferral and hope". I'm glad they told me, otherwise I might have just thought it was a curtain stuck on the wall. What hope do you have of seeing a message like that in a curtain?

Next we have the ultimate child painter -- Jackson Pollock. He is the only bloke I know who carried the skills he learnt as a toddler into his full-time profession.

I love the next room. Let me describe it to you in detail so you can appreciate how dumb it is (I have totally abandoned my attempt to keep an open mind by this point -- a few rooms in and I'm already pondering on the emperor's new clothes): it's a pitch black room with a couple of poofee seats inside, and a row of black and white TVs lined-up on the floor. And you're supposed to sit here on the seats and watch an endless loop of faces and crowds and clouds and cars on these muted TVs. That is what passes for art these days -- watching a black and white TV in the dark.

The next floor is full of sculptures. Well, I say sculptures... but imagine that you are at the office and the workmen have come along and taken all of the strip lights off the ceiling, and left them propped against the wall and buggered off home. Next to those are eleven panes of glass. These represent "literal reflections on the nature of pictorial representation".

That is what passes for sculpture in this place.

Oh my Lord... this one is just a piece of guttering. A piece of metal guttering that might have fallen off the roof -- I'm being serious! And next to that is a flat-pack piece of furniture. (Have I wandered into a joke?)

There's far too much filler. They've got three Coke bottles inside a box. Another artist has glued some of her plastic fingernails to a canvas and the Tate saw fit to hang it on a wall. How about these ones: four blackboards? Ninety-five fire hoses? Two white triangles? Some clay turds? I could go on and on and on, because they've got floors and floors of this stuff.

My all-time favourite has got to be *Untitled Painting 1965* which is... wait for it... a mirror! I kid you not, folks. It's just a plain old mirror -- exactly the same kind that you might buy in your local branch of B&Q. "Viewers are confronted by themselves," it waffles on, "thereby questioning the long-held notion of painting transcending reality". [Note: I would have included a picture of that as well, but because it's a mirror I would have appeared in the photo -- which would have made it even worse!]

Okay... so the art is mostly rubbish, but at least there is one saving grace: the cafe on the 6th floor. They've got a little bar and a restaurant up there that looks out over the Thames. And it's a great view as well: you've got the Millennium Bridge and people messing about on the mudflats, the City skyscrapers to your right and the dome of St. Paul's right across the river. Now *that* is art. Forget all the cr*p on the wall downstairs -- if you want to look at something truly impressive then just come upstairs and look out the window.

So just in case you haven't worked it out already... I'm not a fan of the Tate Modern. I would enjoy it a lot more if it actually had some art inside. Here is my honest opinion: imagine if London Zoo had run out of lions and tigers and just filled up the cages with cats, dogs, chickens and ants, and then tried to pass them off as exhibits. That is basically what we've got here. There are plenty of big names that I do recognise: people like Picasso, Dalí, Miro, Mondrian, Klee and Kandinsky, but the rest is just a random assemblage of wood, wire, lightbulbs and bathroom mirrors -- stuff that you'd struggle to sell at a car boot sale.

If you like modern art then try the Saatchi Gallery and Hayward Gallery.

Temple Bar

ADDRESS The Victorian monument is in Fleet Street (map 4e), and the original is next to St. Paul's (map 4f) **TRAINS** Fleet Street: Chancery Lane, Holborn, Temple (all zone 1) -- St. Paul's: Blackfriars, Cannon Street, Mansion House, St. Paul's (all zone 1) **BUSES** Fleet Street: 4, 11, 15, 26, 76, 172, 341 -- St. Paul's:

4, 11, 15, 23, 26, 100, 242 **TIME REQUIRED** 5 mins each

Easy to get to? ★★★ Good for kids? ☆☆☆
Value for money? free Worth a visit? ★★☆

A little over 250 years ago we still had all of the original gates in place from the Roman city wall, but then somebody had the bright idea of knocking them down to help speed up the traffic flow, and all seven of them came tumbling down practically at once. We still had Temple Bar though, which survived in place until 1878.

Temple Bar was not quite the same thing as a city gate -- it actually stood a fair distance outside the Roman wall and marked the official limit of the city's power (the closest Roman gate was up Ludgate Hill, closer to Old St. Paul's). It was given a makeover in the 1660s by Christopher Wren, but two hundred years later the Victorians kept bashing their horses and carts into it, and the authorities decided to pull it down and replace it with an ornate obelisk-type monument with a big black dragon on top -- and that's what we can see in Fleet Street today. It's called the Temple Bar monument, and it stands on the original site of Temple Bar.

But that's not the end of the story... because the original Temple Bar lives on! Luckily for us a rich Victorian called Henry Meux stepped in to save all of the original stones before somebody could bundle them into the river, and transported them to his posh pile in the country, where he had them re-erected in his garden. In 2003 somebody then had the splendid idea of returning them back to London again. So Christopher Wren's re-build has now been re-built itself at the entrance to Paternoster Square. If you stand on the front steps of St. Paul's Cathedral then you can see it over the road.

I'm guessing that 95% of Londoners haven't got the faintest idea what this building represents when they walk through it, because it looks too new. They seem to have given it a thorough clean but I think they have spruced it up too much -- the bright white shining stone looks too fresh to be three centuries old.

But try and imagine how this gate used to look in its original location... barricading back the traffic in Fleet Street... with the severed heads of traitors grinning down at you.

Temple Church

ADDRESS Temple Church, The City (through a black wooden door in Fleet Street) - map 4e
TRAINS Chancery Lane, Holborn, Temple (all zone 1) **BUSES** 4, 11, 15, 23, 26, 76, 172, 341 **PRICE** Adult £5; Senior £3; Child (under-19) free **OPEN** Usually 10 AM to 4 PM (Mon-Fri); Closed (Sat-Sun, except for Sun services) **DENOMINATION** Church of England **WEB** templechurch.com **TEL** 0207 353 3470 **TIME REQUIRED** 45-60 mins

Easy to get to? ★★★ Good for kids? ★☆☆
Value for money? ★★★ Worth a visit? ★★★

Temple Church is a mysterious old place. When you first clap eyes on the knights' effigies lying on the floor you'll come over all-Indiana Jones and want to smash up the flagstones to find the treasure underneath. I'm almost certain that there's something interesting buried under there -- there must be. I've never seen the *Da Vinci Code* but I can understand why people come looking for clues -- it's that kind of place.

You need a bit of guts to find it, though, because you can't see it from the street. You have to walk through a big wooden archway opposite Chancery Lane, which looks like it was built to keep people out. You'll pause there for a few seconds, and wonder whether you're really allowed inside. You'll probably stand there for a while until you see somebody else go through first. (That's how we Brits like to enter scary places: on the coat-tails of somebody more important -- because then we can blame them if anything goes wrong.) Most of the people who step inside are suited up lawyers and solicitors from the Royal Courts of Justice over the road, because the Temple area is where they have all their chambers. So just hide behind one of those guys and you'll be fine. Head through the arch and down the alley, and you'll see the Round Tower looming up behind some spindly little trees. Keep walking past the front door and you'll get a great view of the entire length, with the entrance door on the side.

You'd never know it from the outside, but large parts of this church are practically new. The Round Tower dates back to the 1180s, but it's all been remodelled, burnt down and bombed ever since. The Victorians had a big fiddle with it in the 1860s, and totally messed up the roof by sticking a big cone on top (straight on top of the Round Tower!). Hitler obviously didn't like it either, because he sent the Luftwaffe along to knock it down in 1941 -- the only bombing raid that ever improved London.

When you get inside you'll see that they've done rather a good job on the restoration, but it's a bit too good for my taste -- I like my churches to be dark and dirty, and there's too much sunshine in here. You can't beg for forgiveness with a shaft of warm sunshine on your face. You need to do it in the dark.

I can hear an organ playing at the moment, whilst I'm writing this, and I can't see a single soul up there. The sound is coming out of the balcony and there's nobody sitting on the seat -- very spooky. Ten minutes later the church is filled with choral voices and an orchestral choir -- and it's just me and a few tourists sitting in the pews. The empty space is making it sound really deep and thick, and I don't know how best to describe it. If you could condense all the notes into a gas-lamp fog then we'd be sitting in the middle of it.

What makes this church different to all the rest is what lies silent to the left. This is what makes it so mysterious... because on the floor of the Round Tower are the weathered effigies of eight stone knights. They are just kipping there, fast asleep, still wearing their pyjamas of armour. These guys have gone to bed with their swords and shields and chainmail nighties.

It would be fantastic if they were still in situ, but, alas, this church has been remodelled so many times over the centuries that they are no longer in the same place. They were definitely interred somewhere around the Round Tower because that's the site of the original Templar church, but as to where their actual bones are: nobody knows for sure. It was the Victorians who placed the effigies where they are today. All eight of them do look amazingly old, though -- Geoffrey de Mandeville is dated 1144. William Marshall died in 1231, and Sir Gilbert is a mere youngster -- he didn't die until 1242.

If you're lucky then they'll let you into the balcony that runs around the rim of the Round Tower (they don't always have the spiral staircase open, so cross your fingers). It provides you with a great view down onto the slumbering knights.

You can learn more about the Knights Templar at St. John's Gate.

Thames Barrier

ADDRESS Thames Flood Barrier, Unity Way, Woolwich **TRAINS** North Greenwich (zones 2&3), and 10 mins on the 472 bus **BUSES** 472 **PRICE** Adult £3.75; Senior (over-60) £3.25; Child (5-16) £2.25; Infant (under-5) free; Family (up to 2 ad+3 ch) £10 **OPEN** 10.30 AM to 5 PM (Thu-Sun); Last entry 30 mins before closing **WEB** gov.uk/the-thames-barrier **TEL** 0208 305 4188 **TIME REQUIRED** 30-45 mins

Easy to get to? ★☆☆ Good for kids? ☆☆☆
Value for money? ☆☆☆ Worth a visit? ★☆☆

I ended up visiting the Thames Flood Barrier twice, because I screwed it up the first time. I didn't realise that the only way of getting there was by bus. The boat from Westminster Pier that says: "This boat goes to the Thames Barrier" doesn't actually stop there... all it does is float up the river and circle around one of the pylons, before heading back the way it came. If you wanted to get off and visit the little exhibition then you'd literally have to dive overboard and swim to shore. And there is no way I'm doing that for you... I'm not *that* dedicated! (And I can't swim either, so I'd probably die.)

I quite enjoyed my little float on the TRS boat though. If you board it at Big Ben then it takes you up the river past the London Eye, Tate Modern, the Globe, St.

Paul's and the Tower of London, under Tower Bridge and past the skyscrapers at Canary Wharf. After that it goes past Greenwich and you come face-to-face with the giant pylons of the Thames Barrier. After sailing around one of them it turns tail 180° and heads back towards Greenwich again. It's definitely the best way of seeing the barrier... and you can trust me on that, because my return visit on the bus today was a complete wash-out.

First of all you have to get the tube to North Greenwich, and then you have to catch a ten-minute bus ride on the 472. I suppose you could walk it from North Greenwich if you were feeling particularly energetic. Once you come out of the station The O2 is right there, looming up on your left, and a little walk to the riverbank will take you to the cable car. I was surprised to find that you can actually see the barrier from here, stretching across the water about two miles downstream. But two miles is a long way with dodgy knees, and I didn't fancy it because the weather wasn't pretty. The riverside buildings are all dull grey concrete rectangles, and with the wind whipping across the water and the rain coming in like icy little darts, I chickened out. So I got the bus.

The bus journey isn't much better. It's all main roads and industrial zones, and out-of-town B&Qs. Big huge carpet warehouses and bedroom furniture shops. Cars streaming down the road with their headlights still on, and lazy ones sleeping in the car parks.

No sooner have we pulled away than a man who's nodding non-stop starts shouting at a pretty woman up the other end of the bus. She ignores him in a nervous manner and starts finding the boring bus advertisements very interesting all of a sudden, and keeps her eyes glued to them. I can completely understand how she's feeling because we all feel it too: we are all looking out of the window at the trees going past. A noisy tin can rolls around the aisle every time we go round a corner. It keeps banging off the chair legs like a pinball machine. The only sound in the whole bus is this tin can rolling up and down.

You have to keep your eyes open for the bus-stop because the route doesn't skirt along the river, so you won't be able to see the barrier. You have to look out for Eastmoor Street and get off there. Then you've got another ten-minute walk down a little nature trail of skinny bald trees and grass verges strewn with crisp packets and crumpled up cans of Coke. It was totally deserted when I went. The only person I saw was a council guy emptying the dustbins into his beeping cart. It's the kind of place that you'd visit if you wished to get mugged.

Then all of a sudden you are there -- the river! And the big barrier stretches out across the water. The view is definitely the best thing about going. You get a nice shot of The O2, The Shard, and the distant skyscrapers at Canary Wharf. The opposite bank is bustling with building yards and big chimneys -- it looks like a sugar cane processing plant with big ships pulling in to offload their stuff. The seagulls are all flapping around like pigeons a few feet off the sea, squawking and fighting over what they've dropped in the water. London City airport must be somewhere over there too, because you get an occasional plane taking off and blowing your eardrums.

The waterfront itself is quite depressing when the weather turns nasty. I was there for thirty minutes waiting for the exhibition to open and I hardly saw a soul; just one lone, crazy jogger getting battered in the wind. He looked like a damp flag battling against the weather. Imagine this depressing scene: a concrete embankment and no one about, just a couple of mangy seagulls sitting on a fence post... sky rumbling like indigestion... rain defying gravity by coming in sideways, and the clouds just tipping more water into the sea. It was just me and the wind and the sound of brown water sloshing up against the side, and old plastic bottles slapping around in the dirty brown bubbles. It's not the kind of river that you'd want to swim in. I don't recommend bringing your swimming trunks.

So that was my morning... standing in the rain getting drenched, waiting for this place to open. I couldn't even sit down because the benches were wet.

The exhibition building didn't exactly fill me with optimism. Put it this way... it's not the kind of place you'd want to take your date on a day out. Not unless you wanted to dump her. For starters, it isn't even by the barrier. You have to walk a little farther down the river, past some kiddie swings and dog sh*t. I was hoping that I might be able to go over to the first pylon and have a look at the machinery, but no. The only way of doing that is by stealing a hard hat and a security pass (and I don't recommend doing that).

I am reluctant to say that the museum was rubbish because that would be totally unfair: it's a museum about the Thames Barrier, so there's a limit as to how exciting they can make it. But even so, it was worse than it needed to be. The whole impression of rubbishyness starts at the door, because you can only get to the museum via the cheapo cafe outside. You have to buy your ticket from the greasy cook at the till, behind all the people queuing to get their polystyrene cups of watery tea.

As soon as you step inside you've effectively seen it all, because it's a one-room exhibit. It should really be free. And I'm not just saying that because I'm tight with my money -- all they've got are some picture boards and a few TV screens on the wall telling you why it was built, plus a model of one of the pylons. That's it. I know it's only a few quid to enter, but when you remember what a trek it was to get here you'd rather have spent it on a sandwich -- I had to get a train and a bus both ways, remember, through the pouring rain and the heartlands of doom, painted in every shade of factory grey. For this? So after fifteen minutes I left, pulling my hood up as I stepped out into the wind, and arrived at the bus-stop just in time to see the next bus leave. Ho hum.

If you really want to see the barrier then do it by boat. Get the TRS boat from Westminster Pier which will show you all the sights along the river too -- then you can spend the rest of the day in Greenwich. Now that is worth doing, but not the exhibition. If you only pay heed to just one solitary piece of advice in this entire book, then trust me -- make it this one.

You can learn a bit more about the barrier at the Museum of London Docklands.

Tower Bridge

ADDRESS Tower Bridge, Tower Bridge Road - map 10b **TRAINS** Tower Gateway DLR, Tower Hill (both zone 1) **BUSES** 15, 42, 78, 100, RV1 **PRICE** If bought online: Adult £8; Senior (over-60) £5.65; Child (5-15) £3.50; Infant (under-5)

free; Family (2 ad+2 ch) £20.30, or £18 with 2 ad+1ch, or £14.10 with 1 ad+2ch -- If bought at the door: Adult £9; Senior (over-60) £6.30; Child (5-15) £3.90; Infant (under-5) free; Family (2 ad+2 ch) £20.30, or £18 with 2 ad+1ch, or £14.10 with 1 ad+2ch **OPEN** 10 AM to 6 PM (Mon-Sun, Apr-Sep); 9.30 AM to 5.30 PM (Mon-Sun, Oct-Mar); Last entry 30 mins before closing **WEB** towerbridge.org.uk **TEL** 0207 403 3761 **TIME REQUIRED** 45-60 mins

Easy to get to? ★★★ Good for kids? ★★☆ Value for money? ★★☆ Worth a visit? ★★☆

The thing that always amazes me about Tower Bridge is its age: it's only 120 years old(-ish). I don't know why I think it's older, maybe I've been fooled by the mock-gothic architecture. But it's a pretty handsome sight, you must admit. This bridge is pure theatre.

What are the chances of somebody building something like that these days? It's all about money and profit nowadays, so we end up with the Millennium Bridge and the two Hungerford Bridges -- *boring bridges*.

The first time I went inside Tower Bridge I wasn't all that impressed, to be honest, but I quite liked it today. Maybe that's because I'm four years older (I feel about ten years older). Maybe it's because I'm more easily pleased. Maybe it's because the sun was out -- *who knows*.

The first thing they do is take you up to the top of the bridge in a lift (or you can walk up the stairs if you're feeling a bit daft). Then they plonk you down in front of a cinema screen to show you a ten-minute film about the guy who designed it. It's not the worst programme in the world, but it's still ten minutes in front of a TV isn't it. Everybody is itching to see the fantastic views from the top, so you're basically just sitting there waiting for it to end so you can move on to the next bit. But it's got some decent information if you're prepared to give it a chance.

After that you are allowed to walk through both of the top-level walkways and take in the views. They've nailed up a load of information boards along the walls with pictures and paintings of the bridge, together with some old black and white photos of the engine rooms. They've got some unnecessary bits and pieces about other bridges around the world as well -- like the Brooklyn Bridge, Sydney Harbour Bridge, and a hundred others that I've never even heard of -- all padded out with Top Trump-style facts like how long they are and when they were built.

They've tried to make the whole thing a bit more exciting by installing some glass floors halfway along the length. (Who's stupid idea was that?) They don't span the entire length of the walkways, just about ten metres-or-so, but it was enough to give me vertigo. The good news is that the glass is capable of withstanding the weight of one elephant and two London black cabs combined. Although how they actually managed to get an elephant and two taxis up there to test it out, I do not know (it's a very small lift). You are supposed to stand there and watch all the thundering missiles (buses and lorries) speeding along the rock solid roadway fifty feet below.

Fortunately they've had the common sense to leave a small strip of normal floor on either side, so you can still get across without bursting into tears. I tried to force myself to walk across the middle to test my manliness but I failed miserably -- I don't care. I don't need to pass a dumb test just to prove to myself that I'm a man. Real men don't need to walk across a glass floor just to impress the ladies. I even saw a few dopey students lying down on it and doing press-ups. *Why?* Why on earth would you do that? Why would you risk it? I didn't stick around long enough to see them plummet to their deaths.

After the first walkway you go into another little movie room but this one is a total waste of time -- it's just five minutes of architectural drawings. If you manage to sit through this one to the end then very well done -- you did better than me. The second walkway is basically the same as the first, with some more pictures of famous bridges and another glass walkway (looking straight down onto the road again).

The views out of the side windows are what you came for. The first one just looks across to Canary Wharf whilst the other one takes in The Shard, City Hall and HMS Belfast, plus the Walkie Scorchie and Gherkin. You can see the dome of St. Paul's and the London Eye as well. See if you can spot The Monument, and the top of Tate Modern too. My favourite bit was looking down into the grounds of the Tower of London. If you know where you're looking then you can actually see Tower Green and the glass monument where the chopping block used to be.

After that you have to come downstairs and walk along the roadway for a bit until you reach the engine rooms. This bit sounds more exciting than it actually is because it's just a load of industrial-sized motors and pistons that have been sanitised and locked off. It would be a lot more interesting if they were feeding coal into the ovens and the machines were going round and round and pumping up and down, churning and coughing and spluttering smoke and dust and flames and fumes, but of course it's all very safe and stale these days. Only one wheel is moving and that's been roped off behind some barriers and made super-safe, so you never really get the feeling of what the engine rooms were like.

Tower Hill

ADDRESS Tower Hill, Trinity Square Gardens - map 10b **TRAINS** Tower Gateway DLR, Tower Hill (both zone 1) **BUSES** 15, 42, 78, 100, RV1
TIME REQUIRED 10 mins

Easy to get to? ★★★ Good for kids? ☆☆☆
Value for money? free Worth a visit? ★☆☆

Have you been inside the Tower of London yet?

If you have, then you've probably seen the spot where Henry VIII beheaded his troublesome wives on Tower Green. You might even have seen inside the chapel where he buried all of their headless bodies. But what happened to all of the non-Royal traitors? Plenty of lesser celebrities got sentenced to death as well, but they weren't allowed inside the grounds of the Royal palace. Their final goodbyes took place over the road on Tower Hill. (If they were a total nobody like you and me then they would have been hanged at Tyburn instead, near modern day Marble Arch.)

What you have to do is walk around to the north side of the Tower and cross over the main road to Trinity Square Gardens (to the west of Tower Hill station). It's only a little piece of green -- which is probably why most people never bother to visit it -- but have a look around and you'll find a plaque on the floor which lists the names of all the traitors. I'd tell you where it is, but I think half the fun is in trying to find it -- it's only a small little area so it shouldn't take you more than a few minutes.

Tower Hill doesn't look like much these days, and it's difficult to imagine how scary it must have been five hundred years ago -- but you've got to try and picture it without all the busy roads and concrete buildings behind. In those days it was just a chopping block or gallows looking down on the Tower. You'd be dragged up here and thousands of people would be crowding around for their bit of Saturday afternoon entertainment. They even had people selling cups of nuts and fruits, like they sell popcorn and Smarties at the cinema.

If you were noble then you were lucky... because they'd hire an axe-man to chop off your head. But if you were unlucky then it would be a thick hood and a scratchy rope looped tight around your neck.

I'm not sure that I'd want to die by hanging. Lots of suicidal people choose that way out but apparently it can take a few minutes if you mess it up (which I would). You just hang there writhing and spitting and fitting until the last breath gets squeezed out of your fat purple face.

When I die I want it to be fun. I have given this a lot of thought and I have decided that it must involve a boom followed by glitter. One minute we will be chatting quite happily and then I will say something like "hang on a minute, I don't feel very well", and then -- *KABOOM!* I will vanish in a cloud of silver glitter. And you will be sitting there showered in the stuff wondering what the hell just happened. My reasoning for this is that God doesn't want people turning up at his front door with fat purple faces filled with blood, or with shattered heads with big bullet holes blown out of them -- he would much rather see some shiny happy people covered in glitter. It's all about first impressions, isn't it -- you don't want to turn up at the Pearly Gates all covered in blood because he won't let you in. So I am going to arrive all sparkly -- that is my tip for you. (That is probably the most useful tip in this book.) Just think how difficult it is to get past a bouncer at the pub when you've got ripped jeans and a t-shirt on -- the Pearly Gates are going to be ten times as hard, so we need to look smart.

Apart from the little plaque on the floor there's not a lot else to see. A lot of the headless bodies were transferred over to All Hallows-by-the-Tower before being carted off elsewhere for interment, so there aren't even any graves nearby. You can still see a large part of the church though -- it's that big green spire over the road. That's about the only part of it that didn't fall down in the Blitz -- the rest of it was rebuilt in the 1950s.

What always amazes me about places like Tower Hill is the way that London does its best to ignore them. For a lot of big cities this would be their absolute highlight, but we just give it a piddly little plaque and forget about it. We've got so much history in this town that we don't need to draw attention to it:

"You want to go and see where Thomas More, Thomas Cromwell and Elizabeth's traitorous toy-boy the Earl of Essex were killed?"

"Oh yeah, okay... it's over there behind the traffic lights. Good luck trying to find it."

Tower of London

ADDRESS Tower of London - map 10b
TRAINS Tower Gateway DLR, Tower Hill (both zone 1) **BUSES** 15, 42, 78, 100, RV1 **PRICE** If bought online: Adult £23.10; Senior (over-60) £17.60; Child (5-15) £10.50; Infant (under-5) free; Family (up to 2 ad+3 ch) £57.40 -- If bought at the door: Adult £24.50; Senior (over-60) £18.70; Child (5-15) £11; Infant (under-5)

free; Family (up to 2 ad+3 ch) £60.70; Price includes a voluntary donation **OPEN** 10 AM to 5.30 PM (Sun-Mon, Mar-Oct); 9 AM to 5.30 PM (Tue-Sat, Mar-Oct); 10 AM to 4.30 PM (Sun-Mon, Nov-Feb); 9 AM to 4.30 PM (Tue-Sat, Nov-Feb); Last entry 30 mins before closing **WEB** hrp.org.uk/ tower-of-london **TEL** 0203 166 6000 **TIME REQUIRED** 3-4 hours

Easy to get to? ★★★ Good for kids? ★★☆
Value for money? ★★☆ Worth a visit? ★★★

They used to shut the gates when hordes of Londoners stormed the Byward Tower. They used to fire arrows at them and hurl rocks from the ballistas. Now they charge them twenty-five quid and give them a pair of headphones and a map. It's a lot easier to storm the Tower these days because they've bricked up Traitor's Gate and drained the moat. They can't fire arrows at us anymore because of health and safety. The only thing that remains the same is the horde of ugly peasants bundling up outside the gates -- there must be five hundred of them at least. The queues are a few families deep all the way down, with reinforcement tourists standing back and waiting to take their place. If you enjoy queueing then this is the place to go.

I was actually dreading going to the Tower of London today because I know how big the place is, and I didn't fancy the walking because my knees are shot. Let me tell you something: this is a tiring place to visit. It is right up there with London Zoo as the most knackering attraction in the city, so you might want to take that into account when you're planning your itinerary. It is massive -- it's like a little city inside the walls, and apart from a few private places where the staff all live you can pretty much walk around wherever you like. You definitely need to get hold of a map because it's a bit of a maze: you will often spy some tourists on top of a walkway somewhere, or coming out of a tower, and see no visible means to follow them. You'll find that you need to enter a building at a certain place and then follow the walkway all the way around the curtain wall, taking in the towers and turrets as you go. But I'm getting ahead of myself here -- I haven't even stepped through the front door yet.

Once you've passed under the Byward Tower you'll enter Water Lane. Halfway up there is the famous Traitor's Gate. That's where they used to boat in all the prisoners and walk them up the stone steps and through the Bloody Tower arch. The water looks nice and still today but it's easy to imagine it steaming with a little green sludge as it floats in off the river. When the lanterns were illuminating the thirty foot wall in front all they could see was the Bloody Tower arch ahead, with a phalanx of foot guards lining the lane, but then it got worse... because when they passed under the portcullis the first thing they saw was the White Tower looming up above and it must have been as scary as hell! It's too sunny to be scared today though -- but I've done a Twilight Tour around here, so I know what this place is like at night.

Stepping through that Bloody Tower arch is a memorable moment the first time you do it. The Norman tower really is impressive the first time you see it up close, and when you clamber up the stone steps at the end to see the Tudor houses around Tower Green, and the church and chopping block with a few Yeoman Guards, then you will instantly forgive them the extortionate entry fee. So many things to see at once... but you have to pace yourself because this place will take you hours to see properly.

You'll probably want to see Tower Green first... because this is where they led out the heads to be separated from their necks. This is where they chopped up Anne Boleyn. There's no chopping block anymore though, just a glass pillow ornament and three million tourists all straining for a see. Behind that is the chapel where they buried the headless bodies.

I always like to start with the little exhibition inside the Bloody Tower, because that's where they keep all of their torture equipment. They've got a rack and manacles in there, and a scary looking iron frame that snaps your bones like pencils. I'm always hoping that they'll ask for volunteers to test them out, so I can push a couple of the annoying school kids to the front, but sadly all of the equipment has been decommissioned.

Every nation had its favourite way of killing people... the French built fantastic contraptions like the guillotine, whilst the Italians just went the DIY route and nailed up their Christians on a cross (after feeding them to the lions, of course). But we preferred to pop people's joints and stretch their bones till they strained in two. And burn them at the stake, of course -- and drown witches in a dunking stool. And hang them at Tyburn. And tie them to a stake and shoot them. We drowned a few pirates in the Thames as well -- we certainly mixed it up a bit. Other nations showed a distinct lack of imagination when it came to torture -- we tried everything. One of the people at the Tower was rammed into a wine barrel and drowned. He died like a cork.

I've always been a bit disappointed by St Thomas's Tower, because even though it's one of the most historic parts of the Tower, it's also one of the plainest. It dates back to the reigns of Henry III and Edward I in medieval times, so not a lot of original items survive -- you're basically just staring at the stonework and the inner wooden walls and floor, plus a few modern reproductions in the bedchamber.

This is a place for your imagination, aided by the whispered snippets of prayer coming out of the speakers -- so remember to bring your imagination along.

The Wakefield Tower is worth a visit because that's where Henry VI met his grisly end. They've got a plaque in the chapel on the exact spot where he died, and that's one of the things that I enjoy most about the Tower: every building seems to have a spot on the floor where somebody famous got beaten up or stabbed or sliced. There are hundreds of little graffitis chiseled into the walls everywhere you go, where the prisoners have spent their final days carving their name into the stone. They must have busted their nails doing that.

Walter Raleigh's cell is the exception, because his prison is actually quite plush. You can't even call it a prison really -- it's more like a 3-star hotel. They've still got all of his belongings in there to show you how nice it was.

If you're following the same route as me then you should be walking around the curtain wall now, with its fine view of the White Tower and Tower Bridge. This will take you through the Langthorn Tower, Salt Tower and Martin Tower. This is where you can stand on the wooden platforms where the archers made rain on the attackers below. These days the only noise is coming from the steady stream of buses and cars passing over

Tower Bridge, but it's not difficult to imagine them as London scum running over the ground towards the wall. I wouldn't mind firing a few arrows from up here myself -- it would be quite fun. There are a lot of targets on the Tower Bridge road.

If you peer down into the street below (the street inside the grounds of the Tower) then you can see the site of the old rifle range where they shot the German spies during World War II. This is where they lined them up against the wall and said auf wiedersehen.

The Martin Tower is where you'll get your first good look at a crown -- but it's not the Crown Jewels. This is where they keep the crowns of old Royals like Victoria and George I, II and III. Most of the precious jewels have been removed so it's just the felt and frames on display, but they will give you a nice idea about what to expect when you see the real deal a bit later.

[Note: Just to give you an idea about how much stuff there is to see and read in this place... it has taken me two hours to get this far, and I haven't even seen the Crown Jewels or been inside the White Tower yet.]

You'll find the Crown Jewels inside Waterloo Barracks. This place always reminds me of a theme park ride, because once you're through the front door you have to walk around a huge queue-line reading little bits of info on the walls whilst you're waiting. There are a few pictures and a movie too, to keep your mind occupied, until finally you walk through a thick vault door into the Holy of Holies.

The jewels are all boxed-up inside bulletproof glass, with a conveyor belt running along the floor to stop people lingering too long. They don't let you try them on either -- so don't get any funny ideas. If you were only expecting to see the Imperial State Crown and a few rings and trinkets then prepare for a surprise, because there is much more than that. It's a bit like Smaug's lair in the Lonely Mountain. They've got swords and sceptres and spoons and plates and bowls and golden goblets, punch bowls, chalices... everything is encrusted with diamonds and sapphires and rubies and jewels. The Queen has got more bling than BA Baracus.

Inside the White Tower itself is a huge collection of arms and armour. They've had a bit of a shift around since the last time I came though, because the famous Line of Kings is now at the start. And it's not much of a line anymore either (they are going to have to change its centuries-old name). But it's still very impressive, and it's quite a thrill to see some suits of armour made for Henry VIII and Charles I. Upstairs is a collection of swords and shields, carbines and flintlock muskets, pistols and rifles, pikes and spikes, daggers and knives, and lots of other boy's toys.

As you're walking around all of the displays it's easy to forget about the building itself, so remember to have a look at the thick stone walls and ceiling. Sadly they don't have any real rooms inside (rooms that have been dressed exactly how they would have been, I mean) -- they have been stripped back to make space for the exhibition. They are basically just empty shells with benches and lights and modern pine planking on the floor, so it's difficult to get a sense of how it must have been in Norman times. The lower level seems to have been sacrificed to make way for the shop -- very disappointing. The only room that still looks like it was is the 800-year-old Chapel of St. John. But that is really the only criticism I can make of the entire place, because what they do have on show is well worth seeing.

So, to sum it all up then: I know it costs a lot to get inside, but I still think it's one of the must-see sights of London.

There are plenty more things to do at the Tower of London... like a Yeoman Warder Tour, Twilight Tour, Ceremony of the Keys and Sunday service at the Chapel Royal.

Tower of London -- Yeoman Warder Tour

ADDRESS Tower of London - map 10b
TRAINS Tower Gateway DLR, Tower Hill (both zone 1) **BUSES** 15, 42, 78, 100, RV1 **PRICE** Included with your entry ticket -- see my Tower of London review for prices **OPENING HOURS** Tours every 30 mins from 10 AM to 3.30 PM (Sun-Mon, Mar-Oct); 9 AM to 3.30 PM (Tue-Sat, Mar-Oct); 10 AM to 2.30 PM (Sun-Mon, Nov-Feb); 9 AM to 2.30 PM (Tue-Sat, Nov-Feb) **WEB** hrp.org.uk/tower-of-london/visit-us/top-things-to-see-and-do/yeoman-warders **TEL** 0203 166 6000 **TIME REQUIRED** 1 hour for the tour, plus 2-3 hours to see the rest after

Easy to get to? ★★★ Good for kids? ★☆☆
Value for money? ★★☆ Worth a visit? ★★☆

If you ever go to the Tower of London then the first thing you'll see when you walk under the entrance tower is a big wooden board by the moat. That tells you what time the next Yeoman Warder tour is starting. They run every half-hour from 10 o'clock (or 9 o'clock), and are included in the price of your ticket. Normally I just skip it and make my way around with an audio-guide instead, but I've never done it before so I thought what the hell: I'll give it a go to see what it's like. The reason that I've never done it before is because of the huge crowds. There always seems to be about five hundred people huddling round this Beefeater guy, and the thought of following the population of a small country around the Tower just did my head in, so I gave it a miss. But it was actually okay -- I was surprised. I estimate that our group swelled up to about 100 to 150 people during the hour, with people joining in and dropping out as we made our way around, but I never struggled to hear the guide.

The Yeoman Warders are better known as 'Beefeaters'. There are about fifty of them in total and they are all ex-military, so you don't want to mess around with them. I remember when I was at school our art teacher always struggled to keep control of twenty kids, but this guy would have had no problems whatsoever; he could have had all 150 of us marching on the spot if he wanted to. Being an ex-soldier, he was also blessed with a fog-horn mouth, so even though the crowd is large you can hear him as clear as a bell.

The tour begins in the moat by the Byward Tower, from whence you'll get a sixty minute speech of pretty detailed history. There are plenty of jokes and laughs along the way, and he loves to tell his gory stories about beheadings, executions and escapes. I wouldn't necessarily recommend it for kids though -- it's an hour of non-stop history. And he doesn't dumb it down either. You'll hear plenty of names that you'll be familiar with, like Henry VIII, Anne Boleyn and the Princes in the Tower, but I'm guessing that your little kid's eyes will glaze over when he's regaling tales about Thomas More and the Duke of Monmouth. Adults will have no such problem though -- I enjoyed the whole lot.

He starts off with who built the tower and the walls, and after that you head up Water Lane to Traitor's Gate. That's where he'll stop and tell you about the prisoners who came in by water. Then you flip around and look at the Bloody Tower, and learn about Richard III and his murdered nephews. You don't actually get to go inside though -- there are far too many people for that. All you do is stand outside and look. But the tour only lasts for an hour, so you've got plenty of time to go back and do the insides later.

Next up is the short walk to Tower Green and the White Tower. This is where Henry VIII liked to chop off his queen's heads. I especially enjoyed hearing about these grisly executions, and the bloody mess that was the Duke of Monmouth's death. (Maybe I have been watching too many violent movies.)

After that comes the undoubted highlight of the tour: you get to go inside the Chapel Royal of St Peter ad Vincula. This is normally closed to tourists during the day (I think it opens for the last half-hour, and for Sunday service), so this is one of the few ways that you can sneak a peek inside. It's quite a plain looking church really, with some wooden pews and a few memorials on the walls, but the real glory is buried by the altar: because this is where they interred the bones of all the headless traitors from Tower Green. When our Yeoman guide pointed out the burial site of Anne Boleyn I was actually a little bit excited. Sad, I know, but what can I say -- I like my Tudors. Two paces over from Anne is the grave of Catherine Howard and the Earl of Essex. Being able to actually go inside the church and see these graves is enough to make me recommend the tour on its own.

And that is pretty much it. After the church you can go on your merry way and do as you please, and have a proper look around all of the towers and walkways. One word of advice though... if you are planning on doing this tour then try and do it at the very start of the day, because it's a really good way of getting an overview of the place. I would also recommend going straight back to the Byward Tower and picking up an audio-guide afterwards, as there is lots of information on there which you will need when venturing inside the buildings.

Why not try a Twilight Tour, watch the Ceremony of the Keys, or attend a Sunday service at the Chapel Royal?

Tower of London -- Twilight Tour

ADDRESS Tower of London - map 10b
TRAINS Tower Gateway DLR, Tower Hill (both zone 1) **BUSES** 15, 42, 78, 100, RV1 **PRICE** Adult £27.50; Under-13s not permitted **DATES** Usually every Sun from Nov-Mar **WEB** hrp.org.uk/tower-of-london/whats-on/tower-twilight-tours **TEL** 0844 482 7799 **TIME REQUIRED** 7 PM to 8.30 PM

Easy to get to? ★★★ Good for kids? Under-13s not permitted Value for money? ★★☆ Worth a visit? ★★★

The sun has scarpered and I'm sitting outside the Tower of London waiting for the Twilight Tour to start. This part of

London is always empty at this time of night, just the occasional worker walking through to Tower Bridge. You can linger along the waterfront and not see a soul for five minutes. It's quite pretty though, sitting on this wet bench with the office lights glowing over the other side of the river. That is where all the life is. People are still working over there -- I can see them moving in the offices. City Hall is all lit up and The Shard is pointing up and up until its pointy top stabs the bottom of the rain clouds. Maybe that is what let all the rain out... it's pierced the water balloon.

If I hadn't been here before then I'd probably be a bit worried by now, because the gift shop is all shut up. The ticket booth is boarded up too and there's not a Beefeater in sight. But you just have to be patient and wait. The Tower has been here for a thousand years and it won't be rushed. Eventually a Yeoman Warder comes along and gathers up his troops (us). I'm trying to gauge how large our group is. When I went to the Ceremony of the Keys a while back it was probably about two hundred people in total, but we are nowhere near that today. I am guessing that there are about fifty people tonight. Some of them count double though.

Skip forward in time... The tour is all over now (I couldn't really write anything down in the dark), and it was pretty much identical to the Yeoman Warder tour that you can do during the day, but with a couple of little extras thrown in. For starters, you actually get to go inside a few of the towers. You can't do that on the Yeoman Warder tour because the crowds are too huge, but this Twilight tour is much more manageable. So you get to hear a little bit of history about the insides as well, which is nice. And the second little extra that you get is the dark. The tower is totally deserted at this time of night (all the tourists have been kicked out) so it's just you and your group and the Yeoman Warder leading you around. What lights they have inside the walls are of the mellow yellow variety, lighting up a piddly little cone of snow below. Everywhere else is very dark and gloomy, so you get a nice sense of how it must have felt when it was still a fortress.

I've already described the Yeoman Warder tour in my previous review, so you might like to read that one as well (it's basically the same), but I will go over the route here too. He starts you off in front of the Byward Tower, where he spends the next ten minutes detailing the history of the site from Norman times through to the building of the moat. He was chuntering along at quite a pace, packing in reams and reams of history, but he sprinkles it with plenty of gags too so it's not boring at all. Then he walks you through the Bell Tower and spends another ten minutes telling you about some of the poor prisoners who lost their heads (quite literally). After that he marches you up to Traitor's Gate and takes you inside St. Thomas's Tower.

It's in here that you get to see Edward III's Royal quarters, and the exact spot where Henry VI was murdered. Then you climb up some winding stairs to the Wakefield Tower and along an elevated walkway to Lanthorn. I particularly enjoyed this bit because it's one of the best viewing spots on the whole tour: you get a truly fantastic shot of the White Tower and Tower Bridge -- both of them lit up in floodlights. I just hope that you have better luck with the weather than I had (I was thoroughly soaked by this point, and my shoes were starting to squidge with water).

Then it's back down to ground level for a walk around the armouries building and hospital block. Our guide proudly pointed out a curtained window where he lives (on the top floor of the old hospital block) and I will happily admit to a pang of jealously.

He skirts around the side of the White Tower now, and past the Waterloo Barracks where the Crown Jewels are kept, but you don't get to go inside either of them unfortunately; and that is why I definitely recommend coming back during the day, because otherwise you'll miss out on two of the highlights.

A little further on are Tower Green and the spot where Henry VIII chopped off the heads of his troublesome wives (is there any other kind?). The guide rattled through another good talk here about all the gruesome beheadings and gory deaths, and he seemed to thoroughly enjoy himself a bit too much. I'm just glad that he didn't have an axe handy, because he might have been tempted to demonstrate the deaths on one of us.

After that came one of my favourites bits... when he took us inside the Chapel of St. Peter ad Vincula. This place is usually closed to the public, and is only accessible on one of these Yeoman Warder tours or at a Sunday church service. It's just a small little church inside, but the real glory is buried in the floor, because underneath the flagstones are the burial sites of Anne Boleyn, Catherine Howard, Lady Jane Grey and the Earl of Essex.

And that's it! After that he walks you to the door and boots you out of the Tower.

So is it worth doing? Well... if I'm being honest then I think I would rather just go during the day. The Twilight Tour is basically the same as a Yeoman Warder Tour, but if you go during the day then you'll also be able to go inside the White Tower and see the Crown Jewels (and visit the gift shop and restaurants too, which are all shut up at night). And as atmospheric as the Twilight Tour is, it didn't give me the goosebumps like the Ceremony of the Keys did (you can read about that in my separate review). So my advice to you is this: go during the day, do a Yeoman Warder Tour, and also apply for some free tickets for the Ceremony of the Keys as well. Then you'll be getting the best out of the Tower. Or, alternatively, you can just totally ignore my advice and do whatever the hell you like, because at the end of the day it's your holiday and you know what you like better than I do. (I never listen to anybody either!)

If you enjoyed this Twilight Tour, then try and get a ticket for Ceremony of the Keys.

Trafalgar Square

ADDRESS Trafalgar Square - map 8b
TRAINS Charing Cross, Embankment, Leicester Square (all zone 1) **BUSES** 3, 6, 9, 11, 12, 13, 15, 23, 24, 29, 87, 88, 91, 139, 159, 176, 453 **TIME REQUIRED** 15-20 mins

Easy to get to? ★★★ Good for kids? ★☆☆
Value for money? free Worth a visit? ★★★

Noise. Traffic noise. People noise. The sound of water falling on the fountains. Flags flapping against their metal poles and the rubber on the bus doors squealing shut. Motorbikes and bikes and cycles and cars... and so many people! Three million kids and six million parents. All standing with their cameras and handbags, rooting around for tissues and maps. It's a very busy place.

Trafalgar Square is where all the crowds come to celebrate. If we ever win the World Cup again (it's never going to happen), then this place will be packed out like we won the war. And whenever the students and unions want to complain about the government and their latest round of funding cuts, then this is where everyone marches to for a big rally at the end. They erect a big stage at the base of Nelson's Column so everyone can stand there listening to the lefties take it in turns on the microphone. They gather with their placards and banners and wave them around for five hours. *Feed the world! Stop the war! Ban the bomb! Free Nelson Mandela! It's all Margaret Thatcher's fault!* Blah blahdy blah. Welcome to Trafalgar Square.

I preferred it when the place was full of pigeons. When I was a kid I remember coming here and getting pecked and attacked and harassed by a bazillion million of the dirty things. It was a big attraction too: *come to Trafalgar Square and see all the pigeons!* They even had an old geezer standing in the corner selling polystyrene cups of bird seed, so you could drop a little pyramid of it on the palm of your hand and let them gobble it off your fingers. Tourists would stand there posing for photos as they flapped around on their hands and heads. Unfortunately the council has banished them as a health hazard now (the pigeons, I mean, not the tourists). They don't allow you to feed them anymore because of health and safety. *You might die!* They would probably lock you in quarantine for three weeks in case you'd caught rabies. Imagine how many people you could sue if a pigeon bit your finger off. Red Ken (a London Mayor) began a campaign to evict the birds in 2000, and started off by booting that old guy off his birdseed stall. A couple of years later they bought a Harris hawk to London to patrol the skies. If you come here early in the morning then you can sometimes see him sitting on a falconer's arm. He lets it fly around the rooftops for a while, just so the pigeons definitely get the message: "If you ever dare to return here then you will DIE!" I don't think I saw a single pigeon the whole time I was there today -- they are probably too scared to show their feathered faces. If any of them slip through the net then they are immediately arrested by the police and locked up in a birdcage for two weeks.

They should try the same thing with the guys who stand outside the National Gallery dressed up as robots and Yoda. It's like a police line-up of stone statues. They've rigged up some kind of scaffolding contraption under their flowing robes and feet, to make it appear as if they're floating in mid-air. Then they stand there all day waiting for a tourist to take a photo and they pounce -- *Ha ha! You took a photo of me! I want five pounds! Give me five pounds!* Other beggars sit there drawing chalk pictures onto the pavement, sketching it out at supersonic speed before the rain comes and washes it away. Tomorrow morning they'll come back and chalk over the whole thing again -- *ad infinitum.*

It always seems to be wet or freezing cold in Trafalgar Square -- it's always one or the other. The sun is shining bright white this morning, but the water spray blowing across from the fountains is like liquid nitrogen -- *no joke!* If you get a bit of that on your skin then it will flash freeze you down to the bone.

I've decided to sit here for sit here for an hour and watch the crowds. Maybe I'll write a few words, or maybe I won't. Everybody seems to be in a tremendous rush to get things done these days. I can seem them marshalling their kids into position and assembling their selfie-sticks and *Snap!* -- a quick picture of Nelson's Column. Then *Snap!* -- a picture of their kids sitting on the lions. Then *Snap!* -- a picture of their husbands looking moody in front of the fountains. *Tick, tick, tick* those three things off their 'Must-do in London' list, then they'll have a quick look at their watch and jump on the bus so they don't fall behind in their itinerary. When they get home their neighbours will ask them whether they went to Trafalgar Square and they'll say, oh yeah... we did that in five minutes on Monday morning.

Slow down, people! Slow down for chrissakes. Slow your heartbeats down and have a look around -- it's not everyday that you're standing in the centre of London. Did you notice those big bronze reliefs of Nelson's battle scenes around the base of his column? Did you stare up at his statue, and zoom in close with your camera? If that's not the world's grandest statue to a half-blind and handicapped man, then I don't know is. I bet you didn't even have a proper look.

There is always something going on in Trafalgar Square to promote some kind of community or national event, and this morning they have a sporty showcase set-up, full of kids in their PE kits doing push-ups and press-ups. They are all very excited, for some reason. I don't understand what is so exciting about jumping up and down in the freezing cold, but hey... maybe that is just my age. I can see some of those crazy 'free runners' dashing along the concrete walls and balancing on metal barriers as well, posing on tippy-toes twenty-feet in the air. I must admit that they are very good, but I don't expect many of them will survive the day. Some of those walls are ten feet high and they are running along them like they are no higher than the pavement.

The four big plinths in each corner of the square are worth looking at. One of them shows George IV, and there are two more for old soldiers from long-forgotten wars. You have to be a military historian to recognise those guys. The fourth one houses a temporary art exhibit that has been changing every six months for the last ten years. At the time of writing it has got a giant rocking horse on it. Don't ask me what the meaning behind that is supposed to be -- I'm sure the artist is trying to tell us something deep and meaningful, but to the everyday man on the street it's just a giant rocking horse. Before that they had a big ship in a glass bottle. I've also seen some truly horrendous performance pieces up there. One of them was just a guy blowing up balloons and letting them go into the sky (that was literally it); another one featured a girl dressed up as *Where's Wally?*. Rumour has it that they are just biding their time for the Queen to die, and then they're going to erect an equestrian statue of her up there. I hope they do, because the old girl deserves a decent memorial.

One thing that really winds me up about London is our generous habit of putting up statues to other countries' heroes in prominent places. Parliament Square is my real bugbear, because that place should be a gallery of our British political greats. And whom have we got lording over us? *Abraham Lincoln*. A fine politician, no doubt. But what has he got to do with England?

The most egregious example is the statue of George Washington in Trafalgar Square, standing outside the National Gallery. Don't get me started on this one, because I could moan about it all day. (Let me just moan for a couple of paragraphs at least, and then I promise I'll shut up.) This guy actually fought against us in the War of Independence (beating us), and vowed " never to set foot in London again". Many moons later the Americans kindly gifted us a statue of our conqueror and had the cheek to ship over some American soil to place under his feet, so he could keep his promise. And of course we just meekly acquiesced! I am sorry America (and I'm sorry if you're American), but if I had three wishes then this would be the very first thing to go. I'd put up a giant statue of a pigeon instead, or a memorial to that old guy who sold cupful's of nuts.

Check out my review of Nelson's Column and the lighting of the Trafalgar Square Christmas tree.

Transport Museum

ADDRESS Transport Museum, Covent Garden - map 8b **TRAINS** Charing Cross, Covent Garden, Leicester Square (all zone 1) **BUSES** 4, 9, 11, 13, 15, 23, 26, 76, 139, 172, 341, RV1 **PRICE** Adult £17; Senior £14.50; Child (under-18) free **OPEN** 10 AM to 6 PM (Sat-Thu); 11 AM to 6 PM (Fri); Last entry 45 mins before closing **WEB** ltmuseum.co.uk **TEL** 0207 565 7298 **TIME REQUIRED** 1½-2½ hours

Easy to get to? ★★★ Good for kids? ★★☆

Value for money? ★☆☆ Worth a visit? ★★☆

I'm always a bit embarrassed when I come to this place because in my head I imagine that it's full of train spotters, so I tell people that I'm visiting the Imperial War Museum instead -- something a bit more manly. Because it's *sort* of the same, isn't it? Both places have got vehicles inside them, except the ones at the Imperial War Museum have guns at the front. Once I'm safely inside I don't mind it so much.

It's arranged like a big warehouse on three different levels, and because the centre is completely open you can look down onto all the vehicles from the balcony above.

It begins with those rickety old stagecoaches that had horses to pull them along. I can see a couple of waxwork passengers sitting precariously on top holding tight to the railing, looking like they're about to fall off and die. That shows you how dangerous they are: they're even scaring the waxwork people. Can you imagine if we still had those stagecoaches today? *Health and safety would have a fit!* We'd all have to sign an insurance waiver and wear an orange bib and a crash helmet. They do look pretty fantastic, though. They are the kind of thing that if they were trundling down the street today, people would stop and point at them and snap a few photos on their mobile phones. Then they'd go home and tell their kids all about it.

The next level has got a couple of full-size carriages from what looks like a 1960s tube train. And at the risk of sounding really sad, I think I much prefer the inside of those old cabins. They're a lot cosier than the plastic crap we have today. I like my tube train seats to have cigarette burns in them, and dirty wooden struts running up and down the floor. I like it when the electric lights flicker on and off every time we run over a bump. They seem to be replacing all of those old trains with new-fangled modern ones now.

There's an even earlier train next-door with a big steam chimney at the end and a skinny little corridor running up the side of some first class cabins -- those chestnut-coloured cabins that you sometimes see in murder movies, where the chubby ticket inspector comes along and raps on the window to stamp your ticket. It's the kind of carriage where husbands kiss their missus through the open window as it chugs off down the platform, smoke curling over the top and covering everyone in smog.

You'll find all the buses on the lower level, starting with a couple of wooden ones that look like they'd blow over in the wind. The last time I came here I was just about young enough to clamber up the stairs, but my knees refused to even try today. They took one look at the stairs and promptly locked up. And there's no arguing with my knees. Once they've made their mind up, that's it. But these stairs are just ridiculous. It's almost like climbing up a castle turret! And you can forget about getting a wheelchair or a pram onboard because the platform is about two feet off the floor! And how on earth did the elderly get on? I suppose they had to walk.

The exhibits that I enjoy the most are actually just the simple little drawings and maps of the old city. They've got plenty of paintings as well. Train travel was a lot more romantic in those days. People didn't barge onto the train in those days -- they stood on the platform waving hankies and flags as it disappeared under an old brick bridge. I can see all the pretty women standing on the platforms with parasols and billowing skirts, and the men are twiddling their moustaches and doffing their hats and caps to everyone within five feet. The platform is almost like a Parisian catwalk, or a promenade for a society show.

They've also got a decent-sized collection of old station signs and London Underground posters, and the history of Harry Beck's London Underground map. You're either going to like this stuff, or you're not. It will either be interesting or tedious. I will just say this: everything definitely looked better in the past, because they actually tried to make their signs and posters look like a piece of art back then, whereas now they just knock up whatever does the job.

After that comes a life-size mock up of how they used to dig out the tunnels -- by hand, with a bucket and spade. With their shirt off and a bowler hat hanging on the gloomy orange lamplight. People came home with a face full of soot in those days. They had to peel their skin off and soak it in the bathtub for two weeks to get it clean.

This museum is a lot better for kids than it might appear on paper, because they've got lots of kid's activities set up all over the place. But I'm talking about very young kids -- definitely not teenagers. It's the kind of museum that attracts primary school classes and three thousand parents with pushchairs and toddlers having tantrums. You have to walk around looking at the ground all the time in case you step on a five year old's foot.

If you're looking for some cheesy London souvenirs to take back home then try the shop: it's full of red double decker buses, black taxicabs and London Underground tea towels. They've got a plenty of retro posters and postcards as well.

How about a ride on a real bus? Check out my reviews of the No.11 sightseeing bus and Marathon Bus Journey.

Victoria & Albert Museum

ADDRESS V&A Museum, Cromwell Road, South Kensington - map 6f **TRAINS** South Kensington (zone 1) and 10 min walk **BUSES** 14, 49, 70, 74, 345, 414, 430, 710, C1 **PRICE** Free, but there may be a charge for temporary exhibitions **OPEN** 10 AM to 5.45 PM (Sat-Thu); 10 AM to 10 PM (Fri) **WEB** vam.ac.uk **TEL** 0207 942 2000 **TIME REQUIRED** 2-3 hours

Easy to get to? ★★★ Good for kids? ★☆☆ Value for money? free Worth a visit? ★★★

I feel a bit ill this morning but don't worry -- that's normal. I'm naturally unhealthy, so I'm not going down the doctor's or anything. I'm not one of those people who take a day trip down the doctor's every time the weather's nice. My idea of medicine is that if you ignore it for long enough then it will eventually go away. Which is more than I can hope for these kids across the road...

I'm sitting here waiting for the Victoria & Albert Museum to open, watching three-hundred school kids piling off a coach. They are drowning out the traffic -- that is how loud they are. And soon they will be running around the museum like a bunch of hyperactive hoodlums. I wish I'd bought my earmuffs with me now. Ah well. You live and learn.

It's certainly a very handsome looking building from the outside. It's more like a cathedral than a museum. I think I'm starting to turn into Prince Charles... I'm starting to agree with a lot of the stuff he says -- that's a bit worrying. And I don't mean all that baloney about talking to the plants... I don't have conversations with my plant pots. I'm talking about when he has a moan about the architects and wants to run around demolishing all of the buildings that they've put up. *He's right!* When I look at buildings like the Victoria and Albert Museum, the Royal Courts of Justice, the Natural History Museum and St Pancras Chambers -- all relatively modern buildings in the grand scheme of things (only 150-ish years old) -- I can't help thinking that these are the end of the line. We are never going to build stuff like that ever again.

What are the chances of somebody building the V&A these days? It just costs too much money. No one wants to spend their money on bricks and concrete. They'd rather spend the lowest amount possible on a steel and glass box, and deposit the rest in the Bahamas earning interest. All the big marquee buildings that have gone up in recent years have been glass and steel skyscrapers. You don't get decorated stone stuff anymore.

We can forget about building something as spectacular as St. Paul's Cathedral. If that had been bombed out during the war then I hate to think what we would have ended up with. If the Houses of Parliament had burnt down this century, instead of the 19th-century, do you think we would have got the gothic-looking Palace of Westminster? Nope... we would have been lumbered with the kind of concrete modern-art piece that the Scots are pretending to love. But who cares anyway. We do have a few good buildings left in London, and I'm staring at one right now.

All I know about this place from the guidebooks is that it is the museum of *fashion and design*, full of tables and chairs and old teapots and china cups and necklaces and dresses; so I don't think I'm the target audience. But I have been surprised before, so maybe my journey down here won't have been a complete waste of time. (Jeez, I'm in a bad mood today!)

I'm inside now, and I'm strolling around the China section. It is nice enough I suppose... if you like teapots and chamber pots. They've got some statues and tapestries in here, plus some of those old blue and white Ming dynasty vases that probably cost a fortune if you smash them. There's not a lot you can say about them really. Here's a teapot. It's old. Here's a vase. It's old as well. Yeah, nice. It would look better with some daffodils in it.

The Japanese section is a bit better. They've got a collection of daggers and swords and intricate leather armour from the days of the Samurai. If I had a suit of armour like that then I would never wear it into battle, that is for sure -- I'd be too afraid of getting it poked. They've got plenty of folding screens and fans too. One thing that I do quite like are those old Oriental watercolours of pretty little bridges and blossom trees and waterfalls. They've got a lot of very pretty scenes like that on show, which are definitely worth a gander. The ink lines are so fine and delicate that if a gust of wind blew through the display then it would probably blow it all away.

Oh... my... Lord. Do you remember when I said that I wasn't looking forward to visiting this museum? Well, ignore all of that, because I was talking rubbish. I have just stumbled into the most amazing room that I have ever seen in a museum. It is full of monuments and statues and huge concrete columns from the wreck of Rome. We are talking full-size tombs of kings and queens and nobles, crucifixes of Jesus looking down, church altars and balconies, huge decorated building fronts twenty-feet tall, all covered in fantastic sculptures of praying saints and angels. They've even got Trajan's Column in here!

Do you remember that scene at the end of *Indiana Jones* when the Ark of the Covenant gets carted off to that big warehouse full of ancient treasures? Well, that room could have been modelled on this one: the Cast Room. The movie has come to life. Alas, none of them are real. They are all plaster cast and concrete impressions, but that doesn't ruin the view though. What a great room!

The Islamic galleries are a bit more sedate. I think they've got a rule that you're not allowed to draw a picture of their God, so all of their art consists of geometric lines and stripes and angled patterns. They've got a lot of plates and pots and carpets, and the centre of the room is dominated by a big Persian rug. They've got quite a large display of bright blue tiles as well, that would look quite nice on my bathroom wall (am I allowed to say that?).

Let me tell you something... they like a nice bit of carpet in India too. Their rooms are full of mats and rugs as well. If the V&A ever gets bored of being a museum then they could open up a pretty good branch of CarpetLand.

I'm not in a bad mood anymore, by the way -- the more I look around this place the more I like it. I have just found a very pleasant courtyard in the centre, all done up in the same style as the Royal Albert Hall -- red and yellow terracotta friezes and carved-columned balconies. They've got a little pool of water in the middle where the pigeons are paddling their feet. That's one of the good things about London: quite often the inside of a building is a total surprise. It's like finding a chocolate box inside a brown paper bag -- you can't tell what you're going to see until you walk through the door.

This next gallery is full of Jesus. If you love Jesus then this is the place for you. They've got stained-glass windows, statues, stone carvings, paintings, delicately crafted wooden crosses... every kind of Jesus under the sun. The only things they haven't got are mouse mats and t-shirts (come back in a hundred years and that's probably what you'll find). The stained-glass windows are certainly intriguing. They are brightly lit from behind and are glowing with brilliantly deep colours. I've never taken the time to stare at a window before, but they are quite beguiling. They've got a statue of St. Peter too, riddled with woodworm.

There are more stained-glass windows upstairs and these ones are even better. A gloomy corridor lit with deep greens and yellows and reds: these things really glow gold when they're six-feet from your nose. The cabinets are filled with golden goblets, chalices, flagons for wine, and plates the size of wagon wheels. Lots of silver pewter too... thick chunky crosses and ornate little boxes for jewellery and keepsakes. A few of them probably had the finger bones of saints inside (chicken bones), or a sliver of wood from the one true cross (someone's garden fence, more likely). The church certainly had a bit of money to spend. If you've ever wondered where your collection money goes every Sunday then here it is... they blew the lot on trinkets.

More rooms full of golden plates and silver jugs. Huge silver shields and swords and candlesticks too, golden guns and rifles. It just goes on and on... rooms and rooms of gold and silver stuff. I'd hate to think how much all of this stuff is worth. There are more treasures inside here than in the whole of King Solomon's Mine! The next time I'm thinking about robbing a bank I'll just make a beeline to this place instead. All they've got for security in here are a few old ladies and suited-up students sitting on a stool by the door.

Now they are taking the mick... as if they didn't have enough treasures already, now I have stumbled across a gallery full of Constables and Turners. And not just a couple of pictures either: but a whole room of them. This one solitary room has got twenty-two different Constables in it. The next one is full of Gainsborough's. Now I'm in a huge cavernous room full of monumental works by Raphael... preparatory studies for his work in the Sistine Chapel. I'm probably surrounded by a few hundred million pounds-worth of art.

Is this place a museum or a gallery? It seems to be making a decent go of each.

The jewellery room is another stunning sight. It is totally pitch black inside like a bank vault, with illuminated cases filled with a woman's wet dream. I can see them all drooling against the glass, nudging their husbands hint hint hint. That is what I want for my birthday please, they are saying, pointing out the rings and things. Do they sell these in the gift shop, dear? Er... no they don't, he says.

Even the theatre section is worth a look. The cabinets are full of outlandish costumes, props for plays, and some old panto posters too. And right in the heart of the darkened room is Shakespeare's *First Folio*. They've got some nice little pop-up theatre scenes too, and famous stagings of *Swan Lake* and the like, complete with tiny little matchstick ballerinas.

The final section I saw was the dresses. Not my cup of tea. But I've already seen more than enough good stuff to recommend a visit. This place has jumped right up to number two on my list of favourite museums (behind the Natural History Museum). And to think that I was a right moody git this morning, and nearly went home!

If you enjoy the V&A then you'll almost certainly like the Wallace Collection.

Wallace Collection

ADDRESS Wallace Collection, Manchester Square, Marylebone - map 2f **TRAINS** Baker Street, Bond Street, Marble Arch (all zone 1) **BUSES** 2, 10, 12, 13, 30, 74, 82, 94, 113, 137, 274 **PRICE** Free **OPEN** 10 AM to 5 PM (Mon-Sun) **WEB** wallacecollection.org **TEL** 0207 563 9500 **TIME REQUIRED** 1½-2 hours

Easy to get to? ★★★ Good for kids? ☆☆☆
Value for money? free Worth a visit? ★★☆

The Wallace Collection came as a total surprise to me. I was expecting just another art gallery but the first two rooms reminded me of Buckingham Palace (no joke). The walls are all velvet reds and warm golds and full of huge oil portraits ten feet across. The antique furniture is overflowing with gilded porcelain and golden trophy plates and statues. They've got urns and clocks and heavy dangling chandeliers -- the marble fireplace looks like it has come straight from the Palace of Versailles!

Honest to God... the first two rooms wouldn't look out of place at Buckingham Palace -- that is how beautiful they are.

The next set of rooms was full of religious treasures. If you've ever been to see the stained glass windows and church exhibits at the V&A then this will be right up your street. The darkened cabinets contain caskets and candlesticks and delicate little reliquaries with the bones of saints inside (chicken bones, more like). There are paintings of angels, glass goblets and altarpieces, and illuminated pages from biblical texts. It's all very beautiful and it's just a shame that I don't believe in God. (I am happy to suspend my disbelief for fifteen minutes when I see a room like this though.)

After that comes a series of rooms stacked full of guns and rifles and suits of armour -- the kind of thing that a chivalrous knight might wear on the Crusades. They've got fantastically ornate helmets and swords and shields and gauntlets, huge maces with deadly metal spikes, cutlasses and crossbows, pistols and scimitars. And they are not clever replicas either... this the genuine stuff from the 1500s. You could start up your own medieval army with the weapons in here. They've even got two full-size fighting horses with two huge sword-wielding knights on top. They look like medieval tanks with a turret on top.

Upstairs is much more like a traditional gallery, with beautiful rooms full of oil paintings. I'm a bit of a dunce when it comes to art (my favourite artist is Tony Hart), but even I recognised names like Gainsborough, Titian, Reynolds, Rembrandt and Rubens. They've got an entire room full of Canaletto's as well. I like the ones he did of London that I saw in the Tate, but these ones all seem to be of Venice.

The famous picture that everyone comes to see is *The Laughing Cavalier* by Frans Hals. I am standing in front of it right now, and yes, he is definitely looking smug about something; but I wouldn't exactly say he was laughing. Have you ever seen the picture? He's not laughing at all! Maybe he's having a laugh on us. I can't work out what he's so happy about... he's imprisoned inside a little square cell of wooden walls directly across from an ugly old nun and a depressing scene of anguished adults. The picture next door is of another ugly bird holding up a dead rabbit. If I had to stare at them all day then it would do my head in. He's got a very pretty lady above him though... but he can't see that one. So what has he got to smile about? He must be drunk -- that is the only explanation.

Just when you think it can't get any better you walk into a suite of rooms where Wallace had his study and drawing room. These are definitely on a par with a royal palace -- there is no question about it. You can't call this place an art gallery, or a museum, or a royal home -- it is all three things rolled into one.

And do you know what the most amazing thing is? *It's free!*

If you like the this then try the Victoria & Albert Museum and Queen's Gallery.

Wellington Arch

ADDRESS Wellington Arch, Hyde Park Corner - map 7d **TRAINS** Hyde Park Corner (zone 1) **BUSES** 9, 10, 14, 19, 22, 74, 137, 414 **PRICE** Adult £5.20; Senior (over-60) £4.70; Child (5-15) £3.10; Infant (under-5) free; Family (2 ad+3 ch) £13.50; Price includes a voluntary donation **OPEN** 10 AM to 6 PM (Mon-Sun, Apr-Sep); 10 AM to 5 PM (Mon-Sun, Oct); 10 AM to 4 PM (Mon-Sun, Nov-Mar) **WEB** english-heritage.org.uk/visit/places/wellington-arch **TEL** 0207 930 2726 **TIME REQUIRED** 30-45 mins

Easy to get to? ★★★ Good for kids? ★☆☆
Value for money? ★★★ Worth a visit? ★★☆

I'm guessing that most people come here for just one reason: to have a sneaky peek over the wall into Buckingham Palace. They're hoping to see the Queen sunbathing on her manicured lawn, or Prince Philip testing out his shotgun on the sparrows. Alas, the view into the gardens is quite disappointing... but more on that later.

The arch is like a Tardis inside, and a lot bigger than you'd imagine from the front. They've got a few rooms on a couple of floors, which they use for temporary exhibitions. At the time of writing they've got a bit about the Battle of Waterloo. I've also seen a collection of old music hall and pantomime posters here. But the most interesting exhibit for me is always the permanent one, which tells you about the architecture of the arch itself. And yes, I know exactly what you're thinking -- *yawn yawn yawn* -- but it's actually a very interesting story.

Wellington Arch originally looked a lot different than it does today, because it started off at right angles, facing Apsley House. When they built the main round they shifted it back and spun it round ninety degrees, so now it faces down Constitution Hill instead. It also had a colossal bronze statue of the Duke of Wellington on top. As soon as they lifted it into position it was obviously too huge for its seat, but nobody wanted to upset

England's greatest-ever general by knocking him off the top of his triumphal arch (especially when he only lived over the road), so they had to wait for him to die before installing the four horses that we see today. Check out the old photos of what it used to look like in its original state -- it's very interesting (if you're a saddo like me, that is).

The highlight is obviously the balcony at the top. There are actually two of them -- one on each side. The first one overlooks Hyde Park Corner and Apsley House, whilst the other one stares straight down Constitution Hill. You can't see Buckingham Palace at all, unfortunately, because it's totally hidden behind the trees. All you can see of the gardens is a little piece of gravel path, and maybe some tennis courts (it's difficult to make them out through the leaves). But there is no way that the Queen ever risks walking around there -- not when people can spy on her from the arch -- so the chances of you seeing her walking her corgis is non-existent. The best you'll get is a gardener raking up the leaves.

If you want to have a game of 'spot the landmark' with me, then try and find The Shard and the London Eye (you'd have to be blind to miss those!). Big Ben is very easy, and so is Westminster Abbey. That's pretty much all you can see.

P.S.: Try and coincide your visit with the Changing the Guard ceremony at Horse Guards. If you stand on the balcony then you'll be treated to a grandstand view of the horses trooping their way down from their barracks in Hyde Park. They'll march straight past the arch at around 10.45 AM, and return the same way at approx 11.40 AM (except on Sundays, when everything takes place one hour earlier).

The West End

ADDRESS Around Shaftesbury Ave, Piccadilly Circus, Leicester Square, Trafalgar Square and Covent Garden - maps 3f, 8a, 8b **TRAINS** Charing Cross, Covent Garden, Embankment, Leicester Square, Piccadilly Circus (all zone 1) **BUSES** 3, 4, 6, 9, 11, 12, 13, 14, 15, 19, 23, 24, 26, 38, 76, 87, 88, 94, 139, 159, 172, 176, 243, 341, 453, RV1 **TIME REQUIRED** 2-3 hours

Easy to get to? ★★★ Good for kids? ★☆☆
Value for money? free Worth a visit? ★★★

The West End roughly encompasses the area around Leicester Square, Piccadilly Circus and Covent Garden. A lot of the biggest theatres can be found down Shaftesbury Avenue, Haymarket and the Strand. This is where you'll get a proper taste of London -- bright lights and terrible traffic. Lots of life, lots of strife. Lots of noise, and six inches of pavement per person.

Shaftesbury Avenue is absolutely heaving with people tonight. You get carried along in the throng, like a fallen leaf in the sea, because there's nowhere else to go. It's very easy to lose your rag in a crowd like this. People clip your ankles and cut you up, and you're forever looking at the backs of coats, and dodging rucksacks that are slung over their shoulders like head-height rocky outcrops. Some people erect gigantic umbrellas and use them as a pavement forcefield, whilst other ones just freeze inexplicably, totally oblivious to the unstoppable mob that is coming up behind. If you want some space then you literally have to step out into the road and take your chances with the buses and bikes, scooters and tooters.

The buses are full of faces peering out of steamed up windows tonight. You can tell which ones are the tourists because they've been excitedly wiping off the condensation with their sleeves, to get a better look at the bright lights of Piccadilly Circus. The locals just settle in behind a net curtain of steam until it's time to get off.

You can really smell the street food at nighttime. All of the food and booze aromas concentrate like a thick sauce in the cold night air, and mix in with the cigarette smoke (plus an occasional whiff of dope) and you're walking along in a fog of lights and nose aromas.

Piccadilly Circus is the kind of place where people wait for something to happen. They sit on the steps and stare at the cars, in a trance, or stand around with their buddies planning what to do next. *Shall we go here? Shall we go there?* Hundreds of couples are just milling around planning their night. They'll probably all end up in a pub or a club or a fight. Some will get laid, and some will get laid out. Which ones are having a good time, and which ones are having a bad time? It's difficult to tell when they've all been drinking.

One of the most amazing things about Piccadilly Circus is the amount of light that is thrown out by the neon sign. It's almost like a second sun. And then you've got the cacophony of tourist chat and traffic and wailing sirens, and people posing for photos everywhere you turn... it's too loud to think! No hermit has ever lived here -- I can assure you of that. No one ever dies at Piccadilly Circus, because the noise would just wake them straight back up again.

I like the bright lights down Shaftesbury Avenue the best, because it reminds me of Christmas. It's all warm yellows and golds, and bright red cherry letters spelling out the prices. But you should definitely have a look down the side streets as well. Rupert Street, Brewer Street and Gerrard Street (Chinatown) are worth a look. It might seem like a slow down after walking through the bright lights of theatre land, but there's much more character in the side streets.

It's after midnight at the moment and the crowds have thinned out. The streets are blowing with cardboard coffee cups and loose sheets of yesterday's papers, which are wrapping around my legs like drainpipe trousers. This is my favourite face of London. The side-street scenes, full of darkened pubs and bolted stage doors.

Once they switch the shop lights off you become part of the scenery. People see you approaching out of the shadows and wonder whether to cross the street. They dress you up in their own fears and turn you into something that you're not. In their heads that businessman on his mobile phone suddenly becomes a drunk man muttering and chuntering to his imaginary friend, and those celebrating students become a gang of rampaging hoodlums out looking for a fight. That little old nun in a habit becomes a fifteen year old kid in a hoodie with a knife.

The spookiest scene is when you see a glowing face in a distant doorway. People stand in the shadows to tap messages into their mobile phones, and the bright white screen lights up the bottom of their chin. Everyone has a phone in London, and they can't go five minutes without checking their messages. Away from the bright lights of Piccadilly Circus there's

Westminster Abbey

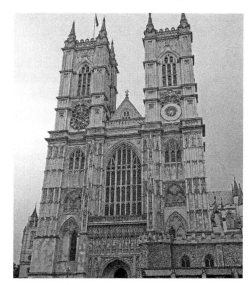

ADDRESS Westminster Abbey, Westminster - map 8d **TRAINS** Westminster (zone 1) **BUSES** 11, 24, 148, 211 **PRICE** Adult £20; Senior (over-60) £17; Child (5-16) £9; Child (under-5) free; Family (2 ad+2 ch) £45, or £40 with 2ad+1 ch **OPEN** 9.30 AM to 4.30 PM (Mon, Tue, Thu-Sat); 9.30 AM to 7 PM (Wed); Last entry 1 hour before closing; Only open for worship on Sun **DENOMINATION** Church of England **WEB** westminster-abbey.org **TEL** 0207 222 5152 **TIME REQUIRED** 2 hours

Easy to get to? ★★★ Good for kids? ★☆☆ Value for money? ★★☆ Worth a visit? ★★★

Everyone who comes to London should visit Westminster Abbey... simple as that. It's the second best building in the capital after Parliament, and contains the single greatest room in the Henry VII chapel. Unfortunately it's also bloody expensive considering that it's a church, but I suppose even God has got his bills to pay.

It's unlike any church that you have ever seen. The tombs and memorials and statues are piled up tight on top of each other and the whole thing is cramped like you wouldn't believe. The walls and floors are littered with them. You walk past ten tombs every two paces so you definitely need to listen to the audio-guide or you'll miss out a lot of interesting material; but I also recommend getting hold of a map beforehand, because the gentleman on the audio-guide (Jeremy Irons) inexplicably misses out a lot of good ones. When you walk in the front door you will pass people like Darwin and Elgar, for example, but neither warrants a mention on the tape. How can you forget someone like Darwin? (Maybe the church still hasn't forgiven him. They sure do hold their grudges a long time!)

Before you reach the standout tombs you have to stroll through a few corridors containing 20th-century politicians like Lloyd George, Attlee, Baldwin, MacDonald and Wilson. Churchill gets a plum spot by the door, but you can definitely see who had the biggest egos: Charles Fox and Henry Campbell-Bannerman -- their tombs are bigger than all the other ones put together!

As you walk through the Abbey it's interesting to see who gets the biggest slab. The explorer David Livingstone has a huge one right in the middle of the Nave, whilst other people have to make do with a little dinner mat off to the side. I suppose it must have come down to whether they had a lot of money or friends in high places. In some places it's almost like walking on a marble carpet. You'll be stepping on bedspread-sized tablets coloured in silver and gold, whilst other ones will have a diamond-shaped slab with their names rubbed off, shined up by the shoes of centuries of sightseers.

The statues around the side are all good enough for the National Gallery. They aren't your usual headstones -- some of them are ten-feet effigies and span two floors in height -- and these are for people that nobody knows! I don't think they had to achieve much to get buried here at the beginning. If they were best mates with the priest then they'd probably find you a shaded spot. But these days they can't even find room for Richard III. It's all protected now and unalterable which I think is a great shame, because what is this place, if it's not an ongoing record of our great and good? Did British history die with Churchill?

It's when you reach the golden screen in the centre of the Nave that you'll start to see how great this place is. It might not have the golden ceilings of St. Paul's Cathedral but there's a lot more atmosphere in this place because it's so cramped and gloomy. I like my churches to be dark and moody. And when you pass under the central screen you'll see one of the most impressive sights in the whole of London -- the dark chestnut coloured wood and stalls of the Quire, with the golden altar and ancient Cosmati pavement.

Just have a look up at that ceiling -- it's almost as tall as most buildings are long! You'll get your first good look at a stained glass window here as well as the light floods down through the smoggy smell of incense onto the hundred-strong throng of a tourist crowd. We are all just standing around with our audio-guide against our ears, staring at this scene. This is where ten centuries of kings and queens have been crowned. When was the last time you spent ten-minutes staring at a floor? I could have done with a bit more Handel on the headphones because when it drums up into Zadok the Priest you get a bit choked up! You know the song that I mean... the famous Coronation tune (and I don't mean *Coronation Street*). They strike that up when you are standing by the altar and if you don't feel something stirring in your heart then there must be something wrong with you. (I'm getting very patriotic in my old age.)

After that you pass round the side of the altar where you can see all the beautiful little chapels and statues. Don't forget to look inside the chapel of St. John the Baptist, because that's one of my favourite places in the Abbey. I think the entrance doorway to this place looks like oldest thing in London (not the chapel itself, but just inside the doorway). Do you agree with me?

On the opposite side to the chapels you will see the tombs of some our most famous kings -- men like Edward III and I (Hammer of the Scots), Henry III, Henry V and Richard II. Right in the centre is the tomb of our only kingly saint: Edward the Confessor. This guy dates back 1,000 years to before the reign of William the Conqueror, and he's been sleeping in that same spot since 1269! Unfortunately the tomb itself is too precious to risk letting the tourist hordes near it, so you can only view it from afar. (The audio-guide provides a little video of what it's like inside.)

At the very end of the Abbey is the single greatest room in the whole of London. No other one even comes close -- not even the State Apartments inside Buckingham Palace. It's called the Henry VII Chapel and contains the graves of Henry, Edward VI (Henry VIII's teenage son), Elizabeth I, Mary I (Bloody Mary) and James I. Round the side of the chapel you'll find the tombs of Mary Queen of Scots and the ultimate mother-in-law from hell: Margaret Beaufort.

It seems almost incredible to me that these tombs still survive -- these are the victors of Agincourt and the Spanish Armada. Edward the Confessor pre-dates the Battle of Hastings! This is the English Valley of the Kings.

Remember to have a look inside the RAF Chapel as well because there's a flagstone on the floor that marks the original burial site of Oliver Cromwell, before Charles II dug up his bones and hanged them at Tyburn.

After that you'll come to the tourist hotspot of Poets' Corner. This place is always packed with Japanese camera-clickers snapping at the statue of Shakespeare (he's only there in spirit, because his body is buried at Stratford-upon-Avon), but it is actually home to more than forty burials and sixty memorials to the likes of Chaucer, Keats, Kipling, Dickens, Tennyson, Shelley, Eliot, Lord Byron, Dylan Thomas... the list just goes on and on. The only big name that I would have liked to have seen there that was missing was Tolkien. I noticed that CS Lewis is there, so why not Tolkien? Maybe we should start a petition up.

After that it's nice to get a bit of peace and quiet in the cloisters. The audio-guide will come to an abrupt end at this point and you will have to hand it in, but there's still plenty more to see outside. You can have a wander around the gardens and the dungeon-like doors in the cloisters where the priests must live. I wouldn't fancy living in those much -- the walls outside your house are covered in graves.

When you get halfway round the cloisters you'll find the tiny Abbey Museum. Considering that the history of this place stretches back a thousand years it's surprisingly small inside, but they've got some wax effigies of old kings and queens that are worth seeing. After that the route will take you back inside the Abbey for a final look at the Coronation Chair.

If you like beautiful old churches then try Brompton Oratory, St. Paul's Cathedral and Westminster Cathedral.

Westminster Cathedral

ADDRESS Westminster Cathedral, Victoria - map 8e **TRAINS** St. James's Park, Victoria (both zone 1) **BUSES** 11, 24, 148, 507, 211 **PRICE** Cathedral: Free -- Tower: Adult £6; Senior £3; Child £3; Family (2 ad+up to 4 ch) £12 **OPEN** Cathedral: 7 AM to 6 PM (Mon-Fri); 8 AM to 6.30 PM (Sat); 8 AM to 7.30 PM (Sun) -- Tower: 9.30 AM to 5 PM (Mon-Fri); 9.30 AM to 6 PM (Sat-Sun) **DENOMINATION** Roman Catholic **WEB** westminstercathedral.org.uk **TEL** 0207 798 9055 **TIME REQUIRED** 1 hour

Easy to get to? ★★★   Good for kids? ★☆☆
Value for money? ★★☆   Worth a visit? ★★☆

Westminster Cathedral is the nuttiest church in London. It's covered in classical columns, checkerboard walls, stained glass windows, Roman mosaics, stripes and spirals, stone statues of saints and angels and birds... and that's just out the front! I don't know who submitted the architectural plans, but they were clearly drunk. I bet they had a lot of explaining to do when they turned up at the Pearly Gates.

"What the hell is this?" asked God. *"I ordered a cathedral, not a Sultan's palace!"*

But don't get me wrong... I do like it. It's one of the few orange brick buildings in the city that doesn't look bland.

When you step inside the front door it gets even better, because it has a ceiling like no other in London. Imagine the interior of St. Paul's, but with soot instead of gold. It looks like the inside of a Victorian chimney. It looks like the inside of a railway tunnel. The entire roof is coloured in nothing but old smoke and charcoal, like a night sky with no stars. The stars are hanging fifteen feet off the floor, on iron chandeliers.

The columns up the side of the aisles are all brightly coloured marble, with those swirling shapes you sometimes see when petrol falls on water. It's when you look inside the chapels that you'll finally find the gold. I'm looking at one right now that has a golden mosaic all over the ceiling, and a lonely old codger slumped over on a seat, catching a few zzz's on the solid stone wall. I can see another old lady checking out her horoscopes in a national newspaper. Obviously God isn't working for her, so she's using astrology as a back-up -- and why the hell not? If God can't help, try Mystic Meg instead. If Mystic Meg doesn't work then give Russell Grant a go. And after that you can start buying packs of magical crystals from QVC.

I've decided to light a candle just for the hell of it -- just because I like the light. Some people light them as an offering to God, but I just want to burn something. I'm not making a wish, though -- forget that. I can see some pious types doing that across the other side of the nave, crossing their foreheads and saying a quick little prayer with their finger on their lips, but I'd feel like a total phoney. Lighting a candle and saying a prayer is just the adult version of blowing out the candles on your birthday cake.

"Blow them out and make a wish!" said your mum.

"Light a candle and say a prayer," says the priest.

You may as well just chuck an old coin in the river, of blow the petals off a daisy. The last time I came in here I saw a young kid lighting a candle with his cigarette lighter -- he was only about twelve. A kid with a Zippo... but using it for prayers.

Because Westminster Cathedral is still relatively new (compared to somewhere like St. Paul's), they haven't yet accumulated much in the way of history. So don't come here expecting to see a lot of historic old tombs inside, because there aren't any. But what they do have is a 273 feet bell tower with an observation platform at the top.

I was just about to psyche myself up for a big trek up the stairs when the nice lady behind the till took me to the lift. *Praise the Lord*, I thought, *a lift! It's a miracle!* She rides it all the way to the top with you and then you have to press a bell when you want to come back down again. That summons her from her slumber, and she rides it back up to escort you back down. So she basically spends her entire life going up and down this tower every time a tourist rings the damn bell. I'm guessing that God must be punishing her for sins committed in a previous life. (She must have done something pretty bad.)

There's not a lot of room on the actual balconies, but you do get a fantastic view of... the rooftops. When you're down on the ground the campanile seems colossal, but when you step out at the summit you'll discover that it's not a lot taller than the surrounding offices, which means that all you get are a lot of boring rooftops and the top half of some famous sights. I saw the top half of the London Eye, the top half of Parliament, the top half of the Gherkin, and a very thin sliver of Buckingham Palace. Put it this way: if I had to climb 273 stairs then I definitely wouldn't do it, but seeing as there's a lift it's just about passable.

If you'd like to have a competition with me then try and find the dome of St. Paul's without looking at the placard -- that should be relatively easy. Nelson's Column shouldn't be too difficult either (just follow the line of The Mall). The giant arch of Wembley Stadium is a little bit harder. And if you manage to spot the Natural History Museum and the V&A Museum without any help, then you're an absolute genius (even I struggled with those).

A word of warning: the bell went off whilst I was up there and it's *extremely* loud! I swear to God that the tower trembled too, because I could feel it swaying from side to side and cupping its hands against its ears. The bell sits somewhere above your head and the sound comes rumbling down like a lightning conductor, racing its way down to the ground. I don't mind admitting that I was a little bit scared, but nobody noticed I don't think.

You should also try St. Paul's, Westminster Abbey and Brompton Oratory.

18 Stafford Terrace (aka. Linley Sambourne House)

ADDRESS 18 Stafford Terrace, Kensington
TRAINS High Street Kensington (zone 1)
BUSES 9, 10, 27, 28, 49 **PRICE** Costumed Tour & Guided Tour: Adult £10; Senior £8; Child £8 -- Self-Guided: Adult £7; Senior £5; Child £5
OPEN Costumed Tour: 11 AM to 12.15 PM (Sat) -- Guided Tour: 11 AM to 12.15 PM (Wed, Sun) -- Self-Guided: 2 PM to 5.30 PM (Wed, Sat-Sun) -- Closed (Mon, Thu-Fri) **WEB** rbkc.gov.uk/subsites/museums/eighteen staffordterrace1.aspx **TEL** 0207 602 3316
TIME REQUIRED Costumed Tour & Guided Tour: 1 ¼ hours -- Self-Guided: 45-60 mins

Easy to get to? ★★★ Good for kids? ☆☆☆
Value for money? ★★☆ Worth a visit? ★☆☆

From the outside this place just looks like a regular townhouse in a regular street -- it's nothing special at all. People must walk past it all the time and not give it a second thought. But if you step inside you'll be transported back to a time when the brightest colour in the world was brown, and the only sound in the house was a ticking clock.

You probably haven't heard of Linley Sambourne, but he was quite famous in his day. He did a lot of cartoons for *Punch*, and the illustrations for Charles Kingsley's *The Water Babies*. I wouldn't have known any of this either, but they make you snooze through a ten minute documentary on his life at the start. He was also a bit of a dab hand at photography, and plastered the walls with shots of his models.

The house has remained pretty much the same as it was at the time of his death. His son took over straight after, but he was clearly too lazy to redecorate because it still contains all of the original interiors and decorations from over a century ago. So what you're looking at is a Victorian house. I wouldn't call it an everyday home, though -- this guy was clearly loaded -- but neither is it a palace. It's just a very fine snapshot of life in the late-19th century.

The decor is all dark greens and chestnut browns. Whatever yellows there are, are just mustard-coloured gloom -- the colour of cigarette-stained fingers. There are lots of china plates and dried flowers, and stopped clocks on the mantelpiece; old photo frames and statues; oval mirrors that make your face look like a dusty portrait painting. Even the stained glass windows do their best to keep the light out. When you get upstairs the walls are covered in his photography -- those early attempts that seem overly posed and ghostly.

It reminds me of a Sunday afternoon round my great grandmother's country cottage -- the one who was born before the age of flight, and still had a picture of Queen Victoria on the mantelpiece. Every room looks like your grandmother either lived in it, or died in it. I'm not sure that I'd want to spend a night there, but it's an interesting way to spend an hour.

If you like this then you might also like the Leighton House Museum, Charles Dickens Museum and Sir John Soane's Museum

Sightseeing Buses & Boats

By Road

Big Bus Tour

ADDRESS Bus stops all over London **PRICE** If bought online: Adult from £24.50; Child (5-15) from £12.50; Infant (under-5) free; Family (2 ad+2 ch) from £61.50 -- If bought on bus: Adult £32; Child (5-15) £13; Infant (under-5) free; Family (2 ad+2 ch) £77 **TIMES** Every 10-20 mins from 8.30 AM to 4.30 PM (Mon-Sun, Nov-Feb), 8.30 AM to 5 PM (Mon-Sun, Mar-Oct), 8.30 AM to 6 PM (Mon-Sun, Apr-Sep) **WEB** eng.bigbustours.com/london **TEL** 0207 808 6753 **TIME REQUIRED** You can hop-on and off the buses all day

Easy to get to? ★★★ Good for kids? ★★☆ Value for money? ★☆☆ Worth a visit? ★☆☆

Whenever I buy a ticket for one of these sightseeing buses it always starts pelting down with rain. And not just a little drizzle either -- I mean a thick drumbeat of dirty grey water coming in sideways, smacking against the side of the bus. It's enough to drive you off the top-deck and into the dry section downstairs. That's not much fun, is it? You want to sit up top, where there are no windows or walls to block your view. Ah well... I think I am just unlucky with the weather. If I went skiing the snow would melt.

After twenty minutes of driving around the rain eventually eases off, and the driver starts handing out plastic ponchos for us to sit on. Otherwise our backsides would get wet from the pool of water on the seat.

I quite like sitting on a bus, driving around town and looking at all the stuff on show. But normally I would advise against spending money on a sightseeing bus because the prices they charge are outrageous: thirty-plus quid for a 24-hour ticket! When you consider that a one-day travelcard is just a third of the price, and that covers all of the tube trains as well, spending so much money on a sightseeing bus seems like a total rip-off to me.

And when you start reading the small print it gets even worse... because you discover that the buses only operate between 8.30 AM and 5 PM. [Note: see above for the exact times, because they change throughout the year.] Now... I'm not much good at maths, but I'm pretty sure that 8.30 AM to 5 PM only adds up to 8½ hours, not 24. How do they get away with calling that a 24-hour ticket? So here is my first piece of advice: if you are planning on using this as a hop-on, hop-off bus throughout the day then watch out -- because your day will be over by 5 PM.

And here's my second piece of advice... well, it's more of a warning really. The Big Bus Tour only operates two real routes, and they only run in one direction. So if you travel from Trafalgar Square to Big Ben, for example, and you decide you want to head back the way you came, then you would have to ride the bus all the way round the loop via the London Eye, St. Paul's, Tower Bridge and The Shard! So if you're planning on jumping on and off the bus throughout the day then you definitely need to study the map on their website beforehand, and plot your route in advance.

If you choose the 'Red route' (2¼ hours) then you will have a live guide talking into a microphone at the front of the bus. The 'Blue route' is longer (3¼ hours), but you have to make do with some headphones instead.

At first sight my guide looks like a student, straight out of university. I don't want to diss the bloke because he is a nice enough fella, but his commentary is a bit hit and miss. He is pointing out silly stuff like a Porsche showroom and a Stella McCartney clothes shop... even the breed of the trees going by. But he's certainly earning his wages though: it is practically non-stop chit-chat. This guy could talk for England -- I think they must have plugged his mouth up to the engine. He's never short of small talk, this bloke. As soon as he fears a lull coming he jumps straight in with an anecdote about the weather. I'm no good at any of that chatty stuff -- I need a reason to talk. I plan my speech a day in advance. I can sit in a room with my sister and not say a word for five minutes. The kind of words that I like are the ones right here on this page -- they leave my mouth in silence and have a kip for six months until a reader wakes them up.

I'm about forty-five minutes into the tour now and it's started to spit with rain again. That is the problem with these open-top buses... they are built for the sun, and this is London. The sun doesn't live in London. It just comes for a quick little look and disappears. Picture the scene: the top deck is full of people wearing see-through plastic ponchos to fend off the rain. We look like a crowd of plastic bags. The sky is greying up and getting very dark, and we need some headlights on to illuminate the gloom -- it's only 11 o'clock in the morning. We've just passed over Waterloo Bridge and seen Big Ben on the left and St. Paul's on the right, all dimmed out in the weather. It must be a bit annoying for the tourists, but I don't care. I have seen it all a million times before anyway. I'd much rather see this stuff in the rain.

We've entered Fleet Street and the City of London now. The guide is finally getting into his stride and is coming out with some interesting pieces of info. He is much better than an audio guide. The last time I came on a sightseeing bus (the *Original Bus Tour*) I ended up slating it as a waste of money, but this time I am actually quite enjoying it. I guess it all depends on the weather and what kind of mood you're in. It's probably a lot better when you haven't seen any of the buildings before as well -- so if a regular Londoner like me can enjoy it then you should have no problem.

My mind is starting to wander every time we enter the traffic, and I end up following the pretty women down the street. I start dreaming about my tea, and what I'm doing tomorrow night, and then all of a sudden a landmark flashes by and I wake up.

After about 1½ hours on the 'Red route' I finally had to get off and have a wee (never drink a can of Coke whilst sitting on a sightseeing bus) and when the next one came along it was for the 'Blue route'. So I ended up doing both routes in one day. This one has got an audio guide instead of a human being sitting at the front. Here is my advice: try and get a human guide if you can, because the audio guide is rubbish. It's just a plummy-voiced posh bloke reeling off a long list of boring facts, intermingled with lots of bombastic *Last Night of the Proms*-style classical anthems. The music seems to kick in every five-seconds (every time you pull up in the traffic) and it quickly outstays its welcome. I'm currently listening to *Rule Britannia* again as we inch our way around Paddington. Ten minutes ago I had *Land of Hope and Glory* blasting out around Notting Hill. And it's not easy listening to headphones on an open-top bus either, with all the traffic noise and cold wind whistling past your face -- it makes it very difficult to hear. In fact, if I had spent the entire day on the 'Blue route' then I would have hated this worse than the Original Bus Tour. Anything that gives me a pounding headache automatically gets a bad review -- that is one of my reviewing rules. But the live guide on the 'Red route' made it worth doing.

So to sum up: the 'Blue route' is the longest one, and actually incorporates the whole of the 'Red route' within it, but it is far too long. Three hours is just too much time to spend on one bus, so I would definitely recommend sticking with the 'Red route'. I still think the price is a total rip-off though.

You might like to look at the Original Bus Tour or London Duck Tour instead.

No.11 Bus -- Sightseeing Route

ROUTE Liverpool Street > Bank > St. Paul's Cathedral > Ludgate Hill > Fleet Street > Strand > Trafalgar Square > Whitehall > Parliament Square > Victoria > Sloane Square - see map 5f for Liverpool St, 5e for Bank, 8d for Parliament Square **PRICE** Normal bus fares apply; See transport chapter for the prices **TIMES** From Liverpool St: Every 7-10 mins from 5.30 AM to 11.55 PM -- From Bank: Every 7-10 mins from 5.33 AM to 11.59 PM **WEB** tfl.gov.uk/bus/route/11/?direction=inbound **TIME REQUIRED** From Liverpool St: 30 mins to Trafalgar Square; 35 mins to Westminster; 45 mins to Victoria; 65 mins to Chelsea -- From Bank: 25 mins to Trafalgar Square; 30 mins to Westminster; 40 mins to Victoria; 60 mins to Chelsea

Easy to get to? ★★★ Good for kids? ★★☆
Value for money? ★★★ Worth a visit? ★★☆

My wallet is a bit threadbare this week so I had a go on the No.11 bus -- London's cheapest sightseeing tour. It's just a normal everyday bus that happens to run through the heart of London, and for a few measly quid you can plonk yourself down on the top deck for sixty minutes of sightseeing.

I decided to do it right, and went all the way to the start of the line at Liverpool Street station. But you might want to pick it up at Bank instead because there isn't really much to see at Liverpool Street. It was quite difficult to find the bus-stop as well, because you have to go right inside the concourse and find the sign. For some bizarre reason known only to them, they have decided not to label it from the outside. So it's like a treasure hunt without any treasure. Just a white-haired old guy smoking his roll-ups by the stop. I think he was on a day out like me, just looking for something to do, and I wondered whether I was looking at myself in thirty years. Ten minutes later the bus turned up and we both clambered up the stairs and sat at the front. It was at this point that I discovered he was a bit nuts, because he started talking to himself every time we stopped at the lights. That is what sixty years of bus travel does to you... it slowly roasts your brain until you lose it like a loon.

Once the bus pulls away from the station it very quickly gets into a routine: you have thirty-seconds of moving forwards, followed by two minutes of standing still. Our trip began at 10.30 AM and within sixty-seconds I was already sitting in my first traffic jam. Welcome to London, folks! But thankfully you soon hit the sights so there are plenty of things to look at. Five minutes after setting off you are already going past the Bank of England and Mansion House. The Royal Exchange is one of London's best buildings, and you'll have to remember to crane your neck to the left to see it. I also quite like staring into the foyers of posh city skyscraper blocks, with their marble floors and modern art on the walls. The city businessmen really do carry umbrellas and briefcases -- it's not a stereotype. I didn't see a single bowler hat though; I guess they must have gone out of fashion.

You have to prepare yourself for the traffic. It's all taxis, beeping cars and buses, and a string of speeding cyclists weaving in and out of the lanes. When the red traffic lights turn green nothing happens. One car manages to sneak through and then it's back to red again. You slowly inch your way forward until a chink of daylight opens up, then the driver puts his foot down for ten-seconds before he's back on the end of another traffic jam. But I don't mind it so much. I quite like watching the world go by on the top deck of a bus. It's all busy shoppers, busy businessman, busy camera-clicking tourists, busy busy busy. Everyone is very busy except for us on the bus -- sitting in the traffic jam watching the world go by.

After Bank you head down Cannon Street towards St. Paul's. You get a perfect view of the Cathedral's dome as you pass it on your right, and then you go round the front as well for a view of the steps. After that you head down Ludgate Hill towards Fleet Street. That's when you pass Temple Bar and the Royal Courts of Justice. By this time it was already half-past 10, so I was twenty minutes into the journey.

The Royal Courts of Justice is quite a grand looking building. While I was sitting in the traffic (again) I saw a black-frocked priest lounging in the doorway. Was he on trial for something? You never know these days. I wonder what his story was.

While we were waiting for the bus to move a woman ran between the cars into the middle of the road, and then coolly strolled across the other lane with a big smile on her face. Her husband was still standing at the kerb wagging his finger at her. He waited until it was safe to cross -- he's not half the man his wife is.

Into the Strand now... heading towards Trafalgar Square. Not content with digging up all of the roads it seems like they have started digging up the pavements too. I think they must be running out of places to put their holes. They will have to start digging up the Thames next. It was a real symphony of beeping horns and bike bells here, quite a musical tune. Everyone trying to get where they're going at the expense of everyone else. It gives you a lot of time to look inside the shop windows to see what they're selling, and I have come to the conclusion that London is 90% sandwich shops, coffee bars and banks. The other 10% is roadworks.

At the end of the Strand comes Nelson's Column and Admiralty Arch, with the National Gallery on your right. Then you turn left into Whitehall, and Big Ben immediately becomes visible above the treetops. It was 10.45 by this time. As you ride down Whitehall you'll get a good look at the tourists standing outside Horse Guards, waiting to have their photo taken with the soldier. I also saw the soggy rain-drenched wreaths at the base of the Cenotaph, and the big black gates of Downing Street. Then you head into Parliament Square, with Big Ben on your left and the gruff black statue of Churchill staring into the top-deck on your right. Then you ride round to Westminster Abbey (remember to crane your neck to the left to get a view of the front).

If you take my advice then you'll get off at this point, because the tour is a lot less interesting once it passes Westminster. But I did my duty and carried on to Chelsea so I could tell you what it's like.

The next bit is severely lacking in landmarks, but the roads around Victoria do contain some nice old buildings. It's a bit of a building site at the moment though, because they're busy erecting some giant glass and steel structures by the station (more roadworks!). The bus continues on past Victoria Coach Station, where it will pick up about fifty-million tourists with their big bags and wheely-suitcases, all looking totally knackered from their ten-hour trips on the continental coaches. I would have got up and offered them my seat but I have a rule: I only get up for pregnant ladies, pretty ladies and old ladies.

It was 11 AM now, and I had been on the bus for fifty minutes -- which is about as long as you want. Any more than that and it becomes a bit boring. There is no real reason to carry on to Chelsea. There are some pretty little brick buildings and bulging baskets of flowers hanging from the lamposts, but that's about it. It's the kind of place where millionaires live. The shops all seem to sell shiny leather chairs for ten grand a pop, and bars of soap for fifty quid. If you stay on to Sloane Square then you can forget about finding Lidl's and the PoundShop -- it's all Hugo Boss and Peter Jones.

The entire journey took sixty minutes from Liverpool Street to Chelsea, or forty minutes to Westminster. The timetable says that it was supposed to take thirty-five, so maybe you'll get lucky with the traffic.

Is it worth doing? Sure! If you like watching the world go by from the top deck of a bus then it's quite a nice way to wile away an hour. And I definitely recommend it over blowing twenty-five quid on a tour bus.

If you want a proper sightseeing bus then try the Big Bus and Original Bus Tour.

Original Bus Tour

ADDRESS Bus stops all over London **PRICE** If bought online: Adult £26; Child (5-15) £12.50; Infant (under-5) free; Family (2 ad+2 ch) £75 -- If bought on bus: Adult £30; Child (5-15) £15; Infant (under-5) free; Family (2 ad+2 ch) £90
TIMES Yellow route: Every 15-30 mins from 8.30 AM to 4 PM (Mon-Thu, Nov-Feb); Every 15-30 mins from 8.30 AM to 4.30 PM (Fri-Sun, Nov-Feb); 10-20 mins from 8.30 AM to 6.20 PM (Mon-Sun, Mar-May); 5-20 mins from 8.30 AM to 8 PM (Mon-Sun, Jun-Aug); Every 10-15 mins from 8.30 AM to 6 PM (Mon-Sun, Sep-Oct) -- Red route: Every 10-15 mins from 8.30 AM to 4.50 PM (Mon-Thu, Nov-Feb); Every 10-15 mins from 8.30 AM to 5.20 PM (Fri-Sun, Nov-Feb); 10-15 mins from 8.30 AM to 6.50 PM (Mon-Sun, Mar-May); 7-15 mins from 8.30 AM to 7.30 PM (Mon-Sun, Jun-Aug); Every 10-15 mins from

8.30 AM to 5.20 PM (Mon-Sun, Sep-Oct) **WEB** theoriginaltour .com **TEL** 0208 877 1722 **TIME REQUIRED** You can hop-on and off all day

Easy to get to? ★★★ Good for kids? ★★☆
Value for money? ★☆☆ Worth a visit? ★☆☆

I was quite looking forward to doing the Original Bus Tour today. What could be nicer than sitting on the top deck of a double-decker bus tootling around the city, relaxing in your seat and learning all there is to know about London? That sounded like a decent way to pass an afternoon, I thought.

Alas I was wrong...

This is now going to turn into a long moany-old review, so if you don't like moany reviews, turn over now.

First of all, it was freezing cold, but that's hardly the bus company's fault. I can't blame them for the weather. But it's not as much fun sitting on the open top-deck when there are icicles hanging off your face. Secondly, and more importantly, the price was a total rip-off: thirty quid for one person! Thirty quid for a bus trip? You can get the National Express all the way to Spain for that price. And what makes it worse, is that they have reduced the ticket validity from two days to just one. I'm pretty sure that you used to be able to use these things spread over two days, but now it appears that you only get 24-hours. When you buy the ticket they give you a whole list of things that you can do with it to make it seem like a bargain: six different bus routes, three walking tours and a river trip, which sounds like great value for money, but I was sitting on the bus for two hours just doing ONE of the routes, so there's no way that you'll want to do two. I reckon the most that you'll feel like doing in a day is one full bus route plus one walking tour (because you'll want to eat and do other stuff as well).

They also make a big play on the fact that you can use the ticket a bit like a travelcard, hopping-on and off the bus whenever you want, which sounds quite handy. But a real travelcard costs a third of the price and you can use it on every bus and tube train in London. Whereas with this one, you are restricted to using it on their sightseeing buses (with very limited routes). And that's not all... because London buses run all day and through the night, but according to my ticket the last sightseeing bus leaves at 5 o'clock in the afternoon! So it's hardly the same as a travelcard, is it? What a swizz!

But what about the actual sightseeing trip? Is that any good? The commentary is not too bad I suppose. You get a little pair of headphones that you plug into your seat, and there are about ten languages to choose from. The lady tells you all the usual touristy stuff as you drive past the buildings. She doesn't have too much time to go into detail, of course, because you are motoring past at twenty miles-per-hour, but at least you get to see most of the major sights.

But that brings me to the traffic... once again, it's not the bus company's fault that the traffic in London sometimes crawls around at a snail's pace, but for large parts of the trip you will find yourself crawling along not at twenty miles-per-hour, but *two*. So you get thirty-seconds of commentary, and then five minutes of listening to lift music as you inch your way to the next destination. I am not kidding when I say that the 'Red route' took me two hours to complete -- because I timed it. Why would you want to do any of the other routes when you've just spent two hours sitting on the first one?

And that leads me to another problem... there is no one route that covers *all* of the sights. The red route does most of them, but doesn't go any farther west than Hyde Park Corner. So you never get to see places like Harrods, the Royal Albert Hall and the major museums. If you want to see those then you have to get the 'Blue route' instead, but that doesn't go anywhere near The City, Big Ben, Buckingham Palace and St. Paul's. So it's basically impossible to see every major sight unless you do two different routes, which means sitting on two buses for four or more hours.

I've got one last complaint (and this is last one, I promise)... because they are touting it as a hop-on hop-off bus service too, you end up visiting places that have no real interest for the camera clickers. The red route takes a little detour to Victoria Coach Station, for example. It even drives right inside it, in case some tourists want to get off and catch their coach back home. So that's a boring ten-minute detour that has no sightseeing interest whatsoever.

If a ticket was half the price, or lasted 48-hours instead of 24, then I might have recommended it. [Note: I've just had a read of the small print on the back of their leaflet and it says: "The ticket is valid for use for 24-hours, or 48-hours on occasions when such tickets are available". So it looks they reduce it down to 24-hours during busy periods. So be aware! Spending thirty quid on this for just 24-hours is a bit nuts.]

Look at the Big Bus Tour as well, or try the cheap version: the No.11 sightseeing bus.

By Rail

Docklands Light Railway

ROUTES Lines start at Bank and Tower Gateway (both zone 1), heading east towards Canary Wharf (zone 2), Cutty Sark (zones 2&3), Stratford (zone 3) and London City Airport (zone 3) - see map 5e for Bank and 11e for Cutty Sark

PRICE Normal train fares apply; See transport chapter for prices **TIMES** See transport chapter for times **WEBSITE** tfl.gov.uk/modes/dlr

Easy to get to? ★★★ Good for kids? ★★☆
Value for money? ★★★ Worth a visit? ★★★

I didn't fancy doing anything major today, so I just had a ride around on the Docklands Light Railway. I went from Bank to the Cutty Sark and back again, which is probably the best little sightseeing route on there.

The good thing about these electric trains is that there are no driver's cabins at the front, so you can sit yourself down by the window and enjoy an uninterrupted view of where you're going. It's a bit like sitting on the front seat of a double-decker bus. The driver's controls are in a little console by left-hand seat, so sometimes you might be unlucky and find him sitting there pushing all the buttons. It doesn't look too complicated. All he seems to do is push one button to start it, and then another for the brakes. That's pretty easy going for forty grand a year. Sometimes I've boarded a train and the driver is nowhere in sight, so Lord knows who's driving the thing: it must be automated or something, like a ghost train. Either that or it's a runaway express on a one-way trip to hell (otherwise known as Lewisham).

If you do want to sit right at the front then take a tip from me: stand right at the end of the platform when boarding it, because it's not possible to walk through the carriages. There's usually a little scrum for the best seats, and you might have to knock a few old ladies out of the way in the rush. Bring a cricket bat with you, that's what I do (no I don't). I don't really knock them out of the way -- I'm far too polite for that. But I did manage to get a decent seat today, which was pretty good going.

I boarded it at Bank where all the busy businessmen get on with their Kindles and iPads for the trip to the big steel and glass skyscrapers of Canary Wharf. I didn't realise that the DLR platforms were so far away from the street, though. You literally have to walk a mile from the entrance before you find them. You go down an escalator, down another escalator, down another few floors in a lift, walk a few miles along never-ending corridors... it's like descending into the bowels of the earth. I swear to God that it heated up a bit, too, from the fiery flames at the core of the planet. Now I know why they call it the Underground. If we walked much further we would have turned into diamonds.

The start of the trip is quite exciting, once it gets going. If you managed to get the plum seat right at the front then you will see the tunnel stretching out before you, twisting and turning as your metal bullet thunders through on the rickety old train tracks. It's a bit like riding a rollercoaster at Alton Towers, but without all those annoying loop-the-loops and death-defying drops. Once you are clear of the Square Mile it gently rises up until a stream of daylight floods in to welcome you back to terra ferma.

Most of the track from this point on is actually above the road -- like a monorail. If you've ever been to America then it will remind you of those elevated train tracks that rattle through the centre of Chicago.

As you get nearer to Canary Wharf you will begin to pass all of the posh boat marinas -- keep your peepers peeled for the O2 Arena. Then you roll through the centre of the skyscrapers into the futuristic stations at Docklands. There's not much to actually do at Canary Wharf, so you may as well stay on to Greenwich. A couple of stations before Cutty Sark it will dive underground again as the train passes beneath the Thames.

So in summary, then... is it worth doing? Well, it's a lot more interesting than catching the dirty old tube, but I wouldn't bother doing it on its own. It's not worth a ride unless you already happen to be going to Greenwich. I still think that the best way of getting there is by boat, though. But a boat will take up a whole hour of your day, whereas the DLR does it in twenty minutes.

London Underground

PRICE Normal train fares apply; See transport chapter for prices **TIMES** See transport chapter for times **WEBSITE** tfl.gov.uk/modes/tube

Easy to get to? ★★★ Good for kids? ★★☆
Value for money? ★★★ Worth a visit? ★★★

I'm standing on the platform waiting for the train to arrive. Everybody is looking into the dingy tunnel for the first sign of the bright lights on the concrete wall. When the train finally comes, it's accompanied by a loud roar and a quick blast of wind as it pushes the air along with it. Then you hear the clacking and screeching of wheels as it speeds past your face at a surprising pace, until it finally comes to an abrupt halt further up the line. The doors will pause for a few seconds and then *whoooosh* -- it's open! -- and it's every man for himself.

Most of the trains in rush hour run every two to five minutes, but nobody wants to wait that long. It's this train, *this* train, *gotta get THIS train;* let me on, outta the way folks -- move down the carriage! Everyone will cram in as tight as they can for fear of being left behind. It's like the last train out of hell before the gates slam shut. The passengers who are disembarking all have to try and squeeze out in the scrum, through a surging crowd that won't allow them any space. Before they've even had time to step out the door we will all be cramming on, sucked into the gaps like a vacuum. Did we make it? Have I still got my hat and bag? What about my arms and legs? Yup, I am safely aboard -- thank Christ for that.

A lot of Londoners take the tube for granted but there is some nice architecture underground if you take the time to look. It's not all rubble, mud, and worms down there. I like a lot of the station tunnels (my God, I'm getting old... I'm turning into a saddo!). The traditional stations all have deep creamy tiles that look a bit art deco, like something out of the 1920s or 1930s. But the new ones have done away with all of that because it's too time consuming and expensive to build -- they just use walls of glass, concrete, and steel. If you travel on the new Jubilee line then it's a bit like entering the body of an industrial machine... walking along its metal veins and down escalator arteries, until it pumps the people out of the other end. I suppose the idea is just to funnel the blood through as quickly as possible -- they don't want people hanging around the ticket halls taking up space.

Once you are safely aboard the train you can take ten seconds to check out your neighbours. Don't stare at them for too long, though, or they'll think you're a weirdo (which I am -- but that's beside the point). Commuters rarely care if they're shoulder to shoulder with strangers on the Underground. There is no personal space on the tube. I've had my face pressed up against the doors before, and morphed my body into the shape of the concave wall -- as long as I get on, I don't care.

If the train is less crowded and you manage to bag yourself a seat, then you'll have the perennial problem of where to direct your eyes. The seats are usually arranged with one row of seats directly opposite another, so you'll always have someone staring straight into your eyes. You can't gaze out of the window because it's underground. So what you need to do is develop a sudden interest in their shoes. Just stare at their shoes for ten minutes, or whip out your mobile phone and start playing around with that instead. One lady near me is applying some blusher in a handheld mirror -- but that's not really an option for me. Or you can read and re-read the boring adverts above their head ten thousand times -- that's what most people choose to do. I just stare at the floor instead. That's what I do. Other people will stare at the route map for five minutes pretending to work out their journey. But anyone who takes that long to read a map is probably lost.

If you aim your gaze down the carriage then you will see a big mix of facial expressions, ranging from total boredom to animated tourist chatter. My favourite faces are the solitary souls (like me) who are replaying old conversations in their head. Sometimes they do the facial expressions that go with them as well, without realising, and you can see them in the middle of cracking a comeback line, or on the verge of a victory smile. I wonder what scene they're re-living? They are probably conversations where their friends have complimented them, or when they've argued with someone and won. But now they have embellished the conversations with words they never said, so they are ten times better than they actually were. Faked memories, puffed up in their heads for their own amusement. I probably do this, too -- I think we all do. I'm in sour need of some new memories myself, because I'm getting bored with my ones. Dreams are just memories that you've made up. I wouldn't have to dream at all if my memories weren't so sh*t.

If you've never been on the tube before then it's probably quite a scary place to be. It's full of terrifying clacks and rumbles as it roars along the tunnel. It's all screeches and sharp wheels grinding on metal. You can see little sparks of lightning illuminate the tunnel walls sometimes, and red lights rushing past the window. Every now and then the electricity will drop out for a few seconds and plunge the entire carriage into darkness.

As the train gets closer to your destination you have to start plotting your escape. If you've been a bit dumb up until this point then you will find yourself stranded halfway down the carriage with a big fight on your hands to get out. You will have to squeeze past about twenty people with big bags and briefcases, whilst another bunch of people are simultaneously surging through the door trying to get on. So you have to plan it like a military operation: recognise your exit route and be ready to move as soon as the opportunity arises. You don't want to get barricaded in behind a phalanx of enemy commuters plugging up the door.

Even when you have successfully exited the train, the battle is still not won because you will find yourself swimming in a sea of bodies all washing along the platform, flowing to the plughole. You just have to hope that the people at the front know where they're going because that's where you'll be going, too, one way or another. Then it's up a mile-long escalator, which gives you plenty of time to ogle the pretty women descending down the other way -- safe in the knowledge that by the time they get to the bottom you will be safely at the top.

There is a well-observed rule in London that you should only stand on the right-hand side of escalators. The left-hand side is reserved for people in a rush -- the ones who want to expend some energy running up the stairs. Every now and then you'll get somebody who doesn't know the custom and will stand there chatting happily to their buddies, blocking up the exercise aisle. But being British, of course, no one will dare say anything to them. We just bundle up behind them and mutter obscenities in our heads. When the blockage is popped at the top everyone will rush across the ticket hall to make up for the lost time. (It probably only wasted ten seconds, but it's surprising how annoying a loss of ten seconds can be!)

The buskers are pretty decent on the Underground. I think they must audition them to make sure that they can actually play. You can usually hear them from 100 feet away -- long before they come into view. The music carries through the tunnels and up the escalators, bouncing back off the brick walls and into the station. The noise gets louder and louder until eventually you'll see them strumming their song; but I wonder why they are always musicians? You never see anybody telling jokes or doing card tricks. I suppose it's because they don't want people to stop and watch, thereby jamming up the tunnels. The buskers are probably secretly wishing for a big crowd to grow, but all they ever get is a never-ending stream of people's fronts and backs, forever on their way to somewhere else. It must be quite dispiriting to see your audience fritter away every time a tube train comes along.

By Sea

City Cruises

ROUTE Westminster Pier (by Big Ben) > London Eye > Tower Millennium Pier (by Tower of London) > Greenwich Pier (by Cutty Sark) - see map 8d for Westminster Pier and London Eye Pier, 10b for Tower Millennium Pier, 11c for Greenwich Pier **TRAINS** Westminster Pier: Charing Cross, Embankment, Westminster (all zone 1) -- London Eye Pier: Charing Cross, Embankment, Waterloo, Westminster (all zone 1) -- Tower Millennium Pier: Tower Gateway, Tower Hill (both zone 1) -- Greenwich Pier: Cutty Sark (zones 2&3) **BUSES** Westminster Pier: 11, 24, 148, 211 -- London Eye Pier: 12, 53, 59, 77, 148, 159, 211, 341, RV1 -- Tower Millennium Pier: 15, 42, 78, 100, RV1 -- Greenwich Pier: 129, 177, 188, 199, 386 **PRICE** See transport chapter for prices **TIMES** See transport chapter for times **WEB** citycruises.com **TEL** 0207 740 0400 **TIME REQUIRED** Between Westminster/ London Eye and Tower Millennium Pier: approx 40 mins -- Between Westminster/London Eye and Greenwich: approx 70 mins

Easy to get to? ★★★ Good for kids? ★★★
Value for money? ★★★ Worth a visit? ★★★

City Cruises operate the most popular boats in town. I think I prefer the TRS boats though -- you can catch them from the same pier and they both go to the same stops, but City Cruises always seems to be packed out from stern to bow. Their boats are bigger and they have a lot more seats on top, but I think you get a much nicer ride with TRS. But hey-ho, I am here now so I will give them a go. I can always jump overboard and drown myself if it gets too much.

I'm a bit paranoid when it comes to boats. When I get on a plane I like to sit by the window so that I can make sure that both of its wings are securely fastened on and that there aren't any screws loose, etc. Likewise, before I step on board a boat I like to give it a quick once over to make sure that it hasn't got any obvious leaks. But you can't look underneath, can you? And when was the last time you saw them send a diver out to check for leaks underneath? That's right, never. I have never seen them do that. So what happens if we capsize? Is it women and children first? Or is it me first and then everyone else after? I need to know the answer to all of these questions before I feel safe.

It's quite nice sitting here on the boat -- it's got a nice seaside feeling to it. There's a fresh sea-salt smell in the air and the sound of seagulls wheeling around the back, and brown water chopping up against the side of the ship as we pull away from the pier.

They do provide a little commentary with City Cruises but it's not up to much. They point out all the obvious sights, but you'd have to be blind as a bat to miss those. They seem to be recycling the same old jokes as the TRS boat (exactly the same jokes!) so they've obviously been spying on their gags.

If you start from Westminster Pier then you'll have Big Ben behind you and the London Eye to the right. Once you've passed under the first bridge you'll have Cleopatra's Needle and the Royal Festival Hall.

When you pull level with the Tate Modern and Globe Theatre you'll have a semi-decent shot of St. Paul's on the left. It doesn't look very tall when you're passing by on the river, but trust me: when you're up there on the balcony, you'll be having panic attacks. I can just about see some ant-sized people walking around the highest dome, probably gripping tight to the railings as the wind buffets them around and bashes them against the side of the wall. They have climbed five thousand steps to get up there, so they'll be clinging on for dear life. No one praises God from the highest dome of St. Paul's -- you do that downstairs by the altar. When you're 285 feet up in the sky you are too busy blaspheming and taking his name in vain.

After that comes London Bridge and The Shard. Keep your peepers peeled for a replica of Francis Drake's Golden Hinde in a dry dock and for Southwark Cathedral hiding amongst the buildings behind. (I will give you some bonus points if you manage to recognise that.) If you look to the left straight after London Bridge then you can catch the golden urn at the top of The Monument, which is close to the spot where the Great Fire of London broke out.

You'll have a nice view of the City skyscrapers here (the Walkie Scorchie, Cheesegrater and Gherkin), before floating past HMS Belfast and City Hall. When you pull up alongside the Tower of London have a search around for Traitor's Gate. The entrance has been bricked up now but you can still see the arch marked out in black where they rowed the poor prisoners inside.

The boat will stop for a short while here for the tourist hordes to disembark and you can take a few pictures of Tower Bridge while you're waiting.

We seem to have picked up a new passenger. A seagull has spent the last two minutes buzzing around our heads in search of somewhere to sit and finally rests his legs on the railing. He has become the star of the show all of a sudden -- forget the landmarks. Forget Tower Bridge and the thousand-year-old Tower of London to our right. Everybody is queueing up to get a snap of this mangy old bird with two toes missing. At least he's not asking for money, I suppose. He hasn't got a fake family and a dog to feed. All he wants is a fish. But all I've got is a packet of Polos. Sorry, mate.

When the boat starts up again it passes straight under the centre of Tower Bridge before heading upstream towards Canary Wharf and Greenwich. This is where the sights start to dry up, and you can just sit back and enjoy the cold and windy river. You really do feel like you're on a boat out here because the guide shuts up and leaves you alone. The only noise is coming from the wind as it slaps you in the face. They finally let the engine have a bit of fun out here, and I can feel its vibrations passing up my elbow and into my chin as I lean upon the rail. Apparently that's how Beethoven used to write his music after he went deaf -- did you know that? He used to wedge a bit of wood between the keys and his mouth so he could feel the piano's vibrations pass into his teeth (I read that in *The Beano* so it must be true). I can't hear any music, though. No sea shanties today -- this boat don't know any tunes.

There are a couple of places worth keeping an eye out for before you reach Canary Wharf. On the right you can try and spy a little pub called The Mayflower (it's quite difficult to spot unless he points it out). This is where the Pilgrim Fathers set out for America. There's another pub on the left called the Captain Kidd. It was around here that the famous pirate was hanged on the beach, although he actually died a little further behind you, in Execution Dock (look for a riverside warehouse with a big 'E' on the top).

I always like the bend of the river that comes up next, which carries you around the front of Canary Wharf. The view of the skyscrapers as you're floating past the pier is one of my favourite shots in London. It's a bit too sunny today though... you really need a fierce wind blowing and a bruised sky to get the best effect. And it needs to be a winter afternoon so you get the office lights lit up. (My favourite-ever view is approaching Tower Bridge from the other direction -- which you will see on the way back.) It's hard to believe that One Canada Square was once the tallest building in London because it looks like a midget these days. If you look past the crap flats on the right, back over your shoulder towards where you came from, you'll see The Shard in the far distance -- that's a proper skyscraper. One that's too high for the sky.

The final stop will see you pulling into Greenwich, right in front of Christopher Wren's Royal Naval College and the tall masts of the Cutty Sark. If you stare through the masts of the Cutty Sark into the trees beyond, then you should be able to see the Royal Observatory perched on top of a distant hill.

One final tip: I never knew this before today... but if you disembark the boat and walk along the riverfront past the Cutty Sark, and past that big brown brick circular building (the entrance to the Greenwich Tunnel), then you can see all the way back to Westminster. There is one particular spot where you can stand that takes in the London Eye, BT Tower, Gherkin, St. Paul's Cathedral, Canary Wharf and The Shard. That's quite a wide view considering that you are still at ground level!

Check out my reviews for the Thames Clippers and TRS boats as well.

Jason's Canal Trip

ADDRESS Little Venice (beside Westbourne Terrace Road Bridge) and Camden Lock - see map 1c for Little Venice **TRAINS** Little Venice: Warwick Avenue (zone 2) -- Camden Lock: Camden Town (zone 2) **BUSES** Little Venice: 6, 18, 46, 187, 414 -- Camden Lock: 24, 27, 31, 88, 134, 168, 214 **PRICE** Adult £9 one-way, or £14 return; Senior (over-60) £8 one-way, or £13 return; Child (4-13) £8 one-way, or £13 return; Infant (under-4) free **TIMES** Little Venice: 10.30 AM, 12.30 PM, 2.30 PM (Mon-Sun, early Apr-early Nov); extra boat at 4.30 PM (Sat-Sun, Jun-Aug) -- Camden Lock: 11.15 AM, 1.15 PM, 3.15 PM (Mon-Sun, early Apr-early Nov); extra boat at 5.15 PM (Sat-Sun, Jun-Aug) **WEB** jasons.co.uk **TIME REQUIRED** 45 mins each way

Easy to get to? ★★★ Good for kids? ★★☆
Value for money? ★★★ Worth a visit? ★★★

Most of the boats I go on head up the Thames to Greenwich, but this one is nice and gentle. There are no waves on the Regent's Canal. No one ever gets seasick on a canal boat. The odds of getting shipwrecked in north London are zero. It's just a nice gentle chug along the waterway past Little Venice and London Zoo to the wooden lock at Camden.

You can find the landing stage by the little blue bridge in Little Venice. There's a canal boat cafe across the other side if you fancy a cup of tea before you start.

The boat is basically a barge -- a houseboat with its sides missing -- and it has about forty plastic seats inside, so it fills up pretty quickly (you might want to book in advance on their website). I'm loving the lady who takes all the money. I don't know if she's having a bad day today, but she's not unlike a pint-sized sergeant. It's all "Stand here!", "Stand there!" and "Don't move until I tell you!" It makes a nice change from all that fake bonhomie you usually find at tourist attractions, because most of the guides you get on the buses and boats act like they're your best mate as soon as they see you -- but she is a proper person; the kind of person that I like writing about. Something bad has happened to her this morning, and I'm wondering what it is.

Now that she's marshalled everyone into position we can finally get going. The boat is totally open to the weather and the wind is really whipping across the top of the water. The sides are only about two feet off the top of the river, so you might want to wear a wooly hat and a scarf and two pairs of underpants. To give you an idea about how low the boat is: I am at eye level with the pigeons walking along the towpath. Whenever we come across a drooping tree the leaves start scraping the roof like creepy fingers through your hair. If there is radar along the lock then we are under it -- we are practically a submarine. We are lower than the Coke cans floating on the water.

The guide is on fine form once we get going. First of all she tells us what to do in case the boat catches fire, then she admonishes the tourists for chatting too loudly and drowning out her commentary (ha ha -- she is my favourite guide of all time!). As we get underway she tells us a little bit of the history of the Regent's Canal and how they used to transport cargos to and from the docks. It's interesting enough if you like that kind of thing, but you don't need commentary when you've got some decent scenery to look at... and there's plenty of that on this trip.

The prettiest houseboats are right at the start, in Little Venice. There are some more pretty houses and churches when you hit the boundary of Regent's Park, but most of it is concrete walls and overhanging trees. My favourite section was definitely when we were chugging through the under-road tunnels. Imagine a long dark arch made of dirty black brick, with the dank sound of water dripping down the sides and the engine coughing off the walls. It's pretty scary stuff actually, and I'm glad we had the guide with us because she would have harangued any hoodlums and scared them away. (Two minutes ago she told off the driver for motoring too fast!) She'll probably start shouting at the fish in a minute.

Once you reach the edge of Regent's Park you get some great riverside mansions and landscaped grounds to look at, before heading straight through the northern edge of London Zoo. This bit is worth the ticket cost alone. You sail straight past a couple of the cages and can peer into the netting of the Snowdon Aviary to see some big-beaked birds.

After that you round the bend into Camden and park up in front of Camden Lock. The whole thing takes 45 minutes from start to finish, and I genuinely hope that you get the same guide as me so you can enjoy some unintentional entertainment -- instead of sitting there listening to one of those fake-happy students you get on the sightseeing buses.

You can learn more about the canal at the London Canal Museum.

London Duck Tour

ADDRESS London Duck Tour, 55 York Road, Waterloo - map 9c **TRAINS** Waterloo (zone 1) **BUSES** 12, 53, 77, 148, 159, 211, 341, 381, 453, 507, RV1 **PRICE** Adult from £24; Senior (over-60) from £20; Child (1-17) from £16; Infant (under 1) free; Family (2 ad+2 ch, or 1 ad+3 ch) from £70 **TIMES** Every 30-60 mins from 10 AM to 2.30 PM (Thu-Sun, Jan), 10 AM to 2.30 PM (Mon-Sun, Feb-Apr), 10 AM to 6 PM (Mon-Sun, May-Sep), 10 AM to 5 PM (Mon-Fri, Oct), 10 AM and 2.30 PM (Mon-Sun, Nov-Dec) **WEB** london ducktours.co.uk **TEL** 0207 928 3132 **TIME REQUIRED** 1¼ hours

Easy to get to? ★★★ Good for kids? ★★★
Value for money? ★☆☆ Worth a visit? ★★☆

I was planning on doing a sightseeing bus today but then I fancied a boat instead, so I thought what the hell: I'll compromise and do a bus and boat together. The London Duck Tour is an amphibious boat so it's half-sightseeing bus and half-river cruise.

Our guide explained that the boat was a bona-fide relic from World War II and actually fought in Normandy in 1944 which sounds a bit far-fetched to me, but that's what he said. Apparently it helped to ferry the men across on D-Day. It's definitely had a paint job since then though, because if it was motoring along the French coast in its bright yellow paint job it would have been shot by the Nazis in two-seconds flat.

Before I go any further let me give you a piece of advice: if you come on the London Duck Tour then bring a coat with you because it is *f-r-e-e-z-i-n-g* cold. Even an eskimo would wear a jumper, that's how could it is. There aren't any windows on the boat, just a load of big gaping holes where the glass is supposed to be, and a bit of roll-down plastic to cover them up. When it gets down in the water the wind is cold enough to solidify your skin -- and I'm not even joking. Two of the passengers on my trip actually froze to death -- I'm being serious! And that is not a joke. (It is a joke.)

The boat is quite small and cosy. There are five two-seaters on each side of the aisle and the windows (holes) are massive, so you don't have to worry about getting a dodgy seat with a lousy view. The guide is only twenty feet away even if you're at the back, and he's got a microphone too, so even if you're deaf you should still be able to hear him. (Unless you're *actually* deaf, of course.)

The tour lasts around 75 minutes and the first 45 minutes-or-so are on the road. You start off near the London Eye and head straight across Westminster Bridge for a look at Parliament, Parliament Square and Westminster Abbey, then it's up Whitehall to Downing Street and Trafalgar Square. Whilst all of this is going on the guy at the front is yapping into a microphone about all of the landmarks that you're passing. I can't remember our guys name but he was okay. He said all of the normal touristy things and told a few jokes, which is all you need. After Nelson's Column you head down Pall Mall and past St. James's Palace, and then up Piccadilly to the Ritz Hotel. A quick steer round Hyde Park Corner takes you past Wellington Arch and towards Victoria

Station. Then you pass by Buckingham Palace and that's about it for five minutes. You just inch through the traffic to Lambeth Bridge.

The best bit of the tour is when you enter the water. The slipway is next to the MI6 building, close to where James Bond shot out of the wall in his speedboat. But of course it's much more leisurely when we do it. There is no fire or flames or gun-toting terrorists running around. You just drive into the water at about 0 miles-per-hour until you're floating along like a duck. The water was quite choppy and the waves were lapping about six inches from the edge of the boat, which was a bit unnerving -- that must be why they've got a load of lifejackets strapped to the ceiling.

You don't have to worry about sinking though, because at one point we were actually driving along on a sandbank, right in the middle of the river. And I'm not making that up either (no jokes this time) -- we were literally driving along in the middle of the Thames because the tide was so low.

The water section was good and a lot of fun, but it doesn't last very long. If you were expecting to float all the way up to Tower Bridge then you are going to go home severely disappointed, because all you do is motor up from Lambeth Bridge to Parliament, and then turn back around again. Once you get close to Westminster Bridge he turns tail and heads back the way he came, so you don't even get as far as the London Eye! You're in the water for no more than thirty minutes -- fifteen minutes each way. Once you're back at Lambeth Bridge he drives back out and returns to Waterloo.

So is it worth it? Yeah, I think so. But I wouldn't choose it over a bus tour. The amount of stuff that you miss out is huge: you don't do anything east of Trafalgar Square, so that basically cuts out St. Paul's, Tower Bridge, the Tower of London, Tate Modern, the Globe, and the whole of the City. You don't go anywhere near the West End either, so there's no Leicester Square, Piccadilly Circus or Covent Garden. No Bloomsbury (British Museum), Marylebone (Madame Tussauds) or South Kensington (Royal Albert Hall). The only things that it does well are the Houses of Parliament, Trafalgar Square and Buckingham Palace -- but even then you don't go up The Mall, so you don't see the palace from the front. And the only things that you can see from the water are Lambeth Palace, Parliament and the MI6 Building. But don't let that put you off... I've made it sound a lot worse than it is! It's a decent enough way to pass a morning, especially if you've got kids.

If you want a real boat tour then try City Cruises or TRS (Thames River Services).

Thames Clippers

ROUTE Putney Pier > Wandsworth Pier > Chelsea Harbour > Cadogan Pier (by Albert Bridge) > St. George Wharf (by Vauxhall) > London Eye Pier > Embankment Pier (by Trafalgar Square) > Blackfriars Pier > Bankside Pier (by Tate Modern) > London Bridge Pier (by Shard) > Tower Millennium Pier (by Tower of London) > Canary Wharf Pier > Greenwich Pier (by Cutty Sark) > North Greenwich Pier (by O2) - see map 8d for London Eye Pier, 8b for Embankment Pier, 10a for London Bridge Pier, 10b for Tower Millennium Pier, 11c for Greenwich Pier **TRAINS** Putney Pier: East Putney (zones 2&3), Putney Bridge (zone 2) -- London Eye/Embankment Pier: Charing Cross,

Sightseeing Buses & Boats | 281

Embankment, Waterloo, Westminster (all zone 1) -- London Bridge Pier: London Bridge (zone 1) -- Tower Millennium Pier: Tower Gateway, Tower Hill (both zone 1) -- Greenwich Pier: Cutty Sark (zone 2&3) -- North Greenwich Pier: North Greenwich (zones 2&3) **BUSES** Putney Pier: 14, 22, 39, 74, 85, 93, 220, 265, 424, 430, 485 -- London Eye/Embankment Pier: 12, 53, 59, 76, 77, 159, 211, 341, 381, RV1 -- London Bridge Pier: 43, 48, 141, 149, 521 -- Tower Millennium Pier: 15, 42, 78, 100, RV1 -- Greenwich Pier: 129, 177, 180, 188, 199, 386 -- North Greenwich Pier: 108, 129, 132, 161, 188, 422, 472, 486 **PRICE** See transport chapter for prices **TIMES** See transport chapter for times **WEB** thames clippers.com **TIME REQUIRED** Approx 1 hour (depending on where you go)

Easy to get to? ★★★ Good for kids? ★★★
Value for money? ★★★ Worth a visit? ★★★

I felt like a boat ride today so I'm getting a day ticket on a Thames Clipper ship. There's nothing like a boat ride in the winter. Forget the sun. Forget the summer. Forget the heat. Cold wind and rain in your face is where it's at. I want my eyes to freeze up and fall out. That is what I call a fun day out.

Let me start off by saying that these aren't my favourite boats in London because they are aimed at commuters really, rather than tourists; and you are supposed to use like them like a bus. They go from Putney in the west, all the way though central London to North Greenwich in the east, which sounds like quite a nice run -- it's nearly 15 miles long. But unfortunately there are about fifty million stops in-between, so they are forever stopping and starting to let people on and off. And there's no one single boat that encompasses the entire stretch either. I'm waiting for the Putney boat at the moment, which takes in Chelsea and Big Ben, but then you've got to disembark at Victoria Embankment and catch another one to Greenwich. And you know how lazy I am (very), so the thought of having to stand up and walk somewhere halfway through the journey doesn't exactly fill me with glee.

But anyway... I quite like Putney. I think it's quite a nice stretch of water, but there's no real reason for a tourist to come here. There are no attractions or landmarks or anything like that, just a high street full of shops. If you're a tourist then you'll probably want to board the boat at the London Eye or Embankment instead -- but I've got a whole day to waste, so I don't care. I am here from sunrise until sunset. I am here forever. I will ride the boat until the water boils off the face of the earth. If I could catch a boat to the edge of the world and drop off the end, then I would do it. I don't think they take you that far, though (not for sixteen quid fifty).

Most of the Thames Clipper ships are totally enclosed, like a glass box on water, but this one has got a few seats at the back where you can experience the noise of the engines. Imagine a farm tractor coughing up blood. It is spluttering and chuntering and spewing out fumes and when the captain kicks open the motors it's like being thrust into the face of a force ten gale. I feel like I've fallen inside an avalanche roaring down the mountainside.

We are under way now and I'm happy. There's something very relaxing about sitting on a boat with the cold wind and seagulls. They are all wheeling around the riverside flats.

A lady has just got on with a troop of dogs -- she's taking them for walkies on a boat (no joke). That's what this service is like... it's more like a floating bus than a sightseeing boat. The rest of the motley crew is made up of mums and dads and pushchairs. I'm sure Horatio Nelson didn't allow pushchairs and prams onboard HMS Victory. The dogs are quite cute though, I suppose. Not as cute as the owner though.

We are passing Chelsea Embankment now, which is where the London landmarks start. You can see the Royal Hospital on the left and the Peace Pagoda on the right -- a big golden Buddha on the edge of Battersea Park. Then you pass Battersea Power Station, which seems to have a chimney missing today (apparently they've taken it down to restore it, which sounds a bit counter-productive to me). Then the riverbank starts to fill up with posh flats and mansion blocks as you get closer to Big Ben and Westminster. I'd hate to think how much these riverside apartments cost, but I'm guessing that it's a bit more than 10p a week, which is all I can afford. I'm not a big fan of all this glass and steel architecture because it makes every building look the same; but that's the way of the world these days. Architects aren't given enough money to build anything in stone. The richer these companies become, the less money they want to spend. Can you imagine what Stonehenge would look like if we built it today? It would just be twenty-five steel girders rammed into the dirt.

We have just passed Tate Britain and Lambeth Palace, and are coming up alongside Big Ben. That's the best reason to get this boat: so you can enjoy a close-up of Parliament from the water. It sails right past the side of Parliament and gives you a fantastic view of the exterior.

And here comes the Victoria Embankment... which is where I have to get off (end of the line). You can either stay on the jetty and catch the next one to North Greenwich, or you can cross over the bridge and catch it from the London Eye instead. It doesn't matter which one you choose because there are boats to Greenwich from both. After five minutes thinking time I finally decide to have a stroll over Westminster Bridge and catch it from the London Eye.

This next boat has only got a few seats at the back and they are already being filled by camera clicking tourists. Luckily I manage to squeeze into the last one left, otherwise I would have had to push one of them overboard when his mates weren't looking. (Don't worry, I would have thrown him a life jacket as well -- I'm not a complete a*hole.)

On we go... past Cleopatra's Needle and Shakespeare's Globe. Tate Modern too, and a so-so view of St. Paul's dome. You can get off here if you like, just past the Millennium Bridge.

Then we come to my favourite part of London -- The City. You can just about get a glimpse of The Monument's golden urn if you know where to look, or disembark at The Shard, or just carry on past Traitor's Gate and the Tower of London (you can get off there too -- there are so many stops!). After that it passes under Tower Bridge and heads into the rough water towards Canary Wharf.

There are no real sights along this stretch of the Thames so you might want to sit inside for a while before you die of frostbite. But I'm a man so I braved it (because I'm an idiot). It's worth sticking around for a little while though, just so you can stare back down the river and see The City, The Shard and Tower Bridge all in the same shot.

The boat certainly doesn't hang around; we must be going about three thousand miles an hour at the moment. The TRS boats are much more leisurely and you can have a nice relaxing ride to Greenwich, but on the Thames Clippers you are pulling 3G at least. When we pulled away from Greenland Pier it felt like we were taking off in a plane.

There's a squadron of seagulls following along behind, and they're like a flock of World War II bombers. They must be attracted by the water churn and smoke coming out of the back, because they don't want to let us go. I feel like a fighter pilot with a load of heat-seeking missiles on his tail. We need to let out some chaff (some breadcrumbs) to lose them. We need some tourists at the back to act as rear gunners, clicking their cameras (their machine guns) at the chasing planes.

I've had a quick look inside the cabin and it's all families chatting and people queuing up for coffee at the counter. They've got a TV playing non-stop adverts as well. The seat backs have got big cards stuck to them saying what we should do in case of an emergency. I love cheery things like that. If the boat starts sinking I don't need a card to tell me to swim.

The final stop before The O2 is at Greenwich, which is probably where you'll want to get off, unless you want to try the cable car by the O2 Arena.

So would I recommend a ride on a Thames Clipper? Hmm... I don't think so. If you're after some sightseeing on the river then I would definitely try a TRS boat or a City Cruise ship first -- because they are much more leisurely and have a lot more outside seating. The Thames Clippers are more like a bus.

If you like boat rides then try City Cruises or a TRS boat from Big Ben to Greenwich.

TRS (aka. Thames River Services)

ROUTE Westminster Pier (by Big Ben) > St. Katherine's Pier (by Tower Bridge) > Greenwich Pier (by Cutty Sark) - see map 8d for Westminster Pier, 10b for St. Katherine's Pier, 11c for Greenwich Pier **TRAINS** Westminster Pier: Charing Cross, Embankment, Westminster (all zone 1) -- St. Katherine's Pier: Tower Gateway, Tower Hill (both zone 1) -- Greenwich Pier: Cutty Sark (zones 2&3) **BUSES** Westminster Pier: 11, 24, 148, 211 -- St. Katherine's Pier: 15, 25, 42, 78, 100, RV1 -- Greenwich Pier: 129, 177, 180, 188, 386 **PRICE** See transport chapter for prices **TIMES** See transport chapter for times **WEB** thamesriverservices.co.uk **TEL** 0207 930 4097 **TIME REQUIRED** 1 hour each way

Easy to get to? ★★★ Good for kids? ★★★
Value for money? ★★★ Worth a visit? ★★★

The river is the same colour as a cold cup of tea. Apparently we have some of the cleanest water in Europe but you'd never know that by looking at it.

Big Ben is slowly ticking his tock behind the trees, counting down the minutes while I'm waiting. That's all he does, all day long: tick tock tick tock tick tock -- it must drive him nuts. It's boring enough just watching it, so imagine what it must be like for him *doing* it. If I were Big Ben I'd start whizzing my hands around at 100 mph just for the sheer hell of it, just to break the monotony and let everybody in London know that I'm still here. I'd ring the bells every five seconds until the MPs came charging out of Parliament demanding that I shut up. He must find it quite cathartic when the hour comes around and he finally gets to scream his head off for twenty seconds. *It's me! I'm still here!*

I feel quite an affinity with Big Ben because he's basically an aged loner with one solitary skill: telling the time (a bit like me). Apparently he's started leaning two feet to the west because of all the tube trains rumbling underneath his feet, so I always picture him as a cantankerous old granddad stooping on his arthritic knees, bellowing at the tourists every sixty minutes while they stand there staring at him.

Twenty minutes later I'm finally sitting onboard the boat, and I've managed to grab myself a plum seat right at the front. These TRS boats have got a flat top deck with a lot of school seats arranged in a row. They don't have much in the way of sides, though, which is a bit disconcerting -- just a few iron railings running along their length. If this boat pitches violently sideways then you can forget about the rest of this review -- I'm going to fall in. If I stop halfway through then you'll know that I'm floating somewhere out at sea. I've noticed that there are only four lifejackets as well, and I'm pretty sure they will be snapped up by the crew as soon as the first wave hits. So where are our jackets? *Er, hello? Excuse me! What about all of us?* I don't give a toss about the tourists, but they'd better at least have one for me.

It's too late to worry about all of that now... because the seat has started vibrating as the engine starts up. The guy unties the heavy-duty rope at the side of the pier and lets us loose. Then we back away from the edge and drift in a full circle, turning around to face upriver. I'm imagining that he's got a big red button in the cockpit marked 'Turbo boost' because he's just done something serious to get us going. The waves are bursting out the back of the boat and churning up the water.

We are under way and motoring past the London Eye and Cleopatra's Needle. It's a bit nippy on the river this morning (I should have brought my coat). There's a stiff breeze icing up my eyes and making them bleed tears.

After that comes the Tate Modern, St. Paul's and The Shard. Keep your peepers peeled for a replica of Francis Drake's Golden Hinde in a dry dock, and Southwark Cathedral hiding amongst the buildings behind (I will give you some bonus points if you manage to recognise that).

Past the City skyscrapers on our left... past the Gherkin and Billingsgate Market. You can just about get a glimpse of The Monument's golden urn glinting off the office tops if you know when to look. Believe it or not that used to be one of London's tallest landmarks, and now it can't even see above its nearest neighbours.

Shortly after that comes the World War II battle cruiser HMS Belfast and the Tower of London. And then you slowly come to a halt past Tower Bridge to let some passengers off. I was hoping that Tower Bridge might sound her horn and open up to let us through, but no... this boat is a midget. We don't even come close to grazing our heads on the concrete roadway. The boat does a slow 180-degree turn into the pier, and off they all get, clambering down the gangway. All you can hear is excited tourist chatter and the clatter of their shoes on the gangplank. We are pointing the opposite way round now, so we can get a good look back towards the City. It is lovely and foggy this morning, so everything is muted in a lick of light grey paint. I can see the muddy colours in the brown bricks of the bridge, but beyond that it's a monochrome world of white and grey.

Off we go again, heading towards Greenwich now. I quite like the noise of the waves sloshing up against the side of the boat. You get sheets of spray coming over the side as the dirty water bangs and slaps up against the bow. Here they come again and again, banging and battering the sides, churning the foam into a dirty mess of bubbles before receding... defeated. The boat ploughs on.

I've pretty much got the top deck all to myself because the tourists have disappeared downstairs for a cup of tea. So that means the wind has only got one target left: *me*. I am on the verge of giving in and going down below. But what the hell? If I die, I die. I will brave it. If I succumb to pneumonia out here on the Thames then that is a decent enough way to say good-bye to the world. And cheap too: it only cost me sixteen quid fifty for a return ticket. Sixteen quid for a boat ride to heaven.

Past the skyscrapers at Canary Wharf now, and the luxury flats worth a few million quid. The river really widens out at this point, and you can almost imagine that you're headed out to sea. They say that London is a crowded city, but they should try coming out on the river first thing in the morning. There's not a soul around, not a face in sight. I can't even see anybody running along the towpath. The only boats that venture out this far are the dredgers, river police, and us. Every now and then we pass a seagull sitting on a fence post poking out of the sand banks, but that's the only sign of life. No traffic, no cars, no buses, no bikes. It's just us and the sea, and the roaring rushing tumbling sound of the wind and water.

It's a very strange sensation out here on the river...it seems as if it's nice and quiet, but the noise is always roaring. The wind and waves and water are bashing my ears, but it still seems totally peaceful and serene. My eyes are really watering too, that's how cold it is. The wind is teasing out the tears from my face, and people will think that I'm overcome with emotion... but I'm just freezing cold.

Now we're floating past the slummy parts of London... past the cheapo flats and wastelands. There are no pretty riverside walks around here, just places where people come to dump their rubbish.

All the boats are busted and what passes for scenery looks dirty, dull, and rusted. I can see a few cranes stooping over half-built houses and a load of old boats chained up in the middle of the river. They are just empty hulks of junk and peeling paint. They look like they've been dumped and abandoned, like scrap metal cars in a breaker's yard.

As we round the corner at the Isle of Dogs I can see what's coming next... Greenwich. Now we're back to beauty -- what a contrast! The tall mast of the Cutty Sark is the first thing you'll see, along with the onion dome of the Greenwich Tunnel. And up high on the hill, almost lost in the fog, is the Royal Observatory. Then you float slowly up to the Old Royal Naval College and get booted off the boat.

You might like to try Thames Clippers, City Cruises and London Duck Tour as well.

By Air

Cable Car (aka. Emirates Air Line)

ADDRESS South bank: Edmund Halley Way (by O2) -- North bank: 27 Western Gateway (by Excel Centre) **TRAINS** South bank: North Greenwich (zones 2&3) -- North bank: Royal Victoria (zone 3) **BUSES** South bank: 108, 129, 132, 161, 188, 422, 472, 486 -- North bank: 241, 541 **PRICE** Adult £4.50, or £3.40 with Oyster card or travelcard; Children (5-15) £2.30, or £1.70 with Oyster or a travelcard; Infant (under-5) free **OPEN** 7 AM to 9 PM

(Mon-Fri, Apr-Sep); 8 AM to 9 PM (Sat, Apr-Sep); 9 AM to 9 PM (Sun, Apr-Sep); 7 AM to 8 PM (Mon-Fri, Oct-Mar); 8 AM to 8 PM (Sat, Oct-Mar); 9 AM to 8 PM (Sun, Oct-Mar); It may close during bad weather **WEB** emiratesairline.co.uk **TEL** 0343 222 1234 **TIME REQUIRED** 10 mins each way

Easy to get to? ★★☆ Good for kids? ★★★
Value for money? ★★★ Worth a visit? ★★★

I went on the cable car today. Have you seen it? It carries people across the river between The O2 and the ExCel Centre. Sometimes I think that London is turning into the world's largest fun fair... we've already got a big Ferris wheel opposite Parliament (the London Eye), and now they've constructed a giant zip-wire cable car across the Thames. What's next -- a giant carousel in Trafalgar Square?

It's surprising how many people still don't know that this thing exists. I suppose it's because it's miles out of the way by The O2, but it's one of the best rides in the capital. If you tried to go on something like this at the funfair then they'd probably charge you five quid a pop and it would only take you up fifty feet. But this thing towers higher than the sky and gives you views all the way to the moon and back. I even saw the Sun from up there once -- and that's millions of miles away.

The only downside is that it is a potential deathtrap, and if the cable snaps then you will plummet to your doom in the icy Thames below, entombed in a glass capsule from which there is no hope of escape. Eventually the Arctic water will seep in through a hole and drown you. But hey, it only costs five quid, so you can't have everything.

When you first come out of North Greenwich station you will have The O2 right next-door, so you may as well go and have a quick look inside (there doesn't have to be an event on -- you can still go inside without a ticket). They've got a load of restaurants and pub-type places under the outer rim, so you can grab a quick bite to eat first if you want to, or down a few beers to pluck up some courage. After that I suggest taking a walk east along the riverfront, where you'll be treated to a distant view of the Thames Barrier a few miles downstream. You can also look up into the sky at the cable cars soaring above your head to see what you're letting yourself in for. (On second thoughts, maybe that is not such a great idea -- you might chicken out!)

Before we get on board let me assure you that it is totally 100% safe. I can honestly say that I have never died on it (and I would tell you if I had). And it's very easy to ride as well. If you've got an Oyster Card then you don't even need to buy a ticket -- you just board it like you're riding a bus or the tube. They've got Oyster card readers at the entrance so you just tap your card down and waltz on. If you need to buy a ticket then you just walk up to the 'check-in' desk window. They've tried to style the whole cable car experience on an airplane ride, so the ride is called a 'flight', and a sexy-voiced stewardess comes on and wishes you a pleasant trip.

When the cab comes round on the carousel you clamber inside and sit yourself down in the plush red seat. It was totally empty when I went so I had the entire carriage to myself both ways, but technically speaking it can hold about ten people -- so there's always a possibility that you might have to share it with somebody else.

Once you are up and away it does wobble around a bit, juddering and shaking and making terrible grinding noises, with metal on metal. It seems like the whole thing is about to shake itself to pieces. I quickly managed to convince myself that the cable was about to snap and send the cabin car plummeting five miles into the icy cold sea beneath me (filled with sharks). I cried. I don't mind admitting it. I prayed, for the first time in my life. If you are of a nervous disposition then you might start sweating and fretting. Another thing that I noticed was that the pod doesn't appear to be watertight (I'm being totally serious now). So if the cable does snap and your cab plummets into the water then you are basically screwed. You're not going to go *bob bob bobbing* along the water -- you will sink. I don't mean to worry you, but things like that are important to me. I like to dwell on my mortality when I'm sitting in a little tin box swaying in the wind. So you might want to bring some scuba-diving gear with you in order to be safe.

But anyway... The O2 looks fantastic below you, and the skyscrapers of Canary Wharf tower up behind it too. You get a great view of London City Airport and the industrial buildings up and down the Thames, but it's too far away from central London to get a good look at the landmarks. You can see the City skyscrapers in the far distance, but you're not going to be able to see the Houses of Parliament, or anything like that.

The whole trip lasts about five minutes each way, and once you get off at the other end there's not a lot to do. And that's the downside... whilst the cable car was certainly useful during the London Olympics, there's practically nothing of interest at either end apart from The O2 and ExCel Centre. And they are only worth visiting if you've got tickets for an event. There are some shops and restaurants dotted around the place, but that's about it. All you can really do is take some photos and get back on, for the short ride back to the other bank.

It's still definitely worth a try though -- and it's something nice and cheap that you can do with the kids.

Plane Spotting at London City Airport

ADDRESS Best viewing spot is on the north bank of the Royal Victoria Docks **TRAINS** Beckton Park, Custom House, Cyprus, Royal Albert, Royal Victoria, Prince Regent (all zone 3) **BUSES** 101, 147, 241, 300, 325, 366, 376, 473, 474, 541, 678 **TIME REQUIRED** 1-2 hours

Easy to get to? ★★☆ Good for kids? ★☆☆
Value for money? free Worth a visit? ★★☆

I'm in a coffee shop (again)... Costa's at the O2 Arena. I'm psyching myself up for a ride on the cable car. I always hate going on this thing because you're basically sixty-seconds from death. Have you ever seen it? It's just a couple of flimsy-looking pylons poking out of the river with a shoelace strung between them, and you have to sit in a ten-tonne ball of steel as it slowly creeps its way across to the other side at about 0 mph, swaying violently in the wind, bouncing up and down and doing loop-the-loops, screeching and crying as the rusty wheels grind each other up. I am being honest... it's a wonder that no one has ever died on it. If that rope snaps then that's it -- you are dead. *End of story.* Down you'll go into the icy cold concrete slab of the sea, trapped inside a glass ball at the bottom of the Thames. They don't tell you any of this beforehand, by the way. There is no mention of dying at the ticket booth... so it's a good job that I am here to warn you about all of this. People think that it's a fun ride, but it isn't: it is terrifying. That is why I am sitting here shaking in the cafe, pouring ten cups of coffee down my neck: to try and buzz me up and get the adrenaline pumping.

Unfortunately it's also the quickest way across the river, which is where I need to go; because I have heard that you can get a great view of the planes taking off at London City Airport from the Royal Victoria Docks. Apparently the runway is a short swim across the water, close enough to blow your eardrums out.

To be fair to the cable car, once you are actually up in the sky and have settled down it's quite fun, and you can sit back and enjoy the view. I only opened one eye though. I kept the other one firmly closed in case something bad happened. I'm not sure why, but it made me feel a whole lot safer.

You certainly get a sky's-eye view of the airport from up there. It's a bit like looking down the barrel of a gun. The runway is practically straight on to your line of sight, so the planes are taking off towards your face. You can also see the long stretch of water by its side, so you can get a decent idea about where we're going to walk (it's a long walk).

It's quite an interesting walk up to the airport. Once you step off the cable car you need to hug the edge of the water, past the shops, past the big cruise ship hotel, and past all those posh flats that no one can afford to buy. For such a pretty place to live it's practically deserted, like a ghost town. There are some nice restaurants and shops dotted along the bank, but none of them have customers. I'm wondering how they manage to stay in business, because as I pass by the windows all I can see are tables and chairs stacked up by the wall like they've never been used. There are car parks with no cars in, and bus stops with no buses. Even the waste paper bins are empty. All I saw for the first ten-minutes of my walk were a couple of cleaners lounging around on a fag break, and two blokes jogging with their dogs. The marinas are all deserted as well: no boats, no floats.

Once you get level with the ExCel Centre you will find yourself directly under the flight path, so when the next plane takes off it will be soaring above your head. If you're wearing a wig then hold tight -- grip that wig so it doesn't blow off into the water. The roar of the engines will come first, long before the plane is bigger than a bird. Then the black shadow will come charging across the tarmac, growing and engulfing you as the aircraft passes high overhead.

I've just passed the ExCel Centre and it's dawned on me that I've still got another mile to go. This walk looks a lot shorter from the cable car. I have just checked the map on my phone and apparently it's one-and-a-half miles from the cable car to a spot that's opposite the airport. I estimate that is a good twenty-five minutes on foot for most people (which is a lot further than I imagined it to be). So you might want to skip my cable car idea and just catch the DLR straight to Royal Albert station instead. That will plonk you down opposite the airport runway. If you do decide to stick with the walk then be prepared for a bit of gloom and doom up ahead, because the next bit past the ExCel Centre turns rapidly glum. It's all litter-strewn paths and concrete wastelands, with big huge roadways lumbering above your head, carrying lorries and trucks out of town. It's certainly not a pretty part of town -- and it's even more of a ghost town than before. This bit hasn't even got ghosts. Even the ghosts have moved out.

I have reached the viewing spot now, directly opposite the airport runway. I can see the whole airport spread out across the water, about 750-feet away. Little trucks are whizzing around carrying pallets and crates, and I can see the planes taxiing around and picking up their passengers. There are four big British Airways planes waiting for permission to depart, plus another couple of Italian ones. There are also a few Lear Jet-type things that probably cost a bazillion quid to run. The control tower is a bit weird: it's not much higher than two storeys, and is dwarfed by the big chimneys of the Tate & Lyle sugar factory behind.

It's quite therapeutic sitting here watching the planes go back and forth, and all the yellow-bibbed workers running around the apron. I wonder what they are doing? Loading up the planes for a foreign jolly, no doubt. Off to Hawaii or the moon... who knows. Maybe it's the south of France today, or a quick ditch in the sea.

The takeoffs are quite interesting. First of all the fire truck races up the runway in case something bursts into flames, then the plane ambles up the taxiway from its parking spot, slowing down for a rest at the end. Then it seems to sit there for a few minutes, waiting, psyching itself up (like I did, before I got on that cable car). Then all of a sudden it kicks open its engines for take off. The power really roars for a second and then it's all motion as it storms up the runway, like a bullet out of a gun, and lifts off into the sky surprisingly quickly. It soars up at 45-degrees and two quick blinks later it has gone... it's just a small dot turning circles in the sky. It's quite a violent goodbye when you're standing on the ground. This is no peck on the cheek and a run for the bus. It's a smack in the face and see you later. I am picturing all of the people inside gripping the sides of the seat, silently praying for their lives whilst the cage rumbles and judders around their ears... trying not to show any outside emotion. (We know that they are scared.)

The flights aren't very frequent at London City Airport. I've been sitting here for an hour now and I've seen a grand total of six planes: three coming in to land, and three more taking off. But it's still definitely worth a look if you fancy a lazy morning without spending any money. And you get to ride the DLR back to Tower Gateway as well, which is a decent way to pass the time. You will get some good views of The O2 and the skyscrapers at Canary Wharf, before it drops you off by Tower Bridge.

Parades, Services & Seasonal Events

Military Parades

Ceremony of the Keys

ADDRESS Tower of London - map 10b
TRAINS Tower Gateway, Tower Hill (both zone 1) **BUSES** 15, 42, 78, 100, RV1 **PRICE** Free, but you must apply for a ticket up to six months beforehand **DATES** Every night **WEB** hrp.org.uk/tower-of-london/whats-on/ceremony-of-the-keys **TEL** 0203 166 6000 **TIME REQUIRED** 9.30 PM to 10.05 PM (precisely!)

Easy to get to? ★★★ Good for kids? ★☆☆
Value for money? free Worth a visit? ★★★

One of the nicest things about going to the Ceremony of the Keys is that you get to see a little bit of London at night. It starts at half-past nine, but if you take the tube to Tower Hill ten minutes before it starts then you really are missing out on a treat. So take a tip from me: Go for a bit of a walk along the river beforehand.

Get the tube to London Bridge and then walk along the south-side of the river towards HMS Belfast and City Hall, with the White Tower illuminated across the water. You can then stroll across the span of Tower Bridge with it all lit-up and have a sit-down before it starts.

There's not much to do around the Tower of London at this time of night. I arrived there at 9 PM and there was absolutely nobody around. Everything was shut up and silent, so it was just me sitting outside the Tower late at night. Just the yellow lamplights and me. That was quite atmospheric right there, before anything had even happened.

As you approach 9.30 PM the Yeoman Warder (or 'Beefeater') will come and open the gate and let you all in. There was around thirty people in our little group, but that rapidly swelled to a couple of hundred once we got inside (as I will explain later). But for the first part of the tour you remain in your little group of thirty, so you don't have to worry about not being able to hear anything. Our guide was an ex-Welsh Guard called Mitch, dressed up in the red tunic and black hat of the Chelsea Pensioners, and being an ex-soldier he had a deep booming voice and we could probably have stood about a mile away and still heard him okay.

The whole thing is extremely atmospheric. The Tower is totally empty of guests at this time of night and the only souls around are the soldiers and you. The cobbled streets are dark and moody with yellow lamplights in the windows. I've been to the Tower plenty of times during the day, but it wasn't until I came to this ceremony after dark that I really appreciated what it must have been like all those years ago. It's a very spooky place.

As he walks you through the Middle Gate and Byward Tower he tells you a quick history of the fortress because he's on a very tight schedule: he has to get it done before the ceremony starts. He had a good line in ghost stories (one of his favourite themes) and he pointed out the rooms where Guy Fawkes was interrogated, Thomas More was imprisoned, and where the two little princes were murdered. You don't actually get to go inside these places though -- he just points out the windows as you tiptoe past. He then walks you down to St. Thomas's Tower and Traitor's Gate, where he assembles you on the kerb ready for show time.

A little piece of advice: if you want to get the best view of the ceremony then it's important that you take up a good position at this point. Your group is only small, but you definitely want to be standing right on the edge of the kerb (which will be at the front of the group). Try and get as close as possible to the right-hand side of the group as well, so you can see through the arch that leads past the Bloody Tower. You want to be able to see through that arch, and all the way back down the road where you've just come from as well... all the way back to the Byward Tower. If you can see both of those places then you have done well.

Once you have lined up on the kerb the Warder will tell you exactly what's going to happen next, and in what order. It's quite a quick little ceremony and it goes on all around you, so you might want to have a proper listen to get the most out of it. It's also at this point that your little bunch might swell with another 200 guests. He explained to us that these interlopers were on a corporate night out, and luckily they were taken to a position across the road and behind us, so they didn't get in the way.

The actual ceremony will begin with a single Yeoman Warder, who enters stage-left carrying an old-fashioned lantern on the end of a pole. You can see him way off in the distance at the Middle Tower (where you came in). He will walk all the way down to Traitor's Gate and wheel left, into the arch by the Bloody Tower, where he picks up an escort of four armed Foot Guards. They will then march back to the Middle Tower again and lock it. Then they'll lock the Byward Tower too, and start marching back. At this point another soldier who has been standing guard to your right will lunge forward, lower his gun and challenge them with a deep and booming shout of "Halt, who comes there!" The Warder will reply: "The Keys!" "Who's keys?" he says. "Queen Elizabeth's keys!" That is the password that lets them through the gate and he says: "Pass Queen Elizabeth's Keys, and all is well".

You have to be quick at this point because you are supposed to follow the soldiers through the arch, and those extra 200 people will try and get ahead of you -- so hot foot it through the arch as quickly as you can. The soldiers will come to a halt a short distance from the stone steps at the end of the path, and you will see the famous old White Tower looming up on your right. The next section takes place in the shadow of the White Tower, and I thought that it was especially atmospheric. Remember that the whole place is dark and in shadow, with just some lazy yellow lamplights to see by, and to have the White Tower suddenly loom up on your right is quite a sight. Another set of soldiers with unsheathed swords will be blocking their path on the stone steps, and after an exchange of words the Chief Yeoman Warder will shout "God preserve Queen Elizabeth!", to which everyone replies "Amen". A lone bugler will then sound the Last Post. The whole place will fall silent at this point, and you'll find yourself standing there listening to this soldier sound his sorrowful tune in the shadow of the White Tower. *I defy you not to get choked up!*

After that the show is effectively over. The soldiers will march off to their barracks and the Yeoman Warder will lead you to the exit. The whole thing takes no more than half-an-hour from start to finish, with the actual ceremony itself lasting just ten minutes. But you've just *got* to do it -- you have to! Just remember to apply for your tickets in plenty of time, because I requested mine in May and was given a date in November -- that's how far in advance you have to plan. Some people have to wait for six months or more.

If you enjoy this then you might like to try a Twilight Tour at the Tower of London.

Changing the Guard at Buckingham Palace

ADDRESS Buckingham Palace forecourt - map 8c **TRAINS** Green Park, St. James's Park (both zone 1) **BUSES** 11, 211, C1, C10 **PRICE** Free **DATES** Usually every day from Apr-Jul, and alternate days from Aug-Mar - see website for dates; It might be cancelled in wet weather **WEB** royalcollection.org.uk/visit/buckingham palace/what-to-see-and-do/changing-the-guard **TIME REQUIRED** 11.30 AM-12.15 PM, but you should arrive from 10.30 AM for a good spot

Easy to get to? ★★★ Good for kids? ★★☆ Value for money? free Worth a visit? ★★★

I finally got around to doing Changing the Guard this week (and last week). I had to go two weeks in a row because I messed it up the first time: *I got there too late!* But it worked out all right in the end because it meant that I got to see the entire ceremony from both inside and outside the gates.

Changing the Guard is one of those things that all the tourists rush to do as soon as they step off the plane, but when you speak to people who have actually lived in London for years they have never bothered to do it. It's too touristy to bother with. It seems a bit twee. That's the camp that I fall into. But I can hardly write a book about London and leave this off the list, can I? (Well, I could -- but I would probably get shouted at.)

I was expecting a crowd about four or five people deep at the gates, assembling about thirty minutes before it started... but boy was I wrong! The first soldiers don't arrive until 11.15 AM, and the actual ceremony doesn't take place until 11.30, so last week I got there just after 10.30 AM -- plenty of time I thought. That would give me nearly an hour to pick a plum spot. But let me give you a piece of advice: 10.30 AM is far too late if you want to grab a place right up against the railings. There was already a mob (or blob) of people by that time. Based on my experience today, when I turned up even earlier, you need to arrive before 10 AM at least. 10 AM is the absolute latest that you should aim to be there if you want the best spot. But don't get too upset if you arrive later, because there are still plenty of decent spots to stand where you can at least see a bit of it. If the gates are already full then take a place upon the Victoria Memorial instead (up the steps). And failing that, take a spot on the road that leads from Birdcage Walk to Buckingham Palace, because they will march straight past you on their way from Wellington Barracks. But even those two spots were full up the first time I came... the crowds were literally all around the Queen Victoria Memorial, all the way around the roundabout, and as far back as the junction with The Mall. That is how busy it was!

Wherever you stand though, you won't be able to see the whole of the parade, so in a way it was lucky that I came twice because I got to see the whole thing from two different angles. The first set of soldiers will come from St. James's Palace (down The Mall), and through one of the side gates into the Palace forecourt. These guys come with a full marching band. The next group sets off from Wellington Barracks in Birdcage Walk, and along the road that links it to the Palace. They will also come with a marching band, past the Queen Victoria Memorial, and straight through one of the side gates. (You can go and watch these guys form up beforehand, in Wellington Barracks, if you like -- on the far side of St. James's Park.)

Once all of the soldiers have assembled on the forecourt you get the ceremonial change over, along with a few tunes by the bands. But you will have to be standing right up against the railings to see any of that, though. Two groups of soldiers will then parade back out of the gate again (the central one this time), back the way they came, towards Wellington Barracks and St. James's Palace.

The entire thing takes an hour from start to finish (11.15 AM to 12.15 PM), but the real meat of it occurs between 11.30 AM and 12 noon. But take it from me: it seems a lot longer when you're standing at the gate for an extra 1½ hours beforehand.

So is it worth doing? Of course! But remember to take a can of Coke with you and be prepared for lots of waiting around.

Another Changing the Guard ceremony tskes place every day at Horse Guards.

Changing the Guard at Horse Guards

ADDRESS Horse Guards, Whitehall - map 8d
TRAINS Charing Cross, Embankment, Westminster (all zone 1) **BUSES** 3, 11, 12, 24, 53, 87, 88, 159 **PRICE** Free **DATES** Every day **TIME REQUIRED** 11 AM-11.30 AM (Mon-Sat), 10 AM-10.30 AM (Sun), but you should arrive 30 mins early for a good spot

Easy to get to? ★★★ Good for kids? ★☆☆
Value for money? free Worth a visit? ★★☆

This ceremony takes place in two different locations: on the Horse Guards parade ground, and also within the little courtyard that faces onto Whitehall; so if you want to see the entire thing on one day then you've basically got no chance, because a succession of horses and soldiers will march back and forth between the two and you'll be running around like a headless chicken trying to keep up. So my advice is to pick a side and stick with it, and just accept that you'll have to miss what's happening in the other section. If you take my advice, then you will pick a plum spot on the parade ground and stay there for the whole duration.

What you need to do is stand right up against the black iron chain that fences off a small square (close to the central arch). The changeover ceremony takes place inside that area. If you stand right up against that chain then no one will be allowed to go in front of you and you will have a fantastic view.

Unlike the Changing the Guard ceremony at Buckingham Palace (which is packed like sardines), the one at Horse Guards is nowhere near as busy because I don't think many tourists know about it; so you can arrive there quite late and still get a decent spot. I turned up at 10.30 AM and still managed to stand up against the chain.

At 10.45 AM you will see a few mounted policeman trot along to keep the crowds in line, and shortly after that you will see the mounted cavalry arrive from their barracks in Hyde Park. They will come along Rotten Row and Constitution Hill, past the palace, and head straight down The Mall. They will then turn right before Admiralty Arch and come towards the parade ground. This is when they will come into view. Some guidebooks suggest that you should stand at Wellington Arch and follow them all the way down The Mall, but I think you'd have to be quicker than Superman to do that. Have you ever tried keeping up with a horse? (There's a reason why jockeys sit on top of their horses and don't run along beside them.) Maybe if you've got four legs like they have then you can give it a go, but if you've only got two legs like me, then stand at Horse Guards and watch them arrive instead. They will ride straight past you and into the fenced-off area.

At the same time as this is happening you will see the old guard come through the central arch (from the courtyard), and occupy the other side of the fenced-off area. The two sets of horses will then stand there for twenty minutes doing nothing -- literally. This is the boring bit, because the action is now taking place inside the courtyard, which you can't see. All you can see are the two sets of horses standing opposite each other in the parade ground. Doing nothing. This goes on for twenty minutes. If you don't mind giving up your good spot in the parade ground then you can head through the central arch and see what's going on.

Luckily for you I decided to visit the ceremony twice, on two different days, so I have seen both bits in full. So let me explain to you what happens inside the courtyard... (this is where it will start to get complicated!).

First of all some horses will ride out from the stables and go through the central arch into the parade ground (they are the same horses that I mentioned earlier). A couple of foot soldiers will do the same, to replace the foot soldiers standing under the arch. After a while some more horses will come out and replace the ones standing in the horse-boxes on Whitehall (where all the tourists gather to have their photos taken). This bit is actually quite interesting, because what they do is open up the back of the boxes to allow the new horses in, which pushes the old horses out the front. They will then do a 180-degree turn through the central gate and head straight into the stables. If you are standing in the courtyard whilst this happens then it will be taking place a few feet from your face!

Now we need to return to the parade ground again (those twenty minutes have passed)... because the ceremonial changeover is about to take place. The old guard will split in two, and half of them will ride out of the parade ground and back up The Mall, towards their barracks in Hyde Park. The rest will head back through the central arch to the courtyard. As soon as this happens you should give up your plum spot in the parade ground and rush through the arch to follow them, because they are assembling in the courtyard for the final flourish. The big boss man will bark a few orders at them, order them to dismount, and everyone will walk their horses into the stables. And that's it... the show's over.

So in summary then, which ceremony is better: the one at Buckingham Palace, or the one at Horse Guards? If you have to choose between the two then you should definitely choose the Palace. There really is no contest. The backdrop is better, the crowds are bigger, and you get some marching bands as well. But the one at Horse Guards is still worth a watch if you happen to be in the area.

Horse Guards has one more daily event called the Dismounting Ceremony.

Dismounting Ceremony (aka. 4 O'Clock Parade)

ADDRESS Horse Guards, Whitehall - map 8d **TRAINS** Charing Cross, Embankment, Westminster (all zone 1) **BUSES** 3, 11, 12, 24, 53, 87, 88, 159 **PRICE** Free **DATES** Every day **TIME REQUIRED** 4 PM-4.15 PM, but you should arrive 30 mins early for a good spot

Easy to get to? ★★★ Good for kids? ★☆☆ Value for money? free Worth a visit? ★★☆

If you've already been to the Changing the Guard ceremony at Buckingham Palace and Horse Guards, then the Dismounting Ceremony will complete your set. There are plenty more parades that take place in London, but these are the only ones that take place during the day, without a ticket. [Note: Changing the Guard at Buckingham Palace only takes place on alternate days outside of summer.]

You can watch the Dismounting Ceremony in the little courtyard at Horse Guards, where all of the tourists gather to have their photos taken by the horse boxes. The reason that I've never been to it before is because it takes place slap-bang in the middle of the afternoon at 4 o'clock -- which is a total pain in the butt.

Compared with the other daily ceremonies this one is just a sideshow. It's extremely short and not a lot happens. All you get are six soldiers and two horses, and a big boss guy who walks around and shouts at them for five minutes. Then they all go inside. That is basically all that happens.

If you're going to do it then try and get there by 3.45 PM -- fifteen minutes before it starts. The courtyard did eventually fill up with tourists, but it wasn't overly busy. I don't think many people know that the ceremony exists, to be honest, so there were probably only about 200 people in total.

Shortly before 4 PM the two mounted sentries who are standing guard in the horse boxes on Whitehall will leave their posts and enter the courtyard, followed by six foot soldiers from the barracks. They will all stand to attention and not do anything for a few minutes... waiting for the clock to strike 4 PM. As soon as that happens the big boss guy will come out of the arch and inspect them, walking around their fronts and backs, checking out their uniforms for spots of dirt and dust and what-not. Once he's satisfied with that he will bark orders at them to go inside. Then he will turn his attention to the mounted sentries, to check whether they have blown their noses and shined their shoes to perfection, etc., then he will order them into the barracks as well. Once they have all disappeared the show is over.

If you like military displays and you've got a soft spot for the Changing the Guard, then it makes sense to see this one too -- because it will complete your set. I was certainly glad that I did it. But it's one of those attractions that you can certainly skip if you want, and you won miss much. If you happen to be down Whitehall at 4 PM, then pop in for a bit of pageantry. But otherwise give it a miss.

Horse Guards also has a Changing the Guard ceremony every day.

Remembrance Day Parade

ADDRESS Horse Guards to Parliament Sq, then back around the Treasury towards Horse Guards - map 8d **TRAINS** Charing Cross, Embankment, Westminster (all zone 1) **BUSES** 3, 6, 9, 11, 12, 13, 15, 23, 29, 53, 87, 88, 91, 139, 159, 176, 453 **PRICE** Free **DATE** Usually second Sun in Nov **WEB** britishlegion.org.uk/remembrance/how-we-remember/remembrance-sunday **TIME REQUIRED** Whitehall opens 8 AM. Ceremony from 10.45 AM. Parade from 11.15 AM-12.30 PM

Easy to get to? ★★★ Good for kids? ☆☆☆ Value for money? free Worth a visit? ★★★

You have to be a bit brave to attend this parade because a week before the date comes round the papers will start churning out scary stories about terrorists wanting to blow up the Queen. This year it's all about ISIS (they are the bad boys at the moment). Before them it was Al Qaeda, and before them it was the IRA. Before them it was probably someone else. Nothing bad ever happens, of course, because with a whole army of coppers and soldiers in attendance it's probably the safest place in England. That doesn't stop you worrying, though. But if the Queen can brave it, then so can I. These soldiers didn't worry when they went off to war for five years, did they? So it's a bit pathetic of me worrying about standing still in Whitehall for a few hours.

This parade has some of the tightest security that I have ever encountered in London. They don't let the public into Whitehall until 8 AM and the queues start forming long before that. I was there before Big Ben even woke up and I didn't get in until 8:15 AM. What they do is barricade both ends with metal fences and a phalanx of police officers, and you have to queue up and be searched by beeping x-ray machines to get inside the cordon. They even make you empty out the contents of your pockets into a see-through plastic bag -- just like they do at the airport.

If you want one of the best viewing spots then you need to get there straight away, when it opens at 8 AM, because the best ones will be snapped up by 8:30, and the whole place will be jam-packed by 9:30.

I ended up picking a spot by the Red Lion pub, but now that I've been here a while I think I've probably picked a crap place to stand, because all of the big wigs stand on the north side of the Cenotaph (on the Downing Street side), and I am on the south side of it (the King Charles Street side). But it's swings and roundabouts... because if you stand on the north side then you will have three rows of soldiers stationed right in front of the barricade between you and the Queen, and those guys are ten feet tall before they even put on their hats. If you stand on the south side then you will have no soldiers at all, so you'll have a great view of the veterans' parade as it passes down Whitehall to Parliament Square. In hindsight I think I would rather stand as close to the Cenotaph as possible.

It's 9 o'clock now and we are squeezed in shoulder to shoulder all the way down the pavement. We are standing here watching the pigeons and the coppers, and the street cleaners sweeping up all the leaves. The TV camera tower has just started broadcasting some classical arias and religious hymns across our heads, which helps to pass the time. And soon after that the Boy Scouts come along and hand out white papers, containing hymns and prayers and the Order of Service. (Who invited God to the Remembrance Day parade? Half of the wars in human history kicked off because of him, so I'm surprised he's got the balls to show his face.)

I have never seen so many coppers in my life. I think they must have the entire Metropolitan police force out this morning. There are hundreds of them everywhere... maybe as many as a thousand -- and that's just in Whitehall alone! Half of them are brandishing automatic weapons and the rest have been issued with an extra pairs of eyes to watch the crowd. A helicopter is doing constant circles in the sky and there are police marksmen on the roof with rifles and binoculars.

While I'm standing here waiting for something to happen I'm going to take a minute to explain the entire parade route from start to finish. Unlike all of the other big parades in London this one is basically just the soldiers on their own, and you don't really see the Queen at all. She doesn't parade down from Buckingham Palace in her coach, or anything like that. All she does is pop out of a building in Whitehall for the wreath laying ceremony, and then disappears back inside again. Before that happens the military bands will come down Birdcage Walk from Wellington Barracks, and form up on the south side of the Cenotaph. The veterans form up on the north side, and also in Horse Guards parade ground, because there are far too many of them to fit down Whitehall at once. Once the wreath laying ceremony is over and the Queen has disappeared back inside, the veterans will parade past the Cenotaph to Parliament Square, and then loop back up to Horse Guards parade ground again, via Great George Street and the eastern edge of St. James's Park. So it's basically just a very small circle -- and you need to be down Whitehall to see anything worthwhile.

I'm still waiting for the parade to start -- there's not long to go now. I've been listening to the crowd's conversation while I'm waiting and I think I'm surrounded by two hundred army wives and patriots. They certainly don't mind a bit of war. If you blurted out that you are a pacifist in the middle of this lot then you would be named and shamed and kicked out into the street. I seem to be the only person here who doesn't have a Silver Star or campaign ribbon on my coat. (I should have brought my cub scout badges along because I had a whole armful of them.) My view on war is this: I'm perfectly happy for people to fight each other, as long as I'm not the one doing the actual fighting. Because without war we would have no war movies. We would have no *Great Escape*, no *Dirty Dozen*, no *Rambo*, and no *Commando* comics. We would have no Churchill and no Nelson and no Marlborough either -- so what the hell.

Let's go for it. A little bit of war never hurt anyone.

The anticipation begins to build around 10.15 AM because that's when the military bands start marching round from Parliament Square. It's all foot soldiers and musicians in this parade, so they are armed with trumpets and tubas instead of guns. I have a perfect view of the back of the band, but unfortunately they have totally blocked my view around the sides of the Cenotaph -- which means that I won't be able to see the wreath laying ceremony.

At 10.45 AM the politicians and military bigwigs start their slow walk up from Horse Guards and take their places level with Downing Street. The Queen just pops out of a building and doesn't really walk anywhere, so unless you have picked a spot level with the Cenotaph then you are highly unlikely to see her. [Note: they erect some big TV screens further up Whitehall for the people with a lousy view.]

Everyone was expecting the two-minutes silence to begin at 11 AM, but they surprised us by starting early. The silence just seemed to descend on us out of the blue, and we had sixty seconds of hush before the first cannon fired. Everyone suddenly becomes motionless at once, and you daren't even look at your watch. It is such an eerie feeling... like time itself has stopped. Everybody's eyes become locked in their sockets. Bones are frozen into position -- we even slowed down our breathing. And it was at that exact moment that I remembered I hadn't put my phone on mute, and with everyone locked in a stone pose I couldn't pull it out to switch it off (I was at the front of the barricade!). I don't mind telling you that the next two minutes were some of the most terrifying moments of my life. I was convinced that my phone was going to blast out its bell and the TV cameras would swing around and focus on this shame-faced idiot in the crowd. I would definitely have made the evening news. I would have been mortified, but luckily nothing happened. The only sound we heard was a flag flapping against its metal pole. Whilst everyone else was praying for the war dead I was praying that my phone would keep asleep.

When the second cannon fires everyone can start breathing again. Then a soldier blows the Last Post and the wreath laying ceremony begins.

I couldn't see any of this bit, but the Royals and politicians basically take it in turns to lay their poppies at the foot of the memorial. After that comes some prayers and readings from the priest, and a sorrowful tune sung by the crowd. Then everyone perks up for the National Anthem -- because you always sing it sweet when the Queen is there to hear it. If you don't choke up and shed a tear at this bit, standing shoulder to shoulder with the cops and soldiers and veterans, shivering in the chilly wind in Whitehall, then you need to get your head and heart examined because there's something wrong with them.

At 11.30 AM a few of the military bands will start to march off, followed by the veterans. This is when the actual parade begins. The Queen and politicians don't bother with this bit -- they all disappear into the warm buildings down Whitehall. But the veterans who have formed up in the northern half of Whitehall will start their slow shuffle past the Cenotaph, and then go round the back of the Treasury towards Horse Guards again. This line will constantly be replenished from the thousands more waiting in Horse Guards parade ground.

If you take my advice then you will bring an extra pair of hands with you for this bit, because you are morally obliged to clap every single soldier as they file past. It goes on for a whole hour... and I am not exaggerating. You will have to clap for an entire sixty minutes as battalions of wheelchairs pass you by. Instead of tanks and horses these guys have got mobility scooters and zimmer frames. Instead of guns and swords they have umbrellas and walking sticks. They will be sporting chests full of medals and tears in their eyes and look as proud as punch. For two hours they become the pride of the nation again -- then it's straight back down the old people's home.

The Gurkhas and the Chelsea Pensioners are the undoubted superstars of the parade. Everybody knows what their uniforms look like so we all break out into a round of cheers and whooping until they disappear out of sight. I enjoyed watching all of the old sergeants as well, still barking out orders at the age of eighty to their platoon of old age pensioners, admonishing them to keep better step with their plastic hips and arthritic joints. (Once a soldier always a soldier!) Those guys would probably march off to war right now if the Queen came out and asked them.

The whole thing comes to an end around 12.30 PM when the last military band walks off to huge cheers.

State Opening of Parliament

ADDRESS Along The Mall and down Whitehall to Parliament - maps 8c, 8d **TRAINS** Charing Cross, Embankment, Westminster (all zone 1) **BUSES** 3, 6, 9, 11, 12, 15, 23, 24, 87, 88, 139, 148, 159, 176, 211, 453 **PRICE** Free to watch from the street. Public are not allowed inside Parliament **DATE** Usually late May or early Jun - see website for date **WEB** parliament.uk/about/how/occasions/stateopening

Easy to get to? ★★★ Good for kids? ★☆☆
Value for money? free Worth a visit? ★★★

The parade was due to march past at 11 AM so I thought I'd better get there by nine at the latest, but it was drizzling with rain all day so maybe that's what kept the crowds away -- the streets were still empty at ten. I could have arrived sixty minutes before and still got myself a decent spot. (I don't recommend that you try that, though -- because you might not be so lucky with the weather.)

With plenty of time in my pocket, I decided to have a walk around the whole route from the Palace down The Mall, through Horse Guards and Whitehall, and all the way up to the Houses of Parliament. Unfortunately you needed a pass to get past Westminster Abbey (the coppers were stopping everyone going any further), so I ended up under the shadow of Big Ben in Parliament Square, right on the corner where Winston Churchill is. It couldn't have worked out any more perfectly: I had lucked myself into the best possible spot.

By the time Big Ben struck at ten it was just me and one other guy standing on this corner, plus ten million billion policeman lining the road. The other guy had brought with him the largest camera I had ever seen in my life -- it was bigger than my head. He was obviously a pro. We had a little moan about the weather (we are British, after all) and had a good old laugh when Danny Alexander went past in a limo. He only works around the corner, you see -- the Treasury is literally two minutes from Parliament -- so much for government cutbacks! Then we had a huge of slice of luck because they started shutting off the roads for the parade, and we ended up being fenced in to Parliament Square, just us and about fifty others. No one else was allowed in from this point on, so we had practically the entire square to ourselves! We happily watched the public cramming up against the barriers down Whitehall, whilst we stood nice and comfy with five-feet of personal space each. So here is my advice: arrive at least ninety minutes before the parade begins and stand on the Parliament side of Parliament Square. With a bit of luck the police will box you in before the tourist hordes arrive.

You know the parade is close when the Foot Guards start pacing down the streets. I noticed this at Trooping the Colour as well: first of all you get a wall of armed policemen staring at you from behind the barrier, eyeing you up in case you look a bit shifty (which I do), and then the uniformed soldiers will come along with their machine guns and ceremonial swords. Their sergeant (or corporal, or whatever he's called), will then march past with his measuring stick to make sure that they are *exactly* ten paces apart, and he straightens up their caps and trousers too -- a real mum. And woe betide any soldier who is slouching! Then they stand there for the next sixty minutes not moving a muscle. They are very disciplined, these soldiers. They don't even move to scratch their nose. The police, on the other hand, just stand around yakking and chatting and joking with the crowd. You can actually have a conversation and a bit of a laugh with them, which helps to pass the time.

Just before 11 o'clock all the limos file past with the foreign flags on. I suppose they must be full of diplomats and visiting dignitaries, but you can't really tell because the windows are all blacked out. And after that the parade starts proper.

After my trip to Trooping the Colour I was expecting to see hundreds of horses, thousands of soldiers and millions of tunes from the marching bands. But I was actually a little bit underwhelmed. The State Opening of Parliament is not on the same scale as Trooping the Colour at all: there were just a couple of bands, one hundred horses at the most, and maybe a few hundred soldiers in their red tunics and bearskins. The whole parade passed us by in two or three minutes -- no joke. I didn't even see the Queen this time because I had the camera pressed up against my face (a rookie mistake). It was only when I got home later and watched the footage that I realised where she was. The Queen was in a closed black carriage with Prince Philip, and that was followed by another one with four more Royals inside. But I haven't got a clue who they are, not even now, even after watching the video with a magnifying glass. They should make them wear name badges or something. Then came an open-top carriage with Princess Anne inside, and that was basically it. I didn't see Charles, William, Harry or Kate, but maybe they were in that closed carriage. It was a very short parade.

After the arrival the Queen disappears into Parliament to deliver her speech, and you have to wait in the rain for forty-five minutes (the public are not allowed inside). I wheedled my way a bit closer to Parliament in the meantime, and got a much better view of them parading out. The whole thing was over by 12.15 PM.

So was it worth it? Of course it was. You can't miss these parades because they are great. But if I had to choose between Trooping the Colour and the State

Opening, then it's no contest -- I'd pick Trooping the Colour every time.

Trooping the Colour

ADDRESS Buckingham Palace to Horse Guards - maps 8c, 8d **TRAINS** Charing Cross, Green Park, St. James's Park, Westminster (all zone 1) **BUSES** 3, 8, 9, 11, 12, 19, 22, 24, 38, 53, 87, 88, 148, 159, 211 **PRICE** Free to watch from The Mall; Seats in Horse Guards must be applied for in Jan/Feb -- see website for details **DATE** Usually 2nd or 3rd Sat in Jun - see website for date **WEB** royal.gov.uk/royalevents andceremonies/troopingthecolour/troopingthecolour.aspx **TIME REQUIRED** Parade at 10 AM. Balcony appearance and fly-past at 1 PM. You should arrive before 8 AM for a good spot

Easy to get to? ★★★ Good for kids? ★☆☆ Value for money? free Worth a visit? ★★★

I went to Trooping the Colour today. This was my fourth parade in a month so the Queen must surely recognise me by now -- she's seen me enough times. It's about time she invited me round for tea.

The parade started at 10 o'clock so I got there about 7.30 in the morning and had a walk up The Mall to Buckingham Palace. After my experience last year of standing halfway down The Mall, I had already decided that the best place to stand was on the bend near Admiralty Arch, where it curves around towards Horse Guards Parade; because that way, I thought, I would see the whole parade approaching down the road. I wished I'd stuck with that plan now, but when I got to Buckingham Palace the whole place was empty, so I decided to stand approximately level with the Queen Victoria Memorial instead. I knew at the time that was a dangerous plan, because the road bends around either side of the memorial -- and which way would the parade go? To the left, or to the right? I ended up asking a friendly copper for advice and she was under the impression that it would go one way on the first journey, and the opposite way coming back. So I thought okay, that sounds all right -- I'll stick with that. *Never trust a copper!*

You can tell when it's getting close to show time because ten million cops turn up, all talking to each other on their walkie-talkies and standing around with their sub-machine bazooka rocket-launcher grenade guns, and then the BBC's Clare Balding stalked past like she owned the place. She wasn't very happy about something -- I don't know what -- but she certainly scared the gun cops.

Then the public started arriving en masse too, and two elderly ladies came and stood next to me and told me everything that I ever wanted (or needed) to know about the Royal Family. Apparently they camped out overnight for William and Kate's Royal wedding a few years ago, down by the Palace gates, and I said oh yeah I came to that as well, and straight away we became best buddies. As soon as I said that I became their honorary grandson and I got the potted history of Buckingham Palace, Windsor Castle, Sandringham and Highgrove -- these two ladies had been to the lot. Apparently they spend their retirement years following the Royals up and down the country taking pics and waving. If the gun cops had been listening then they probably would have got a bit nervous. *Stalker alert! Stalker alert!*

Then the soldiers started marching down the road and lined the street. The policemen were just slouching around in twos and threes, not minding too much where they were positioned, but these soldiers were pacing out their places to the centimetre. Legs spread ten inches apart, no more and no less. Legs at five degrees and eyes front. Lip of the hat hanging just above the eyebrows. Then their scary sergeant came marching down barking out orders and picking stray strands of hair off their hat. Then a few bands came down playing military tunes, with drums and guns and bagpipes. Then a few cars with the lowly Royals who couldn't be bothered to walk. Then some more bands. Then a regimental dog, then the troops on horses. Then there was a huge cheer which could only mean one thing... no, not the Queen, but Prince William and Kate. Everyone goes nuts when they turn up. Kate was in the carriage with Harry and Camilla and one more who I think was Prince Andrew. Everyone started screaming out for Prince William but I couldn't see him at all. It was just a sea of waving arms all around me, trying to get his attention. It was only when he disappeared down the road that my two old ladies said he was actually on horseback with Princess Anne and Charles. I thought he was just one of the troops!

Then the Queen went past in a carriage with Prince Philip all done up in his military uniform, complete with a two-feet tall bearskin on his head. It must have weighed a tonne, the poor fella. He's about 200 years old -- I'm surprised he didn't pass out.

Unfortunately for me the entire parade chose to go around the opposite side of the memorial, blocking 50% of my view. But that was okay, I thought, because I'd have a great view of them coming back. Once the parade passes by the first time you have to stand locked in position for another hour, whilst they do their duty on Horse Guards Parade. If I'd stayed at the other end of The Mall then I might have been able to hear this, or even seen a little piece of it, but of course I was miles away now, so I had no chance.

This is the hardest part of the parade -- the waiting. You can't sneak off for a toilet break or a cup of tea or anything like that because you'll never get back in line again. The crowd by this time will be jam-packed solid and up to ten people deep in places. If you're lucky then you will get some decent neighbours and you can spend some time chatting with them.

I had already been on my feet for a few hours by this time and was seriously starting to wilt, but I toughed it out -- I should have got a medal like all the soldiers. When the Queen came past on the return journey I think she waved at me to acknowledge my bravery. I couldn't really tell though because she disappeared the same way that she came -- around the other side of the memorial again! Did I mention that you should never trust a copper? If it wasn't for the fact that the policewoman had a big truncheon and a pair of handcuffs on her, I would probably have tried to arrest her myself.

So let me give a piece of advice for next year: whatever you do, do not stand in front of Buckingham Palace, or either side of the Queen Victoria Memorial. Because you'll only have a 50-50 chance of the Queen passing by on the right side. The best place to stand now, in my humble opinion, is at the top end of The Mall, just on the bend where it approaches the Queen Victoria Memorial. So don't go near the Admiralty Arch end -- stay at the Buckingham Palace end, but plonk yourself down at the very start of the bend. Not halfway round the bend, like me -- but right at the start. Unfortunately this will give you a lousy view of

Buckingham Palace, but that doesn't matter because you'll have to move for the balcony appearance anyway (for reasons that I will reveal in a minute).

The next bit is quite good: after the Royals have passed by the Queen will get out of her carriage in front of the Palace gates, and stand on a little step to watch the troops parading past her. Unfortunately I couldn't see the Queen (blocked by the gate -- it wasn't my day!), but I had a decent view of the troops. Whilst all of this is going on, the rest of the Royal Family come out onto the balcony to see what is happening down below. Because I couldn't see the Queen, I thought she had somehow managed to hot-foot it inside the palace and up the stairs at supersonic speed, and come out on the balcony too, but she wasn't there. *Where was she?* Has she had enough and gone to have a lie-down? It wasn't until after the troops had passed by that I finally saw the Queen's bright yellow hat get into the carriage again, and disappear inside.

So that was bad thing number two that happened to me today. But there was more to come... bad luck always comes in threes. The only thing left now was the balcony appearance (the proper one, with the Queen) and the fly-past. And because we were already situated quite close to the Palace I naturally thought that we'd get a plum position by the gates. But the police decided to march everybody up from The Mall before they let us out from behind the barriers! So the thousands of people who had been standing further down The Mall managed to fill up the entire area directly in front of the Palace whilst we were still kept caged behind the barriers at the Queen Victoria Memorial. I didn't think that was very fair. Did I mention that you should never trust a copper?

I did end up with an okay view though, but you should have heard some of the language that was being used (it wasn't very nice). Have you ever been to the cinema and had someone super tall sit directly in front of you, blocking your view? Well, that is what it was like in front of the Palace. People were putting up umbrellas because of a few spots of rain, whilst other people were hoisting their 10-year old kids onto their shoulders to get a better view. Lots of people were shouting behind for people to get down, but of course they wouldn't -- everyone pretends to be deaf all of a sudden. It's a dog-eat-dog world in front of the Palace. The fly-past was okay though. Once the Red Arrows had buzzed past, that was it. Time to go home.

I still had an okay day, but it wasn't half as enjoyable as some of the other parades I've been too. I think it all boils down to what kind of view you get. If you have a lousy view then you'll have a lousy day. So my advice is to get there early, and pick yourself a decent spot.

You can also see the Queen during the State Opening of Parliament and Remembrance Day Parade.

Church Services

Evensong at St. Paul's

ADDRESS St Paul's Cathedral, Ludgate Hill, The City - map 4f **TRAINS** Blackfriars, Cannon Street, Mansion House, St. Paul's (all zone 1) **BUSES** 4, 11, 15, 23, 25, 26, 100, 242 **PRICE** Free, but you'll need a ticket to see the whole cathedral - see my St. Paul's review for the prices **DATES** Usually Mon-Sun, but check their website **DENOMINATION** Church of England **WEB** stpauls.co.uk/worship-music/worship/choral-evensong **TEL** 0207 246 8348 **TIME REQUIRED** 5 PM to 5.45 PM (Mon-Sat), and 3.15 PM to 4 PM (Sun)

Easy to get to? ★★★ Good for kids? ★☆☆
Value for money? free Worth a visit? ★★☆

After attending an Evensong service at Westminster Abbey last week, I thought I'd give the one at St. Paul's a try as well. I was totally prepared for the entry scrum this time but it turned out to be a lot more civilised in The City -- everybody queues up in an orderly line. At the Abbey it was a huge free-for-all as everyone fought tooth and nail for their spot.

If you happen to turn up a bit early then you can wile away some time in the Crypt downstairs, which is open to the public without an entry fee. They've got a little restaurant and a shop down there, and you can get a sneaky look at Nelson's black marble tomb through the big iron gate; just don't make the same mistake that I did and come out with only thirty minutes to spare... because you'll discover that half of the congregation have already gone in.

Once you're inside you'll find that there are still quite a few tourists walking around with their audio-guides on. The bouncer-priests don't seem to mind the mass-goers sightseeing for free at St. Paul's, because I was able to walk around a large part of the Cathedral without restriction... all the way up to the dome in the centre. You can't go up the stairs to the domes though, and you can't walk past the halfway point of the building; but even so, that is still a fair-sized chunk of the place to see for free. When I went to Westminster Abbey last week they kept you cocooned in a little line up the side of the nave and you could hardly see a thing, but at St. Paul's they don't seem to mind as much.

I don't like the seats much at St. Paul's. Considering the scale and the grandeur of the place they should have some bought in some intricately carved oak, but they are basically just a load of wooden school seats arranged in a circle by the altar, plus a load more stretching back in rows. They could have nicked them straight out of someone's school assembly. I took my seat right at the front, directly under the centre of the dome. That gives you a fantastic view of the mosaics and the golden finery festooned above the arches. They had a visiting choir from Boston USA today, and I watched them doing their tune-up in the Quire. I swear to God that some of the kids were no more than eight. And I'm not even exaggerating... the front row of the choir was straight out of playschool -- still sucking their thumbs. They still sounded very good though: I've got no complaints about the noise they were making. Even their tune-up sounded like the real thing.

Whilst you are sitting there listening to them warming up their tonsils and tuning their teeth you have to put up with about a bazillion tourists walking around with their audio-guides on. It's not until it gets closer to 5 o'clock that they finally get kicked out of the church (*good!*). That's when the choir disappears too -- out the back for a dress change. Most of the remaining congregation seemed to disappear at this point too. I guess they suddenly realised that an actual mass was going to take place and lost interest. They heard that God was coming on and thought better of it. Imagine stepping out onto the stage only to discover that all of the theatre seats are empty... that is what happened to God today. I reckon the crowd size dropped from about four hundred to two hundred in five-seconds flat.

Whilst I was sitting there a nun came out and started adjusting her hat, or whatever it's called -- a wimple? She was surprisingly young, and I watched her from my uncomfortable seat. A strand of hair was poking out of her hat, and she wiped her fingers under the band to tuck it in. But she wasn't satisfied and took it off, and *christ man* -- was she beautiful. And I mean *properly* beautiful. Too beautiful to put into words. All this brown hair came floating out and I wondered why she was a nun. She could have been a model, a poem, a painting -- anything she wanted. She put it back on, and for five seconds I saw a hair-do that nobody had ever seen except her eyes in the mirror.

Then a priest shuffled out who must have been about ninety years old. Only the co-operation of God was keeping him alive. She took him by the elbow and placed him gently against the wall, like a doorstop. Then she bounded away with a pile of prayer books, and he was left to do battle with his bones on his own, the poor fella.

I was all ready for the service to start at this point, sitting happily in my seat with a great view of the altar. But I got a nice surprise now: because they called about sixty people up to go and sit in the Quire. (The Quire is that set of dark wooden stalls that face each other by the altar, decked out in lampshades and cushions.) It turned out that the Quire was too big for the kindergarten choir and they had a load of spare seats going, and lucky old me got the chance to sit in it. I ended up perched in a stall reserved for Cadington Major (that was the ancient name chiseled into the back of the stand). And it meant that I got to see the second half of the cathedral for free -- with the best seat in the house! To be honest it made me feel like a total phoney... sitting in the seats reserved for God's best mates when I don't even believe that He exists, so I thought I'd better look a little pious and put on a straight face and pretended to pray.

In Westminster Abbey the Quire is situated in front of the altar, but at St. Paul's it is situated directly behind (and behind the choir, even). So if you can imagine the layout... you end up looking down the entire length of the church towards the choir, and then the altar, and then the congregation behind.

Once everybody has settled into their seats the choir files back in and take their seats underneath the organ, and then they start singing their songs whilst the priests parade in. Everyone is issued with a proper little prayer book and a music sheet, but it's a totally different service to the one at Westminster Abbey. For starters... nobody has to sing. There are no hymns for the audience. Only the choir sings. The congregation just sits there and shuts up whilst they bellow out their God songs. And there is no Holy Communion either. So you don't have to chow down on the body of Christ. It's basically just a couple of readings from the Bible, prayers, and songs from the choir. Fifty minutes later it's all over and you can have another little look around before dropping a couple of quid into the offering box.

So how does it compare to the service at Westminster Abbey? If you've only got time for one then I would definitely choose the Abbey. Not that there's anything wrong with the service at St. Paul's... it's still definitely worth attending if you've got an hour to spare. But I just prefer Westminster Abbey as a building because it's a lot more... intimate. St. Paul's is a very wide-open space, and very white and bright inside. Whereas Westminster Abbey is a little bit darker and a lot more... *cramped.* Everything seems to be crowding around you in Westminster Abbey, including the sounds coming out of their mouths, and I just think that a church service is better held in the dark.

Westminster Abbey also has that spectacular altar with a golden screen, and the famous Cosmati pavement. St. Paul's top table was basically just a block of wood with a dinner cloth on. Granted, the ceilings are a lot more impressive in the Cathedral... but I suppose it just comes down to personal taste at the end of the day. If you're just a tourist who doesn't care what flavour of Jesus he's tasting then I'd go for the Abbey.

You might also like the Evensong service at Westminster Abbey.

Evensong at Westminster Abbey

ADDRESS Westminster Abbey, Westminster - map 8d **TRAINS** Westminster (zone 1) **BUSES** 11, 24, 148, 211 **PRICE** Free, but you'll need a ticket to see the whole abbey - see Westminster Abbey review for prices **DATES** Usually every day except Wed, but check their website **DENOMINATION** Church of England **WEB** westminster-abbey.org/music/choral-services **TEL** 0207 222 5152 **TIME REQUIRED** 5 PM to 6 PM (Mon, Tue, Thu, Fri); 3 PM to 4 PM (Sat-Sun)

Easy to get to? ★★★ Good for kids? ★☆☆ Value for money? free Worth a visit? ★★★

You know you're getting old when you'd rather go to a choral evensong at Westminster Abbey than have a night down at the pub, but ah well -- I am at that stage in life now. I am officially an adult.

Let me just start off by saying that I am not religious in the slightest. I make Richard Dawkins look like the pope. I totted up all the evidence for God and Father Christmas once, and Santa came out on top -- so that gives you some idea of what I think about Jesus. But I don't think it really matters when it comes to enjoying a service at Westminster Abbey. There certainly isn't any pressure to convert: the bouncer priests don't look deep into your soul before they let you in; you don't have to sing the hymns if you don't want to (which is pretty hard when you don't know the tunes), and you don't have to shout amen or take Holy Communion or anything like that. As long as you sit quietly and respect what's going on then I reckon even the devil himself could get in.

The whole thing begins at the Great West Door (near the shop), and I recommend that you start queuing up after 4 PM. The tourists all get kicked out of the abbey between four and half-four, and a gargantuan gathering quickly grows at the gate waiting to be let in for mass. (Note: even if you have paid to go sightseeing in the abbey beforehand then you will still get turfed out -- you will have to queue up all over again.) I am guessing that around three hundred to four hundred people attended our little evensong, so you can imagine what the scrum was like when they opened the gate -- people were surging through like they were cramming into a tube train. It was quite an unsightly scrum for a church service... women, children, old ladies... they all got kicked over and trampled on. And it was the old ladies who were doing most of the kicking! So bring some extra-large elbows with you if you want a seat near the front.

If you survive the journey inside then you get ushered past the Grave of the Unknown Soldier, and up the left-hand side of the nave past Isaac Newton's memorial. Then you have to stand there for five minutes and wait for them to open the pews. It is during this lull that you can have a quick look at the vast ceiling and the memorials on the walls. You can't actually go anywhere, though. You are all herded behind a rope into a very small area -- so don't go thinking that this is a cheap way of doing some sightseeing; it's not. If you want to see the abbey properly then you're going to have to stump up the money for a tour.

The service takes place in front of the golden altar in the heart of the abbey, with the seats arranged in the north and south transepts. The altar and quire stretch out on either side, and it's certainly impressive. The choir for our service is from Queen's College, Oxford, and they're standing in the quire to my right, in a set of wooden stalls with dusty red lampshades. I've managed to bag a seat right near the front, so I've got a great view of the famous Cosmati pavement as well, where William and Kate sat during their wedding service, and upon which the queen was crowned.

Unfortunately I haven't been so lucky with my neighbours, who have been blathering on about *Candy Crush* for the last five minutes. One of them has even kicked off her socks and shoes to waggle her toes. The rest of the congregation seems to be a mix of old ladies trying to pray, two hundred tourists straining to see, some young kids being dragged along by their mums, and an old guy hacking up the contents of his snuff box. It's a mixed bunch.

While all of this is going on, we've got the organ playing ethereal tunes in the background. The music then suddenly bellows up into a bone-shaking rumble as the parade of priests marches in. In they come with their crosses held high -- swinging their smoky incense jug around -- a load of old nuns in black dresses and bespectacled men in white gowns. It reminds me of when the footballers come out of the tunnel before kick-off. I must say that the chief priest looks incredibly young -- he's probably only about thirty. How on earth did he get to play at the religious equivalent of Wembley Stadium when he's barely out of university? He must have friends in high places.

The service is underway now with gospels and prayers, and every now and then the crowd will launch into a sing-song with the choir. You get issued with a little hymn sheet beforehand, but there is no pressure to sing. Not every song is sung by the congregation; most of the time it will be performed by the choir alone, and that's when the singing truly shines -- the choir sounds absolutely fantastic. The noise they make is echoed all around the abbey, and it seems to bounce back at you from every direction. If my local church sounded half as good as this then I would have converted ages ago -- it's a lot easier to believe in God when you're standing in Westminster Abbey with the Queen's College choir sounding out.

Even when the singing stops and the priest is droning on, you can still enjoy the surroundings. I was looking up at the stained-glass windows and the ceiling soaring six-storeys above us, and it was actually quite moving. You don't get the full effect when you're on a normal sightseeing tour. It's not the same walking around with an audio guide plugged into your brain. But sitting here with the choir in the quire and the thick, smoky smell of incense in your throat really brings it home what this place is all about.

The whole event lasts for about an hour, and it was over by six. Then the priests parade out again and you are very quickly ushered out of the door. There is no time for sightseeing. You end up on the front steps where the priest is waiting to say good-bye, wishing everyone peace on earth and all of that kind of thing, etc. The bells are pealing high above your head ringing out the end of mass, until the ringing slowly gets drowned out by the beeping traffic and motorbikes roaring round to Parliament Square. Then you can smell the hot dog burger van that is parked ten metres from the gate.

It is definitely worth doing, without a doubt -- even if you're not religious. There's a lot to enjoy, and be moved by, if you let it.

You might also enjoy an Evensong service at St. Paul's Cathedral.

Sunday Service at Hampton Court

ADDRESS Hampton Court Palace **TRAINS** Hampton Court (zone 6) **PRICE** Free, but you'll need a ticket to see the whole palace - see my Hampton Court review for prices **DATES** Every Sun **DENOMINATION** Church of England **WEB** hrp.org.uk/hampton-court-palace/visit-us/religious-services **TEL** 0203 166 6000 **TIME REQUIRED** 11 AM to 12 noon

Easy to get to? ★★☆ Good for kids? ★☆☆ Value for money? free Worth a visit? ★★★

It looks like they've had a funfair on at Hampton Court Green because it's in the middle of packing up and going home. That's a sad sight isn't it: a funfair going home on a Sunday. There are lots of lorries parked around the edge with strip lights and neon signs poking out of the trailer-trucks. I'm surrounded by closed tents and trash, and birds eating hot dog buns on the grass. One of them is pecking at a burst balloon and a crosshair target.

I'm off to church at Hampton Court Palace... I think I go to more church services than religious people do. But this one is well worth a visit because it's in the same place that Henry VIII used to pray with Anne Boleyn before he chopped off her head. It was his own private chapel in the heart of the palace, and it opens up to the public every Sunday for nothing, because you can't charge people to pray. Oh goody, you're thinking... *does that mean I can pretend to be religious and do a bit of sightseeing for free?* That is what you're thinking, right? (Shame on you!) But let's be honest... that's what we're all thinking. Well, the answer is... you're not supposed to. At least, that's what the guard told me when I asked him point blank this morning. If you want to see the rest of the palace then you're supposed to buy an entry ticket. But more about that later...

It's definitely worth turning up an hour early for a stroll along the river. You can get a pretty good look at the back of the palace and the ornamental gardens through the fancy iron railings, and if you walk across the face of the palace to the left-hand side, then you can ramble through another acre of wild plants. There is a huge man-made lake and a fountain out the back -- all of which is totally free to see. The only gardens that you have to pay for are those ornamental ones that you can see through the fence.

After that I recommend seeking out the Tiltyard cafe for a cup of pre-church tea, before making your way to reception at half-past ten.

Reception can be found down the left-hand side of the palace. Just walk up the long drive and take a left before the gatehouse. Then turn right towards the cop's cabin and barrier. Reception is right next-door to that. If you tell the nice lady that you are there to attend the chapel service then she will let you in for free (seriously!). It only works on Sunday mornings though because that's when the service is, and you do actually have to attend it. But I must say that their security is totally rubbish, because they trust you to make your own way to the chapel totally unescorted. So what's to stop you walking wherever you like? No one bothers to ask for your ticket. But it wouldn't be a very Christian thing to do though, would it? You can't very well attend church and then start sinning five minutes later. And if someone did happen to stop you and ask for your ticket then you'll be in trouble, because you won't be able to produce one. So my advice is this: don't risk it. You'll deserve to get caught for being so tight! [Note: I should probably point out that I'm a member of Historic Royal Palaces which gives me free entry into the palaces, so I could walk around totally guilt free. I didn't actually tell them that though, just so I could see how the process works. And it does work, trust me.]

Even if you don't stump up the money to see the rest of the palace, then the Chapel is well worth visiting in its own right anyway. It's a very small and intimate space: all deep reds, blues and chestnut coloured wood. The ceiling is just about the most fantastic roof in England, decorated with golden stars and cherubim. And high up above your head is the ornate Royal balcony where Henry used to sit.

About ten minutes before the service begins they'll start letting people through to the pews and if you're lucky then you'll be allowed to sit in the Quire. (They are the side-facing stalls directly behind the choir, all warmly lit with yellow lamplights.) They seem to separate all the men from the women though -- men on the left and women on the right -- so you might get split up from your family. If that's a problem then don't worry, because they've also got a load of front-facing pews behind. Whilst this game of musical chairs is going on the organ will be playing songs up in the balcony, and then the lamplights will dim down for the choir and priests to parade in...

The choir is the real deal, not a load of lollypop ladies and hen-pecked husbands. It's a mix of sixty year-old blokes and eight year-old boys, all dressed-up in red tunics, white frocks and ruffles. They look like the kind of kids who are never-ever naughty, *ever*. They've probably got names like Tarquin and Cuthbert, and sing higher than the ting of a tuning fork. They wouldn't look out of place on the centre of a Christmas card.

When you're a non-believer like me there's something very strange about a church service... because you're basically standing in a room with fifty other people, chanting about a fella that doesn't even exist. You may as well be chanting about Darth Vader or the Wizard of Oz. I actually made an effort to listen to the readings today but I couldn't make head nor tail of it. It was like a cryptic tale from yesteryear, spoken in words that no one ever says. And judging by the looks on most of the peoples' faces, I don't think a single thought of God went through their heads either. What do you actually learn at these things? If you're not there to learn about God then what exactly is the point? It's just an excuse for a sing-song every Sunday.

My head was filled with other things... thoughts of Henry VIII and Anne Boleyn staring down from the balcony. It's quite something to imagine them sitting up here in this exact same place, looking down on the exact same seats where we're sitting right now. It was probably quite similar to how it looks today. The organ is still playing, the choir is still singing, and the candles are still burning. It's just 500 years later, that's all.

It's very easy to get lost in your thoughts with all the sounds around your head.

You might also enjoy an Evensong at St. Paul's Cathedral or Westminster Abbey.

Sunday Service at the Tower of London

ADDRESS Tower of London - map 10b **TRAINS** Tower Gateway, Tower Hill (both zone 1) **BUSES** 15, 42, 78, 100, RV1 **PRICE** Free, but you'll need a ticket to see the whole Tower - see Tower of London review for prices **DATES** Every Sun (except Aug, and the Sun following Christmas and Easter) **DENOMINATION** Church of England **WEB** hrp.org.uk/tower-of-london/visit-us/religious-services **TEL** 0203 166 6000 **TIME REQUIRED** 11 AM to 12 noon

Easy to get to? ★★★ Good for kids? ★☆☆ Value for money? free Worth a visit? ★★☆

It's amazing how many places you can get into for free by pretending to be religious: St. Paul's, Westminster Abbey, Hampton Court... and now the Chapel Royal at the Tower of London. If I knew that London sightseeing was so cheap for Christians I would have converted ages ago. It must be one of the perks: not only do you get entry into heaven, but you also get free entry into a load of tourist attractions too. *Praise be to Jesus!*

All you have to do is walk up to the Beefeater by the main gate and say you're there for the church service, and he'll let you straight through -- past all the people who paid for their ticket. Yup, I know it sounds totally daft, but trust me -- I've done it. *It works.* It only works on Sunday mornings though, because that's when the service is. And you do actually have to attend the service, so it's not a total free pass. Once you're through the gate you are basically on your own. They'll let you walk to the chapel all by yourself, totally unescorted. They certainly are very trusting, these Christians.

I know exactly what your next question is: *Can I have a look around the rest of the Tower for free as well?* Well the answer to that is... no. You're not supposed to. If you want to see the whole lot then you're supposed to buy a full-price ticket. But there doesn't seem to be a lot to stop you miscreants from trying. Just don't blame me if you end up in the dungeon (or a police cell). Because quite frankly you'll deserve it, for sinning so soon after attending church. Luckily I'm a member of Historic Royal Palaces anyway which gives me free entry into the palaces, so I could walk around totally guilt free. (I didn't actually tell them that though, just so I could see how the process works. And it does work, trust me.)

You get to see a quite a lot of the Tower just by walking to the chapel anyway, because it's situated right inside the grounds. Once you've come through the main gate the route takes you down Water Lane to Traitor's Gate. Then you turn left through the Bloody Tower arch and up the stairs to Tower Green. The famous White Tower will loom up on your right as you stroll up the steps, and then you'll get a glimpse of Waterloo Barracks as well, where they keep the Crown Jewels. The chapel itself is situated right behind the execution site, where Henry's Queens all knelt and lost their head.

At 10.45 AM they'll start letting you in for the 11 o'clock Matin. It's a very nice compact little chapel, but the decoration isn't anything to write home about. It's basically just a big box with a few columns down the middle. There are no stained glass windows or anything like that. The altar is a very simple affair with a few candlesticks, a crucifix, plus a plain table and cloth. There are a few memorials around the walls and along the floor, and one of them is encased behind some metal spikes. They've also got a fine wooden organ with golden pipes. But the real glory is buried beneath the altar: because this is where the headless corpses of all the traitors lie -- people like Anne Boleyn, Lady Jane Grey and the Earl of Essex. (It seems a bit harsh calling them traitors these days... but that's how they went to the chopping block.)

The service is about to start any minute now, so I'm quietly writing this in a pew. Not even God can see me scribbling. It's a Sunday service so everyone is dressed up to the nines like they're going out on a date. Suits and scarves and jackets and ties are the order of the day. I get the impression that the same congregation comes every single week, made up of people who live inside the Tower -- there are not a lot of tourists here (I think I'm probably the only one). It's all old folks and couples in their Sunday best, chatting to each other like they're best buddies. I'm trying to tot them up in my head and I reckon there's about fifty in total, plus another ten for the choir. The choir is all decked out in white robes and red dresses, parading in behind a Yeoman warder.

Because it's such a small place the singing really fills the chapel and it's some of the nicest sounds I've heard. They are doing choral works by Haydn at the moment, standing in a group by the altar. They've got one bird singing solo lines above the bearded blokes and it really is very pretty. Very pretty indeed.

Uh-oh... *drama time*. A little old lady has just shuffled sideways out of her line and ran out crying, weeping down the aisle. The Yeoman warder by the door stood up to comfort her but he is a big burly bloke about ten feet tall, which would have been a difficult shoulder to cry on. I wonder what her story was? I guess it's between her and God, and we'll leave her be.

After an hour it's all over and they've set up a few tables for coffee. Most of the people stay behind for a chit-chat and a cake, but I head out the door into the pouring rain. That is probably God's way of thanking this non-believer for infiltrating his house: sending me home with a wet coat and a cold.

Of all the church services that I've been to in London, this was easily the least popular with tourists. The ones at St. Paul's and Westminster Abbey probably consisted of about 80% tourists, Hampton Court less so (about 20%). But this one was basically just me and the locals -- them in their suits and shoes, and me in my t-shirt and jeans. It was also the only service where I felt like I was intruding on their do, which is silly really because of course it was very friendly. I even had a chat with the vicar by the door.

You might also like the Sunday service at Hampton Court Palace.

Christmas Events

Christmas Ice Rinks

ADDRESS Broadgate: map 5f -- Hyde Park Winter Wonderland: map 7a -- London Eye: map 8d -- Natural History Museum: map 6e -- Somerset House: map 9a -- Tower of London ice rink: map 10b **DATES** Note: not all of the rinks open each year, so check first -- Broadgate: Usually mid-Nov to late-Feb -- Canary Wharf: Usually late Oct to late-Feb -- Hyde Park Winter Wonderland: Usually late-Nov to early Jan -- London Eye: Usually mid-Nov to early Jan -- Natural History Museum: Usually early-Nov to early Jan -- Somerset House: Usually mid-Nov to mid-Jan -- Tower of London: Usually late-Nov to early Jan **WEB** Broadgate: broadgate.co.uk -- Canary Wharf: canary wharf.com -- Hyde Park Winter Wonderland: hydeparkwinterwonderland.com -- London Eye: londoneye.com -- Natural History Museum: nhm.ac.uk -- Somerset House: somerset house.org.uk -- Tower of London: hrp.org.uk/toweroflondon

Easy to get to? ★★★ Good for kids? ★★★
Value for money? ★★★ Worth a visit? ★★★

It's incredibly windy today. The wind is lifting the fallen autumn leaves straight up into the sky, and swirling them around at head height. I've had to fend a few off with the back of my hand.

The best ice rink at Christmas is the one at Somerset House. This is how a winter rink should look, all lit in brilliant blues with a giant Tiffany Christmas tree up the front. It gets dark early in the winter when we put the clocks back so it's pitch black at five-thirty, and people have packed it out already. They are half gliding and half sliding, and they all look scared stiff to me. Once you are in the conga chain you stay in it forever, because you can't get out -- it's a big runaway train of skaters. Some of the mums (I'm guessing they are mums) want out right now, in this exact instant, and yank their husbands to the side. *Don't let go! Don't let go of me!* Down she goes like a sack of spuds.

Big smiles coming round on this lap. This guy clearly knows what he's doing. He's even spinning round 180 degrees in mid-flow to grab hands with his other half. Oh please God, please let him fall over -- *please!* I am begging you. Nope. He is too damn good. Sometimes you get a girl who looks happy and content, and totally in control of her herself, and then *wham!* down she goes like a battleship being bombed. People nudge you from behind and clip your ankles whilst you're turning, or they'll grab hold of your arm to stop themselves falling, and then it's curtains for you as you follow them down to the ground. I think I'll stay watching from the side.

The second best rink in London is the one at the Natural History Museum. They stick it outside the front with a big

Christmas tree and a fairground carousel. They've usually got the best bar as well, nicely decorated and overlooking the ice. This is probably the one that I'd recommend if you've got kids, because you can take them to the museums as well.

The Tower of London's ice rink is quite popular because they stick it in the moat, but they don't have much in the way of decorations though, just a few flashing disco lights. They've got a little cafe selling coffees and bottles of beer, but it's not very Christmassy. It's a bit of a wasted opportunity really.

The ice rink by the London Eye is tiny. It's barely got room for a couple of penguins! You could build the entire thing out of a few ice cubes. But they also have a Christmas market along the Southbank, so you might want to go and have a look at that at the same time.

Broadgate is another little rink, but it's more for the adults than the kids (the business suits who work in The City). You'll find it around the back of Liverpool Street station in Exchange Square. It does have an interesting view down into the train shed though (looking straight down onto the platforms). I always get horribly lost around here though, so you might want to factor in an extra few hours so you can find your way home (at least).

Normally I wouldn't bother with the rink at Canary Wharf, because it's foo far away for tourists, but I'm going to send you on a fifteen minute walk which will make it worth your while. You have to promise me that you're going to do this walk at nighttime, though (and preferably at Christmas), because it's not half as good during the day.

What you need to do is get the DLR to Limehouse, and then take a stroll along the river. The first five minutes are a bit ugly, but stick with it, because it gets better as you go along. Come out of Limehouse station and find Branch Road. Head down there and take a left into Horseferry Road, follow it around to the right, and then head left over the bridge. Hopefully you should see the tall towers of Canary Wharf up ahead. Keep going until you see The Grapes pub on the right. Believe it or not, this crappy-looking pub is part owned by the Hollywood actor Sir Ian McKellan and it's worth a quick look inside, because you can see Gandalf's staff behind the bar -- the same one that he used in *The Lord of the Rings*. Keep walking along the road a little bit further until you find a white office building labelled Dunbar Wharf. Turn right straight away (past those metal pipe barriers) and you'll be on the river. Now you can continue walking left all the way to Canary Wharf.

Check out that river view to the right! If you followed my advice and came here at night then you're in for a treat. Keep going until you get to the ferry stop, and then head left up the steps. Now just keep walking in a straight line towards the base of that tall tower in the distance (called One Canada Square). You will pass Cabot Place on the way, with its round pool of water and spurting fountains. If you come during December then all of these trees with be festooned in fairy lights.

The ice rink is situated on the other side of that tower, in a place called Canada Square Park, so you can either walk right around it, or delve straight through the shopping centre which is situated underneath (the entrance is on the other side of that spurting fountain).

I quite like this ice rink, because it is bang in the shadow of three tall skyscrapers. There's usually a lot of fairy lights on the ring of trees around it as well. And when I say a lot, I mean a lot.

Christmas Lights

ADDRESS The best lights are in Carnaby Street (map 3e), Covent Garden (map 8b), Oxford Street (map 2f), Regent Street (map 8a), Somerset House (map 9a), Southbank (maps 9a, 9c) and Trafalgar Square (map 8b) **DATES** Carnaby Street: Usually late Nov to Twelfth Night -- Oxford Street: Usually mid-Nov to Twelfth Night -- Regent Street: Usually late-Nov to Twelfth Night -- Somerset House: Usually mid-Nov to mid-Jan -- Southbank: Usually mid-Nov to Twelfth Night -- Trafalgar Square: Usually early Dec to Twelfth Night

Easy to get to? ★★★ Good for kids? ★★★ Value for money? free Worth a visit? ★★★

We're lucky in London because we always have plenty of Christmas lights up for six weeks at least. I'm standing down Oxford Street at the moment and the place is dripping in strings of six-foot snowballs. Lots of cherry-sized silver spots too, and electric icicles hanging off the trees like frozen bolts of blue. They've even got some fake snow blowing out the top of HMV. I let some land on me (just to see what it is), and it seems like soapy bubbles.

Have you ever watched that *Christmas Lampoons* movie starring Chevy Chase, when he blankets his house in a billion bulbs? Well, come down to Oxford Street in December and find the House of Fraser, John Lewis and Selfridges, because there must be a zillion lights on those three shops alone. It's as if someone has chopped up the sun and scattered it down the street. They're so bright and white they're giving me sparkles in my eyes when I shut them.

One of my favourite trees is the one they put up in the centre of Leadenhall Market. This is probably the most Dickens-esque tree in The City... a real traditional looking fir, with red and green baubles and bows. It looks like something on a Victorian Christmas card.

I think that Regent Street has become a bit too commercial these days... They've got some big white antlers up there at the moment with Ricky Gervais's face staring out from the centre, plugging his new Hollywood movie. What a sell-out! And it's like that the whole way down the street... Jesus and Father Christmas have been given the boot this year, and replaced by David Brent.

Carnaby Street has gone for some giant headphones, all wrapped up in white fur from Santa's suit. I guess it must be harping back to its Swinging Sixties heyday.

I think the nicest lights in town are the ones outside Somerset House. If you go inside the courtyard you'll find the prettiest tree in the city standing at one end of their outdoor ice-rink, all wound around in strings of winking lights. Now that is a pretty scene (if you only see one tree in London then make it this one)... people are whizzing around the ice with their breath clouding out of their mouths because it's so damn frosty. The place is bathed in a brilliant blue light tonight with old-style lamplights strung up around the sides.

They always have a little cafe overlooking the rink as well, selling hot chocolate and coffee and mulled wine (proper mulled wine with sticks and twigs and berries inside). It's a really nice place to visit even if you can't be bothered to step on the ice. It's usually packed full of mums and grandmothers who are too scared to skate, pressing their noses up against the misty window to make sure their kids are still standing on their feet. Someone definitely needs to buy them a new CD though... because their Christmas tunes are too new. They need some Nat King Cole and Bing Crosby.

Covent Garden has got the second-best tree in town, but it's even bigger than the one at Somerset House -- it must be forty or fifty-feet at least, with cherry red tomato lights and bright white buttons, sitting in a big wooden pot that is bigger than a boat. The market hall roofs are groaning under the weight of baubles fifteen feet across (no joke!), all mirrored up in bright reds, whites and gold. They've got big sheets of white lights strung across the street as well, with little droplets racing down like a shower of snow.

Have a walk across Waterloo Bridge and then check out the festive market on Southbank. Most of it has moved into the big grassy area this year (it usually runs along the river between the London Eye and Royal Festival Hall). This is where they have all of the festive huts and Swiss-style chalets selling hot sausages and Bavarian beer. They've got burgers and steaks and pancakes too -- it's worth walking around just for the smells! There's nothing like the aroma of fairground food on a pitch black night with Christmas lights. They've got one of those funfair carousels pumping out some Wurlitzer tunes as the horses bounce round and round and up and down, and even a little steam train chugging past the Royal Festival Hall (true!).

If you fancy going on a Christmas tree hunt one afternoon, then they usually have another outside the Royal Exchange, one in front of the Byward Tower at the Tower of London, and outside the Dickens Inn at St. Katherine Docks.

I've written a separate review for the Christmas tree in Trafalgar Square.

Christmas Shopping

ADDRESS There is usually a Christmas market outside City Hall (map 10d), inside the Covent Garden piazza (map 8b), Hyde Park Winter Wonderland (map 7a) and along the Southbank (maps 9a, 9c) -- Popular shopping areas include Bond Street (maps 2f, 7b), Knightsbridge (map 7c), Oxford Street (maps 2f, 3e), Piccadilly (map 8a), Regent Street (map 8a) and Sloane Square -- Department stores include Fortnum & Mason (map 8a), Hamleys (map 8a), Harrods (map 7c), Liberty (map 3e) and Selfridges (map 2f)

Easy to get to? ★★★ Good for kids? ★☆☆
Value for money? it depends what you buy!
Worth a visit? ★★★

Fortnum & Mason is the closest that a shop ever gets to being a 5-star hotel. The staff dress up in red tails and shiny shoes at Christmas, with a bit of Bing Crosby and Frank Sinatra on the speakers -- proper Christmas music.

When you step inside from Piccadilly it's all posh chocolates and teas. It's like Santa's sweet factory in there, with decorated tables full of sugar-coated bon-bons, stone-sized toffee chunks, and slabs of fudge as big as bricks. Glass bottles filled with colourful liquids (I don't know what they are, but they are flecked with glitter), tin biscuit-caddies with shortbreads and savouries, huge wooden advent calendars with chiseled out drawers for little gifts, pipe-sized Christmas crackers with silver ribbons and bows. Fat glass jars full of nuts and jams. Downstairs is where you'll find all the booze -- the chestnut coloured whisky bottles and frosted bottles of vodka. They are shining fairy lights through the back of them, so they look like smokey potions in a wizard's bottle shop.

Don't miss their Christmas decorations display upstairs, because it's the prettiest one in London -- they do it in a cozy Victorian style, with a roaring fire and wooden library-style cabinets overflowing with baubles and forest sticks and twigs from alpine firs. They've got wooden cribs with religious figures. Glittery tin drums and trumpets hanging off the parlour tree, and thick woollen stockings on the mantlepiece.

Harrods is more of the same. The rooms are probably nicer but the prices are nicer as well (higher!), but I don't think it's quite as homely as Fortnum's. But if your partner is partial to a bit of champagne fudge instead of Quality Street, then this is the place. If she likes sherry jellies instead of wine gums, then check it out. They make sweets out of saffron and sea salt, cinnamon and goats milk. You can tell that they're expensive because they sell them individually. You see people at the counter saying "I'll have two of those and three of these," and then they say, "that will be fifty pounds, please". It's pick 'n' mix for millionaires.

You can get ginger sticks, berries in a wicker-style box, dates and nuts in a picnic basket, and fruit jams in a glass jar that should really be for roses. They've got teabags in a silver caddy that I'd happily have for my grandmother's ashes.

Their Christmas decorations department isn't a patch on Fortnum's, but they've still got some nice items. A lot of it looks contemporary, though -- and too much like modern art. I see giant eyes on copper-coloured balls, and huge glass orbs with a dollop of purple paint on top. They've got silver moons and chiselled squirrels, duck's heads and dalmatians. Where are all the reindeer? Where are the snowmen? If you're looking for a ball of partridge feathers, or a porcelain relief of an unnamed queen, then Harrods is your place.

If you want to buy some toys for your kids, then there's only one place to go: Hamleys.

The ground floor is where they keep all of their stuffed animals and teddy bears -- I've never seen so many cuddly toys in my life. It's a bit like visiting the zoo, or the Natural History Museum -- they are just sitting there stuffed, spilling off the shelves. Cats and dogs, frogs and bugs, lions and tigers, monkeys, donkeys, snakes and snails, seals and penguins, dragons and unicorns. They've got sheep, stuff that goes cheep, stuff that growls, howls, owls, hand puppets, Paddington Bears... they have basically got everything, for all ages. From toddler toys and little girl's dolls houses, to board games, spaceships, railway sets, remote-controlled cars, PlayStation games, robotic dogs, bathtime frogs, ping pong guns and jigsaws. Downstairs is where they keep all of the boys toys -- gadgets and electronic gear (I wouldn't mind some of it myself).

Hamleys is always cheerfully chaotic because they encourage the staff to play with the toys -- people blow bubbles outside the front door, and chuck hovering helicopters above your head. You'll find people doing card tricks and zooming around on neon roller skates. And amongst all of that are the parents and drooling kids, running around from shelf to shelf with eyes like lightbulbs and touching everything they can see. Picking up stuff, dropping stuff, kicking stuff (and peoples' shins), crying and whining and begging their mums to buy whatever they want. *I want this! I want that!* To sum it up in two words... it's a f*cking nightmare (excuse my French). It's the kind of place that makes you swear in French -- that's how busy it is at Christmas.

I'm not a big fan of their Christmas grotto, though. It's obvious that they don't want kids sitting on Santa's knee anymore (not after Jimmy Saville), so you have to book a breakfast or dinner with him instead, alongside fifty other kids. Then they all sit around the table for thirty minutes whilst his six-foot elves serve them bread rolls and biscuits. It doesn't seem very Christmassy to me.

Do you remember the fantastic grottos that we used to have as kids? We would walk through a dimly lit cave studded with fairy lights and snow, and then step through an icy tunnel into his red velvet throne room, where Santa would be sitting with some genuine 'short persons' (I'm pretty sure that's the correct PC term to use). And then you'd tell him what you wanted, and he would look at your parents for a confirming nod, before saying something like, "Well, er... how about this instead?" And then he'd give you a wooden whistle or a Kinder Egg and tell you your two minutes is up, and point you towards the door. Those were the days! And you went home genuinely believing that he was real -- because you just met the fella. But what do the kids get these days? A couple of sit-down sandwiches with him. They've turned him into a glorified waiter.

Liberty is another shop worth visiting... you can find it on the junction of Oxford Street and Regent Street. It's worth a visit just to stare at the front. It looks like something out of Tudor times (it's not genuine Tudor, but it still looks great). The inside is all wood and worth a look too, but it isn't quite as grand as Harrods and Fortnum's.

Their Christmas decorations section is nice. They've probably got more glass ornaments in here than anywhere else in the world -- there are thousands of different baubles (literally thousands!). You can get dangling fruits and food, animals, people, trees and flowers, stars and cars, ships in a bottle, crowns, houses, hamburgers, eyes, flies (ok, maybe not flies), solid stone ones, ones that glow, ones with snow... hand on heart I have never seen such a huge collection of baubles as I have seen at Liberty.

Selfridges is another big store worth looking at, but it's a bit too posh for me. You come through the front door and straight into their perfume counter with its forcefield of smells. Women in tight ponytails are standing behind brightly lit desks, wearing white lab coats and filing their nails. Every ten steps is a demonstration desk, where the staff do their best to tart up anyone who comes along. It's always the ugly ones who sit down first, hoping for a miracle. They sit down looking like a scarecrow, and want to walk away looking like a Barbie doll. The staff are good, but they're not that good -- jeez!

When I think of a Christmas market I think of a Bavarian mountain. I think of an alpine forest with little ski chalets made out of wood, lit by a string of fairy lights round the door. We don't have many of those in London (we don't have any Bavarian mountains either). The really big one is down Southbank, stretching from the Hungerford Bridge to the Royal Festival Hall. They line them up along the river -- about fifty huts with decorations. But they are basically sheds with a bit of tinsel on top, so don't expect too much. There is usually a big area set aside in Jubilee Gardens as well. That's where they do most of the food -- mulled wine and German sauerkraut, burnt sausages, pancakes and jam. Waffles and hot dogs and chargrilled burgers. They've got a big cider house as well -- I think it's supposed to be a German-style beer hall. It makes a change from going down the pub.

There is a similar sort of thing outside the Tate Modern this year (the same sort of stalls selling the same sort of tat), and there's usually another little market further up by Tower Bridge. They stick it outside City Hall so the Mayor can pop out on his lunch break and buy some Christmas gifts for his mistress (allegedly).

The other big market is in Covent Garden. They spruce it up with some decent decs at this time of year, but the piazza is full of 'arty shops'. It's where you buy knick-knack presents for twenty quid a go. If you want some proper high street shops then try Oxford Street, Regent Street, Piccadilly and Knightsbridge, and the area around Sloane Square in Chelsea.

Christmas Tree in Trafalgar Square

ADDRESS Trafalgar Square - map 8b
TRAINS Charing Cross, Embankment, Leicester Square (all zone 1) **BUSES** 3, 6, 9, 11, 12, 13, 15, 23, 24, 29, 87, 88, 91, 139, 159, 176, 453 **PRICE** Free **DATES** Usually the first week of Dec. The tree stays up until Twelfth Night - check website for the exact date **WEB** london.gov.uk/events

Easy to get to? ★★★ Good for kids? ★★★
Value for money? free Worth a visit? ★★★

I come to see the Trafalgar Square Christmas tree every year, but this will be the first year that I've actually seen the tree-lighting ceremony. Lord knows how they managed to ship the thing over from Norway -- *it's huge!* It must have been a bloody big boat. The ship is probably covered in pine needles now.

I can't see any bulbs or baubles on it, but it's a very grey and gloomy day. The sky doesn't look very happy. The clouds are all clumping up and merging into a dirty great sheet of grey. I think the rain is holding off on purpose, so it can wet our heads come show time. The weather is sneaky like that: it's always plotting and dreaming up ways to ruin our day. There are still two-and-a-half hours to go until they light it up so we're just sitting here waiting, waiting and waiting. Waiting for the button-pushing bigwigs to arrive.

It's 4 o'clock now... two hours to go. One of the singers has just stepped out onto the stage for a little tune-up and a practice. The marshals are busying themselves setting out all the seats for the invited guests. I hope they've checked all the fairy lights work -- there's nothing worse than stringing them around the tree only to find out that one bulb doesn't work. I wonder who untangled them all? Imagine trying to find the dodgy bulb on the Trafalgar Square tree.

I've had to take cover in the National Gallery for a while because some idiot has just done something to upset the sky -- the whole damn lot emptied onto our heads and cleared the square in ten-seconds flat. Every drop of water in the world has come to London to die. There is a storm of water coming in sideways and waves of water are rolling across the roads. It's impossible to brave it and everyone makes a beeline for the insides, in the cafes, into the church, or sheltering under bus stops. It looks like Christmas might be cancelled.

I have ventured out again. The rain has ceased but there is worse to come: *bagpipes!* A fake Scottish man (a Geordie in a kilt) has obviously got his eye on the big crowd and thought he could make a tidy sum of money. So he's set up his pipes right underneath the National Gallery steps and is treating us to his wailing tunes, blowing and droning and whining and crying and making a hell of a racket. Where are all the carol singers? We want *Silent Night* and *Jingle Bells*, not bagpipes!

The square is starting to look very pretty now with the National Gallery all lit up, and St. Martin's all bathed in yellow light. There are no lamplights on Nelson's Column though. He's standing up there all alone and soaking wet. Is this how we treat our heroes? Someone fetch him a coat for chrissakes! If I was in charge I would have wrapped a bit of tinsel around the column and hung some baubles off his hat. Filled the fountains with ice and snow. The Christmas tree is still black as coal. No spotlights on it either. Dead bulbs on an empty stage, waiting for the show. The marshals are hovering around in their fluorescent yellow bibs, hoods done up tight to fight off the wind. It's real winter weather tonight...

It's 4.30 now (we're getting closer), and the roads around the square are clogging up with cars and cabs and buses and bikes. We're surrounded by a bright ribbon of headlights weaving their way around to Whitehall and the Strand. Jesus Christ it is cold. I'm glad I've got a crowd around me because they're keeping off the wind. It is freezing. I don't think I'm going to make it to 6 o'clock because my hands are turning blue. I hope you appreciate what I'm doing here... I am slowly turning solid from the outside in, like a frozen turkey. Only one more hour to go... and still no signs of life on the stage.

Sod this... I am seriously considering jumping over the barrier and switching it on myself, just so we can all go home. I can see the big button on the table... there it is... it's only thirty feet away. I could easily make it if I ran. Shall I do it? I watch the marshal's patrol path and wait until he's out of range and looking the other way... I feel like Steve McQueen in *The Great Escape*, waiting for the Gestapo guards to swing their searchlight away. Have I got the balls to do it?

Nah... I'd just get arrested by the elves and carted off to the North Pole for crimes against Christmas. So I chicken out. I have decided that I will just stand here until 6 o'clock and if I die of cold, then so be it. I have accepted my fate. Either I witness the lights being switched on, or I die. At the moment I don't even care which.

It's 5.30 PM now and the square is still 50% empty. I think the torrential rain has scared everyone away. It's just going to be me, the bagpipe man, Boris Johnson and the Mayor of Oslo at this rate.

5.45 PM now, and at last we have some action! The Salvation Army has got its band in place and is playing some Christmas carols by the tree. Then a crowd comes marching across from St. Martin-in-the-Fields and takes a position in front of the stage. They must be the bigwigs because some of them are wearing fancy hats.

I should probably take a moment to describe the scene to you... so you know the best position to stand for next year. At the moment I am standing directly in front of the tree, at the top of the steps in front of the National Gallery. They have roped off the entire area in front (including the steps), and the stage is in front of that. Unfortunately it looks like I have picked a lousy place to stand, because the bigwigs from the church have been allowed through the barriers and are standing on those exact same steps. So if you go next year then take my advice... don't stand at the top of the steps. The best vantage point is actually on one of the balcony areas either side of the steps, looking down onto the square below. That will give you an uninterrupted view towards the stage and the tree.

The show is over now... it only lasted for thirty minutes. I couldn't really write anything whilst it was going on because I was crammed in elbow-to-elbow with everyone else. But this is what happened: the Sally Army band played a few festive tunes (no bagpipes, thank God), and then the Mayor of Oslo and the Lord Mayor of London took their places on the stage. No sign of Boris Johnson anywhere though. I thought that he was turning up but it was actually the Lord Mayor of London -- the ceremonial one that lives in Mansion House. She said a few nice words, and then handed over to the Norwegian guy.

The Mayor of Oslo started off with a little potted history of the tree... about how we saved their butts during the war... and how grateful they are, etc., blah blah blah, but then he went off on a not-very-Christmassy political tangent about how Norway supplies a large part of the UK's power, and what a great trading partner they are... I think he was trying to drum up a bit of overseas business. But I suppose he does give us a free Christmas tree every year, so you can't begrudge him that.

And then he switched it on and *oooh! aaah!* Christmas has come to London at last. What a pretty tree. It's got a wavy line of white lights running up and down the length of it, with a whopping great star on top -- about the same size as the sun. It really is very pretty. It certainly produced plenty of ooohs and aaahs from the kids in the crowd. Then we had the national anthems playing from the Sally Army band, and that was it. The guests went off to warm their cockles and the crowd went home to dry out their socks. But if you stuck around for a little while longer then you were treated to a traditional carol sing-song with a conductor waving his hands about to urge them on. Very festive. Unfortunately it was also bloody cold so I left them to it. Happy Christmas!

Places Further Afield

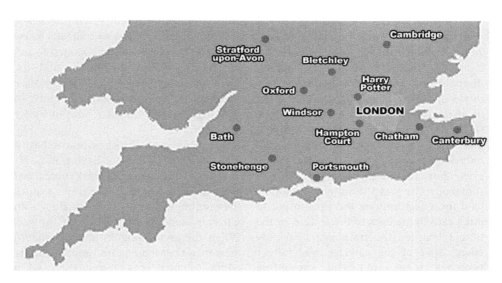

Bath

JOURNEY 1½ hour train from Paddington (zone 1) to Bath Spa (outside zones) **ADDRESS** Roman Baths: Stall Street -- Abbey: 12 Kingston Buildings -- Sightseeing bus: High Street (by Bath Abbey) **PRICE** Baths: Adult £15 (£15.50 in Jul-Aug); Senior (over-65) £13.25; Child (6-16) £9.50; Infant (under-6) free; Family (2 ad+up to 4 ch) £44 -- Abbey: £2.50 donation -- Bus: Adult £14; Senior (over-60) £11.50; Child (5-15) £8.50; Infant (under-5) free; Family (up to 2 ad+3 ch) £39 **OPEN** Baths: 9.30 AM to 6 PM (Jan-Feb); 9 AM to 6 PM (Mar-Jun); 9 AM to 10 PM (Jul-Aug); 9 AM to 6 PM (Sep-Oct); 9.30 AM to 6 PM (Nov-Dec); Last entry 1 hour before closing -- Abbey: 9.30 AM to 5.30 PM (Mon); 9 AM to 5.30 PM (Tue-Fri); 9 AM to 6 PM (Sat); 1 PM to 2.30 PM, and 4.30 PM to 5.30 PM (Sun); Last entry 15 mins before closing -- Bus: Every 30 mins from 10 AM to 3.30 PM (Jan-Feb); Every 20 mins from 10 AM to 5 PM (Mar, Dec); Every 15 mins from 9.30 AM to 5.30 PM (Apr-May, Oct-Nov); Every 6-12 mins from 10 AM to 5 PM (Jun-Sep) **WEB** Baths: romanbaths.co.uk -- Abbey: bath abbey.org -- Bus: city-sightseeing.com/tours/united-kingdom/bath.htm **TEL** Baths: 0122 547 7785 -- Abbey: 0122 542 2462 -- Sightseeing bus: 0122 533 0444 **TIME REQUIRED** 8-9 hours (including travel time from London)

Easy to get to? ★☆☆ Good for kids? ★★☆ Value for money? ★★☆ Worth a visit? ★★★

I'm sitting in Paddington station waiting for the train to Bath. Apparently I went there when I was a little kid but I can't remember a thing about it. (I can't even remember what I did last week.) So this is like the first time for me.

The train journey wasn't the greatest. I wish they would bring back British Rail. At least with British Rail you already knew it was useless, so you weren't disappointed; but they promised me two things on this train and I got neither. First of all I booked a window seat but they stuck me next to a partition (that big plastic strut between two windows) so the only way of looking out was with X-ray eyes. But that didn't matter because somebody else was sitting in it anyway! I paid for a seat number but they forgot to put a card in the back of the seat, so by the time I boarded the train it was already taken. Half of the carriage was full of people arguing about who was sitting where. Nobody wants to move once they are settled, do they -- so you are stuffed. *Ah well...* such is life. What do you expect for a seventy quid ticket? (I'm serious! That is how much it costs for a return ticket to Bath.)

I ended up sitting next to a woman doing her makeup. She was at it the whole way from London to Bath applying about ten different coats like she was waterproofing an exterior wall. First of all came the brush and blusher powder, then some shiny stuff and a dab on her eyes, then under her eyes then her eyebrows then her lips then her hair then a touch up on her face again... *Jesus Christ* I'm glad I'm not a woman! By the time she had finished she looked exactly the same as when she started, except her skin was five inches thicker.

The first thing you notice when you pull into Bath are the pretty sandstone-coloured houses perched precariously on the side of a hill. That's the first thing that I liked about Bath -- the colour of it. It looks like the colour of a beach on a rainy day.

I did a bit of research beforehand (always handy when you're visiting a new town for the first time) so I already knew of at least three places that I wanted to see: the Roman Baths, the Abbey and the Royal Crescent. Happily the first two are right next-door to each other anyway, so you might as well do them both one after the other.

The Romans really knew how to have a bath. Can you imagine us having an hour-long soak before going to work these days? We wouldn't have time! For us it's a quick five-minute shower and out the door with our shirt hanging out to run for the bus. When the archaeologists dig up modern man in a thousand years time all they're going to find is a toothbrush and a stainless steel sink. No murals or mosaics for them. Just a tatty bit of lino and a plastic bog brush with the bristles missing. The Romans had cold rooms, warm rooms, hot rooms, dip pools, massage tables... they really went nuts with it. But I suppose when you live in an age without computers and TV what else are you going to do? It's either that or throw some Christians to the lions.

As soon as you've handed over the entrance money and picked up your audio-guide you head straight towards the main bath, looking down at the pea green water. That's where I am right now, peering down at the pool (writing this). I can see a few fake Roman soldiers down there dressed up in their centurion togs, and some six-foot statues of Roman emperors balancing on the balcony. It looks quite impressive standing up here on the balcony, with the Abbey towering up behind. But then you start listening to the audio guide and discover that a lot of it is modern. Everything above ground level seems to have been built by the

Victorians (including those brown sandstone columns around the edge). The Roman stuff is basically just the plunge pool itself and some stubs of wall up to about six feet in height. You'd never know that by looking at it though -- it still looks very old and I almost wish they hadn't told me the truth!

After that you head down into their little museum space which is full of old coins and busted bits of brick and bones -- the usual kind of fare that you'd expect to find in a museum. Further on are the remains of a room that reminded me a lot of the Billingsgate Bath House in Lower Thames Street (read my review earlier in the book) -- it's a sizeable area of stubby stone walls, Roman drains and pavement that you can examine from the walkway suspended above the floor. It's quite atmospheric down there in the dark.

Then you descend down another level... down to the thermal spring itself. The bubbling water is spewing out of a stone arch and splashing over the orange rocks, with the steam bubbling up into a mist. I'm not sure I'd want to have a bath in it -- it still seems quite powerful even now, two thousand years after the Romans first dipped their toes in it.

They've also got the remains of various plunge pools, warm rooms (tepidarium) and hot rooms (caldarium) -- they really do have it all in this place: the ruins are huge. After that you can walk around the main bath at ground level (and have a chat with that Roman soldier). If you were quick enough then you could probably strip off your clothes and jump in for a swim whilst he wasn't looking, but I have a steadfast rule in life: I never jump into anything that is bright green -- and this water is bright green.

Don't forget to seek out the little drinking fountain at the end of the tour (where you hand in the audio-guide), because you can take a sip from the miracle spring. The Romans believed that one sip from these waters and you'd be cured of all ills... so obviously I had a taste. It tasted a bit weird to me but I'm going to live forever now so I don't care. *I am immortal!* It reminded me of that scene at the end of *Indiana Jones and The Last Crusade* when he splashed some holy water over Sean Connery.

Next up... Bath Abbey, which is next-door to the Roman ruins. You have to donate a few quid to get inside but it's well worth it. I'm a sucker for a stained glass window and this place has got some of the best I've ever seen. Most of the cathedrals that I've been to have just got one at either end and a few piddly ones in the middle, but practically every window in here is a solid slice of rainbow. They really are impressive. The ceiling towers up above the boundaries of the sky. You could probably trap the sun and the moon and the stars underneath. I'm still ranking Westminster Abbey and Brompton Oratory as my all-time favourite religious buildings, but this one definitely comes an honourable third. God certainly does have some nice holiday homes.

If you fancy a bit of exercise then you can climb up the Abbey tower and look out across the whole of Bath; but unfortunately my knees are playing up today so I had to give it a miss (there's no lift).

After that... time for lunch and a gentle stroll around town. The town is surprisingly big if you try and do it all in one day, but I think a couple of hours should be plenty for most people. Pretty much all of the streets around the Roman Baths and Abbey are worth a look, and especially behind the Abbey near the Parade Gardens. They've got an impressive bridge across a thundering weir that is quite a nice sight -- the

Pulteney Bridge. If you are feeling particularly energetic then take a long walk up Great Pulteney Street to the Holburne Museum. Even if you can't be bothered to walk the entire length then it's still worth having a quick look from the beginning -- you can see the museum standing proud way off in the distance.

Now head past Queen Square to The Circus. This place will knock your socks off -- it's a big round ring of Georgian houses encompassing a green with two huge trees in the middle, and I thought it was more impressive than the next bit... which is the famous bit that everyone comes to see: the Royal Crescent.

Whenever you see a picture of Bath on the telly the chances are they'll show you a picture of the Crescent. It is Bath's equivalent of Big Ben -- that big semi-circle of houses on top of a hill. But it's not until you actually get up close that you realise they are actually quite grotty -- I'm serious! I don't mean grotty in a rundown council house kind-of way. They probably still cost a bazillion quid to live in. But they don't seem to be making much of an effort to keep them Georgian. Half of the front doors are bright white and modern. They've all got modern-looking windows too. And if you want a real shock then head round to the back and view them from behind. The phrase "back end of a bus" comes to mind. They remind me of those photographs of models without their makeup on. When you see the Crescent on the telly it's all airbrushed with a bright blue sky, but when you walk down the street you can see the pimples.

If you want to fill up a bit more time then check out the museum at No.1 (the house on the far end). They've decorated it with Georgian-era furniture to give you an idea of what it must have been like in its hey-day. But boy-oh-boy do they need to get rid of the guides! They have a different person lurking in each room and every time you enter one you have to stand there for five minutes and listen to a little monologue. You end up just standing there politely smiling whilst they do their bit. It wouldn't be so bad if it was all in-situ history, but it's just stuff that they've shipped in from other houses, so it's not even original to the house. Ten rooms later you are finally allowed to leave (if you are still awake).

Another thing that you might be interested in is the Jane Austin museum, but that's more for the girlies -- I gave that a miss. Apparently she used to live in Bath. There are also a few bits and bobs about Charles Dickens and Mary Shelley, because they lived in Bath as well.

I decided to fill up my final hour with a sightseeing bus around the city (you can catch it outside the Abbey). It was fourteen quid a go and lasted for just under an hour, and I thought it was well worth doing. You get to see all of the best-looking buildings again, and hear a lot of interesting history without having to wear out your shoes.

If you like Roman archaeology then try the the Billingsgate Roman House, Museum of London and Guildhall Art Gallery.

Bletchley Park

JOURNEY 35-50 min train from Euston (zone 1) to Bletchley (outside zones) **ADDRESS** Bletchley Park, Milton Keynes **PRICE** Adult £16.75; Senior (over-60) £14.75; Child (12-16)

Places Further Afield | 325

£10; Child (under-12) free; Family (2 ad+2 ch) £38.50 **OPEN** 9.30 AM to 5 PM (Mon-Sun, Mar-Oct); 9.30 AM to 4 PM (Mon-Sun, Nov-Feb); Last entry 1 hour before closing **WEB** bletchleypark.org.uk **TEL** 0190 864 0404 **TIME REQUIRED** 4-4½ hours (including travel time from London)

Easy to get to? ★★☆ Good for kids? ★☆☆
Value for money? ★★★ Worth a visit? ★★★

Bletchley Park is where they cracked all of the Enigma codes during World War II. Unfortunately I can't tell you anything about it because it's a top-secret code breaking facility, and they would kill me if I told you where it was. They make you sign the Official Secrets Act before you go inside, and then wipe your brain of all memories when you come out (seriously).

I can't even remember who I am now.

Ha ha... *only joking;* it's a big tourist attraction now so you don't have to worry -- they even let the Germans in. Seventy years ago they would have had to slip in under cover of darkness. Now they get a guidebook and a map.

If you know anything about Bletchley before you arrive then you will probably walk up to the front door expecting to see that old brown-brick mansion. But what you actually see is a load of modern-looking flat buildings -- a bit like an industrial business park. The first few rooms are very bland looking... but stick with it, because they contain a lot of interesting introductory material. You get a good dip into what they achieved here, and can see some old black-and-white photos of how the rooms used to look before the tourists turned up. It looks very cold and draughty filled with computer banks and messy desks. There are lots of handwritten notes and computer ticker tapes too, covered in pencil scrawl and workings out, and papers stamped with "Top Secret" in big red letters. There are even a few letters from Churchill himself, enquiring about the Enigma intercepts.

There is lots and lots and lots, and lots (and lots) of information about how the machines were captured, how they were finally cracked, and which military operations directly benefited from their work. One minute you are looking at a string of random letters and numbers, and the next minute you are looking at troop movements and tank formations in northern France. Imagine how exciting it must have been to read that stuff inching out of the machine! And it's not all about the Germans either: you've got plenty of Japanese and Russian stuff too, biographies of our spies, and even a little bit about Montgomery's double, and how we used him to trick the Italians. In fact... there is more stuff about spy work and code breaking on display at Bletchley, than there is about the entirety of World War II in the Imperial War Museum (and that is *not* an exaggeration).

I've only ever seen one Enigma machine in real-life (at the Science Museum), but they've got a whole cabinet-full in here. If you were under the impression that we only stole one then prepare to get a shock! They practically take one to bits and do an autopsy on it, displaying all of the wiring diagrams and schematics, showing how the keyboard worked the wheels -- it's very detailed stuff.

They provide a lot of information about Colossus as well -- the world's very first large-scale computer (an achievement later claimed by the Yanks, but actually invented by us in secret).

After that comes a little exhibition about the code breaking/computer/maths genius Alan Turing, showing how poorly he was treated by the Government. If you explore all of the huts outside then you will eventually come across his office, complete with a messy desk overflowing with paperwork and pens.

The huts outside are well worth exploring because that's where most of the important work was done. A lot of them have been redecorated to look exactly how they were during the war, with fag packets in the bin and hats and coats roughly stuffed on the hook. They project some actors onto the walls and play some animated chatter and typewriter clacks out of the speakers as well, to bring the place alive a bit. It reminded me of the Churchill War Rooms, because both places are like a time capsule. But the big difference is that the War Rooms were sealed up tight at the end of the war, so everything you see in there today is exactly as they left it, whereas Bletchley is more of a reconstruction.

The rest of the grounds reminded me of a *Boy's Own Adventure*. You can go round the back of the house, for example, and see the gate and sentry box where the dispatch riders roared in to race the intercepts up and down the country. You can have a nose around the garages too, filled with period bikes and vintage cars. They've even got a few cycle sheds filled with rusty old pushbikes with bells and baskets on.

It's not until you get halfway round the campus that you'll finally see the pretty lake and famous brown brick mansion beyond. The mansion is probably the least interesting of all the buildings, which is a bit weird. There's not a lot to look at inside -- just a few function rooms laid out with tables and chairs. Two of the rooms still contain artefacts though, including a very nice-looking library, and there's a little bookshop in there too: so make sure you have a good look around.

So is Bletchley Worth a visit? I think so. But it all depends on whether you like the war. This place is all about the information boards. If you can't be bothered to read those then it's hardly worth going.

As for the town centre... do yourself a favour and give it a wide berth. There's absolutely nothing to see in the town of Bletchley itself. It's just a load of boarded-up windows and billboards. It's all concrete shops and bin bags on the pavement. But now that I come to think of it... it was probably the perfect place to try and hide a top-secret facility, because no one is going to bother bombing Bletchley -- it looks like it's been bombed already!

If you're interested in World War II then try the Churchill War Rooms, RAF Museum and HMS Belfast.

Cambridge

JOURNEY 50-80 min train from King's Cross or Liverpool Street (both zone 1) to Cambridge (outside zones) **ADDRESS** Corpus Christi: King's Parade -- Fitzwilliam Museum: Trumpington Street -- King's: King's Parade -- Queen's: Silver Street -- Sedgwick Museum: Downing Street -- Sightseeing bus: Bus stops all over town -- St. John's: St. John's Street -- Trinity: Trinity Street **PRICE** Corpus Christi: Free -- Fitzwilliam Museum: Free -- King's: Adult £8; Senior £5.50; Child (12-16) £5.50; Child (under-12) free -- Queen's: Adult £3; Child (10-16) £3; Child (under-10) free -- Sedgwick Museum: Free -- Bus: Adult £14.50; Senior (over-60) £11.50; Child (5-15) £8.50; Infant (under-5) free; Family (up to 2 ad+3 ch) £36 -- St. John's: Adult £7.50; Senior £5; Child (12-16)

Places Further Afield | 327

£5; Child (under-12) free -- Trinity: Adult £2; Child £1 **OPEN** Corpus Christi: Mon-Sun -- Fitzwilliam Museum: Closed (Mon); 10 AM to 5 PM (Tue-Sat); 12 noon to 5 PM (Sun) -- King's: 9.30 AM to 3.30 PM (Mon-Fri, mid Apr-Jun, Oct-Nov); 9.30 AM to 3.15 PM (Sat, mid Apr-Jun, Oct-Nov); 1.15 PM to 2.30 PM (Sun, mid Apr-Jun, Oct-Nov); 9.30 AM to 4.30 PM (Mon-Sun, Dec-mid Apr, Jul-Sep); Last entry 30 mins before closing -- Queen's: 10 AM to 4.30 PM (Mon-Sun, first half of Apr, Jul-Sep); Closed (2nd half of Apr-Jun); 10 AM to 4 PM (Mon-Sun, Oct-Mar) -- Sedgwick Museum: 10 AM to 1 PM, and 2 PM to 5 PM (Mon-Fri); 10 AM to 4 PM (Sat); Closed (Sun) -- Bus: Every 20 mins from 10 AM to 5 PM (Mon-Sun, mid Mar-Sep); Every 40 mins from 10 AM to 3.30 PM (Mon-Sun, Oct-mid Mar) -- St. John's: 10 AM to 5 PM (Mon-Sun, Mar-mid May); Closed (mid May-mid Jun); 10 AM to 5 PM (Mon-Sun, mid Jun-Oct); 10 AM to 3.30 PM (Mon-Sun, Nov-Feb) -- Trinity: 10 AM to 4.30 PM (Mon-Sun) **WEB** Corpus Christi: corpus.cam.ac.uk -- Fitzwilliam Museum: fitzmuseum.cam.ac.uk -- King's: kings.cam.ac.uk -- Queen's: queens.cam.ac.uk -- Sedgwick Museum: sedgwickmuseum.org -- Bus: city-sightseeing.com/tours/united-kingdom/cambridge.htm -- St. John's: joh.cam.ac.uk -- Trinity College: trin.cam.ac.uk **TEL** Corpus Christi: 0122 333 8000 -- Fitzwilliam Museum: 0122 333 2900 -- King's: 0122 333 1212 -- Queen's: 0122 333 5511 -- Sedgwick Museum: 0122 333 3456 -- Bus: 0122 343 3250 -- St. John's: 0122 333 8600 -- Trinity: 0122 333 8400 **TIME REQUIRED** 9-10½ hours (including travel time from London)

Easy to get to? ★☆☆ Good for kids? ★☆☆ Value for money? ★★★ Worth a visit? ★★★

In this country you either cheer for Oxford or you cheer for Cambridge -- it's a bit like loving The Beatles or the Stones. When the University Boat Race comes on we are all secretly hoping that the other side will sink (or is that just me?). I'm actually not that fussed, to be honest. I wasn't much of an academic at school so the only way that I was coming here was on a day-trip on the train.

Your first view of Cambridge when you pull into the station will be disappointing, to say the least... it's the same bland flats and concrete office blocks as everywhere else. What you need to do is escape from the station as quickly as you can and head up Station Road and then Hills Road... towards that big church steeple you can see in the distance. That's the church of Our Lady & English Martyrs -- the first decent building in Cambridge. Then take a left down Lensfield Road and right when you get to Trumpington Street.

You'll have been walking for a good 15-20 minutes by this point, but don't worry because things will start to pretty up considerably now. Once you pass the Fitzwilliam Museum (you can't miss it -- it looks like the British Museum) then you'll be in the touristy part of Cambridge. I'm going to save this museum for the end because it's on the way back to the station.

A visit to Cambridge is all about the colleges and the architecture -- that's why you've come here. You need to step inside all of the colleges and have a good nose around, otherwise there's no point coming. That's what most of your day is going to be from this point on -- having a look around the colleges. And the road you're on right now is the one you have to remember -- Trumpington Street. It changes its name as you go along (to King's Parade and Trinity Street), but you'll be following the line of it for the rest of the day. It's basically impossible to get lost -- just keep coming back to this road and make your way up to the end. The colleges are dotted along either side of it, and whilst they might seem out of bounds to the public, they do actually let you inside most of them for free (sometimes you have to pay a few quid). You won't be allowed to enter any of the university buildings though (apart from an occasional chapel), so stick with the open courtyards and paths around the greens -- don't go charging through all of the doors for chrissakes because you'll end up in a bit of bother.

The first college on the left is called Peterhouse. It's not the best in town but it's worth a quick five minutes to get you in the mood. They've got a nice little green underneath the arch, and some pretty little lampposts and flower boxes hanging off the windows.

Pembroke is next, and it's a beauty inside -- but you'll have to brave it through the arch because it does look a bit intimidating. Poke your nose in far enough to see the building in the far corner with the grey spire and brown brickwork. They've got a little chapel too.

Now take a detour down Silver Street and find the entrance to Queen's College. You have to pay a few quid to get into this one but I think it's worth it. This is the first college that will really knock your socks off. It's 550 years old and they've got some very nice timber-framed Tudor buildings inside -- the proper wonky ones with sloping walls. You can peek inside their Old Hall as well, which dates back to the 1450s.

If you continue walking down Silver Street to the river then you can see the famous Mathematical Bridge (you will already have walked over it if you paid the entrance fee into Queen's). There's a myth that Isaac Newton designed this, but he didn't -- it's just a plain old wooden bridge. If you're feeling adventurous then you can pick up a punt from here if you like, and have a lazy float along the river (they have people to do the actual punting, so you don't have to steer them yourself). I witnessed about three crashes whilst I was standing there watching -- no joke! They don't seem to mind nudging the others to clear them out of the way, so it's a good job those boats are flat and wide otherwise they would have tipped the poor tourists into the drink.

Now head back out into Trumpington Street because the next college is a blinder -- Corpus Christi. You have to pay a few quid to enter this one as well, but you'll get to see a couple of the courts, a tiny little courtyard garden and the inside of their chapel. It was whilst I was walking around this place that I realised how young the students are -- I guess I'm getting old. I had a picture in my head of Cambridge being full of bespectacled Alan Turing-type geniuses, tall and lanky and weighed down by a satchel full of papers, but of course it's nothing like that at all -- it's all twenty-year-old kids fresh out of secondary school, bouncing around with chunky headphones and marijuana t-shirts. Twenty years from now these kids will probably be running the country -- god help us!

If you thought that Corpus Christi was nice then wait until you get to King's College further along. The sixty minutes that you spent snoozing on the train will have been worth it as soon as you clap eyes on the exterior of this place. This is the most expensive college to enter but it's worth it for the grounds alone. You can also have a wander across the parkland at the back and see them punting on the river. The only building that you are allowed to enter is the famous King's College Chapel, which is home to the famous choir of angelic-looking schoolboys who sing Christmas carols at the Royal Albert Hall (they are probably chain-smoking hoodlums in real life). Imagine twenty kids who look like Aled Jones, with names like Cuthbert, Tarquin and Hugh, all wearing white ruffs and singing higher than a baby's whistle -- that's the King's College Choir.

You're supposed to say that you like the interior but I guess I must be spoilt, because it just seemed like a big empty box to me. I genuinely loved the outside, but the inside was a bit of a letdown. If you unwrap a present this big then you expect to see something fantastic inside, but it's the sheer size alone that impresses (and the vaulted roof too, if you can bend your neck high enough). There are no columns or statues or tombs or interesting side chapels to focus on, and the stained glass windows are too bright and high up to provide a light show. It hasn't even got a proper altar -- just a plain wooden table at the far end. I would describe it as looking like the shell of Westminster Abbey with all the columns and decorations taken out. Sorry God -- but I am not impressed at all. I'll stick with Westminster Abbey thank you very much. I must be the only tourist in town who was disappointed by the inside of King's.

The big church opposite King's College is St Mary's, which looks quite promising from the outside, but once again it is decidedly average inside (sorry God -- you're not having much luck today!). But you still need to go in there if only to climb up the tower. If you stump up a few quid you can climb up the windy stone stairs to the platform at the top. It's a bit of a climb though -- and I'm being serious. There are a couple of places to sit down and have a rest on the way up, but it's still a heart-thumping workout. Assuming that you don't die on the way up you'll be treated to a fantastic view over Cambridge. You can see right down onto King's College and Clare's College next-door, and all the way up to Trinity College and beyond. It really is a great view and it's definitely worth half-killing yourself up the stairs. (And it's just as scary coming down.)

The next big college to visit is Trinity's, which has a gatehouse very reminiscent of the one at Canterbury. You have to pay a few quid to get inside this one too, but the interior courtyard is worth stumping up a few bob. This was the only chapel I saw all day that actually had some decent statuary inside, with marble works of Cambridge's favourite sons -- Newton, Macaulay, Tennyson and Bacon. The altar is quite nice too, but they've roped it off for the devoted (club members only).

St. John's is another nice college to visit. This one has a very generous selection of courtyards and a chapel to nose around, some of which remind me a little bit of Hampton Court. Unfortunately they've also decided to stain one of the courtyards with a truly horrendous piece of modern architecture. Why do they do that? It's like painting a boil on the Mona Lisa's nose. Go and have a look at the Fisher Building and the Cripps building behind the back of New Court... and tell me that's not the most horrendous piece of architecture you've ever seen in your life. Apparently that building won a lot of prizes (that's what they tell you in the guide). Presumably they were booby prizes. Luckily there's a lovely old bridge just before it to lighten the mood -- the Bridge of Sighs. Oxford built a bridge like this too, but I think Cambridge has won this contest hands down.

Carry on walking down the road until you get to the Round Church. This is a poor man's version of Temple Church in London, and is definitely not worth the entrance fee -- sorry God. In fact, when I get up to heaven I'm going to ask him for my £2.50 back.

The only other college that you might want to visit is Christ's -- but only because of who is associated with it: Margaret Beaufort (the mother-in-law from hell). It's got a nice little green and a tiny chapel inside, but nothing that will knock your socks off.

So that's about it for the colleges... all we've got left to do now is head back to the Fitzwilliam Museum on our way back to the train station. You might want to have a little stroll around the side streets before you do, because there is plenty of old architecture around town (it's everywhere!). The actual city centre itself is a bit bland (where all the high street shops are), but you can still find some interesting things down most of the streets.

You might like to pick up one of those city bus tours as well, which will fill in the history of Cambridge and show you what you've missed. There are bus stops all over the city and it takes about 1 hour 20 minutes from start to finish, and I think it's worth doing.

Now... you're probably wondering what the Fitzwilliam Museum is like, and I would love to tell you but the damn place is shut! It seems that it doesn't open on Mondays so I am stuck outside the front door. I've tried banging on it and kicking it but there is no answer -- sorry about that. It's probably a load of rubbish anyway. I will make up for my error by visiting the Sedgwick Museum of Earth Sciences instead... which turned out to be about as interesting as it sounds. Imagine the Natural History Museum without any of the good stuff. It's just endless cases of shells and stones and tiny bits of bone embedded in the rock. They've got some fossilised leaves and rocks of coral as well -- flints, axe-heads, crystals, minerals and meteorites. There are thousands of these things in dusty wooden cabinets. It's okay if you've already got an interest, I suppose. But don't take your kids there or you'll have to carry them out fast asleep in your arms.

So here comes the million-dollar question: is Cambridge Worth a visit?

Yes, I think so. But it's all about the architecture. If you can't be bothered to walk from college to college and check out the buildings then it's hardly worth going. And all you're really going to see inside are some courtyards and an occasional chapel (and the huge one at King's College), but the town doesn't seem to have the variety of attractions that Oxford does. So if you've only got time for one then I'd definitely pick Oxford (or even Bath).

If you enjoy Cambridge then you'll probably also like Oxford and Bath.

Canterbury

JOURNEY 1-2 hour train from Charing Cross, St. Pancras or Victoria (all zone 1) to Canterbury West (outside zones) **ADDRESS** Cathedral: The Precincts -- Canterbury Tales: St. Margaret's Street **PRICE** Cathedral: Adult £10.50; Senior £9.50; Child (under-18) £7; Family (2 ad+up to 3 ch) £28.50, or £20.50 with 1 ad+2 ch -- Canterbury Tales: Adult £8.95; Senior £7.95; Child (5-15) £6.95; Infant (under-5) free; Family (2 ad+2 ch) £27.75 **OPEN** Cathedral: 9 AM to 5.30 PM (Mon-Sat, summer); 12.30 PM to 2.30 PM (Sun, summer); 9 AM to 5 PM (Mon-Sat, winter); 12.30 PM to 2.30 PM (Sun, winter); Last entry 30 mins before closing -- Canterbury Tales: 10 AM to 4.30 PM (Mon-Sun, Nov-Feb); 10 AM to 5 PM (Mon-Sun, Mar-Jun, Sep-Oct); 9.30 AM to 5 PM (Mon-Sun, Jul-Aug) **WEB** Cathedral: canterbury-cathedral.org -- Canterbury Tales:

canterburytales.org.uk **TEL** Cathedral: 0122 776 2862 -- Canterbury Tales: 0122 747 9227
TIME REQUIRED 6-8 hours (including travel time from London)

Easy to get to? ★☆☆ Good for kids? ★☆☆
Value for money? ★★☆ Worth a visit? ★★★

Canterbury is a long way from London, but it's a very pretty train ride. Most of it is through fields and distant hills, past brown-brick country stations with names like Sevenoaks, Pluckley and Wye. If you want to sit back and enjoy a bit of English countryside then this is the route to do it.

The sun is out today as well. Normally it is raining when I do these long trips, but she's in a good mood today. She's brushed her bright blue hair too -- there's not a cloud in the sky. Everyone seems to be in a good mood today, *even me*. That's because I'm off to see where Thomas Becket got murdered. Nothing cheers me up quicker than a murder scene -- that's the kind of guy I am. I know he's supposed to be a religious martyr, but I'm a royalist through and through so I'm siding with the king. Becket was a pain in the butt and he deserved a knock on the head. (Probably not with a sword though.)

Before you head towards the cathedral you should definitely allow yourself a couple of hours to walk around the town because it's a really pretty place; full of old houses with crooked wooden walls, cobbled streets and crumbling stumps of stone. And it's small enough to walk around as well: you can literally do the whole thing in two hours flat.

Check out the ruined Norman castle on the western edge. It's bordered by a busy road and modern houses nowadays, which is a bit unfortunate, but once you step inside the quiet walls you can block out the traffic noise and sit and wonder what it must have been like. It's just an outer shell now with some birds roosting in the window arches, and shrubs and weeds poking out the bricks, but you get a real good feeling sitting inside that spooky place. See if you can find the spiral staircase that takes you up to the ruined first floor window.

The main road runs in a straight line from the West Gate, down St. Peter's Street, and past the High Street and St. George's Street. If you check out all the side streets once you cross over the canal, then you will come across some really picturesque scenes. There are lots of Tudor-style houses with black-beam timbers and whitewashed walls, and rickety old pubs with overhanging arches. There are a few stone chapels with flints on the front too, and people punting and larking about on the river. This is how *all* of England should be -- this is England from a picture postcard, before the builders got their hands on it.

The best moment will come when you round a corner and find yourself staring at the cathedral gatehouse (directly opposite the entrance to St. Margaret's Street). It's the most fantastic looking thing you'll see all day, standing in a pretty little square with open-air cafe tables. It is wonderfully ornate and obviously old, and covered in heraldic shields and statuary, and it sets the scene perfectly for what you'll find inside.

I must admit that the cathedral wasn't as large as I was expecting (nothing ever is), but inside it opens up like a huge cavernous tube. It is long and narrow and amazingly tall. They could do with sticking a few curtains up on the windows though, because it's a bit too bright for my tastes. I like my churches to be dark and gloomy (and even a bit spooky), but this one is bright brown.

Halfway up the aisle is the place where Thomas Becket was bludgeoned to death. And whilst it is certainly interesting to look at, I think they've blundered by hanging a bloody great big modern art piece on top. It looks like three jagged swords dripping with blood -- like something you'd see in a B-movie poster. Is that really necessary? They should have just stuck with a simple rack of candles and left you to ponder the scene.

I am staring at it right now, as I'm writing this: the spot where Tom got butchered. I am trying to imagine the knights' footsteps stamping up the nave and Tommy's screams as they kicked his head in, but it's not easy with fifty-thousand people all crowding around the crime scene. They should rope it off with yellow police tape and get the forensics down here. Get Gil Grissom down here, or Columbo, or that that perm-haired old granny (what was her name again?) -- they'll work out who did it.

And where was God when Tommy needed him, huh? You would have thought that he might have intervened when the Archbishop of Canterbury was getting set upon by violent murderers, but no -- *not interested*. He just sat back and watched whilst his main man in England got his throat slit. Thanks God. Thanks a bunch! I wonder how that conversation went when Beckett got up to the Pearly Gates. Heaven must have heard a few new words that day.

After the central screen comes the real heart of the church: the Quire and that altar. To the right of those is a treasure that you might walk past if you're not paying attention: a real piece of armour worn by the Black Prince -- the guy who beat the French at the Battle of Crécy (shortly before Agincourt). If you know your medieval history then you'll know that he was quite a cool dude: the Rambo of his day. Next to that are two of the most vibrant and colourful stained-glass windows that I have ever seen in my life. I wish you plenty of sunshine when you come, because when those windows are backlit by the sun you'll be treated to a picture show.

If you carry on around to the end then you'll see a rather poignant candle sitting solitary on the floor. This was where the original shrine to Thomas Becket stood, before it was pulled down on the orders of Henry VIII. It's amazing to think that this was already hundreds of years old before Henry kicked it in 450 years ago.

My favourite part of the cathedral is the crypt downstairs, because they've turned the light level down a few notches. You can't really appreciate the candles upstairs because it's too bright, but down here they glow gold. If I was going to do some praying then this is where I would do it... where no one can see me. I suppose I could do some praying while I'm here. What's the harm? But I'm not in the slightest bit religious though, so I don't know what to do...

1) Kneel down (I'm not doing that with my dodgy knees)

2) Put your hands together into a triangle shape

3) Mind meld with the Almighty (that's the difficult bit). Has anyone ever actually got through to the big fella and had a chat? I doubt it.

I'm not praying for world peace -- sod that. I'm praying for rain. Let's keep it nice and simple seeing as it's my first prayer. Let's see if he can drum up a thunderstorm on a sunny day, and then maybe I'll start believing in him. I don't care if he *did* create the entire universe in one week: unless it rains in the next five minutes I'm not buying it.

I probably shouldn't be saying all of this down here... just in case he is listening.

So then... is Canterbury Worth a visit? ...hmm. As much as I enjoyed it (and I did enjoy it), I'm not sure that I'd want to spend a whole day of my holiday on it. The town certainly is pretty, and the cathedral is definitely worth seeing, but it's nothing compared to Westminster Abbey or St. Paul's Cathedral. So if you want to see something religious on your holiday then I'd stick with one of those.

Chatham Dockyard

JOURNEY 1¼ hour train from Victoria or Charing Cross (both zone 1) to Chatham (outside zones), and a 30 min walk (or the 140 or 141 bus) **ADDRESS** The Historic Dockyard, Chatham **PRICE** Adult £19; Senior £16.50; Child (5-15) £11.50; Infant (under-5) free; Family (2 ad+2 ch, or 1 ad+3 ch) £49.40 **OPEN** Closed (Dec-mid Feb); 10 AM to 4 PM (Mon-Sun, mid Feb-Mar); 10 AM to 6 PM (Mon-Sun, Apr-Oct); 10 AM to 4 PM (Mon-Sun, Nov) **WEB** thedockyard.co.uk **TEL** 0163 482 3800 **TIME REQUIRED** 6-7 hours (including travel time from London)

Easy to get to? ☆☆☆ Good for kids? ★★☆
Value for money? ★★☆ Worth a visit? ★★☆

I'm sitting in Charing Cross station waiting for the choo-choo train to Chatham. It's a bit of a trek from London -- 1¼ hours -- but they've got something worth seeing at the other end, because that's where you'll find the old historic dockyards where they built the wooden ships from the days of Oliver Cromwell right up to the Battle of Trafalgar and beyond. They didn't shut it down until the 1980s, so they even built a few battleships and submarines.

I hope the weather cheers up a bit, because at the moment it's in a worse mood than me. Our grey train is rumbling along with grey faces staring out of grubby windows, all struggling to stay awake (it is 7.30 AM). Looking around my carriage I can see lots of half-closed eyes and lolling mouths, and heads nodding and knocking on the window as the train inches down the tracks. Some people are flicking through their paperwork, whilst others play with their noses and wonder whether they should catch up on a bit of work before they get to work, but then deciding... *nah*... can't be arsed. We'll just sit here and have a snooze instead. Which is what I am going to do...

I nearly didn't bother getting off the train when I woke up in Chatham because we were slogging through a torrential downpour... and I mean torrential. Real end of the world kind of stuff. There was enough water coming out of the sky to sink the sea. No wonder they chose to site the naval dockyards here: you can't float a boat without water.

If you get caught in the rain then let me give you a piece of advice to save you some time: don't bother visiting the town for chrissakes, because it's rubbish. I don't know if it got flattened during World War II, but I was expecting Chatham to be an old historic town full of Tudor timber fronts, hanging bags of flowers and pretty cobbled streets. Well, it's not like that at all -- it's a modern concrete place full of tatty shops and office blocks. It's the kind of place where the Pound Shops sell stuff for 50p. The shopping centre is full of thrift stores and clearance sales, and everyone seems to be sporting a tracksuit, a tattoo or a limp.

Things get better as you approach the Medway (the stretch of the Thames where the docks are located). The river really starts to widen out at this point as it heads towards the sea, so you've got broad flats of mud and sand, and seagulls squawking and squealing around the industrial chimneys and cranes. After half-an-hour of walking I finally reached the dockyards. (It was my first time in Chatham so I decided to walk it from the station, but in hindsight it's probably better to catch the bus -- it's a long way.)

Once you step inside the docks you'll be transported back in time at the first smell of wet wood. They've still got all the old boat sheds and warehouses and the exhibits are housed inside those. The first one is called 'Hearts of Oak', and it's definitely worth seeing. It's a bit like a walk-through movie... narrators are projected onto the wooden walls and lead you from scene to scene through full-sized streets, around the docks, and into the actual room where they designed HMS Victory. You'll hear the sound of creaking planks and shot and thunder of a gun battle on board the boat -- great big booms and lightning flashes fill up the room. It is very atmospherically done and a good introduction into how they built the boats.

After that you'll head out into an open-air square and be surrounded by big ships and masts, metal cranes and anchors, brick chimneys and clock towers, and huge wooden warehouses filled with all kinds of ships. This is actually how I imagined Chatham town would be: straight from the pages of the early 18th-century. They've got a few costumed guides dotted around the place as well, dressed up as old washerwomen and sooty-faced dockhands, and even the seagulls are chipping in with a few lines of their own, bringing the sounds of the sea to the sheds. If they had a Royal Navy guy walking around taking names then I probably would have signed up for a stint there and then.

The 'No.1 Smithery' is where they keep all the naval paintings and intricate little models of boats throughout the ages. It's like a little gallery I suppose, and worth a quick look inside. I was expecting the 'RNLI Lifeboat' shed to be a bit boring, but it was actually pretty decent too. They've got some full-sized lifeboats set-up with a waxwork crew, and you can board a few of them to see what they look like inside. Even the shed itself is worth a look: it's *huge!* It's almost bigger than St. Paul's Cathedral, with a mezzanine level looking down on all the boats below.

When you get to the dry docks you'll find three big boats that you can step aboard and explore. The first one is a cold war submarine called HMS Ocelot, and they actually let you climb down the hatch and explore it (by guided tour). If you've ever seen the movie *Crimson Tide* then you'll know exactly what it's like inside: cramped. The hatches are about the same size as dinner plates, which you somehow have to swing your big feet through whilst gripping a tiny bar above (it's not easy!), and a lot of the corridors are thinner than a lollipop stick. The bed bunks are about the same size as a shoebox, and every inch of wall space is busting with pipes and dials and buttons and beams. It was at this point that I decided that I didn't want to join the navy after all. But I definitely think that it's worth coming to the docks for this one tour alone. How often do you get the chance to explore a genuine 1990s cold war submarine?

The next dry dock along has got a World War II destroyer called HMS Cavalier, and they let you explore this one all by yourself. You can poke your nose into the captain's quarters, the equipment rooms and bridge, and walk around the deck. It's nowhere near as good as HMS Belfast, but it's still definitely worth a look.

The only part of the docks that I didn't really enjoy was the 'Victorian Ropery' -- that was one hour of my life that I will never get back. If your idea of fun is listening to someone talk about rope for sixty minutes, then check it out. But by the end of the speech I was seriously thinking about stealing a piece so I could hang myself with it.

You might like HMS Belfast as well, or a trip to Portsmouth to see HMS Victory.

Chessington World of Adventures

JOURNEY 35 min train from Waterloo (zone 1) to Chessington South (zone 6) **ADDRESS** Chessington World of Adventures, Leatherhead Road, Chessington **PRICE** If bought online: Adult from £27 if dated, or £47 undated; Child (12 and over) from £27 if dated, or £51 iundated; Child (3-11) £27 if dated, or £43 undated; Infant (under 3) free -- If bought at the door: Adult £47; Child (12 and over) £51; Child (3-11) £43; Infant (under 3) free; Note: Children under 0.9m are not allowed on all rides **OPEN** During school term: 10 AM to 5 PM (Mon-Sun, mid Mar-Oct only) -- School holidays: 10 AM to 6 (Mon-Sun) -- Note: The park closes from Nov to mid-Mar, but the zoo and SeaLife Centre may open during the holidays and selected weekends (usually 10 AM to 3 PM, but 10 AM to 5 PM over Christmas) - see website for dates **WEB** chessington.com **TEL** 0871 663 4477 **TIME REQUIRED** 6-8 hours (including travel time from London)

Easy to get to? ★★☆ Good for kids? ★★★
Value for money? ★★★ Worth a visit? ★★★

The last time I went to Chessington World of Adventures it was still called Chessington Zoo -- that was thirty years ago. The most exciting ride they had back then was sitting on the donkeys, but it's more like Disneyland now. They've got rides and rollercoasters, shows and hotels, and the animals have been demoted to a sideshow.

I'm not really looking forward to the rollercoasters, by the way. I am willing to give them a go, but I am at an age now where the ground is my friend. I've had a quick look around and I can already see about twenty different ways to die. I don't mind ending my days in a theme park, but I'm not spending my last five minutes on planet Earth being whizzed around a tubular track in a plastic bat. If I'm going to die here today then it will be in the lion pit, or by being ripped up by tigers, or something like that -- *something manly*. A man shouldn't die with a smile on his face; he should die in battle, fighting and flailing in the jaws of a big cat.

Why am I talking about death already? I've only been here for five minutes! That's why I'm such a good reviewer, you see. If an attraction can break through my wall of doom and gloom, then you'll know it's worth a visit.

I've bought myself a two-day ticket because I'm not sure you can complete it all in one day. I am expecting big queues for every ride... but we'll see how it goes. You can get something called a 'Fastrack' ticket, which allows you to jump the queues, but it will make a big dent in your wallet. Check out these prices: If you want to jump the queue on every single ride then that's another seventy quid on top of your entry cost (no joke). A Fastrack ticket for each individual ride is three to six pounds, depending on the ride; this could easily drain another thirty quid from your wallet over the course of the day. It seems like a bit of a con to me, so I will take my chances with the queues. It's not a school holiday today, so it should be all right. But I can still see a lot of kids running around... why aren't the little blighters in class? They can't all have been expelled, surely? I might try and find out which school they go to so I can grass them up to the headmaster and free up some more queues.

I've decided to start off with a nice easy ride on the Monorail (the 'Safari Skyway'). Now this is my kind of ride... nice and gentle, not too high up, no loop the loops... just a nice trip around the treetops. You go over a few enclosures as well, past the gorillas and the tigers, but it only covers a quarter of the park, so it's not much use as an overview. But it's a pleasant enough way to start the day. And it's *safe* (very important). The chances of you dying on this one are very slim.

Next up is the SeaLife Centre, which is like a mini-version of the London Aquarium. They've got a lot of jellyfish and piranhas in there, and those little orange guys from *Finding Nemo,* but that's about it -- there are no sharks. But they've got a nice underwater tunnel with a sunken plane that you can walk through.

My first proper ride of the day: the 'Scorpion Express'. I remember this one from when I was a little kid (I still have nightmares about it). It used to be a runaway mine train, but they've stuck a big scorpion in the centre with flames coming out of a chimney pipe. The queue is about ten miles long around a rickety old wooden path, but thankfully it is empty this morning. It's just me and a few happy couples wondering what's coming next (death?). But it turns out that it was actually quite easy. I used to be scared stiff of this ride when I was a little kid, but I must have steeled myself as I've grown older, because I hardly even broke a sweat this time around. No tears. No screams. I didn't even wet my trousers. I'm quite proud of myself.

After that comes the 'Rattlesnake', which is basically a little tin bucket rocking and rolling over some old iron pipe. You start very high up and then barrel your way down, shaking from side to side and pitching quite violently, too... I was worried that the cart was going to break free and launch me into the nearest tree. It didn't seem very tightly secured to me, but I am still alive so I guess it was okay. If you've got some kids with you then you might want to test it out on them first, just to make sure it's safe. If you've invited your kids' friends along as well, then that's even better. Send them up first. They are expendable. If they come back crying then you can make your excuses and move on to something else.

'Tomb Blaster' gets the prize for being the worst ride in the park. On paper it sounds quite exciting: an Indiana Jones -- style trip into an ancient Egyptian tomb filled with mechanical snakes and robot mummies, and you have to zap them with your ray gun as your bejewelled cart trundles past. But in reality it is very slow, the robots are about as scary as a fairy, and it kills your finger pulling the trigger ten thousand times. After two minutes I thought, *Sod it, let the mummies kill us, I don't care.*

If you've ever been to Chessington at any time during the last twenty years then you will definitely remember 'Dragon Falls'. This is their log-flume water ride, where you sit in an open-top coffin as it bounces down a raging torrent of bright blue water. They've got a little jump halfway along, and then a very big one at the end that will soak you to the bone. It's actually quite a nice gentle ride until you get to the drop, and then all of a sudden it turns into a living nightmare as it inches towards the top and it's too late to back out. Screaming doesn't help (I tried that) -- crying doesn't either, because nobody takes a blind bit of notice. They just stand at the side laughing and pointing at you.

'Dragon's Fury' is probably the scariest ride in the park. They stick you in a little four-seater turntable that spins around and around as it loops and swoops along a tubular track. It's a real twisty-turny one, up and down and round and round, and it's totally relentless. I actually threw up straight in somebody's face (no I didn't). I would still have happily had another go, though, but the queues were so long they put me off.

If you've ever met somebody who's been to Chessington before then I bet you ten pence the first thing they'll mention is 'Bubbleworks'. For some strange reason everybody seems to love this one, but it's just a kiddie ride (I was a bit embarrassed getting on it). You sit in a circular bathtub and then off you go, along a very gentle river of water, past all the plastic characters in the Bubble Factory. It's a bit like watching scenes in a movie... you see them measuring out the size and strength of the bubbles, building all the rubber ducks, etc., and your little kids will love it. At the end you go down the gentlest incline of all time ('Bath time!') and through a colourful tunnel of dancing fountains, which spurt and spray water over the top of your boat. You will definitely get wet, but you will also leave with a big smile on your face.

The good thing about Chessington is that they've made a real effort to theme the zones. They've got a nice medieval square with a castle gatehouse, a Wild West town with saloon-style shops and funfair games (including those rifle ranges -- I love those!), an old Oriental zone, and an Aztec jungle, too. My favourite area is Transylvania... as you walk around the Dracula-style mountain shops the air will rip with screams as the 'Vampire' flies above your head. This is also where you'll find the best restaurant: Vampire's Burger Kitchen. It doesn't look very exciting on the map, but when you go inside you'll find a medieval dining hall with two huge indoor trees with lights and lanterns strung between the branches -- check it out.

The 'Vampire' is definitely my favourite ride, and I think it will be your favourite, too. I like it for two reasons: firstly, because I am actually a vampire in real life (I haven't told you that before, but it's true). And secondly, because the seats are hanging from the rail so your feet are dangling down. As it roars around the track your legs get forced out at ninety degrees, and your feet seem to get awfully close to the rooftops and treetops; you actually think that you're going to kick the chimneys and instinctively raise your knees up! The quick whip through the tunnel will make your stomach jump out of your mouth. It's also got one of the best queues in park. You line up through a pine forest and make it into the pitch-black tunnels of the castle. When you get to the big hall you are greeted by a demonic Beethoven-like guy pounding out his scary tune on a smoking, glowing organ.

Once you've had a go on all of the rollercoaster rides you can finally check out the animals. The old zoo does still exist, by the way (it's easy to forget about the poor animals with all the rollercoaster rides), and they've got quite a good collection. They've got some lions, tigers, a gorilla, a children's zoo, plus the penguins and aquarium at the beginning. But the biggest surprise of all is the 'Zufari' ride. What they do here is stick you in a safari-style truck with open sides, and ride you through a desert terrain of tall grasses, dusty mud, and water. Your truck rumbles right into the animal enclosures so you can get up close and personal with the zebras, giraffes, and rhinos. And here is the unbelievable thing: *there are no fences!* Three big rhinos were standing twenty feet from the side of the seats, with literally nothing between them and us -- not even a ditch. If one of them had been in a bad mood, I would not be here to tell the tale. The giraffes wouldn't have cared. They would probably have joined in as well, just for something to do: let's eat all the humans, yeah, *come on fellas!* Someone give Mr. Lion a ring and get him over here as well. I'm telling you the truth: if the rhinos had charged across in a blind fury then you would now be seeing horrific pictures of me on the evening news. My truck was full of kids and little old ladies as well, so of course it would have been down to me to fight them off single-handedly. I'm not saying that I couldn't have done it (I could have, easily), but it's not the kind of thing you want to do on a day out. And then if that wasn't bad enough, the truck then drives straight into a cave with a waterfall inside, and you get soaking wet, too!

Now that I've spent an entire day here, I can confirm that it definitely is possible to see the whole place in one day; but you have to be a bit lucky with the queues (which might be difficult during the school holidays), because you can easily spend thirty minutes waiting in line for the big rides. They had some scary signs up suggesting that sixty minutes isn't out of the question either (although I didn't have to wait any longer than thirty, myself). So my advice is to stock up on sweets and cans of Coke and try and do the biggest rides first. I managed to go on all of the major rides at least once; I did the 'Scorpion Express' and 'Vampire' rides twice, plus the monorail and zoo animals too, in a little under five and a half hours (plus I had some dinner as well). And that still left me with an hour and a half to spare before the park closed, so a whole day should be plenty.

Now that I think about it... I would probably rate this as one of the best value attractions in the whole of London. (Okay, so technically it's not actually in London -- but it's only a thirty-five-minute train ride from Waterloo to Chessington South.) When you consider that Madame Tussauds, the London Dungeon, and London Zoo are all practically the same price, and don't last anywhere near as long, whilst this place includes a zoo, an aquarium and lots of rollercoaster rides as well, it should definitely be near the top of your list.

Hampton Court Palace

JOURNEY 35 min train from Waterloo (zone 1) to Hampton Court (zone 6) **ADDRESS** Hampton Court Palace **PRICE** Palace & formal gardens: If bought online: Adult £17.10; Senior

Places Further Afield | 339

(over-60) £14.30; Child (5-15) £8.60; Infant (under-5) free; Family (2 ad+3ch) £43.50 -- If bought at the door: Adult £18.20; Senior (over-60) £15.40; Child (5-15) £9.10; Infant (under-5) free; Family (2 ad+3ch) £46.80; Price includes a voluntary donation -- Formal gardens only: Adult £5.80; Senior (over-60) £4.90; Child (under 15) free; Price includes a voluntary donation -- Informal gardens only: free **OPEN** Palace: 10 AM to 6 PM (Mon-Sun, Apr-Oct); 10 AM to 4.30 PM (Mon-Sun, Nov-Mar); Last entry 1 hour before closing -- Formal gardens: 10 AM to 6 PM (Mon-Sun, Apr-Sep); 10 AM to 5.30 PM (Mon-Sun, Oct-Mar) -- Informal gardens: 7 AM to 10 PM (Mon-Sun, Apr-Sep); 7 AM to 6 PM (Mon-Sun, Oct-Mar) **WEB** hrp.org.uk/hampton-court-palace **TEL** 0844 482 7777 **TIME REQUIRED** 4-5 hours (including travel time from London)

Easy to get to? ★★☆ Good for kids? ★☆☆ Value for money? ★★★ Worth a visit? ★★★

I thought I'd venture a bit further afield today, so I ended up at Hampton Court Palace. It's not too far away from London, only about half-an-hour on the train. I used to go on cross-country runs down by the river when I was still at school so I've got unhappy memories of this place. I nearly died a few times on the towpath... out of breath with two more miles to run. A few of the kids used to sneak off to the bus-stop and ride one back, but I braved it (I was too scared of being caught!).

I've been to the palace more times than I care to remember, so I skimmed it pretty quick today -- but it still took me the best part of three hours to complete. I don't think it's possible to do it any quicker than that: and that is super quick speed. That took in every single room and the gardens out the back, including the maze. But if you actually take the time to stop and listen to the audio guide from start to finish, and have a cup of tea too, then I reckon you'll be there for four or five hours. Lots of people ask me if it's possible to do Hampton Court and Windsor Castle on the same day, but take it from me: you can't. It's *impossible*. Even Superman couldn't do it. You'd end up running around both places at the speed of light and it would be a complete waste of time. You need to take your time with great places like these, otherwise it's hardly worth going.

The first thing that you need to do is pick up an audio guide from a little room in Base Court. They've got narration for pretty much every room in the palace giving you the history of the building, the people who built it, who lived there, who died there, plus some dramatisations of famous events too. A lot of the time you will enter what looks like a tiny little cupboard and then stand there for five minutes listening to the guide. In my opinion, it sometimes gets a bit boring, and after a while you might be tempted to pick and choose which bits you listen to. But you really do need to make an effort if you want to get the best of the place; otherwise you might end up walking through Henry VIII's State apartments and not have a clue what they are.

Here is my second piece of advice: the palace spans a few hundred years of history and you need to try and do it in order, going from king to king, otherwise the stories won't follow on from each other. So grab a map and start with the Tudor section. First up are a couple of exhibitions about Henry's life and how the palace came to be built. Then you'll come across his wine cellars and kitchens, and on to the Great Hall and Chapel.

The Tudor kitchens are very well done. The wooden tables are all laid out with thick crusty pies and bloody butchered meat. They've got a real roaring fire crackling smoke up the chimney too, and Tudor-looking staff lugging big heavy logs on to the flames to keep it burning. You can really feel the heat coming off it and get the smell of thick smoke licking up the walls. Things get even better when you wander into the political rooms. The Great Hall comes first, with its fantastic hammerbeam roof and tapestries hanging all around the walls. Then comes the Great Watching Chamber, where people queued up in the hope of seeing the king. After that you have a very memorable corridor that leads to the Chapel Royal. If you listen to the guide then you'll discover that it's haunted: Henry's missus Catherine Howard was dragged out kicking and screaming when she learnt that she was getting the chop (literally). The first time I visited this corridor many moons ago they actually had a lady dressed up as Catherine fleeing down the carpet, which frightened two old ladies half to death. I didn't see her this time around, but they still had plenty of characters dressed up around the grounds. Much like Disneyland has Mickey Mouse and Donald Duck... when you visit Hampton Court you'll catch a glimpse of Anne Boleyn and Henry VIII wandering around the grounds, stopping every now and then for photo snaps.

The Chapel Royal is one of the few room in the palace where you're not allowed to take a photo, which is a shame because it's probably the best space in the place. It's still a working church, you see, so you have to doff your cap and pay your respects. But you can still wander around inside and see the King and Queen's private pews and the amazing blue and gold vaulted ceiling. (I have actually attended a Sunday service in this chapel, which is well worth doing -- check out my separate review.)

After that you leave the world of Henry VIII and jump forward a couple of hundred years to Charles II and William III. I thought this was one of the best areas, because you can follow the entire route that the privileged did: from the watching chamber all the way through to the Throne Room, taking in their private bedrooms, bathrooms, and where they sat and ate their dinner. All the rooms are decorated exactly as they had them back in the day, and some of the paintings on the walls and ceilings are quite monumental. After that it's on to Mary II and the Georgian apartments. If time is pressing, then you can probably skip this bit and you won't miss much.

Now you can have a stroll around the ornamental gardens out the back. Being a bloke, the gardens and flowers don't excite me very much, but even I can see that the plants are very nicely laid out. The gardens are full of marble statues and spouting fountains, and a lake that stretches as far as the eye can see -- it would take you thirty minutes just to walk around it (and that's not an exaggeration). They've even got a horse and cart to take you round the gravel paths, pulled by two huge shire horses.

As well as the formal gardens, they've also got acres of wild ones outside the palace. These ones are actually free to enter, and you can come and see them for nothing if you want. I have never seen so many daffodils in my life. There must be fifty-million of them at least -- and that is not an exaggeration either. It's as if they've replaced all of the green grass with daffodils. They are stuffed tight around the trees and bushes, plants and paths... just millions and millions of white, yellow and orange daffodils. I actually preferred the wild gardens to the formal ones.

After that there's just one more thing to do: the world famous maze. The last time I tried this I was about eight years old, and I remember the bushes towering above my head and blocking out the sun. But now that I'm a lot older (I'm eight-and-a-half) it just seems small and pokey.

The bushes measure about seven feet, and it took me all of three minutes to find the centre. [A clue: it's in the middle.] It's highly unlikely that you will be trapped in there all night, crawling out on all fours begging for food and water, so don't go worrying about that. Once you reach the middle you can take a photo and then skid-addle out of there, to the restaurant for a cup of tea.

You might like to visit Buckingham Palace, Kensington Palace and Windsor Castle.

Hampton Court Palace -- Ghost Tour

JOURNEY 35 min train from Waterloo (zone 1) to Hampton Court (zone 6) **ADDRESS** Hampton Court Palace **PRICE** Adult £27.50; Under-15s not permitted **OPEN** Usually 7 PM to 9 PM, or 8 PM to 10 PM (Fri-Sun, Nov-Feb only) - see website for dates **WEB** hrp.org.uk/hampton-court-palace/whats-on/adult-ghost-tours **TEL** 0844 482 7777 **TIME REQUIRED** 3½ hours (including travel time from London)

Easy to get to? ★★☆ Good for kids? children under-15 not permitted
Value for money? ★★★ Worth a visit? ★★★

This is pretty spooky already... and it hasn't even started yet. I'm sitting by the river next to Hampton Court listening to the bangs and crackles of Bonfire Night. There is a battle of booms and rifle shots going off in the sky, but I can't see a thing because of the wall of trees before me. There are no lamplights along the river so everything is dead dark. I can't even see where the water meets the mud. The only lights are from a distant drizzle of cars heading across the bridge.

The cracks are really something now. It's like a fight in the sky. Loud booms and explosions are echoing off the buildings behind me. Now I've got some dog walkers coming up the path with torches, shouting out *"Charlie! Charlie! Charlie!"* The poor mutt has obviously got scared stiff from the bangs and had a heart attack, or scarpered off sharpish down the path. I can hear the lady holding back her tears as she's screaming for her dog, whilst the husband is acting like he's got everything under control. I can still hear them shouting five minutes later, a little distance down the towpath, desperately searching for their dog.

I walk a bit farther down the river myself, until the billowing smoke blows over from the fireworks. They have obviously lit a big bonfire on the other bank, and the bright sparks are spiriting up and over the bushes. The dog walker's torch is still darting left and right as they search around the bushes.

A final rat-a-tat of bangs and whistles signals the end of the display and I make my way to the palace. They never did find their dog.

I'm hoping that this ghost tour will be good. It takes place late at night after all the tourists have left, and we're getting led around the courtyards by a guide. I'm half-hoping that we'll see some ghosts for real. I paid for a ghost tour so I want to see some real ghosts.

The tour starts off in the Tiltyard Cafe, so you have to walk up the long entrance driveway in the dark, past the front facade of the palace, past a few pretty gardens (too dark to see), and then they give you a free hot drink so you don't freeze to death outside. Even the cafe is in darkness. It's just a little low light from the tea machine. I reckon the tour crowd probably numbers about thirty people; made up of oldies, young couples and me. No ghosts, though. Then you get a little pep talk from the boss who tells you what you can and can't do (no photos, no running off screaming through the palace, no dying of fright please). Then you zip up your coat and head out into the wind.

Two hours later...

Okay, I've done it... the tour is all over now. (I couldn't write anything down whilst it was going on because it was pitch black). It was really good!

It was a really generous tour which lasted for a couple of hours, and you get to walk around a fair chunk of the courtyards and rooms, and even a little bit of the gardens out the back. The whole thing was done in total darkness, which greatly added to the atmosphere... there were a few ruby red lanterns hanging on the walls, and an occasional lamplight illuminating one corner of a courtyard, but other than that it was really just some dim little electric candles and the bouncing beam from the lady's torch as she tiptoed round the corners. If you weren't walking around in a group of thirty people then you'd probably run away in tears after five minutes.

The guide provides the only moving light on the whole tour, and it's just a dim little torch which she keeps firmly focused on the floor -- that's how deep down she keeps the dark. If you've ever been to the palace during the day then you will already know that some of the corridors around the courts can be quite dark and gloomy, even on a sunshine day. So just imagine what those exact same corridors are like when there is no light at all! I have been to Hampton Court Palace numerous times during the day, but even I was struggling to recognise the rooms in the darkness. I found myself walking through the State Rooms and only becoming aware of where I was when the guide turned her flashlight onto the wall. And there are lots of stairs and steps and skinny little passageways too. I am telling you right now... health and safety has gone right out of the window on this tour. I am surprised that they are allowed to illuminate it so low, given how easy it could be to trip up and crack your head on the concrete; because you can hardly see the feet at the end of your legs. Unless the ghosts were glowing gold you probably wouldn't be able to see them standing five feet from your face. But dark is scary, isn't it? Black is the colour of death. Dead like that dog on the towpath.

As she walks you from place to place she tells you a few ghost stories, pointing out all the doors and windows where the corpses might burst out. I don't believe in ghosts myself, by the way (I'm not an idiot), but even I found myself staring down the dark arch corridors as we passed by, wondering whether an apparition might float into view.

Let me see if I can remember all of the rooms that we passed through before it fades from my memory... you start off in Base Court, and you definitely enter Clock Court and Fountain Court too. One of the best bits was when we exited a door and found ourselves entering the ornamental gardens out the back. It was like passing from one kind of darkness into another, and it took me a few seconds to realise that I was now standing outside (that is how dark the insides are!). When I saw the garden laid out before me it was a really special moment. You don't often get to see a sheet of stars when you live in the city, because the street lights drown them out, but because the gardens back onto the lightless river and your eyes have already become accustomed to the gloom, the stars suddenly fill the sky like sequins. It's funny how the best bit of the tour turned out to be just walking through a door.

Later on in the evening you exit the east side as well, where they have all the gravel paths and man-made lake, and that was where she told one of the best ghost stories. (I won't spoil it by telling you what she said, but when you are standing out there in the cold it is very easy to get the shivers!)

You also enter the wine cellar (spiders) kitchens (bats) and parts of William and Mary's apartments. The standout room is the Great Hall at the end, but it's bathed in such a low light that you can hardly appreciate it. I actually wish that they would have lit it up a bit brighter, because I know how good this room can be, but that is a very minor criticism. (And it's for this reason that I still recommend coming during the day, because you can hardly see a thing by night.) The only top-notch room that you don't get to see is the Chapel Royal. Unfortunately that is also the best room in the entire palace, so that is one more reason why you should definitely come back during daylight.

Along the way she stopped at the big double doors where 'Skeletor' was caught on CCTV. If you don't know what I'm talking about then check it out on YouTube before you go: he is probably the most famous ghost in Hampton Court. She projected some of the footage against a whitewashed wall and then took us out to the actual double doors themselves. This was the only spot on the tour where I genuinely got a fright... but once again, I will keep my mouth shut so I don't spoil the surprise.

The spookiest and probably the scariest part of the tour was upstairs in the 'Haunted Gallery'. That's the corridor that passes in front of the Chapel Royal, where Catherine Howard was dragged out kicking and screaming when she learned about her death sentence. What they do here is really rather special... they force you to walk the entire length of the corridor alone (or in groups of two or three). They literally shove you in one end and shut the door behind you, and then you are totally alone for the entire length of the pitch-black gallery. And I mean *totally* alone -- you haven't even got the guide to accompany you. It's just you, some flickering candles on the carpet, and the same space that Catherine Howard ran screaming down all those years ago. As you tiptoe through the darkness, past the centuries old paintings with their shapeless faces and shadows for hair, you suddenly wonder where the end is... only to find that it turns a few more corners: the corridor is a lot longer than you think! I don't mind admitting that I was walking a lot faster at the end than when I stepped in.

It's a very special tour and you will learn a lot of Tudor history along the way, but if you are an old cynic like me then obviously the ghost stories are a load of pants. I didn't believe a word of it... but that didn't stop me staring down the corridors expecting to see something. If a ghost jumped out, then I wouldn't have been very surprised. If they are going to jump out of somewhere, then this is where they would do it.

You might also like a Jack The Ripper Tour, or a Tower of London Twilight Tour.

Kew Gardens

JOURNEY 30-45 min train from London (zone 1) to Kew Gardens (zones 3&4) **ADDRESS** Royal Botanic Gardens, Kew, Richmond **PRICE** If bought online: Adult £14; Senior (over-60) £13; Child (4-16) £2.50; Infant (under-4) free; Family (2 ad+2 ch) £32, or £18 with 1 ad+2 ch -- If bought at the door: Adult £16.50; Senior (over-60) £15.50; Child (4-16) £3.50; Infant (under-4) free; Family (2 ad+2 ch) £37.50, or £21 with 1 ad+2 ch; Price includes a voluntary donation **OPEN** Gardens: 10 AM to 5.30 PM (Mon-Sun, early Feb-Mar); 10 AM to 6.30 PM (Mon-Fri, Apr-Aug); 10 AM to 7.30 PM (Sat-Sun, Apr-Aug); 10 AM to 6 PM (Mon-Sun, Sep-Oct); 10 AM to 4.15 PM (Mon-Sun, Oct-Jan); Last entry is 30 mins before closing, but greenhouses and attractions close 30 mins earlier -- Palace: 10.30 AM to 5.30 PM (Mon-Fri, Apr-Aug); 10.30 AM to 6.30 PM (Sat-Sun, Apr-Aug); 10.30 AM to 5 PM (Mon-Sun, Sep); Closed (Oct-Mar) -- Note: Temperate House closed until 2018 **WEB** kew .org **TEL** 0208 332 5655 **TIME REQUIRED** 4-5 hours (including travel time from London)

Easy to get to? ★★☆ Good for kids? ★☆☆
Value for money? ★★☆ Worth a visit? ★★☆

It looks like I've picked the wrong day to go to Kew Gardens: it's raining again. I reckon if I totalled up all the reviews in this book then I'd find that at least half of them were written in the rain. I've been trudging across their lawns for the last half-an-hour, and now my trouser cuffs are drenched in wet and hanging like lead weights around the tops of my shoes. But I quite like this place, so I don't care about the rain today. I'm a big fan of the Royals and Royal palaces, you see, and I quite like zoos too, and this place has got a bit of both (sort of).

Before I talk about all of that though, let me talk about the price. I used to think that the entry cost for Kew Gardens was a total rip-off, because you're basically just walking around a park, and who wants to stump up fifteen quid just to see some trees? But I have mellowed a lot since then and have decided that it's actually quite fair. When you take the time to look around the whole place then fifteen quid doesn't seem so bad -- it's not all plants and trees. They do have some interesting attractions too.

It can be quite nice walking through a park. A lot of it is very woody. Everything is covered in soaking wet dew at the moment, topped off with a bucket of rain. You've got squirrels and birds singing, fountains and coots in the water, and even a few menacing geese patrolling the path. When the trees are all wet they become every shade of green: deep greens and bright, light greens. It's like turning up the contrast on your telly.

The main reason that I came here today was because I saw an episode of *Time Team* on the telly (yes, I'm a saddo -- I watch *Time Team*). They were digging up the grounds of Kew Palace where George III used to live when he went a bit nuts. Unfortunately a large part of the building has disappeared now, knocked down in the 1820s. The bit that's still standing is the four-story old palace -- the so-called 'Dutch House' -- plus some kitchens and a few associated buildings round the side. They shouldn't really call it a palace though. If you come here expecting one of those then you're going to go home extremely disappointed -- it's more of a posh house in a park.

There is a nice little ornamental garden out the back which fronts on to the river, with neat little privet hedges and a team of gardeners raking over the stones, sweeping up the twigs and picking dead leaves off the plants with tweezers. The fountain is gurgling away whilst I'm writing this... I'm sitting on a wet stone bench listening to the birds. Everywhere you go in this place there is a chorus of birds doing karaoke cheeping tunes. This is adult entertainment, isn't it. We can pass the time just sitting here and chilling, but no kid is going to thank you for dragging him along to Kew Gardens. (Don't worry, there is some better children's stuff to come.)

It's definitely worth a look inside the palace. All of the staff are dressed up in period costume and hand over a little leaflet guide, and then you can walk around the rooms at your leisure. You can see where the King ate his dinner and lounged around, playing cards and taking meetings with his politicians. Most of the rooms are decked out with period furniture too, and they're playing some narration out of the speakers to tell you a little history of the place.

A lot of the best rooms are missing, of course (because the building has gone), but you still get the King's library, dining room and breakfast room. You also get a few of the Queen's rooms too: her bedroom, boudoir and drawing room. There are also a couple of bits and pieces belonging to the Princesses and the staff. But there are no big State Rooms. There are no gold fittings, or jewels, or anything like that. Everything is quite plainly decorated -- you probably have to be a history nut to appreciate it.

I suppose I'd better just say something about the plants... because that's why the majority people are going to want to come here. I'm not much into plants myself. I don't do gardening. I mow the grass every once in a while, but that's about it. All I want to know about plants is whether you can eat them or not. But I can certainly understand why people would get enjoyment walking around Kew Gardens. Apparently they are supposed to have every kind of English tree and plant in here, and they might be right. I didn't count them up, but I am guessing that there are at least a bazillion millionoid different flowers on display. The place is absolutely colossal -- they even lay on a few bus carts to drive the oldies from place to place. And they definitely need them too (even for the young ones), because you could easily spend all day walking around here and still not see it all.

One very pleasant walk that you might like to check out is through the 'Rhododendron Dell', where they've got big huge Rhododendron bushes towering up double-height above your head. Bright pinks and purples, deep creamy whites and reds, around a winding woodland path... and the inevitable soundtrack of birds playing out the treetops.

I've just wandered across a fantastic view... it must be a mile long at least, stretching all the way down a long line of trees and firs. And right at the end is a ten-story Chinese Pagoda with overhanging eaves.

...I walked all the way to the end only to discover that you can't go inside: it's locked. And it's made of brown brick instead of wood, so it's not as Oriental looking from close-up. So that was a complete waste of time. *Ah well*. But it was good exercise, I suppose.

I'm sitting on a wet bench by the central lake now -- having a lazy moment with the swans. We are just sitting here together, waiting for the world to end. I am quite similar to a swan, I think. Not in looks -- I don't mean in looks. What I mean is this: *we eat, we sleep*, and in between we just sit around waiting for something else to happen. We float this way, then that way, and invariably end up at exactly the same place, another day older. And with a few less feathers.

I think these birds have hit the jackpot. They are living in the human equivalent of

The Ritz. If I was a bird, then this is definitely where I would come. Forget all those pigeons scraping a living in Trafalgar Square stealing crisp crumbs from the tourists -- what are they doing? They have got wings, haven't they? Why don't they use them and come and live by this lake? This is definitely my favourite part of the park: by the Sackler Bridge. They've got a woody trail of fir trees, and the floor is littered with deep green pine needles and cones. You can look out across the water to the cobblestone islands where all the little baby birds are living, whilst the big white swans patrol the place like bouncers.

I'm in the Marianne North Gallery now... full of wildlife paintings of plants and trees. It sounds quite boring when I describe it like that, but trust me -- you have definitely got to see inside this place. Just poke your nose through the door for two minutes, and you will be glad you did. The walls are covered in hundreds of little picture paintings -- and I mean totally covered. It's only a little two-room exhibit, but there must be a thousand pictures at least (no joke!). They are wedged in six or seven high, so tight that you can't even get a butter knife between them. It's almost like being inside a greenhouse, surrounded by real jungle plants. Even the backs of the chairs are pasted up with them.

I've finally found something that is good for the kids (but no so good for adults)... the Treetop Walkway. I'm sitting at the bottom of it right now looking up, wondering if it's safe (I don't think it is). I'm trying to decide whether it's going to fall down in the next ten minutes whilst I'm on it. Let me describe it to you: imagine a load of skyscraper steel girders poking out of the ground, rising up to the tops of the trees and beyond, with a see-through walkway strung between them. And it's one of those iron lattice walkways... which you can see through, all the way down to the woodland floor. This thing is as tall as the trees, *literally*, and you are supposed to climb up the stairs and walk around it. Are they totally mad?

Okay... *I did it!* I'm back down on the ground now and I'm still alive -- thank Christ for that. Thank you God. Thank you Jesus. Thank you Mary and Joseph and Judas and all those other holy geezers. If you are wondering why I didn't take any photographs whilst I was up there then that's because I was too scared to let go of the rail. To be honest, I don't even want to talk about it anymore in case I have a panic attack, so let me just say that it was a) high, and b) it had good views, and leave it at that.

I've entered my favourite part of the whole place now: the Palm House. It reminds me of the Rainforest Room at London Zoo. As soon as you walk through the door you are hit by a sheen of heat that buffs up your face and hands with a shine of sweat. It's warm and humid and full of tropical plants and palm trees. I'm half expecting some monkeys to come swinging through the trees, like they do at the zoo, and see some colourful humming birds flitting around, but there's none of that -- it's just a greenhouse full of plants and trees. It's still nice though.

The best bit is the iron spiral stair that takes you up to the roof. They've got an iron lattice balcony running around the top (not so high this time!), and you can look through the palms at the plants and people down below. There's a nice surprise waiting for you downstairs as well, because if you follow the spiral stairs all the way down to the basement they've got a little one-room aquarium. It's not the biggest exhibit in the world (it's only about twenty small tanks in total) but it's quite nice to see a few fish after overdosing on flowers for two hours.

The Princess of Wales Conservatory is worth a look on the way out. This is another hot greenhouse filled with prickly cacti, orchids and ferns. There are lots of desert rocks and water fountains and bird sounds too (I'm not sure whether they were real or not -- I might have seen a few sparrows flying around). In the middle is a big Amazon pond with water lilies and five-feet fish -- they were bigger than the ones in the aquarium. See if you can find the little tanks filled with tropical fish, turtles and frogs (they are very well hidden). There's an underwater window somewhere too, where you can see all of those five-feet fish swimming around.

If you enjoy Kew Gardens then you will almost certainly like Wisley.

London Wetland Centre

JOURNEY 20 min train from Waterloo (zone 1) to Barnes (zone 3), or 25-35 min train to Putney Bridge (zone 2) **ADDRESS** London Wetland Centre, Queen Elizabeth's Walk, Barnes **PRICE** Adult £12.75; Senior (over-65) £9.50; Child (4-16) £7; Infant (under-4) free; Family (2 ad+2 ch) £35.55; Price includes a voluntary donation **OPEN** 9.30 AM to 6 PM (Mon-Sun, Apr to mid-Oct); 9.30 AM to 5 PM (Mon-Sun, mid-Oct to Mar); Last entry 1 hour before closing **WEB** wwt.org.uk/wetland-centres/london **TEL** 0208 409 4400 **TIME REQUIRED** 3-4½ hours (including travel time from London)

Easy to get to? ★★☆ Good for kids? ★★☆
Value for money? ★★☆ Worth a visit? ★☆☆

I'm not into birdwatching(too cold, too lazy, got no patience) but if you don't mind sitting in a bush for two hours wearing a pair of waders, and holding a pair of binoculars that weigh more than a fridge freezer, then get yourself down to the London Wetland Centre, because this place is birdwatching heaven.

Common sense suggests that you should get a train to Barnes and walk from there, but if you don't mind a leisurely 30-40 minute stroll then I reckon it's a lot nicer getting a train to Putney, or Putney Bridge, and then heading up Putney High Street to the bridge. Then you can have a nice stroll along the river past half-a-mile of boat yards and boat clubs. It's a very pleasant little stretch with racks and stacks of rowing boats all piled up outside, and the sound of hammers and saws coming out of the wooden double doors.

The river is quite wide around here, all dirty brown and slow, with grey stony beaches and slimy mud flats, and a floating row of pleasure craft all chained up in the middle. The second half of the walk is quite dark and woody, and if you keep your peepers peeled then you can spot the white arch of Wembley Stadium curving above the treetops.

The London Wetland Centre is a bit of a strange place. It's not quite a park, and it's not quite a zoo. It's more like a bird sanctuary, I suppose. I think they are trying to return the land to nature and let it grow wild (which is handy, because that means they don't have to do any weeding). Normally you would pull all these plants up and chuck them on the compost, but this is their stronghold, and Mother Nature is the boss. It is like a no-mans land of nature... she has barricaded herself in behind a wetland of ferns and grasses and dykes and marshes, and criss-crossed it with wooden walkways and lookout posts.

Parts of it is quite nicely done though: they've got a lot of pretty little ponds and waterfalls, and some forest-style fences and log cabins. As for the animals... well... it's pretty much all ducks and geese (and flies and midges). They've got a few otters to spice things up a bit, but it's basically a holiday home for ducks.

I'm not much into ducks, myself. I prefer them sliced up on a plate surrounded by peas and carrots and roast potatoes. The only ducks I ever see are wrapped in plastic in the fridge. So I had a good look at them today, to see if they have any redeeming features, but all they seem to do is quack. That is it: *quack*. That is the only word they know. *Quack quack quack quack quack.* They've got a one-word language. How about some cheeps and clucks as well for a bit of variety? They just sit on the water pecking at the ripples, preening themselves, and looking at their reflection in the water. And there are hundreds of them as well -- thousands! -- all walking up and down the paths like they own the place. I don't trust them. And they're not exactly the prettiest of birds either. The most beautiful bird I saw all day was six-feet tall with long blonde hair.

The layout is supposed to take you on a trip around the world... through Iraqi marshes and a Siberian tundra. They have little information boards up saying: "This is what the Siberian tundra looks like", but of course it doesn't. It's just a different colour grass. And the birds don't stick to the correct zones either; so you've got the same old coots and ducks and pigeons in the Orient as you've got in the American forest. What they need to do is chop their wings off so they can't escape, or staple their feet to the floor; so they actually stick to where they are supposed to be. Or put some electric barb-wired fences up to stop them wandering off. No zoo would allow a lion to walk around the petting zoo, would they? And it should be the same rule here: if a duck walks into the wrong zone then they should get a shotgun out and shoot it. That is what I would do if I was in charge. (That's probably why I'm not in charge.)

I quite like all the *Jurassic Park*-style gateways they've got dotted around the trails. They are ten-feet high and protected by chains and chicken wire, with big signs up shouting: "Shut the gate! Don't let the animals out!" But it's all birds. It's like the world's worst prison -- they can just fly over the top.

The best bit about the place is the hides. As you walk around the lake you will come across five or six birdwatching hides, in which you can grab a pair of binoculars and a book about birds and see how many you can spot. I had a little go but I didn't have a clue what I was looking at. It was all just ducks and geese to me. I might have seen a heron as well... or it might have just been a duck with long legs. How can you tell the difference? They don't have name badges on. It might be the same bird with different clothes on.

Most of the hides were busy with birdwatchers. They looked like proper pros as well, with chunky black cameras on tripods and binoculars and a pair of waterproof waders. It was all very quiet and serious, with lots of jottings being entered into their notebooks (no one daring to say a word in case the birds all heard and scarpered).

A lot of the land is incredibly wild, with stony paths walled in with nettles and berries. Some of the grasses are six-feet high at least, and a lot of the water seems to be topped off with a layer of bright green algae. I saw a duck just sitting in it fast asleep. He must have been in there for ages, because the algae had settled around his waist like a duvet.

It's quite a big place, and if the weather is grey like it was today it can even seem desolate; especially when you get out amongst the marshes and grasses. You can be walking around for five minutes and not see a soul. It's just you and the noises that nature makes: wind and water, and strange squawks and screams coming out of the treetops. The birds don't shut up for a second. You might think that it's quiet, but if you actually stop and have a listen for a while then it's a never-ending stream of whistles and trills and cheeps.

This is how I would sum the place up: If you're into birds and birdwatching then you will definitely love the hides (they've got a decent shop as well, full of birdwatching equipment and books), but for everyone else it's just a nice walk. If you're after some flowers then forget it -- you'd be better off going to Wisley or Kew, because the only colour here is green.

If you like birds then you might like to visit the walk-in aviaries at London Zoo.

Oxford

JOURNEY 1 hour train from Paddington (zone 1) to Oxford (outside zones) **ADDRESS** Christ Church: St. Aldate's -- Bodleian Library: Broad Street -- Museum of Natural History: Parks Road -- Ashmolean: Beaumont Street -- Sightseeing bus: Outside railway station **PRICE** Christ Church: Adult £7 (£8 Apr-Jun, £9 Jul-Aug); Senior (over-60) £6 (£7 Apr-Jun, £8 Jul-Aug); Child (5-17) £6 (£7 Apr-Jun, £8 Jul-Aug); Infant (under-5) free; Family (2 ad+2 ch) £17 (£19.50 Apr-Jun, £22 Jul-Aug) -- Bodleian Library: Standard tour £7; Extended tour £13 -- Museum of Natural History: 10 AM to 5 PM (Mon-Sun) -- Ashmolean: Closed (Mon); 10 AM to 5 PM (Tue-Sun) -- Bus: Adult £13; Senior (over-60) £10; Child (5-15) £7; Infant (under-5) free; Family (up to 2 ad+3 ch) £36 **OPEN** Christ Church: 10 AM to 5 PM (Mon-Sat); 2 PM to 5 PM (Sun); Last entry 45 mins before closing -- Bodleian Library: Standard tours at 10.30 AM, 11.30 AM, 1 PM, 2 PM (Mon-Sat); 11.30 AM, 2 PM, 3 PM (Sun); Extended tours at 9.15 AM (Wed, Sat) -- Museum of Natural History: Free -- Ashmolean: Free -- Sightseeing bus: Every 20-30 mins from 9.30 AM to 5 PM (Mon-Fri, summer); Every 15-30 mins from 9.30 AM to 5 PM (Sat-Sun, summer); Every 20-30 mins from 9.30 AM to 4 PM (Mon-Fri, winter); Every 15-30 mins from 9.30 AM to 4 PM (Sat-Sun, winter) **WEB** Christ Church: chch.ox.ac.uk -- Bodleian Library: bodleian.ox.ac.uk -- Museum of Natural History: oum.ox.ac.uk -- Ashmolean: ashmolean.org -- Bus: citysightseeingoxford.com **TEL** Christ Church: 0186 527 6150 -- Bodleian Library: 0186 528 7400 -- Museum of Natural History: 0186 527 2950 -- Ashmolean: 0186 527 8000 -- Bus: 0186 579 0522 **TIME REQUIRED** 8½-9½ hours (including travel time from London)

Easy to get to? ★☆☆ Good for kids? ★★☆
Value for money? ★★☆ Worth a visit? ★★★

I briefly thought about attending Oxford University as a student but they wouldn't let me in -- I'm too stupid. I'm so stupid that when I went to playschool I had to repeat a year -- that's how stupid I am. So I ended up getting my education at the school of life instead (I failed). So here I am, sitting at the station waiting for the 8 o'clock train to Oxford, dreaming of what might have been.

This station is probably full of people dreaming about what might have been -- you can see it in their tired faces. We all want to be somewhere else... and I don't mean sitting on the train. Hopefully this train journey will wake me up a bit because I am dozing off here; I'm not used to these early mornings. You either have a good train journey in this country or a lousy one. You either get a good seat with a window, and a bit of peace and quiet, or you get wedged next to a big mouth and his fidgety kids.

So that is the kind of mood I'm in this morning... like a collapsed rainbow, or a cloud too close to the ground. But at least the weather is nice (it's raining). Someone has put the sun on half-power this morning. Do you think it's running out? Oh I hope so! I wonder if it's going to be like this in Oxford. I doubt it: Oxford is the kind of place where it's permanent springtime. Whenever you see Oxford on the telly it's full of blokes in boaters and summer shirts. The only kind of rain they have in Oxford is butterflies and apple blossom. That's why I could never live there -- it's too damn beautiful.

But anyway... I have arrived now. And yes, it is sunny. The sun miraculously came out as soon as we pulled into the station (and I'm not even joking). I've got a long list of things to do here today and I'm going to try and squeeze them all into six hours. The idea is that I will then be able to tell you how much you can realistically cram into one day, and which things are better being skipped.

Your first impression of the city when you step out of the station will not be very good (you can trust me on this). It's not like Oxford off the telly -- it's more like concrete town and roadworks. But don't worry, just have a ten-minute stroll up Park End Street and then New Road and you will come to the castle. (Did you know that Oxford has a castle?). It's got a big Norman mound out the front and a ruined tower behind, and you can have a walk around the prison courtyard. If you take my advice then you will skip the guided tour because it's sixty minutes long. If you're only here for a day then there are plenty of better things worth seeing, and you don't want to lock yourself into sixty minutes of this. So have a quick look around outside and then continue down New Road and Queen Street. Now you are starting to enter the "pretty Oxford".

If you'd like to have a quick aerial view of the town then you can climb to the top of Carfax Tower (on Queen Street). I was expecting something on a par with The Shard by the way they were talking in the guidebook, but in reality it's just a stubby little church tower. I still think it's worth a quick climb though. The view isn't all that amazing, but hey, it's only a few quid to get in so what the hell -- let's live a little! And it gives your heart a nice work out because you have to clamber up several flights of very tight and windy iron and stone stairs. (I made it okay with my busted knees, so you shouldn't have any trouble.)

Now have a stroll down St. Aldate's and past Christ Church College. Enter the gate at the far end (past the main facade) and get your camera out. This is the Oxford that you came to see. This is the Oxford of *Inspector Morse*. You can see quite a lot of nice architecture out the front for free but I definitely recommend stumping up the money to enter. It reminds me a little bit of Hampton Court and Westminster Abbey inside with all the cosy little courtyards and cloisters, and you can have a nose around the cathedral too. You're not allowed to walk around the entire grounds (large parts of it are only open to the staff and students) but there's definitely enough there to make it worth your while.

You'll probably be lost when you come out of the exit, but try and find Merton

Street. There are lots of very beautiful houses down there -- it's all stone cottages and cobbles and gaslight lampposts. When it bends around the corner you can check out Magdalen College (pronounced 'Maudlin') -- another beautiful building. You can't go inside it unfortunately (at least, not without a scholarship!), but it's near here that they do the punting on the river -- keep going over the bridge and you will see them all lined up in the water.

Now double-back down the High Street (called 'The High') and turn right down Catte Street towards that interesting looking round building. That's the Radcliffe Camera. You definitely need to have a nose around this whole area because it is well worth seeing. I recommend stumping up some money for the Bodleian Library tour as well (which includes the Radcliffe Camera). But first of all you need to find the ticket office... so prepare yourself for the best looking courtyard in town. Walk around to the other side of the Camera and through the central door in the building behind (signposted to the shop). I won't say any more. I don't need to -- the courtyard through here will do all the talking for me. Aren't you glad you came to Oxford now? This place is on a par with Clock Court at Hampton Court Palace.

The Bodleian Library tours book up pretty quickly so you have to be lucky with the times (the first one I could get was for 3 PM, and that was at 12 noon). There are three different options available: cheap, cheapish and not so cheap. All three of them take you into the Divinity School and Duke Humfrey's wooden library (the ancient place with the ancient books and ancient readers reading them), but if you want to see inside the Camera then you have to splash out on the most expensive one. That's the one that I did (but I still recommend doing the cheap one if that's all you can get).

Once you've finished with the tour find Catte Street again and have a look down New College Lane at the famous Bridge of Sighs.

If you fancy a long walk then you can continue in a straight line up Parks Road to Oxford's equivalent of the Natural History Museum. This place reminds me of taking a plant cutting when I was a kid, when the teachers made us slice off some stalk and stick it in a yoghurt pot. Someone has done a cutting of the Natural History Museum and planted it here -- it even looks the same inside with the same style of bricks and arches, and the same towering dinosaurs in the entrance hall.

Upstairs they've got all the stuffed birds and rocks and gemstones. I very nearly strolled out at this point but luckily I wandered into the room at the back (confusingly called the Pitt Rivers Museum, even though it's in the same building) which is totally fantastic -- it's like Aladdin's cave! It's full of cramped up cases packed with all kinds of treasures: oriental armour and Eskimo suits, to old Egyptian canoes and flintlock muskets. They've even got a few shrunken heads and Indian scalps. It might not sound very exciting on paper but it's one of those rooms that you definitely have to see -- it's the way they've dressed it that makes it great. Don't leave Oxford without seeing this room -- it was one of the highlights of my day. If I discover that you left Oxford without seeing this room then I will be very unhappy with you.

Now all you've got to do is find the Ashmolean Museum (head back down Parks Road and turn right down Broad Street). You can pop into the Museum of the History of Science along the way if you like but I don't recommend it. It's full of old telescopes and watches and clocks, and it's pretty boring unless you've got a particular interest in that kind of thing. That impressive-looking round building next-door is the Sheldonian Theatre, built by Christopher Wren.

The Ashmolean Museum is basically a baby-brother version of the British Museum. If you like the British Museum then you will love it, but if you don't then you won't. Personally I can take it or leave it, but I know that for a lot of people this will probably be the highlight of their day. It's quite good on Egyptian and Assyrian history, with cabinets full of statues and mummies and busted bits of brick, etc. And there are plenty of pots and pipes and plates and slates (yawn). Then you repeat all of that for the Greeks: more pots pipes plates slates. Then you repeat it all again for the Romans: bones stones bricks sticks beads seeds (yawn yawn). Then you do it all again for Asia, etc. (You can tell that I'm a total philistine when it comes to this kind of stuff -- the Ashmolean is supposed to be one of the country's great museums!) My favourite exhibit was actually downstairs in the art gallery where somebody had painted a bright green neon Hitler next to what looked like the two motorbiking cops from *Chips* (remember them: Ponch and Jon?) -- I thought that was quite amusing. That was more on my level.

And oh yeah... they've got some Picasso's and Van Gogh's as well (the neon Hitler was better).

And that's about it really. That's all of the must-see stuff in Oxford. It might have only taken you ten minutes to read it, but that's more than enough attractions to fill up five or six hours. If you still have some time left over before your train leaves then you might like a stroll around the shops in the old town. If you want to take a picture of the famous 'dreaming spires' then you'll find them halfway up The High (look up!). There are a few Tudor-style houses down Cornmarket Street which are quite nice as well. The guidebooks always mention the Covered Market but I thought it was a bit of a letdown to be honest -- it's just a normal everyday market and I didn't even bother to take any photos of it.

I used up the rest of my time with a city sightseeing bus. You can catch it outside Christ Church College and pay for a ticket on the bus, or buy one in the little shop at the bottom of Carfax Tower. It only takes an hour to complete the entire circuit and it's an easy way of seeing all of the colleges and learning about the city's history.

If you enjoy this, try Cambridge and Bath.

Portsmouth Historic Dockyard

JOURNEY 1½-2 hour train from Waterloo or Victoria (both zone 1) to Portsmouth Harbour (outside zones) **ADDRESS** Portsmouth Historic Dockyard, HM Naval Base, Portsmouth **PRICE** If bought online: Adult £25.60; Senior (over-60) £23; Child (5-15) £18.40; Infant (under 5) free; Family (2 ad+up to 3 ch) £68, or £51.60 with 1 ad+up to 3 ch -- If bought at the door: Adult £32; Senior (over-60) £28.80; Child (5-15) £23; Infant (under 5) free; Family (2 ad+up to 3 ch) £85, or £64.50 with 1 ad+up to 3 ch **OPEN** 10 AM to 5.30 PM (Mon-Sun, Apr-Oct); 10 AM to 5 PM (Mon-Sun, Nov-Mar); Last entry 1 hour before closing **WEB** historicdockyard.co.uk

TEL 0239 283 9766 **TIME REQUIRED** 6-8 hours (including travel time from London)

Easy to get to? ★☆☆ Good for kids? ★★★
Value for money? ★★★ Worth a visit? ★★★

I'm trying to remember the last time I saw the sea... Do you remember when your parents drove you down to the seaside in the car and everyone went: "The first one to see the sea gets 10p!" Well, that is what I am doing right now, sitting on the train to Portsmouth... trying to spy the sea. I'm too old for sandcastles though. I'm off to see HMS Victory in Portsmouth Harbour -- that's the boat that carried Admiral Nelson at the Battle of Trafalgar. It seems almost miraculous to me that it still survives, and I'm quite looking forward to stepping inside it, if I'm honest, because Nelson is one of my heroes (I'm getting very patriotic in my old age). Apparently he was a bit of an idiot in real life though. He was the kind of guy who talked about himself in the third-person, and filled his house with paintings of his own face. He insisted on wearing all of his medals too -- all fifty-thousand of them at once, jingling and jangling like a one-man band. He didn't do modesty, that is for sure. He knew he was good, and he told everyone worth telling.

The other standout boat in Portsmouth Harbour is even older: Henry VIII's flagship from 1545 -- the Mary Rose. That's the one they managed to pull from the sea in 1982, 440 years after it got sank by the French.

As soon as you get off the train you will be glad you came. There is nothing like the fresh smell of the sea and the sound of seagulls wheeling around in the wind. Portsmouth Harbour is a bit of a misnomer because it seems more like the sea -- it is colossal! You can't even total up the boats on the other side of the bay because they are too tiny to see. It's just a distant picket fence of bright white needles sticking up out of the water. On this side I've got a big boat that I don't know the name of (yet) and a messy yard of upturned fishing boats and fish nets, with piles of coiled up rope rotting in the rain. It's a proper seafront... with grubby seaside pubs and the smell of seafood and seaweed. There are a couple of tanker-sized car ferries too, probably off to the Isle of Wight.

The historic dockyard is just a short stroll from the train station, and I don't mind admitting that I choked up a bit when I first clapped eyes on the Victory. I am standing in front of her right now, with a little tear in my eye. *There she is...* I can hardly believe it. And she looks exactly like she's been described as well (which makes sense I suppose -- seeing as she's the same thing). She's missing her sails, of course, but half of the masts are up and every porthole sports a cannon. When you step inside you'll see her dressed exactly as she was on the day of the battle. But here's the caveat: she looks like she did *before* the battle. There is no damage on her at all. It's like looking at Bridget Bardot after sixty years of plastic surgery. I would have quite liked them to have left some of the damage intact, so I could see her battle scars and wrenches and tears, but I can't see a single scratch or scrape on her. There are no shrapnel scars, no splinters, no smashed up planks. Everything has been replaced and made to look like new. And notice that I said *replaced*, and not *repaired*. I had a chat with one of the navy guys onboard and he reckons that only 25% of the wood is original. It's a bit of a shame really, because it makes her into a clone. But who cares anyway... *it's HMS Victory!*

The whole boat is decorated with historical objects and artefacts: from cannons and cannonballs and reddy-gold lanterns, to wooden buckets, linen beds and tables filled with biscuits and barrels of grog. It's almost as if they lifted her straight out of time and plonked her down in Portsmouth Harbour.

You can explore all of the gun decks and galleys, the Admiral's cabin (which wouldn't look out of place on a 5-star cruise ship), and see where the surgeon patched up the wounded. You get to walk along the top deck too, and stand in the exact location where Nelson got shot (they've nailed a plaque down on the plank to mark it). The most moving bit is down below, where they've set up a little shrine to mark the place where he passed away. It's all dark and creaky down there in the hold, with the sounds of the sea piped in through the speakers.

The Mary Rose is situated just ten steps away from the Victory, in a very modern-looking museum that was built especially to house her.

The actual ship is a bit disappointing though, if I'm honest, because there's not a lot to see. It is immediately obvious that they are still hard at work restoring her, and trying to dry her out, because the whole frame is criss-crossed with great big pipes pumping in and sucking out the air, obscuring the timbers beneath. You can't get into the actual room either... all you can do is peer through some tiny little windows. The windows are ridiculously small -- like letterboxes. They are so small, in fact, that there must be a reason for it, otherwise it is just ridiculous. Maybe they don't want too much light getting in and damaging the wood? But when you remember what these bits of timber actually represent -- the flagship of Henry VIII, no less -- then I suppose we are lucky to even see a sliver of her. It's probably the most historic thing in the dockyard.

The most impressive part of the museum is not the ship's timbers themselves, but the thousands of artefacts that they've pulled up with them. It really is amazing what they've managed to retrieve from below the seabed. The glass cases are stuffed full of cannons and cups and combs, bows, bellows, brooms and flutes, and everything from a backgammon board and the skeleton of a dog, to a whole shoe shop of Tudor footwear. They've even got a full-size skeleton of one of the archers on show.

The last boat that you can board in the main yard is HMS Warrior. Apparently it was one of the very first ironclads from the 1860s. It's certainly worth a look, but it lacks the interesting history of HMS Victory and the Mary Rose. There are also a couple of other boats to visit across the bay, including a WWII submarine; but you have to board a waterbus to see those. Unfortunately I ran out of time at this point and had to give them a miss -- I'd already spent close to four hours looking around the boats and associated museums, and I couldn't squeeze in a waterbus ride plus another boat (plus the waterbus back), followed by a two-hour train ride back to London. So here's my advice: check out their website and plan your day in advance, and decide which boats you want to board beforehand; otherwise you will run out of time like I did. But in hindsight I probably spent too much time on the Victory, inspecting every nail and speck of sawdust, so you might have better luck squeezing them all in than me.

So that's about it really... The rest of the port is home to the Royal Navy's modern-day fleet, but you can't go anywhere near those without getting arrested. I was quite surprised to learn that over 50% of Britain's entire fleet can now fit inside these docks -- which shows you how small our navy is these days. But it does look pretty formidable though: some of the ships I spied from afar looked like they could blow a hole in the world.

You might also enjoy a trip to Chatham Dockyards, where HMS Victory was built.

RAF Museum

JOURNEY 25-35 min train from London (zone 1) to Colindale (zone 4), and a 10-15 min walk
ADDRESS RAF Museum, Grahame Park Way, Colindale **PRICE** Free **OPEN** 10 AM to 6 PM (Mon-Sun); Last entry 30 mins before closing
WEB rafmuseum.org.uk/london **TEL** 0208 205 2266 **TIME REQUIRED** 2½-3 hours

Easy to get to? ★★☆ Good for kids? ★★☆
Value for money? free Worth a visit? ★★☆

I saw *Band of Brothers* on the telly last night so I'm in the mood for World War II. I love a bit of World War II. I love it so much, in fact, that I might start World War III so we can have a re-run. We wouldn't have much chance of winning it now though -- our army these days consists of six guns, two tanks and a clapped-out jeep. Instead of telephoning America two years after it started we'd be begging them to bail us out before we'd even fired a shot. That's why you need to come to a place like the RAF Museum and see what it was like in our glory days... when the pilots still had moustaches and names like Rupert, Hubert and Hugh.

The museum is made up of a few hangar-sized buildings around a big patch of grass. You can do them in any order you like but the first one I tried was 'Milestones of Flight'. It was full of famous planes like a Hawker Hart, Harrier Jumpjet and Eurofighter Typhoon, plus a De Havilland Mosquito and a Mustang too (listen to me... I'm talking as if these names actually mean something to me, but I'm bluffing -- the only planes I've ever heard of are a Concorde and Spitfire!).

You can view them from several different floors and walk around them 360 degrees, but they are the aeronautical equivalent of a stuffed animal. All they do is hang there like an iron chandelier. You're not allowed inside any of them. You can't sit in them. You can't fire up the engines and take off. You can't fire the machine guns at all the noisy school kids. So I think they have missed a trick there -- imagine how much money they would make if they let you fire off a live missile! They could charge 50p a go -- they'd make a fortune.

The next hangar was my favourite because it was full of World War II equipment (I like World War II), and it wasn't until I got a few minutes into the hangar that I realised how vast it was -- it's huge! This is not a piddly little museum that we're talking about here -- they've got more planes than an airport. They've got a Spitfire (of course), and a Messerschmitt (that's probably not how you spell it), and a Flying Fortress and a Focke Wulk. Plus the rusting hulk of a Halifax bomber, dredged up from the bottom of a Norwegian lake.

Halfway through the hangar you come to the absolute beauty of beauties: a pristine Lancaster that looks as good as new. It is easily the most beautiful thing in the building after one of the blonde dolly birds in reception. They've also got a laser-guided missile and a bunker-busting bomb on display, and a huge nuclear-carrying Vulcan, suspended ten feet above the ground with the bomb bay open, so you can walk underneath and see inside.

That thing is a *beast*. They've got a little video playing of him taking-off and the noise is wrecking the sky (and my eardrums) -- it is tearing great big rips in the clouds.

After that you come to a little section filled with rescue helicopters and a Chinook, and they got some flying boats and early Sopworths too -- and some of those ancient planes from yesteryear that are held together with wood and string and prayers.

The whole hangar was so good that I decided to do it twice: once on my own and then once again with the free guided tour that they lay on with an old Air Force guy. He took us around the whole lot in 45 minutes flat and explained the history of each plane with some bits and pieces about the war. The tour starts underneath the gun turret of the Lancaster if you're interested (I think it is definitely worth doing); or you can just sneak into the group as he's walking around -- just look for the posh old guy who looks like he's ex-Air Force.

The next hangar was full of aircraft from the First World War, but I must admit to loathing World War I. It bores me silly -- I don't know why, but it just does. So I skipped most of the Grahame White Factory. (My knees were playing up by this time and I needed to pace myself, so I hope you forgive me.)

Then it was on to the Battle of Britain Hall. This place has got even more Spitfires and Messerschmitts (did I spell it correctly that time?), and also a load of dodgy-looking waxworks acting out scenes from the Home Front. They've got a fat waxwork of Hermann Goering in there as well, plus a frankly terrifying one of Churchill, who looks more like a porcelain ghost.

It's worth having a good look around this area because some of the stuff is quite hard to find -- check out the life-size mock-up of the Operations Room, for example (where they shuffle planes across the map with sticks). It also houses the only plane that you're actually allowed to step inside: a Sunderland Flying Boat. To be honest, I was totally knackered by this point and probably didn't give it enough time (I was dead on my feet) -- but this place is huge! I reckon you need at least three hours to see it all. I personally took 3½ -- but that included the doubled-up guided tour as well.

I can't believe that this place is free. I am genuinely amazed that they don't charge an entrance fee because I would happily stump up fifteen quid.

There are more planes at the Science Museum and Imperial War Museum.

Richmond Park

JOURNEY 25 min train from Waterloo (zone 1) to Kingston (zone 6) and a 20 min walk, or 35 mins on the tube to Richmond (zone 4) and a 30 min walk **ADDRESS** Richmond Park **PRICE** free **OPEN** For vehicles: 7 AM to dusk (Mon-Sun, summer); 7.30 AM to dusk (Mon-Sun, winter) -- For pedestrians: 7.30 AM to 8 PM (Mon-Sun, Feb, Nov); 24 hours (Mon-Sun, Jan, Mar-Oct, Dec) **WEB** royalparks.org.uk/parks/richmond-park **TEL** 0300 061 2200 **TIME REQUIRED** 4-6 hours (including travel time from London), depending on how far you walk

Easy to get to? ★☆☆ Good for kids? ★☆☆
Value for money? free Worth a visit? ★★☆

Richmond Park is big. It's very big. In fact, it's huge -- you could build a new town inside it and still have room left over for another one. People do sponsored runs around it and when they finish five days later their foot bones are showing through their shoes.

I used to come here when I was younger to take a few photos on the expensive camera I got for Christmas. I used to have to drag it around (because it weighed about ten tonnes) in search of some deer, and then I'd sit there for three weeks waiting for them to inch a bit closer. I'm not doing that today, though -- sod that. I am still going to take some photos of the deer but my little camera phone zooms in about ten miles now, so I can snap a few photos without having to walk anywhere. Isn't technology wonderful!

When you enter the park the first thing you need to do is make a beeline for the woods to get away from the roads. You can really get lost in the woods here if you know where to go, but you need to screen out any sight of the cars. There's not much point in me giving you detailed directions because there are hardly any signposts, but what the hell -- let's give it a go anyway. You'll have to print off a map from the web if you want to follow along.

I am starting in the southern tip by Kingston, and walking up the hill towards King's Clump. What we are doing is looking around for deer. This park is famous for them, and if you're lucky then you'll come across a hundred-strong herd. But the trick is in finding them -- this is not the kind of park where you can scan across the fields and see what's happening half-a-mile away -- this is a real woody parkland with fields and hills and a lake. It's like being in the countryside.

If you keep walking north from King's Clump, with the flat fields on your right, you should see a building up ahead. It's actually two houses, one behind the other, and if you walk through the centre of them then you'll be treated to a nice view down the hill. You're supposed to be able to see Windsor Castle from up here, but I'll be blowed if I can see it -- maybe you will have better luck. There's not a lot else that you'll recognise -- maybe just the control tower at Heathrow airport.

It's the end of September as I'm writing this so everything is changing into shades of ruddy muds and orange. All of the trees are in the twilight of their days, shedding their green leaves for bare tree trunks and autumn pyjamas. There are so many toppled logs at this time of year -- you are crunching along on cardboard leaves and empty acorn cups. Imagine if they were all dried up bones and human skulls instead of dead trees and leaves -- we'd be having a heart attack.

I like the wide variety of landscapes you get in Richmond Park: along with the forests and muddy ponds and stepping-stone streams, you've got a huge lake and a yellowing plain that looks like the titles of *Little House on the Prairie*.

Hopefully you are heading back down the road towards Ham Cross, after which you need to clamber back up the steep slope on the other side -- we are aiming towards Pembroke Lodge.

I've just come across some tree trunks which I recognise from my youth -- hollowed out coffins of bark, eaten by weevils, and gnarled up totem poles that must have been struck by lightning. The trees have been stripped of their clothes and are just standing there with bony arms twisting around each other. They are three arthritic grandads frozen in stone. The mud has dried up all along the brow and the tree roots look like leg bones in an archaeological dig. This is Bear Grylls country -- knotted grass and six-foot ferns that are bending over the road to run their fingers through my hair. Some of the brambles are snatching at my trousers and refusing to let go. Don't stray too far from the path for chrissakes, because you'll be taken by the wildlife.

I am on the trail of the deer... I am getting closer. I have just discovered a pile of fresh deer dung. If I were Bear Grylls then I would put some on my finger and eat it, but I am normal, so I don't. Have you seen any deer yet? I would love to be able to tell you to just go to a particular place, where you will definitely see them, but of course it doesn't work like that because they are wild animals; and they can wander wherever they like. That is why zoos are so good, you see... because you can just keep all of the animals locked up in prison and save all this stupid walking about. They don't mind being caged up like inmates -- I'm sure of it. They get a roof over their heads and free lettuce every day. Give a monkey a banana and a stick to wave about and he's happy.

I have just discovered the scariest bench in the world. It is buried alongside the ferns at the side of the path, and if you sit down for a rest then we will find you five months later with the nettles and blackberry brambles wrapped tight like chains around your face. There are some bright white spiderwebs too, looking like handkerchiefs covered in phlegm (covered in dew). And somewhere around here there is an old rook with no feathers, because he has shed them as an offering to the mountain.

Pembroke Lodge is where you can stop for your first cup of tea. There is a little garden attached but it's not a lot different to what you can see outside the fence (just more grass and trees). The inside of the lodge is very posh though, and if you sit on the veranda outside then you'll get a great view down the hill. I tried to find Windsor Castle again but it must be hidden behind the trees -- maybe the Queen has knocked it down.

The only real 'garden' part of the park is the Isabella Plantation, which is an enclosed area full of heathers and flowers and firs. Outside the plantation it's all beetles and spiders and snails, but inside it's butterflies and ladybirds. They've got some pretty little ponds and rockeries in there too. It's nice enough if you like that kind of thing I suppose.

When you reach Richmond Gate turn right and walk along Sawyer's Hill. If you keep looking towards the left then you should eventually catch sight of the London skyline. It might seem a little hard to believe, but you can easily see the dome of St. Paul's and the London Eye from here -- plus the Walkie Schorchie, Canary Wharf and The Shard. I'm pretty sure that if you can see the London Eye then you should be able to make out Parliament too, but the colours are just a little bit too faded today -- maybe you will have better luck (maybe you have got better eyes than me). If you walk far enough along the road then you can see the white arch of Wembley Stadium as well.

Where the hell are all these deer? I feel like I'm a big game hunter out on safari. Maybe someone has beaten me to it and shot them all already. There was a story in the papers a while ago about an American trophy hunter going over to Kenya and shooting a famous lion called Cecil -- do you remember that? He shot him with a bow and arrow and he wasn't very popular (especially with the lion). I seem to remember that he had to go into hiding for a couple of weeks until it all blew over. Well, I am planning on going one better today, because -- I haven't told you this yet -- but I am actually hunting for Rudolph. *The* Rudolph -- of Rudolph the Red-Nosed Reindeer fame. I am going to hunt him down and shoot him and mount his luminous nose on the front of my car. Can you imagine the international uproar if I succeed in doing that? -- I will be world famous! My book will go straight to the top of the bestseller list for sure. Obviously it will put me straight onto Santa's naughty list as well, but I don't care. If I see Rudolph then he's getting a bullet between the eyes. And if Blitzen gets in my way then he'll get one too, and Dasher, Dancer and Prancer... I'm taking them all out. Christmas is cancelled this year.

Keep walking along Saywer's Hill (bearing a little to the right), and you will be treated to the finest view in the park: looking down into the distant Pen Ponds. It's when you're standing up here in the wind that you will finally appreciate how vast the park actually is -- you're looking down onto a few square miles of jutted, muddy hills and woody parkland.

Walk towards the Pen Ponds and straight through the land bridge in the middle, and then head towards the Isabella Plantation.

Wait a minute... hold the front pages... I have just spotted my first deer! There is a whole bunch of them sitting underneath a tree. It looks like one stag is guarding about fifty of his women. Jesus Christ he is huge! He is mooing like a cow -- I haven't got a clue what he is saying. His wails are carrying across the wood like a loudhailer. Hold on a minute... do me a favour and keep quiet for a minute, so I can listen... I think I can hear some more mooing in the distance. It's almost as if they are talking back and forth to each other like that scene in *Crocodile Dundee*. Or maybe it's just the wind -- maybe he's talking to the weather.

So to sum it all up, then... Richmond Park is for walkers. It's all wild woods with dips and hills, rather than pretty parklands full of flowers, so it's perfect for people who enjoy a long walk. Bring your dog as well -- because he will love it more than you.

You could combine a trip to Richmond Park with a visit to Kew Gardens.

Stonehenge

JOURNEY 1½ hour train from Waterloo (zone 1) to Salisbury (outside zones), and a 35 min tour bus **ADDRESS** Stonehenge: Salisbury Plain -- Salisbury Cathedral: 6 The Close, Salisbury **PRICE** Adult £16 (or £27 with tour bus); Senior (over-60) £14.40 (or £27 with tour bus); Child (5-15) £9.60 (or £17 with tour bus); Infant (under-5) free; Family (2 ad+up to 3 ch) £41.60 (or £78 with tour bus); Price without tour bus includes a voluntary donation -- Cathedral: Free, but suggested donation is £7.50 **OPEN** Stonehenge: 9.30 AM to 5 PM (Mon-Sun, mid-Oct to mid-Mar); 9.30 AM to 7 PM (Mon-Sun, mid-Mar to May); 9 AM to 8 PM (Mon-Sun, Jun-Aug); 9.30 AM to 7 PM (Mon-Sun, Sep to mid-Oct); Last entry 2 hours before closing; Note: Tour bus leaves Salisbury every hour between 10 AM and 2 PM, and takes 30 mins. Last tour bus leaves Stonehenge at 4 PM -- Cathedral: 9 to 5 PM (Mon-Sat); 12 noon to 4 PM (Sun) **WEB** Stonehenge: english-heritage.org.uk/visit/places/stonehenge -- Tour bus: thestonehengetour.info -- Cathedral: salisburycathedral.org.uk **TEL** Stonehenge: 0370 333 1181 -- Tour bus: 0120 233 8420 -- Cathedral: 0172 255 5120 **TIME REQUIRED** 6 hours just for Stonehenge (including travel time from London), but allow more if you visit the cathedral

Easy to get to? ★☆☆ Good for kids? ★★☆
Value for money? ★★☆ Worth a visit? ★★★

It's 6 o'clock in the morning and I'm sitting on a seat in Waterloo station. I've got practically the whole place to myself. There are just a couple of early risers, binmen and train station staff pottering around doing nothing... just adjusting stuff until their bones have woken up. Normally I would go upstairs for a coffee but the darn place is still shut. All I can do is buy my train ticket and wait for the clock to drag its heavy hands round to the top.

It's forty quid to Salisbury -- that is how much a return ticket to Stonehenge costs from Waterloo. And even that doesn't get you the whole way. Salisbury is the closest train station to the monument but that's still nine miles away; you have to get a tour bus after that -- but more about that later. All you need to know at this point is that it is 6 o'clock in the morning and I am sitting here still half-asleep waiting for the day to start. Me and the cleaners. Me and the pigeons. Me and the moon.

Thirty minutes later... it's starting to come to life now. The tannoys have crackled into action and workers are pouring off the trains and spilling out over the concourse. They have brought a lot of noise with them. I've only got another ten minutes before my carriage comes so I sip up, chuck my cup across the table and get going.

The 7.10 AM train to Exeter Central is what I need, which pulls into Salisbury 1½ hours later -- so it's quite a lengthy ride. It's definitely a day-trip, put it that way -- so don't go thinking that you can visit Stonehenge and be back home in time for lunch.

When you're on a long train trip you have to be prepared to fight for a window seat -- and I mean actually 'fight' (to the death, if necessary). There is nothing worse than having to stare at your shoes for two hours, whilst the English countryside whizzes past the window out of sight. I used to order my tickets online but I don't bother anymore because the whole thing is a swizz. If you ask for a window seat they always seem to stick you in the one where the window splits in two: with a big plastic spine running down the middle (do you know what I mean?). A window seat to me, is one that has actually got some glass in it -- you know, that stuff that you can *see* through. Not one inch of window and then three feet of plastic. So now I just take my chances and grab what I can -- beating up a few old ladies and kicking a few kids if I have to. I don't care. I am prepared to commit crimes to get a window seat. I don't care about peace in the Middle East, the disappearing rainforests or worldwide famine -- just give me a decent window seat on the train; which is silly really, because I spent most of the journey in the land of nod!

From what I saw, though, it was quite a pleasant spectacle outside the window: miles and miles of brown-brick suburbia merging into the countryside, followed by vast expanses of green and trees, hills beyond hills, more hills behind them, all rolling over the end of the earth as far as your eyes can see... decorated with a billowing ribbon of fast-moving clouds. If it's not green, then it's grey. That is my view of England today: green, grey and raindrops on the window. The perfect weather for Stonehenge: *Stone Age* weather.

I have arrived. It's 8.45 AM and I'm sitting in Salisbury station. That's not bad progress when you consider how far away it is from London (about ninety miles). I never expected to get here this early. But the trek isn't over yet though... because now I have to find the tour bus.

Stonehenge is nine miles away from Salisbury station, and there are no local buses. The only way of reaching the stones is to splash out £27 quid on the

'Stonehenge Tour Bus', which includes entry into Stonehenge. That is your only option. It's either that or walk (or get a taxi, but I wouldn't like to guess how much that costs). Why couldn't those lazy cavemen just have dragged the stones another ten miles into town, closer to the train station? They'd already dragged them all the way from Wales, so I'm sure another ten miles wouldn't have hurt.

The tour bus stops right outside the train station if you want to play it super-safe, but I think it's much nicer to walk ten minutes into town, and use their shop in New Canal Street (called 'Salisbury Reds'). It's quite a pretty little place once you get over the first bridge, and you can check out Salisbury Cathedral too, which is five minutes from the centre. The buses depart every sixty minutes-or-so, so you can easily stop for something to eat before it leaves.

It was at this point (drinking my tea) that I totalled up how much money I'd spent so far, and realised that it's quite a pricey day out. You're looking at 40 quid for the return train ticket, plus another £27 for the bus and entry into Stonehenge. So that is £67 quid straight away, before you've even splashed out on food and souvenirs. If you're thinking of taking your missus with you then that's the best part of £150 quid! (Maybe it's best to leave her at home.)

The tour bus was a lot of fun -- maybe the best part of the day. They do a little commentary as you drive along, pointing out all the old buildings and cathedral. Then you head out into the countryside and very soon you are surrounded by green. I'm from London, remember, so the only shade of green I've ever seen is one that's covered in mud. But this is a rolling wave of dips and hills, past miles and miles of tree-coloured carpet. And all the time your eyes are continually scanning the horizon for your first sight of the stones. The atmosphere was greatly improved today by the grey rain bashing against the windows of the bus. But then all of a sudden you arrive at the Visitor Centre and you are there -- with *no sign of the stones!* Where the hell are they? Well... what they have done is very clever, because they have located the centre more than a mile from the monument, totally out of sight and behind a crest of trees. You then have to ride a little fleet of minibuses up the hill.

But before you do that though... it's worth having a look around the little museum and exhibition space. They've built a few Stone Age huts to poke around in, and there's a cafe and a gift shop too.

The seven-minute minibus ride is the last stage of your journey, but if you want to drag it out even longer then you can opt to walk up the hill yourself. My head was willing, but my knees weren't -- so I took the bus. I thought the ride had quite a nice *Jurassic Park*-style feeling to it, trundling up the tree-lined path in a chained-up row of jeeps. I was half-expecting a big Brontosaurus to come bounding out of the hedgerow but instead I got... stones.

I hate to say this, because I really wanted it to be fantastic, but my first good look at Stonehenge elicited a... *huh, okay.* There they are: some stones. In my mind's eye I was expecting them to be colossal blocks of granite carved out of the earth, like a ten-tonne slice of mountain. But they were disappointingly average. (It takes a lot to impress me!) The largest one didn't seem to be any higher than a house. But I admit that it's difficult to judge their size because you can't approach them close. You are not allowed to walk amongst them. What you have to do is walk around the perimeter on a roped-off bit of tarmac and grass, with about three million other people right beside you (which is a slight exaggeration, but not by much). You are all bundled in together with your cameras and your sandwiches, bottling up the queue behind as you try and take your photos. You've also got the distant rumble of lorries and coaches on the A303 right behind you. If they got rid of that and buried the road in mud then the scene would be pristine: it would be 360-degrees of green hills and trees as far as the eye can see. But it's decorated with a distant string of power lines on the cusp of the hill, a conveyor belt of trucks and buses on the motorway, and a cacophony of camera-clicking tourists five feet from your face.

The most impressive thing that I saw all day was the angry sky. And I don't mean that as a joke either... it's not often that you can look in every direction and follow the sky all the way down to the joint, unencumbered by buildings, skyscrapers and cranes. Imagine standing on top of that windy hill with the clouds as close as a coat. It was almost like the wind and rain were whipping up a painting in the sky: all gloomy blues and sheets of black and grey. It was better than the world's worst watercolour, with a bucket of dirty slop washed over the top.

It's difficult to grade an attraction like this because... well, what does it do? *Nothing.* You just look at it, and then you go home. But I feel a bit guilty telling you not to bother because it's the world famous Stonehenge. So of course it's worth going! But this was my day: I spent over two hours getting there, another hour looking at some stones in the rain, and then another three hours getting home. If that's worth seventy quid to you, then go for it.

Stratford-upon-Avon

JOURNEY 2-2½ hour train from Marylebone (zone 1) to Stratford-upon-Avon (outside zones) **ADDRESS** Shakespeare Centre: Henley Street -- Anne Hathaway's Cottage: 22 Cottage Lane, Shottery **PRICE** Shakespeare Centre: Adult £16.50; Senior (over-60) £15.50; Child (5-17) £9.90; Infant (under-5) free; Family (up to 2 ad+4 ch) £43 -- Anne Hathaway's: Adult £9.90; Senior (over-60) £8.90; Child (5-17) £5.90; Infant (under-5) free; Family (up to 2 ad+4 ch) £26 -- Holy Trinity: £2 donation to see the grave **OPEN** Shakespeare Centre: 10 AM to 4 PM (Mon-Sun, Nov-mid Mar); 9 AM to 5 PM (Mon-Sun, mid Mar-Oct); Last entry same as closing time -- Anne Hathaway's: 9 AM to 5 PM (Mon-Sun, mid Mar-Oct); 10 AM to 4 PM (Mon-Sun, Nov-mid Mar); Last entry same as closing time -- Holy Trinity: 9 AM to 5 PM (Mon-Sat, Mar and Oct); 8.30 AM to 6 PM (Mon-Sat, Apr-Sep); 9 AM to 4 PM (Mon-Sat, Nov-Feb); 12.30 PM to 5 PM (Sun, Jan-Dec); Last entry 20 mins before closing **WEB** Shakespeare Centre: shakespeare.org.uk/visit-the-houses/shakespeares-birthplace.html -- Anne Hathaway's: shakespeare.org.uk/visit-the-houses/anne-hathaways-cottage-amp-gardens.html -- Holy Trinity: stratford-upon-avon.org **TEL** Shakespeare Centre: 0178 920 4016 -- Anne Hathaway's: 0178 920 4016 -- Holy Trinity: 0178 926 6316 **TIME REQUIRED** 9-10 hours (including travel time from London)

Easy to get to? ★☆☆   Good for kids? ★☆☆
Value for money? ★★☆   Worth a visit? ★★☆

The first thing that you need to know about Stratford-upon-Avon is that it's a totally different place to Stratford. If you catch the tube to Stratford then you'll end up by the old Olympic Village in east London. But the Stratford-upon-Avon that we're talking about is 100 miles away and two hours on the train -- a slight difference!

The only reason that you'd want to spend a whole day here is if you're the world's biggest William Shakespeare fan. That is literally the only reason for coming here (you can trust me on this). Stratford is where he was born, so they've got his old house, a couple of exhibitions and a theatre.

Did they make you read Shakespeare at school, like they did with me? Jesus christ... it's like learning another language. I'd rather learn Latin... I'm coming out in a cold sweat just thinking about it. They made us slog through *Macbeth* because it's full of blood and fighting, and presumably they thought that might keep the pupils interested (pupils love a bit of blood and fighting -- especially at break time). I think we did *Othello* as well... was that the one where she dropped a tissue and he stabbed her in the face? *King Lear*... old fella went nuts and his daughter jumped in the canal. *Romeo and Juliet*... everybody says that is romantic but all I remember is Romeo committing hari-kari and Juliet sucking up a toxic miasma. If that's romance then I think I'll stay single, thank you very much. I'm actually thinking about re-writing that play with me in the lead role; but I'll have to make a few changes in case they make it into a movie. For starters, I don't care how pretty she is, I'm not climbing up a balcony to sing her a song -- not with my knees. She'll have to bloody well come down here if she wants a kiss.

My first impression of Stratford when I pulled into the station was that it was just like any other town, but with fancy lampposts. Things start to look up when you walk five minutes down Greenhill Street to the market (on the corner of Wood Street and Rother Street). That's when you'll see your first few Tudor houses with rickety wooden beams. They've got a nice thatched pub on the corner that looks like it might fall down if you lent on it. I'm assuming that the houses are genuinely old judging by the sloping walls, because they'd never let them get away with building anything that shoddy these days.

If you fancy a walk before visiting the exhibitions then there are some more Tudor-style houses down the High Street, Chapel Street and Church Street. All three roads run in a straight line and they've probably got the best architecture in town -- especially the ones down Church Street.

Now head up Windsor Street and turn right into Henley Street. This is the Holy Land of Shakespeare, and you can see his original house just past the Shakespeare Centre. I am finding it very difficult to bite my lip here, because ten feet next to that little gem is a modern monstrosity that is about as in-keeping with the street as a tutu at a funeral. Just shut your eyes and join the mile long queue of tourists (that's the only way to get into the house).

Once you've whizzed through the first few rooms of the piddly little exhibition -- they've got a copy of the *Folio* and a few theatre props, but that's about it -- you'll enter the back garden of Shakespeare's home. This was the first bit of the day that I actually enjoyed -- a whole hour after stepping off the train. It's like an English country garden with pretty flowers and a pear tree, and they've got a little stage set up for impromptu performances. It was quite pleasant having a sit down in the sun whilst they did their little scenes in period costume. They even had an old geezer limping around playing the lute. They don't perform a whole play though... they just do his 'greatest hits': the famous bits that everybody knows, taking requests from the crowd and shouting out the lines across the garden. Obviously I didn't understand a word of it (it's Shakespeare!), but when you're sitting five-feet from the lupins and tulips and lavender it's certainly worth the entry fee. Unfortunately they've also got a load of kids running around on the lawn having mock sword fights with wooden sticks -- they were giving them sword fighting lessons with their mums and dads watching on. So in one ear you've got "to be or not to be" and in the other ear it's all "clack clack clack clack clack ow!".

When you get inside the actual house you can have a walk around every room from top to bottom. It's certainly a creaky old place, but I'm not sure that it's 100% legit... they seem to have restored a lot of it with bits they bought from B&Q (that's what it seemed like to me). Amongst the whitewashed walls and Tudor beams are modern tables and chairs and IKEA-style coat hooks. The highlight is supposed to be the room where he was born, but it looks like a modern bed with one of those electric fireplaces in the hearth: the ones with crappy fake flames and glowing red embers. They've sprinkled some kids' mittens and toy mice on the tables too, and a few pottery pots and jugs. I appreciate that none of his original possessions have survived the passage of time, but come on guys! You could have at least *tried* to make the objects look original. I thought the whole thing was a bit amateurish, to be honest. It was nice to see the outside of the house and hear the floorboards creak, but that's the best thing that I can say about it.

The bit that saved my day was Anne Hathaway's cottage (Shakespeare's wife). It's about a mile outside of town and I walked the entire way, but in hindsight I definitely recommend getting a bus. You have to march down an ugly main road for fifteen minutes... past the car wash, past the job centre, past the B&Bs and suburban semis... the last half mile is down a country lane with roadside nettles and berries and a couple of pretty little thatched cottages. They've got a few fields full of sheep as well which is quite pretty, and then you come to her chocolate box cottage that is too good to be true.

It's like something out of a movie -- it could have been set-dressed by Disney. It's like something that Hansel and Gretel might stumble across in the woods. The cottage is thatched with cream-coloured walls and chocolate beams like sticks of Flake in vanilla ice cream, and outside the front is a country garden in a paint box full of colours. Inside the house is even better -- in fact, it is everything that Shakespeare's house should have been. It is dark and moody with low-slung ceilings, big thick oak everywhere you go, floorboards that talk to you as you walk across them... moaning and creaking with the weight of your toes. The only people who could live in here without bending over are stooped-over old grannies. It's got rickety old chairs and beds and kitchen cupboards hanging with black pans and long-handled pots. It's like something lifted out of time and it's amazing that it still survives. If I had to visit just one thing in Stratford then this would be it. Forget the Shakespeare stuff... Anne Hathaway's house is definitely worth seeing.

If you still have some time left over then have a walk along the river to Holy Trinity Church. Once you've made it past the tourist boats and ice cream stands it turns into a very nice woodland path that takes you down to the 13th-century church where Shakespeare is buried (you have to pay a few quid to get into the burial chapel). All that's left of the fella is a faded slab of stone set against the altar, plus whatever bones are kipping in his coffin. Most holidaymakers fly home believing that they've seen his grave in Westminster Abbey, but that statue in Poets' Corner is actually just a monument -- his real bones are buried underneath this stained-glass window. And very pretty it is too.

To sum up it then... unless you're really into Shakespeare and you're desperate to see his home, I would give it a miss. You're looking at two hours on the train, each way -- so you're basically giving up an entire day of your holiday. If you take my advice then you'll just visit the Globe Theatre exhibition instead. If you want to see a copy of the Folio then you can do that at the British Library or the V&A. Anne Hathaway's cottage is definitely worth a look, as are the original Tudor houses in town, but they're not good enough to make me recommend the lengthy train trip.

If you're interested in Shakespeare then you definitely need to visit the Globe Theatre.

Warner Bros. Studios (aka. Harry Potter Tour)

JOURNEY 20-50 min train from Euston (zone 1) to Watford Junction (outside zones), and a 15-min shuttle bus **ADDRESS** Warner Bros. Studios, Leavesden **PRICE** Adult from £33; Child (5-15) from £25.50; Infant (under-5) free; Family (2 ad+2 ch, or 1 ad+3 ch) from £101; You must pre-book tickets before arrival **OPEN** 10 AM to 7.30 PM (Mon-Fri, Jan); 10 AM to 8 PM (Mon-Fri, Feb-Mar, May-Jun, Sep to mid-Dec); 9 AM to 10 PM (Mon-Fri, Apr, Aug, 2nd half of Dec); 10 AM to 10 PM (Mon-Fri, Jul); 9 AM to 10 PM (Sat, Jan-Dec); 10 AM to 10 PM (Sun, Jan-Dec); Last entry 3-3½ hours before closing **WEB** wbstudiotour.co.uk **TEL** 0845 084 0900 **TIME REQUIRED** 4-5 hours (including travel time from London)

Easy to get to? ☆☆☆ Good for kids? ★★★
Value for money? ★★☆ Worth a visit? ★★☆

This is what I know about Harry Potter: he's a swotty little school-kid with glasses and a wand. That's it. I have never seen any of the movies, and never read any of the books. So getting up at seven o'clock in the morning and jumping on two trains and a bus and stumping up thirty-five quid for a ticket to the Harry Potter film studios doesn't exactly fill me with glee. To be honest I'd rather have just stayed in bed.

The Warner Bros. Studios are quite a trek from London. Harry had it easy, because all he had to do was catch the magical Hogwarts Express from Platform 9¾ at King's Cross station, but in the real world you have to get a twenty minute chug from Euston. And instead of ending up at a gothic castle in the countryside you end up in... *Watford.* And the fun doesn't end there, because after that you have to sit on a tour bus from Watford Junction as well, which takes up another fifteen minutes of your life. (They lay on a £2 shuttle bus from the station, or you can catch a local bus every 15-20 minutes.) So that's one train and a bus, plus whatever bus or train you had to get to arrive at Euston -- so this had better be good! If Harry was half the magician that he's supposed to be then he would have just magicked me there in a lickety-split.

I quite like Euston station. It's got a bit of an airport-style feeling to it. And it's a posh train to Watford too, not a dirty old tube. People are boarding it with big suitcases and luggage labels, off to Manchester airport probably. It almost feels as if I'm going abroad. I can sit here and pretend that I'm off to Oz for the week. [Handy hint: Even though it's situated 18 miles from London you can still use a pay-as-you-go Oyster card to Watford Junction.]

The train ride isn't the prettiest in the world. It's all concrete car parks and out-of-town shopping centres. The track is fenced in by power lines and motorways, and ribbons of dreary terraced houses snaking their way up and down the contours. And then you get to Hogwarts... sorry... I mean Watford. Don't bother having a look around Watford for chrissakes because that will be a total waste of time -- just jump straight on the tour bus that's parked up outside the front of the station as fast as you can, and get the hell out of there. You can't miss the bus: it's plastered with pictures of Harry Potter.

The tour bus was absolutely heaving with tourists and about fifty of them didn't even get on. We just left them standing at the bus-stop waiting for the next one (true!). After the big bundle through the door it was standing room only, shoulder to shoulder with peoples' armpits in your face. Think of a busy bus, and then double it. And then double it again. Then imagine a long drive out of town, past the motorway, and into the middle of nowhere. If you've got any delusions about being able to walk it from the station then forget it -- you've got *no* chance. It's this busy bus or nothing.

I have arrived at the studios now and it looks like a big film lot. The buildings themselves are colossal... like giant airplane hangers. Apparently they used to house an old Rolls Royce engine factory during the war, and this is what's left over from the airstrip. We are surrounded by open fields as far as the eye can see, and it looks like they are building a few new hotels nearby too, so maybe they are turning the whole place into a theme park.

Right inside the front door is a massive gift shop selling every Potter-themed piece of tat known to man. You can get everything from a stuffed owl and carved wooden wand, to Harry's old school jumper, scarf and tie, and even some sports balls for a game of Quidditch (although you'll have to supply the flying broomstick yourself). Obviously it is all *horrendously* expensive... but that is to be expected in a place like this.

All of the tickets are timed so I'm sitting in the cafe at the moment, waiting for my 'show time'. The queues are stretching halfway around the block already, and are filled with visibly excited kids, excited adults, and a few old people too (not quite so excited). But the most excited people of all are the staff. I reckon they must plug them into the mains for thirty minutes before letting them loose on the public, because it looks like they have been charged up with ten-thousand coffees. Their smiles are stretching right round the back of their heads. There's a sweeping film score blasting out of the speakers as well, and I am actually quite looking forward to it now (but don't tell anyone I said that). Let's hope the inside lives up to the build-up.

Once you have snaked your way round the queue and got through the big double-doors, you are herded into a little room with two hundred other people. Then you have to stand there and watch a little introductory movie playing out of the TVs on the wall. Then you get led into a little cinema where you sit down and watch a big budget intro, compered by Dan Radcliffe himself, plus the other two (I forget their names -- that ginger-headed fella and skinny posh kid). If you are like me, and have never seen any of the movies before, then it's actually quite handy to watch this film because you get to see what all of the big sets looked like on celluloid. But here's the interesting thing: even though it's only a very small cinema, all the time you are watching it you are very conscious of the fact that you are sitting inside a film studios; and given that the room is very boxlike and bland you have just one thought in your head... (which I guarantee that you will have too)... which is this: what exactly is hiding behind that wall?

You will be hoping that the entire cinema screen will fall away any moment to reveal that you are actually sitting inside a monumental film set. *And it does!* (Well, sort of...) It's definitely a highlight of the tour, but it's not quite as fantastic as my imagination hoped it would be. The guide invites you down from your seats and then creaks open the heavy blocking door to reveal the Great Hall beyond -- the exact same one that they used in the movies. It's got everything from the flagstone floor and imposing stone fireplace, to the dining tables laid out with silver plates and goblets. As you are walking around the Hall looking at all of the props and costumes from the likes of Professor Dumbledore and Snape, the very excitable guide continues to jabber on at a million miles per hour. You will have to have very quick ears to hear her though, because she talks faster than the speed of sound. Luckily she doesn't accompany you beyond the next-door, so you can enjoy the rest of the tour walking around at your own leisure.

The next room is a vast hangar-like space filled with thousands more props and life-size sets. But first of all you have to negotiate a boring bit of corridor which introduces all of the movie producers, designers, writers and artists. And also the make-up ladies... hair stylists... camera operators... model makers... it's like a walk-through version of the film credits, where they get to write little quotes about how fantastic their movie is. It's basically a big love-in where everyone gets to pat themselves on the back for five minutes.

The hangar is filled with original film-sets and life-size reproductions of the characters' homes. It has got lots of props and costumes too. They've got the Boy's Dormitory and Gryffindor Common Room, for example, complete with its tapestries and stone stairs winding up to the second floor. Then you come to Professor Dumbledore's Office, filled with stacks of dusty tomes and old oil paintings of long-dead wizards hanging on the walls. Next up are the rattling bottles and pinches of powder in the Potions Classroom, complete with little cauldrons billowing blue smoke into the crowd. Then you pass by Hagrid's Hut and Umbridge's Ministry of Magic, decked out in the purples and pinks of a Sultan's palace.

There are a few interactive exhibits as well, like when your kids can test out Harry's wand in a magic mirror. There are plenty of TV screens and info boards explaining all about the special effects as well, but they are aimed more at the adults I think (they are quite technical).

I must just quickly tell you this... After spending the last two years visiting London attractions I have come to realise that when you've got a lot of human beings in a crowd, they are basically like lemmings. Do you remember that scene in *Dead Poets Society*, when Robin Williams orders all his kids to walk around the courtyard, and they end up doing it in unison? That is very much like real life, I think. Because if one tourist stops to take a photo of the floor, then you can bet your life that everyone else will stop and take photo of it too. If one person gets their buddy to snap them standing in front of

Harry's favourite jumper, then ten more people will barge their way up and grab exactly the same shot, just in case the jumper suddenly disappears. One day I am going to try and do a Pied Piper... and walk everyone out the exit.

And speaking of exits... after the hangar you head outside for a quick look at some exterior sets. They've got Harry's house in Privet Drive and the Potter's Cottage (both full-size) and the rickety old wooden bridge that took them up to Hogwarts. You can also have a look inside the three-story knight bus.

Next up is another highlight: *Diagon Alley*. This is a life-size version of the Victorian-esque street, all twisting and turning with shop fronts and doors. You can have a peer inside the Apothecary window at all the bowls of snuff and seeds. They've got Gringott's Bank and Ollivander's Wand Shop too, and Weasley's Wizard Wheezes and Quidditch Supplies. You can't go inside any of these places unfortunately... all you can do is press your nose up against the coloured glass and sneak a peek at the goodies within.

Then it's back to movie-making school again (yawn), with a section on concept art and their architectural plans. As I'm writing this I'm sitting here watching another little TV programme about the different roles of a designer and illustrator, and I'm thinking: there is no way in the world that a little kid is going to be interested in this. Even adults are strolling past without giving it a second look. And the only reason I'm watching it is because I want to sit down and write this review. This whole place has surprised me actually... with how much serious stuff there is inside. I reckon it's probably split about 50-50 between the stuff that will interest kids (big props and monumental sets) and educational skits that are better aimed at the parents.

The final room is another highlight, and even a little bit magical. It's a gigantic model of Hogwarts Castle about fifty-feet across and thirty-feet high. They've carved out the entire mountain and you can walk around the whole lot, and when the room periodically darkens you can see all the little lamplights glinting in the windows. I wish that I could shrink myself down and have a walk around it for real: that is how good it is! If this castle existed in real life then I would be running down the station right now, and jumping on the first train towards it.

And that's it! Then you get herded through the shop again so you can spend a bit more money.

So what did I think of it? Well... despite my initial reservations I think it is definitely worth doing (as long as you don't mind the trek across town to Watford). But I also think that it's worth repeating that there is a hell of a lot of stuff inside aimed only at adults. There are no rides or anything like that. It's basically just a lot of static sets, costumes and props, plus a few documentary-like movies about the film-making process. A lot of the sets are satisfyingly huge (especially the Great Hall at the start), but they don't actually do anything. All you do is stand there and look at them. So whether your kid will enjoy that or not, I will leave that up to you to decide.

I enjoyed it though, if that helps.

Windsor Castle

JOURNEY 40-55 min train from Waterloo or Paddington (both zone 1) to Windsor & Eton Riverside (outside zones) **ADDRESS** Windsor Castle, Windsor **PRICE** On dates when the State Apartments are open: Adult £19.20; Senior (over-60) £17.50; Child (5-16) £11.30; Infant (under-5) free; Family (2 ad+3 ch) £49.70

Places Further Afield | 369

-- When State Apartments are closed: Adult £10.40; Senior (over-60) £9.40; Child (5-16) £6.70; Infant (under-5) free; Family (2 ad+3 ch) £27.80 **OPEN** 9.45 AM to 5.15 PM (Mon-Sun, Mar-Oct); 9.45 AM to 4.15 PM (Mon-Sun, Nov-Feb); Last entry 1¼ hours before closing -- Note: State Apartments and Chapel sometimes close whilst the grounds remain open - check website for the dates **WEB** royalcollection.org.uk/visit/ windsorcastle **TEL** 0207 766 7304 **TIME REQUIRED** 5 hours (including travel time from London), but allow more if you visit the town

Easy to get to? ★☆☆ Good for kids? ★☆☆
Value for money? ★★★ Worth a visit? ★★★

Windsor Castle is a bit of a trek from London. If you're travelling from Waterloo then you're looking at the best part of an hour on the train. I don't normally go that far out, but it's Windsor isn't it. I've come to pay homage to our leader -- the Queen. Let's hope she's home or it will have been a wasted journey.

This is actually my very first visit to the castle. I've never been here before in my life. I saw Tony Robinson dig it up on *Time Team* on the TV, but that's about it. It certainly looks pretty on the telly, so let's hope it lives up to my expectations.

I got my first good look at it coming in on the train, and the place is absolutely colossal. It is huge! It is sitting up high on the hill with big turrets and battlements -- exactly how you want a castle to be. It looks like something out of King Arthur's day. It has straight away become my favourite place to visit, and I haven't even stepped off the train yet. When you exit the station you have to walk a winding path around the old town to get up to the entrance. It skirts around the bottom of the hill and the castle wall, so every step you take you get a little higher up the slope and closer to the stone gates. It's a very picturesque little town full of Ye Olde shoppees selling shortbread and tartan knitwear, with cafes and cobbles and country-style pubs with hanging flower baskets. Eventually you come to the gun cops on the gate and stump up your money to get in.

Once you're through the ticket desk and security scanners you pick up an audio-guide and walk around at your own leisure. The big difference between this place and Buckingham Palace, is that the palace is just one building, whereas here you get to explore the castle grounds and gardens, chapel and State Apartments too. So you're looking at a good three hours to get it all done.

The prettiest bit is the central tower (that big round turret on top of the hill). One whole side of that has been done up like a garden rockery, with crooked stone steps and little river waterfalls running down it. I get the impression that the castle has never been used for defence. All of the military stuff looks a bit twee... like Walt Disney has had a hand in building it. It has all of the usual thick brick walls and arrow slits, but the moat has been drained away and decorated with daffodils and cherry blossom.

St. George's Chapel is right up alongside Westminster Abbey in terms of beauty. As soon as you round the corner of the Quire I guarantee that it will knock your socks off. This is where all of the

Knights of the Garter come and hang their banners and heraldic shields. Some of the greatest names in British history had a stall here, all "ready to defend the Queen" with their swords and shields (the audio-guide says) -- although I'm not sure how much use John Major would be in a fight.

A lot of well-known monarchs are buried here too, including George V and VI. The best of the bunch though, is King Henry VIII -- who gets a plum spot in the heart of the Quire. No big monumental tomb for him though: all he gets is a big black slab in the floor. It's not every day you can place your foot on the grave of the greatest English king, but here he is, lying quietly in the chapel without any fanfare; whilst half of the tourists walk by without even realising he's there. And if that isn't spectacular enough, he also shares his tomb with Charles I. Strange bedfellows, those two. How did Charlie manage to bag a bunk with him?

The altar is just about the most fantastic one in London. It's all peach marble and gold, with the brightest stained glass window I have ever seen in my life. There's an intricately carved wooden stall hanging high over the side, where Henry VIII's missus sat to hear the mass, with the golden plaques and banners of chivalrous knights, dating back 650 years to the reign of Edward III.

As you make your way to the State Apartments you can walk around the curtain wall at the very top of the castle. That's when you really start to appreciate how high up you are... the view must stretch for twenty miles at least. It's just miles and miles of country parks and treetops. Everything going hazy in the bright light as it stretches out to the horizon. If you steel yourself for a peek over the curtain wall then you will discover that you are actually above the tree line, looking down on the boughs that climb up the hill. I'm not very good with heights, so I quickly give up on that and headed inside...

You enter the State Apartments through the Grand Staircase, bristling with swords and canons and silver-suited knights on horseback, all set up to defend against the tourist hordes pouring through the door. There must be a thousand daggers and swords on show, plus another couple of hundred guns and rifles pinned against the wall in spiral patterns. I can't see any bullets though, so I'm not sure how useful they would be. It would take you half-an-hour to climb up and prise one off its place. By the time you'd wrenched it off the wall the tourists would already be through the door and causing mayhem.

The military theme continues into the Waterloo Chamber, which is a very wide room of chestnut walls and honey-coloured carvings on the roof. Fine paintings of Wellington and his generals stare down at the diners (these are the guys who beat Napoleon, so if you're French you might want to skip this room).

I think the King's Drawing Room must have designed by committee because they couldn't decide on a colour. "Sod it," they said: "Let's just use all of them" -- they've got every hue from red and black and brown and blue, to green and white and oodles of gold all over the place (you can never have enough gold). His bedroom is another busy scene, filled with oil paintings, chandeliers, chestnut desks and a gaudy ceiling that will wake you up as soon as you fall asleep.

The next room contains some very famous portraits of Richard III, Edward IV and Henry V (you will recognise these faces because they appear in every book ever written about them). Then you walk through the next-door and see Henry VIII, Edward VI, James I and a young queen Elizabeth (the one where she looks like a redhead in a crimson dress). You will recognise all of these paintings too because they are the de facto portraits of some of our most famous monarchs. And oh yeah... there are some pictures by Bellini, Raphael, Rembrandt, Van Dyck, Holbein as well: this place is better than the National Gallery!

The King's Dining Room is just... I don't know how to describe it... it's just knocked my socks off again. The whole ceiling is done up like the Sistine Chapel, with dark oak woods carved with fruits and berries cascading down the walls. A few candles around the edges bathe the place in golden brown... I would sit in here all day if I could. Forget McDonalds, forget Starbucks -- this is where I want to eat my meals from now on.

More great art in the Queen's Apartments... starting with some large portraits of Charles I by Van Dyck.

St. George's Hall will knock your socks off too -- in fact, you may as well just take your socks off and chuck them away, because they will get continually knocked off from this point on. This is where they hold all the big State Banquets. The room is over 150 feet long and it would be a great place for a joust (you'd have to clear away all the silver plates and tables first though). The roof is covered in hundreds of heraldic shields whilst silver suits of armour tilt iron pikes over the diners' heads. It's exactly like a Disney castle -- this is English history in the style of Arthur's Camelot.

If you're sick of gold then get ready for an overdose: the Semi-State Apartments are like Aladdin's cave. This was the part of the castle that burned down in the 1990s, so to see them looking so spectacular is quite a surprise. I didn't realise that we spent taxpayer's money on stuff like this anymore, but I'm glad that we do. I can see why the Queen prefers this place to Buckingham Palace... I think I prefer it too.

You might also like to visit Buckingham Palace and Hampton Court.

Wisley Gardens

JOURNEY 30 min train from Waterloo (zone 1) to Esher (outside zones), plus 20 mins on the 515 bus (only one bus each hour) **ADDRESS** RHS Garden Wisley, Woking **PRICE** Adult £13.20; Child (5-16) £6.60; Infant (under-5) free; Family (2 ad+2 ch) £32.75; Price includes a voluntary donation **OPEN** Gardens: 10 AM to 6 PM (Mon-Fri, summer); 9 AM to 6 PM (Sat-Sun, summer); 10 AM to 4.30 PM (Mon-Fri, winter); 9 AM to 4.30 PM (Sat-Sun, winter); Last entry 1 hour before closing -- Glasshouse: 10 AM to 5.15 PM (Mon-Sun, summer); 10 AM to 3.45 PM (Mon-Sun, winter); Last entry 15 mins before closing **WEB** rhs .org.uk/gardens/wisley **TEL** 0203 176 5800 **TIME REQUIRED** 4½-5 hours (including travel time from London)

Easy to get to? ★☆☆ Good for kids? ☆☆☆
Value for money? ★★☆ Worth a visit? ★☆☆

I thought I'd better go to Wisley before all the flowers start dying: it's nearly winter. The cold is coming. I don't want to go there and find a load of weeds and rotting autumn leaves, and a stack of sparrow bones on the lawn. I want to see sunshine and flowers. (If I'm honest I'd rather see the weeds.)

The first time I came here was about thirty years ago when I was still a kid. They used to hold open-air concerts by the lake (classical music, opera, that kind of thing) and I was dragged along by my parents. I am guessing that I didn't enjoy it very much, but the truth is that I can't remember. Actually, come to think of it... it might have been Claremont Gardens instead. Remind me to check whether there is a big lake in the middle when I get there... which will probably be in another five hours because this place is a pain to get to. They have built it right in the middle of nowhere. The nearest train station is over four miles away (West Byfleet), and there are no buses to the park. The next closest station is Woking (7 miles), but that doesn't have any buses either. All they've got is one bus that goes via Guildford and Surbiton (the 515), and that trundles up just once every hour. You'd expect them to lay on some better transport links seeing as it's a tourist attraction -- but no. If you want to come to Wisley then the best thing to do is get a car and drive (seriously).

Unfortunately I don't have a car, so I ended up braving the bus, and it's a very difficult bus stop to spot if you've never been here before. You might want to enlist the help of the bus driver if you don't have a map to follow on your phone. You need to get off along a busy dual carriageway and cross over a giant motorway bridge. It's not exactly the prettiest of entrances to a horticultural garden.

I'm not much into plants myself, so I'm probably not the best guy to review a place like this. All I do at home is mow the lawn. I don't do any planting or pruning or any of that other stuff. The only plants that I can recognise are the ones that hurt: nettles and roses. So when I look at a flower I am basically looking at the colour, and if I like the colour then I like the flower, simple as that. And my favourite colour is black.

When you walk through the gate you'll see an old Tudor-style house with manicured lawns, and waterspouts dropping into a fish-filled pond. There are little benches dotted around as well, full of old people eating sandwiches. Unfortunately they don't let you go inside the actual house itself -- that's where they have their offices -- but it doesn't appear to have much history associated with it anyway: it was only built in 1915. It certainly looks a few hundred years older than that though. That is what every new building should look like -- *old*.

I've been walking around for thirty minutes now and I think I've got the gist of the place. It's full of plants and trees that you've never seen. Trees with orange bark and ruby red leaves. Plants that are pink from head to toe, bright blues and purples too. Some of them look like they have had a paint pot tipped on top. They've all got little labels around the base so you can check out which is which, but of course they are all in Latin. Why do they do that? We are not Romans are we, and we don't speak ancient Italian. Nobody goes into B&Q and says can I have a box of Caragana Brevispina please. Doctors do that as well. And the Catholic church. They bamboozle you with classical language.

They've got a nice little pond in the middle where you can have a sit down and ponder the pointlessness of life. It's got some ducks and herons, and some noisy kids and a club of mums with six-wheel pushchairs. It is full of big fat fish that come up out of the water like beaching whales -- they literally flop up onto the pebbles like a circus seal with their mouths puffing in and out for oxygen. I am staring at one right now... he's fed up of living in the water. He doesn't want to be a fish anymore -- he's having a mid-life crisis. He wants to live on the land like me. You'll have to get some legs first, mate, I say. Let's meet again in a million years when you've grown some feet.

A section of the park is done up like an Alpine forest -- the kind of pines that are fifty feet high and covered in a lollipop of sharp green needles. The place is littered with pine cones on the carpet, and a bed of heather and mushrooms too. Obviously there are a lot of birds and squirrels running around -- you can't escape nature in this place. I actually heard a bird say *cock-a-doodle-doo* around here -- I thought they only did that in the cartoons. And there are millions and bazillions of little insects too. That is why I could never be a gardener: because I would constantly be at war with the wildlife. My advice is this: bring a newspaper with you so you can swat God's creations. Or bring a spare shoe so you can squash the bugs. The ladybirds are the worst. Lots of people think that ladybirds are cute, but they are not. When I see a ladybird coming, I run... I leg it. The ones at Wisley have got massive big teeth and the best thing to do is smash them up into little pieces before they can get the first bite in. Here is something strange: some of the ladybirds at Wisley are painted back to front. Instead of having black spots on red bodies, they have got red spots on black bodies. And that is not even a joke! It looks like they've put their coats on inside out.

If you walk right round to the end then you'll find a little birdwatching hide (like the ones they've got at the London Wetland Centre). It's just a wooden shed by a pond really, with a big window inside so you can watch the ducks doing nothing. The ducks float in the pond doing nothing, and middle-aged blokes stand at the window watching them. That is about as good a definition of birdwatching as you can get. If they were watching proper birds (women birds) then I could understand it. But feathered birds? If you stood there watching dogs and frogs all day, people would think you were a bit daft. But for some reason bird watching is considered fun.

The birdwatchers are supposed to chalk up which species they've seen on the blackboard, but there is a lot of silly stuff on there today like penguins, dodos, lions and tigers. I am assuming that somebody just wrote those for a laugh... but it didn't stop me looking out of the window to check.

My favourite part of a horticultural garden is always the big greenhouse. (I don't think you are supposed to call it a greenhouse though -- you are supposed to call it a glasshouse.) Sometimes they've got a few fish tanks inside, but this one is all about the plants. It's nowhere near as big as the Palm House at Kew, but it's still definitely worth a walk around. They've got a little underground exhibit with TVs and push button displays, and the rainforest section is about as hot and humid as can be without it becoming uncomfortable. I am guessing that the greenhouse (sorry, the *glasshouse*) is probably the only exhibit in the whole place that your kids might like to see. Everything else will bore them silly.

And that's about it. So this is how I would sum it up: It's a sunny Sunday afternoon kind of place -- a nice place to go for a stroll. And they've got quite a nice shop and a garden centre as well, if you're into that kind of thing.

P.S.: I never did find that lake... so I guess I must have been thinking of Claremont Gardens.

If you enjoy Wisley, then you will almost certainly enjoy Kew Gardens as well.

Example Itineraries

About the itineraries

Trying to write an itinerary for somebody you don't know is pretty difficult, because we all like different things. Some of us love art galleries, and some of us don't (me). Some of us like visiting Royal palaces (me) and some of us want to burn them down and turn England into a republic (traitors!). Some of us enjoy browsing around the shops, and others prefer sitting on their butts for two hours watching a movie at the cinema. So what I have tried to do is put together lots of different itineraries, taking in a wide variety of different places, so you can mix-and-match which ones you please. I have also tried to offer a few choices *within* the itineraries themselves, so you can swap out any attractions that you don't fancy.

I've lost count of the number of itineraries I've seen on the internet which rely on you running around like a nutter at supersonic speed. I'm actually looking at one right now which suggests a trip to the Tower of London (or St. Paul's Cathedral), followed by a visit to the Museum of London and then back to Tower Bridge again -- and that's just before lunch! Even Superman would struggle to get that one done. The only way that you could get all of that done before lunch is by having lunch at teatime. So I promise that you won't have any such problems with my ones. I have personally visited all of these attractions myself so I know exactly how long they take, and I have even included the journey times between each location. I have also tried my best not to cram too much stuff into each day, to give you time to stop and blow your nose if necessary (note: a maximum of 2x nose blows per day, depending on the size of the nose).

If you are going to try and plan your own itinerary then a good rule of thumb is to limit yourself to an absolute maximum of three attractions each day (three attractions that you actually want to go inside) -- but two is definitely better. Obviously if you are only planning on walking past and taking photos, then you can include a lot more; but if you try and enter any more than three then you will struggle. Bear in mind that most attractions don't even open until 10 AM, and their last entry is usually 30-60 mins before closing time; which means that you can't get inside most places after 4.30 PM. That only gives you 6½ hours in between -- which makes it very difficult to include any more than three places when you factor in travel time and lunch.

Itineraries aimed at everybody

Idea 1: Sightseeing bus, look around Westminster, meal in Leicester Square

This day includes: Sightseeing bus, Houses of Parliament, Westminster Abbey, Churchill War Rooms, Downing Street, Horse Guards, and a meal in Leicester Square or Covent Garden

A popular way of starting off your holiday is with a sightseeing bus. Everyone is impatient to see as much as possible on the first day, and a bus tour is a great way to get you interested in all the things you can see later in the week. Personally I'm not all that enamoured with them (read my reviews), but I think I'm probably in the minority here, so I'll just give you this tip: If at all possible then try and do this on a Sunday, when the traffic isn't so bad, because you might end up sitting in the traffic for two hours.

The most popular tour in London is the Original Bus Tour, and I suggest catching their 'Red Route' from Trafalgar Square. Their main office is on the southwest corner of the square.

The route will take you up the Strand and Fleet Street, past the Royal Courts of Justice and St. Paul's Cathedral, and straight over London Bridge. You will then get a great view of The Shard before passing back over Tower Bridge and round the back of the Tower of London. You will then catch a glimpse of the Globe Theatre and Tate Modern as you cross over Southwark Bridge, before re-crossing at Blackfriars and heading down Victoria Embankment to Trafalgar Square again. A left turn will take you down Whitehall past Horse Guards and Downing Street, ending up at Big Ben and Parliament Square, which is where I suggest you get off (allow for 70 mins in total, but much depends on the traffic).

If you don't fancy sitting on a sightseeing bus (and it's quite pricey too), then maybe you'd prefer an amphibious boat instead? The London Duck Tour has a shop and bus stop in York Road (near the London Eye) which takes 75 mins in total. Unfortunately the route isn't nearly as extensive as the bus, but the water aspect makes it a lot more fun for kids. It starts at the London Eye and crosses over Westminster Bridge to Parliament Square. It then goes up Whitehall towards Trafalgar Square and down Pall Mall (for St. James's Palace). It will then pass The Ritz and Wellington Arch before going round the side of Buckingham Palace (you won't get a very good view of it). It then crosses over Vauxhall Bridge and dives into the chilly Thames, bobbing up to Westminster Bridge (alongside the Houses of Parliament) before heading back to Vauxhall Bridge again. You will then end up back at the London Eye, where you can make your own way across Westminster Bridge to Parliament Square (10 mins walk).

Whether you decided to take the bus or the boat, you should now be in Parliament Square. So whip out your camera and start taking some pictures of Big Ben and the Houses of Parliament (allow for 30 mins). Then stroll over to Westminster Abbey on the south-side of the square.

Westminster Abbey is London's most prestigious religious building. It's the setting for coronations, State funerals, and the burial place of many of England's greatest kings and queens. It is well worth a visit (allow for 1½-2 hours). Note: If you do this itinerary on a Sunday then you won't be able to do any sightseeing inside, because the Abbey is only open for worship on Sundays.

If you're a Second World War buff then you might prefer to visit the Churchill War Rooms instead (10 mins walk away). You can find it opposite the southern corner of St. James's Park, at the end of King Charles Steps. This huge underground bunker was home to Winston Churchill's wartime government in World War II (allow for 1½-2 hours).

Now head down Whitehall and stop outside Downing Street (just after the Cenotaph). You might like to spend 10 minutes in front of the gates to see if you can spot the Prime Minister. (I must have stopped there about a million times myself and I've never managed to see him once -- so good luck!)

A little farther up Whitehall is one of London's most popular photo-spots: the sentry boxes outside Horse Guards. You'll probably find about ten million tourists snapping away at the horseboxes and trying and make the stony-faced soldiers laugh. Remember to have a quick look through the central arch too, where you'll find the huge parade ground that borders St. James's Park.

The walk along Whitehall will probably take about an hour (including all the photo stops), so it should be middle or late afternoon by now -- the perfect time for a meal.

At the end of Whitehall is Trafalgar Square again, but we'll explore that properly tomorrow. All we're trying to do now is find somewhere to eat. There are plenty of great restaurants around Leicester Square (5 mins walk), or how about an authentic Chinese meal in Chinatown? (10 mins walk). You can also try Covent Garden to the east (10-15 mins walk). This is where I would go if I had to choose myself, because there are plenty of good restaurants inside and around the central piazza. The easiest way to get there is by walking up the Strand, and then taking a left-turn into Southampton Street.

The rest of the evening is yours to do with as you please. I have provided a slot for theatre shows later in the week, so you might prefer to just have a wander around instead, and have a drink. (If you took my advice and did this on a Sunday, then you'll find that most of the big West End shows don't even open on a Sunday anyway.) You are right in the busy heart of London here, and there is plenty of nightlife around Leicester Square and Covent Garden.

Idea 2: National Gallery, London Dungeon, Aquarium, London Eye

This day includes: Trafalgar Square, National Gallery, London Dungeon, London Aquarium, ending with a ride on the London Eye

Let's start off in Trafalgar Square again -- the centre of London. This is home to one of London's most famous landmarks: Nelson's Column.

On the north-side of the square is the National Gallery, containing the country's finest collection of old art works. Inside are pictures by Vermeer, Cézanne, Monet, Rembrandt, Rubens, Titian, Turner and Van Gogh. Not everybody enjoys tip-toeing around art galleries, but if you only see one gallery in London then definitely make it this one (allow for 1½-2 hours). Bear in mind that the gallery doesn't usually open until 10 AM, so you'll have a bit of time beforehand to take some pictures in Trafalgar Square. If you are really nuts about art then you can try the National Portrait Gallery next-door as well (allow for 1-1½ hours).

Now walk down Northumberland Avenue and cross over Hungerford Bridge (15-20 mins walk). The impressive building on the other bank, past the London Eye and close to Westminster Bridge, is County Hall. That is where we are heading.

Try and avoid the temptation of riding the London Eye because we are saving that for later in the day, and there are two more attractions that are worth doing first. The first one is the incredibly popular London Dungeon, which uses a mixture of costumed actors and scary rides to make you wet your pants (allow for 1½ hours). The second one is right next-door -- the London Aquarium -- complete with a two-story shark tank and underwater sea tunnel (allow for 1½-2 hours).

Now you can enjoy a ride on the London Eye. It stays open until quite late in the evening, so you should still have plenty of time left. The 30-minute ride will give you some great views of Big Ben, Parliament and the distant city, especially when all of the early-evening street lights come on.

Here comes a word of warning: All three of these attractions are extremely popular, and they will likely have big queues outside (especially the London Eye), so you should be prepared for some waiting time -- maybe as much as 1-1½ hours in total. But here's the good news: You can buy a combo ticket online which includes all three places together: the London Dungeon, London Aquarium and London Eye (that is why we are doing them all on the same day, you see -- aren't I clever!). And it will work out a bit cheaper too. Check out their websites for details.

It should be quite late in the day by now, and if you haven't already eaten then you will be starving hungry. Try walking along the river towards the Royal Festival Hall, because there are a few restaurants past the Hungerford Bridge that are quite nice. There are also a few more on the top-level (go up the stairs by the Hungerford Bridge). Or you could walk even further along the river and stroll across Waterloo Bridge for some great evening views of St. Paul's and The City. If you cross over the main road at the end (the Strand) then you will find yourself back in Covent Garden, where there are plenty more good restaurants.

Idea 3: British Museum, St. Paul's, Tate Modern, Globe or The Shard

This day includes: British Museum or the Museum of London, St. Paul's Cathedral, Tate Modern, Globe Theatre or The Shard

There's a choice of two different museums today, depending on which one you prefer (just choose one).

The British Museum is the most famous museum in London and contains exhibits from all over the ancient world: Egypt, Greece, Italy, Africa and the Orient; including some colossal works by the Romans, Greeks and Persians. Highlights include the Rosetta Stone, the Parthenon Marbles and the world-famous Reading Room (allow for 2 hours).

The second option is the Museum of London, which tells the history of our city all the way back to prehistoric times. You'll find a lot Roman and medieval artefacts inside, a little bit about the Great Fire of London, a life-size Victorian shopping street, and objects all the way up to the present-day (allow 2 hours).

No trip to London would be complete without a trip to St. Paul's Cathedral, so that's where we're heading next. If you decided on the Museum of London then you will be able to walk straight to the Cathedral in ten minutes, otherwise you will have to get the 521 bus from Holborn (20 mins). Don't forget to visit the crypt downstairs and climb up the domes for a fantastic view of the skyline (allow for 2-2½ hours in total). They also have a nice cafe/restaurant downstairs where you can stop for some lunch. *Important note:* If you are planning to do this on a Sunday then you'll have to swap some stuff around, because the Cathedral doesn't open to sightseers on a Sunday (only worshippers).

Now you've got another choice to make... there are three different options coming up, but you will only have time to do one -- so take your pick. All three of them will involve a 15 minute walk across the Millennium Bridge.

On the other side of the river is the Tate Modern art gallery, home to

London's largest collection of modern art (allow for 2 hours). If you're still hungry then maybe you can try the restaurant at the top, which has some great views up and down the Thames (it's that glass level on the roof, if you're looking from the outside). *Note:* late meals are only available on Fridays and Saturdays, otherwise you'll have to stick with the bar.

Or how about a guided tour of Shakespeare's Globe Theatre instead? (allow for 90 mins). Be aware that the tours finish as early as midday between April and October, because that's the theatre season and the space will be used for plays instead -- which means you won't have enough time. But you can still visit the exhibition downstairs, because that usually remains open until 5.30 PM. If you come during the summer months then you might be able to catch a play instead, which often run as late as 7.30 PM (allow for 2-3 hours). You will have to book your ticket at least a month or two in advance though, because they sell out pretty darn quick. Whatever you choose to do, I definitely recommend checking their website first -- because there's nothing worse than a wasted trip.

The third choice is to continue walking along the river towards London Bridge, where you'll see London's tallest building rising up into the sky -- The Shard (25 mins walk from St. Paul's). This is the highest observation deck in the city, and is well worth 1½ hours of your time -- assuming that you can handle the height of course! It looks high from the ground, but trust me when I say that it looks a lot higher when you're actually up there. It's a nice posh place to enjoy an evening meal too. They've got a couple of restaurants halfway up the tower; but remember to check their website first because you'll definitely have to book in advance, and they've got a dress code as well.

Idea 4: Tower Bridge, Tower of London, Cable Car and O2 or The City

This day includes: Tower Bridge or HMS Belfast, Tower of London, followed by either the cable car and O2, or a walk around The City

This day starts off with a choice of two different places (just pick one). The first one is Tower Bridge -- one of London's most iconic landmarks. There is an exhibition inside which takes you up to the top walkway, but I don't recommend doing that. They've installed a glass floor to try and pump up the excitement a little bit, but I still don't rate it all that much, and I suggest that you give it a miss; but if you really want to give it a try then allow yourself an hour. A much better alternative is HMS Belfast next-door. You can explore all of the decks of this World War II battlecruiser in a couple of hours.

Now make your way to the Tower of London (a short walk from either attraction). This world heritage site was started by William the Conqueror in the 11th-century and is home to the Crown Jewels, the Bloody Tower, and the world-famous Traitor's Gate. I recommend starting off your visit with a Yeoman Warder tour (which is included in the cost of your ticket), where you'll get led around by one of the actual Beefeaters themselves (allow for 3 hours in total).

Now you have a choice of two things to do: the cable car and The O2, or a walk around the Square Mile (just pick one).

The O2 will involve catching a train from Tower Gateway to Royal Victoria (Tower Gateway is a 5 min walk from the Tower of London). But it's not a normal train ride... this is a driverless DLR train on an elevated track. There is no cabin at the front so if you're lucky you'll be able to sit right up against the windscreen for a great view of where you're going (journey time 20 mins). It sounds a bit boring, but trust me -- it's good fun. It is especially good if you've got kids.

When you exit Royal Victoria station head towards the water, where you'll find a cable car stretching across the Thames. It's extremely high up, and it even shakes a bit as it goes along, but the view from the top is fantastic. You can look right down the barrel of London City Airport and see the Thames Barrier upstream, plus the skyscrapers of Canary Wharf off in the distance (ride time 10-15 mins).

The ride will deposit you on the other bank about a 10-minute walk from the O2 Arena. There are a few decent restaurants outside the dome, but the best ones are inside (under the outer rim of the tent). I suggest that you go inside for a meal, and then spend the rest of the evening watching a concert. Obviously this will all depend on whether there is something on that you want to see -- so you need to check their website first and book up. You can also try looking for tickets at the Indigo, which is smaller music venue located inside the dome.

If you don't fancy the cable car and O2 then the second choice will involve a fairly lengthy walk into the heart of the Square Mile. Come out of the Tower of London and walk down Byward Street and Lower Thames Street, all the way to London Bridge. Then turn right until you find The Monument. This stone column was built by Christopher Wren after the Great Fire of London, and offers some decent views of the City skyline from the platform on the top (15 mins walk, plus another hour climbing up the column).

Now head down Gracechurch Street to Leadenhall Market (5 mins walk). This ornate Victorian market looks like it came straight from the pages of a Charles Dickens novel. There are some nice pubs and restaurants inside for a bite to eat (allow for 1 hour if you are eating).

After that turn right, and then left into Cornhill. This will take you down to Bank, where you'll find three of the City's most famous buildings: the Royal Exchange, Bank of England and Mansion House (10 mins walk). The only one that I recommend going inside is the Royal Exchange (the other two will be closed by now anyway). It's full of bars and very expensive shops, but bear in mind that the shops close a lot earlier than the bars (6 PM, as opposed to 11 PM); and if it's a weekend then I would advise swapping the days around. The City streets tend to be empty and deserted at the weekend. Hardly anyone lives in The City, and come the weekend all the workers have returned to the suburbs.

It should be very late in the day by now (perhaps as late as 7 PM), so you can either head back to your hotel or have a stroll around looking for somewhere to eat. If it was me I would probably walk across London Bridge and then east along the river (towards Tower Bridge), stopping at one of the riverside pubs.

Idea 5: Two museums, Harrods, concert at the Royal Albert Hall

This day includes: Either the Natural History Museum, Science Museum or V&A, Harrods, and then a concert at the Royal Albert Hall

Today is museum day. Take the tube to South Kensington and then pick two of the following three museums. My recommendation would be the Natural History Museum followed by the Science Museum (especially if you've got kids), but the Victoria & Albert Museum is worth a look too (I suppose you could see all three if you don't mind rushing around, but I'd prefer to take my time with two). All three museums are within 5 minutes walking distance of each other, and just 10 minutes from the station.

The Natural History Museum is called the 'dead zoo' because it is full of stuffed animals from all around the world. They've got an extinct Dodo in there, plus a life-size lion, tiger, elephant, rhino and giraffe; but the most popular exhibits are the old dinosaur bones off the main hall. They've even got an animatronic Tyrannosaurus Rex, which swings its massive head around and roars at you (allow for 2-3 hours).

The Science Museum covers everything from the earliest steam machines and cars, to modern-day computers and the Apollo moon landings. They've also got a cavernous roof-space full of airplanes and an IMAX cinema showing 3D movies (allow for 2-2½ hours).

The Victoria & Albert Museum explores the history of art and design. It is full of furniture, fashions and jewellery, and the world-famous Cast Room -- containing plaster-cast replicas of some of the world's greatest monuments and statues (allow for 2-3 hours). It sounds quite boring on paper but this is actually one of my favourite places -- make sure you read all three of my reviews before making up your mind.

All of these museums are free, so hopefully you will have plenty of money left over to splash out at Harrods -- the world's most famous department store. You'll find it a short walk down the Brompton Road. Allow for 15 mins walking time, plus another 1-1½ hours in the shop, depending on whether you do some shopping and stop to have something to eat.

A great way to finish off the day is with a concert at the Royal Albert Hall. You can catch a number of different buses from Harrods, including the 9, 10, 52 and 452 (allow for 15-20 mins ride time). They don't just show classical music, they have plenty of pop concerts, sports events and comedy gigs too. And if it's Christmas time then you're in luck, because they have some of the nicest seasonal shows around. Check their website first and remember to book up in advance (*do it right now!*). They've got a couple of nice restaurants inside as well, so you might want to save your meal for here.

If you don't fancy a concert then how about a theatre show instead? There are a couple of big theatres around Victoria station (catch the 16, 38, 52 or 73 bus from Harrods, 20 mins ride). Or maybe you'd prefer to have a meal in an expensive restaurant? Check out Chelsea, and the area around Sloane Square for that (19, 22, 137 or C1 bus, 15 mins ride time).

Idea 6: Tussauds, Sherlock Holmes, Zoo, Primrose Hill or Camden

This day includes: Madame Tussauds, Sherlock Holmes Museum or Regent's Park, London Zoo, and then Primrose Hill or Camden Town

Take the train to Baker Street for one of London's most popular attractions -- Madame Tussauds. It is surprisingly big inside and can easily take up a couple of hours. It's filled with waxworks and a sit-down ride, plus a 4D movie at the end. You should definitely buy your tickets in advance because the queues can get totally nuts (allow for 30-60 mins queue time, and 2 hours for the visit).

You've got a choice of two things to do now (just pick one). The first one is just a couple of minutes away around the corner in Baker Street -- the Sherlock Holmes Museum. It's a decent enough way to pass

1½ hours, but it's only really worth it if you're already a fan of Arthur Conan Doyle. The house has been decorated exactly as he described it in the books, and there's a collection of waxwork characters in the attic. After you've finished at the museum catch the 274 bus from Dorset Square to Primrose Hill (20 mins ride). You will then have a 5 minute walk to London Zoo.

Your second choice is a walk through Regent's Park, ending up at London Zoo on the northern edge. You can easily spend an hour or two in the park, strolling around the boating lake and Queen Mary's Gardens. They've got a couple of nice cafes as well (the best one is by Queen Mary's Gardens), and a hamburger/coffee shop too, if you fancy something to eat.

Whatever you chose to do, hopefully you will find yourself at London Zoo by 2 PM at the latest. That will give you a good 2-3 hours to introduce yourself to the animals (try not to get eaten by the crocodiles). I usually recommend 3-4 hours at the zoo, but 2-3 hours should be plenty for most people. My favourite areas are Gorilla World, Rainforest Life, Penguin Beach, the Snowdon Aviary, and the Butterfly House (don't laugh... check it out before you mock me!).

When you exit the zoo it should already be late afternoon, so you might like to walk along Regent's Canal to Camden Lock (20 mins walk). Once you get past the floating Chinese restaurant there should be some nice houseboats along the towpath, and plenty of good pubs and restaurants once you reach Camden Lock.

Alternatively, you might prefer to cross over Prince Albert Road and walk up to the summit of Primrose Hill instead (15 mins walk). It doesn't look like much of a hill when you first clap eyes on it, but believe me, as soon as you start walking up it your legs will start complaining (or maybe I am just very unfit). The view from the top offers one of the finest views of the London skyline from anywhere in the city. Unfortunately there are no cafes nearby, so after you've swapped some stories on the summit you should make your way into Camden for a meal (25 mins walk, or 15 mins on the 274 bus).

Idea 7: Changing the Guard, tea at The Ritz, shopping and a show

This day includes: St. James's Park, Changing the Guard, tea at The Ritz or Fortnum & Mason, Piccadilly Circus, shopping in Regent Street and Oxford Street, plus a show in the West End

Now for one of the must-see sights in London... Changing of the Guard at Buckingham Palace. The ceremony starts at 11.15 AM but I recommend getting there by 10:30 AM for a decent spot (you will need to get there by 10 AM if you want a perfect spot right up against the railings). The ceremony usually takes place every day between April and August, but alternate days at other times -- so remember to check their website to make sure you get the right day.

Unfortunately most of the big attractions don't open until 10 AM, which means that you won't have enough time to do anything beforehand (especially when you remember it's a 10-15 min walk down The Mall to Buckingham Palace), so you can fill up an hour beforehand by having a stroll through St. James's Park. This is easily London's prettiest park, and you can get some great photos standing on the central bridge over the lake. If you look one way then you'll have a great shot of the palace, whilst the other way looks past a fountain to Horse Guards Parade.

When the ceremony ends at 12 noon take a stroll through Green Park to Piccadilly (5 min walk). There's not much to see in the park itself, but Piccadilly has the world-famous Ritz Hotel. How about stopping for some Afternoon Tea? You will have to book up at least three months in advance and observe their dress code, but this is the kind of event that will impress your friends back home with. If you don't make it then don't fret -- try the tea at Fortnum & Mason instead (you only have to book 1-2 weeks in advance for that). Fortnum & Mason is second only to Harrods as the most prestigious store in London.

Keep walking down Piccadilly and you will come to the neon lights of Piccadilly Circus (10 min walk). No trip to London would be complete without a photo of yourself standing underneath the Eros fountain.

You are right in the heart of the West End now, and we will be returning here tonight. But I'm giving you the rest of the afternoon to do some shopping. Every decent itinerary has to build in some time to buy gifts, and I suggest walking north up Regent Street, followed by a left down Oxford Street. You'll find Selfridges right up the end (near Marble Arch), and Carnaby Street close to the junction with Oxford Circus. If you've got loads of money (and I mean *loads* of money -- more money than sense!), then check out Bond Street as well. Burlington Arcade has got lots of little nice shops inside, and corny tourist gifts can be found around Piccadilly Circus and Leicester Square (tea towels, mugs and magnets -- that kind of thing). Covent Garden is only a short 15-20 min walk away as well, and there are lots of nice shops inside the piazza.

The evening can be spent at a West End show. You can get tickets from the little shops around Leicester Square, and the cheapest ones can be bought from the TKTS booth on one side of the central square. Most of the big theatres can be found around Covent Garden, Shaftesbury Avenue and Piccadilly Circus -- but bear in mind that most West End shows are closed on a Sunday, or only open six days a week, so you might want to swap your days around. Check the listings first!

If you don't fancy the theatre then how about a big blockbuster movie instead? Leicester Square is home to three of London's largest cinemas, and there are plenty of pubs around for a pre-movie beer. My favourite cinema is actually one of the smaller ones -- the Prince Charles Cinema -- which shows classic old movies like *Annie Hall, Alien, Ghostbusters, Pretty Woman and Jaws*.

Idea 8: Cutty Sark, Nat. Maritime Museum, Royal Observatory, boat ride

This day includes: Cutty Sark, National Maritime Museum, Old Royal Naval College or the Royal Observatory, and a boat back to Westminster

Let's go a bit further afield today... with a train ride to Greenwich. We will travel from Tower Gateway (near the Tower of London) to Cutty Sark on the Docklands Light Railway (allow for 20-25 mins ride time). The DLR uses electric trains on an elevated monorail, and they don't have a cabin at the front; so if you're lucky you can bag yourself the front seat right up against the windscreen. Be aware that you can't walk between the cabins though, so if you want to try and nab the best seat then you need to board the train right at the front.

There are quite a lot of things to see and do in Greenwich, so I am going to give you a choice. You won't have anywhere near enough time to do them all though, so just choose two out of the following four.

The first one is the famous old Cutty Sark clipper ship (allow for 90 mins). You can explore this ship from deck to deck, walk along the top, and even stroll underneath its suspended hull. They have lifted the entire ship ten metres off the ground, and to see it hanging above your head is quite a sight. It's certainly worth a look, but given the time constraints you might want to give it a miss in favour of the other options.

If you're into naval history then check out the National Maritime Museum. One of its highlights is the actual uniform that Admiral Nelson was wearing during the Battle of Trafalgar -- you can even see the ripped fabric where the fatal bullet entered his shoulder. Remember to check out the Queen's House as well, which is home to the museum's collection of naval paintings (allow for 2 hours in total, and a 10-15 min walk from Cutty Sark).

The most energetic option is at the top of Greenwich hill -- the Royal Observatory. It's a very steep hill, and if you are unfit like me then it will probably totally knacker you out, but luckily they have a very nice food stall at the top selling hot dogs and posh burgers (allow for 20 mins walking time). The Royal Observatory is where you'll find the Meridian line (the line which separates the eastern hemisphere from the west), and the museum covers everything from the earliest clocks and watches to modern-day telescopes. The most popular attraction is the state-of-the-art planetarium, where you can sit back and relax underneath the night sky and watch as the stars and planets streak across the screen (allow for 2-3 hours in total).

Whichever two options you decided to pick you can probably make time for a walk around the Old Royal Naval College -- one of Christopher Wren's most beautiful buildings. You can't get inside all of it, but don't miss the famous Painted Hall and Chapel (allow for 1 hour).

At some point you will want to stop for a spot of lunch, so head into the historic town centre. Greenwich is a World Heritage Site that dates back hundreds of years (all the way back to Henry VIII) and there are plenty of traditional little pubs and tea rooms (10-15 mins walk from the Old Royal Naval College).

After you've finished exploring Greenwich head back to the Cutty Sark for a boat trip back to Westminster. The 60 minute ride from Greenwich Pier to Westminster Pier will give you great views of Canary Wharf, Tower Bridge, the Tower of London and The City. Note: the last boat can depart anytime between 4 PM and 6.30 PM, depending on the time of year you go -- so plan your day carefully. There are three boat companies which operate from Greenwich: City Cruises, Thames Clippers and Thames River Services (TRS), and I recommend reading my detailed reviews for each.

Itineraries aimed at families

Idea 9: London Eye, London Dungeon and Aquarium, NAMCO

This day includes: London Eye, London Dungeon, London Aquarium, Namco Centre

Dragging your kids around London on the busy bus and underground can sometimes be a nightmare, especially when it's hot and they are tired and start whining and crying and dying on their feet. So this day does away with all the travel time, and focuses on three attractions which are right next-door to each other -- *literally*.

The London Eye is the perfect place to start your day. Kids are rarely into sightseeing and taking photos like adults are, so this will at least allow you to point out some famous landmarks like Big Ben, Buckingham Palace and the Houses of Parliament without having to drag them around the streets (allow for 30-45 mins queuing, and 30 mins on the actual wheel).

Now take a ten-second stroll over to the County Hall where you'll find the London Dungeon, which uses a combination of costumed actors and short rides to explain the history of London (allow for 1½ hours). It covers such cheerful subjects as the plague, Henry VIII's headless wives, Jack the Ripper and the Great Fire of London. Bear in mind that the recommended age limit is 8-and-above, and there are some height restrictions on the rides as well -- so check their website first. I have been there myself and I don't think that there's anything too scary inside, but you should be aware that it is extremely dark and there are lots of very loud bangs and screams throughout -- so if you've got a very nervous kid then you might want to think twice. (Or just take them anyway, for a laugh!)

The next attraction is another ten-seconds along the path -- the London Aquarium. I love this place. The standout exhibit is a huge shark tank that spans two whole floors. They've installed a glass walkway across the top if you fancy dicing with death, and there's an underwater sea tunnel as well (allow for 1½-2 hours). They've also got some penguins and a crocodile in there.

At some point you will want to stop for something to eat, and I recommend the Namco Funscape next-door to the London Aquarium. It's a bit like an indoor funfair I suppose, with three floors of arcade games, driving games, bumper-car dodgems and ten-pin bowling. They've got lots of fairground games that you used to play as a kid as well -- do you remember that one where you bounced a penny down the slot and hoped that it pushed a stack of them off the ledge? They've got some of those, plus some cuddly toy cranes. You will find a McDonalds right inside the front door.

Important note: You can save a lot of money by buying a combo ticket for the London Eye, London Dungeon and London Aquarium. You should be able to get one from whichever attraction you decide to visit first, or you can order one online in advance. The price will should be a lot cheaper if you do it online in advance -- and you won't have to queue up at the ticket desk either.

Idea 10: Madame Tussauds, London Zoo

This day includes: Madame Tussauds and London Zoo

Take the train to Baker Street for Madame Tussauds.

You should definitely buy your tickets in advance because the queues can get totally ridiculous (allow for 30-60 mins queue time, and 2 hours for the visit). To be perfectly honest I don't understand why this place is so popular, but everyone else seems to like it so I think I'm in the minority -- maybe I'm just getting old (I'm over three thousand years old). Your kids will probably recognise more celebrities than you do, because they've got everyone from Lady Gaga and Justin Timberlake to One Direction and Rihanna. They probably won't enjoy the politicians and Royal Family so much, though, but will perk up when they reach the Chamber of

Horrors (they must be at least 12-years-old to enter).

Their *Spirit of London* ride is quite fun as well -- you board a time-travelling taxicab and drive through five centuries of the city's history (height restrictions apply, so check their website first). Even the adults will enjoy this bit -- this was my favourite part of the visit.

If you have very energetic kids then you can take a stroll through Regent's Park to London Zoo. Otherwise you can do what I did -- catch the number 274 bus from Dorset Square to Primrose Hill (25 mins ride, plus another 5 min walk at the end).

London Zoo will take up the rest of your day, so allow for 3-4 hours in total. This is just an old-fashioned zoo, full of lions and tigers, giraffes, zebras, Gorilla World, Rainforest Life, creepy crawlies, tropical birds and Penguin Beach. They've got lots of reptiles and an aquarium as well, and you can watch some live animal feedings and a trained-bird display. There are no rides inside (not even a monorail), so it's just the animals and nothing else; but I still rate this as one of my favourite attractions in the whole of London.

Idea 11: Hamleys, Ripley's, Rainforest Cafe, movie at the cinema

This day includes: Hamleys, Piccadilly Circus, Ripley's Believe It Or Not!, Rainforest Cafe, cinema in Leicester Square or the BFI IMAX

If you want to treat your kids to some toys then there's only one place to go: Hamleys in Regent Street. This is the biggest toy store in London, and they've usually got a few live demonstrations going on as well. They also have more cuddly animals than a zoo.

After that head south down Regent Street to Piccadilly Circus, where you can show your kids the famous neon lights and Eros statue (10 mins walk). Then it's into Ripley's Museum of Believe It Or Not! for a couple of hours.

This museum is filled with weird and wonderful objects from around the world. They've got waxwork models of the world's smallest and tallest man, for example, and the world's ugliest guy (no, it's not me). Or how about the world's hairiest woman? They've got shrunken heads, two-headed goats, five-legged sheep... and a portrait made out of burnt toast. If your kids are starting to play up then check out the torture chamber, filled with gruesome punishments and a smoking electric chair.

After that it's probably time for lunch. I recommend the Rainforest Cafe, which is just a short walk around the corner. There are lots of McDonalds/Burger King-type restaurants around here as well, because this part of London is tourist-central -- try walking down Coventry Street towards Leicester Square.

A great way to spend the afternoon is with a big blockbuster movie in Leicester Square, which is home to three of the capital's largest cinemas. The Empire, Odeon, and West End Vue have got twenty-two screens between them, so they're bound to have something suitable on. Or maybe you'd prefer the BFI IMAX cinema instead? This place shows all the latest 3D movies, and you can find it at the other end of Waterloo Bridge (20-25 mins walk). If you don't fancy the walk then just catch the 176 bus from Charing Cross Road and it will take you straight past Trafalgar Square and Nelson's Column, up the Strand and across Waterloo Bridge (25 mins ride).

Idea 12: Natural History and Science Museum

This day includes: Natural History Museum's dinosaurs, and Science Museum's rockets

When I was a little kid we always used to get taken on a school trip to the big museums in London. Sound boring? *Nope!* The two museums that I'm going to mention now are just perfect for kids, and they are handily situated within a five minute walk of each other. And the best thing of all: they are completely free!

Take the train to South Kensington and then walk to the Natural History Museum. There is a long tunnel that takes you straight from the tube station to the corner of the museum (the entrance is just past the ticket barrier), but I actually prefer the walk above ground because South Kensington is quite nice when it's sunny (10 mins walk).

If your kids are into dinosaurs then they're in for a treat... they've got a full-size Diplodocus in the entrance hall. They've also got a huge mechanical Tyrannosaurus Rex that swings around and roars -- and tries to bite your head off. The Natural History Museum is called the 'dead zoo' because it is full of stuffed animals from around the world. You name it, they've got it: lions, tigers, elephants, rhinos, polar bears, pandas, dodos, eagles... and a life-size blue whale suspended from the ceiling. It's almost like going to a real zoo, except everything in it stands still so you can take a photo (allow for 2-3 hours).

The Science Museum is a five minute walk around the corner (allow for 2-2½ hours). If your kids like space then head for the ground floor, where they keep all their rockets and moon landers. They've got a full-size replica of the Eagle lander which took Buzz Aldrin to the moon (*let's give some love to Buzz for a change -- Neil always get the glory!*), plus some bits about Sputnik and the modern-day missions. The rest of the museum contains early steam machines and cars, and big galleries full of boats and full-size airplanes.

The whole place is packed with push-button displays for the kids to press, and there is also a little IMAX cinema showing 3D movies.

Idea 13: Playground, boats, Natural History or Science Museum

This day includes: Princess Diana's Memorial Playground, pedal boat on the Serpentine, Natural History Museum or Science Museum

This day starts off at the Princess Diana Memorial Playground. You'll find it in the north-west corner of Kensington Gardens. They are super-safe at this place and only little kids under the age of 12 are allowed inside (with their supervising adults), so you don't have to worry about them being jumped on by a ten tonne teenager. They've done it out in a *Peter Pan*-theme and there's a big pirate ship in the middle. They've also got plenty of swings and slides and a sand-pit beach (allow for 1 hour).

A short stroll across Kensington Gardens will take you to the Serpentine Lake (allow for 20 min walk). On the north bank you will find a little shop with some pedal boats for hire (allow for 1 hour, Easter to the end of October only). They can carry up to six people each and presumably dad will be doing all the pedalling, so you might want to have a sit-down and a rest afterwards in the little restaurant on the south-side of the lake (it also has some toilets). If dad doesn't fancy doing all that pedalling then they've also got a large SolarShuttle boat, that glides across the water powered by the sun (summer only).

The rest of the day can be spent at either the Natural History Museum or the Science Museum (just pick one). They are both next-door to each other and can be found on the south-side of Kensington Gardens, past the Albert Memorial and Royal Albert Hall, and down the end of Exhibition Road (25-30 mins walking time).

Both of the museums are good for kids, so which one should you pick? Well... if your kid likes dinosaurs then definitely take them to the Natural History Museum. They've got a full-size Diplodocus in the entrance hall, a huge Stegosaurus skull and a mechanical Tyrannosaurus Rex which moves around and roars. The rest of the museum is full of stuffed zoo animals: lions, tigers, elephants, rhinos, polar bears, pandas, eagles, fish and tropical birds... even a life-size blue whale suspended from the ceiling. If your kid is a big fan of natural disasters then he'll love the stuff about earthquakes and volcanoes (allow for 2-3 hours).

If your kid is more interested in spaceships, planes and cars, then check out the Science Museum instead. It covers everything from the earliest steam machines (boring) to the Apollo moon landings (better!). There are plenty of interactive displays for them to play with, lots of buttons to press, and they've also got a 3D IMAX cinema inside (allow for 2-2½ hours).

Idea 14: Cable car, show at The O2 or a boat ride

This day includes: A trip on the driverless DLR train, a ride on the cable car, and a show at The O2 or a boat ride back to Westminster

This day really relies upon there being a suitable show at The O2, so check their website to see what's on before you go (and buy a ticket!). It's not just a music venue -- they also have plenty of kid-friendly shows. In the past they've had shows like *Disney On Ice, Walking With Dinosaurs* and *WWE* (wrestling). They also host a few big-name tennis tournaments and American NBA games.

Assuming that there's something decent on and you've bagged yourself a ticket, start the day off by getting a train to the Excel Centre. Sound boring? *Nope!* Because this is not a normal train... I'm talking about one of those driverless DLR trains. There are no cabins at the front of these things, so if you're quick and lucky then you can grab a seat right in front of the windscreen for a great view of the elevated track. I recommend boarding the train at Bank, where it begins, and then you can watch it tear through the tunnel before coming up above ground for the rest of the route. The journey to Royal Victoria takes about 20-25 minutes.

Come out of the station and head towards the water, where you'll see a cable car stretching across the Thames. If this is the very first time you've seen the cable car then I will forgive you a little tremble, because it is probably a lot higher than you imagined. It is *extremely* high up, and shakes a bit as it goes along -- but what a ride! The view from the top takes in everything from the Thames Barrier and skyscrapers at Canary Wharf, to the planes coming in to land at London City Airport (ride time 5-10 mins).

The white-knuckle ride will end on the other bank, where you'll see the O2 Arena dead ahead. There are a couple of decent restaurants outside the dome, but I recommend going inside for a meal because there are lots of good ones underneath the rim.

Note: Even if you don't buy a ticket for a show, then you can still have a look around inside and use the restaurants. And instead of watching a show you can do something that's just as good: catch an open-top boat back to Westminster. The Thames Clipper service operates a ferry every half-hour until late in the evening, and the 60-minute ride will take you past Greenwich, Canary Wharf, Tower Bridge, the Tower of London, The Shard, St. Paul's Cathedral... all the way back to Big Ben and Parliament. To be perfectly honest, I would probably prefer the boat ride to a show.

Idea 15: Shard, Golden Hinde, lunch at Borough Market and HMS Belfast

This day includes: The Shard, Golden Hinde, lunch at Borough Market and HMS Belfast

This day starts off with a climb to the top of London's tallest building -- The Shard. But first a word of warning: this is the highest observation deck in the city, and I'm being serious when I say it might be too scary for very young kids. It scared the pants out of me, and I'm a fully grown bloke! The viewing levels have got floor to ceiling windows and if you suffer from vertigo then you will feel a little giddy. The highest level even has a few bits open to the sky, so you can feel the chilly wind in your face. But it's well worth spending 1-1½ hours there if your nerves are up to it.

We are going to spend the rest of the day exploring two very different boats. The first one is a quick 5-10 minute walk away, past Southwark Cathedral. It's called the Golden Hinde II, and it's a full-size replica of the ship that carried Francis Drake around the world. This is how you should sell it to your kids: It's an Elizabethan pirate ship with a deck full of cannons, and they can clamber around every inch of it trying out the wooden steering wheel, lying in the captain's bunk, and making their dad walk the gang-plank (allow for 1 hour).

You will probably want to stop for a bit of lunch after that, and I recommend popping into Borough Market, which is a big indoor market with a lot of lively food stalls (it's on the other side of the road to where The Shard was). It might not sound very exciting on paper, but trust me -- you can get some really nice flame-grilled burgers and hot dogs in there (allow for 45 mins-1 hour eating time).

Now head back towards the water and walk east along the river, towards Tower Bridge. After 15 minutes you should reach HMS Belfast -- an old World War II battlecruiser that has been moored up opposite the Tower of London. If you ever dream of sending your kids off to join the navy then this will give them a taste of what it's like. They can explore everything from the gun deck, engine room and missile room, to the mess deck and captain's quarters. The whole place is staffed by waxworks -- plotting courses on the radar, peeling potatoes in the kitchens, playing cards in the bunks, having their teeth pulled out at the dentist -- and the sounds pumped through the speakers give it a real atmospheric and claustrophobic feeling (allow for 2 hours).

Top 10 Lists

Top 10 Must-Dos

① Have a ride on the London Eye
② Buckingham Palace Summer Opening
③ Houses of Parliament Saturday tour
④ View from the top of The Shard
⑤ Watch Changing the Guard
⑥ Ride a boat underneath Tower Bridge
⑦ Whispering Gallery at St. Paul's
⑧ Ride on the London Underground
⑨ Watch a play at Shakespeare's Globe
⑩ Do some shopping at Harrods

If I had to recommend just ten things that every tourist should do in London, then these are the ones. We could probably sit here and argue about this list all day, because everybody is going to have their own likes and dislikes -- I'm not a big fan of art galleries, for example, so there's no place for the National Gallery. And the British Museum is missing too, because I find it quite dull looking at a load of broken stones and bones all day. But I appreciate that there are plenty of people out there who find all of that stuff fascinating. But not me though... *and it's my list!*

I always recommend starting off your holiday with a ride on the London Eye (preferably on your very first day), because *a)* it is quite an exciting thing to do, and *b)* it will also give you a good overview of the city in a short space of time. With a bit of luck you can be on and off it inside an hour, which will give you loads of time to do other things on your first day. The Shard is quite pricey for what it offers... but what a view! The Whispering Gallery inside St. Paul's Cathedral is worth a look too, and if you climb up another flight of stairs then you'll get another great view of the skyline from outside the dome.

Take a tip from me: try and come during the summer when Buckingham Palace and the Houses of Parliament throw open their doors to the public. A guided tour of those two places will definitely make your trip. If you can't make the summer then Parliament also offers guided tours on most Saturdays (the ticket office is across the road in Portcullis House).

Some of the other places are on here because... well... you can't come to London and miss Changing the Guard at Buckingham Palace, can you? Because that is the first thing that people will ask you when you get back home: *"Did you see the Queen at Buckingham Palace?"* And it's the same with Harrods: no one wants to receive one of those crappy *"My brother went to London and all I got was this lousy t-shirt"* t-shirts; what they want is an expensive gift from Harrods in a dark green carrier bag.

If you're wondering why I've included a ride on the London Underground, then that's because it's an experience in itself. When you're descending into the bowels of the earth on a ten-story escalator, wedging yourself into a tightly-packed tube train at rush hour, then you'll know what it's like to live in London. Another of my personal favourites is a boat ride from Big Ben to Greenwich. It can sometimes be a little cold and choppy on the water, but you'll get some fantastic views of the London Eye, St. Paul's, the city skyscrapers and the Tower of London, then under Tower Bridge, and on to Canary Wharf and the Cutty Sark.

Top 10 Things For Free

① Ceremony of the Keys
② Prime Minister's Questions
③ Climb to the top of Big Ben
④ Visit some museums: Natural History Museum, Science Museum, V&A, British Museum, Imperial War Museum, Sir John Soane's Museum, Museum of London
⑤ View from the top of Sky Garden
⑥ Changing the Guard
⑦ Evensong at Westminster Abbey
⑧ Visit some galleries: National Gallery, National Portrait Gallery, Tate Britain, Tate Modern and Wallace Collection
⑨ Church service at Hampton Court
⑩ Street entertainers at Covent Garden

Apparently the best things in life are free -- that is what they tell me anyway. But obviously those people have never been to London before because it is one of the most expensive cities in the world! But happily there are still a few things worth doing that won't break the bank, and I will share my Top 10 with you now.

Ceremony of the Keys at the Tower of London is definitely at the top of my list, but unfortunately you have to book up a few months in advance. It's the same with Prime Minister's Questions and climbing up Big Ben -- you need to post off a letter at least 3 or 4 months in advance. But all three of them are definitely worth the effort -- they could easily end up being the highlight of your stay.

[Note: Before the pedants start writing me letters correcting my mistake: yes, I am aware that 'Big Ben' is the name of the bell and not the tower, and it is therefore not possible to climb up it. But if I suggested climbing up the Elizabeth Tower then no one would have known what I was talking about!]

London is famous for letting everyone into the big museums and art galleries for free. And not just the rubbish ones either: the National Gallery, Natural History Museum, British Museum, Science Museum, Tate Britain and Victoria & Albert Museum are some of the most popular attractions in the capital. And don't forget about the Imperial War Museum, Museum of London, Sir John Soane's Museum, the National Portrait Gallery and Guildhall Art Gallery (with the remains of London's Roman amphitheatre in the basement). You could literally spend your entire holiday just looking around the free museums and galleries.

You can enjoy some decent views of the skyline for free, but the best of the bunch is undoubtedly at the Sky Garden. That is the big walkie talkie-shaped skyscraper in The City. If you print off a ticket from their website then you can ride the lift all the way to the top and see their indoor garden. You might also like to ride the lift to the top of One New Change as well (a shopping centre round the back of St. Paul's).

Attending a choral Evensong service at Westminster Abbey and St. Paul's Cathedral is also worth a try, and you can sneak a peek inside Hampton Court Palace and the Tower of London as well -- provided that you promise you're only there to see the church service (you are supposed to buy a ticket to see the rest of them).

Top 10 For Kids

① Chessington World of Adventures
② London Eye
③ Cable car across the Thames
④ London Zoo
⑤ London Dungeon
⑥ Warner Bros. Studios (Harry Potter)
⑦ London Duck Tour
⑧ Science Museum (if they like space) or Natural History Museum (for dinosaurs)
⑨ London Aquarium
⑩ Madame Tussauds

This is another hard list to write -- primarily because I am not a little kid anymore. But luckily I still act and behave like a child, so I have an advantage.

You can't go wrong with Chessington World of Adventures -- there isn't a kid in the world that won't like that place. (I am prepared to stake my life on that.) It is full of rollercoasters and rides and there's a decent aquarium and zoo too. The Harry Potter Studios could also be a holiday highlight -- but only if your kid actually likes Harry Potter (give it a miss otherwise, because it's just a load of stage sets).

If your kid can handle the height then try them on the London Eye, or even better: a ride on the cable car. If they are super brave then you might try them on The Shard as well (but that even scared *me!*). If they can't stomach the altitude then maybe you can treat them to a London Duck Tour instead -- an amphibious boat that rides around the roads before diving into the chilly Thames.

A lot of the family attractions in London have become tourist traps and are horrendously over-priced (and yes, I am thinking of *you* Madame Tussauds). Ripley's Believe It Or Not is another one that you will find in all the guidebooks, but take a tip from me: save your money with that one. I didn't enjoy the London Dungeon much either, but I am prepared to accept that was probably just me being a miserable old git. Your kids will probably enjoy it a lot more than us adults do; hence its high position on the list.

If you've got kids then the chances are that you will end up at Madame Tussauds, and that is why I have included it on the list; but to be perfectly honest I would give that a miss as well. Why would a kid enjoy looking at Elvis Presley? Or Adolf Hitler? Most of the kids these days don't even know who Adolf Hitler is (they probably think he plays in goal for Bayern Munich). And whilst your wife might enjoy looking at Brad Pitt, to a kid he's just another fifty-year-old bloke whose last decent movie was made before they were even born. The only bit that they will truly enjoy is the Spirit of London ride; but is it really worth stumping up all that money just for that? (I think not.)

Some of the attractions in my top ten I rate a lot higher than I have placed them (like the London Aquarium and Natural History Museum, for example), but I am trying to put my kid head on, and see it through their eyes; and walking around a load of fish tanks and staring at some stuffed animals inside a glass case is a bit boring when you're only eight. One of the problems with being an adult, is that we tend to mix up 'educational' with 'fun', and whilst walking around a museum might be educational, let's face it: it's rarely fun, in the way that a child would see it. They would much rather see a real lion at the zoo, than a stuffed one at the Natural History Museum. They'd much rather watch a planetarium show at the Royal Observatory then visit the Science Museum.

Top 10 Art Galleries

① National Gallery
② Buckingham Palace or Queen's Gallery
③ Victoria & Albert Museum
④ Wallace Collection
⑤ Tate Britain
⑥ Courtauld Gallery
⑦ Old Royal Naval College
⑧ Banqueting House
⑨ National Portrait Gallery
⑩ Tate Modern

If you've fought your way through the rest of the book then you will certainly know by now that I am no lover of art, but even

I can tell a good gallery when I see one, and the National Gallery, Wallace Collection, Tate Britain and Courtauld Gallery are the best of the bunch (in that order). The first three have the advantage of being free, so you might want to skip the Courtauld (it's basically a cut-down version of the National).

I'm slotting Buckingham Palace in at No.2, though, because even though it's obviously not an art gallery, it does contain a large part of the Royal Collection. As you walk around the rooms you'll be looking at works by Rembrandt, Rubens, Vermeer and Canaletto. Unfortunately you can only visit it when it opens up to the public during the summer, so you might have to settle for the Queen's Gallery instead. Windsor Castle is also worth a look, but that's a long train ride away. Kensington Palace has some decent pieces on show, but nowhere near as good as the other two.

Strictly speaking the V&A is a museum and not a gallery, but I've put it at No.3 on my list because it has a surprisingly good collection of art inside: huge pieces by Raphael, and lots of British art by Gainsborough, Constable and Turner. It also has a very fine collection of stained glass.

Banqueting House and the Old Royal Naval College are not galleries either (*what kind of art gallery list is this?*), and they both contain the grand total of one picture each -- but what a picture! Banqueting House has a very famous Rubens on the ceiling, whilst the old Royal Naval College has one by Nicholas Hawksmoor wrapped right around the room. I'm guessing that you don't really want to visit ten galleries in one holiday, so these two places might be a way of indulging your love of art whilst trying something a bit different.

An honourable mention must go to the National Portrait Gallery (next door to the National Gallery). The quality of the paintings sometimes takes a back seat to the importance of the sitter, but if you like history more than art then maybe you'll enjoy it -- it's basically a *Who's Who* of famous Brits.

If you prefer modern art then by all means try the Tate Modern, but it's the kind of place that puts a mirror on the wall and calls it a picture.

Top 10 Museums

① Churchill War Rooms
② Natural History Museum
③ Victoria & Albert Museum
④ Science Museum
⑤ RAF Museum
⑥ Sir John Soane's Museum
⑦ Museum of London
⑧ Imperial War Museum
⑨ British Museum
⑩ National Maritime Museum

The first thought that might enter your head when you look at this list is 'Why is the British Museum at No.9?' Surely there must be some kind of mistake? Well, no, there is no mistake -- I am not a big fan of the British Museum. There... I said it. String me up and shoot me if you wish, but I don't care. Walking around three hundred rooms looking at different coloured stones and bones is not my idea of a fun day out. *Here are some broken plates from Rome... here are some broken plates from Greece... here are some broken plates from Asia... boring!*

The kind of museums that I like are the ones that give you goosebumps... the ones that make you stop in your tracks and go *woah!* And that's why the Churchill War Museum makes the top of my list, because when you first clap eyes on the rooms where Winston plotted the war, whilst the bombs were dropping on London and raining dust and debris on Whitehall, then that is a genuinely spine-tingling moment. That is *real* history -- not some busted bits of pot they dug up in a desert.

The Natural History Museum and Science Museum are both worth a visit. The Natural History Museum is almost like a zoo -- they've got lions and tigers in there, polar bears, elephants and giraffes... and that's before you even get to the dinosaurs. The Science Museum has plenty of big machines and push-button contraptions, and if you're into space then you will love it, because they have some full-size rockets and moon landers. They also have a floor upstairs containing some full-size planes hanging from the ceiling.

The Victoria & Albert Museum sounds quite boring on paper (a museum about art and design?), but if you read my review then you will see how a visit changed my mind. I walked in believing it was rubbish and came out thinking it was great -- that is the sign of a good museum. The Wallace Collection did that to me as well (which is in my art galleries list).

Sir John Soane's Museum is one of the nuttiest houses that you will ever see. You have to be super-skinny to walk down some of the corridors, because the walls are cramped up with every kind of knick-knack in Christendom. He went around the world and stuffed his bag full of stones and bones and plates and slates, and glued them to every shelf and spare inch of wall space he could find. It is a duster's nightmare -- but a must-see for everyone else.

I don't think it will come as much of a surprise if I tell you that I like London, so that's why the Museum of London is down there. I think it's probably more interesting for the locals though, rather than the tourists. And the Museum of London Docklands is the same -- skip it if you're on holiday, but give it a try if you know London. The Guildhall Art Gallery is another place that Londoners will like -- especially when you discover what's in the basement!

I've put the RAF Museum and the Imperial War Museum down here because I like World War II, so they hold a special interest for me. I personally think that the RAF Museum is one of the most amazing museums around -- they've got more planes in there than your average airport. The Imperial War Museum isn't anywhere near as good as it used to be when I was a kid, but it still contains some interesting bits and pieces.

The final spot on my list goes to the National Maritime Museum... but only because of their Nelson memorabilia. They have lots of original items on show, including the actual jacket that he was wearing when he got shot (complete with the musket hole). The rest of the museum is a little bit disappointing, if I'm honest, but the Nelson exhibits more than make up for it.

Top 10 Royal Sites

① Buckingham Palace
② Windsor Castle
③ Hampton Court Palace
④ Crown Jewels at the Tower of London
⑤ Royal burials at Westminster Abbey
⑥ Kensington Palace
⑦ Clarence House
⑧ Kew Palace (in Kew Gardens)
⑨ Royal Mews
⑩ St. James's Palace

I'm a big fan of the Royal Family, so I could happily walk around these places all day. But I have been careful to list them in the order that I think will appeal most to a tourist.

At the top of the list has got to be Buckingham Palace. If you come during the summer then you can get a ticket to look inside... and it really is worth looking at. Buckingham Palace is the kind of place that you'll remember ten years after coming. It's the same with Windsor Castle... you can't come all the way to London and not see one of the Queen's two grandest palaces. If you've only got time for one or the other, then definitely choose Buckingham Palace; but Windsor has got the advantage of being open all year round, rather than just during the summer. [Note: I actually prefer Windsor Castle myself, but I still put Buckingham Palace at the top because Windsor is a pain to get to.]

Hampton Court and Kensington Palace are also worth a look, but you can definitely skip Kensington if you are short on time (it's okay, but it's nowhere near as impressive as the others). Kew Palace is only worth a visit if you want to see Kew Gardens as well. And Clarence House is more of a Stately home than a palace, full of rooms that look like they have been decorated by your grandma.

The Royal Mews is home to the Royal Family's collection of State coaches and posh cars, and if you're lucky then you might see some horses trotting around as well. But you probably need a particular interest in those things to make a visit worthwhile, because there's not a lot about the Royals themselves.

There's not much that I can say about the Tower of London that I haven't already said about a million times before -- *so just go!* You won't regret spending half a day at the Tower. There can sometimes be big queues outside Waterloo Barracks, where the Crown Jewels are kept, but it's definitely worth the wait. Other highlights include the armoury exhibit inside the White Tower, the historic Line of Kings,

and the Bloody Tower where the two little princes were murdered by Richard III -- allegedly. (I have to say that because I don't want the Richard III Society on my case.)

St. James's Palace is a very important building, and is actually the chief building of the Royal court, but sadly it's not open to the public. All you can do is walk around outside and sneak a peek -- hence its low position on my list.

Top 10 Religious Sites

① Westminster Abbey
② St. Paul's Cathedral
③ Evensong at Westminster Abbey
④ Highgate Cemetery
⑤ Church service at Hampton Court or the Tower of London
⑥ Brompton Oratory
⑦ Evensong at St. Paul's Cathedral
⑧ Temple Church
⑨ All Hallows by the Tower
⑩ St. Bartholomew-the-Great

If you're into religion then you're spoilt for choice in London -- we have a lot of sinners in this town so we have a lot of churches too. You're probably going to run out of prayers before you see everything. Are you allowed to say the same prayer in each church? God might get a bit bored hearing the same old prayer each time, so maybe you can offer up some prayers for me instead (Lord knows I need them).

It's a toss up between Westminster Abbey and St. Paul's for the best religious building in London. Obviously they are both fantastic, and if you've got the time then you should definitely see both; but I must admit to having a soft spot for the Abbey. I like my churches to be dark and moody. They have to be cold stone and quiet, and Westminster Abbey is a lot darker than St. Paul's -- St. Paul's is almost bright white like daytime. The statues and monuments inside the Abbey are also a lot more interesting than the Cathedral's. But it's a pointless conversation really, because both of them are definitely worth seeing.

If you'd like to see the buildings in action (although 'action' is probably the wrong word!) then try and attend an Evensong service. After they've kicked out all the annoying tourists they let everybody back in for an evening mass (including all of the annoying tourists), so you can sit down in the seats and listen to the choir. It's also a sneaky way of seeing inside the two buildings for free. The Sunday service at Hampton Court is also worth attending, if only to see inside the Chapel Royal. There is another Sunday service at the Tower of London that you might like to visit, but the chapel is lot less interesting than Hampton Court's (although it's certainly more historic).

Christopher Wren is famous for building fifty-one churches in the City of London, but the only other places that I recommend visiting are nothing to do with him: Brompton Oratory, Temple Church and Westminster Cathedral.

If you agree with me that churches are best seen in the dark, then you simply have to visit the Brompton Oratory. Sunlight is banned at this place. The only light they let in here comes out of the candles. Westminster Cathedral is another one that's dark and gloomy (they seem to have used soot in place of paint), but the best reason to go is to get another 273-feet closer to heaven. You can ride a lift all the way to the top of the bell tower and look out across London.

Temple Church is an intriguing little place that is famous for its slumbering knights. You might recall them from Dan Brown's *Da Vinci Code* movie. St. Bartholomew-the-Great is one of the nicest small churches, because it's very old and dark inside, which is how I like my churches. But don't miss a visit to All Hallows by the Tower, because that will knock your socks off. It's not the church itself that impresses, but rather what they've got hidden in the basement -- they've got some real Roman remains down there, including a piece of mosaic pavement!

Highgate Cemetery appears to have given up on the gardening -- either that or their gardeners have been on strike for fifty years -- but it's the trail of overgrown green that gives it its atmosphere. Some of the tombs and monuments are so grand that you'll think they're home to kings and queens.

Top 10 Political Sites

① Houses of Parliament
② Prime Minister's Questions
③ House of Commons public gallery
④ No. 10 Downing Street
⑤ Churchill War Rooms
⑥ House of Lords public gallery
⑦ Mayor's Question Time at City Hall
⑧ Common Council at the Guildhall
⑨ Parliament Square
⑩ Mansion House

Just because our politicians are a bunch of liars and crooks and two-timing cheaters (probably), that doesn't mean that you should skip the political sights. London has plenty of historical attractions that date back 1,000 years and more, and you should definitely make some time in your itinerary to see a few of them.

Start off with a guided tour of Parliament. You will not believe the opulence and splendour inside that place -- it gives Buckingham Palace a run for its money. The building opens up to the public for two months in the summer, but it also run tours every Saturday if you can't make August and September. (The ticket office is across the road in Portcullis House).

Number four on the list is also number ten; because I'm talking about No.10 Downing Street. Standing outside that big black iron gate and peering over the shoulder of a mammoth copper trying to get a glimpse of the Prime Minister as he steps out of the front door is a must. If you manage to see him then very well done -- because I haven't seen him once in over twenty years of trying.

Just around the corner from Downing Street is the Churchill War Rooms. This is where Winston Churchill directed the Second World War from his bombproof bunker underneath Whitehall.

If you want to try something a little bit different then how about watching a debate inside the House of Commons? If you plan your holiday plenty of time in advance then you might be able to get a free ticket for Prime Minister's Questions instead. (You will need to write a begging letter to your local MP a few months in advance).

If you enjoy listening to the back and forth banter of political debates, then there are a couple of others worth watching in London. The first one is inside City Hall, by Tower Bridge, where the Mayor of London gets grilled by the Greater London Authority. And the second one is inside the historic Guildhall, where the Lord Mayor of London (a different person) attends the Common Council meeting in his traditional robes and hat. You can also go on a guided tour of his ceremonial home at Mansion House.

Top 10 Military Sites

① Churchill War Rooms
② Tower of London
③ RAF Museum
④ Chatham Dockyard
⑤ Imperial War Museum
⑥ HMS Belfast
⑦ Ceremony of the Keys
⑧ Bletchley Park
⑨ Changing the Guard
⑩ National Maritime Museum

The Churchill War Rooms is one of the best attractions in London. End of discussion. The whole place just oozes with history and 1940s nostalgia. It's the kind of place that sends a tingle up your spine. (And I'm not the kind of person who says that something is good when it isn't -- so trust me, it is good!)

I always put the RAF Museum right up there at the top as well because the place is huge. But it's full of planes (millions of them) and not much else; so unless you've got an interest in planes you might want to give it a miss.

Tourists rarely visit Chatham Dockyard and Bletchley Park either because they don't know about them, or they consider them to be too far away. And whilst it is certainly true that they will take up the majority of your day, if you have a particular interest in military history then I think they are worth the effort (Bletchley Park is where they cracked the Enigma codes). If you can't be bothered to travel to Chatham then HMS Belfast is a good alternative.

I used to rate the Imperial War Museum a lot higher than I do now, because I think the place has become a bit too pacifist. I know that sounds daft (a pacifist war museum?), but if you enjoy watching old war movies and reading *Commando* comics, then you'll be a tad disappointed. They don't celebrate our big victories anymore -- they wring their hands and wail about the loss of lives. They have also shipped most of the Second World War exhibits over to the Churchill Museum (inside the Churchill

War Rooms), so there's not a lot about WWII anymore. But I still recommend giving it a try.

If you want to see some real-life soldiers then how about watching a military parade? The Ceremony of the Keys is my favourite, but you have to write a letter to the Tower of London a few months in advance to secure a ticket (it's well worth it). Changing the Guard at Buckingham Palace is the easy alternative, but you'll have to contend with the huge crowds. The Changing the Guard ceremony at Horse Guards is usually a lot less packed, but not quite as impressive.

The National Maritime Museum is worth a visit just to see the Nelson memorabilia -- and it's also a good excuse to catch a boat ride to Greenwich (which is probably more enjoyable than the actual museum).

Top 10 Maritime Sites

① Chatham Dockyard
② HMS Belfast
③ TRS (aka. Thames River Services)
④ Thames Clippers
⑤ London Duck Tour
⑥ City Cruises
⑦ Jason's Canal Trip
⑧ National Maritime Museum
⑨ Cutty Sark
⑩ Golden Hinde

I wasn't sure whether to include Chatham Dockyard on here because it's a long way outside central London, and it will eat up practically an entire day of your holiday. But it's so good I just had to stick it in. Not only can you explore the decks of a World War II battlecruiser, but you can also have a guided tour around a genuine Cold War submarine! [Note: Portsmouth Dockyards would have been my *real* No.1, because that's home to both HMS Victory and the Mary Rose; but I couldn't bring myself to include Portsmouth on a London list -- but check out my big review of it if you're interested.]

If you can't face the train ride to Chatham then HMS Belfast is a good alternative. Of the three boats that you can board in London (the others being the Cutty Sark and Golden Hinde), it is definitely the best. You can walk around all the decks and see the mess, the cabins, the bridge and the engine rooms, and then go up top and stand underneath the colossal guns.

I've included three ferry services on the list (TRS, Thames Clippers and City Cruises), and all three of them are worth a ride. But if I had to plump for my favourite then I'd definitely go for TRS. The Thames Clippers have the longest route, but they stop at too many places and don't have very many outside seats. The City Cruises have got the most outside seats but they've also got three billion tourists filling them up. The TRS boats just seem to have a happy medium between everything -- they have good boats, good seats, and they're not too crowded.

Another nice boat ride is Jason's Canal Trip, which runs from Little Venice to Camden Lock. It takes you down the Regent's Canal and straight past London Zoo, where you can see some birds in the Snowdon Aviary -- the biggest bird cage in London.

If you have some kids with you then you might prefer an amphibious London Duck Tour instead, because that drives around Westminster before diving into the chilly river by the MI6 building. Unfortunately it only goes as far as Westminster Bridge though, before turning tail and heading for home, so you don't get much of a river ride. (It's still fun for the kids though.)

I'm not a massive fan of the National Maritime Museum and the only bit that interests me is the Nelson exhibition, where you can see his bloodied clothes and possessions from the Battle of Trafalgar. But obviously if you've got a special interest in boats then you'll probably love it.

Top 10 Places To Take A Photograph

① Next to a soldier at Horse Guards
② Big Ben from Westminster Bridge
③ View from the top of The Shard
④ Neon lights at Piccadilly Circus
⑤ St. Paul's from Waterloo Bridge
⑥ Tower Bridge from beside City Hall
⑦ Buckingham Palace, from the bridge in St. James's Park
⑧ Sitting on a lion in Trafalgar Square
⑨ From the top of Parliament Hill
⑩ Meridian line at the Royal Observatory

Standing next to a mounted soldier in Horse Guards is the No.1 photo-spot in London. But those horses are pretty big beasts and a little bit scary (if they trod on your foot then you would definitely know about it), so if you want to play it safe then try the foot soldiers standing in the courtyard. Everybody knows that the soldiers aren't allowed to smile or laugh or have a chat, so you always see tourists telling jokes in front of them, and doing daft dances, in an attempt to make them giggle. It never works. Those fellas have seen action in foreign wars (they are real soldiers), so a few dopey tourists aren't going to faze them.

The best shot of Big Ben is from the end of Westminster Bridge, but you'll get a better one of Parliament from the top of the London Eye, which looks right down on top of it. The dome of St. Paul's can be seen from loads of different places, but I think the best shot can be taken from Waterloo Bridge. That view is so celebrated that Ray Davies even wrote a song about it. (Well, that's not *quite* true. He actually wrote a song about the bridge, but let's not quibble.)

If you can handle the height then it's definitely worth a ride up to the top of The Shard. The view up there is amazing. But it's so high that it's genuinely terrifying -- it took me fifteen minutes to psych myself up just to stand next to the window (true!).

You can get a great shot of Buckingham Palace by standing in the centre of the bridge that crosses over the lake in St. James's Park. And if you spin around 180 degrees then you can capture a pretty shot of Horse Guards behind a fountain (they don't always switch it on though, so you'll have to get lucky).

The best view of Tower Bridge is from the pavement next to City Hall (if you do it from the Tower of London side then the leafy trees will get in the way). If you walk past the bridge towards the Design Museum then you'll get another great shot with the city skyscrapers behind.

Tourists always seem to want to snap their buddies sitting astride a lion at the base of Nelson's Column -- but I think you have to be a bit daft to do that one. Those things are absolutely colossal and if you fell off then you would have a couple of broken bones. I think that I would actually prefer to climb onto a real lion, because it's probably safer.

If you want a good shot of the skyline then how about a stroll up Parliament Hill on Hampstead Heath? You can get a similar shot from the top of Primrose Hill (north of Regent's Park), or from the top of Greenwich Hill by the Royal Observatory. And whilst you're up there you can straddle the Meridian line, and tell everybody that you had a foot in each hemisphere.

Top 10 Viewing Spots

① At the top of The Shard
② From the cable car across the Thames
③ From the highest dome at St. Paul's
④ London Eye
⑤ From the belfry at the top of Big Ben
⑥ Inside the Sky Garden
⑦ Greenwich Hill
⑧ Parliament Hill
⑨ From the top of One New Change
⑩ Primrose Hill

I hate heights. I *hate* them. I don't want to die, you see; and there is always a danger that one of these skyscrapers will fall down whilst you're riding up in the lift. Of course they always try and assure you beforehand that it is totally safe -- but they have to say that otherwise they wouldn't sell any tickets. But all you've got to do is use your brain: what happens if you balance a toothbrush on a table? It falls down. And that is what will happen with the Shard one day. You mark my words.

Now that I have got that off my chest, let me share with you the best places to go for a great view of the skyline. The most obvious one is The Shard. Because it's the tallest. And it certainly doesn't disappoint -- you almost feel like you are coming in to land on an airplane, that is how high it is. It is so high that I almost floated off the top due to a lack of gravity. Unfortunately it is also seriously scary, and you might want to think twice if you've got very young kids with you because it has floor to ceiling windows -- it was scary enough for me, and I'm an adult! But then again I was scared on the London Eye as well.

The cable car is frightening too. It takes you across the Thames from The O2 to the ExCel Centre, and the darn thing swings in the wind like it's about to fall off.

Your kids will absolutely love this ride. The dads will say they do (but they don't really), whilst the mums will just refuse point blank to get on.

It wasn't the domes of St. Paul's that scared me... it was the stairs. The first set of stairs you go up are easy-peasy, and so is the second, but the third set is just plain terrifying! But I hear the view from the top is superb (I wouldn't know though, because I chickened out).

Not many people realise that it's possible to have a guided tour of Big Ben, which includes the belfry at the top of the tower (the room that contains the actual bell); but you have to write a letter to your local MP begging for a ticket first, so you have to put in a degree of forward planning. Maybe you can just settle for a visit to the Sky Garden instead, which is higher, greener, and most importantly... they have a lift.

I much prefer sitting on a bench at the top of Greenwich Hill, Parliament Hill and Primrose Hill, because the view is just as good and there is absolutely no danger of a hill falling down (unless there's an earthquake). If I had to pick my favourite one out of the three then I would definitely go for Greenwich Hill. Parliament Hill is a lot farther out from the centre of London and will take up more of your day, so you might decide to plump for Primrose Hill after that.

An honourable mention must go to The Monument (which would be No.11 on my list) but you might want to do some training before you climb it -- just to make sure that your heart can take it. The stairs are totally enclosed inside the column so it's not very frightening, but the steps just go on and on forever until you eventually drop dead from exhaustion. I actually died twice on the way up (not once, but twice), plus another two times on the way down.

Top 10 Day Trips

① Windsor Castle
② Bath
③ Oxford
④ Chessington World of Adventures
⑤ Cambridge
⑥ Stonehenge
⑦ Portsmouth Historic Dockyard
⑧ Hampton Court Palace
⑨ Chatham Dockyard
⑩ RAF Museum

Windsor was always going to come at the top of my list because I'm a big fan of the Royals (...even Charles). I actually rate this place above Buckingham Palace because the State Rooms are every bit as impressive, plus you've got the castle, the chapel (with the tomb of Henry VIII) and the parkland as well. Even the town is worth a walk around. If you're a fan of the British monarchy then you really do have to go to Windsor.

The other Royal palace on my list is Hampton Court. The rooms aren't anywhere near as grand as Buckingham Palace or Windsor, and the town is a waste of time (it's tiny), so I'd probably only recommend it if you're a fan of the Tudors and Henry VIII. It does have some very nice gardens out the back though, if you like walking through the daffodils.

The five cities that every tourist wants to see are Oxford, Cambridge, Canterbury, Stratford-upon-Avon and Bath, and they are usually stuck between choosing Oxford or Cambridge. Well, here is my advice: choose Bath instead. If you've got oodles of time then by all means do all three. But if I had to choose just one then it would definitely be Bath... or Oxford (it's so difficult to choose!).

A trip to Cambridge is all about the architecture and the colleges, and you will spend practically your entire day looking at the outside of the buildings. There's not a lot else to do in Cambridge (the museums aren't up to much). You could do some punting on the river, I suppose. Oxford has got a bit more variety with the colleges and extra attractions, but it still can't compete with Bath -- Bath has got the Roman remains, the Abbey, plus famous places like the Royal Crescent. I also think that Bath is the prettiest city of the three.

Stratford-upon-Avon didn't even make my Top 10, because I found it quite disappointing. Shakespeare's house looks great from the outside but as soon as you step through the door it goes rapidly downhill (check out my full review if you still fancy going). Canterbury is okay, but not worth using up a precious day of your holiday.

Chessington World of Adventures is great if you've got kids, but probably not so great if you're sixty-years-old and riddled with arthritis -- it's a theme park with rollercoasters and a zoo. Imagine Disneyland... but built on a British budget.

Everyone knows about Stonehenge and everyone wants to see it. Well, I have been there myself and I can sum it up for you like this: it's a big pile of stones. I don't know what I was expecting really... something more magical and mystical? I think I enjoyed the trip more than the monument to be honest; but I'm still definitely glad that I did it. Stonehenge is one of those places that the whole world knows about, and it will probably be the only photograph that your friends will want to see when you get back home.

If you like boats then you're spoilt for choice... how about a day trip to Portsmouth to see the remains of Henry VIII's flagship, the Mary Rose? Or Nelson's boat at the Battle of Trafalgar? (You can even stand on the spot where he was shot!) If you take the train to Chatham then you can have a guided tour around a Cold War submarine. I also thoroughly recommend the RAF Museum, but you probably need to have an interest in planes to enjoy it -- it's just a load of hangars stuffed full of military planes.

My Personal Top 10

① Prime Minister's Questions
② Ceremony of the Keys,
③ Evening tour of Buckingham Palace
④ Boat ride from Big Ben to Greenwich
⑤ Windsor Castle
⑥ Watching a play at the Globe Theatre
⑦ Proms concert at the Royal Albert Hall
⑧ London Zoo
⑨ The Shard
⑩ Evensong at Westminster Abbey

I couldn't end this chapter without indulging myself with my own personal list. Everybody has their own special interests and favourite places to visit, and what I enjoy most you might think is a total load of rubbish, so I won't mind if you skip over this one. Not everybody is like me. Not everybody enjoys bad weather, cemeteries and death. But if you fancy following in my footsteps then here are my top ten favourite places...

Prime Minister's Questions is the most exciting thing that you can do in London. If you can wangle a free invite from your local MP then you will be treated to one of the noisiest and most raucous and entertaining debates you will ever see. If you've ever seen it on TV then I will tell you right now that it doesn't compare -- it doesn't even come close. You need to be sitting inside the noise to get the best out of it.

My second favourite event is the Ceremony of the Keys at the Tower of London: it actually choked me up and brought a tear to my eye. Luckily it was pitch black at night so no one could see my cry. But imagine this: you're standing in the shadow of the White Tower two hours before midnight, when everyone else has gone home, and the soldiers are up there dusted in yellow lamplight and blowing out the Last Post. There is no shame about losing a tear over that. It doesn't mean that you are any less of a man. It's nothing to be embarrassed about (I'm not embarrassed). But don't tell anyone I said that for chrissakes because I won't forgive you.

If you're a fan of the Royals and you've got more money than sense, then try an evening tour around Buckingham Palace. Most people plump for the Summer Opening, but an evening tour is definitely better. It's quite pricey, but the big advantage is that you get led around by a human guide after everyone else has left, and you get the whole place to yourself. They even let you sit on the throne (no they don't).

Windsor Castle is another great place to go if you like the Royals, but it's a long train ride away, so you probably have to be a fan, but I personally think it's even more impressive than the palace. The State Rooms are every bit as good, whilst you also get the castle, the chapel and the grounds of the Great Park. I've still placed it underneath Buckingham Palace in my list, though, because I'm basically too lazy to get the train. If they moved it closer to London then it would appear higher up in the list.

I really enjoy boat rides from Big Ben to Greenwich. You get some great views of the city from the deck of a boat, but you need to wait for a day with driving rain to get the best out of it. I realise that I'm probably alone in this thinking, but if you are anything like me (weird) then you will much prefer the wind and rain and falling skies. I like it when the sky comes down to earth like big books falling off a shelf. I like it when the wind is battering me around like damp pants on a washing line. 99% of the tourists will give up and head downstairs to the bar at this point, and leave me alone doing battle with the elements -- one day they will come back up to find me frozen solid at the front with an icicle smile on my face. They will have to get a pickaxe to chip me out of the seat. That will be my final review. That is how I am going to check out of this world: with a sixteen quid boat ride to Greenwich.

You can't come to London and not see a show, and I've seen a few musicals in my time (I've done all the big ones like *Phantom of the Opera* and *Les Miserables*), but given the choice I would much rather see a play at the Globe Theatre. It might be a lot colder inside, and the seats are solid wood, but if you read my review then you'll understand why it's so much better. A Proms concert at the Royal Albert Hall is another experience that is well worth doing.

London Zoo is a good day out because I like animals. Some people think that I actually look like an animal, so maybe that's why I like it so much. I've got more hair on my face than most of the monkeys. I can quite happily stand outside the gorilla pen and watch them shifting about for half-an-hour. I watch them and they watch me. Most of the time they don't even do anything -- they just sit there staring back, but it's the way that they do it that is so intriguing. Underneath all of that hair they are just the same as us, I reckon -- they still get bored and annoyed at all the people watching them. I wouldn't mind climbing over the fence and shaking hands with them (obviously I'd have to take a machine gun with me, just in case they get angry and I have to shoot them -- I'm not totally stupid).

If you've read most of the book up until this point then you will already know that I hate heights, but I still get a thrill at the top of The Shard -- it's the highest that you can go without being a spaceman. If they built another couple of floors on top then you'd be bumping your head on the moon. How it doesn't just topple over in the wind I do not know -- I can't even make a pencil stand up on the carpet, so how does it stay standing? It must be magic.

Top 10 Most Overrated

① London Dungeon
② Madame Tussauds
③ Tate Modern
④ Ripley's Believe It Or Not!
⑤ Carnaby Street
⑥ Saatchi Gallery
⑦ Design Museum
⑧ London sightseeing buses
⑨ Speakers' Corner
⑩ Princess Diana Memorial Fountain

These are all things that I consider to be either overrated or overpriced (or both). But bear in mind that this is my own *personal* list, and lots of people will disagree with it -- you might think they are fantastic.

Lots of people love the London Dungeon. But I don't. (I'm going to sound like Victor Meldrew now... sorry about that!) I don't like the way that they drag shy punters up onto the stage and make them say stuff to the crowd. It's almost like you become part of the show, and have to put on a performance yourself. But I realise that a lot of people will absolutely love being the centre of attention, so let me just say this: there is a danger that you will have to do some public speaking at the London Dungeon.

The problem that I have with Madame Tussauds is twofold: the cost and the queues. For what it offers, the price is totally outrageous -- it's a tourist trap. All you do is walk around from room to room looking at five hundred shop mannequins. If they were proper robots jumping around and singing and dancing, like they did at the old Rock Circus, then that would be fair enough. But they are just stuffed humans. They are just dummies. And we are dummies as well, for queuing up for an hour and handing over a bazillion quid just to see them. And the whole attraction is so obviously set-up to relive you of as much cash as possible: they try and flog you stuff as you walk around, even whilst you're sitting on the ride... I could go on and on. Just read my review and you will understand. And while you're at it read my review for Ripley's Believe It Or Not as well. It's the same thing, only worse.

Carnaby Street would probably be fantastic... if you built a time machine and travelled back to the year 1967 to watch all the pretty women walking around in miniskirts. So unless you can lay your hands on Marty McFly's DeLorean then I would give it a miss. And as for the Saatchi Gallery and Tate Modern... I hate modern art. But maybe you like modern art. If you do then give them a try. Or if you fancy a good laugh, give them a try as well, because that's how bad the art is. At least they are both free, I suppose -- which is more than I can say for the Design Museum. The Design Museum actually has the cheek to charge people to see a display case full of teapots, potato peelers and bricks.

Sightseeing buses are over-priced and they take up way too much time. I like them better when they've got a live guide on board, giving some commentary, but when you're just sitting in the traffic for two hours listening to bombastic classical anthems on your headphones you start to wonder why you wasted thirty quid. I'm also very cynical of the way they pile on as many freebies as they can to make it seem like a good deal: ten walking tours, ten boat tours, ten of this and ten of that, and cheap entry into two million attractions... but only eight hours to do them all in! And what really winds me up is the way they describe it as a 24-hour ticket, when the buses only run for eight or nine hours a day.

And then we come to the Princess Diana Memorial Fountain... *oh dear*. If the Prime Minister announced that they were going to honour me like that, then I would refuse to die. Seriously! Or I would come back to life as a zombie and demolish it. I was no big fan of Princess Di when she was alive, but even I thought she deserved something better than that.

Speakers' Corner is usually full of Bible bashers, angry young men and weirdos.

Hotels

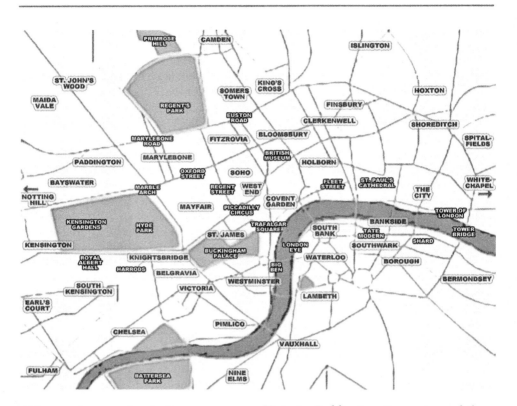

Choosing a hotel area

London is a *very* expensive city to sleep in, and I would expect to pay anything between £35 and £110 for one night in a cheap room (B&Bs, 1★ and 2★ hotels). Medium-cost rooms (3★) can be up to £230 (seriously!). And for an expensive room (4★ and above) the sky is the limit -- you could pay from £200 to £2,000.

If you're looking for something *really* cheap then your best bet is around Victoria/Pimlico, Bayswater/Paddington, and Earl's Court/Kensington. You should be able to find some pretty decent B&Bs there, and plenty of 1★, 2★ and 3★ hotels. If I had to stay in one of those areas myself then I would probably plump for Victoria, Paddington, Bayswater and then Pimlico (in that order).

Mid-priced hotels can be found all over the capital, but I would suggest trying Southwark first, and then Bayswater/Paddington. If you can afford to splash out a little bit more money then try the West End (the area around Piccadilly Circus, Soho and Covent Garden); because despite being right in the centre of town, there are a surprisingly high number of mid-priced hotels available there. They might not be the nicest places in the world, and come with shoebox rooms as standard, but you can't be too fussy if you want something relatively cheap and centrally located.

If you can afford to splash out on a 4★ or 5★ hotel then just go straight for the centre. Don't even bother looking at the other places. I would be happiest around Covent Garden, Bloomsbury, Holborn, Fitzrovia, Soho and The City. Marylebone is also worth a look, and maybe Mayfair, St. James and Westminster if you can afford it.

One final piece of advice: Don't stay in airport hotels (the main airports are 15-35 miles away), and if you come across a hotel in Docklands, Canary Wharf or Greenwich, then just forget it. Those locations are often advertised as being in 'London' (which technically speaking they are, I suppose), but you will end up spending far too much time and money on the trains and buses. Anything that requires the Docklands Light Railway to get home should definitely be avoided, because you'll have to be home by midnight in order to avoid the night buses. Ideally, I wouldn't want to stay anywhere further east than Tower Bridge. I wouldn't go any further west than the Royal Albert Hall either, or north of the Marylebone/Euston Road; and south London begins and ends in Bankside and Southwark as far as I'm concerned -- anything further south than those may as well not exist. Even Chelsea is too far away for me. If you try and stick within those bounds then your location will be fine.

Hotel prices and facilities

This should be taken as a rough guide only because several different companies have the power to dish out star-ratings in London, and they all use different criteria.

In my experience a hotel with a higher star rating is no guarantee that it will be of a higher quality -- only that it will have a higher price. If you read my reviews then you'll see that there are several 3-stars that I would happily rate higher than some 4s -- so don't fall into the trap of choosing a higher rating over a cheaper place in a better location.

I have also provided an *approximate* indication of the cost. The prices are based on one person for one night in a standard room, but a lot will depend on the day of the week, and the time of year that you are travelling (prices are always higher on a Friday and Saturday, and during the holidays). The way I did it was to look at four different dates over the next 12 months, and write down the lowest and highest prices. So hopefully most of the other dates will fall within that range.

Lots of people believe that prices are cheaper if you leave it till the last minute (...because the hotels are supposedly trying to offload the rooms), but in my experience the complete opposite is true: the rooms are usually at their cheapest when you book them at least a month in advance.

Hostels -- £25 to £40 -- Although it's certainly possible to find a private room in some London hostels, it's much more usual to end up in a dormitory sleeping 2-12. The toilet and shower will be shared, and there will also be a kitchen where you can do your own cooking. They will probably have a space where you can go and watch TV or play pool with the other inmates (sorry, *residents*). A lot of hostels these days also have their own breakfast room and restaurant, where you can buy ready-cooked meals. As far as in-room facilities are concerned, *forget it*. You won't have a TV, a telephone or even a hairdryer. The only in-room entertainment is what you can make yourself. But there will probably be an alleyway nearby where everyone goes to smoke some pot (only joking). Sometimes they have an upper-age limit too... but if you are still backpacking around the world at the age of thirty then you are probably having some kind-of a mid-life crisis.

B&B hotels -- £35 to £80 -- Simple little hotels (pokey hotels) that include a breakfast within the price. Most of them don't have a proper restaurant (only a breakfast room), so you will probably have to eat out for lunch and dinner. A few of them might have a tiny little bar area though. Rooms will either have an ensuite bathroom or a shared bathroom in the hall. If it's not ensuite then you'll probably have a sink in the room instead (so if you're a bloke you can have a wee in that). Most B&Bs provide a kettle and teabags in the room, with a TV and a telephone. But that's about it as far as the facilities are concerned.

1★ hotels -- £30 to £60 -- Budget hotels. Economy hotels. Most of them are all right for one or two nights sleep, but I wouldn't fancy staying in them any longer than that because you'll go stir-crazy. The rooms will be the same size as a shoebox and have a shared bathroom that you can access with a key. You might get a sink and a TV in the room, or you might not. You might get a kettle and a hairdryer, or you might not. The lobby might have a small breakfast room if you're lucky, or more likely a vending machine in the corridor. The hotel will almost certainly be outside of the main touristy areas, so remember to budget for a bus ride or a tube ticket every day.

2★ hotels -- £30 to £110 -- A decent hotel with clean (but small) rooms. The bedrooms will most likely have an ensuite shower and toilet. If they don't then you will have to share a bathroom down the hall. The rooms will most likely have a TV and a hairdryer, plus a kettle and teabags. If you're lucky then you might even get a biscuit. You might be able to request an iron from reception if your wife fancies doing a bit of ironing, but there is unlikely to be one in the room. The safe will most probably be in reception too. The hotel should definitely have a breakfast room, and might also have a restaurant for lunch and dinner. Most of the 2-stars are just beyond walking distance of the main tourist attractions, so you will either have to catch a bus or go a few stops on the tube every day.

3★ hotels -- £90 to £170 -- Good quality, comfortable rooms with an ensuite bathroom as standard. They will also have a kettle, telephone, Freeview TV channels and Wi-Fi access (which you will have to pay extra for). You might get a minibar. You should get a personal safe. The hotel will definitely have a breakfast room and will probably serve lunch and dinner as well. It might even have a small gym and concierge services. Many of the 3-star hotels are very centrally located, and it's possible to find a few right in the centre of town. This is the first grade of hotel where you can safely take your girlfriend and not have her dump you within the first five minutes.

4★ hotels -- £140 to £240 -- As above, but with porters and a good-quality restaurant and bar inside the hotel. Rooms will be comfortable and probably spacious (although in my experience some 4-star hotels seem a lot like 3-stars). They will probably have a minibar and room service. You might get complimentary Wi-Fi, or you might have to pay for it. You might get a bowl of fruit and a posh coffee machine instead of a teapot. The hotel will have business facilities, conference rooms and concierge services, and half of them will have a little gym attached. The hotel location should be perfect. Note: 4 and 5-star hotels have the annoying habit of freezing an extra £50 to £100 quid on your card when you first check-in, just in case you empty their minibar or make a phone-call to Peru, etc. So that is something you might have to budget for.

5★ hotels -- £240 to £475 -- As above, but with larger rooms and fantastic views. It will probably have more than one top-quality bar and restaurant inside the hotel to give you a choice of places to eat. Room service, DVD players and complimentary Wi-Fi will come as standard. They might provide a turn-down service as well. They will probably offer a few of these: gym, sauna, spa, swimming pool, in-room massages, business facilities, valet parking, limo service and laundry.

Hotel reviews

If you're wondering why there are so few hotels listed below, then that's because I don't like including places that I haven't tried myself. I could have just done what most guidebooks do, and given you a long list of names and addresses (the kind of information that is easily found on the internet), but I decided to write some genuine reviews instead. Hopefully they will give you a feel for what it's like to stay inside a London hotel.

3-star hotels

Citadines, South Kensington

ADDRESS Citadines South Kensington, 35a Gloucester Road, South Kensington - map 6c **RATING** ★★★ **TRAINS** Gloucester Road (zone 1) **BUSES** 49, 70 **PRICE** £125 to £195 (standard room for one night) **FACILITIES** Car park, laundry, fitness centre **ROOM** Wi-Fi, TV, telephone, hairdryer, ensuite bathroom, ensuite kitchen with hob, microwave, fridge, freezer and kitchen utensils, iron, air-conditioning, safe

WEB citadines.com/en/uk/london/south_ kensington.html **TEL** 0207 543 7878
Centrally located? ★★☆ Nice rooms? ★★★
Value for money? ★★★ Worth a stay? ★★★

I think I've just found my new favourite hotel. This place is great -- it's almost like renting a flat! You get a bedroom, bathroom, and even a little ensuite kitchen.

Here's all the stuff you get in the kitchen: a microwave and hob, saucepan, toaster, plates, bowls, cups, saucers, sieve, tin opener, bottle opener, knives, forks, spoons, sponge, tea towels, and a bottle of washing up liquid (totally wasted on me), plus a proper fridge and a freezer for your food.

The ensuite bathroom comes with a bath, shower, hairdryer, and even a little string washing line to hang up your socks.

The rest of the room has got an TV, iron, ironing board and safe.

The only downside is the lack of restaurant and bar, but seeing as you've got your own kitchen in the room it's no big deal (you can just eat Pot Noodles all week). They supply a big menu of meals and drinks that you can have delivered to your room, if you want, and there are plenty of pubs and restaurants in the surrounding streets. Kensington High Street is only a short walk away.

You also need to pay a supplement if you'd like a maid to come in and make your bed everyday, which means your soap and teabags will rapidly run out if you stay beyond a couple of days. Obviously I'm a bloke, so I wasn't bothered in the slightest that my bed remained unmade every day, and I just bought some extra teabags and stuck them in the cupboard in the kitchen. I bought a bottle of milk and stuck it in the fridge as well. You need to think of it as a flat, rather than a hotel room.

The surrounding area is nice enough, but it's a tiny little bit farther out than where I'd normally like to be. It's within easy walking distance of the Natural History Museum, Royal Albert Hall and Kensington Palace, but that's about it. You could have a walk up to Harrods as well, but there are only a couple of buses that run between Trafalgar Square and South Kensington, so if you want to go anywhere else then you're going to be using the tube all the time, or chopping and changing routes at the bus stop.

But do you know what? The room is so great that I think I'll still recommend it anyway.

Comfort Inn, Westminster

ADDRESS Comfort Inn, 39 Belgrave Road, Pimlico - map 8e **RATING** ★★★ **TRAINS** Pimlico, Victoria (both zone 1) **BUSES** 24 **PRICE** £150 to £200 (standard room for one night) **FACILITIES** Breakfast room **ROOM** Tea & coffee, Wi-Fi, TV, telephone, hairdryer, bathroom, fan **WEB** choicehotelsuk.co.uk/en/comfort-inn-westminster-london-hotel-gb209 **TEL** 0207 834 8036

Centrally located? ★★☆   Nice rooms? ★★☆
Value for money? ★★☆   Worth a stay? ★★☆

If you want a cheap 3-star then this is the kind of place you're going to end up with. It's not great, but it's not rubbish either. Ideally you'd want to be living a bit closer to the centre of town to save on bus fares, but this is London, and for that you have to pay a premium. They call it the *Comfort Inn Westminster* on the website, but it feels more like Pimlico to me. "Westminster" makes it sound like it's next door to Big Ben, but it's actually five minutes away from Lambeth Bridge and a ten-minute walk to Victoria.

The area is nice enough though -- Pimlico is where you find all the cheapo 2-star, 3-star and B&B hotels -- but the houses are all balconied with big white columns out the front. You're not going to bump into anyone famous, but you're not going to bump into any muggers or murderers either -- it's a perfectly nice part of London.

The room is small (as you would expect for a 3-star), but not as small as some of the 4-stars I've stayed at. You get a shower and a hairdryer, but that's about it. The view is all right if you like staring at bricks. You get a kettle and three tea-bags, plus a couple of bottles of mineral water in case you don't trust the taps. Here's something funny: if this was a 4-star hotel then you can bet your life they'd be charging three quid each for those bottles of water. That is how the world works: the more you pay for a room the more expensive everything else becomes. The more money you have, the more money they want. At a 3-star hotel you get complimentary tea bags and a pot of milk, but at The Ritz you don't even get a kettle: you have to order it from room service for £6.50 a go! We all eat and drink the same stuff, but rich people pay five times the price for it. But they can afford it I suppose.

The breakfast isn't up to much. It's just a piece of toast and some fun-size cereal boxes, plus a pot of Ski yoghurt and a croissant -- not exactly the breakfast of champions. But the room is cheerful enough.

My only real criticism of this place is that the walls are a bit thin, and I heard a few things that made me go blind (if you know what I mean).

To sum it up then... it's not the kind of place that you're going to go home raving about, but it's a perfectly decent little 3-star hotel that will keep you happy for a few nights.

Days Inn, Hyde Park

ADDRESS Days Inn, 148-152 Sussex Gardens, Paddington - map 1f **RATING** ★★★ **TRAINS** Lancaster Gate, Paddington (both zone 1) **BUSES** 7, 23, 27, 36, 205, 332, 436 **PRICE** £155 to £170 (standard room for one night) **HOTEL** Breakfast room, bar, laundry **ROOM** Tea & coffee, Wi-Fi, TV, telephone, hairdryer, ensuite bathroom, air-con, safe **WEB** daysinn hydepark.com **TEL** 0207 723 2939

Centrally located? ★★☆ Nice rooms? ★★☆ Value for money? ★★★ Worth a stay? ★★★

I was staying in the cost-a-fortune Waldorf last week and I didn't really warm to it, but then I came to this pokey little 3-star in Paddington and I liked it straight away. That's why you should never spend a few hundred quid on a 5-star, because you're just wasting your money. You may as well spend a bit less on a less stuffy hotel, and then blow what's left on beer. 5-star hotels are for proposing in, or for business meetings, but not holidays. You can trust me on this. I have been to plenty of 3, 4 and 5-star hotels now to know what makes a happy holiday -- and it's something like the Days Inn.

You tend to get more for your money at a 3-star hotel as well. I know it sounds daft, but you actually get more stuff when you spend less money. I had to pay £26 quid for the WiFi at the Waldorf, but in here it's free. They gave me four teabags and two milks at the 5-star, but in here you get seven. The room is a lot nicer too. It's all warm pines and burgundy red, and the staff are just normal people instead of unsmiling supermodels. If you need a bathroom that's bigger than a football pitch then go to a 5-star, otherwise you'll be perfectly happy here.

They've got a little bar and a lounge downstairs behind reception, but I get the impression it's not used much. When I asked the guy for a coffee he looked at me like I was an apparition. I don't think he knew how to work the machine. Then he pressed a few buttons and the coffee came out. *Phew!* When he realised that I actually had a room at the hotel he let me have the coffee for free -- you wouldn't get that happening at the Waldorf.

The breakfast room is a lot better -- it's actually quite nice. They don't do any cooked food though, it's just a lot of yoghurts and hams, cheeses and toast.

410 | London: A Visitor's Guide

They have some of those fun-size boxes of cereals too.

I personally don't mind the streets around Paddington, but I know it won't be to everybody's taste. If you're trying to impress a date then it's probably not the place to go, but if you're just a lost and wandering soul like me, tramping around London until your knees say no, then you'll be perfectly content. Paddington can sometimes look a little grotty if you catch it on a bad day, but a lot of the side streets around there are actually very grand. But I will say this: you do need to be comfortable catching a bus, because you will rapidly tire of walking up from Marble Arch each day. I wouldn't bother with the tube though -- stick with the top deck of a double-decker bus. *See a bit of London!* You can catch buses outside Paddington station to practically anywhere in the city. If you insist on getting the tube then Paddington is a quick two-mins walk.

Ibis Hotel, London City

ADDRESS Ibis London City, 5 Commercial Street, Whitechapel **RATING** ★★★ **TRAINS** Aldgate, Aldgate East (both zone 1) **BUSES** 15, 25, 40, 42, 78, 100, 115, 135, 205 **PRICE** £90 to £165 (standard room for one night) **FACILITIES** Restaurant, bar **ROOM** Tea & coffee, Wi-Fi, TV, telephone, hairdryer, ensuite bathroom **WEB** ibis.com/gb/hotel-5011-ibis-london-city/index.shtml **TEL** 0207 422 8400

Centrally located? ★★☆ Nice rooms? ★★☆
Value for money? ★★★ Worth a stay? ★★☆

The Ibis City Hotel lobby was packed solid when I arrived: it was like a Bethlehem census on Christmas Eve. They've situated the cafe and bar area right next to reception so everybody was sitting around eating and drinking and there were piles of bags and suitcases all over the place. It was like a madhouse. But a happy madhouse. Are they coming or going? Are they waiting for taxis or waiting to check-in? Can I bump in front of you, madam? -- I hope you don't mind. Is it all right if I squeeze in here, sir, because I've got places I need to be and people I need to see.

Everything went smoothly at check-in and my room is all right. And you get free Wi-Fi as well, so I'm happy.

The room is okay for a 3-star hotel... or is it? I've been staying at a lot of 4s and 5s recently, doing these reviews, so I have been spoiled and I'm not sure what to expect anymore. You get a shower (no bath), Freeview TV channels, a kettle and teabags, a hairdryer... what else... that's about it. There is no personal safe. No iron. No minibar. No butler. No masseuse. No limo service. (I told you I've been spoiled.) I'm not sure that I trust the lock on the door though because I'm paranoid about my stuff getting stolen. I want a proper chain and a padlock on the door, preferably with 10,000 volts attached, but all they've got is a piddly little double-latch. So I have to resort to that old 'chair wedged up against the door' routine.

Let's deal with the teabag situation... I always like to count up the number of teabags in my room because I believe that is a surefire way of gauging the quality of a hotel: by the number of tea bags and milk cartons they provide to the guests. This place has done okay: they give you two tea bags, four coffees and four milks. But they give you two flimsy little plastic spoons that look like tooth picks, which is a bit annoying. Have you ever tried to eat a Pot Noodle with a plastic spoon about four inches long? The tub is bigger than the bleedin' spoon! (So remember to pack your own spoons.)

The view outside the window isn't the best I've ever had... it's one of those interior views that looks out into a cube of windows. I'm on the eighth floor so there are probably about sixty-odd rooms to peer into. They've all got net curtains, of course, so there's nothing much to see: just a solid wall of windows and air vents with brown drip stains coming out.

After yesterday's madhouse at check-in I thought breakfast would be heaving with hundreds of people so I went down nice and early and it was just the cook, the waitress and me, plus a couple of Chinese ladies chatting about their kids. The breakfast room doubles up as the restaurant (Fogg's) and has a strange collection of bar stools, sofa seats, office chairs and garden furniture -- it's like they couldn't make up their mind which chair to buy and just bought the entire shop. It's like an IKEA showroom.

You get all the usual kind of stuff for breakfast: sausage, bacon, eggs and beans, toast and ham, cheeses, cereals, yoghurts, etc. (All the stuff that you never have at home.) It's funny how we accept fruit salad and vanilla yoghurt as being a breakfast at a hotel. On any other day of the week it's a pudding. Beans, sausage and scrambled eggs is a dinner in my house. We only have that for breakfast on Christmas Day.

One of the things that I like about hotel living is that after a few days in the same place you start to recognise who's checked-in and who's checked-out. People tend to be creatures of habit and always occupy the same seats at breakfast, so when Mrs New Face is suddenly sitting in Mr Blue Shoes' seat you can say to yourself: "A-ha, it looks like he's packed his bags and left."

Oh wonderful... a load of Americans have just walked in so that's the end of the peace and quiet. Wherever Americans go, noise comes too. The whole room is listening to their conversation and by the time I leave I feel like I know them.

As for the hotel's location... well it's not too bad. It's a ten minute stroll to the Tower of London and Tower Bridge, and you can get to the Gherkin in ten minutes too. But anywhere else is going to be a bus ride or a tube ride away. Luckily it's right next door to Aldgate East tube station (District line straight to The City, Westminster and South Kensington) and the Hammersmith and City line (straight to Baker Street and Paddington). The area itself is quite ugly though -- but I'd still happily stay here again.

Premier Inn, Leicester Square

ADDRESS Premier Inn, 1 Leicester Place, Leicester Square - map 8b **RATING** ★★★
TRAINS Charing Cross, Leicester Square, Piccadilly Circus (all zone 1) **BUSES** 14, 19, 24, 29, 38, 176 **PRICE** £150 to £160 (standard

room for one night) **FACILITIES** Restaurant, bar **ROOM** Tea & coffee, Wi-Fi, TV, pay movies, telephone, hairdryer, ensuite bathroom, air-con, safe **WEB** premierinn.com/gb/en/hotels/england/greater-london/london-leicester-square.html **TEL** 0871 527 9334

Centrally located? ★★★ Nice rooms? ★★☆
Value for money? ★★★ Worth a stay? ★★★

There's no way that Lenny Henry stays at the Premier Inn. He's been on the telly advertising it for the past year or two, having a snooze in their beds and sipping coffee in their bar; but come on: who do they think they are kidding? He's a TV star for chrissakes so he stays at The Ritz or The Dorchester or The Savoy -- not in some pokey little 3-star place with two tea bags and a soap pump on the wall.

There are quite a few Premier Inn hotels in London, but I plumped for the most central one -- in Leicester Square. It's about ten steps from the central square, right behind the Empire cinema -- so you couldn't get much more central if you tried. At the other end of the road is Lisle Street, which is in the heart of London's Chinatown. At the moment Chinatown is all decked out in red lanterns strung across the street -- I think they must be celebrating something. So if you want somewhere cheap and cheerful in the middle of the West End then the Premier Inn is a pretty good deal. In fact, I would go so far as to say it's a brilliant deal.

I'm too old to be staying in 3-stars though. I am well past having a power shower in a stand-up coffin. I need a bath for my knees. They haven't got a bath because the rooms are too small. And I need a teapot too -- but at least they have got one of those. They've also got a TV and a waste paper basket, but that's about it. And a Gideon's Bible, of course. But there's not a lot of room left to fit in anything else. Even the ceiling is a lot lower than usual, so they can cram another floor on top.

The hotel is a bit like Fort Knox inside. When you step inside the front door there is nothing there. No reception desk, no rooms, no people to meet you -- nothing. All they've got is a sign which says go to the second floor. That's where you'll find the restaurant and the receptionist, who will issue you with a swipe card to go anywhere else. It's a bit like having a military pass into the restricted areas. If you want to go down the hall then you have to open the fire doors with your swipe card. If you want to use the lift... swipe card. Turn the lights on in your room? Swipe card. Watch the telly? Swipe card. Enter the hotel after 10 o'clock? Swipe card. Want to blow your nose? Swipe card. I couldn't get the darn thing to work the first couple of times I tried it and I had to wipe it on my sleeve to bring it to life. I'm sure a lot of people must get locked behind the doors with no hope of escape, simply because their card won't work. They stand trapped between a glass door and an unresponsive lift, pounding on the buttons to no effect. *Help me! Help me someone! My card doesn't work!* What they should do is issue everyone with Lenny Henry's home phone number in case of emergencies, so he can come along and rescue us.

But it's okay. I'm not complaining. I actually quite like this hotel and I'd happily stay here for a few days. I thought it was a bit cheeky of them charging for Wi-Fi access though. Even McDonald's offer free Wi-Fi, and you don't even have to buy one of their cheeseburgers. I wonder if Lenny Henry has to pay for his Wi-Fi? And it's rubbish too: it keeps dropping out every five minutes -- presumably because everybody in the hotel is using it at the same time.

I've just noticed that there's a big picture of Lenny in my room, grinning at me from the desk. He's all curled up in bed with a big smile on his face. Underneath his sunny mug it says: "A great night's sleep guaranteed". I wonder what that means? If I have a nightmare tonight does that mean I'll get my money back? In the small print it says: "No questions, no quibbles... We're so confident that you'll have a great night's sleep that if, for any reason, you don't, we'll give you your money back". So the first thing I'm going to do in the morning is march downstairs and test that out. "No questions, it says here," I will say, jabbing my fingers at the small print. I want my money back and I'm not answering any questions! I am exercising my right to silence -- as per the terms on your Lenny Henry manifesto. If they refuse to pay up then I will demand they get Mr Lenny Henry on the phone to sort it out.

I'm in the bar now. No sign of Lenny Henry anywhere. This place doubles up as the restaurant and breakfast room, and it's quite dim and dark and cosy -- I like dark places. The breakfast is just your usual help-yourself fry-up with bacon and eggs and baked beans, with some cereals and rolls too. I don't usually eat breakfast at home but I can't help myself in a hotel. When someone has gone to all that trouble of cooking it, the least you can do is eat it. I'm not doing the washing up though.

Travelodge, Covent Garden

ADDRESS Travelodge Covent Garden Hotel, 10 Drury Lane, Holborn - map 3f **RATING** ★★★ **TRAINS** Covent Garden, Holborn (both zone 1) **BUSES** 1, 242 **PRICE** £75 to £100 (standard room for one night) **FACILITIES** Restaurant, bar **ROOM** Tea & coffee, Wi-Fi, TV, telephone, ensuite bathroom **WEB** travelodge.co.uk/hotels/318/london-central-covent-garden-hotel **TEL** 0871 984 6245

Centrally located? ★★★ Nice rooms? ★☆☆
Value for money? ★★★ Worth a stay? ★☆☆

As soon as I arrived at the Travelodge Covent Garden I knew I wouldn't like it. It took me approximately five-seconds to decide that I'm never coming back here ever again. It looks like an ugly concrete office block... like a 1960s tower block. The kind of residential tower block that sports some kicked over dustbins, a busted lift and stinks of p*ss (it doesn't -- but that is the first thought that entered my head).

When you walk through the door it gets even uglier -- like a student union office and bar. It took me ten minutes to check-in and then I tried to go upstairs and the stupid keycard wouldn't work (you have to use a pass card to work to the lift). So I trooped back to reception and she fixed that, and then I went upstairs again and discovered that she hadn't given me a Wi-Fi code either, so back down I went and she sorted that out. And when I finally had a look around the room I found it to be darker than dark. Of all the hotel rooms that I've stayed in during my life, this one is totally unique in that when you open the curtains, absolutely nothing changes. It is still the same gloomy room that it was before. It is 3.30 in the afternoon at the moment and it is too dark to read without switching on the light.

I hate this place already and I've only been here thirty minutes. I wonder how many people have passed through this miserable excuse for a room in the past twelve months? We were all lying here watching the car lights creep across the ceiling. I think I might go and sleep under a bridge instead. I'll find the nearest homeless guy and offer to swap places with him and he'll say: "What, at the Travelodge? Are you having a laugh?"

I was staying at the Ibis earlier this week (another 3-star hotel) and a Premier Inn before that so I know exactly what a decent 3-star is like. The only saving grace is that I'm here to do a review so I don't really care if it's rubbish, because at least that gives me something to write about.

I suppose I'd better do my duty and tell you about the facilities, in case you actually want to come here. The bathroom has got a shower in it (no bath) and a towel... which reminds me... have you ever noticed those signs in hotel bathrooms which say: "Help save the planet! We will only wash your towel if you leave it on the floor." Well that annoys me as well (everything is annoying me now). *We're not idiots!* Everybody knows that has got sod all to do with saving the planet, and everything to do with keeping the hotel's laundry bill down. They just slap all of that eco-nonsense on there to guilt trip us into doing it. Well, I'm not falling for it this time... I'm sticking the whole damn lot on the floor: the towels, the bed sheets, the pillow cases, the curtains, the carpet... I'll make them wash the lot.

You get a TV with a lousy choice of channels. There's no Sky News. They don't even bother to give you the Freeview channels like Dave. And there's no way of bringing the time up either (so no wake-up alarms). Now I know why rock stars throw their TVs out of hotel windows -- it's because they stayed at a Travelodge.

You get a waste paper bin. You get a chair. You get a mirror. You get a kettle with four milks and two teabags. You get a fan. That's it. You don't even get a bedside table! The nearest table is the desk -- five feet away. So if you want a cup of tea or a can of Coke or something, your only options are to balance it on your head or sit at the desk.

What else don't I like about this place? (I'm just trying to find different things to moan about now because I'm in a bad mood.) This picture is crooked. This coat hangar is bent. I don't like the colour of the carpet. This drawer is a bit stiff.

The restaurant reminds me of a staff canteen. I used to work nightshifts at Sainsburys and we came down at 2 AM for a cup of tea -- it's a bit like that. It has plastic chairs and a silver tea urn and a big metal serving desk full of dried-up scrambled eggs which are curling up at the corners because they've been sitting under the hot lights for too long. Yum yum. They have beans and bacon and sausages too, and bread and cereals.

The only decent thing about this hotel is its location, because it's ten-seconds from the top end of Shaftesbury Avenue. Covent Garden is about five minutes away, and you are within easy walking distance of Piccadilly Circus and Leicester Square. It's also right next door to my favourite shop in London: Forbidden Planet (geek megastore -- sells a lot of *Star Wars* stuff).

4-star hotels

Holiday Inn, Regent's Park

ADDRESS Holiday Inn London Regent's Park, Carburton Street, Fitzrovia - map 2d **RATING** ★★★★ **TRAINS** Great Portland Street, Regent's Park (both zone 1) **BUSES** 18, 27,

30, 88, 205, 453, C2 **PRICE** £100 to £215 (standard room for one night) **FACILITIES** Restaurant, bar, concierge **ROOM** Room service, minibar, tea & coffee, Wi-Fi, TV, pay movies, telephone, hairdryer, ensuite bathroom, air-con, safe **WEB** hilondonregentsparkhotel.co.uk **TEL** 0871 942 9111

Centrally located? ★★☆ Nice rooms? ★★☆
Value for money? ★★★ Worth a stay? ★★☆

This is my first time staying at a Holiday Inn hotel. I wasn't expecting much to be honest, but it's actually quite nice inside. The reception area is quite swish, like a posh hotel. They had a pretty bird behind the desk when I walked in, which is always nice when you step through the door; and she gave me a Jacob's Club biscuit bar as well -- do you remember those little bars of biscuity chocolate that you had in your lunch box when you were a kid? She gave me an orange one of those -- no joke! Apparently they give one to all of their hotel members. So that's the Holiday Inn for you... at a fancy 5-star hotel you get a bowl of fruit and a pot of tea and a bottle of something bubbly, but in here you just get a Jacob's Club biscuit bar -- *ha ha*. I think I prefer the biscuit bar.

I definitely think they should change the name of this hotel though... before I forget to mention it. Because calling it the Holiday Inn Regent's Park makes it sound as if it's north of London Zoo, or up near Camden Town somewhere, but it's actually south of Great Portland Place station. That is quite a nice place to be. But when I say 'nice', I don't mean pretty. This area is definitely not pretty. I just mean that is within easy walking distance of Madame Tussauds, King's Cross and Oxford Street.

The bedrooms are almost within walking distance as well -- the corridors are colossal! They are about a mile long. I am in room 432, which gives you some idea of the size of the place. Every time you turn a corner you see a never-ending cream carpet stretching all the way over the horizon. I am reminded of that shot they do in horror movies, when a victim walks down a tunnel only for the tunnel to continuously expand before them, disappearing into the distance. That is exactly what it's like -- only without the horror. If you replace the horror with a bit of cream carpet then that is what it is like.

The room is okay. It will do. Put it this way: you are not going to die in here, or anything like that. It's not exactly The Ritz but it's got a toilet and a TV, so you can't complain. Give me a bath and a Jacob's Club biscuit bar and I am happy. It's also got a bed, some carpet, a ceiling, a desk, a window, a dustbin, some handles on the doors so you can open them, some lights, a floor for you to stand on, a mirror so you can look at yourself, a spy hole in the door so you can check for hoodlums, an emergency exit leaflet in case the hotel bursts into flames, a Gideon's Bible in case you want to say some prayers, and a menu for the minibar. I think that just about covers it. And oh yeah, a teapot and some cups and an ironing board for the wife, a hairdryer, some toilet paper, and a safe to keep all of your valuables (what valuables?).

I always like to record the number of teabags and the minibar prices when I stay at a hotel (I'm starting to go mental).

Because then you can see how tight and stingy the owners are. The Holiday Inn is better than most. A can of Coke is only £2.04, and a Kit Kat is £1.85. I have stayed in places that charge triple that. You get four teabags, four milks and a few sugars too -- hallelujah! I think this is the very first hotel that I have stayed at that actually provides the same number of milks as teabags. That is my number one hate in a hotel -- when they give you four teabags but only two milks. So the Holiday Inn has straight away found a home in my heart (if I had a heart, which I don't).

The view out of the window is fantastic. And I am saying that in a very sarcastic voice, by the way. They have given me a room on the inside of the building, so it just looks out into a little prison-like courtyard of concrete walls. A load of other rooms are staring into exactly the same spot, so it's just a ring of five floors and seventy-five windows (I counted them) all looking into this zone of nothing. Imagine if we all stood and stared out of our windows together... one hundred and fifty eyes pressed against the glass... what a scary scene that would be... all holding onto our Jacob's Club biscuit bar.

I am going to have to mark them down for the bar because they are playing Simply Red on the radio, followed by Wham and The Bangles. Oh dear. The only people who listen to Mick Hucknell and Wham are big sisters from the 1980s.

The restaurant room is nice as well. It's a bit like a branch of IKEA -- it's all pine woods and spotlights. Everything is either grey, yellow or wood. The breakfast is all right too. It's all self-service so you get your normal cereals, rolls, bacon, scrambled eggs, sausage, coffee and fruit juice, etc. It wasn't the best breakfast I've ever had, but it will do. It was very busy though. I went down there at 6:45 AM and the place was already fit to bursting with business types -- not many tourists about. It was all suits and shoes and shirt cuffs. I'm guessing that the Holiday Inn is the highest hotel that their bosses can put on expenses.

I've been here for two days now and I must say that their Wi-Fi is totally rubbish. Everyone in the hotel must be using it at once because it's like being back on dial-up twenty years ago. I'm sitting here eating my Jacob's Club biscuit bar waiting for it to work. If this page doesn't come up soon then I am going to storm downstairs and shout at the first person I see (no I'm not). I'm going to start smashing things up (not doing that either). I'll tell you what I will do... nothing. Absolutely nothing. Because I'm British. I'm just going to sit here and eat my Jacob's Club biscuit bar.

So in summary... it's all right. It will do. It's nothing special. I wouldn't rate it as a 4-star though. Apparently that is what they call themselves on the front door, but for me it's just a 3-star. But it's a perfectly nice 3-star and I would happily stay here again.

The Kingsley (Thistle)

ADDRESS The Kingsley Thistle, Bloomsbury Way, Bloomsbury - map 3f **RATING** ★★★★
TRAINS Holborn, Tottenham Court Road (both

zone 1) **BUSES** 1, 7, 8, 10, 14, 19, 25, 38, 59, 68, 73, 91, 134, 188, 242, 390 **PRICE** £150 to £215 (standard room for one night)
FACILITIES Restaurant, bar, concierge **ROOM** Room service, minibar, tea & coffee, Wi-Fi, telephone, TV, hairdryer, ensuite bathroom, air-con, safe **WEB** thistle.com/en/hotels/united_kingdom/london/thistle_holborn **TEL** 0871 376 9006

Centrally located? ★★★ Nice rooms? ★★☆
Value for money? ★★☆ Worth a stay? ★★★

I've just checked into The Kingsley Hotel and it's pretty posh. Or maybe it's not posh, because I don't really go anywhere that's posh. But by my lowly standards... it's posh. Even the cleaner I bumped into is nice and polite and posh. Every time you pass a member of staff they smile and say hello like they've met you before.

When you walk inside there's a little desk by the door and a bloke behind it who smiles and says hello... I think he's the concierge. He's all dressed up in a suit like he's about to go out for the night. The lady behind the reception desk was nice and pretty too (very important). She also said hello.

I must say that the decor is pretty plush. It's all purple carpet and chandeliers, tall white walls and two-story drapes. The other night they put some little flickering candles on the stairs as well.

I'm sitting on my bed writing this, so let me describe the room to you. It's pretty pokey. Are all 4-star hotels this pokey? It's no bigger than some of the 3-stars I've stayed at. It has all the usual TV, satellite channels, radio, Wi-Fi, kettle and a cup of tea... but this always winds me up big time... this is my pet hate... they give you a bazillion tea-bags and coffees and sugars, but only two milks! How are you supposed to drink all of those other tea bags when you've only got two milks? If I ever own a hotel then that's the first thing I'll do -- I'll supply a load of extra milks to the rooms. They give you a piddly little biscuit too. It's like a fun-size one. Have you ever seen those little fun-size cans of Coke, that are about as much fun as a boot in the nuts? Well, I never knew before today that it was possible to buy a fun-size biscuit, but here it is... I actually lost it under my tongue, that is how small it is. The crumbs are bigger than the biscuit.

I've got a nice view out of the window... let me describe it to you. It's basically a fire escape and a big brick wall, with some black netting all over the place to stop the birds crapping on the windowsill.

Okay, now I'm sitting on the toilet (yeah I know... too much information). This is a good example of how posh this place is -- they've got a bar of "green tea and ginger soap" on the sink. *Green tea soap?* What is that all about? I might try and melt it in the teapot once I've used up all the milks. They've even got a flannel in here. I've never been to a hotel that gives you a flannel before. Usually you get two towels that are about the same size as a flannel, but this place gives you a few towels plus a flannel. Luxury!

You get a proper ironing board as well (I'm a bloke, so that's a complete waste of time) and a snazzy white dressing gown. When you open up the wardrobe a little light comes on, like it does in the fridge. That is what separates the two classes... the working class light up their food, whilst the rich light up their clothes. You also get a pair of flip-flop slippers and... look at this! The hairdryer hasn't been bolted to the wall. Normally you need a screwdriver to get it off but this one can be sneaked into your suitcase nice and easy.

I'm sitting in the downstairs bar now. The kind of places that I normally go to have a bowl of peanuts on the bar, but this place has got a bowl of bananas and soft jazz playing in the background. There are a few business types dotted around all suited up and chatting to their business buddies.

I don't really get the etiquette of posh places. I asked for a "cup of coffee" but I can't have that apparently. I've got to have an espresso or an americano or a mocha or a latte or some other foreign sounding concoction that everyone knows is basically just a coffee with bubbles in it. And she doesn't want my money either. I have to sit down and then she'll bring it over and then she'll take the money later. Jesus Christ what a palaver! I suppose they must trust the customers that come in here. The kind of people who stay at The Kingsley don't run off without paying their bill. At the Premier Inn they want the money up front. *No money, no coffee!* But at the Kingsley everyone is very friendly and trusting. And then when she finally takes my money she brings me the change on a little silver platter like she's serving up a slice of cake. My little 20p piece has never felt so important. I take the 20p and give her the tray back. Then she takes it out the back and probably has to put it in the dishwasher.

The restaurant is nice enough and the staff are friendly too. Breakfast is a self-serve affair with baked beans, scrambled eggs, sausages, bacon, hash browns, toast, muesli, cereal, fruit... whatever you want.

As for its location, that's pretty good to. It is literally sixty-seconds from the British Museum. If you walk along the road it will take you all the way down Shaftesbury Avenue to Piccadilly Circus (12-15 min walk). Leicester Square is very close too, and Covent Garden is within stagger distance. St. Paul's and Big Ben are probably at the absolute limit of where I'd want to walk to (half-an-hour at my pace)... any further than that and I'd have to get the bus.

To sum up then... it's a nice hotel. It's not my all-time favourite, but I'd happily stay here again.

Mercure, Paddington

ADDRESS Mecure, 144 Praed Street, Paddington - map 1f **RATING** ★★★★
TRAINS Paddington (zone 1) **BUSES** 7, 23, 27, 36, 205, 332, 436 **PRICE** £130 to £230 (standard room for one night) **FACILITIES** Restaurant, bar, concierge, laundry **ROOM** Room service, tea & coffee, Wi-Fi, TV, radio, telephone, hairdryer, trouser press, ensuite bathroom, air-con, safe **WEB** mercure.com/gb/hotel-8062-mercure-london-paddington/index.shtml **TEL** 0207 706 8888

Centrally located? ★★☆ Nice rooms? ★★☆
Value for money? ★★☆ Worth a stay? ★☆☆

Let's get straight down to business: number of teabags = two (but one of them is apple flavour); milks = two; biscuits = three. So straight away that is more than you get at The Ritz, which is a good start. You also get a wardrobe without any walls -- just a load of coat hangars on a pole -- but there is a very good reason for that: because there isn't enough room for a cupboard!

This is without any shadow of a doubt the smallest room that I have ever slept in -- and it's supposed to be a 4-star hotel. If they put two single beds in here then the room would be totally full up. It's a good job that I'm skinny otherwise I would never have squeezed in.

I'll give you an example of how small the room is: they've stuck a trouser press on the wall, but you can't lower it down because the mattress is in the way. The plug socket is literally flush against the sheets and if I turned it on then I'd be worried about setting fire to the bed. (Luckily I never do any ironing, so it's a moot point.)

And here is something that I've never seen before: a hotel window with frosted glass. All of the interior rooms look out over a concrete courtyard so they've obviously decided to frost up all the glass to stop people perving on each other. So that basically means that I've got a window I can't look out of. I can't see a bleedin' thing through it... it's like living with cataracts.

So how are we doing so far? Let's have a quick little re-cap... it's a 4-star room about the same size as my shed with a frosted window in it. And it's got a wardrobe without any walls -- just a metal stick with coat hangars on it. And an apple flavoured teabag.

I might steal one of the golden stars from the sign outside because they are taking the mick calling this a 4-star room. The only thing that you'd have to do to turn this into a 2-star room is take out the teapot and hairdryer and trouser press, and chuck out the shampoo, and that's it. Then you can knock a hundred quid off the room rate.

Oh yeah, and there's no bath either -- a 4-star room with no bath.

It gets better... because the next day the cleaner didn't bother washing the cup up or replacing any of the teabags. I know they are only piddly little problems in the grand scheme of things, and who really cares about a dirty cup (I'm perfectly capable of washing a cup up myself!), but it's supposed to be a 4-star hotel... and when they take a load of money off you for a shoebox room the least they could do is replace a 2p teabag.

As for the bar... well that is even smaller than my room (no joke -- I'm being serious). It's just a desk next to the reception with two tables in front of it. If two other people are using it then you'd have to stand up. Maybe I'm an old cynic but I reckon they just shoe-horned that in there so they could claim their fourth star.

The one redeeming feature was the breakfast room/restaurant, which turned out to be the Garfunkel's next door (they've got their own door into it from the reception). They give you a voucher for breakie and you can go in there and choose straight from the Garfunkel's menu. Seeing as it was a proper high street restaurant and had nothing to do with the hotel it turned out to pretty good. If the hotel ran it then they'd probably give you two baked beans on a saucer.

Here is my review: I'm not coming back here ever again. I'd rather stay at home -- and that is the truth! Luckily I don't mind when I get a lousy room because I'm only here to write a review, and having a lousy room at least gives me something to write about (bad moods are a wonderful cure for writer's block).

Strand Palace Hotel

ADDRESS Strand Palace Hotel, 372 Strand - map 8b **RATING** ★★★★ **TRAINS** Charing Cross, Charing Cross, Embankment (all zone 1) **BUSES** 1, 4, 6, 9, 11, 13, 15, 23, 26, 59, 68, 76, 87, 139, 168, 171, 172, 176, 188, 243, 341, RV1 **PRICE** £140 to £220 (standard room for one night) **FACILITIES** 2 restaurants, 3 bars, concierge, gym **ROOM** Room service, tea & coffee, Wi-Fi, TV, pay movies, telephone, hairdryer, ensuite bathroom, air-con, safe **WEB** strandpalacehotel.co.uk **TEL** 0207 379 4737

Centrally located? ★★★ Nice rooms? ★★☆
Value for money? ★★☆ Worth a stay? ★★★

Do you know what the nicest sight in the world is? It's walking over Waterloo Bridge bent over double, wind biting into you as it whips along the river, rain tipping down on your head, and the Strand Palace Hotel coming into view as you walk around the corner. They've even got a bowler-hatted gentleman on the door to hold it open for you.

The lobby is colossal. They've got four or five women behind the desk, all suited up in ponytails and very nice and friendly, and quite pretty too, which always helps. There are a few restaurants coming off the lobby, a jewellery shop and a cafe, bar, the obligatory aquarium, and a few computers for surfing the net. The lobby is always very busy when I walk in here, packed out with people queuing at the concierge, the reception desk, or just milling around with their bags and suitcases strewn about their feet.

I've actually stayed here a few times now, but this is the first time that I've bothered to review it. Luckily I already like the place or I would have moaned about the room. This is probably the smallest one I've ever had, but all the others have been pretty decent so I'll let them off. It's got all the normal stuff in it - - TV with Freeview, telephone, desk, a little safe, hair dryer and free Wi-Fi. It's also got a bin, a window, some carpet, four walls and a door (I like to be thorough).

The bathroom is quite roomy with a shower and a bath. I know from previous visits that not all the rooms have a bath -- so I made a point of asking for one on my booking. That's a sign of getting old apparently -- needing a decent bed and a bath in the room. When I was younger I used to go to Australia and some of the pokey old rooms I stayed in didn't even have a TV. I didn't care though -- I used to stay in hostels too. You wouldn't catch me doing that these days. I'm like the princess and the pea these days. Even the Ritz has trouble keeping me happy.

Do you get a little bar of soap? Yes you do.

What about those little bottles of shampoo? Yes you do.

But here comes a moan... and it's about the tea. You don't mess around with a British bloke's cup of tea. Don't you find it annoying when a hotel gives you five sugars, four tea-bags and three coffees, but only two milks? If you've only got two milks then you've only got two drinks -- it doesn't take a genius to work that out. So if you drink two cups of tea you may as well chuck the rest of the stuff away. But at least you get a biscuit. I'll give them an extra point for that. But you only get one cup though... which means you have to wash it up every time you want a drink. And I'm a lazy bloke, so that is a big no-no. So I'm taking the point away again.

One thing that is quite handy is the vending machine on each floor. If you're posh then you probably think that's a bit common -- having a crisp and Coke machine right outside your door -- but who wants to dress up and go downstairs for a can of Coke?

I'm sitting in the little bar area now and it's not too bad. It's only a little place full of businessmen and old ladies squinting at the menu trying to work out what to eat. It's the kind of place that sells bottles of red and white for twenty quid. There's a nice bottle of champers too, if you've got £55 pounds burning a hole in your pocket. I don't have anything to celebrate that's worth 55 quid, so I settle for a glass of Pepsi. That is more my level. I have a little read of the menu and, *jesus christ!* -- even the coffee will set you back £4. A cup of tea is £3. I'd want it served up in a 2-litre bottle for that price.

Breakfast is an all-you-can-eat, self-service type of affair in the Strand Carvery. They've got baked beans, sausages, fried eggs, scrambled eggs, hash browns, black pudding, a load of cheeses, cereal, and fruit salad too. And then there's your fruit juice, tea and coffee. I had dinner in there as well which is £16 for two courses. It's a bit annoying that they don't let you sit wherever you want though. The restaurant was half empty and she kept leading me to a crappy seat by the door. I don't suppose she would have minded if I'd asked to be moved, but she sounded Russian and I'm scared of Russians.

One of the best things about the Strand Palace Hotel is its location. It's down the Strand (obviously), right at the end of Waterloo Bridge. Covent Garden is right around the corner, and Trafalgar Square is a quick five-minute stroll down the road. You can easily walk to Parliament, Buckingham Palace and Piccadilly Circus. St. Paul's is probably a bit too far, but there are about a bazillion buses right outside the front door which will take you anywhere in London.

So, to sum it up, then... would I stay there again? Yes, I would. And I have! I've been to quite a few London hotels and this is definitely one of my favourites.

The Tower Hotel (Guoman)

ADDRESS The Tower Guoman Hotel, St Katharine's Way - map 10b **RATING** ★★★★ **TRAINS** Tower Gateway, Tower Hill (both zone 1) **BUSES** 15, 25, 42, 78, 100, RV1 **PRICE** £135 to £225 (standard room for one night) **FACILITIES** 2 restaurants, bar, concierge, gym, car park **ROOM** Room service, minibar, tea & coffee, Wi-Fi, TV, telephone, hairdryer, ensuite bathroom, air-con, safe **WEB** guoman.com/ en/hotels/united_kingdom/ london/the_tower **TEL** 0871 376 9036

Centrally located? ★★☆ Nice rooms? ★★☆ Value for money? ★★☆ Worth a stay? ★★★

I'm staying at The Tower this week (the Guoman Tower Hotel, not the Tower of London). I stumped up a bit extra for a "fantastic view of Tower Bridge", although I wasn't expecting much. I am the world's biggest cynic, you see, so I was assuming that I'd get a little glimpse of a pylon through the trees, or six inches of roadway through a crack in the door, or something like that, but it's actually quite a nice view. I can see one whole tower (the one closest to the Tower of London), plus the entrance roadway too, all lined with cabs and vans and buses. I'm not high up enough to see further down the river though, which is a bit of a shame. They've stuck me on the very first floor, with a big air vent outside, and I've got a mountain wall of nine floors staring straight down into my room. There are probably about seventy different windows all watching what I'm doing... all laughing and taking photos on their mobiles so they can have a good laugh at the ugly bloke in room 133. That is my No.1 hate in a hotel... having a load of other people staring down into my window. My No.1 love is when I'm the one doing the staring.

The building is pretty ugly. It's not exactly a looker. Check out my photo of the hotel. It looks like a brown brick car park... like one of those places that Prince Charles is always complaining about. I can see his point though. On one side you've got Tower Bridge and the Tower of London -- a World Heritage Site, no less -- and on the other side you've got a pile of brown breeze-blocks.

But the inside is nice. You've got all your pretty women lined up behind the desk in their air-hostesses uniforms, all smiling and being nice. And a load of smartly dressed gentlemen to open the doors and press the button on the lift (in case you can't manage it yourself). Then when you get up to the room you've got all the usual stuff in there: a bed, some carpet, some wallpaper and some lights, etc., even a smoke alarm in case you accidentally set yourself on fire.

I hate reviewing hotel rooms because what can you say that you haven't already said before? It's got a door... tick. What about a window? Yeah, tick that too. Is the mattress a bit lumpy? Are there any hairs in the bath? Can you hear the couple playing in the room next door? No, no and no.

I'm getting close to middle age now, so as long as I've got a toilet and a TV then I'm happy. When I was younger I used to stay in Australian hotels that had neither. I didn't have any money so I had to settle for shared bathrooms as well, so I had to wander out into the corridor and knock on the door to see if anyone else was using it. If somebody was having a shower then that was it -- no p*ss for you for half-an-hour at least. But when you're young, you don't care -- it doesn't matter. But these days I have an inviolable checklist of two: I need a TV, and a toilet. And a bath. And a teapot. (Okay, so that's four.) And a proper lock on the door so I don't have to wedge a chair against it. (Five.) If I get all of those then I'm happy. Plus a desk and preferably a radio. Apart from those I'm not fussed. (And a restaurant and a bar.)

This room has got a widescreen TV, a drawer full of tea and coffee (hooray!), an iron and an ironing board (I didn't come here to do the housework), a posh ballpoint pen which you can steal if you are feeling brave, a Gideon's bible in case you want to do some praying, and some posh bottles of soap and shampoo.

The only things that I don't like are the little fun-size biscuits on the tea tray. This is my second pet hate in a hotel -- when they serve up biscuits that are the same size as a crumb. And then they give you twelve tea bags and packets of coffee... but only four milks. Aaargh! What is the bleedin' point of that? That is like asking for a sandwich and getting a load of butter with no bread. You need two to tango, don't you? You don't have to be a genius to see that twelve teabags and four milks won't work. Maybe they want us to use three teabags per cup? Yeah, that is a good idea... let's all have a cup of tea so thick and black and stewed and brewed that we can stand our spoons up in it. And that is not all... because they have got a fun-size teapot too. Have you ever heard of such a thing? You have to literally fold the teabag up to fit it inside. You can't even fit two cups of water in it! So that is basically a complete waste of time -- you may as well just make it in the cup. I'm going to open the window and chuck the damn silly teapot in the river... that is how stupid it is.

I'm in the bar now. It looks like one of those wine bar places that you go to after work when somebody is retiring, with plank pine floors and wicker basket seats.

But it's got a nice view out of the window, straight onto Tower Bridge. The coffees cost three quid fifty though, and come with a head that's bigger than my head. It's got three-feet of foam on top. That's the problem with posh places... they serve everything up in a tiny cup and then clobber you for twice the price. I'm still going to drink it though. And I'm still going to smile and say thank-you to the waitress. Because I'm British. I'm a pushover. You can slap me in the face and I'll thank you for that as well.

They have two restaurants at this hotel: The Gallery and The Brasserie. I'm in The Gallery at the moment having my breakfast, looking out over St. Katherine Docks. The windows on the other side of the room look out over Tower Bridge. The breakfast bar has got everything you could possibly want... apart from Coco Pops. If you want Coco Pops or Sugar Puffs then you are out of luck. But if you want bacon and eggs, fruit salad, cereals and toast then you are laughing. They've got a very weird conveyor belt-like toaster which I am too scared to use in case I blow it up -- it looks a bit like an electric mangle. You feed your bread in one end and it comes out golden brown.

I quite like the sound of hotel restaurants in the morning. It's all clink clink clatter clatter as they put the plates out, with tourists wandering in half asleep planning what they are going to do with their day. Young couples wracking their brains trying to remember what they did (or didn't) do last night. City businessmen yakking on their phone and punching numbers into their laptop (do they really start work at 7 in the morning?). And pretty waitresses running around being as nice as pie. That is my favourite thing about hotels, I reckon -- everyone is nice to you, all the time. In my real life it is the total opposite: I can't walk five feet down the street without getting punched and kicked and spat at, but when you walk through the hotel lobby all of a sudden everybody knows you and wants to say hello. Obviously they are all being paid to do that and wouldn't give a hoot if you dropped down dead, but hey, it's nice to pretend.

I don't think I'd come here again, if I'm honest. It's supposed to be a 4-star hotel but it doesn't seem a lot different to the 3-star Strand Palace, which is closer to Trafalgar Square (and a lot cheaper too). But one thing that I will say about this place is this: it has got a very nice location. You can fall out of bed and bump your head on Tower Bridge, or take a two-minute stroll over to the Tower of London. And you've got St. Katherine Docks out the back too, which is a nice place to eat and have a drink.

P.S.: I was wrong about the Coco Pops. I had breakfast before I checked-out and saw some fun-size boxes of cereals on the bar -- one of which was Coco Pops! No sign of any Sugar Puffs though.

The Trafalgar (Hilton)

ADDRESS The Trafalgar, 2 Spring Gardens, Trafalgar Square - map 8b **RATING** ★★★★ **TRAINS** Charing Cross, Embankment, Leicester Square (all zone 1) **BUSES** 3, 6, 9, 11, 13, 15, 24, 29, 139, 159, 176, 453 **PRICE** £215 to £265 (standard room for one night) **FACILITIES** Breakfast room, 2 bars (including rooftop bar), concierge, gym **ROOM** Minibar, tea & coffee, Wi-Fi, TV, DVD, telephone, hairdryer, ensuite bathroom, air-con, safe **WEB** thetrafalgar.com **TEL** 0207 870 2900

Centrally located? ★★★ Nice rooms? ★★★
Value for money? ★★★ Worth a stay? ★★★

You can generally tell whether you're going to like a place within the first two minutes; and it took me even less time for The Trafalgar Hilton -- because I loved it as soon as I saw it. This hotel is situated on one corner of Trafalgar Square (I can see into Canada House from my bedroom window). So it's literally sixty-seconds to the National Gallery and five minutes from Big Ben. If you want a good location then you can't get any better than that -- it's absolutely perfect.

I was under the impression that Hilton hotels were always 5-star, but it turns out that this place is only a four. It still feels like a 5-star when you step inside, though. It's what I call an 'arty' hotel, rather than a cosy one -- full of mood lighting and eight-foot tall blondes behind the desk. All the staff are super smart and say hello to everyone they meet -- even me. I was staying at a Mercure last week (another 4-star hotel) and the difference is like night and day. That place was a 3-star masquerading as a four, whereas this place is a 4-star that should be a five. The price I paid was practically identical, but that one was overlooking the traffic in Paddington whilst this one is two minutes from Downing Street. So it just goes to show you that you shouldn't put too much faith in the star-ratings because they don't tell you the whole story.

The bedroom is quite large with a sitting area and a desk, plus a big bathroom and a bath. You even get a set of scales to stand on (I stood on it, but I'm not telling you how much I weigh -- I think they must be broken anyway). You also get a widescreen TV with a DVD player, minibar and safe, plus an ironing board and an iron, and something called a shoe mitt (I haven't got a clue what this is).

But how many teabags do you get? That is what we all want to know.

Well, they have been super generous... they give you more tea than I can drink in a day. You get eight teabags (but two of them are peppermint, so they don't count), plus three coffees, two hot chocolates and six milks. And two biscuits. And one of the biscuits is banana flavour. (Have you ever heard of a banana flavoured biscuit? -- I told you it was an arty hotel.)

I always like to price up the minibar so you can see how expensive it is. All hotel minibars are expensive, of course -- that is just the way of the world. And anybody who drinks the minibar dry is a total mug because the hoteliers know we'll be sitting here at midnight listening to the clock ticking quicker than the raindrops on the window. That's when you break open the mini bottles and try and speed up time. But you'd have to be loaded to get drunk in here, because it's £7 quid for just one shot of vodka. Another £7 quid for rum and £3.75 for Coke. Even the water costs three quid.

I've just noticed a sign on the minibar which says (and I quote): "Please be aware that any items moved will be charged using motion sensor technology." *Now they tell me!* I've just been shifting the whole lot around to see what was on offer -- I'll probably get billed an extra fifty quid now. Ah well. I may as well drink the whole lot now.

They don't have a proper restaurant in this place, only a breakfast room (which is basically the same as the downstairs bar). But they do have a rooftop bar which overlooks Trafalgar Square. And when I say a rooftop bar that is exactly what I mean... if it's raining then you will get wet. It is literally on the roof. Apparently they only open it during the 'seasonal months', so if you come over during the winter then expect it to be closed. It is a totally unique view that looks straight down onto Trafalgar Square at the National Gallery, Nelson's Column and St. Martin's church. Unfortunately you have to reserve a table and they won't let you have a simple coffee on its own -- you have to actually sit down to eat or drink (it's not like a pub bar). But it's well worth popping along just to have a peer over the edge -- the guy said he didn't mind.

I wasn't too fussed about their breakfast. I'd much rather they just put out a big pan of baked beans and hashed browns and sausages and eggs, and let us help ourselves. But it was just a load of fancy yogurts, origami hams and chiseled bread rolls. Then you have to wait while the egg chef makes you an omelette. That is literally the only hot thing that they have on offer: an omelette. But this is no ordinary omelette -- he doesn't just crack an egg into a pan and flip it over a few times. This omelette is a work of art, with mushrooms and peppers and meat and all the trimmings, all coloured like a folded pillow of gold. It was perfectly nice to eat, but where are the beans? Where are the sausages? Where are the Coco Pops?

So that was my only tiny criticism. The location = great. The room = great. The omelette = great. The breakfast = not so great.

5-star hotels

Andaz Liverpool Street

ADDRESS Andaz, 40 Liverpool Street - map 5f
RATING ★★★★★ **TRAINS** Liverpool Street (zone 1) **BUSES** 8, 26, 35, 42, 47, 48, 78, 135, 149, 205, 242, 344, 388 **PRICE** £190 to £360 (standard room for one night) **FACILITIES** 2 restaurants, two bars, concierge, valet parking (at a local car park), laundry, health club, spa

ROOM Room service, no alcohol minibar, tea & coffee, Wi-Fi, TV, telephone, hairdryer, ensuite bathroom, air-con, safe **WEB** london.liverpool street.andaz.hyatt.com **TEL** 0207 961 1234

Centrally located? ★★☆ Nice rooms? ★★☆
Value for money? ★★☆ Worth a stay? ★☆☆

I don't like it. End of review.

I'm too old for a hotel like this. It's for people under thirty, and people who love style over substance. It is immediately obvious as soon as you walk through the door that they are trying too hard to be cool. (That shows you how old I am -- I'm still using a word like *cool*.) I'd like to send the manager of the Andaz over to The Ritz, or the Royal Horseguards, so he can see what a proper 5-star hotel looks like. They need to turn some lights on, for a start, because the reception area is darker than space. Where's the bleedin' reception desk? They haven't even got one! They are too cool for that. Reception desks are what other hotels do -- what you have to do at the Andaz is introduce yourself to one of the suits who are just standing around in the dark, who will then lead you over to an office desk with a laptop on it, and start punching in some numbers. This is where it started to go downhill for me, because the very first thing he did was try to upsell me to another room. I'd just spent a bundle of money on a 5-star hotel --

which is supposed to be the bee's knees -- and the first thing out of his mouth was that he had something ten times better. No thanks mate, I said.

Next problem: There's no bath. I've got a shower and a sink, but no bath, and I'm too big to have a bath in the sink. Bear in mind that this is supposed to be a 5-star hotel, and every house in the country has got a bathtub in it -- so where is it? Maybe they've hidden it in the cupboard... let me go and have a look... nope. That's where you'll find a pair of slippers in a plastic bag, and a dressing gown that looks like a karate costume.

The Andaz is the hotel equivalent of that Stealers Wheel song, *Stuck In The Middle With You*, where they wonder if it's cool to go to sleep on the floor. The hotel spends too much time worrying about whether something is cool, and not enough time wondering if it's any good. They give you pencils instead of pens. They give you Chinese news, Russian news, French news and Al Jazeera on the telly, but no Sky News. They give you a copy of *Wired* magazine instead of a paper. You get an IKEA-style pine desk and metal office chair instead of an armchair. You get peppermint tea and glutton-free crisps. They even advertise the fact that their eco-friendly toilet uses 80% less water. Who honestly cares about that? When was the last time you booked a hotel room because the toilet uses less water?

Another thing that wound me up was this: the promise of a complimentary minibar. The guy downstairs made a big deal about that, but when you get up to the room all you'll find inside the fridge is a bottle of water, a tin can of Coke and a little plastic bottle of Tropicana orange juice. All the booze has to be purchased separately from room service. That's hardly a minibar, is it? That's more like the contents of a child's lunch box.

There's no ironing board either, and no iron -- you have to order those from reception. But at least they give you free Wi-Fi, I suppose -- which is more than most hotels do.

They have a couple of restaurants and a couple of bars onsite. One of them looks like a traditional British pub, and the other one is a champagne bar with mood lighting and sofa seats lower than your ankles. They certainly love the dark in this hotel -- thank Christ it had candles in it, otherwise I wouldn't have been able to see what I was drinking.

The only good thing that I can say about this hotel is that it's situated nextdoor to Liverpool Street station, which is a very busy and lively part of London. But I'd rather stay at the Premier Inn in Leicester Square -- and that's the honest truth. Maybe you'll like it better if you're under thirty.

The Ritz

ADDRESS The Ritz, 150 Piccadilly - map 8a
RATING ★★★★★ **TRAINS** Green Park, Piccadilly Circus (both zone 1) **BUSES** 9, 10, 14, 19, 38, 52, 452, C2 **PRICE** £395 to £475 (standard room for one night) **FACILITIES** 2 restaurants, bar, concierge, chauffeur, valet parking, laundry **ROOM** Room service, minibar, tea & coffee, Wi-Fi, TV, movies, telephone, hairdryer, ensuite bathroom, air-con,

safe **WEB** theritzlondon.com **TEL** 0207 300 2222

Centrally located? ★★★   Nice rooms? ★★★
Value for money? ★★☆   Worth a stay? ★★★

Oh my Lord. So this is how the other half lives!

I must be honest and say that I was a little bit intimidated before I walked into The Ritz. I know it sounds daft, but I wasn't really looking forward to my stay here. I'm basically a slob, you see. I wear the same shirt all week, shave once a fortnight, and the only suit I own is my birthday suit. So the thought of walking into the poshest hotel in London filled me with foreboding. I'm definitely going to get chucked out, I thought. There is no way they're going to let me in. They'll just stand around laughing at me, or have me arrested for impersonating a rich bloke. Then I'll be tied to the back of a limo and dragged around town whilst people chuck mouldy old cabbages at me... these are the kind of thoughts that were going through my head this morning.

But I've made it past check-in now and I'm well happy... my fears have disappeared.

As soon as you walk through the door everyone is very nice and polite and treat you like you actually deserve it (which I don't). They are probably used to getting a two grand tip from everybody they meet. The guy in reception was like an extra from *Downton Abbey*. He had about a bazillion questions to make me feel more welcome... would you like a paper sir (er... can I have *The Sun*?). Would you like a wake-up call? Would you like your bag carried up? Would you like a tour of the hotel? When would you like dinner, sir? What about room service? It was a blizzard of questions, and I aimed a whirlwind of nods back at him. But the one that flummoxed me the most was the turn-down service. I haven't got a clue what that is mate, I said. Apparently a lady is going to come into my room tonight and get it ready for bed, he said. Er... okay. That sounds like something for five-year-olds... pumping up my pillow and tucking me in. I wonder if she'll read me a bedtime story too? We will have to wait and see!

After I checked-in I was given a guided tour of the hotel by a pretty blonde bird (apparently they do this for everybody). She showed me the Rivoli Bar and Palm Court. It looked pretty plush. It was all round tables and gigantic flower arrangements, with posh people suited and booted and sipping their china cups of Oolong tea. Waiters waltzing around with silver trays of teacakes, and a penguin suit tapping out the tunes on his piano. Then it was up to my room and she even gave me a little tour of that. *Jesus Christ*, I thought, as I walked into the room... trying my best not to look too impressed. (I didn't want her knowing that I normally stay at the Ibis.) There were so many cupboards and electronic gizmos around that it took her five minutes to point it all out. Classical music was playing on a loop too... I think it was Chopin's *Raindrops* but I don't really know. It was something like that. All I know is that it was posh. That is what greets you as you walk through the door.

What a room! If you knocked together all of the downstairs rooms in my house, then I'm pretty sure that the Ritz room is bigger. First of all you've got a little sitting area with a sofa, two armchairs and a glass coffee table groaning under the weight of big books about cocktails and Van Gogh. They've also got a few papers and the latest issue of *Tatler* magazine. Then you've got acres of space to the bed in case you want to have a ballroom dance, and then another acre to the window with another set of table and chairs. Then you've got a separate dressing table and a mirror for the ladies, a big chest of drawers, a writing desk and a chair, two bedside tables... a marble fireplace with a Ming dynasty vase on it and a DAB radio with iPod dock. And then another huge cabinet with a Sky HD box inside, and a huge widescreen TV that is bigger than the bed. Then you've got another massive mirror on the wall, five paintings, an umbrella stand (complete with umbrella), a proper ironing board, two pairs of slippers, a minibar and a fridge with six crystal glasses and a tumbler of ice... I think that's about it

The bathroom is decorated in red marble and gold. You've got his and hers of everything... his and hers fluffy white towels, his and hers dressing gowns, his and hers taps. You even get two toilet rolls in case you want to have a crap together. You get a bath and a shower, plus a separate shower too. The mirror is bigger than my dining room table. And of course it's got a phone in there as well in case you want to order a pizza whilst you're having a wee.

Have you ever been in a room with three telephones in it? That gives you an indication of the room's size. There's one in the bathroom, one in the sitting area and another by the bed. And bear in mind that this was one of the *cheapest* rooms. But when I say cheap what I actually mean of course is that it was bloody expensive -- 350 quid per night. So lord knows what the suites are like. They must be like Buckingham Palace.

I'm heading down to the Rivoli Bar now to check that out. But I've got to put my jacket and tie on first though, otherwise they won't let me in...

Okay, I'm in. They let me in, which is a good start. You get met by a waiter who of course is very friendly and polite and speaks in la Français, sits you down and asks you what you want. I'll have a coffee please mate (£6.50!). It comes in a china cup on a solid silver tray, and the iceberg-sized lumps of sugar have a silver set of tongs to pick them up. He's handed me a broadsheet paper to read as well and a couple of slices of cinnamon cake. Frank Sinatra singing softly in the background -- it's like being transported back to the 1950s. It's all art deco browns and golds, with waiters in sharp white suits and slicked back hair.

The bar is full of posh wives and widows. There are a few decorated ladies spending their dead husband's money, and a couple of perm-do oldies who look like they are used to this kind of thing. One of them is the perfect stereotype of a posh old doddy with dripping earrings and thick gold rings on her fingers, talking in a voice that's posher than the Queen.

I'm trying to catch a few snippets of their conversation and it sounds like they are bitching about someone they know. Just two gossipy old women at the Rivoli Bar. Two more next-door are celebrating a birthday -- maybe her last, judging by the wrinkles on her face. What do you buy a woman who's ninety-years-old? Another ten years? It must be sobering knowing that your clock is ticking down... it's a bit like counting down the days to Christmas except when Christmas finally comes, you go up the chimney instead of down it. Now a crazy old professor has walked in with a wispy white beard and five aerials of hair sticking out the top of his head. I'm just sitting here drinking my £6.50 coffee, unwrapping the blanket that is my broadsheet paper. Why do they have to make these things so large? It's like reading a roll of wallpaper.

An assortment of black suits, posh frocks, and a fancy blue bow-tie walks in. Everyone gets met by the waiter who attentively asks them how their day has been. "What would you like, sir?" he says, and he gets met by a question this time: "What is the best drink for a sore throat?" I would probably go for a Lemsip, mate, is what he should say, but he suggests a whiskey and water instead. Huh? A whiskey and water? It's a good job this guy is not a doctor or he'd be giving out beer on prescription.

If you're lucky then you'll get met by the waitress instead, in a tight black dress and ponytail. The ultimate posh totty. I've just realised something... I haven't seen a single ugly person since I walked through the door. The last time I saw someone ugly was when I looked in the mirror.

Okay... I've found out what the turn-down service is. Imagine that you have hired a servant to do a load of unnecessary things for you... that is basically what it is. First of all she peels back the bed covers, then she puts a fresh pair of slippers by the bed and a glass of iced water on the table. Then she goes and hangs up your jacket that you've lazily dumped on the sofa. It's all highly embarrassing... I'm a grown man for chrissakes. She's like a mother and a nurse all rolled into one, making sure that there are no monsters under the bed. But she's getting well paid though so I guess it's all right, she doesn't mind. I wonder if she's going to kiss me goodnight as well... (no).

Do you know what I've just realised... you are not going to believe this... there is no kettle in here! Oh my god -- this is England -- the land of tea, so where the hell is my kettle and tea bags? *This is an outrage!* This is the first hotel that I've ever stayed at that doesn't provide a kettle and teabags in the room. Even the 2-star dumps that I've kipped in do that. So, finally, at last I have found something that I can moan about. I was going to give them a 5-star review, but they're not even going to get one now (that is how strongly I feel about my tea). Apparently you have to order your tea from room service instead. Rich people don't pour out their own tea, you see... it would do the butler out of a job.

I don't normally stay in places where you have to wear a suit and tie to dinner. I eat at McDonalds. That is my kind of level. The breakfast doesn't cost £36 quid at McDonalds (that's how much it costs in here). And the evening meal doesn't cost £50 quid (that is how much it's costing me to eat in the restaurant tonight -- and that's before you even order any food!). So if you spend one night in here you are approaching £500 quid for two meals and a room (plus £6.50 for a cup of coffee, of course).

Have a look at these minibar prices: packet of crisps £4.50, can of Coke £6, peanut M&Ms £10, shaving kit £28, scented candle £30, bottle of bubbly £50 to £150. I've stayed in rooms that cost less than the scented candle! I think that's a bit cheeky, to be honest. I don't mind paying a fortune for dinner in the restaurant, because you're basically paying for the glorious surroundings as much as the meal. But why is there a 600% mark-up in the minibar? That is just a swizz. There's a caravan outside Green Park tube station that sells the same stuff for a sixth of the price. But I don't suppose rich people give a toss.

I'm sitting in the restaurant having breakfast now. Very nice. Lots of round tables all pink and white, flowers everywhere and waiters in their tails. Lots of chandeliers and a big mirror wall at the end with pastel frescos and a giant gold statue. You have to dress up to get in. I've never dressed up for cornflakes before. (I'm being serious -- if you don't wear a jacket then they insist on lending you one from their wardrobe round the back.)

All of the food is wheeled out on a silver service with pots and plates and jugs and little bowls of jam and pans of sculpted butter. I've got three thousand knives and forks and big spoons and little spoons too. Plus a few glasses and cups. I've got a bread knife, a butter knife, a cheese knife with a curly tip, plus two more knives that I haven't got a clue about (a Rice Krispies knife?). That is a hell of a lot of washing-up to do just for one person. The waiters are just about the most helpful people on the planet: pouring out the coffee, pouring out the milk, putting a napkin on my lap, fetching the newspaper. If I asked them to blow my nose I reckon they'd do it. My waiter is just about the nicest person I have ever met, and he has boundless enthusiasm. I get the impression that he never stops smiling -- like someone has smacked him round the face with a bunch of flowers.

A steady stream of sleepy suits and grey-flecked hairdos walk in with the *Financial Times* hooked over the crook of their elbow. They look like the captains of industry -- the movers and shakers of the business world. Two guys behind me are currently discussing emerging markets in the third world, in between mouthfuls of bacon. They all look totally at home, like this is a regular part of their day. Then a middle-aged couple walks in, all goggle-eyed and smiling like they are in a dream. Oh my lord, they are saying, this sure beats breakfast at McDonalds.

Evening meal now... *this is the life*. If you ever want to take a girl out on a date then dinner at The Ritz will seal the deal, for sure. Talk about glamour! You've got a quartet playing outside the Palm Court and it's back to the golden days of Hollywood. Waiters in their buttons and tails. Lamplight yellow and flickering candles setting the mood. All the diners are waltzing in with posh frocks and jewellery. They are almost dancing to the tables.

I'm reminded of that scene in the *Blues Brothers*, when they go inside that posh place and start flicking bread rolls about. That is me. I am the lowlife. I am the one who doesn't belong... but maybe no one does. Maybe we are all playing the same game.

The waiter starts me off with three little canapés and they are like a work of art, it's almost a shame to eat them (but I do). Then some coffee and wine and fancy little toasts. Then he's like a one-man Red Arrows display team as he swaps all the knives and forks around in a flash (you've got to use the right ones for dinner). Everything has its own antique silver pot: the salt, rock salt, pepper, white sugar, brown sugar, milk, butter... I've got about three thousand pots and plates on my table and he hasn't even served up the meal yet.

When dinner finally arrives it is what I call a modern art meal... it looks like it should be on the wall instead of the plate. A pencil-sized piece of fish, three slices of carrot (not a joke -- I counted them) and a few spots of colourful sauce dribbled artistically around the plate. Very nice though -- one of the best meals I've ever tasted -- but if you were starving hungry then you would be going home with a rumbling stomach. They could have fitted it all on a saucer, but they served it up on a wagon wheel.

The evening ends with a string quartet playing jaunty waltzes in Palm Court. Then it's off to bed and back to reality.

The Royal Horseguards

ADDRESS The Royal Horseguards, 2 Whitehall Court (behind Whitehall Gardens) - map 8b **RATING** ★★★★★ **TRAINS** Charing Cross, Embankment, Westminster (all zone 1) **BUSES** 3, 11, 12, 24, 53, 87, 88, 159 **PRICE** £220 to £280 (standard room for one night) **FACILITIES** Restaurant, bar, lounge, concierge, laundry, gym **ROOM** Room service, minibar, tea & coffee, Wi-Fi, TV, telephone, hairdryer, iron, ensuite bathroom, air-con, safe **WEB** guoman .com/en/hotels/united_kingdom/london/the_ royal_horseguards **TEL** 0871 376 9033

Centrally located? ★★★ Nice rooms? ★★★
Value for money? ★★★ Worth a stay? ★★★

If you want to impress somebody then show them a photo of the Royal Horseguards hotel from the outside. Book a weekend away, and then show them a photo of where they're staying -- I guarantee that they will be impressed. They'll probably agree to marry you on the spot. If you look at the hotel from across the river then it's all turrets and spires and golden lamplights in the leafy trees. It really is a beauty (although some of it is private apartments). Unfortunately the front door is around the other side, and isn't nearly as impressive, but the reception area, restaurant and bar are all luxurious.

My bedroom is good, but not great. And the only reason I say that is because it doesn't have a bath. I don't understand how a 5-star hotel can have a bathroom bigger than a bedroom, and still not find room for a tub. The shower in my room is bigger than my shed. *It's huge!* You can probably fit about six people in it, so why not rip it out and stick a bath in there? It's supposed to be a 5-star hotel for chrissakes. I am sure that this is the real reason why rock stars smash up their hotel room -- just ask Jimmy Page. Ask Led Zeppelin why they wrecked their bedrooms. It's because they didn't get a bath. And the only reason why I'm not smashing up this one is because I can't afford to replace everything.

Now that I've got all of that off my chest, let me assure you that everything else is fantastic. This is the kind of hotel that I'd happily like to live in forever. I'm even tempted to die here, if they'll let me. When it's time to check out, I'm actually going to check out for real (permanently). I'll stick a tenner on the table as a tip for the cleaner, and leave a suicide note complaining that there was no bath.

I'll tell you what you *do* get, though -- a TV in the shower. I'm being serious! There is an actual TV screen inside the shower cubicle. When was the last time you wanted to watch *Coronation Street* in the shower? And the marble bathroom floor must have under-floor heating, because it's like walking on a piece of warm carpet. It's a very nice bathroom (apart from the bath -- did I tell you that there's no bath?).

There's no bath!

The room has all the usual goodies inside it: a bed, a desk, chair, another chair, a big armchair, lots of drawers with nothing in them, a Bible, a very posh box of tissues, an ice cooler with no ice in it (so it doesn't cool diddly squat), a safe, a pair of slipper flip-flops, a dressing gown, an ironing board, an iron, a shoe horn that is about a foot long, some padded coat hangers, three telephones (one for each ear, plus one for your mouth?)... and some carpet. But no bath. And you get free Wi-Fi as well, which isn't always the case with 5-star hotels.

They also kindly provide you with a copy of *Business Traveller* magazine, which has interesting articles like "Business start-ups are flourishing in the

Indian city of Bengaluru" and "The Savoy's American bar reveals new cocktail list". Nothing about baths, though.

They have been pretty generous with the teabags. You get a little wooden casket full of Twinings tea, and plenty of coffee and sugar and milks, plus a few biscuits. They actually give you more tea than I can drink in a day -- and I can drink a lot of tea. The minibar is full of booze and crisps and nuts, but you'd actually have to be nuts to eat them, because the prices are outrageous (as they always are in hotel minibars). Everything is triple the price it is in the shops.

The restaurant is very nice. It's all white china and marble columns, marble floors, polished tables and portraits of old soldiers on the walls. All the flowers are fresh and starched and standing up straight like old soldiers, posing for photos. The bookcases are filled with leathery old tomes too old to open, and all the staff look like they've stepped off a Parisian cat-walk. They all have red ties and buttoned up waistcoats, and walk around with silver trays balanced on upturned fingers. It's far too posh for cornflakes, of course. You shouldn't be listening to Mozart over a bowl of Kellogg's cornflakes. You don't need a napkin when you're eating Rice Krispies, but that's what you get. You could practically have a four-course meal just for breakfast. You could start with fruit and yoghurt, follow it up with a plate of sausages, eggs, boiled potatoes and a bowl of olives, and finish it off with a croissant and five triangles of toast.

The customers who frequent this place all have very important things they need to do today. The old toadies next to me are currently discussing the market's reaction to their new portfolio share options, and every other sentence contains a phrase like 'forcing audience direction'

or 'company communication channels'. I'm just sitting here thinking, *Come on, guys*. At least wait until 9 o'clock before you start talking about work -- you're not getting paid for this, you know! Eat your damn cornflakes and talk about the football. They are probably the kind of guys who make daily use of that TV in the shower, so they can catch up on the Bloomberg news. Other people are sitting here with folded legs in starched trousers, and a broadsheet newspaper. One guy is studiously adjusting his floppy fringe in the mirror.

The bar is nice and dark and gloomy (I like dark and gloomy). It's the kind of place where you can think dark and gloomy thoughts over a ten quid thimble of coffee. It's so dark and gloomy that I'm actually wondering whether all the lightbulbs are broke. It's not the kind of place where you'd want to have a party, that's for sure, but if you want to treat your missus to a romantic bottle of candlelight wine before you take her for a slap-up meal at McDonalds then it's perfect.

They've decorated it with lamps and candles and golden horse heads, and the staff are all shaved and well behaved. They say things like "Yes, sir" and "You're welcome, sir", and lots of other things that you don't really deserve.

Let me be honest: there's no way that anybody can truly mistake me for a *sir*. I'm not even a *mister*. I'm barely even a *guv*. I should be calling *them* sir. But that's part of the fun of staying in a posh hotel, isn't it? -- you can pretend that you're somebody worth knowing; and for all they know, maybe you are. As long as you keep paying then they'll carry on playing the game.

As for the hotel's location... it's pretty much perfect. It's on a very grand road that runs parallel with Whitehall, and you can walk to Downing Street in about three minutes. Horse Guards is just across the street. Trafalgar Square is two minutes down the road. I might give the Prime Minister a ring and ask him if I can borrow his bath. If he starts running the taps now, I reckon I can be round his house before the tub fills up.

Shaftesbury Premier, Piccadilly

ADDRESS Shaftesbury Premier, 65-73 Shaftesbury Avenue, Soho - map 8a **RATING** ★★★★★ **TRAINS** Leicester Square, Piccadilly Circus (both zone 1) **BUSES** 14, 19, 38 **PRICE** £235 to £255 (standard room for one night) **FACILITIES** Restaurant, concierge **ROOM** Tea & coffee, minibar, Wi-Fi, TV, movies, telephone, hairdryer, iron, ensuite bathroom, air-con, safe **WEB** theshaftesbury.com/hotel-the-piccadilly-london-west-end-109.htm **TEL** 0207 871 6000

Centrally located? ★★★ Nice rooms? ★★★
Value for money? ★★☆ Worth a stay? ★★★

The problem with most 5-star hotels is there's too much pressure to be posh. You can't relax and have a walk around because you feel like you're on trial. You have to press your shirt and shine your shoes and straighten your tie for breakfast, and I hate all of that. I don't like people striking up a "how are you today, sir" conversation every time I get in the lift. It's all right if you're trying to impress somebody, but I'm not -- it's just me. (It's always just me.) And that's why I like this place -- because it's a bit more normal and homely and there's no pressure to be posh. It's a posh hotel for non-posh people.

The room is quite small though (it's actually tiny), and it hasn't got a bath either, but I don't care. Everything else is nice. You get a big TV about the same size as my dining table, a fat bed that is deeper than a swimming pool, and a Nespresso machine. But let's check out the tea bags... that is how you gauge the true quality of a hotel.

You get six tea bags, four coffees and a hot chocolate too... but only four milks. But some of the tea bags are of the watery oriental kind, like green tea and lemongrass. Are you supposed to put milk in those? They've got Jade Sword and Ginger too -- I haven't got a clue what that is. It comes in a net instead of a tea bag. I guess I've still got some learning to do if I want to be posh. I think I'll just stick with the Nespresso machine, because I know where I am with that.

You also get a minibar full of booze and mineral water. Let's have a look at the prices: £2.50 for a fun-size can of Coke, £5 for a tiny bottle of red or white, £5 for a tiny bottle of vodka, whiskey or rum, £6 quid for a peanut-sized tub of peanuts, and another £3.50 for a cup-sized tub of Pringles. So... *yeah*. There you go. Those are the prices -- if you've got money to burn then it's perfect.

The bathroom is nice enough. It's got a toilet and a sink to brush my teeth -- that is all I need. And some soap. And a bottle of shampoo. And some scales. And a mirror. And some towels and a flannel and a few rolls of toilet paper. What else can I find in here... a shower cap and a vanity pack. Do you want to know what is inside a vanity pack? Some circular cotton wool things that I presume are for wiping the make-up off your face, plus some ear buds and a nail file. So that is what vain people spend half-an-hour doing in the bathroom every morning -- sticking ear buds up their nose and filing down their toenails.

Do you want to know how much I weigh? I may as well stand on the scales seeing as they are here. This is not the usual kind of thing that you get in hotel reviews, is it? But what the hell... eleven stone and a little bit. That's not too bad is it? I'm quite proud of that -- I might have that tub of Pringles in the minibar now.

You also get plenty of pillows and a safe, an iron and an ironing board, a sewing kit (safety pin, needles and thread and a couple of shirt buttons) and a shoe mitt. This is the second time that I've stayed in a hotel with a shoe mitt, and I still haven't got a clue what it is, so I'm going to open it up and have a look... it looks like a cross between a glove and a hanky. I think you are supposed to buff up your brogues with it.

Their 'restaurant' is really just a breakfast room that is no bigger than a little office -- it only has seven tables in it. But the breakfast is okay. You get all the usual kind of stuff: sausage and beans, scrambled eggs and hash browns, mushrooms, cheese and hams. And some cereal and toast too.

The best thing about this hotel is its location. It's halfway up Shaftesbury Avenue, about two minutes from Piccadilly Circus. So you can walk to Leicester Square in five mins, Trafalgar Square in ten mins, and Big Ben in fifteen.

Just to show you how screwed up the hotel rating system is in London: half of the websites call this a 4-star hotel, whilst the other half call it a five. The hotel unsurprisingly calls itself a five-star as well... but I think it probably warrants a four.

Shangri-La at The Shard

ADDRESS Shangri-La Hotel, The Shard, 31 St Thomas Street, Southwark - map 10c **RATING** ★★★★★ **TRAINS** London Bridge (zone 1) **BUSES** 43, 48, 149, 521 **PRICE** £405 to £450 (standard room for one night) **FACILITIES** Restaurant, bar, concierge, valet parking, laundry, gym, swimming pool **ROOM** Room service, minibar, tea & coffee, Wi-Fi, TV, movies, telephone, binoculars, hairdryer, ensuite bathroom, air-con, safe **WEB** shangri-la.com/london/shangrila **TEL** 0207 234 8000

Centrally located? ★★★ Nice rooms? ★★★
Value for money? ★★☆ Worth a stay? ★★☆

If you've ever wondered what it's like staying in a 5-star hotel then let me just say one thing: heated toilet seats. The Shangri-La has got a heated toilet seat and it's like sitting on a warmed up oven. You don't even need toilet paper because they've got little sprays of water that fire up from the toilet bowl (I know this is uncouth, but this is important information that I'm giving you here). And you can angle the sprays by manipulating a computerised control panel on the wall -- it's a very hi-tech toilet. I've never sat on a toilet that has to be plugged into the mains before. That is why the room costs £450 quid a night -- you are paying £200 quid just for the toilet!

I like this bathroom better than the one at The Ritz. Forget the bedroom. Forget the restaurant, and the bar and the bed... who cares about all of those. Let's just focus on the bathroom for a little while longer.

They've got some electronic scales in here and a space-age telly floating in the middle of the mirror. It's a bit like one of those hologram screens you see in *Star Trek*. So you can look at yourself in the mirror and watch TV at the same time -- useful. It's got two fluffy white rugs and a couple of dressing gowns and a pair of flip flops too. I think I'm just going to stay in this toilet for two days.

The Shangri-La is halfway up The Shard, by the way. (Did I not mention that? I was too busy talking about the toilet.) It spans floors 34 to 52, and my room is on the 45th. (The public observation decks are on 68 to 72.) When you first enter the hotel you have to say hello to the welcome desk, where you'll get met by a nice lady who whisks you up 35 floors in the lift. Then you've got all of your form filling and signing to do at the reception, where you'll get met by another nice lady who will take you up to your room. I don't know if this is standard for 5-star hotels, but every time I've stayed in one so far I get a little guided tour of the place. The first time it happened at The Ritz I thought I was special, but now I just think they do it for everyone.

The room is a bit of a knockout. It's not that big for a luxury hotel but the view is something else entirely. I paid for a 'City View' room, so it looks out over Bankside and the Square Mile. I can see everything from Big Ben and Parliament in the west, right round the bend of the Thames to the Gherkin, with St. Paul's slap bang in the middle. It doesn't quite go far enough around to see Tower Bridge, but I'm certain that some of their other rooms do (but then you wont be able to see Big Ben). The farthest thing that I can recognise is the tall arch of Wembley Stadium.

If you've ever been up to the top of The Shard then you will know the view already, because you're only about twenty floors further down. If you thought that the London Eye was high then you are wrong. Compared to this place it is a midget. And the windows are all floor-to-ceiling as well, so it really is scary when you walk up close. I don't think I'd like to live here forever because of the height, but I'm brave enough to handle a couple of nights.

I thought it was a nice touch that they've provided a pair of binoculars in the room and a seat by the window, so you can just sit and relax, and watch the trains snaking their way into London Bridge. I can follow their entire railway journey from Waterloo East to Cannon Street station from my seat in the sky -- if you're a train spotter then this is your dream come true. I'm probably looking at a million people up here. A million people and fifty-thousand rooftops. A quick count reveals eight river bridges and three different cathedrals -- St. Paul's, Southwark and Westminster Cathedral. Plus Westminster Abbey as well. The binoculars bring out Whitehall and maybe Buckingham Palace too, but the sunlight is starting to make it hazy. Imagine being able to see all of that, plus the Bank of England, Royal Courts of Justice, Tate Modern and Nelson's Column -- all in the same view. (You will need the binoculars and some good geography knowledge to see Nelson -- so good luck!) I can see some people using the telescopes at the top of The Monument as well -- not realising that there are people even higher up spying on their lives.

The view at night time is amazing. And instead of the quick thirty minutes that you get on a visit to The Shard, in a hotel room you can literally sit here all night with your floor to ceiling panorama.

It makes you realise how big the city is when you can see all the lights come to life -- they cover every speck of land to the wide horizon, like a load of dodgy pixels flashing on and off. And then you look down close and see a snake of cars and buses, and tiny little ants walking home across the bridge. I feel like a spy satellite, sitting here, nosing down on people's lives whilst they wander along oblivious.

So what else is there? Well... the first time that you enter the room they will have warmed up a pot of tea for you, all ready to pour. I thought that was quite a nice touch, until I discovered that it was Chinese tea, with no milk and a load of herbal weeds in it (I poured it down the sink). They've put a little Pot Noodle in the cupboard too (but with a posher sounding name than Pot Noodle, of course -- but we all know that it's a Pot Noodle) and a few tubs of nuts and shortbread. I daren't eat any of this stuff yet because I don't know how much it costs -- I haven't found the minibar menu.

Okay, I've found it now... here we go... have a listen to this. Nuts = £7. Plain packet of crisps = £7. A normal sized can of Coke = £4. A tiny little bar of chocolate about the same size as a credit card = £5. A little minibar-sized bottle of Jack Daniels = £9.

This is the first 5-star I've stayed at that that actually gives you free tea and coffee, which is nice. And you get a little Nespresso machine as well, with a load of complimentary capsules, which is probably the only thing I will drink all week.

There's a little school set in the desk drawer as well... in case you've got any homework to do. It's got a pair of scissors in it, plus a stapler, a pencil, a pencil sharpener, and Tipex tape in case you make any mistakes. And here's something weird: I've just discovered a chunky torch in the drawer. I'm assuming that must be for emergencies, in case we have to climb down the skyscraper stairs in darkness. That's a bit worrying! I immediately start thinking of the *Towering Inferno* starring Steve McQueen.

But here comes the bad bit... I've been here for two nights now, and I must admit that I don't like the restaurant and bar very much. Silly old me just kind-of assumed that because it was a 5-star hotel, it would always have a place to eat and drink. But it turns out that you have to book well in advance for both, because they are so busy (because of the view). They've stupidly decided to let in people off the street, and no preference is given to the guests; so if you decide to go down there in the evening, on a whim, then you may as well just forget it -- you've got no chance. I got turned away myself, and heard another guy complaining at the desk when he suffered the same. Another couple had one eye on the clock because they'd been given a deadline to leave. Who's ever heard of booking time slots in a hotel bar? It doesn't seem like a very friendly way to treat your high-paying guests.

The breakfast the next morning was useless too. I went down there at 7 AM, which was half-an-hour after it opened, and waited an age for the waitress to turn up, only to be told that the hot buffet (bacon, sausages, eggs, etc.) wouldn't be out for another fifteen minutes -- which would have been twenty-five minutes after I sat down (and nearly an hour after it was supposed to have opened). So I switched to a continental breakfast instead, only to be told that the bread and rolls weren't ready yet either... but I could have a cup of fruit juice and a bowl of cornflakes. Now bear in mind that a continental breakfast in this place costs a ridiculous £28 quid. Would you want to spend £28 on a bowl of cornflakes? That was when I gave up and went to Starbucks.

Oh yeah... and the bar latch on my hotel door fell off. Do you know that thing that you flap across the door to stop thieves getting in? Well, that was screwed on so tightly that it just fell off when I shut the door. So if you want to burgle some rooms you should go to the Shangri La. Give the door a big shove and the lock will probably fall off. (Although to be fair to them, they did send somebody up to fix it pretty quickly.)

And one last thing to be aware of: they do that cheeky thing of pre-authorising a load of extra money on your credit card, in case you decide to make any phone calls or ring down for room service. And it's a very hefty charge = 200 quid a night (on top of the £450 a night that you've already paid for the room). That 200 quid a night becomes frozen money that you can't spend until your holiday is over. Why are they confiscating money for something that you might not even buy? Why can't they just charge you at the end, like everyone else?

Here is my final advice: this hotel is all about the view, which is fantastic, but it's not worth staying overnight for. If you want to see the view then just come as a tourist and stay in a different hotel.

And if you don't like heights then don't even think about it -- this hotel is higher than the clouds!

Waldorf Hilton

ADDRESS Waldorf Hilton, Aldwych - map 4e
RATING ★★★★★ **TRAINS** Covent Garden, Temple (both zone 1) **BUSES** 1, 4, 6, 9, 11, 13, 15, 23, 26, 68, 76, 87, 91, 172, 188, 243, 341, 521, RV1, X68 **PRICE** £260 to £320 (standard room for one night) **FACILITIES** Restaurant, bar, concierge, laundry, gym, pool **ROOM** Room service, minibar, tea & coffee, Wi-Fi, TV, movies, telephone, hairdryer, iron, ensuite bathroom, air-con, safe **WEB** waldorfhilton.co.uk **TEL** 0207 836 2400

Centrally located? ★★★ Nice rooms? ★★☆
Value for money? ★☆☆ Worth a stay? ★★☆

I thought I would really love this place, but do you know what? I don't think I do. I don't like the Waldorf (I'm very hard to please). Once you've stayed in The Ritz then nowhere else comes close.

But before I explain why, let me get all of the plaudits out of the way first. The location is great. It is situated right on the bend of Aldwych, five minutes from Trafalgar Square and two minutes from Covent Garden. You can even walk to St. Paul's if you're feeling energetic. Big Ben is walkable as well... so the location is pretty much perfect. And the outside looks fantastic, with its warm yellow lamplights and fancy black iron work (especially on a rainy night).

The room is big. It's probably the second largest room that I've ever slept in after The Ritz. But it's all white. It has white walls, white doors, a white bed... a bottle of water and clean glasses on the side. Mirrors absolutely everywhere (seven of them). It's like sleeping in a goddam hospital! It's like sleeping in a doctor's clinic. Any minute now the doc is going to come up and give me some bad news. He's going to deliver my brain scan results. *I'm very sorry, sir, but I'm afraid you've only got two days to live. And you're going to have to spend them in the Waldorf.* There are a couple of black and white photos of Marlene Dietrich above my bed as well (or somebody like that -- I don't know exactly who)... and in my hospital frame of mind I'm imagining them as being backlit x-rays of my skull.

The bathroom is white. Everything is white. This entire room is white. Whenever you see a lunatic locked up in a padded room, the room is invariably white.

I'm probably being a bit harsh... if the only thing that I can complain about is the whiteness of the walls then it can't be too bad, can it? I'd be no good as an eskimo, that's for sure. *This igloo is too damn white!* You do get plenty of extras, though. A big TV, a clock radio, ironing board, teapot, dustbin, carpet, wallpaper, teabags and coffee, minibar, dressing gown and slippers (both white), a personal safe and air conditioning. You also get about ten light switches but only seven lights. I wonder what the other ones do? That is one of the annoying joys of moving into a new hotel room -- trying to work out which switch does what. Sometimes they try and confuse you with a master switch, which toggles off all the other ones before you've even had a chance to turn them on. It was whilst I was standing there doing this that I discovered that this room has got something I've never seen before: a night light. It's just a dim little lightbulb by the skirting board, about six inches off the floor. Have you ever seen such a thing? You literally have to get down on your hands and knees to see it. It's a light for the mice. It looks a bit daft to me... but if it scares away the monsters from under the bed, then I'm leaving it on.

One thing that really winds me up about 5-star hotels, is the crazy amount of money they want for trifling things. For example, (you are not going to believe this), for two-days access to the hotel's Wi-Fi they want £26 quid. No joke! You get free Wi-Fi in McDonalds and Starbucks for chrissakes, so why is a 5-star hotel asking for twenty-six quid? That is a total rip-off. There are no other words to describe it. (Obviously I still paid it though, because I'm an idiot.)

Luckily things pick up considerably when you get out of the room and into the bar. It's just a tiny little bar decorated with dark wood and pretty women, low lights (barely on), soft jazz (acoustic guitars and Spanish singing), and I definitely don't belong. But I can just about blag it as a smart man, because I'm wearing my funeral trousers and job interview shirt. I can be smart when I have to (when I'm forced to). They very nearly ruined my mood by serving up the coffee in a thimble, but I am even prepared to forgive them that because the atmosphere is so great. The coffee is super-strong though. *Jesus Christ!* It's almost like smoking a cigarette, and I have to do my best not to cough.

The waitress must think I need cheering up, because she's just lit a candle and brought it over. I seem to be the only person in here with a romantic candle. *Er... thank you* (what else can you say?). Normally I would blow it out, but I'll leave it burning tonight. I'll leave it burning on the table top, like they do at the foot of a tomb. Like they do in the churches. Like they do at a wake. I hope it doesn't set fire to this rose that they've placed inside a vase. That just about sums up my love life: a romantic candle burning down the flowers.

I can hear a conversation a few tables away with four equally unhappy women, all bemoaning the fact that they are still single. One of them thinks she is too ugly. Another one thinks she is too fat. The third one thinks that all men are useless (which, to be fair, we are), and the fourth one... well, I haven't got a clue what she thinks, because she's just sitting there in total silence. Maybe she's shy. Maybe she's dead and they haven't noticed yet. Maybe she's got the most to say, but can't find a way to say it. Who knows. I will never know. But I think she's the most memorable thing in this hotel. I'm going to remember the girl who didn't say a word.

The breakfast is nice. It takes place in a big dining hall with faux-Roman columns down the side (imagine a mini-Banqueting House, but without the Rubens on the roof). There are lots of pretty staff floating around, lots of business types in smart shirts and ties, talking business over breakfast, and that soft Spanish jazz playing in the background again. Then you help yourself to all the usual stuff: sausages, eggs, bacon, beans, toast, cereals, yoghurts, etc. No Sugar Puffs, though. I can't see any Coco Pops either -- it's all cornflakes and muesli. One day I will find a 5-star hotel that serves up Coco Pops, and my quest will be complete.

So that's about it, apart from one more gripe: they didn't bother to replace the milk and tea-bags. And you don't mess with my tea -- hence why I'm never coming here ever again.

Using London Transport

How to Pay a Fare

Oyster cards

An Oyster Card is made out of plastic and looks like a blue credit card. It comes in two different types: a *pay-as-you-go* version, which you can keep loading up with credit however many times you like, and the correct fare will be deducted every time you touch it on a reader, and a *travelcard* version, which you buy for a one-off fee and remains valid for a set period of time: either one day, one week, one month, or one year. (Note: It is also possible to combine the two, and load a travelcard straight onto a pay-as-you-go card, but I'll talk about that in the travelcard section.)

The big advantage in choosing a pay-as-you-go Oyster card over a 1-day travelcard, is its 'daily price cap' feature. This will freeze your maximum daily spend at a level below the cost of a 1-day travelcard. So even if you jump on ten million buses in one day it will still end up being cheaper than a 1-day travelcard -- *handy!* But it doesn't do the same thing with weekly, monthly or yearly travelcards unfortunately, only 1-day travelcards.

Where can I get a pay-as-you-go Oyster card?

There are four ways to get hold of a pay-as-you-go Oyster card. The easiest way is just to order it online and have it delivered to you. You can do this at the Transport For London website: *https://oyster.tfl.gov.uk/oyster/entry.do*. This will henceforth be known as the 'TFL' website, to save me the trouble of having to type it out every time (because I'm very lazy). This website is only suitable for people who live in the UK, though. If you want it delivered abroad then you will have to get a Visitor Oyster card instead (which is explained in the section below).

The second way to get one is from a manned ticket window or a self-service machine at a train station. For some crazy reason the manned ticket windows are currently being phased out of all the Underground stations, so you'll have to visit a big National Rail station if you prefer talking to a human. (National Rail stations are the big overground hubs: Euston, Liverpool Street, London Bridge, King's Cross, Marylebone, Paddington and Waterloo.)

The third way is to find a London Travel Information Centre. There is one at Euston station, King's Cross, Liverpool Street, Piccadilly Circus, Victoria and Heathrow Airport (there are actually two at Heathrow: one inside Terminals 1-3, and another one inside the Underground station).

The fourth and final way is to look for an 'Oyster Ticket Stop'. These are basically just high-street shops (usually newsagents), which have a blue Oyster card symbol showing in the window.

Important note: You always have to pay a refundable £5 deposit the first time you purchase an Oyster card. This will go on top of whatever credit you want to load on. So if you want £20 quid credit, you'll have to spend £25.

Visitor Oyster cards

Visitor Oyster cards are primarily aimed at tourists, but you don't have to be a foreigner to buy one -- UK tourists can use them as well (even Londoners), because they are basically the same as pay-as-you-go Oyster cards. The biggest difference is that they come with their credit pre-loaded onto them, to save you the trouble of having to load it on yourself. They come in the following amounts: £10, £15, £20, £25, £30, £35, £40 and £50. You can then top them up whenever you like, in exactly the same way as you would with a normal pay-as-you-go card (I'll explain how to do this later).

Normal Oyster cards are always blue, but Visitor Oyster cards usually have a snazzy picture on the front to advertise various different events. Don't worry if your card looks different to the one shown above, because the picture changes all the time.

Visitor Oyster cards also come bundled with a booklet of discount vouchers. These discounts are constantly changing all the time, so I can't tell you what they are right now, but they might include something like 10% off a boat ride, or 20% off a meal in a particular restaurant.

Where can I get a Visitor Oyster card?

Visitor Oyster cards can either be bought overseas (here's a list of agents: *https://tfl.gov.uk/fares-and-payments/where-to-top-up-and-buy-tickets/overseas-travel-agents*), or ordered online and posted to your home. UK delivery typically takes between 2-4 days, whilst overseas can be as long as 1-2 weeks. Visit their site for details: *https://tfl.gov.uk/travel-information/visiting-london/visitor-oyster-card*.

You can also buy them from the 'Gatwick Express' and 'Stansted Express' ticket office at each airport, and the 'National Express' office inside Gatwick, Stansted and Luton airport. You can also buy them onboard a Eurostar train.

For some bizarre reason it is not possible to buy a Visitor Oyster card once you arrive in central London. And, yes, I know that sounds totally ridiculous -- but it's true. You have to purchase one *before* you arrive in the city. If you forget then you'll have to buy a normal pay-as-you-go Oyster card instead.

Important note: You always have to pay a non-refundable £3 admin fee the first time you purchase a Visitor Oyster card. This goes on top of your credit. So if you want £20 quid credit, you'll have to spend £23.

How can I top-up an Oyster card / Visitor Oyster card?

Topping up an Oyster card with extra credit is easy-peasy. (Note: Pay-as-you-go Oyster cards and Visitor Oyster cards are basically the same thing, so whenever I talk about an Oyster card from now on you can assume that I'm also talking about a Visitor Oyster card.) The quickest way to do it as it a self-service machine at a train station:

All you have to do is wave your Oyster card in front of the big round yellow reader in the middle, and select 'Top Up' on the touch-screen. You can either pay by cash, debit or credit card. Some ticket machines are only set up to take cards, though, so make sure you check before you press any buttons. If you look at the photo then you can see that one machine only takes 'Card Payments', whilst the other accepts 'Cash and Card Payments'.

The second way to do it is at an 'Oyster Ticket Stop'. These are basically just high-street shops (usually newsagents), which have a blue Oyster card symbol showing in the window. Just hand them your card and tell them how much you want to add on. The big advantage of doing it at a newsagent is that you can buy some sweets at the same time.

The third way involves a bit more work, because you have to register your card on the TFL website first. You can do that here: *https://oyster.tfl.gov.uk/oyster/link/0004.do*. Once you've set it up you will be able to log on and top it up online whenever you like.

Bear in mind that the maximum amount of money that a pay-as-you-go Oyster card can hold at any one time is £90 -- it's not possible to go above that.

If you can't be bothered to keep topping it up yourself then there's one more thing that you can do. Oyster cards come with an 'auto top-up' feature, which will automatically draw another £20 to £40 from your bank account every time your credit drops below a certain amount. You can set this up at *https://oyster.tfl.gov.uk/oyster/link/sso/0002.do* (you will have to buy a card first, though, because you'll need the serial number on it).

How much credit do I need?

This will obviously depend on how long you're staying for, and where you're planning on travelling to. But here are some tips...

Unless you fly in from Heathrow (zone 6), you will likely spend your entire holiday inside zone 1 (the touristy bit), but may enter zone 2 for places like Greenwich, Camden, Canary Wharf and The O2. Zone 3 is for places like Kew, Wimbledon and Highgate. I have provided the zones for each attraction within my reviews. What you need to do is go through all the attractions and work out which zones you will be travelling through each day, and then write them down. Each zone has something called a 'daily price-cap', which limits the amount of money that is taken from your Oyster card each day. The daily price-cap for zone 1, for example, is currently £6.50. This means that you can use as many trains or buses as you like within zone 1, and the maximum amount that will be taken from your Oyster card in any one day will be £6.50. Zone 2, and zones 1&2 combined, also have a daily price-cap of £6.50, making it very easy to work out your sums.

Therefore, if you're staying for just one day then £10 will be more than enough (because you won't be spending any more than £6.50). If you are staying for two days then £15 will be plenty. If you are staying for three days then £20 should just about cover it (but only just!). I always recommend sticking an extra couple of quid on, just in case you stray into another zone for whatever reason. And don't forget about the £5 deposit that you have to pay when you set it up, either. You can't use that money as part of your fares, so whatever credit you decide to load on you will have to pay another five quid on top. The same thing applies to the £3 admin fee that you have to pay for a Visitor Oyster Card.

I have provided the daily price-caps for each zone in the train fares section. If you limit yourself to the buses then the daily price-cap will be slightly lower.

Can you share an Oyster card?

It depends. If you are travelling together, then definitely not -- each person in your group will require their own pay-as-you-go Oyster card, because it's not possible to take multiple fares from one card. But if you are travelling at totally different times then that is okay -- provided that you each have the card in your sole possession. Oyster cards do not have your name or photo on them, so it doesn't matter who originally bought it.

Important: This rule only applies to pay-as-you-go Oyster cards. If the Oyster card contains a travelcard, or a concessionary entitlement (maybe because of your age, or a disability), then it can only be used by *you*. You are not allowed to lend it to anybody else.

How can I refund the credit?

At the end of your holiday you can claim back the £5 deposit, plus any credit that you haven't yet spent, up to a maximum of £10, at a self-service ticket machine at a London Underground station. All you have to do is touch the Oyster card against the big round yellow reader and select 'Oyster Refund', and then follow the on-screen instructions. Note: It's not possible to claim back the £3 admin fee for a Visitor Oyster Card.

If you wish to claim back more than £10 then it's a bit more complicated. The easiest way to do it is on the TFL website, but this only works if you set up an online account beforehand (see *https://oyster.tfl.gov.uk/oyster/entry.do*).

If you haven't got an account with them then you will need to give their Customer Service team a ring on 0343 222 1234. Unfortunately they can only make payments to a UK bank, which isn't much use if you're a tourist, so the final way is to download an application form from *https://tfl.gov.uk/fares-and-payments/replacements-and-refunds/oyster-refunds-and-replacements*. Unfortunately there's another catch if you do it this way, because they can only send you a check in British currency. So you may as well just let them keep your money -- just call it a tip.

Note: If you can't be bothered to claim back your credit then it's still worth keeping hold of the card. The credit never expires, so you can carry on using it the next time you come to London.

Travelcards

Travelcards last for a set period of time: either one day, one week, one month, or one year, and you can travel as many times as you like during that period. Tourists tend to prefer travelcards because they are a lot easier to understand than pay-as-you-go Oyster cards. You simply choose which zone you want (probably just zone 1, but maybe zones 1-2), then pay a one-off fee, and that's it -- *job done*. You don't have to keep topping it up with credit, or anything fiddly like that. You just carry on using it until the date expires.

You can get them in two different versions. The first version just covers the bus/tram network, and the second version includes the trains as well. (Note: There are no trams in central London, only in places like Beckenham, Croydon and Wimbledon -- places that you will never go.)

A travelcard will either come as a paper ticket, or be put onto a blue Oyster card. This is *extremely* confusing, because it's basically impossible to tell the difference between an Oyster travelcard and a pay-as-you-go Oyster card. Underground stations also have a different coloured paper roll to the overground stations -- so don't be surprised if your paper travelcard looks different to your mate's, if you bought them at different stations. I have shown you the two types of paper in the picture above.

You might want to look at the prices before you buy one, though, because tourists usually assume that travelcards are the cheapest way to travel. Oyster cards and contactless payment cards are *always* the cheaper than 1-day travelcards, but weekly travelcards usually work out cheaper than seven days on pay-as-you-go Oyster -- but it depends on how many journeys you make. If you are planning on making two or more journeys for seven days, or three or more journeys on five or six days, then a weekly travelcard is probably cheaper.

Where can I get a travelcard?

This is where it gets confusing...

It is not possible to buy a 1-day travelcard for the bus/tram network in advance. You can only purchase it on the day of travel from a train station, a London Travel Information Centre, or an Oyster Ticket Stop.

1-day travelcards for the bus/tram/train network, plus weekly travelcards, can also be ordered from their website: *https://visitorshop.tfl.gov.uk/tfl/london-travelcard*. These ones will be issued as a paper ticket. If you get them from a train station, a London Travel Information Centre, or an Oyster Ticket Stop, then they will be put onto a blue Oyster card. (Note: The usual £5 deposit will apply if you require a new Oyster card -- which comes on top of the travelcard cost.) If you buy a weekly travelcard from a National Rail station then you will also need to supply a passport-style photo -- so just get them from an Underground station, London Travel Information Centre or Oyster Ticket Stop instead.

Monthly and annual travelcards can only be bought from a train station, a London Travel Information Centre, or an Oyster Ticket Stop. They cannot be ordered online because you definitely need to provide them with a passport-style photograph. They will always be issued on a blue Oyster card. (Are you following all of this? It's a bit complicated isn't it!)

You can also have a weekly and monthly travelcard loaded straight onto an existing pay-as-you-go Oyster card. That might sound a bit daft, but it can actually come in quite handy. Most tourists will spend their entire holiday in zone 1 (or maybe zones 1-2), but might wish to enter zone 3 for a one-off day-trip. Buying a zone 1-3 travelcard for an entire week would therefore be a waste of money, so they can just buy a zone 1-2 travelcard and load some extra credit on to cover that extra day. The computer will recognise that their travelcard already cover zones 1-2, and only charge them for zone 3. It also comes in handy if a tourist is planning to stay for longer than seven days, because they can still purchase a weekly travelcard and load a bit of extra money on to cover the final few days.

Note: It is not possible to load a travelcard onto a Visitor Oyster card, or a contactless payment card.

Can you share a travelcard?

No. And this applies even if you have the travelcard loaded onto an Oyster card.

Is there a family travelcard?

No. (There used to be, but not anymore.)

Contactless payment cards

A contactless payment card works in exactly the same way as a pay-as-you-go Oyster card, but you have to use your own bank card (and yes, I mean the exact same card that you use to do your shopping). Contactless payment cards have one big advantage over Oyster cards: you don't have to remember to keep topping them up -- they just drain the money straight out of your bank account until you have none left.

Personally, I'm still at the stage of not entirely trusting their system with my bank card, so I still use an Oyster card; but of course I'm just being paranoid. (New technology has to be around for at least twenty years before I start trusting it -- I'm still using cassette tapes.)

Unfortunately not all bank cards are suitable. UK-issued cards should be okay if they carry the following symbol: but only a few foreign cards are currently accepted: some Visa and MasterCards, and American Express -- but you should be extremely careful about the charges: your overseas provider might add on a hefty transaction fee for anything purchased abroad, which will include individual bus and train tickets. You can check if your card is suitable on the TFL site: *https://tfl.gov.uk/fares-and-payments/contactless/what-are-contactless-payment-cards.*

The 'daily price-cap' feature works in exactly the same way as it does with an Oyster card, but with a contactless payment card you also get the added bonus of a weekly cap. This will freeze your maximum weekly spend at the same level as a weekly travelcard. But it only works from Monday through to Sunday, though, which is a bit of a pain -- so if you're travelling between Friday and Thursday, for example, then you'll just end up paying the normal rate for seven individual days. Presumably their computers still aren't clever enough to realise that seven consecutive days constitutes one week.

Note: Contactless payment cards suffer from something called 'card clash'. Lots of people keep their Oyster cards and bank cards in the same wallet, so when they touch their wallet onto the reader the computer will get confused about which one to charge. It will then end up rejecting both, making the person panic that they don't have enough credit. If this happens to you then don't fret... just separate the cards and try again. If it still doesn't work then *that's* the time to panic.

Can you share a contactless payment card?

No. I often see people tap their card down on the reader twice, making the perfectly reasonable assumption that it will subtract two fares (they try and do this with pay-as-you-go Oyster cards as well), but the system doesn't work like that. The first time you tap down the computer will think that you are entering the station, and the second time you tap down it will think that you are leaving the station. Only one fare will be deducted, so if you get stopped by an inspector then you will be in a bit of trouble. (You will have to decide which person gets arrested for fare dodging -- you or your missus.)

Luckily there is an easy solution... just walk up to a manned ticket window or a self-service ticket machine, and use your card to buy two separate tickets (or just buy one ticket and continue to tap down for the second one).

Do seniors get cheap fares?

Not if you're a tourist, no.

UK citizens can get a 'Senior Railcard', and local Londoners can get a 'Freedom Pass' (see below), but you can't get them if you live abroad.

Senior Railcards

If you have a UK address and you're aged over 60, and you don't mind stumping up an annual fee of £30 quid, then check out the 'Senior Railcard' from *http://www.senior-railcard.co.uk*.

This entitles you to a third off standard and first class train fares throughout Britain, and a third off a 1-Day Travelcard in London (zones 1-6, off-peak only, and subject to a minimum fare). You can also get the discount loaded onto your Oyster card, and save a third off single off-peak pay-as-you-go fares.

Freedom Passes

If your principal home is in London, and you are old enough to receive a woman's state pension (regardless of whether you are a man or a woman), or you have an eligible disability, then it's worth looking into a Freedom Pass. Freedom Passes are supplied by your local council, and you will need to fill in an application form and provide a passport-sized photo to get one. Check out their website for more details: *http://www.londoncouncils.gov.uk/services/freedom-pass*.

A Freedom Pass entitles you to free travel on all TFL buses, plus many local bus services beyond the TFL network. You can also travel on the whole of the London Underground, Overground and Docklands Light Railway (DLR). National Rail trains within London can be boarded any time except during the very busiest period (4.30 AM to 9.30 AM, Mon-Fri).

London Underground

When is peak-time?

Train fares are usually more expensive during 'peak time'. If you want the cheapest fares then you will need to avoid travelling between 6.30-9.30 AM and 4-7 PM, Mon-Fri. Weekends and public holidays are always classed as off-peak.

'Rush hour' is slightly different: it's when all the workers are travelling to and from their jobs. It runs roughly from 7-10 AM, and 4-7 PM.

Adult train fares

Adult fares on the train	
For journeys inside zone 1 only	
Cash	£4.80
Oyster	£2.40 (daily cap £6.50)
Contactless	£2.40 (daily cap £6.50, weekly cap £32.40)
1-day travelcard	£12.10
Weekly travelcard	£32.40
Monthly travelcard	£124.50
For journeys between zones 1 and 2	
Cash	£4.80
Oyster (peak)	£2.90 (daily cap £6.50)
Oyster (off-peak)	£2.40 (daily cap £6.50)
Contactless (peak)	£2.90 (daily cap £6.50, weekly cap £32.40)
Contactless (off-peak)	£2.40 (daily cap £6.50, weekly cap £32.40)
1-day travelcard	£12.10
Weekly travelcard	£32.40
Monthly travelcard	£124.50
For journeys between zones 1 and 3	
Cash	£4.80
Oyster (peak)	£3.30 (daily cap £7.60)
Oyster (off-peak)	£2.80 (daily cap £7.60)
Contactless (peak)	£3.30 (daily cap £7.60, weekly cap £38)
Contactless (off-peak)	£2.80 (daily cap £7.60, weekly cap £38)
1-day travelcard	£12.10
Weekly travelcard	£38
Monthly travelcard	£146
For journeys inside zone 2 only	
Cash	£4.80
Oyster (peak)	£1.70 (daily cap £6.50)
Oyster (off-peak)	£1.50 (daily cap £6.50)
Contactless (peak)	£1.70 (daily cap £6.50, weekly cap £24.30)
Contactless (off-peak)	£1.50 (daily cap £6.50, weekly cap £24.30)
1-day travelcard	£12.10
Weekly travelcard	£24.30
Monthly travelcard	£93.40
For journeys between zones 2 and 3	
Cash	£4.80
Oyster (peak)	£1.70 (daily cap £7.60)
Oyster (off-peak)	£1.50 (daily cap £7.60)
Contactless (peak)	£1.70 (daily cap £7.60, weekly cap £24.30)

Contactless (off-peak)	£1.50 (daily cap £7.60, weekly cap £24.30)
1-day travelcard	£12.10
Weekly travelcard	£24.30
Monthly travelcard	£93.40
For journeys between zones 1 and 6 (Heathrow)	
Cash	£6
Oyster (peak)	£5.10 (daily cap £11.80)
Oyster (off-peak)	£3.10 (daily cap £11.80)
Contactless (peak)	£5.10 (daily cap £11.80, weekly cap £59.10)
Contactless (off-peak)	£3.10 (daily cap £11.80, weekly cap £59.10)
1-day travelcard (peak)	£17.20
1-day travelcard (off-peak)	£12.10
Weekly travelcard	£59.10
Monthly travelcard	£227

In order to work out your fare, you will need to know which 'fare zone' your train (or trains) pass through. The more zones you pass through, the higher the fare.

Most underground maps will show the zones as a series of concentric grey/white rings, with the smallest ring at the centre of London. That is zone 1 (the touristy bit). Just to confuse things, sometimes a station might be in two different zones at the same time. For example, Earl's Court is in zone 1 *and* zone 2. If you disembark at one of those stations then the fare will be based on your direction of travel. It will count as zone 1 if you came from the direction of zone 1, and it will count as zone 2 if you came from the direction of zone 2.

And just to confuse things even further, you need to remember that it's the zones you *pass through* that matter -- not the ones you begin and end at.

The table only shows the prices for zones 1, 2, 3 and 6, which is what 99.99% of tourists will use. If you need to look up the prices for zones 4 and 5 then check out the official TFL website at *https://tfl.gov.uk/fares-and-payments/fares*.

Child train fares

Child fares on the train (under-11)	
Free when accompanied by an adult (maximum of 4 children per adult), or when using a '5-10 Zip Oyster photocard'	
Child fares on the train (11-15, with a photocard)	
For journeys inside zone 1 only, or between zones 1 and 2	
Cash	£2.40
Oyster (peak)	£0.85 (daily cap £3.25)
Oyster (off-peak)	£0.75 (daily cap £1.50)
Contactless (peak)	£0.85 (daily cap £3.25)
Contactless (off-peak)	£0.75 (daily cap £1.50)
1-day travelcard	£6
Weekly travelcard	£16.20

Monthly travelcard	£62.30
For journeys between zones 1 and 3	
Cash	£2.40
Oyster (peak)	£0.85 (daily cap £3.80)
Oyster (off-peak)	£0.75 (daily cap £1.50)
Contactless (peak)	£0.85 (daily cap £3.80)
Contactless (off-peak)	£0.75 (daily cap £1.50)
1-day travelcard	£6
Weekly travelcard	£19
Monthly travelcard	£73
For journeys inside zone 2 only	
Cash	£2.40
Oyster (peak)	£0.85 (daily cap £3.25)
Oyster (off-peak)	£0.75 (daily cap £1.50)
Contactless (peak)	£0.85 (daily cap £3.25)
Contactless (off-peak)	£0.75 (daily cap £1.50)
1-day travelcard	£6
Weekly travelcard	£12.20
Monthly travelcard	£46.90
For journeys between zones 2 and 3	
Cash	£2.40
Oyster (peak)	£0.85 (daily cap £3.80)
Oyster (off-peak)	£0.75 (daily cap £1.50)
Contactless (peak)	£0.85 (daily cap £3.80)
Contactless (off-peak)	£0.75 (daily cap £1.50)
1-day travelcard	£6
Weekly travelcard	£12.20
Monthly travelcard	£46.90
For journeys between zones 1 and 6 (Heathrow)	
Cash	£3
Oyster (peak)	£0.85 (daily cap £5.90)
Oyster (off-peak)	£0.75 (daily cap £1.50)
Contactless (peak)	£0.85 (daily cap £5.90)
Contactless (off-peak)	£0.75 (daily cap £1.50)
1-day travelcard (peak)	£8.60
1-day travelcard (off-peak)	£6
Weekly travelcard	£29.60
Monthly travelcard	£112.80
Child fares on the train (11-15, without a photocard, but with a 'Young Visitor Discount')	
Pay-as-you-go Oyster fares are half the adult fares, but only for a maximum of 14 days	
Child fares on the train (16-18, with a photocard)	
Pay-as-you-go Oyster fares and contactless payment card fares are half the adult fares	

Child fares on the train (11-18, without anything)
Same as the adult fares

Child fares are extremely confusing on the London Underground, and I actually think it's easier just to leave your kids at home. Lock them in the garage for two weeks, or get their grandparents to look after them -- that's what they're there for. Or sell them. Put them up for adoption. I don't care what you do with them, just get rid of them! But I suppose I'd better try to explain the fares anyway, just in case your wife decides that you *have* to take them.

Children under the age of 11 can travel for free on the London Underground and DLR, provided that they are accompanied by an adult (up to a maximum of 4 children per adult), or have a *5-10 Zip Oyster photocard*.

11-15 year olds pay a child fare on the London Underground and DLR, provided that they can show an *11-15 Zip Oyster photocard*. If they cannot show a photocard, then they will have to pay a full adult fare.

16-18 year olds pay half the adult fare when using a pay-as-you-go Oyster card or contactless payment card (there are no discounts for cash fares or travelcards), provided that they can show a *16+ Zip Oyster photocard*. If they cannot show a photocard, then they will have to pay a full adult fare.

You can apply for all of these photocards here: *https://tfl.gov.uk/fares-and-payments/travel-for-under-18s/zip-oyster-photocards*. Unfortunately you have to pay quite a hefty fee for them, which will probably wipe out any savings that would have been made.

But wait! If you're a non-Londoner then you're in luck... because TFL have realised that getting hold of a photocard is a pain in the backside when you're only here on holiday, so children aged between 11 and 15 who don't have a photocard can get something called a *Young Visitor Discount* instead. This entitles them to 50% off the adult fare for a maximum of fourteen days.

What you have to do is buy your child a normal adult pay-as-you-go Oyster card (not a travelcard) and then ask a member of staff to apply the 'Young Visitor Discount' to it. You can do this at a London Underground station, a National Rail station (within London), or a London Travel Information Centre. You child must be with you when you do it (up to a maximum of four children per adult), and they will probably ask for proof of age if your kid looks like Chunk from *The Goonies*. As soon as the fourteen days are over the card will revert back to charging adult fares again. See *https://tfl.gov.uk/fares-and-payments/travel-for-under-18s/travelling-with-children* for full details.

How do I use an Oyster card, contactless payment card or travelcard on the train?

When entering a station, you won't be able to use every single ticket barrier. You can only use the ones that are showing a yellow or green arrow on the LCD screen. If it has a red or yellow cross then it won't accept your ticket.

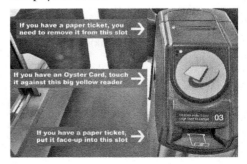

Using London Transport | 451

To get through the barrier all you have to do is place your Oyster card or contactless payment card near the big round yellow reader at the front of the gate, and wait for the green light to appear (you can usually hear a beep as well, if it's not too busy). You don't even have to remove the card from your wallet or pocket if you don't want to, because the machine is usually sensitive enough to read it right through your clothes. (If you're worried about pickpockets then this is a handy tip to remember, because it saves you from having to get your valuables out.) The gate will open automatically if it worked okay.

If the gate refuses to budge then try getting your card out of your wallet and touching it flush against the reader. If that doesn't work then you are probably out of credit (there is usually a little LCD screen nearby which will tell you the reason).

If you have a paper ticket then it's slightly different: you have to insert the ticket face-up into the slot at the front of the gate -- it's usually situated just underneath the big round yellow reader. The same ticket will then pop out of a slot at the top. The gate won't open until you remove your ticket from this slot (...something that catches a lot of people out). Bear in mind that if the ticket is no longer of any use (because it was for a single journey, and that journey is now over), then the ticket will instead be retained by the machine and the gate will open straight away; so you don't have to remove anything from the slot.

Important: Do not throw your paper ticket away after you've passed through the barrier! Because you will need it to open the gate at the other end of your journey. Similarly, if you have an Oyster Card or contactless payment card, then you will need to touch it down again at the other end of your journey to open the gate. The reason that you need to touch it down at the beginning *and* the end of your journey, is because the computer needs to work out what your journey was. If you forget to touch down as you exit then it won't know where you went, and it will just charge you whatever the maximum journey was on that line as a penalty (ouch!).

You'd be surprised at how many people forget to touch their Oyster card down as they exit, because not all stations have exit barriers (especially the suburban stations and DLR). Some of them allow you to walk straight out of the station without going through any gates at all, and hide their Oyster readers on the wall, or at the bottom of the stairs -- which are extremely easy to miss (especially if you've got your head in the clouds, like me). Likewise, the train station staff will sometimes open all of the exit barriers to speed the flow of people towards the door. Whenever that happens I see countless people marching straight through the gate without touching down, thinking that they've managed to blag a free ride -- *but they haven't!* They touched down on the way in, remember, and if they don't tell the computer where they got off then it will just whack them for whatever the full fare was on the entire line. Personally I think this is a very lucrative scam, designed to catch people out, and I don't think they should be allowed to do it.

And finally... you might be wondering how to get your kid through the barrier if they are travelling for free (because they won't have a ticket). Well, the easiest thing to do is to just pick them up and hurl them over the top. You grab their arms, get your wife to grab their legs, then whirl them around a few times and let go. Try not to smack their heads on the concrete ceiling though, because that would be quite painful. Or you could just leave them at home... just lock them in their bedroom for two weeks and tell them that you don't love them anymore -- that is what I do. Alternatively, you could ask a member of staff behind the gates to let them through. That is what you are *supposed* to do. He has a special pass which he can use to open the gate (he may ask to see your child's photocard first, if they are of an age to need one). You can also look for one of the extra-wide gates and use that, which should give you enough space to kick them through.

What are the pink Oyster card readers for?

Just to confuse things, you might sometimes come across a pink Oyster card reader instead of a yellow one. They only exist at fifteen stations: *Blackhorse Road, Canada Water, Clapham Junction, Gospel Oak, Gunnersbury, Highbury & Islington, Kensington Olympia, Rayners Lane, Richmond, Stratford, Surrey Quays, West Brompton, Whitechapel, Willesden Junction* and *Wimbledon*.

The first time I saw these things I thought they were installed for the girls, but they're not. They exist because some journeys are cheaper if you avoid travelling through zone 1. For example, if you want to travel from Epping (zone 6 on the Central line) to Richmond (zone 4 on the District line), then you would normally go straight through the centre of zone 1. But if you don't mind a slightly longer journey then you can change onto the London Overground line at Stratford, and bypass zone 1 completely -- thus saving you a few pennies. Unfortunately the computer has no way of knowing you did this, because you don't have to pass through any barriers when changing trains at Stratford -- so it will continue to charge you for zones 1-6 regardless. So what you have to do is touch down on the pink reader at Stratford, and then it will know to only charge you for zones 2-6. If you forget to tap down then it's not the end of the world... you'll just be charged the higher fare.

Pink readers can usually be found on the platforms, up against a wall, or at the entrance to the platform stairs.

Note: you still need to tap down on the yellow readers at the beginning and the end of your journey.

Do I have to pay twice if I change trains?

If your journey involves a change of trains then you only pay one fare -- provided that you don't exit any of the stations in-between. For example, if you are travelling between Waterloo and South Kensington, then you will need to change trains onto the District (or Circle) line at Westminster. But there is no need to exit the station at Westminster -- you should be able to walk between the platforms without passing through any barriers. As long as you remember to tap the card down at Waterloo and South Kensington then the computer will recognise that you only made one journey, and charge you accordingly.

The only exceptions are the fifteen stations that have a pink Oyster card reader.

Do the trains run all night?

The London Underground typically operates from 5 AM to 00.30 AM (Mon-Sat), and 7 AM to 11.30 PM (Sun). The DLR runs from 5.30 AM to 00.30 AM (Mon-Sat), and 7 AM to 11.30 PM (Sun). But the times are going to differ depending on the date, and which line you're using.

A 24-hour service was supposed to kick-in from September 2015, but they had to postpone it after all the drivers went on strike. When it finally does begin in late 2016 we have been promised a 24-hour service on the Jubilee, Piccadilly, Victoria, and most of the Central and Northern lines -- but only at the weekend.

But this is where it promises to get a bit complicated: because the all night service on the Central line will only be operating between Ealing Broadway and Loughton. It will not operate from North Acton to West Ruislip, from Loughton to Epping, or from Woodford to Hainault (although it *will* go between Leytonstone and Hainult). The Northern line will only be operating from Morden to Edgware, and Morden to High Barnet (both via the Charing Cross loop). It will not be operating on the Bank loop. The Piccadilly line will be running all the way from Cockfosters to Heathrow Terminals 1-3, and Terminal 5 -- but not Terminal 4. And it will not be operating between Acton Town and Uxbridge.

How often do they run?

Obviously this will all depend on which route you're using... but a good rule-of-thumb is every 5-10 minutes in zone 1, and every 2-5 minutes during peak time. Trains outside zone 1 can be anything from 10 to 30 minutes.

The all-night services will run every 10-20 minutes, and every 10 minutes between London and Heathrow.

The big exception is the 25th December, when pretty much the entire system closes down for the holidays. A lot of tourists are somewhat surprised to find that there is no service at all on Christmas Day -- you can't even catch a bus. But that's all right... because none of the attractions will be open either! So that's something to bear in mind if you're planning a Christmas break: remember to bring your walking shoes. Because you'll be doing a lot of walking.

Where can I get a timetable?

You can look up an exact time on the TFL website: *https://tfl.gov.uk/plan-a-journey/*. You can print off timetables at *https://tfl.gov.uk/travel-information/timetables/*.

Understanding the London Underground map

The first thing to bear in mind when looking at the London Underground map is that it is not drawn to scale. The distance between each station bears no relation to its distance on the ground. Some of the stations are so close together that it's actually quicker to walk between them. Charing Cross is only a few minutes stroll from Embankment and Leicester Square, for example, and you'll save yourself some time walking between Leicester Square and Covent Garden. Bank, Cannon Street and Monument are all within five minutes of each other as well, and I would always walk between Bank, Mansion House and St. Paul's.

You shouldn't really rely on the map for directions either. St. Paul's is shown to the north of Mansion House, but in reality it is due west. The most notorious one is Regent's Park, which is shown to the south of Baker Street. But everyone who has ever been to Madame Tussauds will know that it is actually to the north -- whilst the station itself is due east! (This is one of the joys of being a Londoner... learning all of these little quirks.)

Once you've got your head wrapped around all of that, then it's actually quite easy to follow (I promise!). There are thirteen different lines on the map, and they each have their own special colour:

Bakerloo - *brown;* Central - *red;* Circle - yellow; District - *dark green;* Docklands Light Railway (DLR) - *aqua blue border;* Hammersmith & City - *pink;* Jubilee -

grey; London Overground - *orange border;* Metropolitan - *purple;* Northern - *black;* Piccadilly - *dark blue;* Victoria - *light blue;* Waterloo & City - *cyan*

Here is a small section of the map:

Stations which only serve one line are shown by a little stub protruding from the line, like *Covent Garden,* which only serves the Piccadilly line (dark blue line).

Stations which serve two or more lines are called interchanges and are shown by a large white circle, like *Leicester Square,* which serves the Piccadilly line (dark blue line) and Northern line (black line).

Stations which include a blue wheelchair symbol inside the circle, like *Green Park,* have step-free access between the train and the street. If they have a white wheelchair symbol then they only have step-free access between the platform and the street.

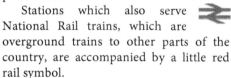

Stations which also serve National Rail trains, which are overground trains to other parts of the country, are accompanied by a little red rail symbol.

How can I find my platform?

Platforms are usually labelled by the direction of travel. So if you want to travel from Piccadilly Circus to Oxford Circus on the Bakerloo line (brown line), then you will need to look for signs that say *Bakerloo Northbound.* If you are returning in the opposite direction then it would say *Bakerloo Southbound.* You can also get trains that head *Westbound* and *Eastbound* (like Chancery Lane to Oxford Circus).

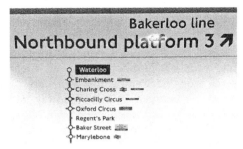

Sometimes one line will split into several different branches, so there may be more than one train heading in each direction. What do you do then? All you have to do is look for the last stop on the line. So if you want to travel from Westminster to Kew Gardens on the District line (the dark green line), then you will need the *District Westbound to Richmond* -- because that's the last stop on the branch that goes to Kew Gardens. If you boarded the *District Westbound to Wimbledon* instead, then that would be the wrong one, because that branch doesn't go to Kew Gardens.

Most Underground platforms will also have a number (like '3', as in the photo above), but I think these are a complete waste of time. No one ever looks for, or knows, where "platform 3" is, but if you ask them for the "Bakerloo Northbound" then they will be able to help you.

Stairs and escalators

Because large parts of the London Underground are very old, a surprising number of stations don't have lifts. A lot of them don't even have escalators. Roughly half of the overground stations are step-free from the platform to the street, but only a quarter of the Underground stations are, so the odds are pretty high that you will find yourself facing a long flight of stairs at some point. (The exception is the Docklands Light

Railway, which is fairly new, so it is totally accessible).

Luckily there are two websites that can help you out. The first one is the official Transport for London website: *https://tfl.gov.uk/plan-a-journey/*. This allows you to search for a journey with extra options like "I need step free access to the platform" and "I can use stairs but not escalators". They also have a very handy online map that contains information about which stations have stairs, escalators and lifts: *http://content.tfl.gov.uk/step-free-tube-guide-map.pdf*.

The second website is called Direct Enquiries: *http://www.directenquiries.com/londonunderground.aspx*. This site allows you to see the route between the platforms and the exit, and shows you how many steps, escalators and lifts there are.

National Rail

If you need to travel a long way outside central London, then you will probably find that the London Underground doesn't extend far enough, and you will have to get an overground train instead -- *National Rail*. National Rail trains are the ones that go to other parts of the country.

There are actually lots of different companies that operate National Rail trains: *Chiltern Railways, East Midlands, First Great Western, Great Northern, Merseyrail, South West Trains* and *Virgin Trains*, to name just a few. But they all come under the umbrella of National Rail.

Here is a list of the main National Rail stations in central London, together with some of their most popular destinations. All of them have London Underground stations attached.

For trains heading north	
Euston	Birmingham, Glasgow, Liverpool, Manchester, Watford
King's Cross	Cambridge, Edinburgh, Newcastle, Nottingham, York
St. Pancras	Brighton, Eastbourne, Gatwick Airport, Luton Airport, Nottingham; (St. Pancras is also home to the Eurostar, which goes to Amsterdam, Brussels, Paris and Disneyland Paris)
For trains heading south	
Blackfriars	Ashford International, Brighton, Luton Airport
Cannon Street	Ashford International, Margate
Charing Cross	Canterbury, Dover, Hastings
Farringdon	Brighton, Luton Airport
London Bridge	Brighton, Canterbury, Hastings
Victoria	Brighton, Dover, Eastbourne, Gatwick Airport, Margate
Waterloo	Bournemouth, Canterbury, Cornwall, Dover, Hastings, Plymouth, Portsmouth, Salisbury, Southampton
For trains heading west	
Marylebone	Birmingham, Glasgow, Liverpool, Manchester
Paddington	Bath, Cornwall, Heathrow Airport, Oxford, Plymouth, Wales
For trains heading east	
Fenchurch Street	Southend
Liverpool Street	Stansted Airport

Where can I buy National Rail tickets?

The easiest place to buy a train ticket is at the station. All mainline stations have ticket windows and self-service machines -- *but be careful!* Train tickets are notoriously expensive if you buy them on the same day of travel: sometimes by as much as four times. So the best thing to do is plan ahead and order them online. The prices drop considerably if you get them at least two or three weeks in advance. If you don't have to time to get them posted to your home address then you can usually print them out at the station on the day (but this will depend on who you book with).

Just in case you don't believe me... I'm looking at a ticket from London to Manchester right now, which would cost me £36 if I book it one month from today. But if I try the exact same thing tomorrow morning then it jumps up to £135. (I could get two nights in Barcelona for that price -- with the hotel included!)

Each train company has their own website, but I recommend using National Rail's website at *http://www.nationalrail.co.uk* -- or Trainline, which can be found at *https://www.thetrainline.com*. Both of these sites sell tickets from all of the train companies combined, which makes it a hell of a lot easier to compare the times and prices.

Can I use an Oyster card or travelcard on National Rail?

This depends on how far you are travelling. If you have a pay-as-you-go Oyster card, and you stay within zones 1-6, then you will definitely be okay -- but there are also a handful of stations within zones 7-9 that are okay as well. You can check which ones are okay on Transport for London's handy map: *http://content.tfl.gov.uk/london-rail-and-tube-services-map.pdf*.

If you have a travelcard, then it all depends on which one you buy. If you buy a travelcard that only covers zones 1-2, then obviously you will only be able to travel as far as zone 2.

What is a 16-25 Railcard?

If you are aged between 16 and 25, or you're a full-time student aged over 25, and you have either a valid international passport or a UK driving licence, then you are in luck! Because you should be able to get a discount of 33% on rail fares with a 16-25 Railcard.

But there are a few caveats to be aware of: there is a minimum fare of £12 for all journeys made between 4.30 AM and 10 AM on Mon-Fri, which renders it useless for daily commutes. And it doesn't work with season tickets, Eurostar tickets or First Class fares either. The rules regarding the Underground are quite confusing, but it should reduce Oyster fares by a third... provided that they are all off-peak, pay-as-you-go, and you have already registered your Oyster card in your own name. It should also reduce the cost of a zone 1-6 travelcard (subject to a minimum fare).

You can apply for a card at *http://www.16-25railcard.co.uk*. The current price is £30 for one year, or £70 for three years.

What is a BritRail pass?

If you're planning on escaping London and seeing a bit more of beautiful England, then you might save a bit of money with a BritRail pass. They have lots of different versions for sale: covering just the south-east of England, the south-west, central Scotland, the whole of Scotland, and the whole of Britain. All you have to do is buy one that combines all of the different destinations you want, and then you can travel as often as you want, whenever you want, just hopping on and off the trains as you please.

So what's the catch? Well... first of all, you can only buy them overseas. They are not available to UK residents. And they only work on National Rail trains -- so you can't use them on the Underground.

You can get them for a range of dates spanning 3, 4, 8, 15 or 22 consecutive days, or one month. You can also get flexi-passes with cover any 3, 3, 4, 8 or 15 days within one month. They cost anything from $222 to $878 per adult, and $116 to $442 for kids, depending on which destinations and duration you choose. (Note: those prices are in dollars, because they're not available to UK residents.)

If you like the sound of a BritRail pass, then check out their website at *http://www.britrail.net*. (Note: They have some fancy IP blocking which prevents British residents from buying a ticket, so you won't be able to checkout or even see the prices if you're in the UK.)

Buses

Adult bus fares

Adult fares on the bus	
Cash	not possible
Oyster	£1.50 (daily cap £4.50)
Contactless	£1.50 (daily cap £4.50, weekly cap £21.20)
1-day bus/tram pass	£5
Weekly bus/tram pass	£21.20
Monthly bus/tram pass	£81.50

There's a flat-fare on London's buses, so it doesn't matter whether you go ten yards or ten miles, it's always the same price. There are no return fares either.

Cash fares were abolished ages ago, so don't go up to the driver with a handful of coins because he will just stare at you blankly. The only way to board a London bus now is with an Oyster card, a contactless payment card, or a travelcard -- all of which have to be obtained before you board the bus.

Child bus fares

Child fares on the bus (under-11)	
Free	

Child fares on the bus (11-15, with a photocard)	
Free	

Child fares on the bus (11-15, without a photocard, but with a 'Young Visitor Discount')
Pay-as-you-go Oyster fares are half the adult fares, but only for a maximum of 14 days

| Child fares on the bus (16-18, with a photocard) | |

Cash	not possible
Oyster	£0.75 (daily cap £2.25)
Contactless	£0.75 (daily cap £2.25)
1-day bus/tram pass	not possible (they can buy an adult one instead)
Weekly bus/tram pass	£10.60
Monthly bus/tram pass	£40.80

Child fares on the bus (11-18, without a photocard)

Same as the adult fares

Children under the age of 11 can travel for free on London's buses. They do not need a photocard. (Note: Children aged between 5-10 might need a photocard if they want to travel for free on the train. See the child train fare section for details.)

11-15 year olds can also travel for free, provided that they can show the driver an *11-15 Zip Oyster photocard*. If they cannot show a photocard, then they will have to pay a full adult fare.

16-18 year olds pay a reduced fare if they can show a *16+ Zip Oyster photocard*. If they cannot show a photocard, then they will have to pay a full adult fare.

You can apply for all of these photocards at the TFL website: *https://tfl.gov.uk/fares-and-payments/travel-for-under-18s/zip-oyster-photocards*.

If your child is aged between 11 and 15 but you can't be bothered to get a photocardfor them, then check out the *Young Visitor Discount* instead. This will entitle them to 50% off the adult fare when using a pay-as-you-go Oyster card. I've already explained how the *Young Visitor Discount* works in the train section, though, and I'm basically too lazy to explain the whole thing all over again (hey, at least I'm honest!), so have a read of the child train fares section, because it works in exactly the same way for the buses.

How do I use an Oyster card, contactless payment card or travelcard on the bus?

Once you've got hold of a suitable card, all you have to do is touch it against the big round yellow reader at the front of the bus. Some buses also have a second reader by the middle door, and another by the rear door, and you will notice a lot of people boarding the bus there instead. But if you are an inexperienced traveller then I recommend sticking with the front door, because the front door will *always* have a reader. With some designs of bus the middle doors don't -- and if you try and board a bus through a door where there is no reader then people will think you are trying to dodge your fare and scream for the police. Eventually you will come to learn which styles of bus have a second reader and which ones don't, but until then... *stick with the front door.*

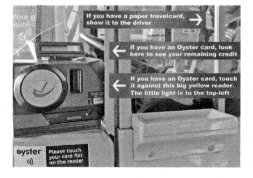

Whichever door you use, it is very important that you touch your card down correctly, otherwise you might get into a bit of bother with the ticket inspector. If it works okay then you should hear a beep, and see a tiny little green light by the reader. If it doesn't work first time then just try again (the machines are useless). If it still doesn't work then try again. And again. And again. And again. Try taking it out of your wallet and holding it flush with the reader, actually touching it.

Eventually the correct fare will be deducted from your card, and the remaining credit will be shown on a small screen above the reader. (If it's an Oyster travelcard then obviously no money will be deducted, because you can just carry on using it until the date expires.)

There is no need to touch the card down again when you leave the bus -- you only have to do that for trains.

If you have a paper travelcard then things work a little differently, because all you have to do is show it to the driver through the glass.

Do I have to pay twice if I change buses?

Yes. Each journey is charged separately. It is not possible to buy one ticket that covers two different buses (unless you buy a travelcard, of course). And there's no such thing as a return fare, either.

Do the buses run all night?

Some of them do, and some of them don't -- it depends on how busy the route is. As a very approximate rule-of-thumb, most of the buses in central London run every 5-12 minutes between 5 AM and 00.30 AM, but the frequency will slow down markedly from 11 PM onwards.

Night buses kick in between midnight and 5 AM, and are always prefixed by the letter 'N'. You usually only get three or four an hour, and after 3 AM you will probably have to wait a whole hour between buses. Most of these routes radiate out from Trafalgar Square -- so if you want to find a bus after midnight then that is a good place to start.

I used to enjoy riding around on the night buses when I was kid, but I try and avoid them now, because they always seem to be packed full of big-mouth kids and tiddly drunks after the pubs have shut. (Maybe I am just getting old.) If you do have to catch one then I don't recommend sitting on the top-deck.

If you do end up on a night bus, then remember that your 1-day travelcard doesn't run out at midnight: it stays valid all the way through to 4.30 AM.

Where can I get a timetable?

You can look up an exact time on the TFL website: *https://tfl.gov.uk/plan-a-journey/*. You can print off timetables at *https://tfl.gov.uk/travel-information/timetables/*.

You can also get paper timetables from a Travel Information Centre at Euston station, King's Cross, Liverpool Street, Piccadilly Circus, Victoria, and Heathrow airport -- but the easiest way is just to look at the bus stop itself:

This timetable appears on a bus stop outside the Royal Courts of Justice, and provides the timings for routes 11 and 23 (...there are many more routes on the real thing, but I've only included two). The timetables are very straightforward to use once you get the hang of them. *For example,* this one tells you that the first No.11 bus on a Monday is at 5.38 AM and they run every 15 mins until 6.08 AM, and then every 7-12 mins until 00.24 AM. The last one is at 00.39 AM. Underneath is a little banner that says "Night bus N11 please see separate panel". If you looked at that timetable (not pictured, but on the same bus stop) then you would see that the No.11 actually continues all through the night, but it's called N11 instead of 11.

Most bus stops provide a little route map as well. I have included the map from the same stop here:

Notice the line at the top which says: 'You are here > The Royal Courts of Justice'. The different bus routes then continue down the page on their own line. So our next stop is Fleet Street, which takes 4 mins, followed by Ludgate Circus, which takes 8 mins. If you wanted to go to Liverpool Street then you've got a choice between three buses -- No.11, 23 or 26 -- and you can see that it will take a total of 23 mins. If you wanted to go to Moorgate then you've only got a choice of one -- No.76 -- which takes 20 mins.

How do I stop a bus?

Most of the buses in central London are fairly busy and will probably pull up at every single stop without you having to do anything. But the drivers are not actually obliged to stop everywhere (especially if they are already full up), so you need to know the difference between *request stops* and *compulsory stops*. The way you tell the difference is by looking at the pole:

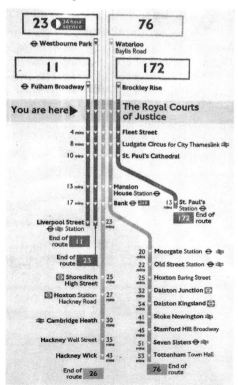

If the top of the pole has a red circle on a white background then it's called a *compulsory stop*, and the driver is supposed to stop every single time without being hailed. But if it has a white circle on a red background then it's called a *request*

stop, and the driver will only stop if you make it clear to him that you need it. If you don't, then he will drive straight past laughing manically.

If you want a bus to stop then it's easy: just stick your arm out horizontally into the street to grab the driver's attention. Make sure that you do it in plenty of time though, to give him time to stop safely. (To be honest, most Londoners don't know the difference between the two types of stop, and will just stick their hand out every single time -- which is what I recommend you do.)

Note: Night buses will only stop if you request them, regardless of which kind of stop you're standing at.

How do I get off a bus?

When you want the bus to stop all you have to do is find a bell and press it. If you can't hear the bell go *bing* (or *bong*) then don't worry -- you are probably just deaf. Either that or it has already been pressed by somebody else and become mute. (Apparently the drivers became annoyed with everyone pressing the bell ten thousand times, and introduced a system where it only rings once.) Just look for an LCD 'Bus stopping' sign near the front. It is usually situated quite high up, by the ceiling.

Prams and wheelchairs

Bus travel is free for wheelchair users, and all modern buses are equipped with ramps beneath the middle doors. The driver will usually let the existing passengers disembark first and then close the doors again. He needs to do this in order to work the ramp. Just wait patiently by the middle doors and you will see the ramp descend onto the pavement. He will then open the doors again so you can get on.

If you have a big pram that won't fit down the central aisle then you should start at the front doors, pay your fare, and then ask the driver to open the middle doors. If there are already a couple of prams onboard then don't be offended if he asks you to wait for the next bus, because there are rules against blocking up the aisle with buggies.

Minicabs and Taxis

What's the difference between minicabs and taxis?

Black taxi cabs used to be a familiar sight in London, but these days they come in all sorts of different colours. They are always the same basic shape though, and will have an orange 'Taxi' light on the roof. They all come equipped with meters, so you can see how much you're spending as you drive along.

Minicabs are different: they use normal looking cars, and rarely have a meter inside. It is therefore imperative that you negotiate a price with the minicab office before setting out, because you won't have any way of knowing how much it is until you get there. You should also reconfirm the price with the driver before he gets underway.

The most important difference between taxis and minicabs is the price. Minicabs are usually cheaper (sometimes a lot cheaper), and minicabs tend to offer a fixed fare between two places, whereas a taxi will charge you on the meter (so if the journey takes longer in the traffic, your fare will go up).

Where can I get a minicab?

It is technically illegal for a minicab to find new passengers in the street, because there are laws in place to protect the taxi drivers' trade. So you either have to phone-up and order one, or pop into a high-street minicab office.

Some drivers simply don't care though, and you will often see them lurking around a busy tourist area hoping to pick someone up. But my advice is this: unless you have actually given the minicab company a ring and ordered it yourself, don't step into a car posing as a minicab -- *ever* (I'm being serious). Not only is the minicab driver breaking the law, but you are also putting your own safety at risk by getting into a stranger's car. How do you know that he's properly licensed?

If you do want to order a minicab but don't have the number of a local minicab firm, then try using Transport for London's online form at *https://tfl.gov.uk/forms/12389.aspx*.

Where can I get a taxi?

Taxi cabs can be picked up from taxi-ranks outside train stations, airports, and popular tourist spots. You can also flag them down in the street.

A taxi should be available whenever its orange 'Taxi' sign is lit upon the roof. Just stick your arm out and wave it down. If the light is out, then it probably already has a passenger.

It is quite common for taxis to drive around at night with their light out. This is so the drivers can pick and choose their passengers and avoid the ones that look like trouble (ie. drunks). So if you see one with its light out at night, then it might still be worth sticking your arm out just in case -- just don't be surprised if it drives straight past.

It is also possible to order a cab in advance, and have it meet you somewhere, but this will add a few pounds onto the meter before you start (the cost will depend on how far they had to travel to get there). The TFL website provides a few telephone numbers for some reputable companies: *https://tfl.gov.uk/modes/taxis-and-minicabs/book-a-taxi*.

Taxi fares

Taxi fares	
Around central London	
1 mile (6–13 mins)	Approx £5.60 to £9
2 miles (10–20 mins)	Approx £8.60 to £15
3 miles (13–25 mins)	Approx £12 to £22
4 miles (16–30 mins)	Approx £15 to £28
5 miles (21–35 mins)	Approx £19 to £31
6 miles (28–40 mins)	Approx £23 to £33
From an airport to central London	
Heathrow airport (30–80 mins)	Approx £55 to £100
Gatwick airport (70–90 mins)	Approx £110 to £150
Stansted airport (60–90 mins)	Approx £135 to £155
Luton airport (60–80 mins)	Approx £115 to £135
London City airport (30–50 mins)	Approx £30 to £90
Note: An extra few pounds is usually added to airport fares to cover their parking costs	

I know exactly what you're thinking... you are probably looking at these fares and thinking that they seem awfully expensive. Well, you are right, because they *are* expensive... if you are travelling alone. You can easily spend a tenner just travelling between Trafalgar Square and St. Paul's. But when you remember that you can fit up to five people inside one taxi -- and you only pay one fare between all five of you -- then a taxi is quite often the cheapest way to travel. You probably need at least three people to make it worth your while though.

The cost fluctuates depending on the time of day and how lucky you are with the traffic, which can be quite horrendous in central London. The cost will always be 10% higher late at night (8 PM-10 PM, Mon-Fri), and during the weekend (6 AM-10 PM, Sat-Sun). And it will be 20% higher in the early hours of the morning (10 PM-6 AM, Mon-Sun). The table above takes all of this into account -- the highest prices shown are the ones that include the 20%. The fare will also increase at a faster rate once you reach six miles (don't ask me why -- it just does!).

There is also a minimum fare of £2.40, which will appear on the meter before you start. Plus another £2 quid if you booked it over the phone.

It is customary to give the driver a 10% tip as well -- although most people will just round up to the nearest pound, or the nearest £5, so he doesn't have to root around for change.

And just in case you're wondering... there is no point trying to haggle with the taxi driver beforehand because all taxi cabs charge by the meter. If you want the certainty of a fixed fare then you should really be using a minicab.

How many people can fit inside a taxi?

A typical taxi can carry up to five people: three on the seat, plus two more on the jump seats (the fold-down seats). But remember that you have to squeeze all of your luggage inside the same space -- so if you've got some bulky bags then you might struggle to sit four.

Taxis do not charge extra for luggage.

What if I have a wheelchair?

All modern taxis are wheelchair accessible, so shouldn't give you any problems, but minicabs use normal-looking cars -- so unless you can actually get in and out of the chair yourself then a minicab might not be suitable. (Minicab drivers might refuse to help you for insurance reasons -- so remember to check before you book.)

Boris Bikes

A 'Boris Bike' is the affectionate nickname for the hire bikes that London Mayor Boris Johnson introduced in 2010. As you travel around London you will undoubtedly come across them at some point because there are about 10,000 of the bleedin' things all over the capital.

If you fancy a bit of exercise then they can be a fun way of getting around. All you've got to do is take a bike, ride it wherever you like, and then drop it off at the next rack. There are 700 racks in central London, which are available 24 hours a day, 365 days a year.

My attempt at using one lasted approximately fifteen seconds, and I can confirm that they are not the most comfortable bikes to ride; presumably because they don't want anybody to steal them.

Boris Bike fares

Boris Bike fares			
For access only		**For time travelled**	
Per day	£2	Under 30 minutes	free
		Every 30 mins after	£2

Note: You must be over-18 to purchase a ticket, and over-14 to ride them. You will have to provide your own cycle helmet as well. All of the bikes must be returned within 24 hours.

How to use a Boris Bike

You will notice that there are two different fees to pay in the table above -- the first one is for 'access only', and the second one is for 'time travelled'. There are two ways of doing the first one. You can either sign-up as a member beforehand at *https://tfl.gov.uk/modes/cycling/santander-cycles/register-for-your-own-key*, or you can just pay on the day with a credit or debit card at the docking station. It is not possible to pay by cash or Oyster card.

After you've paid for access you should receive a 5-digit release code, which you can type into a keypad on the rack (press any button on the panel first, to wake it up). Before you type it in remember to check that the tyres, brakes and bell are okay -- but don't take too long because you need to enter the code within ten minutes to free the bike. When the green light comes on, pull out the bike. If the bike is being a bit stubborn then try bouncing the back wheel up and down a bit. If that doesn't work then try kicking it. If that doesn't work then you're on your own (blame Boris).

The second fee will now kick in, which changes depending on how long you use the bike. Happily the first thirty minutes of each journey are free, but you have to pay an extra two quid for every thirty minutes after that (or part thereof).

Once you have completed your journey, it is very important that you correctly return the bike to a rack. It doesn't have to be the same rack that you got it from (in fact, that's the whole idea -- you are supposed to ride the bike between different places). Just push the bike in and the light should turn green once it has been successfully accepted.

If all of the racks are full (quite a likely occurrence), then you can use the 'No docking point free' option on the terminal to find out where the nearest free space is. You will then be given an extra fifteen minutes to ride the bike to the next rack (hopefully it will only be a couple of streets away). Don't just leave it in the street and abandon it for chrissakes, because you will be charged up to £300 in 'lost fees' -- they have your bank card remember!

Where can I find a map of all the docking stations?

There's a docking stations map online: *https://tfl.gov.uk/modes/cycling/santander-cycles/find-a-docking-station*.

River Cruises

Thames Clippers

Thames Clippers fares	
Single tickets	
Adult (cash)	£7.50 to £8.20
Adult (with travelcard)	£5 to £5.45
Adult (with Oyster)	£6.30 to £7.20
Adult (with Freedom Pass)	£3.15 to £3.60
Child (5-15, cash)	£3.75 to £4.10
Child (5-15, with travelcard)	£2.50 to £2.75
Infant (under-5)	free
Note: Single tickets vary in price, depending on how far you wish to travel	
River Roamer tickets	
Family (2 ad+up to 3 ch, cash)	£36
Adult (cash)	£17.35
Adult (with travelcard)	£11.55
Adult (with Freedom Pass)	£8.65
Child (5-15, cash)	£8.65
Child (5-15, with travelcard)	£5.75
Infant (under-5)	free
Note: River Roamer tickets start at 9 AM and can be used as hop-on, hop-off tickets	

Thames Clippers are supposed to be a bus service on water, aimed at commuters rather than sightseers. But that doesn't mean that tourists can't use them.

They sail from Putney to Woolwich, but the stops that will most interest tourists are *London Eye Pier* (for London Eye and Big Ben), *Embankment Pier* (for Trafalgar Square), *Bankside Pier* (Tate Modern), *London Bridge Pier* (The Shard), *Tower Millennium Pier* (Tower of London and Tower Bridge), *Canary Wharf Pier*, *Greenwich Pier* (for the National Maritime Museum and Cutty Sark) and *North Greenwich Pier* (for the cable car and O2).

Putney Pier (towards Greenwich): Approx every 30 mins from 6 AM to 9.30 AM, and then every 25-45 mins from 5.30 PM to 9.10 PM (Mon-Fri).

Embankment Pier (towards Greenwich): Approx every 30 mins from 7 AM to 9.10 PM, and then every hour until 11.10 PM (Mon-Fri), and roughly every 30 mins from 9.30 AM to 9.10 PM, and then every hour until 11.10 PM (Sat-Sun).

London Eye Pier (towards Greenwich): Approx every 30 mins from 7 AM to 9.15 PM, and then every hour until 11.15 PM (Mon-Fri). At the weekend it's every 30 mins from 9.35 AM to 9.10 PM, and then every hour until 11.10 PM.

Bankside Pier (towards Greenwich): Approx every 30 mins from 7.10 AM to 9.20 PM, and then every hour until 11.20 PM (Mon-Fri), and roughly every 30 mins from 9.45 AM to 9.20 PM, and then every hour until 11.20 PM (Sat-Sun).

London Bridge Pier (towards Greenwich): Approx every 30 mins from 6.50 AM to 9.30 PM, and then every hour until 11.30 PM (Mon-Fri), and roughly every 30 mins from 9.50 AM to 9.25 PM, and then every hour until 11.25 PM (Sat-Sun).

Tower Millennium Pier (towards Greenwich): Approx every 30 mins from 7.20 AM to 9.30 PM, and then every hour until 11.30 PM (Mon-Fri), and roughly every 30 mins from 9.55 AM to 9.30 PM, and then every hour until 11.30 PM (Sat-Sun).

Tower Millennium Pier (towards Westminster): Approx every 30 mins from 6.35 AM to 8.45 PM, and then every hour until 10.45 PM (Mon-Fri), and roughly every 30 mins from 9.10 AM to 8.45 PM, and then every hour until 10.45 PM (Sat-Sun).

Canary Wharf Pier (towards Westminster): Approx every 30 mins from 6.30 AM to 8.40 PM, and then every hour until 10.40 PM (Mon-Fri), and roughly every 30 mins from 9 AM to 8.30 PM, and then every hour until 10.30 PM (Sat-Sun).

Greenwich Pier (towards Westminster): Approx every 30 mins from 6.15 AM to 8.30 PM, and then every hour until 10.30 PM (Mon-Fri), and roughly every 30 mins from 8.50 AM to 8.30 PM, and then every hour until 10.30 PM (Sat-Sun).

North Greenwich Pier (towards Westminster): Approx every 30 mins from 6.10 AM to 8.20 PM, and then every hour until 10.20 PM (Mon-Fri), and roughly every 30 mins from 8.45 AM to 8.20 PM, and then every hour until 10.20 PM (Sat-Sun).

Their website can be found at *http://www.thamesclippers.com*.

City Cruises

City Cruises fares	
Westminster/London Eye ↔ Tower of London	
Adult (single)	£9.90
Adult (return)	£13.15
Senior (over-60, single)	£6.93
Senior (over-60, return)	£9.21
Child (5-16, single)	£4.95
Child (5-16, return)	£6.58
Westminster/London Eye ↔ Greenwich	
Adult (single)	£12.25
Adult (return)	£16
Senior (over-60, single)	£8.58
Senior (over-60, return)	£11.20
Child (5-16, single)	£6.13
Child (5-16, return)	£8
Tower of London ↔ Greenwich	
Adult (single)	£9.75
Adult (return)	£13
Senior (over-60, single)	£6.83
Senior (over-60, return)	£9.10
Child (5-16, single)	£4.88
Child (5-16, return)	£6.50

Red Rover tickets	
Family (2 ad+up to 3 ch)	£36
Adult	£18
Senior (over-60)	£12.60
Child (5-16)	£9

Note: Red Rover tickets can be used all day as hop-on, hop-off tickets

City Cruises are very popular but they don't stop at so many places. You can catch them at *Westminster Pier* (for Big Ben), *London Eye Pier* (for the London Eye), *Tower Millennium Pier* (for the Tower of London and Tower Bridge) and *Greenwich Pier* (for the National Maritime Museum and Cutty Sark).

Westminster Pier (towards Greenwich): During summer: Approx every 30 mins from 9.30 AM to 7.30 PM (the last boat to Greenwich is at 4.50 PM) -- During winter: Approx every 30 mins from 10 AM to 5.50 PM (the last boat to Greenwich is at 2.40 PM)

London Eye Pier (towards Greenwich): During summer: Approx every 30 mins from 9.45 AM to 7.45 PM (the last boat to Greenwich is at 5.05 PM): During winter: Approx every 30 mins from 10.15 AM to 6.05 PM (the last boat to Greenwich is at 2.55 PM).

Tower Millennium Pier (towards Greenwich): During twinter: Approx every 30 mins from 10.55 AM to 3.35 PM.

Tower Millennium Pier (towards Westminster): During winter: Approx every 30 mins from 9.50 AM to 5.10 PM.

Greenwich Pier (towards Westminster): During summer: Approx every 30 mins from 10.10 AM to 6.40 PM -- During winter: Approx every 30 mins from 10.50 AM to 4.30 PM.

Their website can be found at *http://www.citycruises.com*.

TRS (Thames River Services)

Thames River Services fares	
Westminster ↔ Greenwich	
Adult (single)	£12.25
Adult (return)	£16
Child (5-15, single)	£6.13
Child (5-15, return)	£8
Westminster ↔ Thames Barrier/Greenwich	
Adult (single)	£14
Adult (return)	£17
Child (5-15, single)	£7
Child (5-15, return)	£8.50
St. Katherine's ↔ Greenwich	
Adult (single)	£9.75
Adult (return)	£13
Child (5-15, single)	£4.88

Child (5-15, return)	£6.50
St. Katherine's ↔ Thames Barrier/Greenwich	
Adult (single)	£12.25
Adult (return)	£16
Child (5-15, single)	£6.13
Child (5-15, return)	£8

TRS is my favourite tourist boat because they usually have a guy standing at the front giving funny commentary as you sail along. But other than that, their service is practically identical to City Cruises -- except they use smaller boats (not always a bad thing, because they don't get so packed out with people).

You can catch them at *Westminster Pier* (for Big Ben and Parliament), *St. Katharine's Pier* (for the Tower of London and Tower Bridge) and *Greenwich Pier* (for the National Maritime Museum and Cutty Sark). They also send boats farther up the river to the Thames Barrier (Apr-Oct only), although you can't actually disembark there -- they just sail around the pylons and head straight back to Greenwich.

Westminster Pier (towards Greenwich): During summer: Approx every 30 mins from 10 AM to 5 PM -- During winter: Every 40 mins from 10.20 AM to 3 PM.

St. Katherine's Pier (towards Greenwich): During summer: Approx every 30 mins from 10.20 AM to 5.20 PM.

Greenwich Pier (towards Westminster): During summer: Approx every 30 mins from 11 AM to 6 PM -- During winter: Approx every 40 mins from 11.20 AM to 4 PM.

Their website can be found at *http://www.thamesriverservices.co.uk*.

Airports

Heathrow Airport

Heathrow is the biggest and busiest airport in the UK. It has got five terminals and is located 15 miles west of central London. If you are arriving on a big international flight with one of the major airlines, then this is where you'll probably end up.

Website: *http://www.heathrow.com*
Telephone: 0844 335 1801

Heathrow Express: The Heathrow Express train is the quickest way to travel between the airport and central London -- but it only stops at Paddington. And Paddington is not exactly the most central of train stations, so unless your hotel happens to be in Bayswater or near Marble Arch then you'll probably have to catch the Underground or a bus afterwards -- which means that it's not as quick as it at first appears. (If you have to buy a London Underground ticket on top, then you may as well just get a tube train in the first place.)

The good news is that it is a direct train, and it only takes 15 mins to get from Terminals 1-3 to Paddington. It takes a bit longer from Terminal 4 (19 mins, and you will have to use a free transfer service to Terminals 1-3). Terminal 5 takes 21 mins (transfer service not necessary).

It runs every 15 mins from 5.07 AM to 11.48 PM (Mon-Sat), and every 15 mins from 6.07 AM to 11.53 PM (Sun). If you're coming towards Heathrow from central London then it runs every 15-30 mins from 5.10 AM to 11.25 PM (Mon-Sun).

Single tickets cost anything between £21.50 and £29.50. Return tickets cost between £35 and £53. Their website is at *https://www.heathrowexpress.com*.

National Rail: National Rail trains go by the fancy name of 'Heathrow Connect'. They follow exactly the same route as the Heathrow Express (into Paddington), but they also stop at an extra few places along the way and take a little bit longer than the express train -- 35 mins instead of 15.

They run roughly every 20-30 mins from 5.07 AM to 11.12 PM (Mon-Sat), and 5.48 AM to 10.48 PM (Sun). If you're coming the other way (from Paddington to Heathrow) then they run roughly every 20-30 mins from 4.42 AM to 11.03 PM (Mon-Sat), and 6.27 AM to 11.12 PM (Sun).

Single tickets cost £10.10, and a return costs £20.20. Check out their website at *https://www.heathrowconnect.com*.

Underground: Terminals 1, 2 and 3 share a single Underground station (all three terminals are within 15 mins walk of each other), whilst Terminals 4 and 5 have one each. All three stations are within zone 6, and you can ride the Piccadilly line all the way into central London without changing trains.

The first train from Heathrow is just after 5 AM and the last one is around 11.30 PM (Mon-Sat). On a Sunday it's 5.45 AM to 11.15 PM. If you are coming the other way (central London to Heathrow) then the first train is approx 5.45 AM and the last one is around midnight (Mon-Sat) -- but of course it will depend on where you catch it. On a Sunday it's approx 7 AM to 11 PM.

The only downside is the amount of time it takes: you'll be sitting on the train for at least 50 mins, and you'll be stopping at roughly 18 different stations along the way (depending on where you get off). You can find the fares in my 'London Underground' section.

Coach: National Express provides a coach service from the main bus station (outside Terminals 1-3) to Victoria Coach Station. They run every 30-60 mins from 7.30 AM to midnight, and take about 35-55 mins to get there.

A single ticket costs £6, and a return will cost £10.50. Visit their website at *http://www.nationalexpress.com*.

Bus: Heathrow's main bus station can be found outside Terminals 1-3. The only bus that goes directly from the airport into central London is the N9 -- but that's a night bus. It runs every 20 mins between 11.35 PM and 4.55 AM, and takes about an hour to get to Trafalgar Square (if you're coming the other then it runs between 11.10 PM and 6.15 AM). You can find the fares in my 'Buses' section.

If you're travelling during the daytime then I seriously wouldn't bother with the bus, because it would be a total nightmare. It would take you 2½ hours and you'd have to change vehicles at least twice. (Why the No.9 doesn't go to the airport during the daytime is a total mystery -- but it only goes as far as Hammersmith.)

Taxi: A taxi from Heathrow into central London can take between 30 and 80 mins, and will cost between £55 and £100.

You might find that a minicab is cheaper, but you'll have to ring around for a quote. You can find some companies here: *http://www.heathrow.com/transport-and-directions/taxis-and-minicabs*.

Gatwick Airport

Gatwick is London's second airport, and is located about 30 miles south of central London. It has two terminals, North and South, but the trains and buses all depart from the South. If you are unlucky enough to be in the North terminal then you can catch a free 24-hour shuttle train over to the South (it only takes about five minutes, but allow yourself at least twenty minutes to find out where it is and ride it).

Website: *http://www.gatwickairport.com*
Telephone: 0344 892 0322

Gatwick Express: The Gatwick Express is a high-speed train that takes 30 minutes to get to Victoria. Victoria is just about within walking distance of Westminster (for Big Ben), but if you're staying anywhere else then you'll probably have to get another bus or tube train. (I don't think I'd fancy walking to Westminster with a suitcase though.)

It runs every 15-45 mins from 4.35 AM to 1.35 AM (Mon-Sun), and every 15-60 mins from 3.30 AM to 00.30 AM if you're coming the other way (from Victoria to Gatwick).

Single tickets are £17.70 to £19.90, and return tickets are £31.05 and £34.90 (the cheaper tickets are only available online). Children's tickets (5-15) are £8.85 to £9.95, and £15.55 and £17.45 for a return.

Check out their website at *http://www.gatwickexpress.com*.

National Rail: Trains run between the airport and London Bridge, St. Pancras and Victoria. They run every 5-40 minutes, 24-hours a day (as long as you don't mind which station you arrive into). The journey takes anything from 40-90 mins, depending on which station you choose. You can reach all of the other mainline stations as well, as long as you don't mind changing trains halfway through.

Single tickets can cost anything from £10 to £25 (depending on the time, date and station you choose). Return tickets can cost anything from £16 to £35.

Their website is at *http://www.southernrailway.com* (although I would recommend *http://www.nationalrail.co.uk* instead).

Underground: Not possible, it's too far away.

Coach: National Express operates a coach service between Gatwick and Victoria Coach Station. They run every 30-60 mins from 00.30 AM to 10.30 PM, and take between 65 and 110 mins to get there.

A single ticket is available from £8, whilst a return ticket costs between £10 and £20. Visit their website at *http://www.nationalexpress.com*.

Bus: There are no local buses from Gatwick to London, it's too far away.

Taxi: A taxi into central London will take around 70-90 mins, and cost anything from £110 to £150. You might find that a minicab is cheaper, but you'll have to ring around the companies and get a quote.

Stansted Airport

Stansted has one terminal and is mainly used by low-cost airlines. If a low-cost airline sells you a "London flight" to Stansted then you'll have a very long walk -- it's nearly 35 miles away!

Website: *http://www.stanstedairport.com*

Telephone: 0844 335 1803

Stansted Express: The Stansted Express will take you into Liverpool Street (close to The City). The journey takes around 45-50 mins, stopping at a couple of stations along the way.

It runs every 15-30 mins from 5.30 AM to 00.30 AM (Mon-Sun) from Stansted to Liverpool Street, and every 15-30 mins from 3.40 AM to 11.25 PM (Mon-Sat) or 4.10 AM to 11.25 PM (Sun) if you're coming the other way.

Single tickets cost between £19 and £30.50 depending on which class you pick, and return tickets are £32 to £49. Children's tickets (5-15) are £9.50 to £15.25 for a single, and £16 to £24.50 for a return. Check out their website at *https://www.stanstedexpress.com*.

Luton Airport

Luton has one terminal and is mainly used by low-cost airlines. It is located 32 miles north of central London. (This is exactly why I hate low-cost airlines... they land you at an airport that is miles away from London and then claim that it's a London airport. Anybody who thinks that Luton is in London needs a better map!)

Website: *http://www.london-luton.co.uk*
Telephone: 0158 240 5100

National Rail: Trains run from the airport into Blackfriars, Farringdon and St. Pancras, but you also have to catch a 10-min shuttle bus from the terminal to Luton Airport Parkway Station.

The journey takes around 45-60 mins, and they run every 15-60 mins, 24-hours a day.

A single ticket costs anything from £15 to £25. A return ticket costs £25 to £35.

London City Airport

National Rail: ...exactly the same as the Stansted Express.

Underground: It's not possible to get the Underground because it's too far away.

Coach: You can get a National Express coach from Stansted to Victoria Coach Station. They run every 15-30 mins, 24-hours a day, and take 80 and 140 mins.

A single ticket starts from £6, and a return ticket costs £19. Visit their website at *http://www.nationalexpress.com*.

Bus: There are no local buses from Stansted to London, it's too far away.

Taxi: A taxi from Stansted airport into central London will take around 60-90 mins, and will cost anything from £135 to £155. You might find that a minicab is cheaper, but you'll have to ring around the companies and get a quote.

Underground: It's too far away for the Underground.

Coach: You can catch a National Express coach from Luton airport to Victoria Coach Station. They run every 15-60 mins, 24-hours a day, and take between 70 and 110 mins to get there.

A single ticket costs around £10, whilst a return costs between £18 and £25. Their website can be found at *http://www.nationalexpress.com*.

Bus: There are no local buses into London because it's too far away.

Taxi: A taxi from Luton airport into central London will take around 60-80 mins, and will cost anything from £115 to £135. You might find that a minicab is cheaper, but you'll have to ring around the companies and get a quote.

London City is the smallest of London's five main airports, and lies just 6 miles east of central London. It is mainly used by business travellers and their private planes, but it does have an increasing number of holiday flights.

Website: *http://www.londoncityairport.com*
Telephone: 0207 646 0088

Docklands Light Railway: The DLR (which is basically the same thing as the London Underground, but runs overground instead), goes from the airport into Tower Gateway (for the Tower of London) and Bank (for The City).

Trains run every 8-15 mins from 5 AM to 00.25 AM (Mon-Sat), and 6.25 AM to 11.15 PM (Sun). The journey takes between 25 and 50 mins. [Note: If you're travelling from central London towards the airport then you need to catch a train heading towards King George V or Woolwich. If you catch one heading towards Lewisham or Beckton then you will miss your plane!]

You can find the adult fares in my 'London Underground' section -- you need the row that says zones 1-3.

Coach: London City Airport is the one airport that National Express doesn't bother with... presumably because it's so close to the centre of town.

Bus: Despite its closeness to central London, there are no direct buses between the airport and the centre of town (and yes, that sounds totally daft to me as well -- but that's the truth!). Luckily the DLR is so simple and easy to use that you may as well just stick with that.

Taxi: A taxi from London City Airport into central London will take around 30-50 mins, and cost anything from £30 to £90. You might find that a minicab is cheaper, but you'll have to ring around the companies and get a quote.

Other Useful Information

Climate and Daylight Hours

Month	Rainy days	Avg. Temp	Sunrise - Sunset
January	10 days	2 - 6°	8.00 AM - 4.20 PM
February	7 days	2 - 7°	7.15 AM - 5.15 PM
March	9 days	3 - 10°	6.15 AM - 6.00 PM
April	8 days	6 - 13°	6.10 AM - 7.55 PM
May	8 days	8 - 17°	5.10 AM - 8.45 PM
June	8 days	12 - 20°	4.45 AM - 9.20 PM
July	6 days	14 - 22°	5.00 AM - 9.15 PM
August	6 days	13 - 21°	5.45 AM - 8.25 PM
September	8 days	11 - 19°	6.35 AM - 7.20 PM
October	9 days	8 - 14°	7.25 AM - 6.05 PM
November	9 days	5 - 10°	7.15 AM - 4.15 PM
December	10 days	4 - 7°	8.00 AM - 3.55 PM

Everyone likes to joke about the English weather, but it's actually not that bad. The warmest time is between June and August (that's when we see a bit of sun), but even during the summer months rain is never more than a week away. Most of our rain is spotty and light, but we do get a few heavy showers and downpours. Britain has earned a bit of a rainy reputation, and I've seen more than a few guidebooks recommend carrying a brolly with you at all times -- what a load of nonsense! Sure, it does rain a lot, but it's not *that* bad.

You shouldn't have to worry about extreme temperatures. The average temperature during the summer is around 20°C, and it rarely gets above 30° for more than a few days. (People will start to wilt and complain once it gets above 22° -- we Brits are not used to the heat.) During the spring and autumn it is more like 12°. The average temperature in the winter will be somewhere around 5°.

The coldest months are between November and March. Falling snow is relatively common in central London, but settled snow is rare because all of the warm buildings and heavy traffic. If snow is going to come, then it will most likely come in January and February.

We don't suffer from any of the more exotic weather conditions. So you won't get ravaged by a tornado, hurricane, earthquake or an erupting volcano. We do occasionally have thunder and lightning though, so it's not all boring.

Time Difference

London is at the centre of Greenwich Mean Time (GMT), so in theory every country is either plus or minus us. Unfortunately it isn't quite as simple as that, because between late-Mar and late-Oct London switches to British Summer Time (BST), which is one hour ahead of GMT. The exact dates when the clocks change can be found in my table of 'Useful Calendar Dates'.

The following table shows the time difference between the world's major cities and GMT -- but remember to minus an extra hour if BST applies:

City	± hours	City	± hours
Accra	± 0	Amsterdam	+ 1
Ankara	+ 2	Athens	+ 2
Atlanta	− 5	Auckland	+ 12
Baghdad	+ 3	Bangkok	+ 7
Barcelona	+ 1	Beijing	+ 8
Belfast	± 0	Belgrade	+ 1
Berlin	+ 1	Berne	+ 1
Bogata	− 5	Bombay	+ 5½
Bonn	+ 1	Brasilia	− 3
Brussels	+ 1	Budapest	+ 1
Buenos Aires	− 3	Cairo	+ 2
Calcutta	+ 5½	Calgary	− 7
Cape Town	+ 2	Caracas	− 4½
Chicago	− 6	Copenhagen	+ 1
Damascus	+ 2	Dar-es-Salaam	+ 3
Darwin	+ 9½	Delhi	+ 5½
Denver	− 7	Dublin	± 0
Edinburgh	± 0	Frankfurt	+ 1
Geneva	+ 1	Glasgow	± 0
Havana	− 5	Helsinki	+ 2
Hong Kong	+ 8	Honolulu	− 10
Houston	− 6	Istanbul	+ 2
Jerusalem	+ 2	Johannesburg	+ 2
Karachi	+ 5	Kuala Lumpur	+ 8
Kuwait	+ 3	Lagos	+ 1
Lisbon	± 0	Los Angeles	− 8
Madrid	+ 1	Manila	+ 8
Melbourne	+ 10	Mexico City	− 6
Montréal	− 5	Moscow	+ 3
Mumbia	+ 5½	Muscat	+ 4
Nairobi	+ 3	New York	− 5
Oslo	+ 1	Ottawa	− 5
Paris	+ 1	Perth	+ 8
Prague	+ 1	Pretoria	+ 2
Quebec	− 5	Reykjavik	± 0
Rio de Janeiro	− 3	Riyadh	+ 3
Rome	+ 1	San Francisco	− 8

Other Useful Information | 475

Santiago	− 4	Seoul	+ 9
Shanghai	+ 8	Singapore	+ 8
St. Louis	− 6	St. Petersburg	+ 3
Stockholm	+ 1	Sydney	+ 10
Tokyo	+ 9	Tripoli	+ 2
Toronto	− 5	Vancouver	− 8
Vienna	+ 1	Vladivostok	+ 11
Warsaw	+ 1	Washington	− 5
Wellington	+ 12	Zurich	+ 1

Useful Calendar Dates

	2016	2017	2018
New Year's Day	1 Jan	1 Jan	1 Jan
Twelfth Night	5 Jan	5 Jan	5 Jan
Chinese New Year	8 Feb	28 Jan	16 Feb
Valentine's Day	14 Feb	14 Feb	14 Feb
St. David's Day	1 Mar	1 Mar	1 Mar
Mother's Day	6 Mar	26 Mar	11 Mar
St. Patrick's Day	17 Mar	17 Mar	17 Mar
Spring begins	20 Mar	20 Mar	20 Mar
Clocks forward 1 hour	27 Mar	26 Mar	25 Mar
Easter Sunday	27 Mar	16 Apr	1 Apr
St. George's Day	23 Apr	23 Apr	23 Apr
Father's Day	19 Jun	18 Jun	17 Jun
Summer begins	20 Jun	21 Jun	21 Jun
Longest day	20 Jun	21 Jun	21 Jun
Autumn begins	22 Sep	22 Sep	23 Sep
Clocks go back 1 hour	30 Oct	29 Oct	28 Oct
Halloween	31 Oct	31 Oct	31 Oct
Guy Fawkes Night	5 Nov	5 Nov	5 Nov
Remembrance Sunday	13 Nov	12 Nov	11 Nov
St. Andrew's Day	30 Nov	30 Nov	30 Nov
Winter begins	21 Dec	21 Dec	21 Dec
Shortest day	21 Dec	21 Dec	21 Dec
Christmas Day	25 Dec	25 Dec	25 Dec
Boxing Day	26 Dec	26 Dec	26 Dec
New Year's Eve	31 Dec	31 Dec	31 Dec

Bank holidays

The UK enjoys eight 'bank holidays' throughout the year. These are basically just days off, when everyone gets to descend on London with their kids. You can pretty much guarantee that it will rain on these days. Practically all of the big shops and attractions in central London remain open, but you might find that they use reduced opening hours. Some of the smaller shops and restaurants might be closed.

Bank holidays always fall on a weekday. If the date would occur on a weekend (like Christmas Day, for example), then the holiday rolls over to the following Monday.

	2016	2017	2018
New Year's holiday	1 Jan	1 Jan	2 Jan
Good Friday	25 Mar	14 Apr	30 Mar
Easter Monday	28 Mar	17 Apr	2 Apr
May Bank holiday	2 May	1 May	7 May
Spring Bank holiday	30 May	29 May	28 May
Summer Bank holiday	29 Aug	28 Aug	27 Aug
Christmas holiday	27 Dec	25 Dec	25 Dec
Boxing Day holiday	28 Dec	26 Dec	26 Dec

School holidays

If you want to avoid all the screaming kids running around causing mayhem, then try and avoid visiting London during a school holiday. The queues will be longer and the prices will go up.

The following dates should be taken as a rough guide only, as they vary greatly from school to school.

Spring half-term	last week of February
Easter holiday	one week either side of Easter Sunday
Summer half-term	last week of May
Summer holiday	late July to early September
Autumn half-term	last week of October
Christmas holiday	mid-December to first week of January

Annual events

Shopping sales	26th Dec to end of Jan
New Year's Day parade	1st Jan
Chinese New Year	last week of Jan or 1st half of Feb
St. Patrick's Day parade	mid-Mar
University Boat Race	last week of Mar or 1st week of Apr
Cricket season	early Apr to end of Sep
London Marathon	usually mid-Apr
Globe Theatre season	usually late Apr to mid-Oct
State Opening of Parliament	usually early May

Royal Windsor Horse Show	2nd week of May
FA Cup Final	usually mid-May
Chelsea Flower Show	3rd or 4th week of May
The Derby	1st week of Jun
Beating Retreat	1st or 2nd week of Jun
Royal Ascot	usually 2nd week of Jun
Trooping the Colour	2nd or 3rd week of Jun
Pride London (LGBT march)	usually late Jun
Wimbledon Tennis	last week of Jun and 1st week of Jul
Hampton Court Flower Show	early Jul
Royal Albert Hall Proms	mid-Jul to early Sep
Buckingham Palace Opening	end of Jul to end of Sep
Houses of Parliament Opening	end of Jul to end of Sep
Football season	mid-Aug to end of May
Notting Hill Carnival	end of Aug (Bank Holiday weekend)
Last Night of the Proms	early Sep
Rugby Union season	early Sep to end of May
Great River Race	mid-Sep
Guy Fawkes Night (fireworks)	week leading up to 5th Nov
Lord Mayor's Show	usually 2nd Sat in Nov
Remembrance Day parade	2nd Sun in Nov
Christmas lights go up	usually 2nd week of Nov
Christmas ice rinks	mid-Nov to early Jan
Christmas markets	mid-Nov to end of Dec
Christmas pantomimes	last week of Nov to 1st week of Jan
Trafalgar Square tree	1st week of Dec to Twelfth night
New Year's Eve	31st Dec

Using the Telephones and Internet

Emergencies	999 (or 112, which is the pan-European equivalent). The operator will say "Emergency, which service please?", and you should answer ambulance, police or fire
Non-emergency police	101 (for crimes that don't need an immediate response)
Non-emergency medical	111 (for non-urgent medical advice)
Speaking clock	123
Operator (local)	100
Operator (international)	155
Directory enquiries (local)	118 118, 118 500, or 118 888
Directory enquiries (international)	118 505, 118 866, or 118 899
Reverse charges	155

How to telephone abroad

If you want to call another country from the UK then you need to start with the international dialling code (00), followed by the correct country code. If the telephone number that you are dialling happens to have an area code that starts with a zero then it is usual practice to drop the zero (but this differs from country to country, so you might want to try both ways).

Country	Prefix	Country	Prefix
Albania	00 355	Algeria	00 213
Argentina	00 54	Australia	00 61
Austria	00 43	Bahamas	00 1 242
Bangladesh	00 880	Barbados	00 1 246
Belarus	00 375	Belgium	00 32
Belize	00 501	Bermuda	00 1 441
Bolivia	00 591	Bosnia-Herze.	00 387
Brazil	00 55	Bulgaria	00 359
Canada	00 1	Chile	00 56
China	00 86	Columbia	00 57
Costa Rica	00 506	Croatia	00 385
Cuba	00 53	Cyprus	00 357
Czech Republic	00 420	Denmark	00 45
Dominican Rep.	00 1 809	Ecuador	00 593
Egypt	00 20	El Salvador	00 503
Estonia	00 372	Ethiopia	00 251
Fiji	00 679	Finland	00 358
France	00 33	Germany	00 49
Gibraltar	00 350	Greece	00 30
Guatemala	00 502	Haiti	00 509
Honduras	00 504	Hong Kong	00 852
Hungary	00 36	Iceland	00 354
India	00 91	Indonesia	00 62
Iran	00 98	Iraq	00 964
Ireland	00 353	Israel	00 972
Italy	00 39	Jamaica	00 1 876
Japan	00 81	Jordan	00 962
Kazakhstan	00 7	Kenya	00 254
Korea (North)	00 850	Korea (South)	00 82
Kuwait	00 965	Latvia	00 371
Lebanon	00 961	Libya	00 218
Luxembourg	00 352	Malaysia	00 60
Malta	00 356	Mexico	00 52

Mongolia	00 976	Morocco	00 212
Nepal	00 977	Netherlands	00 31
New Zealand	00 64	Nicaragua	00 505
Nigeria	00 234	Norway	00 47
Pakistan	00 92	Panama	00 507
Paraguay	00 595	Peru	00 51
Philippines	00 63	Poland	00 48
Portugal	00 351	Puerto Rico	00 1 787
Romania	00 40	Russia	00 7
Saudi Arabia	00 966	Serbia & Mont.	00 381
Singapore	00 65	Slovakia	00 421
Slovenia	00 386	South Africa	00 27
Spain	00 34	Sudan	00 249
Swaziland	00 268	Sweden	00 46
Switzerland	00 41	Syria	00 963
Taiwan	00 886	Thailand	00 66
Trin. & Tobago	00 1 868	Tunisia	00 216
Turkey	00 90	UAE	00 971
Ukraine	00 380	Uruguay	00 598
USA	00 1	Venezuela	00 58
Vietnam	00 84	Zimbabwe	00 263

If somebody wants to call *you* from another country (whilst you are still in the UK), then they will have to start with the correct international dialling code (*00* from China, Europe, India, Middle East, New Zealand and South America; *001* from Hong Kong, Korea and Thailand; *0011* from Australia; *010* from Japan; *011* from the USA and Canada), followed by the UK's own country code: *44*. And remind them to drop any zeros at the start of the number as well.

Finding a free Wi-Fi spot

Most hotels offer Wi-Fi these days, but there is actually a pretty decent free service that operates in large parts of London. It's called 'The Cloud', and you can sign-up at *http://www.thecloud.net/ free-wifi/join-the-cloud*. They've also got a handy mobile phone app, which will automatically log you on every time you are in range of one of their zones. Find out more at *https:// service.thecloud.net/assets/ fastconnect*.

Unfortunately there's no such thing as a free lunch, and they will try and get an address and postcode out of you when you sign-up -- so just give them your hotel's address. They will also need your mobile phone number and email address. (Unfortunately you'll have to use your real ones this time, because your account will be tied to your phone.)

Once you have a username and a password then you should be able to access it in the City of London (the so-called 'Square Mile', which runs roughly from Fleet Street to the Tower of London), plus hundreds of pubs and food shops like Caffe Nero, PizzaExpress, Pret a Manger, Wagamama and more. You will know that you are 'in their zone' when 'The Cloud' page pops on your browser as you try to surf the web. That's when you need to enter your username and password. If you download their mobile app then it's supposed to log you on automatically.

'The Cloud' isn't the only free Wi-Fi service in London. London Transport also provides 15 minutes of free Wi-Fi at 150 of their train stations, but only if you've already got a mobile phone account with one of the big British providers: *O2*, *EE*, *Virgin*, *Vodafone*, *T-Mobile* and *Orange*. If you're not already a customer then you can buy temporary access from *https://wifipass .virginmedia.com/w/register.aspx*.

A better bet is the free Wi-Fi inside the British Library (*http://www.bl.uk/aboutus/ stpancras/wifi*) and along the Southbank (*http://www.southbanklondon.com/our- guide-to-free-wifi-in-south-bank*). This one is quite extensive and covers the Southbank Centre itself, the National Theatre, London Eye ticket hall and BFI IMAX cinema. If you're really desperate then you can make your way to City Hall (by Tower Bridge), and sit down in their cafe. They have free Wi-Fi throughout the building under the name of 'GLA Guest'. And there's always good old McDonalds as a last resort... because, let's be honest, that's where you're going to spend most of your lunchtimes anyway. Lots of their London branches offer free Wi-Fi if you don't mind registering your details first (*http://www.mcdonalds.co.uk/ukhome/ restaurants/free-wifi.html*).

Useful websites

http://www.visitlondon.com -- the official tourist website for London

http://www.timeout.com/london -- info about upcoming gigs, concerts and shows

http://www.tkts.co.uk -- cheap theatre tickets from TKTS in Leicester Square

https://tfl.gov.uk/plan-a-journey -- TFL's handy planner for buses and trains

http://ojp.nationalrail.co.uk/service/planjo urney/search -- National Rail sells train tickets to places outside central London

http://www.directenquiries.com/default.asp x -- information about travelling around London if you're mobility impaired

http://www.hrp.org.uk -- the official website of the Royal Palaces

http://www.bbc.co.uk/weather/2643743 -- 10-day weather forecast for London

and last, but not least...

http://www.londondrum.com/blog -- it's my own London blog -- check it out!

Posting letters

Letter	*Weight:* Up to 100g -- *Max size:* 24cm x 16.5cm x 0.5cm -- *1st class:* 63p -- *2nd class:* 54p
Large letter	*Weight:* Up to 750g -- *Max size:* 35.3cm x 25cm x 2.5cm -- *1st class:* 95p to £2.42 -- *2nd class:* 74p to £2.05
Small parcel	*Weight:* Up to 2kg -- *Max size:* 45cm x 35cm x 16cm -- *1st class:* £3.30 to £5.45 -- *2nd class:* £2.80
Medium parcel	*Weight:* Up to 20kg -- *Max size:* 61cm x 46cm x 46cm -- *1st class:* £5.65 to £33.40 -- *2nd class:* £4.89 to £28.55
International letter	*Weight:* Up to 100g -- *Max size:* 24cm x 16.5cm x 0.5cm -- *Europe:* £1 to £1.52 -- *Rest of world:* £1 to £2.25

International large letter   *Weight:* Up to 750g -- *Max size:* 35.3cm x 25cm x 2.5cm -- *Europe:* £2.45 to £6.60 -- *Rest of world:* £3.15 to £10.75

International parcel   *Weight:* Up to 2kg -- *Max size:* Height+width+depth less than 90cm, and no side greater than 60cm -- *Europe:* £3.45 to £13.46 -- *Rest of world:* £4.10 to £21.50

There are two classes of mail in the UK: *1st class* and *2nd class*. First class is supposed to arrive the next day if it's posted before 5 PM, but that's just for local letters (e.g., from London to London). If you want to post it to another part of the country then you need to get it inside the letterbox by 1 PM. Second class letters take a bit longer: up to three days.

Stamps can be bought from post offices supermarkets and newsagents (look for a red Royal Mail sign in the window). They usually come in books of four or ten. If you want a single stamp then you will have to get it from a post office.

The cost of a letter rises with its weight and size, so don't just stick a 1st class stamp on and hope for the best. Anything A4-sized, for example, is classed as a 'large letter' and will cost extra. If you want to play it safe then take it up to a post office counter and ask them to tell you the cost.

International mail (previously known as 'Airmail') usually takes around three days to reach Europe, and 4-6 days to reach the rest of the world.

Poste Restante

If you don't have a local address but you still need to receive a letter, then you can take advantage of the UK's *Poste Restante* system. If the sender writes your full name, 'Poste Restante', and the address of a post office branch on the envelope, then you should be able to pick it up by showing a recognised photo ID (e.g., your passport).

Mail is kept for a maximum of two weeks, or one month if it's sent from abroad. I'm not sure what they do with them after that, but I'm guessing that they burn them.

Most travellers address their Poste Restante to the big branch by Trafalgar Square (24-28 William IV Street, London, WC2N 4DL), but you can actually send it to any post office you like, as long as you know its address. You can find some more big branches in Regent Street (11 Lower Regent Street, London, SW1Y 4LR), Aldwych (95 Aldwych, London, WC2B 4JN) and Holborn (181 High Holborn, London, WC1V 7RL).

You can find your nearest post office on the Royal Mail website: *http://www.royalmail.com/branch-finder*

Spending Money

British currency

Britain's currency is the pound sterling. There are 100 pence (or 'pee') to a pound.

Coins are issued in bronze denominations of 1p and 2p (called 'coppers'), and silver denominations of 5p, 10p, 20p and 50p. There is also a gold-coloured £1 coin (commonly called a 'quid'), and a silver and gold £2 coin.

Paper notes come in denominations of £5 (called a 'fiver'), £10 (a 'tenner'), £20 and £50. If your wallet is full of £50 notes then good luck trying to spend them in a shop (nobody ever sees those!).

Sometimes you might be surprised to receive a Scottish banknote, which looks totally different to the usual ones. Technically speaking they are legal tender throughout the UK, but in practice many shops refuse to take them because they can't tell whether they are fake (because they don't see them very often). If that happens to you then don't worry, just spend it in one of the big high-street stores or train stations instead. Or try and find a local Scotsman who will start ranting and raving at the shopkeeper on your behalf.

Exchange rates

This should be taken as a rough guide only, as exchange rates fluctuate from day-to-day. You can get an exact rate from http://www.xe.com.

Currency exchange rates (approximate)		
British pounds	£1 = €1.38	Euros
Euros	€1 = 73p	British pounds
British pounds	£1 = $1.50	US dollars
US dollars	$1 = 66p	British pounds
British pounds	£1 = $2.04	Canada dollars
Canada dollars	$1 = 49p	British pounds
British pounds	£1 = $2.09	Australian dollars
Australian dollars	$1 = 48p	British pounds
British pounds	£1 = ¥185	Japanese yen
Japanese yen	¥1 = 1p	British pounds
British pounds	£1 = ¥9.67	Chinese yuan
Chinese yuan	¥1 = 10p	British pounds
British pounds	£1 = ₽104	Russian rubles
Russian rubles	₽1 = 1p	British pounds
British pounds	£1 = ₹100	Indian rupees
Indian rupees	₹1 = 1p	British pounds

Using credit and debit cards

The following credit and debit cards are widely accepted in London: *Cirrus, Delta, EuroCard, Maestro, MasterCard* and *Visa*. *American Express* and *Diner's Club* are not as widely accepted as they once were -- it's really just the big expensive places that accept them.

Cash machines (also known as cashpoints, or ATMs) can be found all over the capital. Be aware that some of them charge a small amount for withdrawals (typically £1.50 -- £2). You should see a warning sign somewhere on the screen, or by the side of it, before you put your card in. The ones that you find inside pubs, shops and tourist attractions are the worst offenders, and will probably charge you a couple of quid each time. If you want to avoid a charge then stick with the ones outside high-street banks, or inside bank lobbies, because those ones are always free.

It is usually a wise idea to give your bank a quick ring before using your card abroad, because they tend to play it ultra-safe these days and block it if they see unusual activity. I have actually fallen foul of this myself: my card packed up without warning, and when I telephoned the bank to see what was going on they explained that it was my unexpected overseas use.

You might also want to get your PIN number changed before you arrive in London. Apparently a lot of the foreign cards have a six-digit PIN number instead of the UK's four. Our cash machines will only accept a four-digit PIN, so you could find yourself with a bit of a problem.

Popular shopping areas

The most famous shopping streets in London are Oxford Street and Regent Street. Both are home to big department stores and **chain stores**. Oxford Street is best-known for Selfridges and the flagship stores of TopShop, Debenhams, House of Fraser and John Lewis. It also has big branches of Primark and HMV (now re-named 'His Master's Voice'). Regent Street has got Liberty, Hamleys, the Apple Store, and lots of big-name clothes stores. You will find plenty more **department stores** in Kensington High Street, Marylebone High Street and King's Road (just off Sloane Square). Knightsbridge is also pretty handy for high-street shops -- that's where you'll find Harvey Nichols and the most famous shop of all: Harrods.

If you're looking for **boutique clothing** stores then try Carnaby Street and the area around Seven Dials (north of Covent Garden). Floral Street is good too (near Leicester Square), and lots of young people like Camden (I wouldn't know, though -- I'm too old). Camden's markets are good for **cheap clothes** and **cheap jewellery**. Lots of guidebooks suggest King's Road for boutique stores, but all I see these days are high-street shops and chain stores.

Expensive **men's tailoring** and custom-fit suits are best bought from Savile Row and Jermyn Street.

Expensive jewellery and antiques can be found in the streets behind St. James's Palace and around Bond Street -- but remember to bring your wallet, because that's where you'll find famous names like Cartier, Rolex and Tiffany's. There are some very expensive little shops in Burlington Arcade and the Royal Exchange as well (near the Bank of England). But if you really want to impress someone, then try the London Silver Vaults in Chancery Lane. This huge underground vault is home to more than thirty silver dealers, selling everything from £25 to £25,000. Portobello Road has a famous **antiques market** every Saturday (it's all fruit, food and clothes on the other days).

The historic town centre in Greenwich has lots of interesting shops selling old **books and antiques**, and the market in the central piazza of Covent Garden is a great place to look for handmade **crafts and gifts**. You can also try Gabriel's Wharf on Southbank (close to the National Theatre), which is home to lots of little craft shops.

If you want some **Royal souvenirs** then try the official Buckingham Palace shop at 7 Buckingham Palace Road (although I actually prefer the Royal Mews gift shop across the road is better). They've also got a little Royal section set-up in Harrods. It was near the toys the last time I looked, but they seem to move their stuff around every five minutes.

The **Houses of Parliament** gift shop is on the corner of Parliament Square (diagonally opposite the Winston Churchill statue). **Sherlock Holmes** themed-gifts can be bought from the big gift shop inside the Sherlock Homes Museum, and if you're after some **Shakespeare books** then try the shop inside the Globe Theatre (it sounds obvious, but you'd be surprised how many people don't think of trying places like that).

The biggest concentration of **book stores** can be found down Charing Cross Road (near Leicester Square). That is also where you'll find Foyles -- the largest bookstore in London. Large branches of Waterstones and Hatchards can be found down Piccadilly. There is another big branch of Waterstones by Trafalgar Square (although I actually prefer the one in Gower Street, because it's more cosy). If you want some **travel books and maps**, then your best bet is Stanfords in Long Acre (Covent Garden). If you're looking for **art books**, then try the gift shops at the National Gallery, Tate Britain and Tate Modern. **Military books** can be found at the Imperial War Museum. The Natural History Museum and Science Museum's shops are good for **children's gifts** and stocking fillers. If you want old **antiquarian books** then there are lots of dusty little shops around the British Museum (start in Great Russell Street and have a wander around from there).

Musical instruments and sheet music can be found in Denmark Street (London's equivalent of *Tin Pan Alley*), just off Charing Cross Road.

If you're after **electrical goods** and computer stores, then head for Tottenham Court Road.

If you want some **fancy food and chocolates**, then try the food halls in Harrods and Fortnum & Mason. Posh English tea can be found in both those shops, plus the historic Twinings Tea Shop down the Strand. Borough Market also has some very nice food... but that's probably more for your lunchtime, rather than gift-buying. Leadenhall Market is another good place for lunchtime food.

And finally... if you just want to buy some simple **souvenirs of London** (T-shirts, postcards, cups and keyrings -- that sort of thing), then there are plenty of shops around Leicester Square and Piccadilly Circus. The biggest one is called Cool Britannia, just a few steps from the Eros fountain.

Business opening hours

This should be taken as a rough guide only, as each business will have its own opening times. If you visit on a Bank Holiday then expect to find many of the small shops shut. Most of the big shops, attractions, pubs and restaurants will remain open, but with reduced hours. The big exception is Christmas Day, when practically everything is closed. Even the buses and trains shut down.

Shops	9 AM to 6 PM (Mon-Sat); 11 AM to 4 PM (Sun); Big stores usually have a late opening night once a week, typically on a Thursday, when they'll stay open until 7 PM or 8 PM
Supermarkets	8 AM to 10 PM (Mon-Sat); 11 AM to 4 PM (Sun)
Attractions	10 AM to 5 PM (Mon-Sun); Last entry is usually one hour before closing; Big art galleries usually have a late opening night once a week, typically on a Friday
Restaurants	12 noon to 3 PM, and 6 PM to 11 PM (Mon-Sun)
Pubs & Bars	11 AM to 11.30 PM (Mon-Sat); 12 noon to 10.30 PM (Sun)
Nightclubs	10 PM to 3 AM (Mon-Sat); 8 PM to midnight (Sun)
Banks	9.30 AM to 5 PM (Mon-Fri); 10 AM to 4 PM (Sat); Closed (Sun)
Post offices	9 AM to 5 PM (Mon-Fri); 9 AM to 12 noon (Sat); Closed (Sun)
Pharmacies	9 AM to 6 PM (Mon-Sat); 10 AM to 5 PM (Sun)

Typical prices in London

Fast food meal (e.g. McDonalds)	£5 to £6
Meal at a pub/cheap restaurant	£8 to £15
Meal at a mid-range restaurant	£15 to £30
Meal at an expensive restaurant	£30+
Supermarket sandwich	£2 to £3
Packet of crisps	55p to £1
Chocolate bar	60p to 90p
Pint of beer	£3.50 to £4.75
Posh coffee	£2.50 to £3.50
Cup of tea	£1.50 to £2.50
Can of Coke	80p to £1.50
Bottled water	90p to £1.20
Cigarettes (pack of 20)	£9
Tourist attraction	free to £30
Theatre ticket	£25 to £120
Music concert	£15 to £100
Cinema ticket	£10 to £18

Tipping

Taxi drivers	10% of the fare is an oft-quoted figure, but it is more usual for people to round up to the nearest pound, or £5, and then wave away any change
Restaurants	10% of the bill—but check the small-print on the bill or the menu first, because sometimes a 'service charge' is automatically included
Pubs & Bars	Nothing. Nobody expects a tip in a pub. If you really want to tip them (ie. because they are pretty) then you can say "and one for yourself" and let them keep the change, so they can buy themselves a drink
Hotel maids	£1-£2 per day, paid at the end of your stay
Hotel porters	£1-£2 per bag, as they leave the room
Hotel concierge	£5, if they have performed a service

Discount Passes

London Pass

Duration	Price	Price + travelcard
1 day (adult)	£59	£72
1 day (child)	£39	£45
2 days (adult)	£79	£97
2 days (child)	£59	£71

3 days (adult)	£95	£123
3 days (child)	£66	£84
6 days (adult)	£129	£172
6 days (child)	£89	£119
10 days (adult)	£159	£212
10 days (child)	£109	£162

Note: Children are aged 5-15

If you spend any time at all planning your holiday, then sooner or later you will come across something called a 'London Pass'. This discount card is sold online through *https://www.londonpass.com*, and at the London Information Centre just south of St. Paul's Cathedral (that weird angular-looking building in St. Paul's Churchyard). You can also get them from a circular booth opposite the Garrick Theatre in Charing Cross Road, and at the Travel Information Centres inside Euston, King's Cross, Liverpool Street, Paddington, Piccadilly Circus and Victoria train stations. (Note: for some bizarre reason known only to them, you can only buy the Pass + Travelcard through their website, or at the booth in Charing Cross Road. None of the other places I mentioned above will sell you a Pass + Travelcard -- only the London Pass on its own.)

The pass provides you with free entry and discounts at lots of London attractions. It sounds like quite a good deal when you read all the blurb on their website. But is it worth it?

Well... *it depends.* It doesn't cover every single attraction in London, so what you need to do is look through their list and see which ones you want to visit. At the time of writing it includes free entry into places like Windsor Castle, Westminster Abbey, Tower Bridge, the Tower of London, Hampton Court, Kensington Palace, the Churchill War Rooms and London Zoo. But you will notice that many of the most popular attractions are missing: places like Madame Tussauds, the London Dungeon, London Aquarium, London Eye, the Shard and St. Paul's Cathedral.

Gaining free entry into 60+ attractions sounds like a good deal, but be careful... what you need to do is compare the entry costs with the price of the pass. I have been sitting here doing my sums, and at the current rate you could purchase a 1-day pass and get into the Tower of London, Westminster Abbey and Tower Bridge for free, but you would save *no money whatsoever*. You would actually be £5.50 down! It's not until you visit a fourth attraction that you start saving. And do you really want to rush around four attractions in one day? I would suggest not -- I wouldn't even want to rush around three.

I wouldn't be bowled over by their promise of a 'Fast Track' ticket either. This allows you to bypass some of the busy queues, but in my experience the only attractions that have a truly terrible wait are the London Eye, London Dungeon and Madame Tussauds (none of which are included on their list). Long queues at the other places are bearable, and not worth the extra expense of a London Pass.

And while I'm busy banging nails into their coffin, here is one more: it is possible to buy a London Pass with a travelcard attached, for use on the buses and trains; but you may as well just buy it yourself -- it's no cheaper getting it through a London Pass. And it's not a proper travelcard anyway (I think they should be a lot clearer about this, as it's not immediately obvious) -- it's actually a pay-as-you-go Oyster card with some credit loaded on. If you buy a 1-day pass then you get £10 loaded on -- even though you paid £13 extra, because there's a £3 fee to set it up. But journeys inside zone 1 and 2 currently have a daily cap of £6.50 anyway, so it's theoretically impossible to spend more than £6.50 in one day. If you bought that 1-day pass I mentioned earlier, then you would now be down a total of £8. And children fare even worse because they get a paper travelcard -- but unlike the adult pass, it's off-peak! So it doesn't even cover the whole day.

It's all extremely confusing, and is best avoided in my opinion. Its one saving grace is that it takes the place of money, so you can avoid having to carry around your life savings in your wallet. And the bundled guidebook is useless as well. It's 180-odd pages long, but a third of it is in French, and another third is in German. It basically just shows you where all their attractions are, and their opening times. But it misses out all the places not included on the pass, so it's probably the only London guidebook in the world that fails to mention St. Paul's Cathedral, Madame Tussauds and the London Eye!

Merlin Pass

If you have kids then you might be better off buying a Merlin Pass instead (from *http://www.merlinannualpass.co.uk*). This will give you 12 months entry to the London Dungeon, London Aquarium, London Eye, Madame Tussauds, Chessington World of Adventures and Shrek's Adventure (amongst others). They also offer combo tickets that combine any 2, 3 or 4 of these attractions together, which are available to buy from the attractions' individual websites. You will save yourself quite a few pennies doing that.

The current price for a standard pass is £169 per person, or £129 per person if it's a family ticket. Remember to read the small print though, because some of the attractions have date restrictions. A couple of them won't let you visit during August.

2-for-1 offers by train

This idea is going to be less useful if you are staying inside central London, because you won't be catching many mainline trains -- but you should definitely check out *https://www.daysoutguide.co.uk/2for1-london* before you go.

They've got a bit list of 150+ attractions which are offering '2 for the price of 1' entry deals when you show a valid train ticket for the same day of travel. All you need to do is print out the relevant voucher from their website first, and then present it at the gate along with your train ticket. But here's the caveat: the ticket has to be for a National Rail train (the overground ones). So travelling on the London Underground doesn't count. And Oyster cards don't count either... nor do Freedom Passes (OAP passes). It has to be a *paper National Rail ticket*. So that basically means you have to travel in, or out, from central London.

The list of attractions is very good and includes popular places like the London Eye, London Dungeon, London Zoo, London Aquarium, Madame Tussauds, Churchill War Rooms, Westminster Abbey, St. Paul's Cathedral, Tower Bridge and the Tower of London. Some of them are already outside central London (like Chessington World of Adventures and Hampton Court), so even if you are staying in central London the chances are good that you will need to catch an overground train at some point.

Historic Royal Palaces

If you're planning on visiting London's Royal palaces, then it might be worth joining Historic Royal Palaces beforehand (see *http://www.hrp.org.uk/support-us/individuals/membership*). This will allow you to visit five of the palaces as many times as you like for the duration of one year, at the cost of just £47.

But there's a caveat: it doesn't include Buckingham Palace, Windsor Castle or Clarence House. The only places that it covers are the Tower of London, Hampton Court, Kensington Palace, Kew Palace and Banqueting House. And there's a second caveat: because you still have to pay the entrance fee into Kew Gardens if you want to see Kew Palace (which seems like a total swizz to me, because it's situated inside the grounds!). If you are just here on a holiday then you'll probably need to visit the Tower of London plus two other places to make it worth your while.

English Heritage

English Heritage members get free entry into more than 350 historic properties all over England. Not all of them are within easy reach of London though, and lots of them will use up an entire day of your holiday. You can view a complete list of their attractions here: *http://www.english-heritage.org.uk/visit/places*.

The best ones in London are Apsley House, Chiswick House, Eltham Palace, Kenwood House and Wellington Arch. You might also want to try day-trips to Dover Castle and Stonehenge.

At a cost of £50 per adult (£41 for the over-60s) it's highly unlikely to be worth it if you're only here for a week-or-two, but if you live in England then it might be worth thinking about, because you can use it over the span of a year.

Cheap theatre tickets

Cheap theatre tickets can be bought from the TKTS booth in Leicester Square. It's open from 10 AM to 7 PM (Mon-Sat) and 11 AM to 4.30 PM (Sun). They also have a website at *http://www.tkts.co.uk*.

If a theatre is having trouble selling their remaining seats for that day, then this is where they will end up. The best prices will always be for that same day, or up to one week in advance, so you won't be able to book much further ahead than that. But there are usually hundreds of discount and half-price tickets available for the big shows. Their typical discounts are between £5 and £40. The only downside is that most of the good seats will already be gone... but you can't be too choosy if you want a cheap ticket.

Voluntary donations

Another way that you can save a few pounds is by keeping an eye out for places that automatically add a voluntary donation onto the ticket cost.

The usual way they do it is through something called 'Gift Aid' -- a tax relief scheme for charities and attractions. It's worth around 25p for every £1 you spend with them, but you only have to pay an extra 10% yourself (and yes, that sounds a bit silly to me as well -- but that's how it works). So if an attraction asks you whether you want to "Gift Aid it?", what they are really asking you is this: "Would you like to add an extra 10% onto the ticket cost?" If they try and reassure you that it won't cost any more money, then that is probably because they have already quoted a price which included it (sneaky!). Whilst it might seem a little embarrassing to ask, it is perfectly okay to get this removed. (They are counting on your embarrassment to keep it on.)

Gift Aid only works with British taxpayers though, so don't be surprised if they ask you where you came from. They will also need your name, address and postcode to process it. Handing over your personal details is always onerous, but sometimes you will get an extra benefit which will make it worthwhile. St. Paul's Cathedral, for example, will let you return for free within 12 months if you keep the same ticket. Other places might give you a percentage discount in their gift shop.

Personally, I think the whole thing is a bit cheeky. Attractions in London are rarely cheap (and often extortionate!), so I have disclosed which ones charge a donation within my reviews -- that way you can make up your own mind about whether to pay or not before you arrive.

Drinking and Smoking

When do the pubs close?

Generally speaking, most pubs open from 11 AM to 11.30 PM (Mon-Sat), and 12 noon to 10.30 PM (Sun) -- but the hours vary from business to business. The law allows some pubs to stay open later if they have the correct license, and some pubs in the tourist hotspots will stay open for the whole 24 hours. Nightclubs usually open from 10 PM to 3 AM (Mon-Sat) and 8 PM to midnight (Sun).

Last orders will normally be called 30 minutes before closing time, which means you have an extra half-an-hour to drink up and leave from when the bell rings.

What is the drinking age?

You have to be over-18 to buy and drink alcohol in England, but a lot of pubs ask for ID if you look under 21 -- so being 19 is no guarantee that you'll get a drink. If you do get turned away then take it as a compliment -- you don't stay young forever!

You will find that a lot of pubs in central London have bouncers on the door once it starts getting late. Large groups of men are more likely to get turned away than a pair (especially if they don't have any women with them), so you might want to try splitting up into little groups to increase your chances.

Can children go inside pubs?

Under-18s who are accompanied by an adult might be allowed to enter a pub during the daytime, but this isn't always the case. Each license holder may be within his rights to ask you to leave, depending on his licensing conditions.

If you are under-14 then you will definitely not be allowed in the bar area. The only places that you can sit as a kid are in the beer garden and any specially designated family rooms (but not all pubs have these).

Most pubs will not allow children anywhere inside the pub during the evening, regardless of their age.

What is the smoking age?

You have to be over-18 to buy and smoke cigarettes in London.

Where can you smoke?

It is illegal to smoke inside a public building, an enclosed workplace, or on public transport (which includes train platforms).

It is also illegal to smoke inside a vehicle whilst there are under-18s present -- even if the window or sunroof is open.

Free public toilets

The days when you could spend a penny to spend a penny (if you excuse the pun) are drawing rapidly to a close, as most of the public urinals in London need 20p to 50p to enter (even the ones inside train stations); but luckily there are still a few free public places dotted around the city if you know where to look.

The most useful one used to be in **Trafalgar Square**, between the fountains and the central steps leading up to the National Gallery, but they've started charging money now, so I think we should all start peeing in the fountains in protest. If you prefer to tinkle somewhere a little less public, then you can try the one inside the National Gallery itself (you will have to go down the stairs, towards the bookshop). There is another set of toilets through Admiralty Arch and further along the Mall, just inside one of the big black gates to **St. James's Park** (roughly opposite St. James's Palace). This is also the closest one to Buckingham Palace.

Another convenient convenience (excuse the pun again) used to be on the northern corner of **Leicester Square**, opposite the Empire cinema. The entrance is next to the barrier that separates the pavement from the central grass area. Unfortunately they've started charging for that one now as well.

The best one near **Piccadilly Circus** is inside the big branch of Waterstones (a short walk down Piccadilly).

If you're caught short by Westminster Bridge and the **London Eye**, then you can pop into the NAMCO Centre and use the one downstairs (go down the escalators, walk past all of the fruit machines, and then follow the signs). Easier to find are the ones inside the basement of County Hall, which you can reach through the London Eye ticket office. If you're really desperate then you could even pop into St. Thomas's Hospital (over the road from Westminster Bridge, near the Florence Nightingale Museum).

If you are a little further down the river then you can make a quick dash for the ones inside the **Royal Festival Hall** or **Tate Modern**.

If you need a wee whilst doing a wee bit of shopping along **Oxford Street** (another terrible pun -- sorry), then your best bet is to pop inside one of the big department stores. Selfridges, Debenhams and John Lewis all have free toilets.

My favourite toilet is definitely the one inside **Harrods**... *gold fittings!*

If you're inside the Square Mile (which runs roughly from Fleet Street to the Tower of London) then you're in luck, because the City of London maintains an interactive online map of every free WC. You can find it at *http://www.cityoflondon .gov.uk/services/transport-and-streets/ clean-streets/Pages/toilet-map.aspx.*

If you can't make it to any of these toilets in time, then keep your eyes open for a coffee shop, because many of the bigger branches of Starbucks and Costas have toilets (although lots of them require you to get a code from the staff these days). And of course you can always rush into the nearest pub. But the problem with pubs is that you invariably have to walk straight past the bar, and the staff may try and stop you if you're not there to buy a drink.

Staying Safe in London

Are the locals friendly?

I think London is a friendly city, but when it comes to simple little things like saying hello we are totally useless. For example, we don't do eye-contact. People don't exchange greetings with people they don't know, and we rarely acknowledge the person sitting next to us on a bus or train. That shouldn't be taken as rudeness -- it's just the way it is. I have sat on foreign trains and planes and had conversations with whoever was sitting opposite, but that doesn't happen very often in London. If you strike up a conversation with a random person on the bus then they will probably think you are a weirdo (which I am... but that's beside the point).

I actually think that that is one of the good things about London: we are very tolerant of weirdos. You can stand on a street corner all day long, spouting out all sorts of rubbish, and no one will bat an eyelid. They will just ignore you and pretend that you don't exist. We are probably one of the most tolerant cities in the world. People don't care what you wear, whose hand you're holding, or which sex of person you're kissing. But it works both ways, because if somebody starts a scene or a shouting match with you in public don't expect anyone to help you out. They are more likely to look at the walls and pretend that nothing's happening.

The one thing that everybody knows about Britain is this: we like a nice queue. Apparently all Londoners love to queue up in orderly lines and get hot under the collar whenever somebody tries to jump the line. When it comes to shops and tourist attractions this is still largely true, but anyone who regularly boards a bus or a train will know different. People don't queue at the bus stops anymore (unless there are only a few people waiting), and when a tube train comes along it's basically just a big bundle through the door.

We do love animals though. If a cute fluffy dog is in trouble then you can bet your life that everyone will come running.

Avoiding crime

London is a very safe place to stay, but common sense rules always apply when you're in a big city (all big cities have their fair share of idiots). As long as you don't do anything daft then you should be fine. I have been visiting London my whole life and I've never met a pickpocket, never been mugged, never been shot or stabbed, never been murdered, and never even felt threatened (I've probably gone and jinxed myself now). Actually that's a lie... a little kid stamped on my foot once whilst I was wedged into a tube train.

Here are some common sense rules to keep you safe:

1) Don't leave your wallet or mobile phone sticking out of your back pocket, or left lying on a pub table. And don't leave your coat or bag hanging on the back of your chair either, as they can easily get rifled. The dumbest way to get your bag stolen is to leave it on the floor in a toilet cubicle, as a lot of them have big gaps under the walls where people can stick their hands (it's pretty difficult to chase a thief with your trousers flapping around your ankles!).

2) Be wary of pickpockets, especially on the London Underground. If somebody appears to be pressing up against you in the crush, then they may be trying to sneak a hand inside your outside pocket. Sometimes they tease open the zips on your bag, or slash the sides with a blade to make a hole. People might try and steal your stuff on the escalators as well. If you notice that somebody is standing close behind you on the next step down, then just be aware of what they are doing. The big crowd around 'Changing the Guard' is another popular spot for thieves, along with the one that forms in Covent Garden to watch the street entertainers.

3) Avoid using any cash machines that look as if they have been damaged or tampered with. Be especially careful of the slot: *if it looks wrong, walk away.* Sometimes they will replace the entire front facade with a fake version, and it can be very difficult to spot whether it's real. I am actually so wary about using cash machines these days that I only use ones situated inside bank lobbies. My advice would be to pick a safe one and stick with it for the duration of your holiday, so you know exactly what it's supposed to look like. (I might be a little paranoid.)

4) Be aware of who is standing behind you when you withdraw some money. One of their favourite tactics is to distract you with a tap on the shoulder or a question, a split second before the money comes out. By the time you have turned around again their accomplice will already have waltzed off with your money. The bloke you spoke to will then feign innocence, as if it was nothing to do with him. They might even try and tempt you by holding out a tenner, and asking if you dropped it -- it's a dumb trick, so don't fall for it!

5) Travelling on the bus or train late at night can sometimes be intimidating, especially if you are unlucky enough to get some dopey drunks on board. 99% of the time it will just be drunken banter and them showing off to their mates, so don't get yourself worked up into a tizzy for no reason. You might want to take your headphones off as well, so you are aware of what is happening around you. And for chrissakes don't fall asleep!

6) Use taxi cabs instead of minicabs, because you can be confident that the driver will be properly licensed. If you do want to use a minicab then make sure you phone up a minicab company and order it yourself -- and ask the controller for the driver's name and description (and check it when he arrives). You can obtain the phone number of a reputable firm directly from the TFL website: *https://tfl.gov.uk/forms/12389.aspx*. You can also download their 'Cabwise' app from the iTunes store and Google Play store, which will not only provide you with some safe cab firms, but it will also let you book one online. But the golden rule is this: never get into a vehicle that is just cruising down the street, claiming to be a minicab, because that is basically the same as getting into a stranger's car. If you decide to risk it then you are a total idiot.

Looking After Your Bags

Left-luggage facilities

If you're looking for somewhere to store your bags, then the first place to try is a mainline train station (I don't mean the underground stations -- I mean the big overground hubs). There are seven stations in London which offer left-luggage facilities: Charing Cross, Euston, King's Cross/St. Pancras, Liverpool Street, Paddington, Victoria and Waterloo. You can also store your bags at the five main airports: Heathrow, Gatwick, Stansted, Luton and London City.

The facilities are provided by a company called the *Excess Baggage Company*, and you can look up their prices here: *http://www.left-baggage.co.uk*. A rough guide is £11 per item, per 24-hours, but the prices differ between locations. Remember to check their opening hours as well, because they don't always open through the night. Their typical opening hours run from 7 AM to 11 PM.

Finding lost property

If you lose something in a London tube train, DLR train, London bus, black taxi (but not a minicab), or at Victoria Coach station, then it will be dealt with by the same place: Transport for London's Lost Property Office at 200 Baker Street.

You can either phone them up at 0343 222 1234, or use their online form at *https://tfl.gov.uk/corporate/useful-contacts/lost-property*. You need to give them a detailed description of the item, say a prayer, and then hope that somebody nice finds it and hands it in (remember to cross your fingers). You may have to wait as long as ten days for a result. If they don't find it within three weeks then they will give up -- there's nothing much you can do after that, you can only pray that somebody belated hands it in.

If you get lucky then you can collect it from their office after paying a small fee and showing some ID (8.30 AM to 4 PM, Mon-Fri). You can also have it couriered to you for an extra cost. If they find it in a black taxi then you will be expected to pay the driver a small reward fee on top (seriously!).

If you don't claim it within three months then it will either be sold off or destroyed.

494 | London: A Visitor's Guide

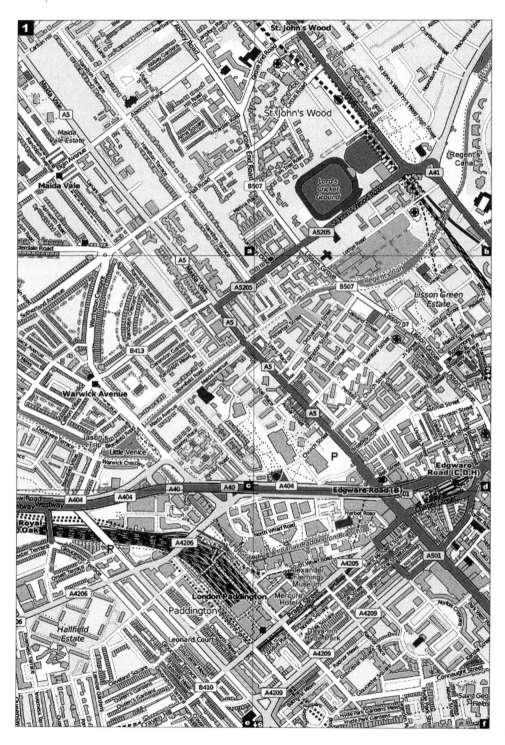

Street Maps | 495

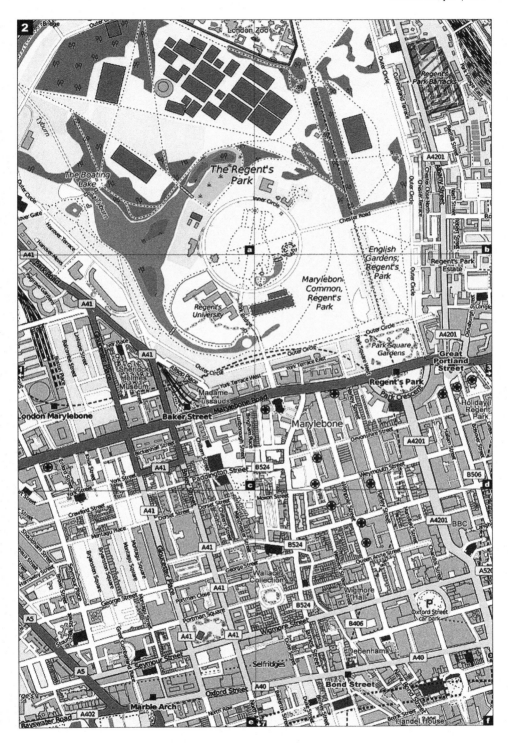

496 | London: A Visitor's Guide

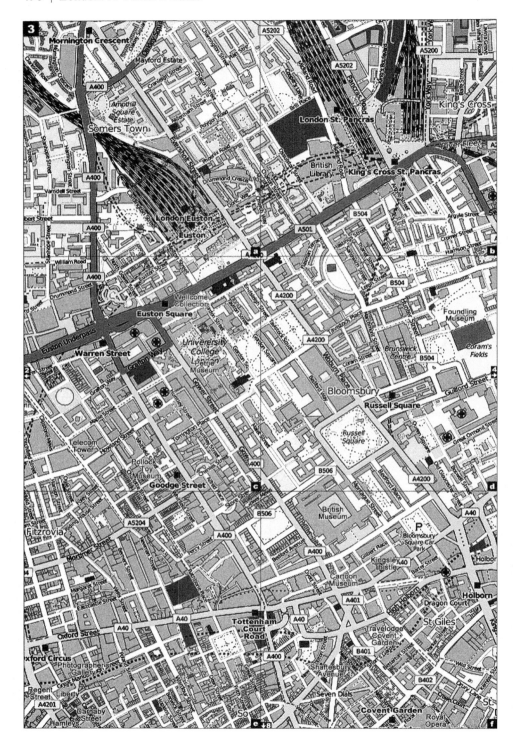

Street Maps | 497

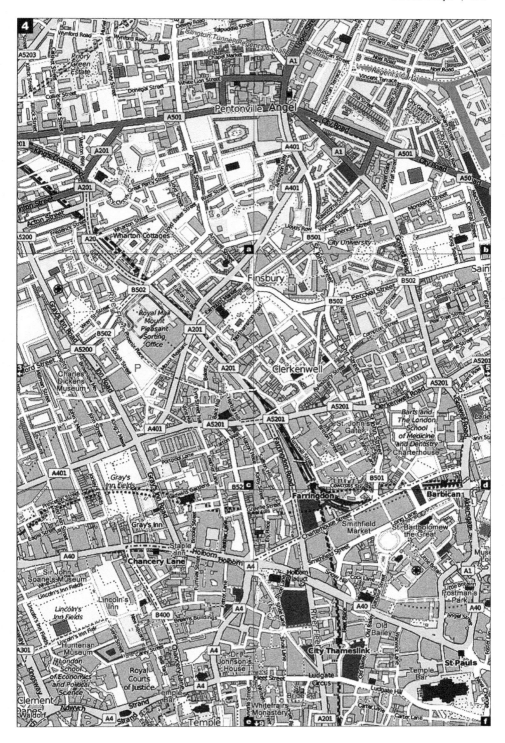

498 | London: A Visitor's Guide

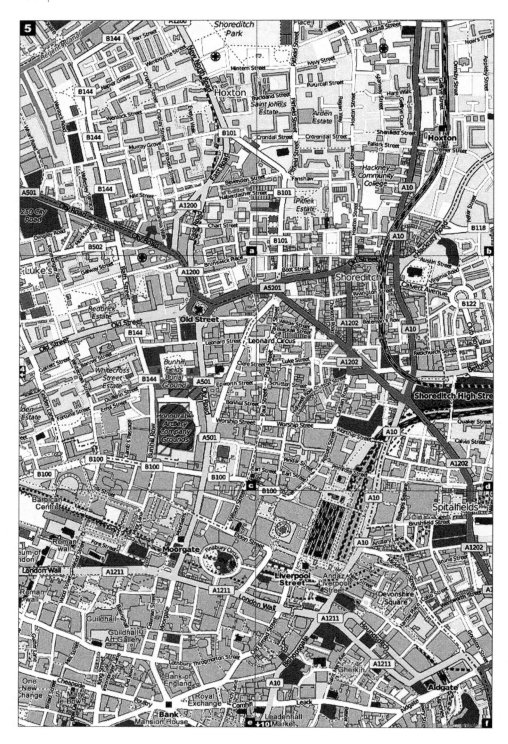

Street Maps | 499

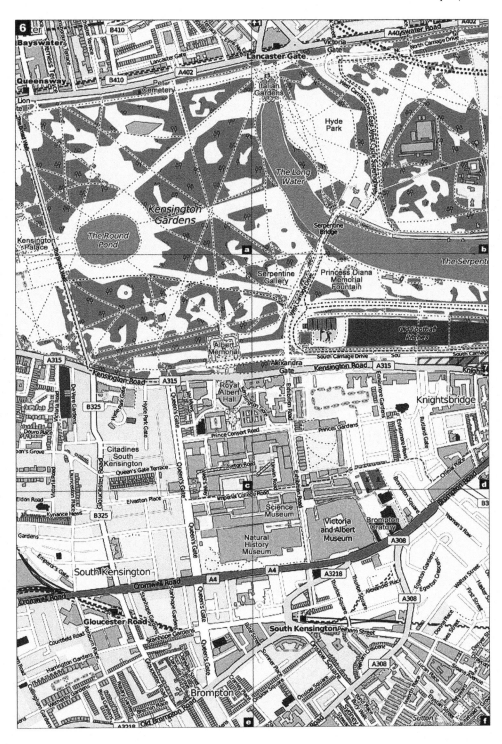

500 | London: A Visitor's Guide

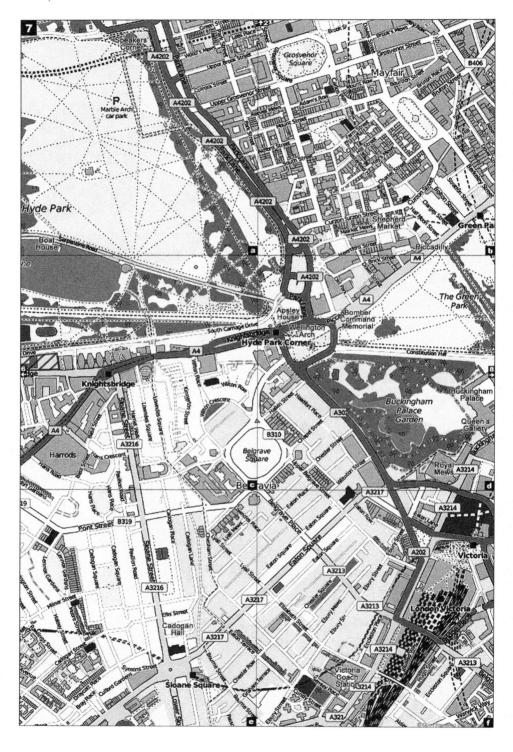

Street Maps | 501

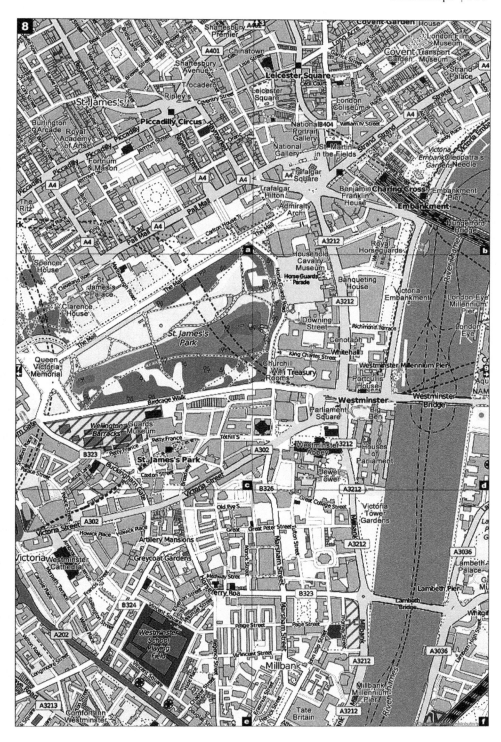

502 | London: A Visitor's Guide

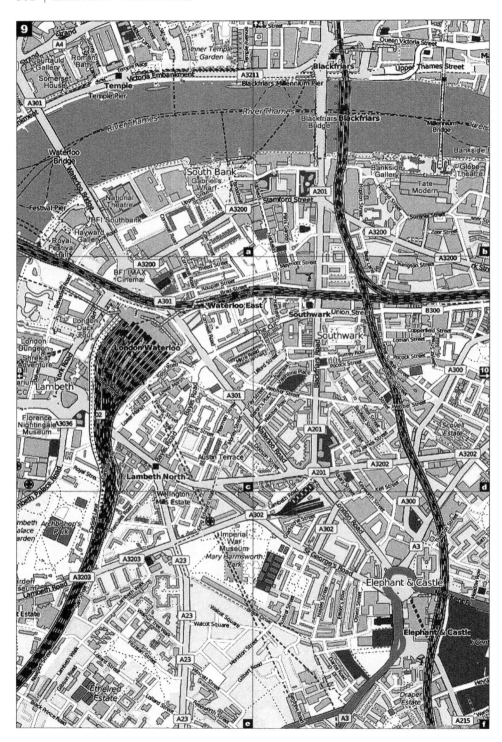

Street Maps | 503

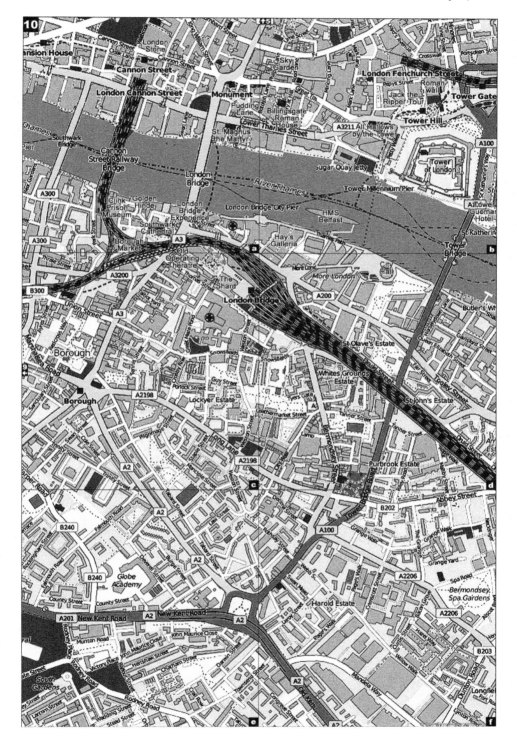

504 | London: A Visitor's Guide

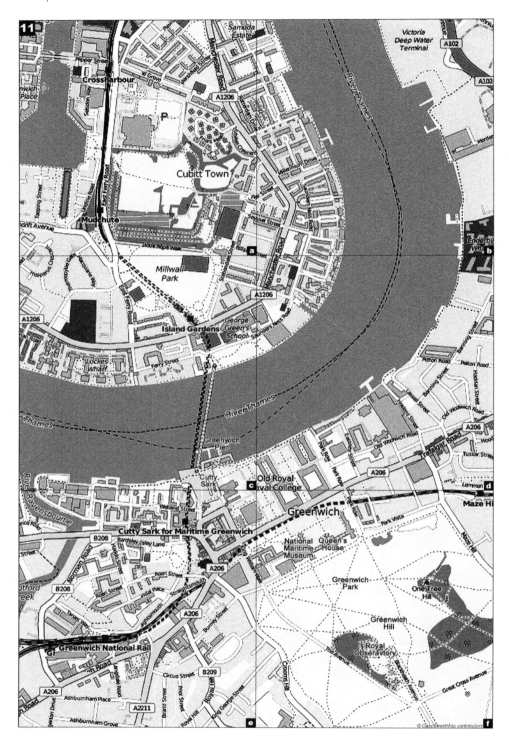

Index

10 Downing Street, 70, *Map 8d*
16-25 Railcard, 456
18 Stafford Terrace, 263
2-for-1 offers by train, 487
4 O'Clock Parade, 295, *Map 8d*
Abbey Road, 7
Admiralty Arch. *Map 8b*
Airports, 468
Albert Memorial, 8, *Map 6c*
Aldgate station. *Map5f*
Alexander Fleming Museum, 8, *Map 1f*
All Hallows by the Tower, 9, *Map 10b*
Andaz Liverpool Street, 425, *Map 5f*
Apsley House, 10, *Map 7d*
ArcelorMittal Orbit, 13
Baker Street. *Maps 2c, 2e*; station. *Map 2c*
Bank of England Museum, 15, *Map 5e*
Bank station. *Map 5e*
Bankside Gallery. *Map 9b*
Bankside pier. *Map 9b*
Banqueting House, 17, *Map 8d*
Barbican. *Map 5e*; station. *Map 4d*
Bath, 321
Battersea Park Children's Zoo, 18
Bayswater station. *Map 6a*
Benjamin Franklin House, 20, *Map 8b*
BFI IMAX Cinema, 21, *Map 9c*
BFI Southbank. *Map 9a*
Big Ben, 23, *Map 8d*
Big Bus Tour, 265
Billingsgate Roman House & Baths, 25, *Map 10b*
Blackfriars: bridge. *Map 9b*; pier. *Map 9b*; station. *Map 9b*
Bletchley Park, 324
Boats, 275, 464; Chatham Dockyard, 333; City Cruises, 275; Cutty Sark, 67; Golden Hinde, 81; HMS Belfast, 98; HMS Victory, 352; Jason's Canal Trip, 277; London Duck Tour, 279; Mary Rose, 352; Portsmouth Historic Dockyard, 352; Thames Clippers, 280; Thames River Services, 283; TRS, 283
Bond Street station. *Map 2f*
Boris Bikes, 463; Fares, 463; Using, 464
Borough Market, 26, *Map 10a*
Borough station. *Map 10c*
British Library, 27, *Map 3b*
British Museum, 28, *Map 3f*
BritRail Pass, 456

Brompton Cemetery, 31
Brompton Oratory, 33, *Map 6f*
Buckingham Palace, 35, *Map 7d*; Changing the Guard, 292; Evening tour, 38; Summer Opening, 35
Burlington Arcade, 40, *Map 8a*
Buses, 457; Adult fares, 457; Changing buses, 459; Child fares, 457; Getting off a bus, 461; Paying a fare, 440; Prams and wheelchairs, 461; Stopping a bus, 460; Times, 459; Timetables, 459
Cabinet War Rooms, 50, *Map 8d*
Cable car, 285
Cadogan Hall. *Map 7e*
Cambridge, 326
Camden Town, 41
Canary Wharf, 43
Cannon Street station. *Map 10a*
Canterbury, 330
Carnaby Street, 44, *Map 3e*
Cartoon Museum. *Map 3f*
Cenotaph, 45, *Map 8d*; Remembrance Day Parade, 296
Ceremony of the Keys, 290, *Map 10b*
Chancery Lane station. *Map 4e*
Changing the Guard: at Buckingham Palace, 292; at Horse Guards, 293
Charing Cross station. *Map 8b*
Charles Dickens Museum, 46, *Map 4c*
Charterhouse, 47, *Map 4d*
Chatham Dockyard, 333
Chelsea Physic Garden, 48
Chessington World of Adventures, 335
Chinatown, 49, *Map 8a*
Christmas, 312; Ice rinks, 312; Lights, 313; Shopping, 315; Trafalgar Square tree, 318
Church services, 303; at Hampton Court, 308; at St. Paul's, 303; at the Tower of London, 310; at Westminster Abbey, 306
Churchill War Rooms, 50, *Map 8d*
Citadines South Kensington, 407, *Map 6c*
City (Square Mile), 53, *Maps 4f, 5e, 5f, 10a, 10b*
City Cruises, 275; Fares, 466; Times, 466
City Hall, 56, *Map 10d*; Mayor's Question Time, 57
Clarence House, 59, *Map 8c*

506 | London: A Visitor's Guide

Cleopatra's Needle, 61, *Map 8b*
Climate, 473
Clink Prison Museum, 62, *Map 10a*
Comfort Inn Westminster, 408
Common Council, 86
Contactless payment cards, 445; Sharing, 446; Using on the bus, 458; Using on the train, 450
Courtauld Gallery, 63, *Map 9a*
Covent Garden, 64, *Map 8b*; station. *Map 3f*
Crime, 491
Crossharbour station. *Map 11a*
Cutty Sark, 67, *Map 11c*; station. *Map 11e*
Dates, 475; Annual events, 476; Bank holidays, 475; School holidays, 476
Day trips, 321
Daylight hours, 473
Days Inn Hyde Park, 409, *Map 1f*
Design Museum, 69
Discount Passes, 485; 2-for-1 offers by train, 487; English Heritage, 488; Historic Royal Palaces, 488; London Pass, 485; Merlin Pass, 487; Removing voluntary donations, 488
Dismounting Ceremony, 295, *Map 8d*
Docklands Light Railway (DLR), 271; Riding, 271; Stairs and escalators, 454; Times, 452; Timetables, 453
Downing Street, 70, *Map 8d*
Dr. Johnson's House, 72, *Map 4e*
Edgware Road station. *Map 1d*
Elephant & Castle station. *Map 9f*
Embankment: pier. *Map 8b*; station. *Map 8b*
Emirates Air Line, 285
English Heritage, 488
Euston Square station. *Map 3a*
Euston station. *Map 3a*
Farringdon station. *Map 4d*
Fenchurch Street station. *Map 10b*
Festival pier. *Map 9a*
Fleet Street. *Map 4f*
Florence Nightingale Museum, 73, *Map 9c*
Fortnum & Mason. *Map 8a*
Foundling Museum. *Map 3d*
Freedom Passes, 446
Garden Museum, 74, *Map 8f*
Gatwick Airport, 469; Coach, 470; Express, 470; Taxi, 470; Train, 470
Gatwick Express, 470
Geffrye Museum, 75

Gherkin. *Map 5f*
Globe Theatre, 76, *Map 9b*; Guided tour, 76; Watching a play, 78
Gloucester Road station. *Map 6e*
Golden Hinde, 81, *Map 10a*
Goodge Street station. *Map 3c*
Great Portland Street station. *Map 2d*
Green Park, 82, *Map 7d*; station. *Map 7b*
Greenwich: pier. *Map 11c*; station. *Map 11e*
Greenwich Hill, 83, *Map 11f*
Greenwich Park. *Map 11f*
Guards' Museum, 84, *Map 8c*
Guildhall. *Map 5e*; Common Council, 86; Guided tour, 85
Guildhall Art Gallery, 87, *Map 5e*
Hamleys. *Map 3e*
Hampton Court Palace, 338; Ghost tour, 341; Sunday service, 308
Handel House Museum, 89, *Map 2f*
Harrods, 90, *Map 7c*
Harry Potter Tour, 365
Hay's Galleria. *Map 10b*
Hayward Gallery, 92, *Map 9a*
Heathrow Airport, 468; Bus, 469; Coach, 469; Express, 468; Taxi, 469; Train, 469
Heathrow Express, 468
Highgate Cemetery, 93
Hire bikes, 463; Fares, 463; Using, 464
Historic Royal Palaces, 488
HMS Belfast, 98, *Map 10b*
HMS Victory, 352
Holborn station. *Map 3f*
Holiday Inn Regent's Park, 414, *Map 2d*
Horse Guards, 100, *Map 8d*; 4 O'Clock Parade, 295; Changing the Guard, 293; Dismounting Ceremony, 295; Trooping the Colour, 301
Hotels, 404; 3-star reviews, 407; 4-star reviews, 414; 5-star reviews, 425; Andaz Liverpool Street, 425; B&Bs, 406; Choosing an area, 404; Citadines South Kensington, 407; Comfort Inn Westminster, 408; Days Inn Hyde Park, 409; Holiday Inn Regent's Park, 414; Hostels, 405; Ibis London City, 410; Kingsley Thistle, 416; Mercure Paddington, 418; Premier Inn Leicester Square, 411; Prices and facilities, 405; Ritz, 426; Royal Horseguards, 430; Shaftesbury Premier Piccadilly, 433; Shangri-La at

Index | 507

The Shard, 434; Strand Palace Hotel, 419; Tower Guoman Hotel, 421; Trafalgar Hilton, 423; Travelodge Covent Garden, 413; Waldorf Hilton, 437
House of Commons, 109; Prime Minister's Questions, 111
House of Lords, 114
Household Cavalry Museum, 102, *Map 8d*
Houses of Parliament, 103, *Map 8d*; Big Ben, 23; House of Commons, 109; House of Lords, 114; Prime Minister's Questions, 111; Saturday audio tour, 107; Saturday guided tour, 106; State Opening of Parliament, 299; Summer Opening, 103
Hungerford Bridge. *Map 8b*
Hunterian Museum, 116, *Map 4e*
Hyde Park, 117, *Maps 6b, 7a*; Speakers' Corner, 226
Hyde Park Corner station. *Map 7d*
Ibis London City, 410
Ice rinks, 312
Imperial War Museum, 119, *Map 9e*
Island Gardens station. *Map 11c*
Itineraries, 374; For everybody, 374; For families, 383
Jack The Ripper tour, 122, *Map 10b*
Jason's Canal Trip, 277, *Map 1c*
Jewel Tower, 124, *Map 8d*
Kensington Gardens, 125, *Maps 6a, 6c*
Kensington Palace, 127, *Map 6a*
Kew Gardens, 343
King's Cross station. *Map 3b*
Kingsley Thistle, 416, *Map 3f*
Knightsbridge station. *Map 7c*
Lambeth: bridge. *Map 8f*; palace. *Map 8f*; pier. *Map 8f*
Lambeth North station. *Map 9c*
Lancaster Gate station. *Map 6b*
Leadenhall Market, 129, *Map 10b*
Leicester Square, 129, *Map 8b*; station. *Map 8b*
Leighton House Museum, 131
Liberty. *Map 3e*
Lincoln's Inn, 132, *Map 4e*
Linley Sambourne House, 263
Little Venice, 133, *Map 1c*; Jason's Canal Trip, 277
Liverpool Street station. *Map 5f*
London Aquarium, 134, *Map 8d*
London Bridge. *Map 10a*; pier. *Map 10a*; station. *Map 10c*

London Bridge Experience. *Map 10a*
London Canal Museum, 136
London City Airport, 471; Taxi, 472; Train, 472; Watching planes, 287
London Coliseum. *Map 8b*
London Duck Tour, 279, *Map 9c*
London Dungeon, 137, *Map 8d*
London Eye, 139, *Map 8d*; Millennium pier. *Map 8d*
London Film Museum, 141, *Map 8b*
London Pass, 485
London Stone. *Map 10a*
London Transport, 440
London Wetland Centre, 347
London Zoo, 143, *Map 2b*
Lord's Cricket Ground. *Map 1b*
Lost property, 493
Luggage facilities, 492
Luton Airport, 471; Coach, 471; Taxi, 471; Train, 471
Madame Tussauds, 147, *Map 2c*
Maida Vale station. *Map 1a*
Mall, The. *Map 8c*
Mansion House, 149, *Map 5e*; station. *Map 10a*
Marble Arch, 151, *Map 2e*; station. *Map 2e*
Mary Rose, 352
Marylebone station. *Map 2c*
Mayor's Question Time, 57, *Map 10d*
Mercure Paddington, 418, *Map 1f*
Merlin Pass, 487
Millbank Millennium pier. *Map 8f*
Millennium Bridge. *Map 9b*
Minicabs, 461; Where to get one, 461
Money, 481; Exchange rates, 482; Using credit cards, 482
Monument, 153, *Map 10a*; station. *Map 10a*
Moorgate station. *Map 5e*
Mornington Crescent station. *Map 3a*
Mudchute station. *Map 11a*
Museum of London, 154, *Map 5e*
Museum of London Docklands, 156
Museum of the Order of St. John, 207, *Map 4d*
NAMCO Funscape. *Map 8d*
National Gallery, 157, *Map 8b*
National Maritime Museum, 160, *Map 11f*
National Portrait Gallery, 162, *Map 8b*
National Rail, 455; Buying tickets, 456; Using Oyster cards, 456; Using

travelcards, 456; Using Visitor Oyster cards, 456
National Theatre. *Map 9a*
Natural History Museum, 163, *Map 6e*
Nelson's Column, 166, *Map 8b*
No.11 bus, 267
Old Bailey. *Map 4f*
Old Operating Theatre, 168, *Map 10c*
Old Royal Naval College, 169, *Map 11d*
Old Street station. *Map 5c*
One New Change, 170, *Map 5e*
Original Bus Tour, 269
Oxford, 349
Oxford Circus station. *Map 3e*
Oxford Street. *Maps 2e, 2f*
Oyster cards, 440; How much credit, 442; Pink readers, 452; Refunding the credit, 443; Sharing, 443; Topping up, 441; Using on National Rail, 456; Using on the bus, 458; Using on the train, 450; Visitor Oyster cards, 441; Where to buy, 440
Paddington station. *Map 1e*
Palaces: Buckingham Palace, 35; Hampton Court Palace, 338; Kensington Palace, 127; Tower of London, 240; Windsor Castle, 368
Parades, 290; 4 O'Clock Parade, 295; Ceremony of the Keys, 290; Changing the Guard at Buckingham Palace, 292; Changing the Guard at Horse Guards, 293; Dismounting Ceremony, 295; Remembrance Day Parade, 296; State Opening of Parliament, 299; Trooping the Colour, 301
Parks: Chelsea Physic Garden, 48; Green Park, 82; Hyde Park, 117; Kensington Gardens, 125; Kew Gardens, 343; Regent's Park, 182; Richmond Park, 356; St. James's Park, 206; Wisley Gardens, 371
Parliament Hill, 171
Parliament Square, 173, *Map 8d*
Petrie Museum, 174, *Map 3c*
Photographers' Gallery. *Map 3e*
Piccadilly. *Maps 7a, 7d, 8a*
Piccadilly Circus, 176, *Map 8a*; station. *Map 8a*
PMQs, 111
Pollock's Toy Museum. *Map 3c*
Portsmouth Historic Dockyard, 352
Post, 480; Poste Restante, 481; Prices, 480

Postman's Park, 178, *Map 4f*
Premier Inn Leicester Square, 411, *Map 8b*
Prime Minister's Questions, 111
Primrose Hill, 179
Princess Diana Memorial Fountain, 179, *Map 6d*
Pubs, 489; Children, 489; Drinking age, 489; Opening hours, 489
Queen Victoria Memorial. *Map 8c*
Queen's Gallery, 180, *Map 7d*
Queensway station. *Map 6a*
RAF Museum, 355
Railcards: 16-25 Railcard, 456; BritRail Pass, 456; Senior Railcard, 446
Regent's Park, 182, *Maps 2a, 2b, 2c, 2d*; station. *Map 2d*
Remembrance Day Parade, 296, *Map 8d*
Richmond Park, 356
Ripley's Believe It Or Not!, 184, *Map 8a*
Ritz, The, 426, *Map 8a*
River cruises, 275, 464; City Cruises, 275; Jason's Canal Trip, 277; London Duck Tour, 279; Thames Clippers, 280; Thames River Services, 283; TRS, 283
Roman amphitheatre, 87
Roman bath, 186, *Map 9a*
Royal Academy of Arts, 187, *Map 8a*
Royal Albert Hall, 188, *Map 6c*; Guided tour, 188; Proms concert, 189
Royal Courts of Justice, 192, *Map 4e*; Guided tour, 192; Watching a trial, 194
Royal Exchange, 196, *Map 5e*
Royal Family: Buckingham Palace, 35; Changing the Guard, 292; Clarence House, 59; Hampton Court Palace, 338; Kensington Palace, 127; Queen's Gallery, 180; Royal Mews, 199; Trooping the Colour, 301; Windsor Castle, 368
Royal Festival Hall. *Map 9a*
Royal Horseguards, 430, *Map 8b*
Royal Hospital, 197
Royal Mews, 199, *Map 7d*
Royal Oak station. *Map 1e*
Royal Observatory, 200, *Map 11f*
Royal Opera House. *Map 3f*
Russell Square station. *Map 3d*
Saatchi Gallery, 202
Science Museum, 216, *Map 6f*
Selfridges. *Map 2f*
Senior Railcard, 446

Serpentine Gallery. *Map 6d*
Shaftesbury Avenue. *Maps 3f, 8a*
Shaftesbury Premier Piccadilly, 433, *Map 8a*
Shakespeare: Globe Theatre, 76; Stratford-upon-Avon, 362; Watching a play, 78
Shangri-La at The Shard, 434, *Map 10c*
Shard, 219, *Map 10c*; Shangri-La Hotel, 434
Shepherd Market. *Map 7b*
Sherlock Holmes Museum, 221, *Map 2c*
Shops, 483; Christmas, 315; Opening hours, 484; Prices, 485; Tipping, 485
Shoreditch High Street station. *Map 5d*
Shrek's Adventure!. *Map 9b*
Sightseeing buses, 265; Big Bus Tour, 265; London Duck Tour, 279; No.11 bus, 267; Original Bus Tour, 269
Sir John Soane's Museum, 223, *Map 4e*
Sky Garden, 224, *Map 10b*
Sloane Square. *Map 7e*; station. *Map 7e*
Smithfield Market. *Map 4f*
Smoking, 489
Somerset House. *Map 9a*
South Kensington station. *Map 6f*
Southwark: bridge. *Map 10a*; cathedral. *Map 10a*; station. *Map 9d*
Speakers' Corner, 226, *Map 7a*
Spencer House. *Map 8c*
Spitalfields Market. *Map 5f*
St. Bartholomew-the-Great, 203, *Map 4f*
St. Bride's, 205, *Map 4f*
St. James's Palace. *Map 8c*
St. James's Park, 206, *Map 8c*; station. *Map 8c*
St. John's Gate, 207, *Map 4d*
St. John's Wood station. *Map 1b*
St. Katherine Docks, 208
St. Katherine's pier. *Map 10b*
St. Magnus the Martyr, 210, *Map 10a*
St. Martin-in-the-Fields, 212, *Map 8b*
St. Pancras station. *Map 3b*
St. Paul's Cathedral, 213, *Map 4f*; Evensong, 303
St. Paul's station. *Map 4f*
Stansted Airport, 470; Coach, 471; Express, 470; Taxi, 471
Stansted Express, 470
Staple Inn, 227, *Map 4e*
State Opening of Parliament, 299, *Maps 8c, 8d*
Stonehenge, 359

Strand. *Maps 4e, 8b, 9a*
Strand Palace Hotel, 419, *Map 8b*
Stratford-upon-Avon, 362
Tate Britain, 228, *Map 8f*
Tate Modern, 230, *Map 9b*
Taxis, 461; Fares, 462; How many people, 463; Wheelchairs, 463; Where to get one, 462
Telephone, 477; Country codes, 478; Directory enquiries, 477; Emergency numbers, 477; Time difference, 473
Temple Bar, 233, *Maps 4e, 4f*
Temple Church, 234, *Map 4e*
Temple station. *Map 9a*
Thames Barrier, 235
Thames Clippers, 280; Fares, 464; Times, 464
Thames River Services, 283; Fares, 467; Times, 467
Theatre tickets, 488; TKTS booth, 488
Time difference, 473
TKTS booth, 488
Toilets, 490
Top 10 Lists, 389; Art galleries, 391; Day trips, 400; For free, 389; For kids, 390; For photographs, 398; Maritime sites, 397; Military sites, 396; Most overrated, 402; Museums, 392; Must-dos, 389; My own personal, 401; Political sites, 395; Religious sites, 394; Royal sites, 393; Viewing spots, 399
Tottenham Court Road station. *Map 3e*
Tower Bridge, 237, *Map 10b*
Tower Gateway station. *Map 10b*
Tower Guoman Hotel, 421, *Map 10b*
Tower Hill, 239, *Map 10b*; station. *Map 10b*
Tower Millennium pier. *Map 10b*
Tower of London, 240, *Map 10b*; Ceremony of the Keys, 290; Sunday service, 310; Twilight tour, 245; Yeoman Warder tour, 244
Trafalgar Hilton, 423, *Map 8b*
Trafalgar Square, 247, *Map 8b*; Christmas tree, 318; Nelson's Column, 166
Trains, 446; 16-25 Railcard, 456; Adult fares, 447; BritRail Pass, 456; Changing trains, 452; Child fares, 448; Contactless payment cards, 445; Finding the platform, 454; Freedom Passes, 446; National Rail, 455; Oyster cards, 440; Paying a fare, 440; Peak

time, 446; Senior fares, 446; Senior Railcard, 446; Stairs and escalators, 454; Times, 452; Timetables, 453; Travelcards, 443; Visitor Oyster cards, 441
Transport Museum, 250, *Map 8b*
Travelcards, 443; Family, 445; Sharing, 445; Using on National Rail, 456; Using on the bus, 458; Using on the train, 450; Where to buy, 444
Travelodge Covent Garden, 413, *Map 3f*
Trocadero. *Map 8a*
Trooping the Colour, 301, *Maps 8c, 8d*
TRS, 283; Fares, 467; Times, 467
Underground, 446; Adult fares, 447; Changing trains, 452; Child fares, 448; Finding the platform, 454; Paying a fare, 440; Peak time, 446; Riding, 272; Senior fares, 446; Stairs and escalators, 454; Times, 452; Timetables, 453; Understanding the map, 453
Victoria & Albert Museum, 252, *Map 6f*
Victoria coach station. *Map 7f*
Victoria Embankment. *Maps 8b, 8d, 9a*; gardens. *Map 8b*
Victoria station. *Map 7f*
Visitor Oyster cards, 441; How much credit, 442; Pink readers, 452; Refunding the credit, 443; Sharing, 443; Topping up, 441; Using on National Rail, 456; Using on the bus, 458; Using on the train, 450; Where to buy, 441
Waldorf Hilton, 437, *Map 4e*
Wallace Collection, 255, *Map 2f*
Warner Bros. Studios, 365
Warren Street station. *Map 3c*
Warwick Avenue station. *Map 1c*
Waterloo: bridge. *Map 9a*; station. *Map 9c*
Waterloo East station. *Map 9c*
Websites, 480
Wellcome Collection. *Map 3c*
Wellington Arch, 256, *Map 7d*
West End, 257, *Maps 3f, 8a, 8b*
Westminster: bridge. *Map 8d*; pier. *Map 8d*; station. *Map 8d*
Westminster Abbey, 259, *Map 8d*; Evensong, 306
Westminster Cathedral, 261, *Map 8e*
Whitehall. *Map 8d*
Wi-Fi spots, 479
Wigmore Hall. *Map 2f*
Windsor Castle, 368
Wisley Gardens, 371

Get the eBook

Did you know that *London: A Visitor's Guide* is also available as an eBook? I have totally redesigned it from scratch to take advantage of all the extra storage space on your eBook reader. It includes a couple of hundred colour photographs, bigger street maps (to cater for the smaller screen on an eReader) plus a bonus chapter full of self-guided walks. It's available to buy from all good eBook retailers.

Contact the Author

Thanks for taking the time to read my book. It took me a few years to research and write it, and if you enjoyed it please consider telling your friends, or writing a short review somewhere (it doesn't matter where). Word of mouth is an author's best friend and is *hugely* appreciated.

If you'd like to talk to me for whatever reason, or maybe share your thoughts about London, then you can reach me through my blog: *http://www.londondrum.com/blog*. I'm also on Facebook: *http://www.facebook.com/london.visitors.guide*.

Some of the reasons why you might like to contact me are, for example:

1) You'd like to invite me to stay in the Presidential suite at your 5-star hotel so I can review it (make sure it has plenty of teabags)

2) You're a literary agent, or a publisher, and you'd like to sign me up (I know it's a long shot, but there's no harm in asking!)

3) You'd like to ask my advice about a personal problem -- I like to think that I'm an expert on most things (except for women, obviously)

Whatever it is, *drop me a line*, and as long as you're not nuts I'll probably reply.

Visit the Website

Visit *London Drum* -- a handy website for tourists, locals, and people who just want to have a wander around town. You can find it at *http://www.londondrum.com*.

It contains a guide to upcoming theatre shows, music concerts, comedy gigs, art and museum exhibitions, sightseeing tours, landmarks and attractions, and information about hotels and restaurants.

You can also look up transport fares, work out train journeys, and bookmark everything on our interactive trip planner.

We've also got a forum and blog (written by the same guy who wrote this book).

My Other Books

If this book made you smile then you might enjoy my totally ridiculous comedy novel: *World War Snow*. I have also written a biography of The Beatles called: *The Beatles: Day-by-Day, Song-by-Song, Record-by-Record*. They're available to buy online from Amazon, Barnes & Noble, Waterstones... *etc etc!*

Lightning Source UK Ltd.
Milton Keynes UK
UKOW05f2018291016
286433UK00021B/675/P